THE LAND BETWEEN:
NORTHWESTERN ONTARIO RESOURCE DEVELOPMENT,
1800 TO THE 1990s

W. ROBERT WIGHTMAN
AND NANCY M. WIGHTMAN

The Land Between: Northwestern Ontario Resource Development, 1800 to the 1990s

UNIVERSITY OF TORONTO PRESS
Toronto Buffalo London

Toronto Buffalo London
Printed in Canada

ISBN 0-8020-0937-9 (cloth)

Printed on acid-free paper

Canadian Cataloguing in Publication Data

Wightman, W. R. (William Robert), 1937–
The land between : Northwestern Ontario resource development 1800 to the 1990s

Includes bibliographical references and index.
ISBN 0-8020-0937-9

1. Natural resources – Ontario, Northern – History.
2. Ontario, Northern – History. 3. Ontario, Northern – Economic conditions. I. Wightman, Nancy M. II. Title.

HC117.05W53 1997 333.7'15'09713 C96-931769-7

The maps in this book were prepared by the Cartographic Section of the Department of Geography, University of Western Ontario.

University of Toronto Press acknowledges the financial assistance to its publishing program of the Canada Council and the Ontario Arts Council.

This book has been published with the help of a grant from the Humanities and Social Sciences Federation of Canada, using funds provided by the Social Sciences and Humanities Research Council of Canada.

Contents

Maps

Tables

Preface

Although rarely appreciated either publicly or politically, northern, or 'New,' Ontario is not an amorphous place but a series of distinct regions. Each is larger than southern, or 'Old,' Ontario and stands in a variant geographical relationship to that core. Each historically has had its economy profoundly shaped by different relationships and by its peculiar balance of natural resources. Sadly, many Ontarians who live in these areas are only vaguely cognizant of their regional heritage, of the notable achievements that mark their particular past, and of the value of their present accomplishments.

Over twenty years ago, the authors began a trilogy of resource-oriented studies covering more-populated northern divisions. *Forever on the Fringe* (University of Toronto Press, 1982) used the Manitoulin Island to typify the developmental balances and patterns of farm, forest, and fishery in Ontario's near-north. It was an experiment that melded what turned out to be rich local records, collected through fieldwork, with traditional sources from major archives, libraries, and other provincial repositories.

The Land Between is a much more ambitious interpretation of the whole of northwestern Ontario but uses the same data-gathering procedures. To Manitoulin themes, it adds the complexities of mining and delves more into tourism as well as the supportive aspects of urbanization, transport, and communications. Like its predecessor, it is conceived as a sequence of free-standing essays, each covering a distinct period of regional development in a context of national and provincial trends. Each essay treats the elements of the resource base and of the supportive infrastructure individually, although emphasis may vary with changing times. As in the previous volume, the approach is descriptive in its examination of economic and social trends. It is aimed at both scholars seeking critical elaboration of northern themes and the general reading public in search of an understanding of the North.

Acknowledgments

This book is dedicated to several groups of people who made its successful preparation possible. First are the many librarians and municipal officers in the region who cheerfully provided space and opened their files to us. Then come those in regional government offices and in industry who patiently answered our questions and tactfully corrected our misconceptions. Among the latter, a special thanks goes to Dick Harkness, Alan Buel, and Ross Silverside, who told us what it was really like to be a forester during the boisterous years of change after World War II. Next are those in the National Library and in the official archives of both Canada and Ontario as well as in major university collections across the province. Special thanks here go to Madame LaFlamme at the microfilm collection of the National Archives. Finally, we would like to thank the staff of the Government Document Section of the University of Western Ontario's D.B. Weldon Library as well as the staffs of the Serge Sauer Map Library and the Cartographic Section of the Department of Geography in that university. To all, a hearty and humble thank-you.

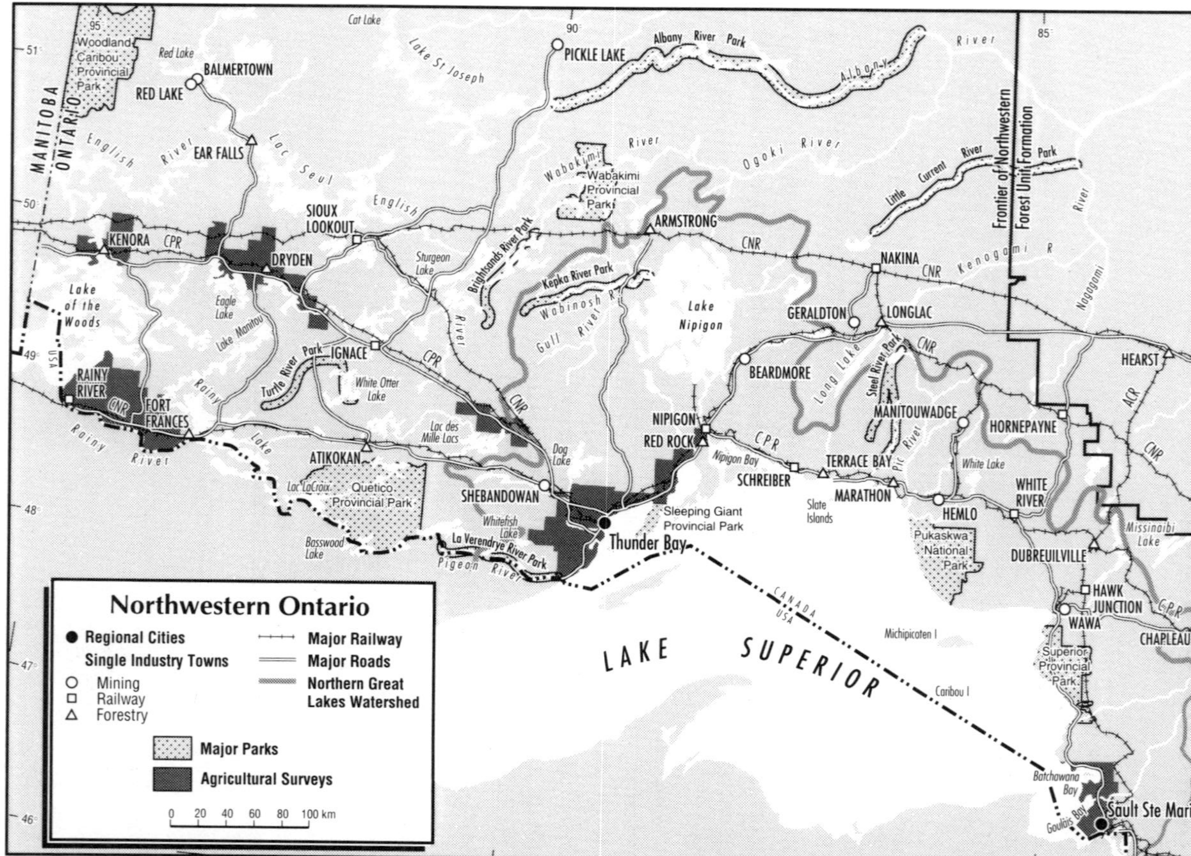
Northwestern Ontario
Regional Cities
Single Industry Towns
Mining
Railway
Forestry
Major Railway
Major Roads
Northern Great Lakes Watershed
Major Parks
Agricultural Surveys
0 20 40 60 80 100 km
MANITOBA
ONTARIO
Woodland Caribou Provincial Park
RED LAKE
BALMERTOWN
EAR FALLS
Lac Seul
KENORA
DRYDEN
SIOUX LOOKOUT
Lake of the Woods
RAINY RIVER
FORT FRANCES
IGNACE
Turtle River Park
White Otter Lake
ATIKOKAN
Quetico Provincial Park
Lac LaCroix
Basswood Lake
La Verendrye River Park
Pigeon River
SHEBANDOWAN
Whitefish Lake
Dog Lake
Lac des Mille Lacs
Thunder Bay
Sleeping Giant Provincial Park
PICKLE LAKE
Albany River Park
Wabakimi Provincial Park
ARMSTRONG
Brightsands River Park
Kepka River Park
Lake Nipigon
NIPIGON
RED ROCK
Nipigon Bay
BEARDMORE
GERALDTON
LONGLAC
NAKINA
Long Lake
Steel River Park
SCHREIBER
TERRACE BAY
MARATHON
Slate Islands
MANITOUWADGE
HEMLO
Pukaskwa National Park
WHITE RIVER
White Lake
HORNEPAYNE
Little Current River Park
Frontier of Northwestern Forest Unit Formation
HEARST
DUBREUILVILLE
HAWK JUNCTION
WAWA
CHAPLEAU
Missinaibi Lake
Superior Provincial Park
Michipicoten I
Caribou I
Batchawana Bay
Goulais Bay
Sault Ste Marie
LAKE SUPERIOR
CANADA
USA
Cat Lake
Lake St Joseph
Ogoki River
Kenogami R
Nagagami River
English River
Sturgeon Lake
Gull River
Wabinosh R
Pic River
Rainy Lake
Rainy River
Lake Manitou
Eagle Lake
CPR
CNR
ACR

THE LAND BETWEEN

The Northwest: A Regional Overview

Northwestern Ontario is an important geographical and historical fulcrum in Canada, a huge intervention of Precambrian Shield that separates western prairie vastness from eastern industrial heartland. More definitively, it is that rugged part of the provincial mid-north extending from Sault Ste Marie west to Manitoba and from the American border north to the English and Albany rivers. A glance at any provincial map underlines its distant relationship to southern Ontario, to which it also stands in sharp economic, social, and cultural contrast. Since the mid-eighties, the authors have driven its highways, prowled its rural concessions, followed its logging roads, and traced many overgrown tracks to forgotten places. The northwest is a fascinatingly distinctive mosaic of primitive scenery, human activity, cultural duality, and environmental wealth.

For many of us the region is a land of varied recreational opportunities. Indeed, it has become a haven for both American and Canadian urbanites in search of a broad range of natural experiences. Formal hunting and fishing lodges and fly-in camps, other rental accommodations related to family vacations, and summer cottages or homes attract people from both the U.S. Midwest and prairie Canada to the region's far western areas. Vacationers from lower-lake states and southern Ontario enjoy its more easterly portions and the varied opportunities there. Many car campers and travel-oriented vacationers sample the region's panoply of pleasures each summer. The younger set have revived an old emphasis of wilderness experience and adventure vacationing by canoe or walking trail. Older tourists, coming to enjoy the region's more traditional pleasures by car or bus tours in spring and fall, have put shoulders on the recreational year. To much of this seasonal pattern the local population is an allied contributor. It is also the leading force in the current development of a range of winter activities that include snowmobile touring, cross-country skiing, and ice-fishing.

The imprints of both aboriginal and non-Native cultures on this landscape have been remarkably widespread. Yet, in modern times, the contrasting activity of these two groups has become less widely dispersed and more focused on selected centres or local areas in this huge region. For many Native people, the gradual retreat to a more sedentary existence on the reserve over past decades has reflected the deteriorating prospects of even semi-dependence on a traditional life off the land. For more northerly and isolated bands, this trend has been exacerbated by the recent collapse of their trap-line economy. On more accessible reserves, the past century has brought many material and social benefits to aboriginal life, some of which have been harmful to traditional culture and folk ways. In recent years, more liberal official policies towards aboriginal self-determination have introduced a refreshing revival of pride in being Native. A renewed vitality in confronting social and economic problems is encouragingly evident on most reserves.

For most whites, the scattered resource and railway towns and focal cities like Sault Ste Marie and Thunder Bay have become home. These dynamic centres of business and industry are uniquely northern in outlook. Their personalities too are distinct from most southern centres, being built on a longstanding tradition of ethnic diversity. These urban places are sewn together by an effective system of transport and communication. The distances along and between the corridors of road, rail, air, and telecommunication are of an order that visitors find hard to comprehend. This is compounded for the uninitiated by the official Ontario road map, which portrays northern Ontario at less than half the scale used to depict the southern regions of the province.

This is a landscape where land competes with water for a share of the area and where bog, marsh, and muskeg represent an uncertain transition. Yet in this realm are two easily definable watersheds. The territory served by rivers flowing to Lake Superior is remarkably limited. These rivers, from the Pigeon to the Michipicoten, are characterized by short, steep gradients. Once intensely used by forest companies for spring log driving, they now are valued chiefly for their enormous power capacity. In comparison, ones flowing to eventual Arctic outlet down the Albany/Moose systems in Ontario or the Red/Nelson via Manitoba have long, usually wide and meandering courses. These rivers, with broad grassy borders, frequently incorporate large water bodies in their watersheds. Some, like Rainy Lake, Lake of the Woods, and Lac Seul, drain westward by way of the English and Red. Others, like Lake St Joseph, are near the modern head of the eastern-flowing Albany system. While the quiet murmur of power installations is not unknown here, such stations in the northwest are small and infrequent compared with those of Superior-oriented flow. Related dams on the latter have drowned the magnificent white water of rivers like the Nipigon. They also have questionably redirected certain arctic supplies down courses such as the Aguasabon to Superior. With mines, pulp and paper mills have capitalized on such power potential, the latter locating at generation sites. Both have added their significant towns to the scene and their inherent problems of environmental management and economic stability to the region.

This being Precambrian country, rugged Shield formations are the basis of its massive scenery. Some landscapes are made up of the tired and rounded forms of old mountain chains, which are noteworthy for their dramatic views. Best-known are those depicted by the Group of Seven, overlooking the vastness of Lake Superior or focusing on the settings of small lakes. Elsewhere, erosion has made deep carvings in immense plains. The results are such majestic vistas as the Lakehead's Sleeping Giant, the neighbouring Ouimet Canyon, and the dentated skyline around Lake Nipigon. However, in certain inland areas, particularly west of Thunder Bay or east from Beardmore, such former plains are of less varied character and prove of modest visual interest. Nevertheless, the sporting opportunities they afford – for example, camping, packing, skiing, and snowmobiling, as well as wilderness adventure – are attractive to many.

The most common heritage of this region, however, is the rich forest cover of highly varied speciation. The more southerly forest includes a strong mix of hardwoods, often at the limit of their range, with an increasingly varied coniferous membership, which extends up the eastern shore of Superior and through the Rainy River country. In contrast is the taiga or boreal forest to the north, dominated by spruce, balsam fur, jackpine, and tamarack and also including birch, aspen, and poplar. In this area, the primary industrial focus is on the production of pulpwood, but even the scrawny jackpine and poplar are harvested, as they are used for veneering and laminating in modern carpentry. Visitors to northwestern Ontario will be struck by the impact on the forests of decades of harvesting. However, they should remember that woodland conditions here, as elsewhere, were never idyllic. Nature's vegetative cover was frequently ravaged by fire and extensively modified by disease – it was often as visually repellent in its wild condition as it can be today after a recent clearcut or burn.

Tracing unpredictable and complex patterns in the geology beneath this vegetation are the famous green stone belts. These have spawned huge iron developments at Wawa and Steep Rock, famous gold fields around Geraldton, Red Lake, and Hemlo, and rich base-metal operations at places like Sturgeon Lake and Manitouwadge. They are the haven of head-frames and related mining communities. Like the ruins of fishing stations along Superior's shore or former fur posts and sawmills in the interior, abandoned mine sites underline the impermanence of much human activity in this region. Indeed, outside major centres with their rural adjuncts and some types of resource towns, the region remains a remarkably transient world of human values and endeavours.

Finally, strewn about the irregular rocky surface of the region are frequent pockets of clay and silt, several of which have promoted important farm-use and related patterns of rural habitation. A few are quite large, such as the broad, level stretch of agriculture down the Rainy River Valley or that of the lowland behind Thunder Bay. Unfortunately, their capacity as farming tracts has declined since the fifties. Their fading landscapes, sometimes complete with silos, gambreled barns, and southern residential styles, are reminiscent of Old Ontario. Yet, equally, they can reflect cultural features of prairie life in neighbouring Manitoba. They are one of the numerous visual reminders that historically, as well as geographically, northwestern Ontario has been 'a land between.'

1

Climates of Northwestern Change, 1800–1850

At the close of the eighteenth century, only the old French endeavour along the St Lawrence could boast any semblance of rural maturity in a British North America under which it had been subsumed in 1763. Indeed, the newer colonial partner, Upper Canada (now southern Ontario), remained in only the early stages of settlement in 1800. Yet about the upper Great Lakes and beyond them to both the Prairies and Hudson Bay, the fur trade, the first exploitive activity under European aegis, was well into its second century. Over the next five decades agriculturally based development adjacent to the lower lakes and St Lawrence would expand steadily. In contrast, the fur trade would suffer marked vicissitudes. These were sharply felt around and beyond Lake Superior in that huge territory later to be called northwestern Ontario. Although the effect of the declining fur trade was mitigated by the initial broadening thrusts of other resource industries, what emerged in this region by mid-century were conditions that were conducive to broader economic development but that hardly promoted its rapid appearance.

An Old Order Ages, 1800–1821

The Ultimate Fur Diopoly

In 1800, the last phase in a continental fight for fur trade supremacy had begun. In British North America, this now was between two legendary firms. The North West Company, an association of Montreal Scots, had re-established and now extended the French thrust, north and west via the upper lakes. This forced the London-based Hudson's Bay Company to expand its active fur pursuit competitively into that same huge, interior domain. In a larger context, this vast drama also included John Jacob Astor's American Fur Company, which was to compete stiffly, but also to struggle to exclude others from western territory claimed by the United States.[1] In this colourful war for peltry, drives west to the foothills and the Athabasca and Mackenzie country grew intense. Separate thrusts to the Pacific and Asian markets were vigorously launched by both British and American interests.[2] The first resource-exploitive wave to wash across North America from east to west was finishing its course.

The principal campaigns of this sprawling, brawling era occupied two fronts. Behind these, the Ottawa-Upper Lakes supply corridor and access inland from Lake Superior was as fundamental to North West Company strategies as was cheap ocean access via Hudson Bay to its adversary. As in earlier years, the territory north of the Great Lakes and west to the line of the Red River–Nelson River system was commonly considered one theatre. This 'Petit Nord' was served by the Hudson's Bay Company, principally up the Albany and Moose rivers from its posts on James Bay. By the Nor'westers it was attainable from Superior rivers such as the Michipicoten and Aguasabon as well as the Wabinosh and other courses from Nipigon to portages across the arctic divide. West of this district lay the second and now more profitable area. Christened 'Le Grand Nord,' it covered the huge territory to the foothills of the Rockies and north to the Mackenzie and Athabasca areas. This more distant west was linked to the trading posts of Hudson Bay down the Churchill or Saskatchewan–Nelson River systems. Similarly, it could be reached from Superior by the Winnipeg–Rainy River route from the Grand Portage.[3] After twenty years of bitter competition, which by 1816 degenerated to open warfare with considerable loss of life and wanton destruction of property, the Colonial Office forced an accommodation.[4] Ironically, this settlement of 1821 ended forever any significant Canadian involvement in the profits from these fur resources. It generated instead a newly constituted Hudson's Bay Company singularly dedicated to the financial advantage of its principally British stockholders.[5]

Regional Ramifications

This spectacular continental competition, coupled with an international boundary agreement through the Lakes country, brought a flurry of new activity to the environs about Superior. There had been twenty fur posts in this area at the opening of the nineteenth century.[6] Of these, three-quarters belonged to the 'Peddlers' from Montreal, who until 1804 were divided into two competing factions. (The above figures exclude several short-lived posts generated by this division as well as a few belonging to independent American traders.) At the time of the amalgamation in 1821, total posts appear to have risen to thirty, about a third being in the hands of the Hudson's Bay Company.[7] Those of the latter firm were concentrated largely in the Albany River watershed, its major entry to this portion of 'Le Petit Nord' (see Map 1.1). In most cases, even those pre-dating 1800 were recent additions, grudging responses to the growing need to establish a network of inland forts and to service them with a fleet of York boats. Their principal purpose was not only to foster a remunerative trade here but to protect this corridor from North West Company use or fur diversion. The exceptions were instances at Michipicoten River, Fort Nipigon, or Red Lake, where Nor'wester posts posed an external or internal threat to this northerly trade sphere. Regardless of its stance elsewhere, the strategy of the Company in this region was clearly one of partition and defence.[8]

The numerous posts of the more aggressive Montrealers in the early nineteenth century hid beneath their broader distribution considerable functional diversity. Those on Superior itself were now limited fur outlets, their hinterlands having been stripped of most peltry over previous decades. The role of these posts now combined trade with the trans-shipment of goods to and from more inland locations in the 'Petit Nord.'[9] Those farther inland were the real producers and were often located in isolated areas where the fur resources were still considerable. West from Superior the region's posts had been involved for years in the growing logistical support of 'Le Grand Nord.' Theirs was the task of promoting both the shipment of huge volumes of goods to the latter and the reciprocal flow of baled fur to Montreal. While each post retained some secondary role in fur production, each was also a prime supplier of local fish, large game, and wild rice to feed the canoe brigades along this transport axis.[10]

Growing recognition of the wealth of 'Le Grand Nord' had by 1800 focused much interest in Montreal on the use of the Grand Portage from Superior's Pigeon River to Rainy River's westward flowing drainage. Indeed, for almost two decades the Grand Portage depot had been next in importance to Mackinac in the trade networks of the entire fur fraternity of the upper lakes.[11] Yet over the same twenty years of rising interest, the future use of both these depots and the Pigeon River route by the Montrealers was increasingly uncertain. By the Treaty of Versailles in 1783, the British had agreed to the Pigeon River as one end of a westward boundary link to the forty-ninth parallel at Lake of the Woods. This placed the depot, with its warehousing at the Grand Portage, in American territory. However, action to implement this border came only in the wake of Jay's Treaty of 1794. Under this agreement, Britain promised not only to vacate the forts such as Mackinac but also to give up use of any other American facilities within two years.[12] In addition, several debilitating U.S. customs regulations and frequently clogged conditions along the Grand Portage by this time were making the Pigeon River route less and less inviting.

As a result, the gradually emerging association of Montreal traders, known as the North West Company, set out to seek another site for their operations on another route to the plains. Actually, an alternate way west had been an earlier

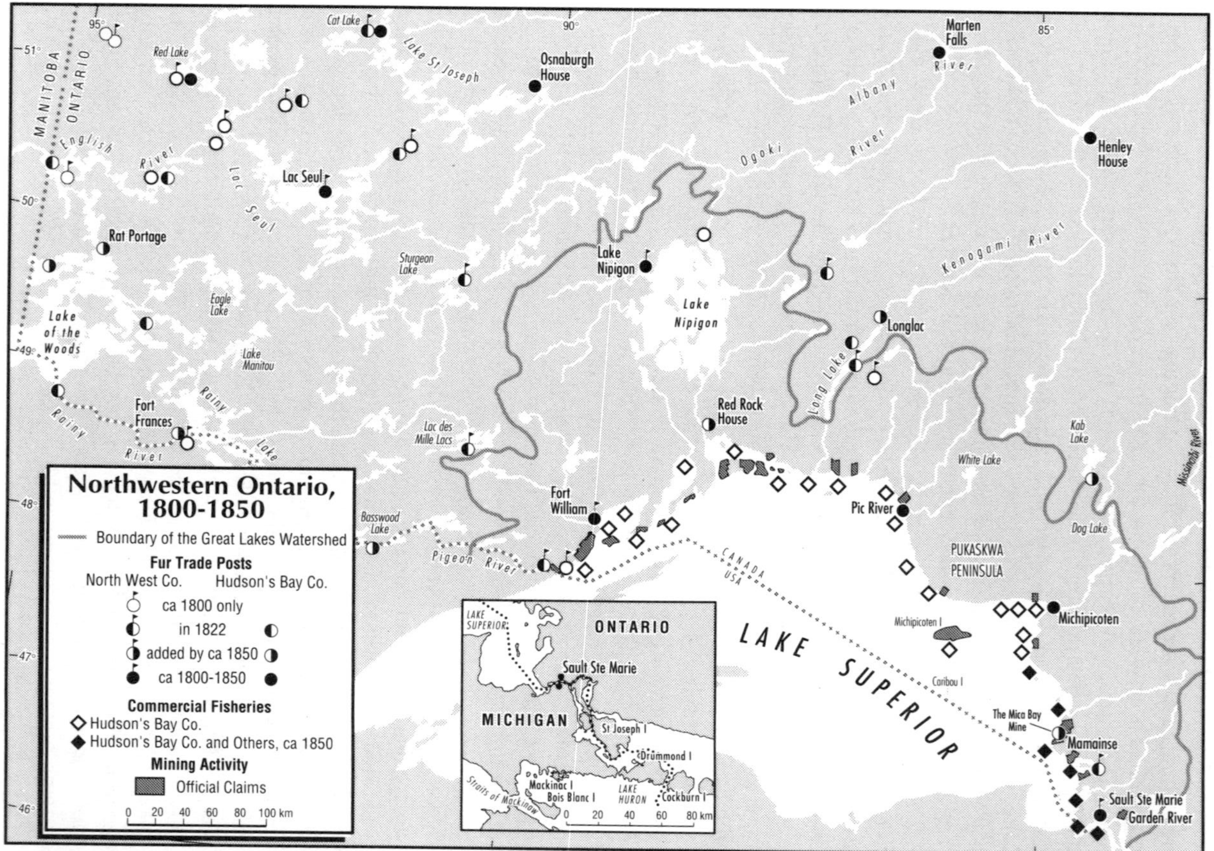

Northwestern Ontario, 1800-1850
Boundary of the Great Lakes Watershed
Fur Trade Posts
North West Co.
Hudson's Bay Co.
ca 1800 only
in 1822
added by ca 1850
ca 1800-1850
Commercial Fisheries
Hudson's Bay Co.
Hudson's Bay Co. and Others, ca 1850
Mining Activity
Official Claims
0 20 40 60 80 100 km
MANITOBA
ONTARIO
English River
Red Lake
Cat Lake
Lake St Joseph
Osnaburgh House
Marten Falls
Albany River
Ogoki River
Henley House
Lac Seul
Rat Portage
Sturgeon Lake
Eagle Lake
Lake of the Woods
Lake Manitou
Rainy Lake
Rainy River
Fort Frances
Lac des Mille Lacs
Basswood Lake
Pigeon River
Fort William
Lake Nipigon
Red Rock House
Kenogami River
Longlac
Long Lake
Pic River
White Lake
Kab Lake
Dog Lake
Missinaibi River
PUKASKWA PENINSULA
Michipicoten
Michipicoten I
Caribou I
The Mica Bay Mine
Mamainse
Sault Ste Marie
Garden River
CANADA
USA
LAKE SUPERIOR
ONTARIO
MICHIGAN
St Joseph I
Drummond I
Mackinac I
Bois Blanc I
Cockburn I
LAKE HURON
Straits of Mackinaw
0 20 40 60 80 km
95°
90°
85°
51°
50°
49°
48°
47°
46°

MAP 1.1

concern among these fur merchants as part of a loose plan to open the central western part of 'Le Petit Nord.' Edward Umfreville had spent several summers after 1784 exploring these rich fur lands to these ends. He finally located a portage-strewn route on the westward course of the English River near Sioux Lookout.[13] But, while his efforts probably resulted in the establishment of posts at both Sturgeon and Red lakes, the difficult nature of this passage doomed it for heavy westward use. Only in 1798, when issues at Grand Portage had become acute, did another employee of the budding Nor'wester organization rediscover an alternate old French trail. It led inland from Thunder Bay via Dog Lake and Lac des Mille Lacs, to rejoin Rainy River drainage far to the west of the Grand Portage.[14] The following summer, a full inventory was taken of goods stored at the Pigeon River depot and plans were laid for New Fort in the delta of the Kaministiquia River (sometimes hereafter called the Kam) on Thunder Bay. Construction of this huge facility was not complete until 1804, but trade goods and operations were shifted here four years earlier. Renamed Fort William, it became the nerve centre and entrepôt for the North West Company's new drive for interior fur[15] (see Map 1.1).

Similar changes reflective of trade needs and treaty requirements also made themselves evident on the St Marys River and adjacent upper Lake Huron. In 1796, in response to the requirements of Jay's Treaty, the British military had erected a new fortification on St Joseph Island, moving its establishment there from Mackinac. On this fort's completion, the Montrealers in 1798 erected an adjacent facility for canoe building to augment another at distant Trois-Rivières.[16] They also applied for and were granted a substantial plot of land on the Canadian side of the rapids at Sault Ste Marie. Here they erected a second new facility, which may have served in some sense as an administration centre, directing the fur trade in the Lake Superior segment of 'Le Petit Nord.' Like New Fort, however, it was dedicated less directly to the trade thrusts of the new century than to the increasing need of those thrusts for efficient transshipment and supply.[17]

Such demands on transport over the difficult and costly route above Montreal had initiated a stream of innovations on the Ottawa and beyond, started by the French. By 1800 two interlocking systems were in place. One employed the large canot du maître between Montreal and Fort William. The other used the smaller canot du nord from western and northern posts to the same Superior depot. Here, during the company's annual meeting in its elaborate council chamber, the yearly exchange of fur bales for trade goods was swiftly accomplished. However, those wintering partners from the distant Mackenzie and Athabasca country, who now would become numerous, were permitted the privilege of making this exchange at Rainy River House (later Fort Frances).[18]

Since about 1790, the more easterly of these systems had been bolstered by small 10–15-ton sailing vessels on both Huron and Superior. On the latter, the much larger *Invincible* now came to serve with the *Athabasca* and the *Otter* in the carriage of bulky loads. It was followed by a sequence of vessels of about 100 tons, one of which, the *Recovery*, was later used by Captain Bayfield, R.N., in the twenties for his charting of Lake Superior.[19] However, the immediate importance of canoes here cannot have diminished, for the new facility at Sault Ste Marie included a lock and canal around the St Marys River rapids which provided for their haulage by ox teams.[20] In addition, on Huron a new route came into some use about this time. Upon a subsidy to the colonial coffers for road improvements, the Nor'westers began to experiment with the Yonge Street–Lake Simcoe supply line to their schooner the *Beaver* on Georgian Bay. Over this route they hauled a certain amount of cheap Upper Canadian food stuffs as well as certain other freight from Montreal.[21] These latter transport developments, coupled with others on the American side, were signs of future change.

However, the ordered and progressive activity which had marked the Superior Northwest, both before and after the turn of the century, now was upset by events beginning with the War of 1812. During that indecisive conflict, the elaborate facility at Sault Ste Marie, along with the property of certain independent traders, was destroyed by American troops. The North West Company post there was never fully restored, nor the canal repaired.[22] After this same conflict the British troops from St Joseph Island, who also had held Mackinac for the duration, were relocated on Drummond Island until their withdrawal in 1828. Their departure from St Joseph seems to have coincided with the closure of the Nor'westers' canoe repair station there, presumably because declining need made its services unnecessary.

More disruptive regional events were sparked by the now furiously cutthroat competition being waged between the Hudson's Bay and Montreal interests in 'Le Grand Nord.' The final stage in this vicious and unprofitable fight was initiated in 1816. It was triggered by the so-called Battle of Seven Oaks between parties affiliated with the Nor'westers and elements among Lord Selkirk's Red River settlement. Selkirk's singular reaction to this altercation, as both a substantial backer of the Hudson's Bay Company and protector of his settlers, came quickly. The following summer he brought sufficient European mercenaries up the lakes to capture both Fort William and the Rainy River post. Although these properties were returned to their owners some months later, this action seriously disrupted the Nor'westers' western trade and, therefore, their finances, which were already in critical condition. These events were followed belatedly by the previously mentioned amalgamation, which was signed on March 26, 1821, bringing this boisterous period to a close.[23]

Harbingers of a New Era, 1821–1850

A Monopolistic Reordering

With the enforced end of competition in the fur trade came monopoly and, with it, startling changes by 1826. Many posts, now redundant or in unprofitable locations in Rupert's Land, were abandoned abruptly, reducing the total active number in 'Le Petit Nord' from 109 to 45 and causing a corresponding loss of employment. Even larger labour cuts came along a transport system no longer geared to speed and other competitive ends. Most spectacular were the results of the cancellation of the highly labour-intensive canoe route inland from Montreal.[24] This caused immediate unemployment problems and financial dislocation in that city and elsewhere along the north-westward axis. All Company trade was now oriented through forts on Hudson or James bays. On western rivers where two fleets had once served, now one sufficed. Wherever practical, the ponderous York boat replaced the more versatile canoe, because of its larger capacity and lower labour costs. Estimates suggest that by such means the transport manpower of the fur trade was reduced to as little as a third of its former level.[25]

All cuts probably were not achieved by the middle of the twenties but any remainder came quickly thereafter. Some of the large cadre of now unemployed were senior officers who returned to Britain or to homes in the Canadas whence several spoke out about the Company and its practices in later years.[26] However, the majority were from the lower ranks of the industry and tended to remain in fur country. Some Europeans with Native wives retired to the Red River settlement or other points in Rupert's Land. Most of those dismissed, however, were Natives or 'engagés' of mixed blood, of whom the former returned to the Native community. The latter most frequently took up a semi-sedentary existence, based on independent trade, part-time agriculture, and, around Superior, employment in the fisheries.[27] However, among such personnel were certain very capable and well-educated people of mixed background, who had once stood as equals among the wintering partners of the North West Company. Now they departed the industry and even the country, foreseeing enforced inferiority and lack of advancement in their future under the new order that would now prevail.[28]

While the new Hudson's Bay Company acted quickly and decisively in such unpopular areas to regain maximum profitability, it failed in its longer-term attack on the largest and most complex problem it faced. During previous years of avid competition, every imaginable extravagance had been condoned and practised in the trade. Now came the time to pay for these ecological follies. Not only were large areas of woodland and prairie trapped out of beaver and other commercial fur, but also much territory had been divested of large game in the drive for provisions.[29] The first promoted Native economic disorder, and the second forced band migration. Both were unsettling for the trade. Formal attempts to conserve what fur stocks remained and to regenerate the beaver populations, as well as those of large game, were initiated by the Company in the early twenties. A variety of schemes were tried. These included such things as the closing of posts in areas with good potential for recovery, the encouragement of hunting, and the search for fur in less ravaged areas. They also involved the re-education of Native trappers to discourage the taking of immature animals or pelts in inappropriate seasons and the refocusing of the harvest on less valuable species through a bounty payment system. However, such measures were unable to prevent the continued use of the very efficient steel trap, which since 1797 had been a growing factor in over-harvesting.

After twenty years, the results of these attempts at conservation were not encouraging. Many employees had failed to support such practices, which did not serve their own narrow financial goals.[30] These schemes also had found little sympathy among U.S. free-traders poaching in border territories, although the American Fur Company complied in boundary zones east of the Red River to Superior.[31] In addition, most former engagés, now turned independent traders but embittered by earlier Company treatment, ignored the potential of such policies. More important, among the much larger aboriginal population many had refused or had been unable for economic reasons to cooperate in the restorative process. Ironically, just when some glimmer of success might have appeared, the central aim of these efforts was shattered by a whim. About 1843 the silk hat replaced the beaver in fashionable Europe. While this popular shift brought immediate despair to the investor, the later result was a more balanced relationship between fur production and the breeding stock on which that depended.[32]

Shifts in Trade and Orientation

All these changes, short-term and long, brought their own particular impact to the region north and west of Lake Superior. By 1825 the active posts had declined from thirty to about twenty-four, with most closures within the limits of the Lake Superior watershed. Those that remained outside the boundaries of Rupert's Land actually were beyond the Company's chartered domain. However, their transferred operation from the old North West interests was condoned by Britain, for want of any other territorial administrative agency.[33]

On paper such forts at Sault Ste Marie and Fort William remained district centres for the reorganized Company in what was termed the Southern Department. However, the discontinuance of the route west from Montreal to the Lakehead and over the portage to Rainy River marked the beginning of their decline. By mid-century the once elaborate facility beside the Kam had been reduced to a blockhouse and main building with residential quarters. Conditions were not much better on the St Marys River. In fact, the Chief Factor for the Lake Superior region was now resident at Michipicoten River, on the base of the prime water link with Company centres on James Bay. His rank rarely denoted much seniority and his responsibilities would later pass, with this role, to Red Rock House. Within his purview fell such other old posts and outposts as Batchawana, Agawa, Pic River, and Lake Nipigon, where fur activity had been long reduced to low levels.[34] The once stormy fur trade era on Superior was now winding down, eventually to reach near cessation by the end of the century.

Across the arctic watershed, things were quite different, for a vibrant fur trade was to continue here for generations. Some thirteen former posts had been retained in this area after amalgamation. Several of these as far west as Fort Frances were made more substantial. Like several others, including Rat Portage (now Kenora) west of the arctic divide, Fort Frances was now linked westward via the Winnipeg and Red to an ultimate headquarters on Hudson Bay at York Factory. Yet most were tributary eastward to the two forts on James Bay. Michipicoten in the context was unique in its ties by the Missinaibi and Moose rivers to Moose Factory. Otherwise the newly prevalent transport system was focused on Fort Albany, often via the Kenogamis tributaries, Henley House, and Marten Falls, or the Albany itself from as far west as Osnaburgh House and Cat Lake.[35] In addition, a series of marine railways carried York boats from Lake St Joseph into Lac Seul and ultimately down the English River, when westward access was required.[36]

This reoriented northern access and egress by 1830 suited Company interests most satisfactorily, but it severely dampened any immediate possibility of further development around Lake Superior. Once part of the link between the Canadas and the West, this lake, along with its littoral and back-shore, was now the southern frontier of a northerly directed trade.[37] This territory was viewed principally either as a buffer against the incursions of independent traders or as a territorial fringe over which the Hudson's Bay Company exercised only loose control.

The Rise of Commercial Fishing

Relief from these economic doldrums and isolated conditions around Superior would come only gradually before 1850, but the Hudson's Bay Company would aid inadvertently in this recovery. The dip-net fishery at the St Marys Rapids, long used by the Natives, had been a source of provisions in the western fur trade for decades before 1800.[38] About this date commercial shipments of salted whitefish commenced from here to Detroit by way of a vibrantly active fishing station on Mackinaw Island.[39] By 1809 this resource of the Rapids had attracted the attention of the growing American Fur Company. However, this firm did not seriously contemplate Superior's huge fishery potential until 1823 and did not pursue it until 1834. Then within two years, they had numerous fishing stations in operation on the western end of the lake. However, the exposed south shore was to remain unused except at the sheltered base of the Keweenaw Peninsula and around Whitefish Bay. To serve the firm's mixed needs of fish and fur, the *John Jacob Astor* was launched on Superior in 1835 and soon was followed by two other sailing vessels.[40] Before the close of the decade, this commercial venture was supplying annually about 8,000 barrels of salted fish (1.6 million pounds) to Detroit. Indeed, the American Fur Company had been forced to increase its U.S. marketing area substantially. Unfortunately, this last endeavour was not yet profitable when the whole company was forced into bankruptcy and ultimate liquidation by an American financial panic in the early forties.[41]

On the Canadian side of the lake the posts of the North West Company had traditionally harvested fish for provisions. So had most posts westward on Rainy Lake and the Lake of the Woods as well as north on Lac Seul and Lake St Joseph.[42] While this domestic activity continued under the Hudson's Bay Company, the latter began to contemplate possible commercial pursuit in 1835, being cognizant of the recent move of its American rival. The following year it arranged construction of the schooner *Whitefish* near Sault Ste Marie to serve this new endeavour on Lake Superior and in 1837 contracted to market its total catch through a Cleveland wholesale house.[43] By 1839 Fort William alone was managing seventeen fishing stations, and the collective shipment by way of Sault Ste Marie was about 2,000 barrels. As in the case of the American Fur Company, the principal species taken were whitefish and lake trout, but others from pickerel to pike and perch were included. The harvest was pursued in all seasons, through the use of spears, hooks and gill, seine and pound nets, as well as weirs. It concentrated on inshore areas, often at river mouths, and the heaviest catches were in the spring and autumn spawning seasons.

After the failure of its Cleveland marketer in 1843, the Company experimented briefly with both Upper Canadian and Montreal outlets but settled on Detroit as the most profitable. In future years it also came to accommodate the local mining demands that appeared after 1845. At mid-century its posts about Lake Superior were all heavily involved in what had become a most lucrative branch of their operation. They were working as many as thirty-five seasonal stations each year for as much as 10,000 barrels of salted catch.[44] Much more important was the fact that this market re-established a peripheral connection with the rest of the Great Lakes region.

Such contact with the lower lakes was not a one-way affair. As early as 1800, the independent general trader with lower-lakes ties had become a fixture on both sides of the St Marys River. As fur resources began to decline, here as at Mackinac, these businessmen dealt more and more in such products as maple sugar, but particularly in fish.[45] While first concentrating on the rich resources of the local rapids, small stations were beginning to appear on the American side of Superior by the early twenties. Such operations were manned by fishermen, sometimes up from the lower lakes or from Huron, but often by local Natives or persons of mixed blood.[46] Employing the now traditional mackinaw sailing skiff, such men were usually under contract to one of the Sault Ste Marie traders. To the intense annoyance of the Hudson's Bay Company, similar small operations, usually backed by Americans from Cleveland or Detroit, began to appear on Superior's northeast shore a decade later. Indeed, the Company used every possible means, from the destruction of facilities and nets to open harassment of stations, to rid themselves of these territorial invaders' and 'fish pirates.'[47]

After 1835, southern corporate operations began hauling schooners over the American portage at Sault Ste Marie to transport supplies of salt, barrels, staves, and personnel up to their stations and to accommodate the pickled product down from such locations about Superior's littoral. These firms were not averse to a bit of trading, which cannot have increased their popularity with fur interests on either side of the border. However, their attention was directed principally along the American shore and their history was generally brief.[48] These activities were paralleled on northeastern Superior by a gradual increase in small operators, despite their continuing abuse by Hudson's Bay personnel. In the middle decade of the century thousands of additional barrels of salt fish from commercial fishermen on both shores passed yearly through the hands of St Marys' merchants. Some sixty mackinaw boats under the control of these traders now served the Canadian shore. However, their registration had to be American, since all fish leaving the Superior basin were otherwise subject to a U.S. tariff on their arrival at Detroit.[49]

Initial Mineral Drives

It was the mineral potential around the upper lakes, not the rich fisheries, that attracted most early public interest in the 1840s. Superior's copper deposits, including some at Mamainse, had been used by the Natives for centuries. Indeed, these had been mined unprofitably at both Ontonigan and Michipicoten before about 1770, first by La Ronde, then Alexander Henry (the Senior) in conjunction with other trade endeavours above Sault Ste Marie.[50] But only in 1842 did Douglas Houghton, new state geologist, begin to publicize the mining possibilities of Michigan's upper peninsula. In a world short of copper to sheath its marine fleets, the effect was electrifying. In 1843 the growing rush caused the American government to cancel all Native title there. By May 1845 demand was so intense that the registration of mining locations was stopped, at least temporarily, for want of available properties.[51] In the interim the U.S. side at the St Marys Rapids had become a very busy place. Its marine railway had witnessed the transfer of several schooners and two steamers to Superior to serve this bustling new industry, while its trans-shipment functions had grown accordingly.[52]

On the Canadian shore matters developed more modestly and slowly. Here, Captain T.G. Anderson and later Captain George Ironside, from the headquarters of the Northern Superintendency on the Manitoulin Island, tried to administer the Native population at Sault Ste Marie. In vague fashion, they also were responsible for those about Superior and west to the Mississippi.[53] No other resident officials complicated this colonial back-country of fur traders and fishermen. However, with the boisterous influx of miners to the new American copper claims, the colonial government felt the need to appoint Joseph Wilson as customs officer at Sault Ste Marie in 1843.[54] So little did authorities know of this regional outpost that in 1844 they were forced to seek local information on its exact location, its population, and its economic base.[55] Their interest was generated in part by the published musings of Sir William Logan, newly appointed geologist for the Canadas. About this time, he speculated that similar mineral potential as found in upper Michigan might exist on the British side of Superior.[56] Officials even may have been aware that this same idea had occurred to many an American copper prospector who had paid these shores a surreptitious visit.[57]

That the copper rush would spread eventually to the north and east sides of the lake was inevitable. However, government administration was quite unprepared for its occurrence. When John Prince and his associates made the first formal application to explore and develop minerals on Lake Superior in 1845, the sole mining policy in the Canadas reserved gold and silver to the Crown.[58] Logan had yet to be directed to explore and report on the region. Joseph Wilson, now official factotum at Sault Ste Marie, was still without instructions for the control of what now must have been a considerable population of prospectors moving quietly about these Canadian shores.[59]

This was the first real colonial experience with frontier mining operations and their regulation. Authorities were forced to proceed by trial and error, sometimes borrowing American ideas on policy, but more often relying on Cornish precedent. All the Executive Council was prepared to grant Prince was a free licence to explore at his own expense. If the year-end report on his findings was satisfactorily detailed, he might expect some preference in location and terms of occupation 'when related matters [had been] determined.'[60] Much to Prince's chagrin, since he believed he had been granted a monopoly, twenty-nine similar licences were sanctioned on Superior over the ensuing weeks of 1845, principally to persons from Montreal, Toronto, and Hamilton. (Americans at this time being debarred from participation).[61] But the required reports on what were most often purely speculative ventures were slow to appear. Where these summaries were not forthcoming by December 12, 1845 licence renewals for claims were refused.[62]

Nevertheless, the next spring a deluge of new and renewed applications for exploration permits generated 100 licences for the shores of Lake Superior.[63] That April the Executive Council decided that all final claims would be a mile on each side, but quickly increased these dimensions to two miles of lake front by five in depth, or 6,400 acres, to satisfy an outcry among prominent applicants.[64] By June, Logan and a team that included John McNaughton P.L.S. had arrived at the U.S. border on western Superior. They worked meticulously eastward, exploring and surveying each desired location, until they completed their task on Huron in September.[65] Subsequently, those holding registered locations were permitted to work their claims. Such persons were given the option of paying four shillings an acre immediately or a £150 deposit and the balance in five annual instalments with interest. The Executive also determined in October that similar size, price, and options for payment would apply to all new locations on submission of a satisfactory report and approval of a suitable survey.[66]

By year's end, large business associations had already acquired the most valuable properties, often through quiet purchase from speculative holders. On Lake Superior, British North American Mining held the Prince Location southwest of Thunder Bay and the Upper Canadian Mining Company owned a scattering of three claims. The Canadian Mining Company had four properties along the north shore, and the Montreal Mining Company held eighteen, grouped principally near Nipigon and about Mamainse[67] (see Map 1.1). However, only the Quebec–Lake Superior Mining Association, which held a total of ten, mostly around Mica Bay and on Michipicoten Island, ever utilized its properties above Sault Ste Marie.

This alliance of Toronto business interests and Quebec lumber money began work near Mica Bay on Superior's east shore in 1848. Here they had established a lavish facility the previous year, including expensive accommodations, numerous mine buildings, elaborate machinery, and water-powered dressing equipment. But while the Quebec interests were speculative in their intent, hoping for a quick and profitable resale to possible British interests, those from Toronto (principally the Macdonell brothers) were intent on serious mining. After a tumultuous altercation and split among the investors, the Quebec group shifted operations to Michipicoten Island in 1850. Three years later, unable to find a buyer and deeply in debt, this former Quebec–Lake Superior Mining Association became as dormant as its fellow companies had been and, for the most part, would remain.[68]

Since the earliest American discoveries, the press had kept the public well informed on these mining developments about the upper lakes. Yet popular interest and involvement among Canadians never touched the heights achieved in the United States by mid-century. This milder reaction was related in part to a continuing colonial preoccupation with more southerly agricultural settlement and to the relative lack of accumulated risk capital in the Canadas. However, it also was coloured strongly by suspicions of shady governmental and bureaucratic management. On this latter count, the *Globe* and politically allied newspapers came loudly and frequently to demand an inquiry into procedures for locating and licensing mining claims.[69] Indeed, the apparent ineptness of government in its approach to mineral policy, combined with claims of Tory patronage, were the basis of a full review of mining administration during a session of the House in 1847.[70] This review was widely reported and certainly revealed how much had been acquired by how few and for how little. No properties at that date had engendered more than the initial deposit of £150 and many were to be abandoned before even that amount was collected. Eventually this down payment would appear for forty-five Superior locations,[71] but the official fight to obtain subsequent instalments would continue into the next decade. Far fewer than this number of properties would ever see patents.

In the end, the entire issue of such frontier mining came to nothing. A largely agrarian public saw it as a badly managed, unsavoury, and expensive experiment in colonial expansion by politically well-connected, urban capitalists that was doomed without a firm, farm base. The time had not yet come when development of the northern resources of Canada West would collect much public support.

Native Roles and Reactions

In this historically colourful drama to 1850, the Native population had been cast in the unfortunate role of community in the middle. Over many decades, contact with the fur trade and with its European goods had substantially altered and homogenized their material culture.[72] Utilization of Native skills in pursuit of fur irrevocably had distorted former aboriginal ways of life and the environment on which these were based.[73] The opening decades of the nineteenth century witnessed the height of the regional fur frontier, subsequently destabilizing basic Native existence about the upper lakes and in the Shield country to the west.[74] By mid-century, around Superior's shores, the introduction of commercial fishing and mining exacerbated Native problems, while also inciting the first stubborn reaction to colonial 'theft' of traditional lands and resources.

Documentary details of Native life, even within the Lake Superior portion of what later would become northwestern Ontario, are scant in these years leading up to 1850. The inhabitants were largely Ojibway, who for about two hundred years had been expanding slowly westward from the Sault Ste Marie area, like a wedge between the northern Cree and the Sioux. They had been squeezing the latter inexorably south and west onto the grassland, but not without resistance.[75] However, as late as 1848 Native numbers and conditions about Superior could be only loosely estimated. Firm information in the hands of the Northern Superintendent of Indian Affairs on the Manitoulin Island, George Ironside, extended only as far as Sault Ste Marie. Neither the scattered missionaries nor the traders beyond the St Marys Rapids seem to have shown much interest in such matters beyond their most immediate flock.[76]

Published material makes it clear that the decline of the fur harvest over much of the region was first felt at a variety of dates between the late eighteenth and early nineteenth centuries. More important, the impact varied in intensity from area to area. As on upper Huron, the Native economy around Sault Ste Marie by 1800 was increasingly linked to salt fish and maple sugar destined for lower-lake markets.[77] North of the Montreal River, where the maple component of the forest disappeared, dependance on the demands of the Hudson's Bay Company for fish assumed increasing importance, particularly after that firm entered commercial harvesting.[78] The same shift to such heavier reliance applied to the bands of the north shore of the lake, where beaver had sometimes been in short supply as early as 1804.[79] On both shores, the expansion of commercial fishing up from the lower lakes often had the unfortunate effect of converting the Native further to seasonal wage dependancy. West of Superior, in Lake of the Woods and Rainy River country, decline in beaver was steep by 1800, and two decades later the trading economy of local bands was rescued only through Company promotion of a regulated muskrat harvest.[80] Yet elsewhere north and west of the arctic divide, fur resources remained demonstrably promising and traders could comfortably press for continuing emphasis on the trap line and on high-quality fur.

Such varied conditions in Native life, as a result of the rapacious fur-trade activity before the early twenties, were also mirrored in the realm of food. All bands in the region remained dependent on some balance of hunting, fishing, and gathering. Only in the Rainy River Valley and on the islands of the Lake of the Woods is there real evidence of simple agriculture. Here, wild rice joined the usual array of wild fruits in the diet, supplemented by the harvest from rich local fishing grounds.[81] Yet prior intense hunting for fur-trade provisions had greatly depleted the large game resources. This situation was so severe that in 1822 sufficient leather was not available for simple moccasins and snowshoe thongs.[82] Here, as on the east and probably the north side of Lake Superior, the dearth of large game and the depletion of small fur-bearers had resulted, before the twenties, in a heavy reliance on rabbits for both food and clothing. This dependence would deepen in most areas, despite the cyclical nature of the rabbit supply. As in the Rainy River Valley, however, this most unreliable source of fat and protein was balanced by an increasing emphasis on the seasonal catch of fish at traditional river mouths and at the old dip-net fishery of the St Marys Rapids.[83] Only in the northern and western interior – often across the arctic divide where large animals like the woodland caribou and sometimes moose still prevailed – were former balances of hunting, fishing, and gathering still to be found.

The first comprehensive assessment of Native circumstances along the Canadian side of Superior was made at the request of the colonial government in the summer of 1849.[84] It was carried out by canoe and was a preparatory step to a possible treaty. The work was undertaken by T.G. Anderson, an experienced Indian officer, and Alexander Vidal, a surveyor knowledgeable about the area. It revealed the existence of almost 1600 people, exclusive of those living west and north of the arctic divide. The largest single concentration was in several locations around Lake Nipigon and along the river of the same name. Other notable groups were to be found in the country around Pic River and Michipicoten, Fort William, and Sault Ste Marie.[85]

At the latter two centres these figures ignore considerable colonies of people of mixed blood. These were composed largely of former engagés who had remained or removed there with their families on their release from the fur trade after amalgamation of the two major companies in the twenties. Precise numbers about Fort William remain unknown, but were small. Around the St Marys Rapids they made up a significant share of the resident population in a revised count of 1852. This tally, including 400 Natives and a 'small white population,' totalled some 850 persons.[86]

Between these two places there can have been little comparison. Fort William was composed of a dilapidated post farm and sparse métis clearings.

Across the river was the new Jesuit mission to a small and yet seasonally migratory population. Both remained beyond the fringe of the colonial world, enmeshed in the economic torpor of Hudson's Bay Company control.[87] In contrast, Sault Ste Marie was adjunct to a vibrant American scene and obliquely involved in its lively, Detroit-oriented commerce.

Community development on the British side at Sault Ste Marie had begun in the twenties. By that date the engagé migration had been joined by a substantial aboriginal population in the wake of the formal delineation of the international boundary through the upper lake country. To remain under the British flag, Shingwauk, a respected leader and veteran of the War of 1812, brought the majority of those Natives previously resident on the Michigan shore across the St Marys River at that time. By 1830, some forty homes, numerous wigwams, as well as the residences and buildings of fur traders dotted the Canadian front at the Rapids.[88]

Under the now finalized boundary definition, however, the recently established British military station and centre for northern Native administration on Drummond Island passed in 1828 to the United States. Its functions, including the administration of all northern aboriginals to the base of Georgian Bay, were removed to Penetanguishene. Not until the mid-thirties would the combined efforts of Lieutenant-Governor Colborne and Bishop Strachan help to redress this inadequate situation in native supervision. Aided by a new imperial policy for aboriginal peoples, they relocated the Northern Indian Superintendency to the Manitoulin Island. Here they created a huge Native refuge dedicated to religious teaching and secular education as well as training in agriculture and practical arts.[89]

Meanwhile, in 1833, on Shingwauk's request, Colborne had authorized the Society for the Propagation of Christian Knowledge to establish a school and mission at the St Marys Rapids. They had arranged the rental of certain buildings from a local trader there and the erection of a necessary residence to these ends. Unfortunately, his successor, Sir Francis Bond Head, summarily cancelled support to this project in 1836, under his plan to concentrate most of the willing colonial Natives on the Manitoulin.[90] Nevertheless, the Society continued its work here, with some help from Sir George Arthur, after Bond Head's short but disastrous term in office. However, after strong cajoling around the end of the decade, the Chief moved his people experimentally to the Manitoulin Establishment, intrigued by the opportunities of education and agricultural training there.

Dissatisfied with what they found, Shingwauk and his people returned quietly to Sault Ste Marie a year or two later, resettling twelve miles below the Rapids at Garden River where the soil was excellent.[91] With the help of both government and missionaries, the Chief resumed his drives here for the education and agricultural conversion of his people, but at a distance from the culturally erosive white world of Sault Ste Marie.

But by early in the next decade, the largest concerns of this perceptive elderly leader refocused on the more immediate protection of territorial rights and resources. These concerns no doubt arose out of early American mining activity and its effect on the land claims of his brethren of upper Michigan.[92] As early as 1843, he organized a petition to the governor general, protesting the actions of Charles Ermatinger. The latter had occupied considerable Native property at the Rapids over two decades earlier and built his large stone house without Native permission or payment.[93] After mid-decade Shingwauk, with his son-in-law, Chief Nebanaigooching of the Batchawana band, became the most active opponent of any property usurpation by whites. In 1846 Mr Alex Vidal, who had been ordered by the Crown Lands Office to survey a town plot at Sault Ste Marie, reported a very heated session with these two about his rights to do so. They argued that the colonial government had not yet purchased the site from their people. He also reported that these chiefs were even more upset about government licences for mining purposes on land that was still untreatied Native domain. Vidal's reply was an ill-conceived threat of official reaction, if they, their bands, or any other Natives were to offer the miners resistance.[94]

Inaction, ineptitude, and ignorance were to characterize the colonial government's approach over the next two years on this issue of land rights and treaties. Meanwhile, Shingwauk and his fellow chiefs from around Lake Superior became more and more agitated about mining activity. At Garden River, a Mr Bristol was even able to obtain a licence that covered all the homes and agricultural acreage, as well as the forested land of the aboriginal community, and to have his activities there upheld by the Executive Council.[95] Elsewhere, Peau de Chat at Fort William and lesser chiefs elsewhere grew disturbed. They added their weight to Native concerns over timber removal, surface stripping, irresponsible use of fire, and other destructive practices. Their displeasure prompted another round of petitions to the governor general in 1845–6. In all these matters, the chiefs asked simply for initiation of the normal procedures of the treaty process and subsequent regulation of individual actions. No official move was made until August 1848.

At that time a Native Council was called at Sault Ste Marie. It was composed of an array of chiefs from as far away as the Lakehead; Bishop Strachan and prominent mission leaders; members from the mining fraternity, including Allan Macdonell; and local interests. In his report to the Executive Council, Anderson, who had chaired this gathering, bluntly stated that the territorial claims of the Natives were sound and their assertions about damage to their land and other resources, caused by mining, were correct. As a result, he recommended a treaty 'to cover all unceded land north and west of the Midland, Newcastle, Home and Simcoe districts as far as the Ottawa ... and following the height of land; the Hon'ble Hudson's Bay Company boundary Line north of Lakes Huron and Superior; until it strikes the frontier line between Lac La Pluie and the Mouth of the Pigeon River.'[96]

Unfortunately, aboriginal patience was running out. Government action was not immediately forthcoming, and by that October Shingwauk, Nebanaigooching, and others had found an unexpected source of support in Allan Macdonell.[97] This son of a well-connected family, a lawyer and former sheriff of the Gore District was an early supporter of northern development. He was also an embittered stockholder in the Quebec-Lake Superior Mining Association and just the visionary colleague the Native leaders needed. Over the winter of 1848, he developed their legal case and set in motion a ninety-nine-year lease of a railway right of way about the Canadian side of the St Marys Rapids. It guaranteed substantial royalties to the Natives on the future ore and mine freight to be carried here. The following summer, he leased, on the same terms, several of the east Superior mining locations. On these he guaranteed quick development, a Native share of profits and both employment and training in mining for the aboriginals who held this territory. He further arranged a potential treaty claim to cover all other mineral locations in this area as part of their reserves. These were to be worked by their own labour and for their own gain in the decades to come.

Macdonell and his allies kept these developments firmly under wraps until the next autumn of 1849. In the meantime the Executive Council created a Royal Commission, made up of Anderson and Vidal, to examine the case further, to discuss treaty arrangements with the Natives, and to carry out their previously mentioned fact-finding tour about Superior. Meanwhile, Macdonell and the chiefs were in Montreal on a carefully orchestrated publicity tour. Press from as far away as London England's *Illustrated London News* reported on their case and on their interview with the governor general, Lord Elgin. Indeed, to the acute embarrassment of colonial officials, Macdonell and the chiefs were briefly the toast of the town, even having their picture painted by Krieghoff.[98]

However, while this visit greatly increased public awareness of Native concerns, it had little impact on the Royal Commission, which met with the Natives and Macdonell that fall. Vidal, on hearing the secret arrangements entered into with Macdonell for the railway and mining leases, determined the latter was simply an adventurer and left the session. Anderson remained to hear Macdonell out but refused to entertain his plans or opinions. To be fair, as an employee of the colonial administration, he could hardly have reacted otherwise. However, both actions inadvertently promoted the violent events that followed.

These events involved the forceful closure of the Quebec-Lake Superior mine at Mica Bay in late November. This was accomplished dramatically by Macdonell, his brother, and a friend, in the company of Shingwauk, Nebanaigooching, and a substantial company of Natives. Colonial reaction was immediate. The initial press reporting was righteously heroic. It depicted aboriginal savages overcome by an intrepid military expedition up by ship from the new railhead at Collingwood and the ringleaders being transported south for trial in Toronto. In the new year of 1850 the press coverage was more balanced, informed, and questioning. It introduced issues of aboriginal rights and questions of Native welfare/protection, and by the attempts by the Macdonells to justify their actions and to clarify Native goals.

In the interim, administrative wheels were turning. In the spring of 1850, negotiations were started by W.B. Robinson for those treaties that bear his name and that cover both upper Lakes watersheds. The treaties' Native financial arrangements and protective clauses for holders of mining claims were much less acceptable than Macdonell had led his followers to expect, and gained only grudging acceptance from the chiefs and their religious mentors, like Father Frémont at Fort William.[99] Yet, the terms were much more liberal than the colonial public would have condoned a few months earlier, before its eyes had been opened and its social conscience stung. Of the resultant treaties concluded in the fall of 1850, one covered Huron's northern watershed and Superior to Batchawana Bay because of the Batchawana band's use of the St Marys River fishery. Another covered the balance of Superior's drainage.

The Stage Is Set

Thus, at mid-century, the initial regional thrust towards colonial occupation and administration came to an uneasy and inconclusive end. The long reign of the fur trade was winding down, its traditional east–west, then tentative north–south axis now slowly being replaced by distant thrusts from south of Lake Huron. Indeed, the Hudson's Bay Company's major interests would now begin retreating quietly northward to beyond the arctic divide, where it would retain importance in the Native economy for decades. Commercial fishing had now supplanted the fur trade as the major economic activity in the region. However, the area still was isolated by distance from southern markets and by transport problems associated with the St Marys Rapids. Meanwhile the Montreal and Upper Canadian rush into copper ventures had proved a short-lived financial disaster, the result of geological ignorance, regulatory inexperience, and official mismanagement. Nevertheless, this second resource-oriented thrust from the Canadian colonial world into Superior territory had attracted to this unknown land its first real public attention. Spirited Native reaction to the miners' activities brought the region more colonial press coverage than the mineral rush itself. It also forced the government to acknowledge its responsibilities to the aboriginals and at the same time to assume Crown title to the huge upper-lakes watershed. However, this new interest in the north had yet to translate itself into firm action by an Upper Canadian society still busily colonizing the last broad acreage in southern townships and only beginning to look at the potential beyond.

2

New Assessments, New Beginnings, 1850–1890

At mid-century the last good land about the Canadian lower lakes and along the St Lawrence was passing rapidly within farm fences. With continuing heavy immigration from the British Isles, the population of Upper Canada came to exceed that of Lower Canada. Each was climbing towards a million, largely rural, people who were as yet looking only tentatively beyond old southern cores. Ontario's lumbering frontier was concentrated on the timber of the upper Ottawa and was soon to move into the pineries of the middle lakes and Georgian Bay. Its commercial fishing community too was contemplating a further northern thrust, into territory where Canadian mineral drives were diminishing rapidly. Its rural youth was turning a speculative eye toward soil pockets in the Shield, but glancing as well at the similarly unproven American grasslands as a possible home for their generation of colonial farmers. Political leaders, along with the financial communities of Montreal and Toronto, were becoming intrigued, not only with possible resources on the Shield, but also with the national potential of the prairie and mountains beyond. Finally, among these larger schemes was the age-old international vision of a direct westward route from Europe to Cathay.[1] Almost in passing, this complex of speculations would contribute to the advancement of the future northwestern Ontario, the region that came to be viewed as the land between a new west and an old east.

To the Brink of Apparent Success, 1850–1870

The first two decades after mid-century witnessed a number of changes in Upper Canada that greatly influenced trends and developments in what was to become its northwestern member.[2] Externally, this was the era of the rising expansionist cause. That movement was most strongly rooted in Toronto and focused on its aggressive Board of Trade. The first manifestation of this new expansionism was a colonial fight to wrestle from the Hudson's Bay Company its control of western British North American and its influence about the upper lakes.[3] Undoubtedly the single most important contribution to these ends was the Hon. Joseph Cauchon's dramatic Crown Lands Report for 1856, published the next year. This report captured public attention and excited popular imagination with its vision of a northern and northwestern colonial destiny.[4]

In addition, the period saw declining rates of immigration and trends towards youthful emigration to the United States with the passage of the American Homestead Act in 1860.[5] Economically, the period witnessed the uneasy era of Reciprocity, the peculiar trade conditions of the American Civil War, and the buoyant times of the late sixties and early seventies. It was also an era both of growing interest in northern resources and of rising agrarian excitement kindled by both the Hind and Palliser expeditions to the vast plains beyond.[6] Finally, the period was marked by the arrival of Canadian steam on Superior, as well as a related mail service, linking the Red River colony to central Canada by way of Fort William and Collingwood.[7] Yet, surprisingly, before 1870 very few developmental footprints of expansionism were made in prairie mud. Instead, they were left tentatively on the rocky landscape of upper-lake watersheds and principally about Superior's littoral (see Map 2.1*).

The Company in Further Retreat

Given the chartered boundaries of Rupert's Land were defined as the arctic divide, the Hudson's Bay Company can never have regarded its inherited territory in the upper-lakes country as more than a transient and peripheral possession.[8] This realization, as well as the already decimated fur conditions the Company found, probably contributed to the lack of interest it displayed in this region after 1821. However, to hold such lands in doubt or to give up control voluntarily remained two different issues.[9] This was particularly true inasmuch as certain early boundary arguments between the United States and Britain could be interpreted to suggest that the Company held some proprietary rights west of Fort William. Such hopes were dashed with the resolution of the modern Minnesota-Ontario border in 1842.[10] Subsequently, the Company sat by as the Robinson treaties claimed the Superior and Huron basins in the name of the Crown. It continued passive while the colonial government moved to survey these lands selectively for settlement, to offer more mining locations,

* Map 2.1 will stand as the general reference for the first major section of this essay, supplemented by more specific maps as necessary. The same pattern of general, followed by specific, maps will be used throughout the book.

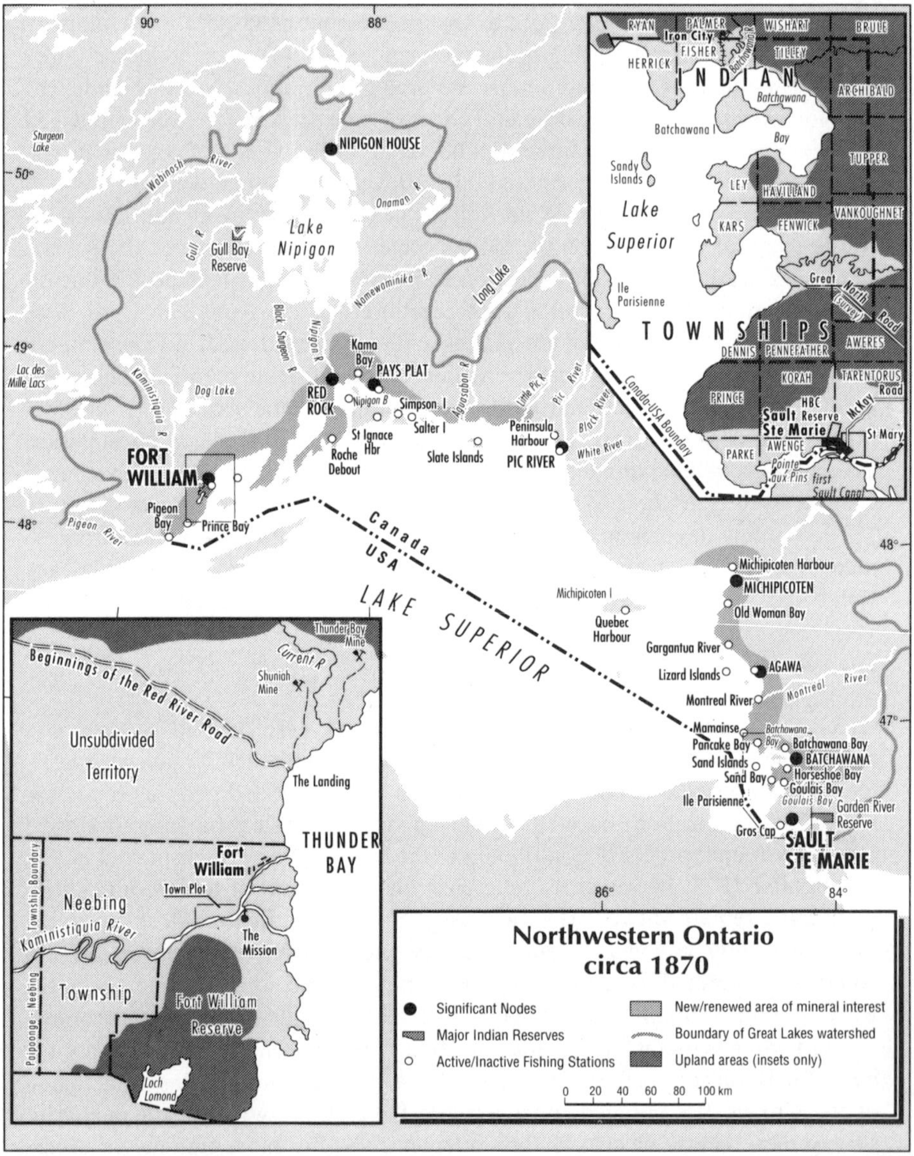
Northwestern Ontario circa 1870
Significant Nodes
Major Indian Reserves
Active/Inactive Fishing Stations
New/renewed area of mineral interest
Boundary of Great Lakes watershed
Upland areas (insets only)
0 20 40 60 80 100 km
90°
88°
86°
84°
50°
49°
48°
47°
Sturgeon Lake
Lac des Mille Lacs
Wabinosh River
Gull R
Gull Bay Reserve
Lake Nipigon
NIPIGON HOUSE
Onaman R
Namewaminika R
Long Lake
Black Sturgeon R
Nipigon R
Kama Bay
PAYS PLAT
RED ROCK
Nipigon B
Simpson I
Salter I
St Ignace Hbr
Roche Debout
Slate Islands
Aguasabon R
Little Pic R
Pic River
Black River
White River
Peninsula Harbour
PIC RIVER
Dog Lake
Kaministiquia R
FORT WILLIAM
Pigeon Bay
Prince Bay
Pigeon River
Canada
USA
LAKE SUPERIOR
Michipicoten I
Quebec Harbour
Michipicoten Harbour
MICHIPICOTEN
Old Woman Bay
Gargantua River
Lizard Islands
AGAWA
Montreal River
Montreal River
Mamainse
Batchawana Bay
Pancake Bay
Batchawana Bay
BATCHAWANA
Sand Islands
Horseshoe Bay
Sand Bay
Goulais Bay
Goulais Bay
Ile Parisienne
Garden River Reserve
Gros Cap
SAULT STE MARIE
RYAN
PALMER
WISHART
BRULE
Iron City
FISHER
HERRICK
Batchawana R
TILLEY
INDIAN
Batchawana
ARCHIBALD
Batchawana I
Bay
Sandy Islands
TUPPER
LEY
HAVILLAND
Lake Superior
KARS
FENWICK
VANKOUGHNET
Great North Road (survey)
Ile Parisienne
TOWNSHIPS
DENNIS
PENNEFATHER
AWERES
Canada-USA Boundary
KORAH
TARENTORUS Road
PRINCE
HBC Reserve
McKay
Sault Ste Marie
St Mary
PARKE
AWENGE
Pointe aux Pins
First Sault Canal
Thunder Bay Mine
Beginnings of the Red River Road
Current R
Shuniah Mine
Unsubdivided Territory
The Landing
THUNDER BAY
Fort William
Town Plot
Township Boundary
Neebing
Kaministiquia River
The Mission
Township
Fort William Reserve
Paipoonge - Neebing
Loch Lomond

MAP 2.1

prepare timber berths, and tender fishing grounds along the Lake Superior shores. In this era, the continuing presence of the Hudson's Bay Company was actually a blessing to the Native economy, by providing stability, and to the logistical success of the early surveyors, miners, and fishermen who relied on the Company for supplies. To retain colonial good will as well as to foster its own ends, the Company even took on the distribution of the annual payment of Native annuities here after 1850.[11]

However, the Company was rightly loath to lose its financial investment in posts and in the land around these sites.[12] As a result, the Company entered on a protracted series of negotiations with, first, the colonial and, later, the provincial government about its establishments and area entitlements.

In response to a request from Governor George Simpson in 1842, the Executive Council of the Canadas refused to honour a Lower Canadian precedent concerning the protection of posts and suitable reserves around them.[13] Matters about Superior then languished until 1847, by which time the Company's management of Native people was under considerable attack by interest groups and other individuals in England and the Canadas. Despite the fact that neither the colonial nor imperial administration was willing to take action on the issue, there was a growing distaste for the Company's suzerainty over aboriginal territory.[14] This no doubt spurred an offer from Simpson to pay the costs of a government surveyor to lay out a set of desired properties about upper Huron and Superior.[15] (Later correspondence reveals, save for a 1,200-acre agreement at Sault Ste Marie, that these generally were conceived as 2-by-5-mile blocks.) These holdings it seems the Company requested immediately and at no charge, either on the basis of traditional occupancy or as a pre-emptive right at the time of surrounding subdivision and settlement.[16] However, the Executive Council took umbrage at this demand. In 1856 a mollified Simpson was still awaiting the expected patents, even after agreeing two years previously to pay for the desired real estate.[17]

That December, 1856, the *Globe* uncovered the affair. Being an expansionist organ now dedicated to the removal of the Hudson's Bay Company from the path of northwestern development, the *Globe* gave the matter wide and disparaging publicity. Along with the rest of the radical press, it immediately dismissed any Company claim to legal jurisdiction and demanded no more than modest recompense be given for posts and improvements.[18] The investigation went on over the ensuing months to ferret out the facts. These revealed that the promised reserves had grown over the years to eight posts and 46,000 acres about Superior.[19] This was the case even after the dismissal of an escalated request for inclusion of a rich agricultural area, 10 miles by 12 miles, behind Fort William.[20] For such reserves the proposed payment was calculated to be about one cent an acre. Public opinion finally led to official withdrawal from any firm promise to the Company beyond the retention of its posts and surrounding improvements. Save for a brief revival around 1870,[21] no more interest was taken until 1880–1. At that time, previous slim allowances of 50 and 68 acres negotiated for Fort William and Sault Ste Marie were grudgingly honoured, and up to 200-acre blocks were offered at each of Agawa, Michipicoten, Pic River, Pays Plat, and probably Red Rock (Nipigon).[22]

The Company's role within Superior drainage was much diminished in other ways by 1870, when even the much more important Rupert's Land was lost to its closed control. While Fort William would remain open until 1881, the old post at Sault Ste Marie would close its doors in 1863.[23] Taking advantage of available steamer service after the opening of the American Sault Canal a decade earlier, the supply line for the upper-lake posts was reoriented to Montreal.[24] This shift considerably reduced the importance of Michipicoten and its former James Bay connection. Indeed, its quasi-administrative function was now moved to Red Rock. Most posts along the lake now faced ever-increasing rivalry from private traders, who were no longer occasional visitors by schooner but land-based neighbours. This annoying development, which fostered a much-increased alcohol problem among the Natives, the tiny cadre of colonial officials in the region found hard to police.[25] The Company's withdrawal from commercial fishing in the mid-sixties, along with the above developments, very considerably reduced the profitability of these centres.[26] Nevertheless, some would last until the turn of the century or later, sustained, not only by Native trade, but partially by white needs in semi-isolated parts of the region.

A Land of Hidden Promise

Despite experience gained during the recent mining rush, popular colonial knowledge of the northern resource base remained thin in the early fifties. Articles in the colonial press, often emanating from the *Globe* and extolling northern expansionism, were more notable for their imaginative rhetoric than for their factual basis.[27] Even a report by a House Committee in 1853 revealed surprising official ignorance. It also reflected the very circumscribed level of knowledge among those with past northern experience.[28] However, none of the regional fur fraternity were asked to contribute what might have proved more cogent and balanced information to this document. This was probably because of territorial tension between the Canadas and the Company.

As the official need for information increased, more competent observers were chosen to visit the region. However, all held a long-standing colonial belief that effective exploitation of any other resource must depend on the proven existence of an agricultural base. About Superior they observed little to convince them that the necessary soil resources existed except in widely separated areas. Yet their observations of the gardens at various fur posts suggested none of the serious climatic problems they may have anticipated.

W.B. Robinson, speaking generally of Canadian Superior in September of 1850, described it as 'notoriously barren and sterile,' attractive only to transient miners.[29] His views were supported subsequently by T.W. Keating, on completion of a coasting reconnaissance of the shore from Sault Ste Marie to Fort William.[30] His companion, J.W. Bridgland, P.L.S., concurred. However, like Robinson, both spoke warmly of the agricultural potential of substantial acreages at both ends of their journey and of the possible dependent growth of fishing as well as mining along the coast between.[31] In these opinions they agreed with the earlier pronouncements of William Logan of the Geological Survey and of Louis Agissiz.[32] Logan, however, went on to evaluate disparagingly the forest cover. This he described as fit only for firewood and pit-props in general, being usually short of hardwoods and pine,[33] a general opinion in which the others may have joined.

In the face of such generally unenthusiastic assessments of soil for farming and of the quality of other resources in the Superior territory, government interest shifted to the lands north of Lake Huron. In June 1855, A.P. Salter was ordered to commence an exploratory survey west from the area of the French River to Sault Ste Marie and was able subsequently to report considerable tracts of good land and timber along his route.[34] The next season, under much tighter instructions, he was ordered to lay out a line at a considerable distance inland from Lake Huron. It was to run due west from the mouth of the Sturgeon River on Lake Nipissing to Batchawana Bay on Lake Superior. At 18-mile intervals he was to survey exploratory lines due south to the lake and north for 30 miles. With the assistance of three other surveyors, his task was completed early in 1857.[35] Salter's report this time was much less positive about most of the huge area examined. However, he noted very fine soils in the valley lowlands back from both Batchawana and Goulais bays as well as some pine and considerable stands of excellent hardwood on surrounding uplands.[36] Indeed, his findings here helped confirm a very positive private report, in the hands of the Commissioner of Crown Lands, from a prospector who had made the same local discoveries a little earlier.[37]

Such news was most welcome to a government being pressed for northern colonial action and reform of its resource policies there. Both the officials and the press were quick to discover that all Superior surveys to date had been limited to conditions proximal to the shoreline.[38] Perhaps in the interior were to be found other fertile valleys and rich timbered uplands. If so, they could generate numerous rural settlements with which to support the steady development of coastal fishing and mining activity.[39] Yet, for the moment, government leaders were prepared only to speculate on these possibilities, their exploratory energies being shifted to a more westerly venture.

This venture related to the contest between a Canadian drive for western dominion and Hudson's Bay Company attempts for continued control over Rupert's land. The real issue centred on legal rights to and countering agricultural opinions about western British North America. However, a subordinate government concern was the uncertain existence of a viable all-Canadian route to this western domain and the possible value of resources for agricultural settlement and other exploitive activity along its course.[40]

The route to be assessed was that one formerly used by the North West Company from Fort William to Fort Frances, then via the Rainy River and the Lake of the Woods to Fort Gary. Instructions were issued to the principals of the expedition in the early summer of 1857, just before their northwestward departure. A former Company employee, George Gladman, was the first espoused leader of the expedition. Science professor H.Y. Hind of Trinity College, Toronto, was assigned the initial duty of exploring and describing the natural resources along this corridor across the Shield.[41] (On these matters he reported after the first season. Later he became heavily committed to more westerly interests and assumed the leadership role.) In his initial evaluations he was aided and later abetted by the ever-practical S.J. Dawson. His principal orders were to assess the practicability of road construction over this often arduous route. While Captain John Palliser, leader of the parallel British expedition to the west, was to claim that no such road was possible, Dawson's more positive view would later prove correct.[42]

The voluminous information on resources produced by Dawson and Hind can be dealt with here only in a brief and combined summary.[43] Behind Thunder Bay in the Dog Lake area and west, they observed the basic elements along the southern fringe of the forest we today commonly call the taiga: birch and poplar, spruce, jackpine and balsam, cedar and tamarack, punctuated by muskeg and bog, and with only the occasional pine of any size. From the base of Lac des Mille Lacs, their descriptions came to include more and more large red and white pine, often in considerable groves, but the gradual addition of southern hardwood elements. However, amid this rich, if varied, cover their comments admitted to much burned and fire-fallen timber. Some of this probably dated back to negligence among the employees of the fur trade over many decades earlier. Only patches of lowland acreage near Lac des Mille Lacs attracted their agricultural attention before they reached 'the open and beautiful but indescribably barren and desolate region of Rainy Lake.'

As at Fort William, at Fort Frances both were able to confirm from the post farm the potential of these northwestern environs for the production of most cereals, roots, small fruits, and clover and hay for livestock. Along the Rainy River each praised the quality of land and the nature of the timber. However, suspicions were raised concerning bogginess in the back-country, and comments underlined the sporadic but destructive effects of fire.

Professor Hind estimated that an area exceeding 260,000 acres was of farmable quality here, extending back from the river as much as 18 miles. The hardwood and softwood complex, described with its substantial pine component, was that of the northern Great Lakes Forest of modern classification rather than the transition to taiga that lay farther north. Neither Hind nor Dawson made much comment about any real colonial potential on the margins or on the islands of the Lake of the Woods. Both however were impressed with the amount of commercial pine they observed in this area, which along its southern and western margins penetrated almost to the prairie park belt. Such positive views, by 1859, were attested to by other prominent and experienced travellers to the area. Among these were William Gibbard, sometime fishery officer, and William Kennedy, a retired fur trade employee. Both these men carried the mail over this route about this time in connection with a first attempt to link the Red River community more closely to the Canadas.[44]

With the completion of this encouraging traverse of the southern Shield by Hind and Dawson, Crown Lands again could turn its attention to the Superior basin. In the spring of 1860 it ordered Thomas Herrick, P.L.S., to run the previously considered line about 20 miles back of the lake shore from Sault Ste Marie to the area behind Thunder Bay. He was also to search on either side of this line for a possible roadway. However, his main assignment was to glean a general picture of the resources and settlement potential across this huge inland territory.[45]

Unfortunately the results of his arduous endeavours were generally much less encouraging than those just achieved to the west of Superior. True, Herrick discovered the northern finger of rich Great Lakes hardwoods and associated pine that stretched over the inland country far beyond the Montreal River in Algoma. But from there, his descriptions were of the poplar/birch/coniferous mix of the taiga, then of no commercial value. This scrubby forest of unimpressive tree-size was concentrated in valley environs and on lower slopes of otherwise barren rock knobs. Herrick was clearly impressed at the size, hydraulic possibilities, and navigable capacity of the numerous rivers he crossed and explored. However, west of the plateau backing Michipicoten he found the country very broken, fire-torn, and disappointing. After the Batchawana/Goulais area, his next reference to soil fertility was along the muddy Pic. Further comments on agricultural potential were rare, until he entered the Nipigon country. Here Herrick spoke carefully of soils about the lake and with more enthusiasm about those in the broad Nipigon River valley. Similarly he was quick to note good pockets to the west behind Black Bay and to spot the productive bright red loams extending from there towards the Kaministiquia Valley.[46]

Desultory exploration north and east of Superior continued in the early sixties. As if government could not believe the uninviting news it continued to receive about the potential for agricultural colonization here, work quickened again after 1865. The following summer, crews were at work between the Michipicoten River and Salter's Line, running a traverse even farther inland than before, with 5-mile offsets at regular intervals to aid in the renewed search for farmable soils and commercial timber.[47] A year later work was started on a more detailed study of the lowland east of Nipigon, and an exploratory tie was ordered from the Michipicoten River to a tributary of the Ottawa.[48] Similarly, in 1870, an ambitious reconnaissance, also about 20 miles inland from Herrick's Lines, was being pursued west from lake Nipigon and east of its shores to the Michipicoten. It ran along what was referred to as the seventh astronomically determined baseline.[49]

This latter work was coordinated with certain mineral exploration and mapping endeavours under Dr Robert Bell of the Geological Survey. In 1869, Bell had completed a general study of the Nipigon watershed. The following year, with the experienced help of two local prospectors, he made a similar initial reconnoitre of all major watersheds of the Superior north shore.[50] His work, combined with these other endeavours, provided a reasonable picture of the relation of Superior drainage to that of the Albany and English river systems across the height of land. These collective accomplishments were highly praised in the *Globe*, which interpreted them as bold strokes towards both the determination of Canada's future northern boundary and one possible route for a Pacific railway.[51] However, Bell's reports tended to confirm the views of limited agricultural potential previously expressed by Herrick. His work contributed little of immediate note to official goals or public hopes of broadened colonial settlement on which to base sound resource development. Indeed, this vast back-country, from Nipigon to Batchawana, would remain largely undervalued until the pulp and paper industry changed the perception of its forest resources a half-century later.

Initial Surveys and Settlements

Following upon these processes of exploration and general evaluation were other initiatives towards the colonization of those few areas where initial assessments had indicated suitable soil. At the St Marys Rapids, the long-standing population of squatter farmers were the first to witness the result. In 1846 a town plot had been ordered on the river-front, accommodating the establishment of the Hudson's Bay Company as well as its reserve at the rear.[52] The surveyor had also established property boundaries to best suit all other agricultural small-holdings, here and along the front of an adjacent square-mile block. Many of the latter were still in the hands of old engagé families. The intent had been to assure firm title to the inhabitants then faced with the uncertain property prospects of the mining boom.[53] However, because of the issue of Native claims, patenting had to be delayed until after the Robinson treaties were executed in 1850. Even then local people were slow to seek ownership. Finally, in 1856, the remaining unpurchased properties of the plot and lots of 50 to 200 acres in the neighbouring block (later the Township of St Mary) were advertised for sale. The auction held that fall was not a major success; a number of squatter farms remained unpaid for in full and some purchases in the plot were mere speculations.[54] However, the results were mildly encouraging to those responsible and to the budding commercial community gradually evolving here.

More important, both public and government interest in the Superior country were now to become better focused and more aggressively spirited. This change came with the Hon. Joseph Cauchon's visionary prognostication about northern and western colonial expansion. In and around Sault Ste Marie resultant changes came quickly. Between the spring of 1858 and the fall of the next year, the new townships of Awenge, Aweres, Korah, and Tarentorus were surveyed. They were advertised for sale in September 1859, at 70 cents an acre cash or $1.00 over five annual instalments.[55] Again the results were not startling but were satisfactory, leading in 1860 to the survey of the remaining lowland townships of Parke and Prince.[56] These subdivisions of land were among the first to recognize that northern soils and draining conditions were often unusually varied, even at the local level. Duplicating an American idea, they were based on the 160-acre quarter section. This provided the aspiring colonial settler with a larger than traditional area on which 'to find a farm.'[57]

Crown Lands was not the only agency at this time to begin thinking more aggressively about the marketing of northern areas under its control. In 1859, two years after the discovery of the rich valley land of the country behind Batchawana and Goulais Bay, the Indian Branch opened its first township there. Eventually, by 1866, it placed a total of thirteen, in part or entirety, on the market in this area as well as the town plot of Asaquosh (now Goulais River). These townships copied in their subdivision the sectional survey system introduced about Sault Ste Marie.[58]

At Thunder Bay survey activity came about the same time but was much less extensive. Only two townships in this fertile lowland were created for agricultural purposes before 1870. These were Neebing and Paipoonge, both laid out by Herrick in 1859. Neebing included a town plot on the Kaministiquia, which would later be settled as West Fort William. Interestingly enough, these surveys were composed of the standard 100-acre lot, reminiscent of southern Ontario. They were therefore unusual among those to be laid out in the provincial northwest.[59] As elsewhere, these lands were put immediately on the market to encourage a hoped-for influx of agricultural settlers.

This anticipated flood did not materialize for a number of reasons. First, the expansionist dreams of persons like Cauchon had been premised on a continuing high rate of immigration as well as a natural increase in the Upper Canadian population base. Instead, after 1860, the immigrant stream went increasingly to the United States. The attraction of free land in the American midwest also syphoned off many colonial youths who might otherwise have sought a rural northern home.

Equally important factors in the failure to attract settlers were the disastrous, officially sponsored experiments at Shield fringe settlement in southeastern Ontario during the earlier fifties. These ill-conceived endeavours made many later farm progeny dubious about a colonial start in any similar environ north of the Great Lakes. They too quietly migrated in gradually increasing numbers to the American midwest frontier. Of those who were determined to settle in the provincial north, many were of the second generation from colonial farms in the maturing counties of Simcoe, Grey, and Bruce.[60] These areas were now served by frequent steamers up the lakes. However, along the route north from Collingwood and Owen Sound were new agricultural townships close to markets and former southern homes. These were open, opening, or would soon open on the Manitoulin Island, along Huron's north shore (particularly about the Bruce and Wellington Mines) and at St Joseph Island.[61] Such developments cut deeply into what otherwise might have been a solid colonial flow to Sault Ste Marie and beyond.

These low immigration levels into the Lake Superior region must have had a disheartening impact on hopeful officialdom. Land prices in all three Superior pockets were soon dropped to 50 cents an acre cash, plus interest for instalment payment. As the degree to which the over-supply of the whole upper lakes land market came to be appreciated, prices fell further to 20 cents around mid-decade, at which levels they remained so as to be competitive with the prices around upper Lake Huron.[62]

At Thunder Bay large acreages of the finest land in both Neebing and Paipoonge were acquired quickly by local and distant speculators, for reasons not often allied to farming.[63] This situation first became problematic in the late sixties when a mineral rush caused these townships and much surrounding territory to be inundated with claims. While such mining activity, as well as seasonal work on a tentative government road to Red River, generated much summer employment, no more than three families in these townships were committed to farming.[64] Indeed, in these years, most food, even hay, was being imported from Collingwood, Sarnia, and Detroit at very high prices.[65] The only self-sufficient elements then around the Lakehead were the numerous employees of the Hudson's Bay Company, with the engagé colonists and the Natives settled up-river at the Jesuit mission. These groups had the produce of gardens and farms to augment their seasonal consumption of fish and game.

About Sault Ste Marie, colonial settlement developed more slowly but achieved much more significance, because of markets at American mines and the closer proximity to outside markets. Even in the mid-forties when a government presence was first established and regular mail was initiated, Thompson's Royal Mail Line proudly advertised delivery from Toronto to Sault Ste Marie in sixty hours. More frequent American boats to Detroit now gave even better access, although, beginning with the opening of the railhead at Collingwood in 1855, Canadian ties to southern centres became very competitive.[66]

During the mining rush of the late forties on both sides of Superior, Sault Ste Marie's location made it a focus of vagrancy and violence. The inhabitants therefore petitioned in 1848 to be made a part of the southern District of Simcoe, under the municipal title of Penrith. (They also banded together to form a rifle brigade in an attempt to deal with their immediate problem.)[67] However, after deliberation, the Executive Council delayed its decision until after the Robinson treaties, when this distant community was instead added to the judicial responsibilities of the former Western District.

Here matters rested until renewed law-and-order problems in 1856 brought a small number of military pensioners to the community as special constables.[68] However, this force was withdrawn in two years on the appointment of a stipendary magistrate. Finally, in 1860, Sault Ste Marie was proclaimed the administrative seat of the enormous Algoma District, extending from the French to the Pigeon River. It thereby acquired all the related officials as well as the promise of a future jail and courthouse.[69] However, the community then amounted to little more than a scattered settlement of 400 to 600 persons, the number depending on one's definition of its spatial extent. It also had a steamer landing below the St Marys Rapids, with regular service from Collingwood. A hotel and three stores, including the Hudson's Bay Company, completed its current functions, while several hydraulic sites were about to be surveyed for potential future development.[70]

In the same year, in response to cross-border trade problems, which hampered commerce, this former customs centre became the focus of a tariff-free area covering all of Canadian Superior and most of upper Huron. However, a later assessment would suggest that this move had little if any beneficial impact on either the regional economy or local commercial prospects.[71] Development over the next decade was marked by the closure of the Hudson's Bay post by 1864 and the completion of the District buildings in 1868. A domestic sawmill opened briefly at the Rapids only to close its doors in 1869.[72] The government's Great North Road came to link the area to that of the Bruce Mines. But while the MacKay branch led into Sault Ste Marie, the continuation from Garden River to Goulais Bay remained unopened.[73] The community added 400 or more people to its population during the sixties, in spite of regional economic malaise, and was designated an incorporated village in 1871.[74] Nevertheless, it remained much smaller and less attractive to visitors than its bustling sister in Michigan, host to the first canal to Superior since 1855.[75]

By 1860 most of the small adjoining Township of St Mary was in private hands, sometimes those of village residents who wanted a garden, pasture or woodlot. Although considerable portions of adjacent Tarentorus remained under mining locations, parts of it and about half the farmable lowlands in Korah and Awenge were quickly taken up.[76] The rocky upland that characterized the northern parts of the former two and most of Awenge remained unclaimed. The same was true of a very considerable band of swamp and fire-torn land back from the river in Awenge. While numerous settlers cleared land for farms here after the opening of the sixties,[77] a considerable acreage remained undeveloped. The same came to be true in the lowland portion of Prince and the better-drained interior of Parke, which townships were withheld from the market until 1862. This tendency, which continued to build with later purchases across the area, was not principally the result of land speculation. As elsewhere about the upper lakes, it was the work of potential colonists from southern farms, who acquired their lots at the low going price some years before they came north to utilize them.[78] As a result, of the over 80,000 acres in these townships, of which under a half had agricultural potential, about 21,000 acres were in private hands by the end of the decade. Yet the Census of 1871 admits that only 8,200 acres were actually farm occupied. These last were home to about 375 rural residents, who by that time had improved over one-fifth of their acreage for farming. However, considerably more acreage consisted of pasture in either cut-over or semi-wooded state. These settlers began to open out their road allowances, founded their first rural school district, and, after the creation of the Algoma Agricultural Society, held their first fair in 1869.[79] However modest these statistics and accomplishments may seem, they made this soil pocket, with its focal village, the most progressive area in what was now northwestern Ontario.

Contrasts in Forest and Fishery

Interest in the forest resources of Superior's littoral was to remain very limited until after 1870. The then-accessible species were of no particular value beyond the limited domestic demands of the region. Huge sources of quality pine for commercial lumber, as well as a broader range of saleable hardwoods and other softwoods for U.S. and Canadian markets, were only now being explored about upper Lake Huron and Georgian Bay.[80]

In the forties and fifties, certain friction developed over timber resources on the Canadian shore of the St Marys River, which local American interests were then prone to borrow. On one occasion a colonial official, while investigating the cutting and surreptitious rafting of numerous Canadian white pine logs to the U.S. side, was arrested and jailed in Michigan.[81] This incident caused a mild diplomatic flurry but otherwise came to nothing. Such trespasses, in combination with Canadian deprivations over past decades, left little lumber for a considerable distance back from the river. Indeed, as early as 1853 in the environs of the Hudson's Bay post, not even good firewood was said to be available within any proximity.[82] In the same decade, local Natives cut and sold several hundred cords annually to fill this void, from their reserve at Garden River. To this they added some 6,000 pieces of long wood for sale to passing steamers.[83] Similar wooding stations at points up-river on both shores also served this growing need.[84] With the increasing appearance of steam vessels on the opening of the American canal, much more steamer wood was marketed from wharves along routes to Duluth and Thunder Bay.

Even on upper Huron no forest administration was in place until the creation of the Huron-Superior Timber Agency in 1856, with its headquarters at Barrie.[85] While prominent persons like the Hon. Casamir Gzowski were then quick to take large timber limits as far north as Michipicoten, they were equally quick to cancel.[86] What is more, there is very little later evidence of applications on Superior for Crown timber licences in the period.[87] The major exception was for the rich pine and hardwood stands behind the Batchawana/Goulais shores. These may have seen some lumbering trespass prior even to their survey. Applications for limits on these retreatied lands and for available mill sites were common after 1860. However, during the early years of attempted sale for agricultural settlement, few if any were accepted.[88] Willingness to entertain tenders came only in early 1869, after which the Native administration received several offers of substantial bonuses per square mile, in addition to rent and dues.[89] A few agreements were then entered upon, but no development of mill sites or cutting of timber had begun by the close of 1870.[90] At that date mild interest in the even more inaccessible forests of the Indian Reserve at Fort William was just beginning.[91]

In comparison, commercial fishing, which already had an increasing presence on Lake Superior, sporadically made more energetic, if little more conclusive, advances. While hampered to some degree on the American side by canal construction, the dip-net fishery in the St Marys Rapids continued to be productive over the period, both for aboriginals and others.[92] At least as early as the mid-fifties some of the catch from here was not salted but sold fresh, iced, and rushed south by steamer to Detroit or even Cleveland.[93]

In addition, a considerable fleet of mackinaw boats under American registry, but often with Canadian crews, continued to man the seasonal fishing stations on proximal parts of Superior.[94] These inshore gill-net fisheries, tributary to Sault Ste Marie, stretched as far as the Batchawana or Goulais areas and such neighbouring islands as Parisienne and Sandy. Served regularly by the supply schooners of their Sault Ste Marie–based operators, these stations, like those on the American shore, were a main source of salt fish through the fifties.[95] This rapidly increasing harvest also continued to move by boat to American lower-lake ports. There it joined a rising proportion of such Great Lakes production being shipped to the southern states as food for slaves.[96] To this latter flow all Hudson's Bay posts as far as Thunder Bay and American fishing stations at such distant western points as the Apostle Islands and Isle Royale contributed modestly. Sometimes shipments from the latter now included numerous barrels of siskwit, which were valued particularly for their oil.[97]

Before the passage of the Fisheries Act of 1857, all harvesting practices on Canadian Superior were free of government interference. The legislation of that year was both regulatory and conservational in its thrust. It set up a licensing system of defined fishing grounds and specified closed seasons, as well as minimum mesh sizes for nets.[98] This legislation was put into effect immediately on the lower and middle lakes. However, such regulation was not scheduled to apply on Superior until the following year and in fact was not enforced there until the end of the decade. Much of this delay resulted from under-staffing, only a single administrative officer being appointed for all upper-lakes waters. It was also due to Inspector Gibbard's almost total ignorance of the Superior fisheries when he was ordered in 1859 to visit and list all stations, their state of occupation and production.[99]

His report and other allied materials reveal conditions on the lake to have been changing at that time. The Hudson's Bay Company still controlled many seining grounds and, like most older occupants of the fisheries, dealt exclusively with American forwarders through Sault Ste Marie. Yet other commercial fishing stations had now been added to the north of Batchawana Bay. These included Copper Mine Harbour (Mamainse area), Montreal River, Gargantua, and the Lizards and Quebec Harbour on Michipicoten Island. However, it would appear that over-fishing at Ile Parisienne, Goulais Bay, and Batchawana by former station operators had caused them to be temporarily abandoned.[100] Equally as interesting, now that the railway was well established at Collingwood, those fishing from that port had expanded onto upper Huron and were beginning to explore for additional stations on the north shore of Superior. Such rising interest also included migrants from far-away lakes Ontario and Erie, where quality catches of whitefish and trout were now in decline.[101]

These distant drives for either new or additional grounds were strongly allied, as of 1858, to the market opportunities offered by the first Canadian steamers to ply Lake Superior from the developing ports of Georgian Bay. These called normally at Michipicoten, Red Rock, and Thunder Bay as well as at other points on request. While serving the periodic needs of the fur trade and the varied requirements of prospectors and other visitors, these vessels willingly transported the numerous barrels of salt fish that awaited them at such stops.[102] The new outlying fishing stations, from which such supplies often came, still had little more than temporary buildings and were irregularly scattered east from the Minnesota boundary. They remained noticeably absent on the coast between the Pic and Michipicoten rivers.

At this point the swelling industry was dealt two severe economic blows, causing the previously mentioned withdrawal of the Hudson's Bay Company from commercial fishing. The first was related to the American Civil War, the commercial effects of which lasted well beyond its end at mid-decade. At the beginning of the war in 1861, the huge demand for salt fish in the southern states evaporated and over-production caused prices to plummet. In addition, the demand for fresh fish in northern U.S. urban centres, decreased. The result was the sudden disappearance of an estimated 70 per cent of the fish market. Several American traders in Sault Ste Marie suspended or severely curtailed their fishing activities. Grave unemployment hit the Superior fishery, with mackinaw boats and outfits lying idle, and many available grounds went unleased and stations unoccupied for a number of years.[103]

The second blow to the fishing industry was related to the lack of coastal service on Superior. For political and financial reasons, no Canadian steamer plied the Superior coastal route in either 1862 or the year following. Instead, the mail service west was assumed by an American carrier out of Detroit. The vessel supplied by the Ward Line for this task deviated only to Fort William from its normal route to and from Duluth. While this lack of coastal service also must have irritated both fur traders and mining interests, it contributed quickly to the closure of many remote fishing locations. Other locations, not served by regular steam access, continued to be worked by small parties of men who were visited twice a year by schooners bringing barrel staves and salt and departing with the catch.[104] The reintroduction of coastal service in 1864 by the Collingwood Royal Mail Line's steamer *Algoma* did not result in substantially increased fishing for some years. This was environmentally fortunate, because these waters were without regulatory policing for most of a decade after the death of the previous fisheries overseer in 1862.

Existing records suggest some of the earliest recovery was along the eastern reaches of the lake near the market at Sault Ste Marie. Before mid-decade surveyors in the Batchawana Bay area were noting good harvests again from stations at Sand and Horseshoe bays.[105] Slightly later, large operations returned to the mouth of the Chippewa River, where Gibbard had reported serious deprivations only a few years before.[106] A similar resumption of activity occurred on Ile Parisienne about the same time.[107] Such developments may have been aimed at the domestic market in Canada, although that small market was probably well supplied from closer fisheries. However, a considerable American outlet seems equally unlikely. As late as 1868, the few statistics available on fishing show a modest 167 persons employed. Only about 1,500 barrels were marketed from sources on northwestern Lake Huron, at Sault Ste Marie, and along the Canadian side of Superior.[108]

Recovery and active expansion in these waters, however, followed quickly. By late summer 1869, the operation on Ile Parisienne had grown to very large size and had converted to the fresh fish trade. This station was served from a coaling and icing focus at Pointe aux Pins by the first steam fish tug on the Canadian shore.[109] Figures for 1870 give the commercial catch for this northwestern region as an encouraging 6,179 barrels. Nevertheless, a very heavy duty now levied by the Americans continued to cripple the Canadian salt fish trade. As a result, total employment rose only to a little more than 200 men. Unfortunately, the names of the stations occupied or yet to be reoccupied are ignored in the slim records of the year.[110]

Shifts in Mining

After the Quebec-Lake Superior Mining Association's episode at Mica Bay, mining enthusiasm about Canadian Superior had flagged, leaving a shoreline punctuated by 288,000 acres of inactive and largely unpatented locations.[111] These big blocks were to remain dormant for most of the next two decades and largely in the hands of the four major consortia that had assembled them in the forties. Through the fifties, both inaction on the mining front and the indolence of these large firms were frequent targets for an exasperated *Globe*. To support its allegations, the paper often drew unhappy parallels between the inactivity here and the rapid advances in mining and supportive infrastructure on the American shore.[112]

These attacks on government were not without justification. Little enough was being done officially either to encourage renewed activity among old companies or to promote new investment. However, the *Globe* continued to ignore the fact that the copper deposits on the Canadian shore were not comparable with the American ones. It also refused to admit that the colonial north in these years was simply not a popular place for foreign mining capital, either American or British.

When criticizing the mining companies the *Globe* and its provincial cohort of radical weeklies were on much firmer ground. The continuing existence of the companies was more a reflection of political connections than financial viability or energetic leadership. Whatever their initial aims, these firms were now speculative enterprises patiently awaiting developments in the region that would enhance the value of their unworked holdings.[113] Only the huge Montreal Mining Company was ever moved to obtain a clear title to its possessions. In 1856, it agreed to pay a paltry sum per acre for patents on 110,000 of an original 130,500-acre holding. The Quebec-Lake Superior Mining Association's disastrous early endeavours forced an assignment of all but 12,800 of its 70,000-acre assets. These it was never able to redeem and it sought belated title to the remainder only in 1865. Neither the Upper Canadian Mining Company, with 32,000 acres, nor Canadian Mining, with 44,800, were moved to patent anything, despite weak government threats of dispossession.[114] Resolution of this situation came with a small provincial tax on such property in 1869. That move was sufficient to promote the sudden sale of all Montreal Mining claims along with the abandonment of most similar holdings by the other original firms.[115]

Nevertheless, desultory exploration, prospecting, and even mining marked the fifties along these shores. The focus of such activity moved away from copper and hinted at possible wealth in other metals. It was mildly encouraged by government recognition that the huge claims of the past were counterproductive. On Crown lands as of 1853, the prospector could acquire a $100 licence and during its two-year run could select a 400-acre claim. This could be patented after a suitable survey, payment of one dollar an acre, and proof of two years' active occupancy.[116]

Although the Indian Branch did not move exclusively to such 400-acre locations, it too was quick to favour both smaller units and immediate, active occupation. In 1852, the management of a now-tenuous Quebec–Lake Superior mining experiment on Michipicoten Island had discovered good iron deposits at the Gros Cap Reserve on the adjacent mainland.[117] These he undertook to develop the next season, and by autumn shipped the first ore for evaluation.[118] While he had the confidence of the Natives, neither his survey nor his financial arrangements with them was approved by government until 1855.[119] The following year marked the first mineral interest in similar deposits inland from Batchawana Bay. Although exploitive endeavours did not begin here immediately, most properties tendered for official approval were of 400 acres and sometimes even less.[120]

Attention at this time began to focus along the Superior north shore, particularly in the Lakehead area. Here silver and lead, long recognized as companions of copper in local ores, started to attract interest. In 1856, the first 400-acre locations were requested under prospector's licence and were ordered to be surveyed.[121] Ten of these were patented over the next three seasons. In 1859 numerous others were laid out when Thomas Herrick created the new townships of Neebing and Paipoonge.[122] The following year, such licences were replaced by a simple system of 400-acre grants at a dollar an acre, on proof of one year's work.[123]

With the sixties came a considerable increase in mineral activity. At the outbreak of the American Civil War, the demand for iron climbed rapidly. The deposits at the Gros Cap Reserve near Michipicoten Harbour, therefore, were put into firm production to augment much larger supplies from upper Michigan and Wisconsin.[124] In addition, the numerous magnetite-bearing blocks behind Batchawana came to the fore under the control of several Americans from New York, Boston, and Detroit.[125] These gentlemen were quick to establish their operations here, and were said to have lavished more than $100,000 on the project. In addition to their mining plant and accommodations, they completed a five-mile tramway to a 300-foot wharf at the mouth of the Batchawana River. They brought in as many as 300 Cornish miners and arranged a weekly steam communication to the U.S. side for the transport of ore. By 1865, three mines were reported here at 'Iron City.'[126] Although the Gros Cap deposits continued to be shipped for only two more years, mining at Batchawana survived until the immediate iron ran out in 1869.[127] By that time, a prospecting rush in the area had come to generate almost 4,500 paid-up and patented acres of locations in the surrounding retreatied townships and Crown holdings inland. Indeed, along the east coast of Superior as a whole, new acquisitions had climbed to a total of over 9,300 acres of iron and copper claims. To these could be added the 12,800 acres patented by the Quebec-Lake Superior Mining Association.[128]

During the sixties, government legislation grew more and more liberal and accommodating in a new drive to promote growth in the industry. At the outset, two issues were key to friction between officials and the mining community. The first was the traditional reserve of gold and silver to the Crown. The second was a matter of policy, which insisted that the public should share in any profits from the harvest of Crown resources. This philosophy of public benefit already had found application in recent licence fees for timber limits and fishing grounds.[129] Since the focus of interest at the Lakehead now had turned to silver, the reserve of silver and gold to the Crown was of considerable moment. A Select Committee of the House was struck to study the matter and led to the ultimate passage of the Gold Mining Act of 1864, which liberalized the rules governing precious metals. That enactment was clarified and extended in 1868, after a fact-finding visit to Thunder Bay by a party of legislators, and was reformed even further under the General Mining Act in the following year.[130]

Solution of the second issue followed a very similar course. The slowly growing mining community, with its increasing component of Americans and American capital, reacted violently in 1862 to a 2½ per cent royalty on all ore prepared for market.[131] To the Americans in particular, this policy of public share was both foreign and unacceptable. They held the royalty to be especially troubling in such financially risky endeavours and under the isolated conditions on the north shore of Superior. The industry remained unhappy even with a reduction in the royalty to $1.00 a ton by the legislation of 1864 and managed to have that charge eliminated the next year. However, the royalty clause was again inserted in the Gold and Silver Mining Act of 1868 and was not finally eradicated until 1869.[132] As a result, public coffers were not to enjoy royalty remuneration from this industry until 1891, but the province was to benefit from vibrant mining activity in the interim.[133]

Despite this wrangling and related uncertainty, prospecting and exploration for silver about the Lakehead continued. By the spring of 1862, government allowed lots in northern agricultural surveys to be acquired as mining locations. The first such block of 405 acres in Neebing was quickly taken up and was followed by a modest rush.[134] By that fall, silver locations were being carefully assessed, from the Nipigon area and the off-shore islands to the Thunder Bay back-country and the old Prince Location on Prince Bay near the Minnesota border. The U.S.-backed Wallbridge mine was in its initial stages and local residents had built a road and also sunk a shaft in the nearby Current River area. Several parties of Americans, often with their own mining engineers, had been summer visitors and some had acquired considerable quantities of north shore property.[135] Over the next two seasons exploration became intense. Many more locations were staked and tentative work reported at isolated sites from St Ignace Harbour west. By the fall of 1865, patented mining claims rose to cover more than 16,000 acres here.[136] An ecstatic *Globe*, reflecting on these as well as the iron developments on the east shore, speculated about a future coast 'fringed with mining villages' as the wealth of the Shield continued to unfold.[137] This now positive mood in the press was reinforced by the continuing growth of Superior's mining population the following year.

However, the real burst of silver activity at the Lakehead came in the same summer as Confederation. That season witnessed an escalated immigration of American miners and prospectors, due in part to a post-war dislocation in mining activity below the border. It resulted in the formation of several large tent camps near the mouth of the Current River.[138] In addition to American capital invested here, a Mr Wither and companions from Toronto commenced work on a local silver vein, and Montreal interests under a Mr Redpath were prepared to do the same.[139] Not only were some 6,000 more acres sold that year, but many older locations rapidly began to change speculative hands. By autumn, the *Lake Superior Mining Journal* was predicting that this area would prove the richest field for silver in the country.[140] Surprised by this sudden increase in interest and worried by the speculation that attended it, Crown Lands stopped all sales that fall in order to fully appraise the situation. Nevertheless, a total of nine owners, principally between the Kaministiquia and Current rivers, made plans to begin mining the following spring. A few even kept crews at preparatory work through the winter.[141]

When land sales were again started in the spring of 1868, a calmer and more balanced atmosphere prevailed. Yet prospecting and exploration continued along the north shore at a steady pace, adding another 20,000 acres of locations by December 1869.[142] The Shuniah and the Thunder Bay Mining companies now controlled the two major operations, previously in the hands of Wither and Redpath. The first was based on American money, the second on British, and each had at least one shaft down 60 feet or more. The Shuniah Mine was linked to the shoreline near a government wharf at The Landing. The Thunder Bay Mine had built a good dock of its own at the base of an access road to the east of the Current River. Each now had a large complement of men and had brought in the first simple shaft machinery. In addition, the Thunder Bay Company had set up a small water-powered stamp mill on the lower river.[143] Despite encouraging assay reports on their ore samples, after two busy seasons both suspended work and their quite extensive establishments stood temporarily deserted in 1870.[144]

Native Problems and Attempted Solutions

These, like decades to follow, were not easy times for the aboriginal population of the Superior watershed. They now found themselves increasingly involved with a colonial society very different from their own and were sometimes taken advantage of by its rough frontier elements. These were also trying times for those with direct responsibility for Native welfare. The philosophy behind the Robinson treaties of 1850 had been new to Canadian experience. These agreements were based on a plan to make the Natives more materially self-sufficient through the institution of annuities.[145] Into these funds all monies derived from the sale of land, mining locations, or other resources were to be deposited and the interest was to be shared annually among the appropriate populations.

The official view was that an arrangement of this type had to be achieved if the upper-lake watersheds were to be added formally to the Canadas and if their Native people were now to be more responsibly treated. Yet, since the peak of aboriginal concern in England during the thirties, Imperial public interest had dwindled.[146] Britain had gradually withdrawn much of its support from Native management and was moving to cancel even its financial commitment to the old tradition of annual gifts.[147] However, the bands of the Upper Lakes could not be left to eke out an uncertain living from their ravaged supply of game and peltry, sometimes augmented by sporadic wage employment.[148] Under the Robinson treaties colonial Upper Canada tacitly recognized a direct responsibility for the future welfare of these Native people.

The fundamental arrangements that these treaties established were not without critics, both aboriginal and white, at the time of their signing. However, even to missionaries like Father Frémont at Thunder Bay, this annuity proposal was preferable to current procedures on the American side of the lake. (There the bands were commonly required to seek new territory west of the Mississippi with little or no payment for what they left behind.)[149] Upper Canada, caught between shrinking Imperial funding and growing colonial responsibility, defended these agreements as joint means to territorial expansion and improved Native welfare. Unfortunately, this official view assumed that the then-current rush for mining lands would be followed by rapid patenting and development and would be to the lucrative advantage of the Natives.

This dream was quickly shattered by events already discussed. Until late in the next decade, only the limited infusion of Montreal Mining money helped bolster annuity capital. Periodic Native queries and complaints about the continuing small size of their annual payments, therefore, gained no satisfactory answer from embarrassed officials.[150] Meanwhile, the survey of the huge original Garden River Reserve was completed by J.S. Dennis in 1852. The following year, J.W. Bridgland completed another exceptionally large one (15 miles long and 10 miles deep) in the Goulais and Batchawana Bay area, a small tract required at Gros Cap near Michipicoten and a more substantial one at Thunder Bay.[151] Because of its extreme isolation up the west side of Lake Nipigon, the modest Gull Bay Reserve was ignored by this survey team of 1853. It was not laid out until after mineral prospecting invaded that area some years later.[152]

Only near Fort William was there any disagreement over the boundaries negotiated by Robinson in 1850. T.W. Keating, who was present at the Lakehead on both occasions, later wrote that 'when first gathered together [on his second visit] the Indians claimed an area 16 miles by 20 miles which was so far from the treaty that it could not be allowed.' Eventually these chiefs settled for a reserve roughly 5 miles by 6 on the south side of the Kaministiquia. It was very similar to that agreed to with Robinson, except that it now was extended to front on the lake.[153] However, Keating's suggestion that the band also be awarded an island as a fishing station was ignored. This was later to cause serious problems when commercial licences were introduced on the surrounding grounds.[154]

By Robinson's count, which he believed to be highly accurate for the Superior watershed, about 1,600 Natives lived between Garden River and Fort William. However, not all of these chose to reside on the reserves provided, preferring instead to retain their seasonally migratory ways. For example, some 385 who traded at Nipigon House, 148 at Pic River, and 269 at Michipicoten elected no such affiliation at this time. Indeed, some of these probably were not eligible for the annuity, since their lands lay north of the arctic divide.[155] There is evidence too of a small American influx to both Garden River and Fort William after the treaties. But except at these two missions and later on Lake Nipigon, there is nothing to suggest that many from migratory bands adopted reserve life over the next two decades.[156] Ironically, the very large reserve set aside about Batchawana and Goulais Bay in anticipation of such later influx was never to count more than 55 families. Most of these spent much of the year at the fishery also reserved for them at the St Marys Rapids. While the numbers at Gros Cap (Michipicoten Harbour area) remained even smaller, those around Fort William and at Garden River had begun to blossom even before 1860. Their growth reflected the strong encouragement of local missionaries for them to adopt a sedentary life of agriculture, which would also encompass education and religious instruction. Nevertheless, the economic conditions prevailing even on these centres led the Special Commission investigating Indian Affairs in Canada to report most critically in 1858.[157]

Probably in direct response to the Commission's widely critical comments of its colonial administration, the Indian Branch initiated a plan to increase the annuity levels under the Robinson Treaties. The next year it introduced a scheme to repossess specific resource-rich areas of the reserves about the Upper Lakes for a nominal payment and then to market these resources to the much greater advantage of the band funds. In July 1859, the Superintendent

General, the Hon. R.T. Pennefather, treatied back from the Natives of Batchawana and Goulais Bay their entire reserve. He also arranged to resume about three-quarters of the once huge Garden River block and some 5,000 acres from the rear of the Fort William Reserve.[158] During these negotiations, an agreement was reached whereby the Batchawana band would in future reside at Garden River, being promised adjacent lands to the west of the existing reserve. They also were to retain their fishing station at the Rapids. However, certain dissatisfied families were later allowed to return to certain small holdings in their former territory and to their mission church on Goulais Bay.[159]

The Branch now set out to sell or lease these resumed lands according to the second part of the plan. Given the rising tide of queries about mineral, agricultural, and forest resources by the late fifties, the Branch proceeded quickly and optimistically to prepare for the task. At Thunder Bay, these lands, being of fine agricultural quality, were surveyed as part of Neebing Township and placed on the market the following year.[160] In the Batchawana and Goulais Bay area subdivision of the aforementioned agricultural townships began immediately, although the latter would not enter the market until 1866. Behind the new Garden River Reserve, preparations were quickly initiated to tender this rugged upland area for its mineral potential and its forest resources.[161]

As in 1850, the material future of the Native communities on reserves around Superior looked bright in 1860, but again this view was to prove overly optimistic. As already mentioned, except in the St Marys lowland, no significant agricultural land purchase was to occur during the sixties. Here, as at the Lakehead where speculation/mining confused the picture, and in the Goulais/Batchawana area, land prices, once at seventy cents an acre, fell to fifty cents and finally to twenty cents before mid-decade. Little revenue was to be derived from such bargain-basement rates. In fact, among the numerous retreatied townships north of Sault Ste Marie, no sale of agricultural property was recorded by the end of the period. However, some new annuity income must have been generated by the speculation in agricultural lots and sale of mineral locations, known to have occurred in the retreatied portion of Neebing Township behind Thunder Bay. In addition, the tiny Gros Cap Reserve benefited from the sale of one square mile for mining purposes, and the iron claims inland from Batchawana (although not the active mines) were partially on property controlled for Native benefit as were the new copper patents behind Garden River. In contrast, very little money was to be contributed by timber licences on any of this repossessed acreage until about 1870. For the Natives and their administrators, as for everyone else working towards the ultimate development of northwestern Ontario, real progress at this date still seemed to lie just beyond their grasp.

The Rewards of Persistence, 1870–1890

In the grand context of the fledgling Dominion, the twenty years after Confederation were colourful, if not remarkable. They began with the Canadian takeover of Rupert's Land, the initial opening of prairie settlement, and the related Riel crisis. They were also marked by the completion of the then longest railway on earth. They closed with a nation of only four million still dreaming of a heavy flow of European immigrants in search of new homes west of the Shield.

The colony of Canada West had championed these dreams and drives. Ironically, the new province of Ontario now found strong need to counter Ottawa's measures to achieve these same ends. These measures it perceived as threatening the future of cherished territorial assumptions and of visionary northern plans. Hence, jurisdictional curbs by federal edict and boundary claims by Ottawa on behalf of a new Manitoba triggered a protective reaction.

On two other fronts the province was to remain stubbornly but ineffectively opposed to federal policy over the decades to come. First, Ottawa's philosophy of free prairie land, espoused in 1870, was copied from the highly successful American legislation of a decade earlier. It was aimed at attracting Canadian youth as well as a tide of immigration to the western grasslands. Like the U.S. move, this one stood in direct conflict with the strategy of Ontario's own Free Grant Act of 1868. This provincial legislation was intended to promote settlement of Ontario's own colonial youth in its own north and to combine that with supportive immigration, as in prior decades. While southern Ontario pressed hard, it was never truly successful in this regard. Second, while Ontario's goals in resource development ran parallel to those of the new Dominion, Ottawa's slow implementation and weak enforcement of its policy was viewed unfavourably by Ontario. The focus of growing irritation on the part of the province was the ineffective federal protection of Ontario's forest economy and its inadequate conservation of Great Lakes fisheries against American deprivation. Yet these issues would bring stormy provincial response only later.

Territorial Alienation, Dispute, and Exploration

During the two decades of 1870–90, the large tract north and west of Superior along the eastern fringe of the former Rupert's Land witnessed fundamental changes in administrative control. The first of these changes involved treaty negotiations for this area west and north of the Robinson Treaty boundary. Here territorial frictions with the Natives already had a considerable history.

During his reconnaissance of the late fifties, S.J. Dawson had encountered the Natives' defensive mood. He tried to assure Native leaders that his explorations and the peaceful passage of the expedition did not compromise their title to the land.[162] He was thereafter to write appreciatively of these bands: 'They are very different from the timid and cringing creatures who are now the sole representatives of the Indian Race in the back settlements of Canada.'[163]

Others a decade or more later were to find reason to agree with this assessment. Such persons included the first squatter on the Rainy River, who was quietly ejected from his clearing, and early railway surveyors in the same valley whose every move the Natives intimidatingly watched. A number of skilled steamboat builders at Fort Frances were frightened into leaving their task. A party assembling boats at Shebandowan for the Wolseley Expedition to the Riel uprising were forcefully dismissed after the confiscation of their tools. Gold miners at nearby Jackfish Lake were pointedly removed back over the height of land.[164] Despite a previous official council with the bands to assure free passage for the troops, even Colonel Wolseley found himself summarily stopped and bluntly questioned at the Rainy River on his way to quell Riel.[165] Clearly these Natives had become fully cognizant of the frontier forces they faced and were firmly determined to negotiate for their lands.

Weymiss Simpson, the knowledgeable Hudson's Bay Company man who had visited these bands in preparation for Wolseley's passage, may also have been the first to raise with them the possibilities of some permanent right of way to Fort Gary. He had been confronted with territorial propositions to which he promised answers from an appropriate negotiating commission within a year. In the interim, after the Rebellion, quantities of needed flour were given to these Natives for past considerations and to assure their continued goodwill over the winter. In the spring Robert Pither, then at Fort Frances, confirmed that these bands would be as willing to treaty the whole of their lands as to negotiate a permanent corridor for passage across them.[166] Nevertheless, the resultant process of alienation was to be a long one. Forceful demands by determined Natives would meet perceptive understanding among negotiators. However, the latter would encounter a wall of resistance from an impecunious bureaucracy and arrogant senior officialdom that refused to accept Dawson's assessment of the Native bands.

In late April 1871, Dawson, Pither, and Simpson were appointed to treat with the bands for land as far west as the Lake of the Woods and north to the area of Lac Seul and the English River system.[167] After long and complex negotiations that August, the talks failed, largely because Ottawa had not anticipated the financial commitment demanded by the Natives. Yet, their demands did not exceed the terms of agreements reached by the Americans with other bands in neighbouring Minnesota. Another attempt the following summer included special sessions at Shebandowan, then Fort Frances, and finally the Northwest Angle of the Lake of the Woods. It also failed, and for the same reasons. So belligerent were the last sessions that thought was given to the provision of a small protective military force at future negotiations.[168]

Finally, after a belated but substantial increase in the government's financial offer and a third season of protracted deliberations, an agreement was reached. A telegram to Ottawa in October 1873 announced the arrangement of Treaty 3 for an estimated 55,000 square miles of rocky wilderness (see Map 2.2). It promised an initial $12 a head for each of the roughly 2,000 inhabitants, as well as some additional perquisites, and subsequent payment of the equivalent of $5 to each person in every following year. No mineral or agricultural sales were to occur until representatives from both sides laid out the various plots and wild lands that were to be reserved for exclusive Native use. Acceptance of this agreement by the absent Shebandowan population was assured by Dawson, and approval by the more distant Lac Seul residents was obtained the next spring.[169] Frontier development could now proceed legally on its usual wide range of fronts, including railway building.

For Ontario these changes were dwarfed in importance by Ottawa's unilateral declaration of 1871 about the province's western and northern boundaries. That decision denied the province the control of all this soon-to-be-treatied territory.[170] According to the Dominion's interpretation of the old Quebec Act, Ontario's northern limit was at the arctic divide, while provincial understanding was that it followed the line of the English and Albany rivers. The western boundary was asserted by Ottawa to be a line due north from the Ohio–Mississippi junction, which passed just east of the Lakehead and would grant the newly formed Manitoba a port on the Great Lakes. This latter claim was particularly unacceptable to the province. Since the pre-Confederation decades, it had been administering justice, laying out surveys, supervising settlement, and regulating resource developments as far west as the Minnesota border country. Indeed, it had just carved the new District of Thunder Bay from western Algoma to better serve these needs.[171] Ontario stubbornly adhered to its previous belief (also based on the Quebec Act) that its western limit was the extension of a line due north from the headwaters of the Mississippi, touching Canada at the Lake of the Woods.

So things remained until after Treaty 3 was signed. An accommodation in 1874 temporarily divided the area in half, allowing provincial jurisdiction west to a line north from Hunter Island and east along the fifty-first parallel. As well, a federal–provincial commission was created to arbitrate the larger issue.

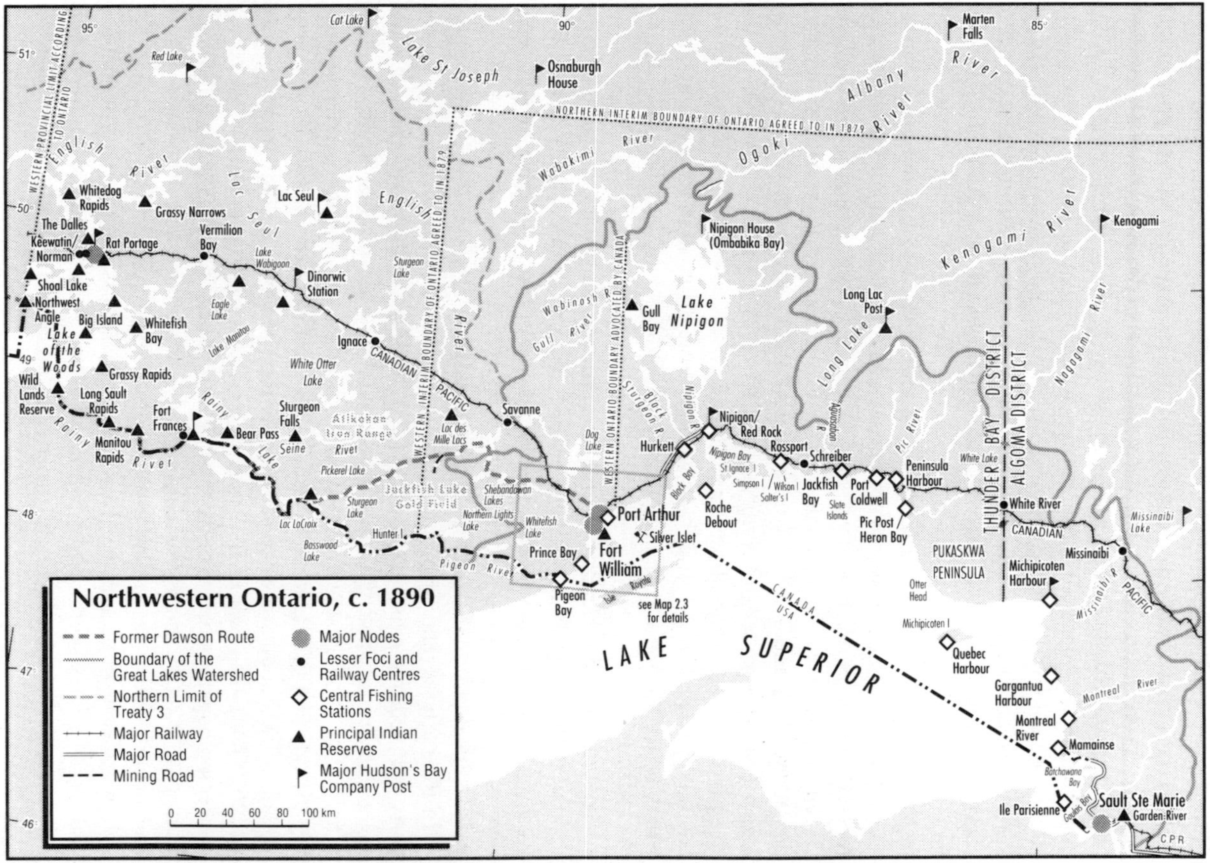
Northwestern Ontario, c. 1890
Former Dawson Route
Boundary of the Great Lakes Watershed
Northern Limit of Treaty 3
Major Railway
Major Road
Mining Road
Major Nodes
Lesser Foci and Railway Centres
Central Fishing Stations
Principal Indian Reserves
Major Hudson's Bay Company Post
0 20 40 60 80 100 km
LAKE SUPERIOR
Lake Nipigon
Lake of the Woods
Lac Seul
Lake St Joseph
Albany River
Ogoki River
Kenogami River
English River
Rainy River
Rainy Lake
Pigeon River
NORTHERN INTERIM BOUNDARY OF ONTARIO AGREED TO IN 1879
WESTERN INTERIM BOUNDARY OF ONTARIO AGREED TO IN 1879
WESTERN ONTARIO BOUNDARY ADVOCATED BY CANADA
WESTERN PROVINCIAL LIMIT ACCORDING TO ONTARIO
THUNDER BAY DISTRICT
ALGOMA DISTRICT
CANADIAN PACIFIC
CANADA
USA
Port Arthur
Fort William
Rat Portage
Keewatin/Norman
Sault Ste Marie
Garden River
Savanne
Ignace
Vermilion Bay
Dinorwic Station
Fort Frances
Nipigon/Red Rock
Schreiber
White River
Missinaibi
Silver Islet
see Map 2.3 for details
PUKASKWA PENINSULA
Osnaburgh House
Marten Falls
Kenogami
Cat Lake
Red Lake
Lac Seul
Nipigon House (Ombabika Bay)
Long Lac Post
Gull Bay
Michipicoten Harbour
Whitedog Rapids
The Dalles
Grassy Narrows
Shoal Lake
Northwest Angle
Big Island
Whitefish Bay
Grassy Rapids
Wild Lands Reserve
Long Sault Rapids
Manitou Rapids
Bear Pass
Sturgeon Falls
Seine River
Hurkett
Rossport
Jackfish Bay
Port Coldwell
Peninsula Harbour
Pic Post / Heron Bay
Roche Debout
Prince Bay
Pigeon Bay
Quebec Harbour
Gargantua Harbour
Montreal River
Mamainse
Ile Parisienne
Atikokan Iron Range
Jackfish Lake Gold Field
CPR

MAP 2.2

In 1879 this small body ruled in favour of Ontario's northern and western claims, but Ottawa refused to concur. Ontario responded with the appointment of W.D. Lyon as stipendiary magistrate for its Thunder Bay District lying east of the now partitioned area under contention. In 1881, the Dominion Parliament extended Manitoba's eastern limits to the height of land. Ontario retaliated by expanding the jurisdiction of its Thunder Bay District to the Lake of the Woods, and the fat was in the fire. Criticisms, cross-measures, and counterclaims quickly followed. The resultant legal, social, and economic turmoil brought the whole matter before the Judicial Committee of the Privy Council in 1884. This British body also ruled in favour of Ontario's contentions. Again, Ottawa made no move towards acceptance and mounted a claim for continuing federal control of all resources west of Great Lakes drainage, because the Dominion had been the official signator to the recent treaty. This claim was denied by the same Judicial Committee in 1888, and the next year Imperial legislation was passed to confirm Ontario in its right to the whole of the 'Disputed Territory and all resources therein.' A serious matter of jurisdiction had finally been resolved, rightly or wrongly from the point of view of Manitoba, which lost both rich forest and mineral potential as well as a possible port on the Great Lakes.

Exploratory and evaluative interest in northwestern Ontario, previously concentrated along the Rainy River corridor, extended more widely across this westerly area in the seventies and eighties. Several recognizable groups were involved in the resultant activity and so became the principal sources of new geographical information and public knowledge.

In the early seventies the most important of these was the railway survey party, ordered into existence in June 1870 'to discover the most practical route for a Pacific railway.'[172] Crews saw preliminary service that same summer, running lines both east and west from the head of Lake Nipigon and determining the position of the arctic divide across northwestern Ontario. That season was also the first of two when such exploration probed the Rainy River country and the area to the east of the Lake of the Woods. More intense work across the region began the next spring when eleven parties, each with several crews, were put on to the survey operation between Mattawa and Fort Gary. These endeavours, under the direction of Sandford Fleming, continued to comb the area northwest of the Lakehead, as well as east across Algoma, through 1872 and 1873.[173] They produced an enormous volume of information on the physical landscape of the Shield and generated three feasible rail routes east from Red River. The most northerly passed above Lake Nipigon. A middle route touched Superior at Red Rock (Nipigon) before again arching north, and the most southerly reached Superior at Fort William and passed eastward along its north shore.[174] Ironically, all these diligent efforts were couched in transcontinental cost-conscious thinking, which ignored all but the most obvious regional transport needs and resource considerations. Not surprisingly, the specific data these surveys produced added only modestly to popular understanding of the geography of northwestern Ontario.

The second group to aid in this broadening exploration was composed of a largely anonymous group of prospectors, timber cruisers, and area residents. Unlike the surveyors, their interests were not in the details of elevation, topography, and drainage but in the general nature of the resource base. From among this cadre came early discoveries of gold near Long Lake and Nipigon as well as westward in the Shebandowan, Seine River, and Lake of the Woods areas. The same was true of iron around modern Atikokan and south toward the Minnesota boundary.[175] Timber cruisers and persons with related lumbering interests were first to appreciate that the considerable pine resources of the northwest often did not occur in large continuous stands as elsewhere, but in smaller, discontinuous, or scattered groves.[176] Their search for the broad range of timber required by railway contractors made them aware of the rich range and wide utility of the taiga for timber. It also revealed to them that very considerable pineries existed as far north as the Lac Seul country, well beyond the limit of the Great Lakes Forest.[177] Finally, from among this group came important public knowledge about the fine sport fishing in Nipigon and other Superior rivers, as well as the navigable potential of inland waters like the Lake of the Woods and Rainy Lake.[178]

Contributors to such expanding awareness and understanding also included those of a scientific bent. They were principally the field parties of the Geological Survey of Canada, who over these two decades reconnoitred and roughly mapped much of this territory.[179] During the seventies, men like Robert Bell worked their way quietly through the back-country east of the Lake of the Woods. They carried out canoe surveys north through the Lac Seul area, down the English River system, and west from Lake Nipigon to this latter area. Bell and other party leaders of the eighties pressed on through Lake St Joseph and down the Albany as well as north and west to Cat Lake and beyond. Their wide-reaching travels were sometimes duplicated by that equally knowledgeable northerner, E.B. Borron, exploring and assessing resources for the province of Ontario. The result of these professional endeavours was a stream of broadly based reports evaluating drainage systems, unravelling a complex geological scene, describing forest conditions, even commenting on Native well-being. While their erudite writings may have attracted only a small public, the essence of their work was frequently incorporated in publications with a much broader readership.

Nevertheless, the main source of popular information remained the provincial press, which sometimes relied on the last-mentioned sources, but as often depended on a reporter's observations during an assignment to the region. When stripped of their frequent political bias, many newspaper accounts were astute and comprehensive in their descriptions and were widely reprinted in small-town weeklies. Sometimes they praised the region's beauty, its rich resources and economic progress. As frequently, they pointed to the landscape of barren rocky ridges, the dismal miles of muskeg, the huge expanses of burn or scorched timber, and the harshness of the environment and of life there.[180] Collectively, their articles presented a bluntly balanced picture to their readers, some of whom were considering lives and careers in northwestern Ontario.

To Span a Region

Colonial interest in direct water transport to Superior extended back to the early copper rush of the forties. At that time, the Americans produced a simple tramway at Sault Ste Marie for the transfer of ore destined for lower-lake refining. On the Canadian side, Allan Macdonell proposed a steam railway about the Rapids as part of his visionary plan for future Native welfare.[181] Next came serious consideration of a canal in which Macdonell and his expansionist friends also took strong interest. While the Canadian side offered the easiest location, this controversial plan was abandoned by a financially strapped colonial government, which at the same time refused to consider private pursuit of the project.

As a result, in 1855, the state of Michigan produced the first canal, linking Superior and its budding ports to the rest of the lake transport system. The dimensions of the first two locks in tandem were 350 feet by 70 feet with a total rise of 18 feet, more than comparable to others down the lakes and quite adequate for passenger vessels and 'canalers' of the day. Rising traffic, particularly the southward passage of American copper and iron and the northward flow of coal, demanded improvements by the seventies and a subsequent transfer to federal authority for expansion by 1880.[182]

While immediate American use was intense, steady Canadian flow came more slowly, despite Cauchon's famous Crown Lands vision for northern and western colonial expansion, which so stirred the public in 1856 and after. Not until 1858 was the Northwest Transportation Company (often called Northwest Transit Co.) in operation with Macdonell again prominent among its Toronto-based membership. This firm held a mail contract to serve Superior points by their powerful steamer *Rescue*, as well as the Red River Settlement by canoe, using the fur-trade route west from Fort William via the Lake of the Woods.

Over the former route, up from the new Toronto railhead at Collingwood, the company faced unexpected, irregular competition from the aging steamer *Ploughboy* in 1859 and 1860. Despite heroic efforts, the Northwest Transit Co. fell to unexpectedly harsh realities and creased operation in late 1861. Not until 1864, with the arrival of the steamer *Algoma* of the Collingwood Royal Mail Line, did regular passage to Superior by a Canadian vessel resume. About 1870, it was joined from the same early railhead of Georgian Bay by the *Chicora*, which introduced scheduled stops at Duluth as well as the Canadian Lakehead. Two years later, this tie from Collingwood first faced staunch competition from the newly built *Ontario* and *Quebec* of the Beatty Line, serving the Grand Trunk Railway from Windsor/Detroit and Sarnia. For over a decade, these rival ports and lines served Lake Superior harbours and docks with a variety of vessels of increasing size and elegance. However, after the introduction in 1884 of the crack CPR steamers – *Alberta*, *Algoma*, and *Athabasca* – between the railhead at Fort William and wharves at Owen Sound, this Collingwood trade collapsed.[183] By that time, Superior's key routes for through freight and passengers were at capacity, and general lake service under sail, steam, and by steam barge with tows was quite adequate to the coasting trade.

Meanwhile, growing public interest in the wake of the Hind and Dawson reports had come by 1860 to focus on a suitable all-Canadian passage west to Red River. This followed the old fur route reintroduced by the Northwest Transit Co. Indeed, early travellers pressing west, including one party of overlanders to the gold fields of British Columbia, had already employed it to avoid an expensive passage through U.S. territory.[184] However, such support for the orderly improvement of the route in the early sixties was forestalled by the lingering territorial dispute over the future of Rupert's Land.[185] Unlike Superior shipping, which was envisioned to serve regional as well as larger ends, this push westward by land, like other schemes to follow, was conceived as a way to leap to western goals beyond.

Work again was begun on this westward road and water corridor in early 1867. As a decade earlier, when the Northwest Transportation Company had built its landing and made a brave start inland, Simon Dawson was the superintendent. By November, crews had reopened much of his previous track to Dog Lake, where a dam was to back water for the next thirty-five miles towards Lac des Mille Lacs (see Map 2.2). Initial colonial finance was soon superseded by federal funding, and the total labour force grew quickly to exceed a thousand men. By 1869, a revised route ran more directly northwest by way of Shebandowan. On the Fort Gary (Red River) end, work was proceeding on a road east to the Lake of the Woods at the Northwest Angle.[186]

When Riel and his followers erupted late that year at Red River, Dawson was commissioned to continue work through the winter. Unrealistic official hopes were that he could complete the many miles of road work at both ends, open out the portages to Rainy River, and construct a good wharf on the shores of Thunder Bay.[187] Ottawa, in turn, commissioned more than a hundred large open boats in ports like Owen Sound and Collingwood to serve as transport on the various lakes between the interior portages.[188] These, with the assembled troops of the Wolseley Expedition and their supplies, were shipped north on break-up. Despite certain delays and diplomatic problems at the American Sault Canal, the Expedition reached what Colonel Wolseley dubbed 'Prince Arthur's Landing' (Port Arthur) in late spring of 1870.[189] However, Dawson's most heroic efforts understandably had fallen short of bureaucratic dreams, and a month and a half was spent by the troops improving the road to Shebandowan and transporting heavy wagonloads of equipment there.[190] Leaving the latter in mid-July, the first brigade reached Fort Frances on August 3 and, because the road west from the Lake of the Woods was still incomplete, proceeded to Fort Gary by the Winnipeg River. It arrived there on August 24 thirty-seven days after its departure from Shebandowan.[191] Finding the rebellion to have collapsed, the core of the Expedition departed again in early September and were back in Toronto within a month. This remarkable sequence of events, given the political and geopolitical implications for western Canadian dominion, drew considerable national and continental attention.

The reaction of a congratulatory Ontario press echoed the old expansionist cause. Hence, even before Wolseley's return south, the *Globe* was already demanding the immediate utilization of the route as an east-west trade corridor to reduce U.S. influence in Manitoba and to promote central Canada's commercial links there. That October the paper continued this theme. It asserted that the Pacific Railway was years way and pressed for 'the completion of Mr. Dawson's plan through the expenditure of sufficient money to carry out the work well.'[192] Ottawa clearly concurred in these views and spent lavishly on what now became known as the Dawson Road or Route. Over the next half-decade in the seventies, the 137 miles of road at both ends and on the portages were brought to good gravelled standard and were supplied with numerous teams and wagons (even tramways were considered for some stretches). Most interior lakes were raised by dams to increase depth and shorten connecting land passages. All such waters were supplied with small steam tugs to tow boats and freight or livestock barges.[193] Substantial paddle steamers were constructed to run both Rainy Lake and Lake of the Woods, joined by a more powerful craft able to negotiate the Manitou and Long Sault Rapids on the Rainy River.[194] At Kouchiching Falls (Fort Frances) an 800-foot canal and lock

(200' × 36' × 7') were driven through solid rock[195] before the entire project was suddenly moth-balled, then abandoned in the later seventies.

Several reasons lay behind the final closure of the Dawson Road (often called the Dawson Route) beyond the commonly cited ones of federal party politics. Seasonality, heavy annual maintenance requirements, and frontier isolation from labour, equipment, and supplies contributed to high operating expenses. A dozen portages, each requiring freight handling at both ends, added considerably to costs and user discomfort. Poor management in the route's early years, which saw long delays for passengers, bad freight handling, and inadequate supply of provisions along the route, tarnished the route's public image.[196] Official attempts to promote the route's utilization through subsidies on rail and water passage to the Lakehead were effectively countered by U.S. price reductions to competitive levels over alternate routes. These problems were gradually eradicated later under private operation, and in its final year, 950 tons of freight and almost 2,000 persons were transported over its length.[197] Despite this, throughout the life of the road, most settlers and travellers preferred to go to Manitoba by Duluth or other American ports from which rail connection, even to Winnipeg, was possible after mid-decade.[198]

Principally however, the cause of the demise of the Dawson Road was the birth of a transcontinental railway that, given the national temper of the day, required a totally Canadian route. Unfortunately, the railway surveys through the Rainy River country found no satisfactory line west without brief passage through Minnesota. With the onset of world-wide depression in 1873, plans for this Pacific railway suffered a brief setback. A new government in Ottawa promoted the idea of steamer service from rail docks at Algoma Mills on upper Lake Huron to Prince Arthur's Landing and the upgrading of this old route from there to Winnipeg. In this way it intended to delay the astronomical expenditure required for rail construction across the Shield until better economic times.[199] Yet Ottawa curiously reversed itself in 1874 and a year later turned the first sod on rail between Fort William and Manitoba, along a line through Rat Portage (Kenora).[200] This move brought the beginning of the end for Simon Dawson's magnificent dream. In the spring of 1876, the road was closed to all but railway-related traffic. This move came much to the surprise of many who had expected its continuance to promote rising agricultural settlement along the Rainy River. Only at Fort Frances did work press on, and even this was abandoned in 1878, with the lock gates ready but still unhung.[201]

The new rail line between the Lakehead and Winnipeg was built under government supervision and made the long-surveyed Plot (West Fort William) on the Kam its official terminus, to the distress of those businessmen at The Landing (Port Arthur). Earlier rail surveys had suggested Nipigon as an alternate focus on Lake Superior, but in an unusual spirit of cooperation, these two contending centres on Thunder Bay joined forces to fight off this possibility.[202] Construction of the link with Manitoba, which was carried out under government supervision, was initiated at both ends. The track laid east was completed speedily after the final location of its route, reaching the Winnipeg River in late 1880 and crossing to Rat Portage the next autumn. Much more serious engineering problems amid muskeg and rock plagued the contractors west of Lake Superior and dramatically delayed final track laying on this section until late 1882. Some service was initiated over the line that winter but final ballasting and actual take-over by the CPR was completed only in May 1883.[203]

By that time the CPR was beginning the second year of its own construction east towards Sudbury. In the process, its contractors used numerous ports and harbours on the Superior shore as supply depots and camps.[204] Indeed, at Michipicoten Harbour, a route was even driven inland to otherwise inaccessible stretches east and west of Missanabie. Over it supplies were hauled by Mormon mule trains, with support from tugs and barges on Wawa and other intervening lakes.[205]

Finally, the entire transcontinental railway was nearing completion when the second Riel Rebellion erupted in the prairie west. On March 30, 1885, military detachments from Halifax and Quebec boarded their trains in Montreal for Winnipeg. Joined by those from central Canada, they reached Red River on April 4, despite their frequent disembarcation and transport by sleigh or travel on foot between finished sections of track on this Superior shore.[206] West and east were finally joined across 'the land between' at Jackfish Bay in mid-October 1885, and the first direct train left Winnipeg for Montreal on November 2.[207] Two years later, the short line from Sudbury to Algoma Mills, once built to avoid immediate construction over the Shield, was pushed west towards Sault Ste Marie and links with American counterparts.[208] About the same time Lakehead interests, which had obtained a charter in 1885 for much more local trackage to link with Minnesota rail near Arrow Lake, began construction of the Port Arthur Duluth and Western Railway (PAD&W). It was open across the Kam at Stanley and to the Silver Mountain mines by late 1890 (see Map 2.3).[209] Unlike the other federally financed modes of transport discussed above, the PAD&W, like the Algoma Central to follow, was regional and provincial in its scale and intended purpose, rather than transregional and national.

Nevertheless, these transport-related events left their mark on northwestern Ontario. The Dawson Route, with its initial labour gangs and later its crews of maintenance people, drovers, artisans, engineers, and other personnel, must

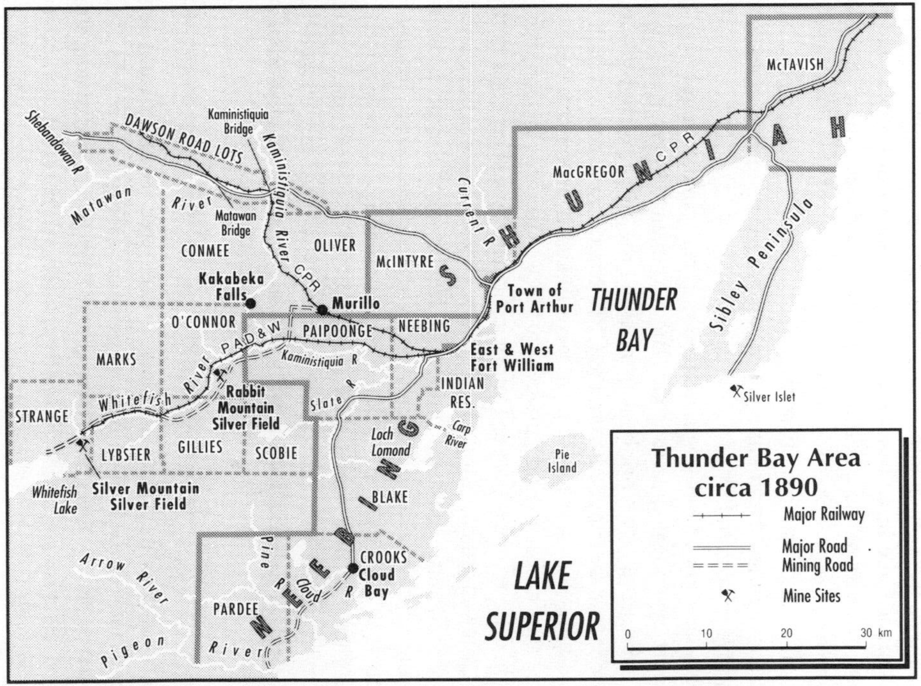
Thunder Bay Area
circa 1890
Major Railway
Major Road
Mining Road
Mine Sites
0
10
20
30 km
THUNDER BAY
LAKE SUPERIOR
McTAVISH
MacGREGOR
CPR
Sibley Peninsula
Silver Islet
Current R
Town of Port Arthur
East & West Fort William
McINTYRE
OLIVER
NEEBING
PAIPOONGE
INDIAN RES.
Carp River
Pie Island
Loch Lomond
BLAKE
CROOKS
Cloud Bay
Cloud R
Pine R
PARDEE
Pigeon River
Arrow River
Murillo
Kakabeka Falls
Kaministiquia Bridge
Kaministiquia River
Kaministiquia R
DAWSON ROAD LOTS
Shebandowan R
Matawan River
Matawan Bridge
CONMEE
O'CONNOR
PAD&W
MARKS
STRANGE
Whitefish River
Rabbit Mountain Silver Field
Slate R
LYBSTER
GILLIES
SCOBIE
Whitefish Lake
Silver Mountain Silver Field

MAP 2.3

have given a considerable boost to the regional economy. However, this effect was highly seasonal (most of these people came up in May and went down in October) and is impossible to measure. With the CPR this seasonality was much less pronounced. Work of varied forms continued on the line throughout the year, although the ranks were very considerably swelled by the summer requirements of the contractors. This variance was countered each winter by the large labour force hired to take out the millions of ties, posts, and poles as well as other timber needed, not only here, but for construction on the western plains. However, transiency was a principal feature of this ethnically diverse construction force. While numbers might temporarily swell the population and commerce of regional communities, few permanent residents, other than operating employees, resulted.[210]

With this new era of rail several interesting and rapid changes also came in the transport system of the Hudson's Bay Company. Many posts, with their outposts once served by York boat from along the Albany–English River system, now came to be supplied from the CPR. Major trade centres such as those on Lac Seul and Red Lake no longer were linked over the arduous system of boat routes and crude marine railways to Moose Factory. Instead, their needs were handled from a new post at Dinorwic Station by a short road north to the English River watershed. Similarly, Red Rock Post (Nipigon) became the rail depot for such north-south movement of freight over the portages to Lake Nipigon and ultimately to posts in Albany drainage beyond. Finally, a road north from Jackfish Bay to Long Lake and Longlac Post now serviced numerous interior traders once supplied by the difficult Pic River route.[211] But in the world away from railway and frontier contact, only these few changes came to the long-standing fur-oriented life of both trader and Native inhabitant.[212]

Northwestern Colonization on Trial

In the post-Confederation decades Ontario attempted to attract rural settlers to its northern lands through three basic provisions: free grants, access roads, and promotional publicity. Over the colonial era, land policy had swung gradually in favour of disposal by sale.[213] Related regulations, therefore, had covered the early lots in both Crown and Indian townships behind Sault Ste Marie and at the Lakehead. However, reacting to declining immigration, growing out-migration, and the lack of further colonial opportunity in southern Ontario, the new province passed its Free Grant and Homestead Act in 1868, with an eye to its Precambrian frontiers. Because of the earlier disastrous attempts at Shield settlement in southeastern Ontario, this legislation applied only to townships in which the surveyors reported substantial proportions of agriculturally suitable land. In such townships it awarded any household head up to 150 acres (160 in sectional surveys), with the option to purchase more, on completion of two years' residence and prescribed settlement duties.[214] But free grant status was not universal among townships opened in the north. For example, such status never applied to retreatied lands or ones awarded to provincially endowed institutions such as the University of Toronto. While some earlier surveys were converted to free grant later, others were not, because their initial settlement had been quite successful. Finally, as late as 1890, the twenty-four townships under this designation in the northwest made up less than a fifth of the provincial total.[215] The overwhelming concentration of free grant townships was, and would remain, on the Georgian Bay/Ottawa upland. Unfortunately, this fact has been lost on historians, who too often have also taken the ugly settler-lumberman experience there as representative of all other free grant areas. In fact, the forest-related colonial abuse, so typical of that pine country, was much less evident across the northwest.

The trans-regional passage effected by the CPR had the side-effect of strengthening and occasionally adding to the pattern of rural nodes, ports and other villages or hamlets of this period. It also initiated the first extra-regional corridor of rapid movement, although the location of its line had paid little attention to regional resources. Yet the provision of a road-and-water-related access within pockets of agriculture or to areas of mineral potential in this frontier era was far more fundamental to northern colonization and economic development. Indeed, national strategies behind this railway and provincial ones related to such resource utilization were, at this time, independently derived and sometimes operationally incompatible. The result was a lack of coordination, which severely hampered transport interchange, except through the scant and ill-distributed number of now rail-related centres.

Much earlier problems of frontier access had generated the colonization road under the Department of Crown Lands during the thirties and forties to open broad tracts of southwestern Ontario to farming. The later unsuccessful use of the colonization road idea by the Agricultural Ministry in the attempt to settle the Shield in southeastern Ontario brought serious reappraisal.[216] The ultimate result was the creation of a Colonization Roads Branch in 1862, under Crown Lands, with a set of practical strategies and guiding tenets suitable to colonial conditions in northern environs. Among these were sectional land surveys, designed without road allowances but with a reserve of five per cent of each property for such purposes. This permitted flexibility where suitable routes, like farmable soils, were irregularly distributed within each township.[217] Promotive mining policies came to incorporate variations on the basic concept of access. They came to provide free road passage across Crown lands for as much as twenty miles and later permitted direct funding of roads into new mining areas.[218] In some instances mine road and farm road were the same road, and in all cases the ultimate aim was union of such local routes with future traffic corridors to major centres and the outside world.

At Confederation, Ontario's continuing intent was to fuel at least part of its northward expansion with immigrants. From the fifties, the former colony had extended its campaign for such newcomers, first focusing on Great Britain, then France, Germany, and Scandinavia.[219] For the most part, these efforts failed, as did certain official publications of the late seventies, exemplified by *The Undeveloped Lands of Northern and Western Ontario* or *North-Western Ontario; Its Boundaries, Resources and Communications*.[220] Through the eighties, these latter printed efforts were abetted in both the Algoma and Thunder Bay districts by similar local endeavours. Their success rate too was dubious, except perhaps among Ontario's own youth.

These younger sons and daughters from southern farms were also the target of much newspaper ink. Such articles were fostered by a popular hope that the increasing migration of this home-grown population to lands of the American West in the seventies and to Manitoba during the eighties could be curbed and redirected to settle Ontario's north. These attempts too were only modestly successful. The earlier-fostered suspicion that northern rural areas were environmentally harsh, agriculturally marginal, and economically uncertain for settlement had grown to be a stubbornly but silently held belief among such provincial youth. As a result, those who could afford to transport themselves and their effects moved to distant grassland homes, while those with lesser finances went north to farm.[221] The result of such trends was a provincial population that grew only slowly after 1870. By 1891 northwestern Ontario had yet to reach a total of 20,000 and a determined farm population of 7,000.[222]

No co-ordinated search for good land across northwestern Ontario was ever officially attempted. Given the emphasis placed by the province, public, and press on northern agricultural settlement, this fact is worth pondering. Many discoveries were by chance, often during the pursuit of some other end. After 1870, most additions to the inventory of good land between Nipigon and Rat Portage came about during the wide-ranging rail surveys, and not all were along the eventually chosen right of way. Of this fact the Rainy River Valley was the prime example.[223] In any case, because of the prolonged federal–provincial boundary disagreement, most colonial activity to 1890 concentrated on the older, known soil pockets.

Algoma West

In the Crown townships adjacent to Sault Ste Marie, problems with undeveloped agricultural holdings persisted into the early seventies. Activity then began to increase in response to the onset of world-wide depression. This brought many people north from Lambton, Huron, or Bruce and others from now terminated work at the Bruce Mines to settle formerly purchased holdings. Further arrivals here were encouraged by the designation of four core townships for free grants. As a result, work on opening out more colonization roads west through this lowland and north-south on its shorter axis were well advanced in 1880.[224]

By that date the Agricultural Society at Sault Ste Marie had held its annual exhibitions for over a decade and drew heavy rural support. Further migrations of settlers followed in the nineties, as did a growing tendency for established farmers to balance or replace their early emphasis on crops with a growing component of sheep and cattle.[225] Later in that decade, the lot of the average settler here improved quickly. Heavy demands for labour on the new locks at the Sault now augmented the usual winter employment of cutting steamer wood and working in or supplying logging camps north along Superior and east on Huron.[226] However, the urban market of a tiny Sault Ste Marie remained limited, and this situation would not begin to improve until the next decade.

To the north in the retreatied townships about Goulais and Batchawana bays, things were really only beginning to improve near the close of the period. By that time all agricultural lots had long been open for sale. In attempts to gain cheap control of the timber on these lands, more than one lumber interest had offered to provide forty or more settlers, but Indian administrators watched each of these schemes fall through.[227] In 1871, the old extension of the Northern Road, once laid out by Salter, was re-examined by the local Indian Agent with an eye to opening it under joint federal and provincial funding. Three years later this project was completed from Sault Ste Marie to the base of the retreatied townships. Six years after that the final bridging of the Goulais River gave potential market access to future farmlands here, all the way to Batchawana Bay. (Indeed by 1882, a winter road, continuing on north to Mamainse, had been built under a cost-sharing agreement with a local mining company.)[228] However, only in the mid-eighties did bona fide settlement begin, when people from the Southampton area arrived by water at the Goulais River. By late 1886, more than twenty families were resident there and by decade's end over 8,000 acres of land in this valley and behind Batchawana Bay had been removed from an existing timber limit for agricultural purposes.[229] However, very little of this new acreage was beyond the most primitive phase of development by the close of the period.

Thunder Bay Area

Behind Thunder Bay and along Superior from Minnesota to the Pukaskwa Peninsula, some twenty-five townships were added to Neebing and Paipoonge by the late eighties. Twelve existed by 1874, but only one of the remainder pre-dated 1885. At least ten were laid out solely to facilitate mining demands, and of the farmable remainder, only seven were designated for free grants.[230] More than half were so labelled only after 1886 and several remained closed to settlement at the end of the decade. To aid in administration, in 1873 the Lakehead core of the active mining and farming townships was organized into the huge Municipality of Shuniah, which came to include the village of Port Arthur (see Map 2.3). In 1881, the southern and western members of this group withdrew to form the sister Municipality of Neebing, which in 1890 still contained the lots of an unincorporated Fort William (East and West).[231]

In the early seventies speculation and mining claims covered much land in the two original townships, particularly in Neebing. This effectively prevented agricultural development on several thousand acres of good soil. The opening of adjacent Oliver and the inland Dawson Road lots in 1873, as free grants, did something to relieve this situation. Within the next two seasons over a hundred families from southern Ontario were reported to have acquired property, and in Oliver some thirty households were actively clearing land.[232] During the second half of the seventies, colonization roads from the Fort William town plot into northern Paipoonge and from the future Port Arthur (Prince Arthur's Landing) into Oliver provided the settlers with local access.[233]

Indeed, the pattern of government-sponsored roads soon began to tie the whole of Shuniah and Neebing together and to adjacent territory. In 1872, local pressure had mounted here for a winter road to the Pigeon River, joining an existing one from Duluth. Over this road mail was to be routed between navigation seasons on Lake Superior. After years of bickering over unsatisfactory work, it was opened near the end of the decade. By 1885 this route was said to be in fine condition, particularly over the first thirty miles to the new rural community of Cloud Bay.[234] A year after its initiation, work was begun on a road in the opposite direction to serve mines east from The Landing to Black Bay, with a winter mail trace on to Red Rock Post (Nipigon). A decade later it was described as a good wagon road, and a branch of similar quality had been added to the mining community of Silver Islet.[235] The third major radial was the Dawson Road, described by a visitor in the fall of 1870 as the equal of any in southern Ontario for its first twenty-one miles to the Mattawin bridge and quite acceptable on to Shebandowan River.[236] This condition it long continued to enjoy.

With the following decade came social organizations in more established rural communities and serious consideration of a grist mill and sawmill for Oliver. The eighties were also marked by the formation of an Agricultural Society and by a provincially financed model farm to sponsor improvement in agriculture.[237] With railway building came new market incentives as well as seasonal employment on construction gangs, which combination brought appropriate rural incentive and further colonization road mileage to established townships.

However, it was at the end of that boisterous period that expansion into new areas began, with the opening of the free grant townships of Conmee, Gillies, and O'Connor. Resultant settlement in the Whitefish River Valley followed quickly and was accompanied by early colonization road building.[238] Near the close of the eighties, silver mining in this same locale produced a further route from the CPR at Murillo. This road was jointly funded by the mines and the province and saw heavy use by settlers.[239]

Rainy River Country

Along the Rainy River, squatters quickly began to assume land with the signing of Treaty 3 in 1873. However, not until the spring of 1876 were most of the first twenty-one townships federally surveyed, under Ottawa's claim to the northwest.[240] The Dominion then was prepared to market these lands, which were subdivided into long-lots extending back from fronts on the river in a manner reminiscent of old Quebec. However, these lands being in the disputed territory, Ontario was tactfully consulted on these matters during the brief truce between governments after 1874. The province agreed that the area should be opened and concurred in the survey design. However, it expressed serious reservations about the depth of the properties (10 chains by 2 miles) and both the high frequency and unusual width of the road allowances (99 feet as opposed to the normal 66 feet).[241]

Ironically, the project received the first of two stunning setbacks about this time. The spring of 1876 witnessed the unanticipated closure of the Dawson Road, which, with the prior decision to route the CPR north by Rat Portage, left this agriculturally promising area in sudden isolation. Settlement faltered, as might be expected, with potential market access dropping to seasonal steamer service to Rat Portage. The second blow fell in 1878 with federal refusal to accept the first western boundary decision in favour of Ontario; its impact was exacerbated by Ottawa's unilateral subsequent extension of Manitoba's eastern boundary to the Lakehead in 1881. Old settlers and new, some of the latter being in groups under the auspices of southern provincial settlement societies, now found no government willing or able to issue clear title to lands on which all requirements had been completed.[242]

Finally in the summer of 1886, two years after the Privy Council again confirmed Ontario's western claim, the province made its first determined move to promote settlement in this Rainy River country. The Colonization Road Branch began opening out the old river road survey and trace made by Dominion land surveyors a decade earlier. Proceeding in four annual stages west from Fort Frances, it completed a good route along the front for settlers to use in the months between navigation and safe sleighing over the ice.[243] Impelled by a controversy in the press, Crown Lands also initiated an exploratory survey of the back country here, to assess supposed problems of drainage which some news articles said prevailed. Although Thomas Bolger, P.L.S., found such concerns to be largely unfounded and an estimated 600,000 acres there to be worthy of colonial consideration, no further township surveys were required until after 1890.[244]

Yet settlement in the Valley had made solid progress by the latter date. Initial colonization around Alberton (Fort Frances) had spread down the front to the Wild Lands Reserve near the mouth of the river. Steamer service to the railway at Rat Portage was increasingly frequent and seasonally adequate.[245] Numerous descriptions noted the scattered clusters of homesteads, each with its boat landing, gradually coalescing along the front by the later eighties when as many as 200 clearings were estimated to be here.[246] In 1889, with the boundary dispute finally settled, Ontario passed a special Free Grant Act for the Valley townships to encourage their rapid future settlement.[247]

In 1890 the rural landscape here, around Thunder Bay, or in the area of Sault Ste Marie was dominated by brulé (burned area) and bush, dotted by log homes and outbuildings in modest clearings, roughly fenced as fields or yet unstumped. Such agricultural progress was the proud achievement of about 1,700 farmers, few of whom were not Ontario-born. Such householders had in crops, hay, and improved pasture some 30,000 acres as well as almost 112,000 acres in woodland and unimproved pasturage (see Table 2.1). However, the greatest increase in both these figures had come over the immediate decade, and many of these properties were probably still subsistent. Outside markets were likely uncertain or periodic for some farmers and hard to find for most, except the best-established ones in older colonial areas. Off-farm work connected with rail building, colonization road work, or bush employment was a seasonal necessity for most in such rural societies.

TABLE 2.1 Northwestern Agricultural Development (in acres), 1871–1891*

	1871	1881	1891
Improved Acreage			
Cropland			
Cereals	530	2,150	7,160
Roots	320	470	2,830
Hay	770	1,390	7,080
Other	30	70	830
Total	1,650	4,080	17,900
Pasture	940	1,110	12,230
Total Improved	2,590	5,190	30,130
Unimproved			
Pasture/woodland	7,840	36,650	111,560
Grand Total	10,430	41,840	141,690

* All tables are for northwestern Ontario (as defined on page 3) unless otherwise stated.
Source: Compiled from Census of Canada, Agricultural tables, 1871 to 1891.

As in the colonial tradition of more southerly townships a generation before, communities here were at only the earliest stages in fostering basic social amenities. Schools, where now available, might also be shared by several religious denominations on Sunday and serve as the first community gathering place for other functions. Rural colonists, often still in isolation or semi-isolation from neighbours, were slowly coming to terms with soil and climatic conditions or problems. These demanded new and different frontier approaches or solutions from those their parents had learned to follow in settling southern Ontario. Experiments and experiences in this very different world had begun to modify approaches to land selection, to crop balances, livestock patterns, and even to the rural way of life. From these advances the next generation would benefit, but for the present this was an agricultural world of trial and error, only beginning to show promise for future success.

Expanding Forest Utilization

On the American side of the upper lakes, these were great years of pine lumbering, a period when wanton harvest in Michigan, Wisconsin, and Minnesota far exceeded in value all gold ever mined in California.[248] On Canadian shores in 1870, the watersheds of Georgian Bay and upper Huron supported more pine than anywhere else to the east. However, the untapped supply of such timber to the west was more sporadic and still largely isolated. Depression through mid-decade dampened exploitive trends, but by the eighties huge booms of logs from Huron limits moved to Michigan mills and on to New York or Chicago lumber wharves.[249] On both sides of Superior and further west, the buoyant eighties also promoted harvesting and milling. In Ontario this economic stimulus was matched by voracious but less discriminating forest harvesting for CPR construction. As in neighbouring American states, the industry here was heavily oriented towards burgeoning demands from the prairie and plain frontier. These growing demands lessened the dampening effects on the industry of uncertain eastern lumber markets. Only from near Sault Ste Marie were log booms rafted down the St Marys Rapids and towed for sawing to Lake Huron or Michigan towns. There is no evidence to suggest that many of these booms had Ontario origins.[250]

On the Superior Watershed

On the Canadian side of eastern Lake Superior, before the onset of tough times in 1873, pine licences were opened on Ile Parisienne and in the vicinity of Michipicoten River. Their duration was undocumented and brief, in comparison with others in the retreatied townships behind Goulais and Batchawana. Here the limits by 1871 were operating busily under three southern Ontario interests sharing two modest mills.[251] Held by a sequence of financially unstable operators, these 86 square miles of now-tattered timber were combined in 1883 with another 29 square miles of property that had been worked only the last four seasons. Divested of its former pine and any useful hardwood, this large holding was a rich source of posts, poles and railway ties. This 73,600 acre limit lost some lots late in the decade to incoming settlers, who worked as winter labour in its camps.[252] Similar seasonal employment in proximity to the home farm resulted from four small timber limits granted to local mills behind Sault Ste Marie, which no doubt also accommodated logs off neighbouring farm properties.

In contrast, the area around the head of Superior was principally mining country in 1870, still almost devoid of agriculture and only beginning to attract interest for its forest possibilities. A serious fire that spring had swept along the first stretch of the road to Red River, adding to the extensive patchwork of burns between the Pigeon and Pic rivers. Many of these fires were attributed to miners and prospectors; many more across northwestern Ontario would be the later product of railway survey crews and construction gangs.[253] The first timber limit here had been created on retreatied land in Neebing Township and was assigned in late 1871 to Adam Oliver and Joseph Davidson. These prominent gentlemen with lumber interests near Barrie erected a steam mill at the mouth of the Kam the next spring. After wrangling with another applicant, they also gained a lease to rich pine on Mount McKay, within the Fort William Indian Reserve. This they also began to timber in 1873, driving their logs down the Carp River from Loch Lomond to the lake.[254] These leases from the Natives seem to have been sufficient to supply the building needs of a tentatively rising Fort William and Port Arthur to the end of the decade.

Also in 1873, the Department of Crown Lands first ordered an assessment of provincial woodlands on Superior and the rumoured pine country towards the Minnesota border. In late 1876, when rail construction from The Plot (West Fort William) was gradually gaining momentum, a selection of timber berths here, north from the border and east to the Nipigon area, were put up for sale.[255] These were not particularly pine limits. Rather, they were the source of the mixed timber needed for ties and other railway purposes, as well as material for the wharves and docks on both the Kam and the lakeshore at The Landing.[256] Not surprisingly, incoming settlers were most willing to contribute to these supplies for cash but received stern warning that they could do so only after patenting their lands. Nevertheless, small-scale trespass cutting for this or other markets would be a frequent charge against farmers here, as elsewhere, during the colonial development phase.

With the eighties, progress on the railway brought interesting changes to forest activity. By then the movement of construction inland had greatly reduced local pressure on timber supplies for the Manitoba branch. Indeed, such demand fell further when federal legislation granting railway supplies from a 40-mile zone astride the right of way east from Rat Portage was extended across the disputed territory to the height of land. This move infuriated the province. Aware that such harvesting of resources, which it held to be its own, was being loosely supervised, Ontario took what limited action it could to minimize the resultant illegal cutting.[257] Happily for the province, subsequent rail construction eastward along Superior confined this highly suspect enterprise to woodlands that Ontario could more satisfactorily police and profitably administer.

After its completion, the CPR continued to require a moderate annual quota from northwestern forests. This was needed for normal maintenance of its line across the region and for the trackage of the eastern prairies. Such modest withdrawals were to add to the income and economic stability of a growing woodland population along its course. The health of the Lakehead forest industry was bolstered by the demands of protective harbour work in front of the wharves of Port Arthur. This was subsequent to the heavy railway expenditure on port facilities and early grain storage along the Kam. Such protective work on the lakefront was begun in 1883, and the 5,000 feet of breakwater required enormous quantities of tamarack piling and other crib timber to contain its rock core.[258] Most of this harvest would be taken from the Kam watershed and the Sibley and Black Bay peninsulas to the east, as would much more harbour materials later.

Other encouraging signs in local woodland endeavours now came with moderate growth in pine lumbering. In the spring of 1881, C.W. Carpenter, who had originally come north to operate the Dawson Road, bought about 40 square miles of the former limits of Oliver and Davidson. To this he added enlarged mills on the Kam and new ones at Carp River. He also took on a new limit to the south on the Cloud River, and from these properties generated a respectable million board feet of pine the following year. During that season, he was joined by Graham, Horne and Co., yet another saw firm up from Georgian Bay.[259] Indeed, the mill towns of Simcoe County would figure prominently at the Lakehead in these early railway years when lumber demands were high in Winnipeg and prices soared. So high did the prices become at the Lakehead that individuals constructing hotels and other buildings in Fort William temporarily stopped or postponed their efforts.[260] Under these profitable boom conditions firms from Parry Sound and Midland even chartered steam barges and tow hulks to carry lumber up the lakes for the Winnipeg market. As much as 50 million board feet of Georgian Bay lumber passed in this way across Lakehead wharves and west to Manitoba in 1883.[261] However, this thrust was to dwindle away about mid-decade in the face of much less certain profits and much more proximal supplies. Ironically, this whole westward trend was countered in December 1886 when the first flat cars of lumber from British Columbia were reported passing through the Lakehead for markets in central Canada.[262]

The inflated prices and opportunities for participation in this lumber boom had not been missed by local entrepreneurs. By the spring of 1883, Carpenter's mills and those of Graham and Horne had been considerably enlarged, while two other businessmen, James Conmee and Thomas Marks, were planning or erecting large new facilities.[263] Crown Lands, anticipating such increased demand for resources, by late 1882 had arranged the opening of new pine limits in parts of the Kam watershed and others both to the south and east. In addition, timber in the remaining long-dormant lease on lands in the Fort William Reserve was put quickly to the axe. Even before the spring of 1884, considerable volumes of logs were being driven down the Slate and Whitefish rivers to mills on the Kam. Booms also were being towed here or to Port Arthur from southern camps on the Pine, Cloud, and Carp watersheds or such eastward ones as those on the Black Sturgeon River at the head of Black Bay[264] (see Maps 2.2 and 2.3).

Some of this enlarged local supply was probably intended originally for the Manitoba trade. Yet most of it would seem to have been utilized domestically to fill the requirements of the two growing Lakehead communities and their ports. In any case, the actual size of the industry seems to have been unexpectedly constrained. While contemporary estimates of reserves (principally of white as opposed to red pine) ran as high as three billion feet, a large tract of white pine in the Pigeon and Arrow River watershed was reserved until the nineties. Moreover, bad fires in the second half of the eighties burned or scorched huge tracts of limits south and west of the Kam. Despite intensive salvage programs sponsored by the province, much of this damaged timber was found to be unusable for lumber, which may explain why the peak labour force in the local camps never reached 500 men.[265]

Across the Divide

By far the most intense and rapid harvesting of regional forests in these years occurred west of Great Lakes drainage. Here real beginnings had to await the arrival of rail, and development through the period was impeded by the Dominion–provincial boundary dispute. W.J. Macauley first asked Ottawa about pine tracts on the Lake of the Woods in 1872. However, his office was reminded that as yet no treaty had been signed for the area and that federal timber regulations were not yet in place there.[266] Richard Fuller and Co. from Hamilton, like Macauley, already had limits and hungry mills in Manitoba and may have made even earlier inquiries of the same nature. Certainly, Fuller was granted first timber selection, and before December 31, 1875, had decided upon all islands in the north half of the lake and a small block along its eastern shore.[267] Macauley was permitted the next twelve months to make his selection, with the additional freedom to choose scattered blocks of less than 20 square miles and to take them on both the Lake of the Woods and Rainy Lake watersheds. In turn, during 1877, S.H. Fowler, also from southern Ontario, settled upon a series of pineries exclusively about Rainy Lake and such tributary rivers as the Manitou and Seine.[268] In this way, these three federal licensees (held by Ontario to be political jobbers who had been unfairly allowed to occupy all commercially valuable stands) each gained a limit of up to 100 square miles for twenty-one years but were warned to expect no protection if the province were to win the boundary case.

Given the sequence of events at both Goulais-Batchawana and the Lakehead, the next developments were predictable. When the railway reached the yet-to-be-completed bridge across the Winnipeg River to Rat Portage in 1880, the stage was set. Fowler, with his new steam mill at Fort Frances, was already into a profitable transfer of his interests to a group of central Canadians calling themselves the Rainy Lake Lumber Co. Fuller in turn had assigned his limits and a water mill at Cross Lake to John Mather and Ottawa associates as the Keewatin Lumber Co. Macauley, who was working to complete his dam and mill at neighbouring Norman, was about to share his collective forest enterprise with Dick and Banning, an established firm from Winnipeg.[269] In spite of all these financial manoeuvres, by July 1881 the first small supplies of lumber began to flow from among these mills to eager wholesalers on the Red River.[270]

In anticipation of the arrival of track at the Lake of the Woods and the track's future progress, mills for railway materials were already rising in 1879 along the eastward right of way as far as Vermilion Bay on Eagle Lake, about 60 miles inland. Others on Lake Wabigoon, in the Ignace area, at the bridge on the English River and near Savanne would follow as construction developed.[271] Blatant misrepresentation of real railway requirements was as rife along this route in the early eighties as Ontario had believed it to be. Contractors, employing several thousand men, cut far in excess of railway needs, often without the required prior surveys and frequently far beyond the zone to which their activity was legally limited.[272] Such actions, abetted by corruption among federally appointed forest rangers, were curbed modestly by the frequent and stiff penalties assessed by William Margash. He was appointed by Ontario in early 1883 as a special timber agent to look after provincial forest interests along this section of railway.[273]

A similar cycle of rail-related activity prevailed about the Lake of the Woods, where the collective communities of Rat Portage, Norman, and Keewatin became a temporary focus for the mills of numerous contractors. Indeed, at one point, suitable land was so limited that two firms found themselves contesting an acreage that was not sufficient for both to use.[274] Huge quantities of rail timber for prairie sections were boomed in from camps down the lake where the same violations of timbering regulations were startlingly common, until dampened by Margash's arrival. With the last spike on the CPR late in 1885 and the subsequent reduction of this once-swollen industry to simpler size, however, most of these mills quietly disappeared, as did the related levels of forest abuses.

Given this colourful but unfortunate interlude, pine lumbering still typified the forest economy of this westerly area over the eighties. When the Rainy Lake Lumber Co.'s large and alternate mill at Rat Portage opened in the spring of 1883, the combined capacity about the outlet to the Winnipeg River reached 250,000 feet per twelve-hour shift. The supply of pine logs to feed this substantial appetite came off combined limits up this watershed, which now totalled about 410 square miles and would grow further.[275]

After early years of heavy exploitation, Keewatin's proximal limits on the northerly islands in Lake of the Woods began to run out. More and more emphasis by all three major contenders became focused on inland limits east of that water body, made accessible by dams and timber slides. To these were added others above the mouth of the Rainy River. Their collective winter camps often absorbed up to 2,500 men, including many local aboriginals and settlers. At Rainy River's outlet a booming, sorting, and rafting complex was established in 1885 to separate and prepare each company's cut before transport to its mills behind one of an increasingly large fleet of lake tugs.[276] The system was not foolproof and in the spring of the following year sudden floods loosed 22 million feet of logs over guard timbers here and scattered them over Lake of the Woods.[277]

During the years to follow, seasonal cuts, often much in excess of 40 million feet, were commonly collected in this river mouth facility and were augmented at the mills by the above-mentioned harvest from east of the Lake of the Woods.[278] Much of the timber down the Rainy River came from legal limits as far up the watershed as the Seine, but the total continued to be significantly salted with illegal logs from Native property and settler cutting. Later in the decade such logs also came increasingly from isolated Minnesota tracts on Rainy Lake and down American tributaries to the Rainy River. The adjacent state, which had yet to settle this frontier, took umbrage on discovery of these illegal activities and was proceeding with a major inquiry into these Canadian infractions as the period closed.[279]

The annual marketing of the resultant volume of manufactured lumber was not without its problems. The demand for pine in Manitoba fluctuated after about 1883, and stiff American competition exacerbated this tendency. This situation, complicated by participation from the distant mills of Georgian Bay, caused the first of several unpredictable periods of high inventories around mid-decade.[280] The ensuing cash flow problems, combined with the loss by fire of a new mill at Rat Portage, put Rainy Lake Lumber in the hands of its bankers in 1886. However, its remaining mills at Fort Frances were soon running again, first under a receiver and then as a reorganized company.[281] Later in the eighties disconcerting lulls left the participants with millions of board feet on hand at one year's end, only to be scrambling for logs to saw by the next summer. Nevertheless, the decade closed on a high note, with anticipated winter cuts of 60 million feet and with forecasts for mill employment the following summer in excess of a thousand hands.[282]

While these lumbering enterprises around Rat Portage were certainly the most spectacular of the period, they were not the only participants in the pine industry to the west of Superior. In 1881, the Dominion Lands Branch had revoked the twenty-one-year clause in most of its earlier timber agreements and introduced a new system of annual rents. It had also adopted a policy that made future limits single blocks of approximately 50 square miles, under a similar system of very modest yearly charges. These new regulations came into effect in 1882 and, without consultation with an exasperated Ontario, were made applicable all the way to the eastern edge of the arctic watershed.[283] By the end of 1884, almost 1,500 square miles of such limits had been taken up, some in the complex country north of Rainy Lake, others on Lac Seul and adjoining reaches of the English River. Most, however, were nearer the railway around Eagle Lake, Lake Wabigoon, and Lac des Mille Lacs.[284] Many more of these popular licences might have been granted. However, their issuance was suspended at mid-decade when the province started related court action in the precedent-setting case of the St Catherines Lumber Co. (This litigation was eventually key to the conclusion of territorial squabbling here between Ottawa and Toronto.)[285] Most of these agreements covered substantial additions to the pool of legally available pine. Such resources were sometimes procured for local mills, like those at Eagle Lake and Lake Wabigoon, which had been purchased by Graham and Horne or other lumbering interests from Port Arthur to supply the prairie. Others, particularly about Lac des Mille Lacs and those of Thomas Marks around Ignace, were taken up as limits from which pine logs could be moved to the tracks and transported to their owners' mills at the railhead on Superior.[286]

On the settlement of its territorial dispute with Ottawa, Ontario moved quickly to assert its control and to bring timber operations in the once-contested area into line with its practices elsewhere. In 1889 it cancelled all federal timber licences that were not being actively worked and issued one-year permits for the balance. By the following July it had arranged for the October disposal of a wide range of timber berths here and across northwestern Ontario. This sale was to include the last modest tract in Crown hands behind Sault Ste Marie, numerous pineries east and north of Rainy Lake, and similar areas near Superior on the Minnesota boundary. As well, it was later to add other stands that had been recently fire-damaged in the Lac des Mille Lacs watershed.[287]

The application of marketing by tender and certain new conditions of sale that were standard provincial policy brought loud protests from Rat Portage interests, who were accustomed to more considered treatment. They demanded continuation of the permit system, threatening to boycott the sale, to buy their logs from Minnesota, and to deny the growing farm population on the Rainy River its accustomed winter employment.[288] Ignoring their cries, the province successfully marketed most of the properties it put up for auction. Indeed, it obtained an unexpectedly high return of almost three million dollars in bonuses for what the *Globe* described as 'often sparse and poorly explored acreage.' In addition to about 20 square miles in Aweres Township inland from the St Marys River, the province sold six berths totalling 44 square miles in the area of the Pigeon and Arrow rivers, a parcel of 38 square miles around Lac des Mille Lacs, and twelve limits encompassing 285 square miles in the Rainy Lake country.[289] Even before this event, a new mood was evident in the industry west of Superior. Here the energetic Mr Margash was already busily engaged in cruising for further pine stands to satisfy Ontario's aggressive marketing intentions.[290]

All That Glitters

Silver and Gold

Silver, more than gold, continued to be the touchstone of mining development in Ontario's northwest region over these decades, which were highlighted by the discovery and development of Silver Islet. This was an offshore portion of the Woods Location on the Sibley Peninsula, one of the acquisitions of the old Montreal Mining Company. Faced suddenly with annual taxes on its lands, that firm ordered Thomas Macfarlane in 1868 to reassess this, along with other of its properties.[291] His discovery of the rich potential of this tiny island led the Company to order him to prove-up this find, while over the next two years a purchaser was quietly sought. Late in 1870, a consortium of New York and Detroit interests, calling themselves the Ontario Mineral Lands Company, took up this location, along with Montreal Mining's other tracts on Superior. Next they isolated this particular parcel for immediate development through an incorporation under New York State law, leaving the rest dormant and later open to rapacious pulp harvesting. Over the following dozen years the resultant mine was to process over $3.5 million worth of silver through the Wyandotte Refinery in Detroit. Its innovative owners were also responsible for the regional introduction of the diamond drill for exploration, the pneumatic hammer for rapid mining, and the use of pressurized ventilation to push their search far underground. Its management also made major contributions to machinery for ore separation and grading. However, by the end of 1882 the commercial potential of its lode was nearing exhaustion, and two years later, when the pumps were halted in late fall by a delay in the arrival of more coal, the shaft was allowed to fill with water.

During its relatively short life, Silver Islet's startling wealth was the frequent subject of comments in government reports, in the press, and in the world's great mining journals. It attracted to the Lakehead area a steady flow of skilled Cornish workers departing the then-failing mining industry in their homeland. To this was added a badly needed supply of experienced American mining men and a much enlarged injection of international capital. It also stimulated much prospecting and the resultant location of thousands of acres of new mining claims within townships laid out for that purpose and across the miles of territory round about. In the shadow of this spectacular find, the older, more marginal mines about the Lakehead, like the Shuniah, limped on. These were joined periodically by new silver finds such as the Beck and 3A, other speculative possibilities among the islands off Thunder Bay, or enthusiastically touted locations to east and west along the lake.

In 1882, closure at Silver Islet and the demise of the Duncan, which was the last of the initial producers, did not spell the end of the local silver boom. During the previous autumn, Oliver Daunais (later styled the Silver King), on information supplied by his Indian friend Weisaw, had located the first rich deposits at Rabbit Mountain a few miles inland from Fort William. He and his partners staked neighbouring rich properties (the future Porcupine, Beaver, and Twin City mines) over the winter and the next spring. Despite newspaper rumours in December 1881, their secret was well kept and the real prospecting rush began only in 1883. By this time senior mine captains and the pick of the Cornish miners from Silver Islet were busily at work at their Rabbit Mountain Mine. As with later properties on which Daunais initiated development, lucrative sale of this mine to a foreign interest followed.

By 1884, again on the advice of his Indian friend Weisaw, Daunais had staked new rich exposures on Silver Mountain, a few miles to the southwest. These finds continued to fuel the heavy rush. It now attracted mining personnel from as far away as Colorado and financial interests from both sides of the Atlantic. The following year saw provincial funds match money from mining firms to produce a previously mentioned road to the CPR at Murillo. Over this combined route to Lakehead docks much ore from a dozen mines soon was passing on its way to smelters as distant as New Jersey. The labour pool, once largely composed of Cornishmen and Scandinavians, now came to include Finns and Italians, as well as some Canadians who had entered the area as rail workers. The close of the decade also saw PAD&W railway tracks reach the neighbourhood and heighten access for ore shipment.[292]

While silver certainly was the continuing mainstay, it was far from unique in regional mining activity. In the autumn of 1871, a total of twenty-four locations were surveyed around Jackfish Lake, west from Lake Shebandowan. Here Peter McKeller, a well-known and experienced prospector and promoter, had recently discovered gold. However, his find was in the still-untreatied land west of the divide, and the incipient rush of American and Canadian prospectors and miners the next spring was turned back by the local Native band.[293] Development work on several sites here began again in 1875 but was hampered by difficult access from the Dawson Road. In the early eighties this situation was eased by a route south from the new railway at Savanne, using scows and a small tug to cross Lac des Mille Lacs.[294] Ottawa interests bought the principal location at Jackfish Lake about this time and, as the Huronia Mining Co., transported a full range of equipment over this route. After deepening the shaft and adding a stamp mill, it obtained with the now-neighbouring Canadian Gold Mining Co. matching funds from Ontario in 1878 to improve the road section of its access to Savanne.[295] However, both these operations fell into temporary inactivity by the end of the decade. Other gold finds east along the Superior shore in the Pic River area, on the Slate Islands, inland from Jackfish Bay, and near Rossport still lay largely unexplored.[296]

Base Metals and Iron

The heavy prospecting drive that marked these years resulted in a much broadened appreciation of the range of minerals associated with the Lakehead. In the Black Bay area the search revealed the existence of rich lead deposits, and by the late seventies generated the development of the large Enterprise Mine there, as well as the Ogema.[297] Beginning in 1882, excellent quarries of red stone, discovered about Nipigon Bay and on the islands offshore, supplied large annual shipments to Chicago building firms.[298] Similarly, good zinc was turned up near the modern town of Schreiber and may have undergone some initial extraction on the later completion of the CPR.[299] However, the early years of these new eastward endeavours along Superior were also marred by a major swindle involving supposed tin deposits near Otter Head on the Pukaskwa Peninsula.[300] Fortunately, while this scam earned some bad American press and no laurels among the investment community, it did little to counter rising outside interest in the area's mineral potential.

To the west and northwest of the Lakehead this knowledge of mineral resources also involved iron. Finds north of Shebandowan along the CPR were uncovered during rail construction in the early eighties but were not effectively explored until the next decade.[301] The McKeller find on the river near Atikokan was patented in 1887 and drew considerable excitement from the professional geologist Robert Bell the next season. Much prospecting followed, with American interests hoping for a continuation of the rich iron ranges of Minnesota.[302] At the close of the decade, Belgians, working through their Canadian consul and their national bank, were busy formulating plans to mine here, to smelt in

Fort William, and to sell to a Chicago iron and steel firm.[303] Such plans were to be revived later, but not before the turn of the century.

On eastern Superior, mining interest returned exclusively to copper, save for an early and improbable flurry by the Victoria Silver and Lead Co. on a location in Prince Township near Sault Ste Marie.[304] High copper prices in the later seventies encouraged renewed interest around both Michipicoten Island and Mamainse (Pointe aux Mines). Promising properties here passed to British companies, who were startlingly lavish in their expenditure on equipment, wages, and facilities. About 1880, the Michipicoten Native Copper Co. started operations, complete with its own steamer, the *Steinhoff*. The following year, the Canadian Native Copper Co. began its spending spree at Mamainse with a previously noted winter road, jointly financed with Ontario, to the Batchawana terminus of the colonization route from the Sault. Neither was to enjoy a long life. After reorganization at mid-decade and a further year of exploratory diamond drilling under strict economy, the last miners at the former were delivered south in the spring of 1868. The latter closed the previous fall, wound up its final affairs in 1888, and stood as an expensive ghost town at the close of the period.[305]

Gold Again

West of the Lake Superior watershed rumours of mineral wealth, particularly of gold, pre-dated 1870. In the area east of Rainy Lake, confirmation came first during the Wolseley Expedition and later from prospectors who gained access to this country from the Dawson Road. Yet, apart from the iron activity around Atikokan, this area remained dormant in 1890.[306]

Farther north and west rumours of minerals did not appear until the era of railway construction. While new gold finds inland at Lake Wabigoon and farther east along the rail survey came with the eighties, in the fall of 1879, rich ones were reported from more westerly points towards Rat Portage.[307] The following June the *Winnipeg Free Press* was eulogizing about 'A Country of Rich Minerals.' By then a Mr. Heenan was resident at his mining property on Hay Island about 15 miles up the Lake of the Woods, and several properties surveyed over the winter were about to see their first exploration.[308] However, the anticipated rush in the spring of 1880 did not transpire, although by then access was no problem by rail or locally by water. The issue then and for the rest of the decade was clear land title. This was necessary to secure stable investment but impossible until the resolution of the territorial dispute between Ontario and Canada/Manitoba.[309] By 1882 there were some 200 mining locations on the islands and about the shores of the lake. Unfortunately, only a handful had seen more than surface stripping, and even those with shallow shafts were 'waiting for something to happen.'[310]

However, that summer saw the first tentative investment of real capital. Winnipeg interests created the Manitoba Consolidated Mining Co. and began to develop several promising properties on Clearwater Bay. The same year also witnessed the first American financial backing for the Sultana Island Mine, after very successful assays in Detroit.[311] The next spring Heenan and his associated, whose mine had a promising shaft, were able to dispose of stock in Toronto and New York. By that autumn at least seven and possibly nine mining companies, most with risk capital from the United States, were assembling imported machinery. Indeed, Manitoba Consolidated had poured its first small gold brick.[312] Newspaper excitement reached exuberant heights.

But here things stopped again. This was blamed by the press on heightened friction in the boundary dispute and on the new federal mining regulations, which had dampened American interest. These regulations included limitations and charges, which investors found as unpalatable as the provincial ones they had helped to overturn on Lake Superior in the sixties.[313] Yet the root of the problem lay elsewhere, partly in the goals of those who had carved out the locations and partly in the allied aims of those now willing to risk their finances. As one professional observer wrote in 1885,

> It would appear that the main object of proprietors of the Lake of the Woods mining locations has been from the outset to sell their claims to capitalists at the highest figure and with this in view have trusted more to sensational newspaper advertising than to the intrinsic value of their properties, which could only be established by systematic development.[314]

Far too many in this mixed population were simply promoters, interested in a quickly profitable flip of holdings now supplied with impressive machinery, not in the sound application of such equipment to the development of these mineral finds.

These combined woes and certain conflicting assessments of this gold field, which now began to appear more prominently in both the Canadian and American press, would continue to retard serious development. By 1888, there were said to be twenty-five to thirty active locations in the area, but only the Sultana and Gold Hill claimed to have begun more than tentative commercial production.[315] Only the former was capable of standing up to the rigorous professional assessment demanded prior to its purchase by Taylor and Sons of London, England, in 1890.[316] More tellingly, a firm incorporated in the late eighties and bonused by the municipality of Rat Portage had struggled to create a central reduction works to treat ore from lesser mines than the Sultana, which already had a refining facility. However on its opening, no smaller mines were operating and no prior ore was on their stockpiles for processing.[317] For many investors, northwestern Ontario remained a land of uncertain or even suspect mineral promise in 1890. Its exploration was as yet tightly confined to areas readily accessible from rail and water communication. Finds within such limited bands along Superior's shore and both the CPR's new trackage and the old fur corridor west to the Lake of the Woods were encouragingly numerous and varied. Even within these circumscribed bands prospectors as yet had made only a quick assessment, and much more wealth might yet be uncovered. Unlike the continuing silver activity about the Lakehead, but like the old copper finds of eastern Superior, the gold field on the Lake of the Woods had still to prove its commercial viability. Elsewhere, and in other minerals, discovery too often had been followed by nothing more than short-term speculative development indicative of finds of low or marginal value.

Growing Commercial Fishing

The fishing industry increased and changed quite remarkably between 1870 and 1890. Late in the period, the Hudson's Bay Company's traditional harvest of post provisions on distant inland lakes, like St Joseph and Lac Seul, was supplemented by small private commercial operations on these and other lakes such as Lac des Mille Lacs.[318] Similarly, on the American side of the Lake of the Woods a commercial ice fishery was begun in 1883, and later pound net owners there came to ship their summer catches west over the CPR.[319] Canadian commercial fishing, however, remained intensively focused on Lake Superior. Total catch on Ontario's side of the lake climbed from slightly over 310 tons to three-and-a-half times that figure in the twenty years after 1870 (see Table 2.2). While the Algoma shore and markets at Sault Ste Marie accounted for slightly more than half the catch in 1871, this share would fall to much less than a third two decades later. The rising importance of Port Arthur as a market centre reflected not only its improved access by steamer to eastern outlets but also the opening of U.S. trackage west from Duluth in 1870 and the subsequent opening of the CPR.[320] Throughout the period the most prized species remained whitefish, followed by lake trout, although harvested proportions of these two varied with time and location. The salted product had dominated in 1871, except around Sault Ste Marie. In 1880 the general proportion of preserved to fresh fish dropped to 68 per cent and plummeted to less than 25 per cent by 1890.

TABLE 2.2 Lake Superior Commercial Fisheries Catch (in pounds), 1871–1891

	1871	1881	1891
Algoma Shore			
Whitefish	179,600	74,400	326,200
Lake trout	138,400	152,200	351,400
Total	318,000	226,600	677,600
North Shore			
Whitefish	290,600	196,600	939,000
Lake trout	13,000	235,600	447,000
Total	303,600	452,600*	1,525,000*
Grand Total	621,600	679,200*	2,202,600*

* These figures for 1881 and 1891 include 20,400 and 139,000 pounds, respectively, of other fish.
Source: Compiled from tables accompanying the Reports of the Federal Department of Marine and Fisheries, 1871 to 1891.

These shifts in production reflected not only changing market demands but also the rise of new fishing methods and more efficient business organization. The seventies, and more particularly the eighties, witnessed the rise of large fishery firms in the area, often with financial backing from the United States. These firms were able to afford the elaborate stations, icing facilities, pound nets, steam tugs, and transport systems that went with the growing fresh fish trade.[321] Since these companies were also the key marketing agencies and the holders of most of the licences, previously independent fishermen came increasingly to assume the role of either wage labourers or contracted tenants. They did not accept this change willingly, fighting unsuccessfully in the seventies for a system of independent boat licences, as opposed to territorial ones, which placed them under company control.[322]

These decades also witnessed considerable international friction over Great Lakes fisheries. In the United States, authority for regulating such resources lay with the individual states, which applied few rules. In Canada, such matters were up to the federal government, which in 1868 had passed legislation to confirm the closed season each November and the commercial licensing system already in place. American fishermen, however, ignoring these rules, poached blatantly and sometimes intensively on the isolated shores of lakes like Superior. This raised considerable Canadian ire in spite of renewed federal emphasis on fishery surveillance and conciliatory cross-border discussions of the problem.[323]

Friction also marked the fish trade between the two nations. By the early eighties certain American interests claimed that they were prevented from fishing under licence in Canadian waters (where the regulations now permitted only Canadian equipment and labour). They also cried foul at a related tariff of a penny a pound to sell their American catch there. They asked for and received an extra half-cent per pound on the existing duty for the huge volume of Canadian fish then entering the United States.[324] However, this attempt by the numerous small American operators suffering financially from a public preference for Canadian fish was to fail in its price-protective intent. The giant fish wholesalers in Buffalo, Detroit, and Chicago now bought heavily into fishing companies in ports like Collingwood, Sault Ste Marie, and Port Arthur to circumvent the above requirement for the use of Canadian equipment in Canadian waters. Through manipulation of U.S. law, a catch in Canadian waters, by Canadians, and using 'Canadian equipment' magically changed nationality during transport in American vessels from one side of the lakes to the other. Other international irregularities in the fisheries on the lakes were also ignored by both governments. For example, the industry at Port Arthur, where the northern open-water period for fishing was short and further curtailed by the fall closed season, was allowed to harvest off American Isle Royale each November. In return, local fishermen from Minnesota were permitted to use certain grounds each spring on the immediate Canadian side of the international boundary off the Pigeon River.[325] However, these comfortable conditions suffered a rude jolt at the end of the eighties, when the McKinley Act threatened not only to heighten the duty on Canadian fish but also to tighten restrictions on their import into the United States.[326]

The recovery of the fishery north of Sault Ste Marie from the doldrums of the sixties was indeed rapid, as the first full statistical report in 1871 reveals. While certain U.S.-backed operators from Sault Ste Marie were ready to return to these grounds, such well-established Collingwood firms as Clark Brothers and the Nobles were also quick to expand their operations here. At least as early as 1874, the Clarks, with their tug *Hathaway* and a dozen mackinaw boats, were working waters about Goulais and Batchawana Bay, as well as the adjacent Ile Parisienne.[327] By that time they had also established a permanent station at Gargantua Harbour and fished extensively from there. Although the record is incomplete, a similar facility on the Lizard was in the local hands of Sherman and Roussain. As well, Endress Brothers from the Michigan side of the St Marys River was established, through Canadian affiliates, at Quebec Harbour on Michipicoten Island.[328] Although some of the labour force on these stations was made up of local Natives or men up from Georgian Bay, much of it was composed of persons of mixed blood, many of whom remained more conversant in French than in English.[329] While the Michipicoten Native Copper

Co. was in business during the seventies, their steamer, the *Steinhoff*, appears to have accommodated the simple needs of salt fish stations along the Algoma shore. However, the strictly scheduled requirements of fresh fisheries kept tugs like the *Hathaway* running busily between the stations here and the major steamer connections at Sault Ste Marie.[330]

With the eighties came a much-enhanced shift to serve the rapidly expanding fresh fish market. This in turn brought heavy infusions of Buffalo capital into Clark Brothers' and Detroit finances into Nobles' operations here, as well as on Lake Huron and Georgian Bay. It also promoted the transfer of Sackett's Harbour money from Lake Ontario to sponsor the Canadian appearance of Ganley and Ainsworth along the east shore, from a headquarters on the St Marys River.[331] With these changes came the introduction of pound nets to the inshore fishery, wherever the coastal conditions would permit, and the increasing use of offshore fisheries under more traditional gill nets. By 1885 a total of fifteen pound nets were being operated in the waters of Goulais and Batchawana bays, and before the end of the decade similar devices were commonly at work near Michipicoten River.[332] By that date, the large tug *Anne Clark*, modified to include cabin and freight space, was running regularly between the Michipicoten River and Sault Ste Marie, serving both the fishing stations and coasting needs of this shore.[333]

On the north side of Superior, east of Nipigon, the early seventies witnessed the revival of the salt fish industry through the activity of numerous independent fishermen. Such persons had reoccupied the rough fishing camps along the coast and on the islands off Nipigon Bay. Large establishments at this time were rare. Early ones included a community of eighteen fishermen on Salter Island and a smaller gathering at Wilson Island. At another, probably off the mouth of the Aguasabon, about 5,000 barrels of pickled whitefish were taken annually.[334] Beyond the range of the three mackinaw boats at Peninsula Harbour, however, the Pukaskwa Peninsula remained unused by fishing interests on this coast and those up the east side of the lake.

Only in the latter part of the decade did substantial business interests and the fresh fish industry begin to invade this area. Here numerous immigrant Norwegians and parties up from lower lakes now joined the existing population of fishermen.[335] In 1877, O'Malley Brothers set up a large station at the mouth of the Nipigon River. With their tug *Mary Hurlbert* they exported 7,250 barrels of whitefish that first season to railheads on the Wisconsin side of the lake.[336] The following year they opened a fresh fishery, using pound nets to good result. However, other operators, who made the same attempt but chose their pound locations badly, lost heavily along this rugged coast. As a result, gill nets remained the choice of most inshore as well as offshore fishing interests here well into the eighties.[337] By then, substantial stations also existed at Nipigon and Rossport, as well as at Jackfish Bay, Port Coldwell, and both Heron Bay and Peninsula Harbour. One of the major proprietors here was Noble Brothers of Collingwood but others had more local roots. Most of these ports had served as supply centres for earlier railway contractors, and the fishermen had benefited from such facilities as abandoned warehousing and sturdy docks. Shipping problems at these ports were solved by the CPR, which also became a steady customer for its dining-car needs. By the end of the period, these were thriving communities, often with as many as two tugs and a dozen or more mackinaw boats steadily at work from break-up to freeze.[338]

Farther west about the Lakehead, a considerable domestic fishery on Thunder Bay and stations offshore was maintained by the Hudson's Bay Company until the closure of Fort William in 1881. Little record remains of what must have been a lively and lucrative era in the seventies. In those years individuals and groups of fishermen, in camps from Black Bay west and south to the mouth of the Pigeon River, found a good income in supplying miners, Dawson Road crews, and full-time residents on Thunder Bay.

In 1879, the Lake Superior Fish Co. was formed at Prince Arthur's Landing and soon had a sequence of formal stations, serviced daily by two tugs. This firm sent the bulk of its fresh fish to Detroit, by way of the Beatty Line steamers, and the balance to Minneapolis via vessels to Duluth.[339] About that time, pound nets were introduced and found instant success in the sheltered coastal waters of both Black and Thunder bays, although gill nets remained widely used elsewhere.[340] In 1882, the rival Thunder Bay Fish Co. was formed by American and Canadian interests from Lake Erie, adding its tug, *Three Friends*, to the trade.[341] Both firms began immediately to ship fresh fish west over the newly opened CPR to Manitoba and swelled the supply down Superior to eastern markets.[342] However, using transport supplied by Cooley and LaVeque of Duluth, they also considerably expanded their midwestern markets. In 1885, these and smaller interests about the Lakehead united as the Port Arthur Fish Co., controlling four tugs, forty-four mackinaw boats, and crews. They required 2,000 tons of ice each year and sponsored both gill nets and pound nets as far east as Jackfish Bay. By the end of the decade, this firm was shipping almost 550 tons of fish each year to suppliers in Buffalo and Toronto as well as Chicago, St Paul, and Winnipeg.[343]

The Beginnings of Tourism

Excursions by steamer to Sault Ste Marie from Sturgeon Bay, at the Georgian Bay terminus of the stage route from Toronto, appear in newspaper ads and vacation diaries from the late forties. Prominent among such visitors were writers like William Kingston and later John Disturnell, who followed the earlier tour by Anna Jameson. In 1857, other sightseeing travellers (including the Toronto painter William Armstrong) chartered the *Collingwood* and journeyed north to the Lakehead with the Hind Expedition.[344] With the opening of rail at Collingwood and a canal at Sault Ste Marie in 1855, such tourists were among the growing number of travellers to the upper lakes who frequented the St Marys Rapids or wrote interesting descriptions of Quebec Harbour, Nipigon, and Thunder Cape on their passage up Superior.[345]

At the beginning of the seventies, the growing passenger traffic was sufficient for the addition of scheduled shipping from Sarnia to the Lakehead, doubling the weekly service.[346] This now included miners and labourers, settlers (including Mennonites and others destined for Manitoba), businessmen, and sportsmen. The commodious Queen's Hotel, an addition to the older boarding houses about Port Arthur docks, was a logical result. It came to be joined by the larger Northern and other facilities in Fort William.[347] These places also came to serve as the first summer resorts. They advertised visits to the neighbouring Indian reserve for crafts, picnic trips by stage to Kakabeka Falls, charter fishing on the tug *Watchman*, and sightseeing cruises on the Kam to Point Demeuron. Such characteristic Victorian delights were in heavy demand here by 1890, when plans for both a pleasure park and resort at Kakabeka were in an advanced stage of discussion.[348]

These decades also saw the growing fame of the speckled trout sport fishery on the Nipigon River, which had seen only tentative use in the sixties. Sportsmen, dropped from calling steamers or coming on their own yachts, were increasingly common, so much so as to require a government fish guardian and permit system by 1873.[349] By the end of the eighties descriptive articles in the press and features in sporting magazines were common. They were attracting both the adventurous and the wealthy, not only from Canada and the United States, but from England and Europe.[350] Suggestions also were being made that the CPR or other interests should erect a good summer hotel here to serve this growing and often very monied trade.[351]

Ironically, the Canadian Sault benefited little from this rising recreational interest. The large population that enjoyed vacations here was prone to go to the American shore for more adequate or lavish accommodation.[352] Like its Michigan competition, the Ontario community also suffered from the alternate attraction of famous Mackinac, where most vessels stopped on their way to these St Marys River communities. Nevertheless, discriminating travellers and diarists, such as William Kingston and John Disturnell, were strong in their praise of the Canadian sport fishing at the St Marys Rapids and the sport to be had on rivers entering Goulais and Batchawana bays.[353] They also made fond reference to Pim's small but comfortable inn on the Ontario shore. By the late eighties, tourist demand at the Canadian Sault finally reached a level sufficient to invite the construction of the International Hotel, with its two to three hundred rooms.[354]

Yet the real surprise in tourism was far to the west. Here earlier sporting claims for the Rainy River were suddenly stifled by Winnipeg's discovery of the railhead town of Rat Portage and its adjacent vacation opportunities on the Lake of the Woods.[355] By 1881, the *Winnipeg Free Press* was boosting Mr Rideout's hotel and health resort and the canoeing, fishing, cruising, and picnicking opportunities in the area. Two years later, a pamphlet promoting the same ends was in wide circulation.[356] In 1884, wealthy Winnipegers were renting summer accommodation in the community or building summer homes in its neighbourhood.[357] For others, annual excursions here by clubs and societies were also available. These exhausting one-day events were complete with bands, games, lake cruises, dinners, and entertainment before late evening departure west again by train. They came to be paralleled each summer by an influx of campers who tented around the area.[358] In 1890, the more than 300 wealthy family members ensconced here for the season mounted their first regatta. This event would later make the area recreationally quite famous.[359]

Resultant Nodal Development

Fuelled by this mix of development, the nodal and neo-urban side of the region began to escalate by 1890. While the old pattern of fur posts continued to prosper beyond the expanding frontier of white activity, their importance elsewhere was generally much reduced. However, in a few instances, such old premises had become large general stores for the new communities now rising about them.

Most of the scatter of new places were very new indeed, being a product of the railway. Ones like Ignace, Schreiber, and White River had in 1890 little more than the raw trappings of the important divisional points they would become. Their clusters of roundhouse, shops, coaling tower, and water tank had been thrown up quickly and now would enter upon a cycle of improvement and enlargement. As yet their hastily surveyed and subdivided plots hosted only such essentials as a rooming house and store, along with a street or two of rough railway housing along the tracks. Such centres, however, were far ahead of the few budding nodes in agricultural areas, to which the business directories of the day rarely ascribe more than a lonely general store.

Yet two places in the extreme west of the region had considerably longer and more active histories. Fort Frances (first known as Alberton) had sprung up about Fowler's sawmills and the old Hudson's Bay Company post at the

Kouchiching Falls on the Rainy River in 1874.[360] It had flourished on the trade of the Dawson Road and on the estimated 250 men employed on the construction of the early canal and related steamers here. Its newly surveyed site came to have about forty houses, several stores, a grist mill, and a newspaper office before the closure of this Dawson Route and the cessation of lock building in 1878.[361] At the beginning of the eighties, nearly half its homes and many of its stores stood empty. The only remaining source of major wage employment was the Rainy Lake Lumber Co., and that firm's financial troubles would close its much enlarged mills here for two seasons at mid-decade.[362] During the era of the disputed territory, its agricultural market functions were slow to expand and at the close of the eighties this village was still regaining its former momentum.[363]

Development at Rat Portage, with its satellite sisters of Keewatin and Norman, was quite different. These colourful saw towns, bolstered by railway construction, buffeted by mining uncertainties, but encouraged by rising tourism, first appeared in 1880. A year later, with a combined population of 500, they were linked by steam ferry across the entrance to the Winnipeg River, and Rat Portage was incorporated as a village. Meanwhile, despite rising competition, the Hudson's Bay Company store had come to thrive on its new retail markets, which it combined with its former business in fur and isinglass (from sturgeon) with the area's Indians.[364] During the rough-and-tumble days of the territorial dispute, Rat Portage gained an Ontario courthouse and jail, which Manitoba threatened to duplicate.[365] With the last spike at mid-decade, the collective community here could boast schools, churches, hotels, and even its first sidewalks. Mill capacity now required ten tugs to tow in booms of logs each season. In addition, two small steamers ran regularly to the increasing landings along the Rainy River and on to a rapidly recovering Fort Frances.[366] Despite the instability of lumber markets, the rest of the eighties witnessed steady growth to a combined population of over 3,000 as well as the construction of a bridge and floating causeway to unite this cluster further. Equally important by 1890 was the opening of the Lake of the Woods Milling Company. This Montreal-based firm was to use the water power potential here to flour prairie grain for eastern markets under its Five Roses label for almost a century. Its huge capacity was later joined by a second mill erected by a competitor, Robin Hood Milling (both burned in this century). At the close of the period Rat Portage had electricity in its major stores and in the homes of its wealthiest citizens.[367]

At the Lakehead, development of the twin towns that were destined to rise here proceeded differently from each other in the seventies. The cluster of wooden structures, homes, and shacks about the Landing (Port Arthur) on the government reserve behind and up the neighbouring slope of the Red River Road were included in a surveyed plot in 1871. With further additions they became the village of Prince Arthur's Landing the following year.[368] Through its service to the growing demands of local mining activity as well as the needs of both contractors and travellers over the Dawson Road, it also became a police village in 1872. However, the federal choice of the original Plot (West Fort William) in 1873 as the Lake Superior head for its CPR touched off a volcanic response from the Landing. That community, as the already rising centre of trade on Thunder Bay and the recognized terminus of navigation there since the days of the *Rescue*, had anticipated this role. As rail work began to stir at the Lakehead, a conciliatory Ottawa built a large new wharf out to the unobstructed deep water on the bay and early contractors built large warehouses and storage facilities here. These were served by tracks laid at community expense to the Plot and linked there to those of the railway without the CPR's agreement. This and later cavalier behaviour by Prince Arthur's Landing was to earn the animosity of the CPR's William Van Horne. His dislike would cost its commercial leaders dearly to the turn of the century. As a result, the railway continued to concentrate its functions and opportunities at Fort William after about 1885.

Meanwhile, through the rail-building era of the early eighties, advances at the Landing were rapid, as its waterfront provided the most suitable depth for vessels transporting loads of railway iron, building equipment, locomotives, and rolling stock. These usually proved too heavy to negotiate a reoccurring bar at the mouth of the Kam and direct transfer to the terminus up-river. The community came to boast a bank, some fifty businesses (including a brewery), churches, and a school as well as a population of about a thousand people by the close of the decade.[369] Further development immediately followed the completion of the CPR link from Winnipeg in 1882. Two years later, under the impetus of breakwater construction to protect this proven port and the rise of its first grain elevator, the Town of Port Arthur was incorporated with a population in excess of 6,000.[370]

Yet, with the transcontinental completion of the CPR in 1885, Port Arthur, now judicial centre and home to a growing labour component, suffered a lull. Unemployment rose and railway jobs were transferred slowly but continually to the rising port of Fort William on the Kam. The commercial economy slowed. Population dipped to less than 5,000 and the tax base shrank alarmingly. Businesses closed and uncertain silver prices caused local mining activity to waver. Boom town became gloom town with resultant paranoia figuring large in the editorials of the local press.[371]

Meanwhile, significant development at the riverside site of the future rival to Port Arthur, Fort William, appeared late, although its site was planned earlier. The original Plot (the modern West Fort William), surveyed in the sixties, was later joined by a subdivision (now East Fort William) nearer the mouth of the Kam. This bifurcated hamlet contained some two dozen dwellings in the early seventies when most of its economic activity centred on the new sawmills of Oliver, Davidson and Company.[372] The limited size and still-sleepy nature of the community made the reaction of its more vibrant neighbour, Prince Arthur's Landing, to the choice of the Plot as opposed to the Landing for the railway depot on Superior very understandable. However, this local reaction to the choice was soon lost on the general public in a din of parliamentary inquiry questioning the selection of this riverine harbour location and charging patronage in the selection of certain of Oliver and Davidson's property there.[373] While that storm would die with time, the local one set off a bitter urban rivalry at the Lakehead that would colour and complicate municipal relations there for almost a century.

Despite this federally initiated furor, by the autumn of 1875 a band of continuously occupied property on the east side of the Kam, including numerous residences, joined the two initial foci. Among other occupants of lots here were five hotels or boarding houses, extensive railway shops, several hundred feet of docks and wharves, in addition to extensive sawmills.[374] In 1877 land was cleared for a roundhouse at Westfort, where a small cluster of stores, businesses, houses, and other buildings had begun to rise and a population in excess of 300 had come to reside. In addition, a good road was opened down river through East Fort William (sometimes called the McKellar Ward) to the aging Hudson's Bay Company post, with a lesser road across the front to Port Arthur.[375] (The basic pattern of these routes survives in the street pattern of today, for anyone who refers to a map.)

Since conditions at the mouth of the Kam still caused problems for deeply loaded vessels, when the first trickle of prairie grain arrived at temporary bunkers, a token cargo was loaded at Westfort, with the balance put aboard at Port Arthur.[376] However, the first significant dredging of the Kaministiquia in early 1884 permitted the passage of the CPR's three huge new lakers to the waiting railway docks on the river. It also opened their use to Beatty Line vessels, which had been previously limited to the use of Port Arthur's wharves.[377] These developments stimulated a building boom accompanied by the rise of numerous new businesses at both East and West Fort William. This boom was also marked by the erection by the railway of the first three huge grain elevators along the river and further shops and roundhouse stalls at yards rising about the site of the former Hudson's Bay Company post. By 1889, the population of a still-unincorporated Fort William had reached a small but comfortable 2,000. However, a slight drop the next year in this more corporately insulated economy perhaps reflected something of Port Arthur's grim problems at the close of the decade.[378]

The mixed events of the eighties at the Lakehead left their mark in other ways on both these communities, but particularly on Port Arthur. Much of the initial growth in each place had come from a rough and youthful influx of Americans, Canadians, and some Europeans, who had built the railway, promoted the mining rushes, and worked in construction of forest-related industries. Yet as soon as employment dropped off, this frontier population abandoned the area as quickly as it arrived. Left behind was a smaller but more permanent community with a considerable commercial/professional component of British background but southern Ontario roots.

As in smaller places like Rat Portage, all the residents, from merchants to millhands, who decided to stay and make a life here, were concerned about the future of their town or village. Each local board of trade and weekly newspaper was loud in boosting the accomplishments and potential of its community to all who would listen. But such communities at this early stage in their existence were overwhelmingly the creation of both commercial capital and industrial acumen with origins elsewhere. As a result, each population also lived with a helpless awareness that the most important decisions about their immediate future were being made, not locally, but in the banks, business centres, and industrial offices in distant southern Ontario.[379]

Developments in the older-established centre of Sault Ste Marie followed a course of their own after 1870. The municipality was incorporated in 1871 but its population, given as 880, seems to have included families living on the Korah Road outside its bounds. At that time it could claim several stores, the courthouse and jail for Algoma, churches, a hotel, taverns, and a plethora of scattered homes. These collectively occupied a loose band within the original plot about three blocks deep extending along the river below the rapids. On the front was a steamer dock that seasonally was served by supply vessels up the North Channel from Georgian Bay. Two years later, steam power quickened the old ferry link with the American side. A newspaper joined the small business cluster, and soon after water-driven grist and sawmills came to be added to the short roster of enterprises in the village.[380]

Yet by the mid-seventies, such encouraging signs of growth ceased for reasons that are not clear, largely because only scattered copies of the *Algoma Pioneer* have survived and few other records fill the gap. Part of the reason may have been the negative effect on copper prices of a world recession that had begun in 1873 and that curtailed any remaining mining and prospecting in the surrounding area. Another reason may have been the continuing lack of energetic colonial development eastward along the river and Lake Huron shore over this decade, which might have aided village income. However, the major cause would seem to have been related to the fact that all canal traffic continued to touch exclusively on the Michigan side. This continued to lead most travellers, services, and new business enterprises to locate in Michigan. Well into the next decade, the population of the Canadian Sault remained unchanged, and contemporary descriptions continued to compare the village unfavourably with the thriving centre on the American shore.[381]

However, by 1886 these clouds began to lift rapidly. That year saw several parties of immigrants from the British Isles and Germany add new blood and energy to the community and its environs. The next year welcomed the arrival of the CPR from Sudbury and both the end of seasonal isolation from direct Canadian contact and the improvement of market access eastward. Yet, too much can be made of the long-term impact of this event on the business sector. CPR interest lay not in Sault Ste Marie, but in a link here by river bridge to American trackage and ultimately the transport of flour from huge mills at Minneapolis/St. Paul to Montreal. Nevertheless, its short-term labour demands and construction needs soon facilitated a newly incorporated town of 1,600 people. A bank, a new high school, a mechanics' institute, and twenty-seven new businesses followed quickly, as did a large resort hotel. Building trades grew frantically busy with these developments and with the rising demands of a population that doubled by September 1888. Most remaining lots in the old survey were quickly taken, and new adjacent properties began to be added both down river and on the slopes behind.[382]

The underlying cause of this rapid development, which later witnessed the first appearance of electric lights and telephones, was not simply the arrival of the railway. It reflected growing anticipation of construction on a Canadian canal around the St Marys Rapids that was to commence early the next year. With its initiation the railway labourers found new employment as did a swelling influx of Slavs, Irish, Finns, and Italians. As events turned out, many from this polyglot group appear to have stayed, joining a basically anglophone community in which there were already those whose first language was French.[383] This was the harbinger of the much more ethnically diverse future, which would also soon mark the personality of northwestern Ontario as a whole, and certainly its urban component.

Impacts on Native Life

The three treaties that had been concluded for the region by 1873 had many similarities but also significant differences in concept. The philosophy of eventual aboriginal acculturation, officially enunciated in the thirties and widely promoted across the British colonial world, was at the core of the two Robinson treaties and Treaty 3. For this reason the fundamental clauses covered education, assumed religious training, and promoted an agricultural way of life that would provide a more stable food supply and economic existence. Acknowledging the immediate needs of protection against unfortunate frontier elements, it placed these ideas within a firm frame of reserved lands and modest monetary subsidy.[384] However, the financial arrangements behind the Robinson treaties had been based on the investment of funds from the sale or lease of local resources and the distribution of the annual interest. As in the subsequently improved model applied to Manitoulin Island in 1862,[385] these remunerative arrangements had not proved more than marginally successful as generators of suitable support. Treaty 3, one of a total of seven western agreements reached after Confederation, incorporated different thinking. Under its clauses, each member of the Native population was given an initial sum, then annually awarded a smaller but specified yearly payment, made usually in the form of ammunition and other necessary goods. This provided a more secure means of assuring basic Native welfare.[386] That fact was not lost on the aboriginals of the Superior watershed, who made loud comparisons between their uncertain financial provision and the security of their western neighbours.[387]

By 1890, scattered reserves had come to cover the country westward to the now-determined Manitoba border (see Map 2.2). These established under Treaty 3 were much more numerous, particularly in the Rainy River–Lake of the Woods area, than under the Robinson agreements for three fundamental reasons. First, the population here was considerably bigger and more scattered over a much larger territory. Second, group affiliations among bands, even within the same community, were less well established. Finally, Ottawa at the time of negotiation was committed to westward access by road, then by transcontinental railway, and at all cost to serving its promise of dominion. A plethora of reserves, often in multiple sections of lavish size and usually accompanied by a further scatter of tiny garden plots, was a price the government was forced to pay to attain its goals. Because of this proliferation, only the largest reserves can be displayed on Map 2.2. On the resolution of the federal–provincial territorial dispute, this large number of reserves caused Ontario to promote consolidation and even reduction in acreage.

However, even the generalized representation on this map can convey a misleading impression of the degree of Native residential stability here, but also across the rest of the region. For example, the small Batchawana-Goulais band, which had negotiated a return to its former Superior shores in the sixties, had grown and negotiated the purchase of more land there in the seventies.[388]

Once-roaming bands, which had previously visited the mouth of the Pic River only seasonally to fish and trade at the Hudsons' Bay post there, had petitioned and been granted a tiny reserve there by 1885.[389] By that time, the Gros Cap band had almost totally abandoned their small reserve near Michipicoten and moved inland to the area of Chapleau.[390] Friction among elements at Gull Bay in the late eighties had caused the departure of small colonies to three other locations on Lake Nipigon. Meanwhile, in common with others in the district, the once-modest community of residents on the Fort William reserve had grown in population to over 1,600 by 1887. Several bands that had initially claimed only tentative ties to the Fort William Reserve and other reserves now had moved permanently in from the bush.[391]

West of the height of land, more recent developments under Treaty 3 displayed certain related features. The numerous reserves in the Rainy Lake watershed, along Rainy River and about the Lake of the Woods, were surveyed by the mid- to late seventies.[392] However, bands elsewhere, still with roving tendencies, were slower to make final decisions on their locations. Reserves in the Wabigoon–Eagle Lake area were finally surveyed during the rail building years in their vicinity. Surveys for ones further north about Lac Seul and west along English River drainage were only sought late in the eighties and were not all complete by 1890.[393] In several cases about the Lake of the Woods, surveyed reserves lay largely unused by the latter date. One band near Rat Portage had asked and been granted the right to move their reserve to the Dalles on the Winnipeg River. Supervision of such choices, shifts, and changes had become part of the duties of the Indian agents. Those at Sault Ste Marie and Port Arthur settled such matters in the Superior watershed, while others at Fort Frances, Rat Portage, and Savanne, where appointments came gradually after 1873, dealt with the rest.[394]

In Algoma the lot of the Indians, while far from idyllic, was much improved from earlier years. Those residing at Garden River continued to find employment in the bush as well as on the river, adding a simple agricultural subsistence from their fields on the reserve. The splinter group in Batchawana-Goulais, while doing little farming, found wage employment on local timber limits, seasonal work in the commercial fishery, and other remuneration from guiding sports fishermen.[395] In addition, the return of land prices to fifty cents an acre in the retreatied townships north of Sault Ste Marie and the sale of the forest resources in western Algoma also added substantially to pertinent annuity funds.

Elsewhere about Superior, advances and opportunities which paralleled the above were complicated by varying degrees of contact with frontier society. Beginning in the early seventies a series of arrangements had been made for the timbering of large portions of the Fort William reserve, as has been noted elsewhere. Despite some trespass cutting, which was not judicially prosecuted, very substantial ground rents and bonuses in excess of $50,000 were added to local Native coffers by 1889 when the last of these licences lapsed.[396] Yet conflicting groups, some in favour of continued cutting, many who claimed they had never been consulted, and others who decided later that such harvesting should cease, caused much confusion and frustration during these years.[397] As in Algoma, these controversial bush operations provided the community with much-needed wage employment. So did the rising fishery and probably both mining and rail construction. However, proximity to the new Lakehead centres also created serious alcohol problems for this reserve and other ugliness for those who sought employment in the white world beyond its bounds.

Natives on other reserves along the north shore of Superior appear to have had less income from such outside sources. A few found brief employment in rail construction or sporadic mining ventures, while a few more gained seasonal work in the fishery or in guiding sportsmen on the Nipigon.[398] However most remained tied to their trap lines and local trading posts for much of their limited income. Their introduction to the changing cultural surroundings, therefore, may have been less intense, brutal, and confusing.

West of the Great Lakes, frontier transgressions generated many problems for Mr Dawson's more spirited bands, who sometimes were hard-pressed to protect their property and retain something of their cultural independence. In spite of firm action by the first Indian Agent, Mr Pither, timber was cut illegally from selected regional reserves even before the action of the surveyors could protect them.[399] Such early theft was practised with the greatest intensity on Native land in the Rainy River Valley and about the Lake of the Woods.[400] As the records show, loud Native complaints here over the years usually resulted in substantial, if grudging, restitution. However, attempts to gain similar compensation for the disturbance of their fishery by the boom company at the mouth of the Rainy River failed. Later, despite a call for Native fishery reserves down the Valley and in the Lake of the Woods, annoyance by certain Americans fishing illegally in these Canadian waters continued. Native reactions culminated in forceful occupation of one company's main station and the destruction of all nets there.[401] Throughout the eighties, the avarice of mine speculators and their impact on Native mineral rights generated many headaches here. These included a long and involved case over title to the rich Sultana Mine. In this instance, the legal ambiguities even led to a dispute over the continuing right of the Keewatin Lumber Company to the timber on this property.[402]

While problems with whisky pedlars remained common, the deleterious impact of intoxicants reached a peak during rail building at Rat Portage. The illicit market was not only the Native population but the much more lucrative construction camps from which alcohol was supposedly banned. This nastiness, along with numerous forest violations on Native land along the railway right of way, at places like Eagle Lake, Wabigoon, and Lac des Mille Lacs, came to scar Native experience deeply.[403] However, as elsewhere west of Lake Superior, such problems sometimes brought firm reaction from proud aboriginals seeking to live freely next to, and benefit from, what the white community had to offer.

Not all regional experiences with either the reserve system or frontier society were negative or punitive in these decades. For example, a combination of religiously sponsored and secularly based government schools appeared, with generally positive response. Large residential ones were the Shingwauk, an Anglican operation near Garden River, as well as the Jesuit boys school and the girls school opened by Catholic nuns at the Lakehead.[404] These introduced training in practical skills as well as religion and academic subjects. Other missionary efforts were focused about Lake Nipigon and at Red Rock as well as along the Rainy River.[405] These, like the federally sponsored day schools now established on most reserves, were aided by government grants for their construction and a small stipend for the support of teachers.[406] Attendance at such facilities was sometimes sporadic or limited. Yet this reflected family needs on garden plots, in wild rice harvesting, the hunt, or the annual collection of blueberries much more than parentally condoned disinterest or delinquency.

In the traditional drive for an agriculturally sedentary life on the reserves, which Ottawa was now promoting with vigour, those west of Superior also showed some interest. Once the Natives chose their reserves and (in all cases save those well north of the CPR) submitted them for survey, they received a supply of seeds, livestock, and implements. While instruction was rarely more than rudimentary and enthusiasm short-lived, most reserves came to produce annually at least basic root crops.[407] Nevertheless, in 1890, reliance on traditional forms of sustenance was still most evident. Indeed, the records suggest that crops like wild rice now were being grown over much broader northern areas than previously.[408] On Lake St Joseph, Lac Seul, and perhaps other northern waters, Indians also fished heavily for themselves as well as for the Hudson's Bay Company posts. More southerly bands remained reliant on sturgeon, among other species, which they also harvested for incoming settlers about Fort Frances and miners about Rat Portage.[409] At Fort William, where agricultural beginnings had been made only years after those at Garden River, farming also was beginning to flourish by the mid-eighties.[410] Elsewhere along northern Superior this interest was very tentative and often nonexistent.

Across the arctic divide, the initially sharp differences in treaty arrangements, reserve numbers, and sizes as well as duration and intensity of white contact had lost much of their significance by 1890. Native people had found their feet in the dramatically altered socioeconomic sphere that had evolved. Reserves had become home to the majority of this indigenous population that formerly had lived a migratory existence. However, income from the trap line and subsistent contributions from the countryside varied in economic importance in most such cultural enclaves. Many household heads had earned off-reserve wages in the mills, on the railway, in the bush, on the docks, or in the fisheries. Their experience had sometimes brought its own problems, including alcohol abuse and demeaning treatment in the workplace, but for those who bypassed the former and conquered the latter, such dollars became an important element in their yearly incomes. The bands that were least affected by white ways and less buffeted by the rough intolerance of the colonial community were the more isolated ones. For the most part, their reserves lay north of the CPR in the western portion of the region or back of the unpopulated shore of Superior, east of Nipigon. Government programs in agriculture, intended to strengthen sedentary drives and promote stability, achieved notable success only on more southerly reserves. Programs in primary education were modestly well received in most communities and encouraged the founding of central mission schools for the more gifted or dedicated young people. Such activities accomplished much of their intended aim over these years.

While the erosion of Native culture over these years was considerable, other social and demographic aspects of Native life experienced remarkable advances. Particularly west of Superior the bands were undeniably more secure from the vagaries experienced under their traditional way of life. Collectively, they not only had the opportunity to be better nourished, clothed, and housed, but to be protected from white diseases, which during the fur trade era had so often ravished their numbers. Several outbreaks of measles and smallpox were reported over these years, sometimes limited to one reserve, but often touching several. Medical treatment, even vaccination that was often not available for the white frontier population, was available when serious epidemics appeared.[411] The results of the general improvement of Native existence were reflected in the population figures. In the area of Treaty 3, by 1890, numbers had increased by over 800 from an initial 2,000. Similar increases of roughly 25 per cent were registered about Lake Superior and at Garden River, where the reserve system and paternal Native policy were longer established.[412] While some element of this growth may have reflected more accurate figures of total population, with the gradual adoption of reserve life, much growth was a response to improved medical care.

Indeed, like the white community of the northwest, the Indian inhabitants of the region profited significantly from the events of these decades, if in their own distinct and simpler ways. However, they still had to endure the second-class status they held before the law and in the society they had been asked to join.

The Emergent Colony

Most regional efforts in the first half of this period were tentative and limited, although they initiated important additions to the range of resource activity. However, by 1890, this youthful economy had come to include substantial contributions from fisheries, forestry and mining with more modest ones from agriculture and even tourism. Experience and study led to a much sounder public understanding of the resource base. Silver finds grew spectacular, attracting foreign mine investment, which encouraged early gold and iron interest along with some revived copper activity. Growing regional demand and subsequent railway construction from the Lakehead west transformed the lumber industry, bringing big pine mills particularly to western watersheds and to the banks of the Kam. The CPR itself needed heavy cuts from northwest woodland for its building and maintenance requirements. It also brought Winnipeg tourists to the Lake of the Woods, while a growing Great Lakes fleet introduced more southern vacationers to Superior's delights. In addition, commercial fishing made a startling recovery since its difficulties in the sixties and now was an intensive and highly capitalized industry with strong ties to U.S. finance and markets. However, agriculture increased in economic importance only gradually, even in older townships, while in new western ones farming was hampered by events related to the closure of the Dawson Road and the prolonged boundary dispute.

This new provincial economy, with its only moderate emphasis on agriculture, had other problems and peculiarities. The region had yet to acquire satisfactory external or internal links. It was now traversed by a national railway built principally to join east to west across the country's rugged expanse. Such year-round passage was linked in season to Great Lakes shipping, which also carried cargoes and passengers whose origins and destinations often ignored this land between. At the same time, provincially promoted colonization roads in the scattered agricultural pockets reached acceptable local levels of effectiveness, as had a modest complex of government mining routes. However, their inter-connection with the railway was still limited to an infrequent sequence of stations and occasional sidings. These as yet were inadequate to encourage effective ties between most farm settlements and between such rural pockets or other foci of resource activity and urban suppliers or market outlets.

Similarly, up from the hamlets and villages at its base, the urban hierarchy remained ill-developed, numbering only two small towns and three larger centres. The latter had undergone only recent and varied degrees of economic stimulation. All five had yet to establish more than modest economic ties with each other or with rural hinterlands. Like the rest of the population in this young northwest, that of nodal places, be they hamlets or villages, remained culturally homogeneous, being still pre-eminently British in background and having Old Ontario roots. The only substantial contrast yet to emerge was the smaller Native population, which still was coming to terms with the material rewards and sometimes ugly shortcomings of a life next to a white frontier society. Varying amounts of time would pass before these unusual characteristics of the economy and society would find resolution or change.

3

Ontario's Emerging Northern Empire, 1890–1930

For Canada, in the period 1890–1930, the dream of continental dominion moved from fledgling claim to vibrant reality. Closure of the American frontier in 1896 redirected European and U.S. homesteaders to Canada's prairies. By 1930, the population there touched 2.3 million. Meanwhile, western grain markets, a reassertive world economy, and a protective national policy turned much Canadian trade from America to Europe. This shift in orientation was aided by two new transcontinental railways linking prairie farms and cities across the Shield to Lakehead docks and St Lawrence ports.

Ontario's previously stunted population rose sharply to 3.4 million with the new century. This augured a shift toward urbanism that reflected growing prairie markets for provincial manufactures and Toronto's increasing commercial/financial interest in the west. Yet new U.S. industrial dollars and trade opportunities sustained the old north–south interests, while traditional ties with Europe were maintained. Behind this countering thrust was the dream of New Ontario as a cornucopia of resources that were to be developed intensively under Old Ontario's profitable stewardship and sold south of the border.

Provincial policies followed these sometimes contradictory thrusts, often with surprising success. In southern Ontario, they engendered enormous public revenues, enhanced Toronto-based financial strength, and also produced notable increases in urban industry and rural material advancement. In northern Ontario, negotiated U.S. tariff reductions prompted gratifying leaps in resource acquisition, harvesting, and processing. However, the northwest's long-known economic promise came to be rivalled or eclipsed by exciting developments in northeastern Ontario. All in all, the sum of such provincial accomplishments did much to return American markets to 61 per cent of Canadian exports by 1930.[1]

Old Drives and New Developments, 1890 to World War I

The pre-war decades in northwestern Ontario were ones of encouraging development along both established courses and newly fostered thrusts within its resource-dependent economy. Provincial population north of the French River climbed from 33,500 to 170,000. About half of this expanded number continued to reside west of the St Marys Rapids. This population grew surprisingly polyglot and increasingly urban, or at least non-farm, in nature. The former characteristic was the result of the long-sought rise in immigration and the latter reflected an encouraging northern share in the province's current industrial growth.[2]

Heightened southerly interest in New Ontario's potential found expression in varied and sometimes conflicting ways. A modest commitment to resource stewardship formed the basis of the rising conservation movement. Firmer official aspirations to regulate and exact a public share from the exploitation of all Crown resources were manifested in attempts at northern policy reform.[3] Growing or renewed popular support for northern agricultural ideals enthusiastically promoted farm settlement and supportive road building programs under an emerging Bureau of Colonization.[4]

Yet the north, and most frequently the northwest in this period, was not always suitably grateful for such attention from Old Ontario. This the Toronto press pointed out on occasion in exasperated but patronizing fashion.[5] Indeed, total or partial northern secession was periodically a hot issue for Queen's Park and late in the 1890s even resulted in a fact-finding and educational legislative tour. People in the northwest often deemed government to lack understanding and its decisions to be unresponsive to their interests. In particular, those west of the Lakehead frequently felt themselves alienated from public regard and identified more with neighbouring Manitoba.[6] Such rumblings of discontent across northern Ontario have recurred sporadically into recent years, mirrored by calls for a separate province or provincial political party. Much of the sincerity of such later movements and the justness of northern complaints has been lost on the larger Ontario public. This usually sympathetic audience has been made sceptical by past abuses of the resource base by private enterprise, most often with the quiet awareness and compliance of the northern community. Such occurrences and the political underhandedness that sometimes facilitated them, however, only began to colour events and public impressions by the onset of war in 1914.

Further Exploring, Spanning, and Expanding

By the early nineties, the main features of northwestern Ontario's natural geography and resource wealth had been established. Most of this evaluative work had been carried out either by the provincial explorer E.B. Borron or by the reconnaissance efforts of the Geological Survey of Canada. However, the provincial creation of its own Bureau of Mines in 1892 brought on years of uncertain relations in this task. The Survey, reticent about appearing competitive with this Bureau, quietly conducted out-of-the-way field studies, principally east of Rainy River and north of the CPR. Robert Bell, in particular, helped extend the Survey's general evaluations onward to the shores of James and Hudson Bay. He, with others, was also involved here in useful reconnaissance for new transcontinental railways at and after the century's turn. Relations between the two organizations were finally reconciled in 1906 when the federal agency agreed to leave the most important aspects of northern mineral investigation to the province.[7] Additional geographical contributions, as of that date, fell to field parties of the provincial Survey Branch in the new Ministry of Lands and Forests. This body also continued to lay out the northern meridians, baselines, even township surveys, on which all ordered territorial registration depended.[8]

Meanwhile, in an attempted appraisal of its northern wealth, Ontario initiated a broad evaluation of the area from the CPR northward to the provincial boundaries of 1899. Ten teams of suitably trained personnel were dispatched in 1900 to accomplish this end. Each was to explore and assess the extant resources in a defined sector of this huge tract south of the Albany and English rivers, between Quebec and Manitoba. Five teams submitted evaluations of northwestern areas, and a sixth did so in the region's eastern periphery. The summary report, lavishly published and carefully staged, was warmly received by both the press and its readership. The text focused much attention on the huge Clay Belt and the unexploited potential of northeastern forest and farm. Yet it also described possible new agricultural acreage, especially to the east of Lake Nipigon towards Long Lake, and the huge taiga resources remaining in the northwest. Although admitting much devastation by fire and disease, here as elsewhere across the north, it championed the still-enormous pulpwood and lumber potential of this dominantly spruce, balsam, and jackpine woodland.[9] In balance, the picture of northwestern Ontario that came out of this assessment was that of a distant but established, sturdy, and potentially productive region.[10]

In these years of continuing exploration and rising interest in evaluative details, dreams of two new transcontinental railways were exciting the national imagination (see Map 3.1). The planners, like their predecessors, viewed the Shield as a hurdle to be leapt, along routes of least cost, to link western and central Canada.[11] Their decisions ignored the economic needs, resource potential, and future aspirations of the northwest itself. However, appreciating the

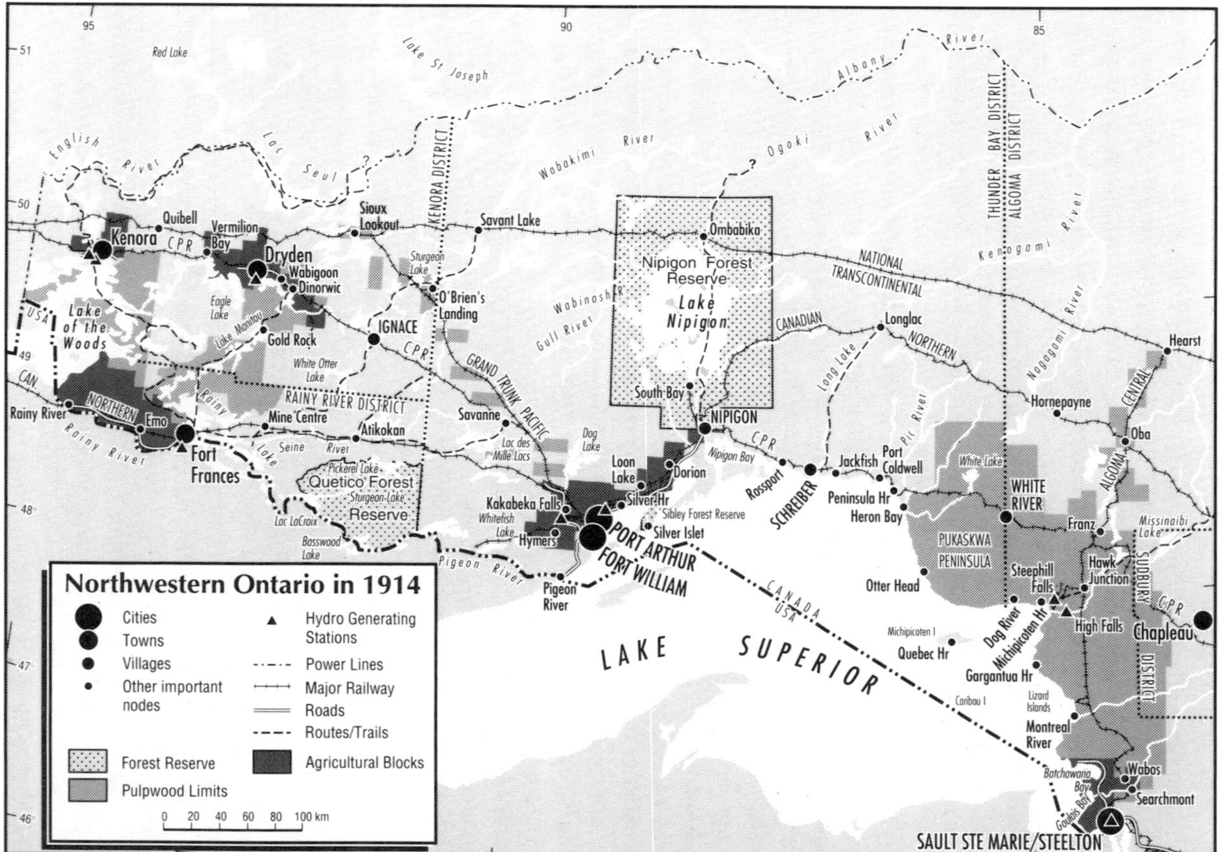

Northwestern Ontario in 1914
Cities
Towns
Villages
Other important nodes
Hydro Generating Stations
Power Lines
Major Railway
Roads
Routes/Trails
Forest Reserve
Pulpwood Limits
Agricultural Blocks
0 20 40 60 80 100 km
LAKE SUPERIOR
Lake Nipigon
Nipigon Forest Reserve
Quetico Forest Reserve
Lake of the Woods
Kenora
Dryden
Fort Frances
IGNACE
NIPIGON
SCHREIBER
PORT ARTHUR
FORT WILLIAM
WHITE RIVER
Chapleau
SAULT STE MARIE/STEELTON
Hearst
Longlac
Sioux Lookout
Savant Lake
Ombabika
THUNDER BAY DISTRICT
ALGOMA DISTRICT
KENORA DISTRICT
RAINY RIVER DISTRICT
SUDBURY DISTRICT
NATIONAL TRANSCONTINENTAL
CANADIAN NORTHERN
GRAND TRUNK PACIFIC
ALGOMA CENTRAL
CPR
PUKASKWA PENINSULA
CANADA
USA

MAP 3.1

profits to be derived from seasonal links over water, both railways were quick to establish trackage to and port facilities on Thunder Bay. The competitive significance of this latter strategy was not lost on the CPR, which moved quickly to double its track between Winnipeg and Fort William.[12]

Yet the first of these new railways, constructed by William Mackenzie and Donald Mann and ultimately known as the Canadian Northern, was not initially intended to extend east of its wharves at Port Arthur.[13] This road was a highly speculative but most popular endeavour that had its roots in prairie dislike of the CPR monopoly in grain handling. By the late nineties, therefore, the Canadian Northern set out to gain competitive eastern access on Superior through a quick assembly of minor trackage and existing rights of way. Already assured of a route southeast from Winnipeg, MacKenzie and Mann in 1898 took over an old lumbering railway, the Minnesota and Manitoba. This provided a link south of the Lake of the Woods to the mouth of the Rainy River. Next they acquired from Thunder Bay interests an ageing charter for the Ontario and Rainy River Railway, conceived in the image of the Dawson Road. With this they had clear access eastward to their chosen Thunder Bay location.[14] However, for the last nineteen miles to the docks, they preferred a route built by the now-languishing Port Arthur, Duluth and Western. This they acquired in 1900 as an alternate right of way to the harbour from the river hamlet of Stanley.

Exact route definition and construction proceeded rapidly. Final surveys through the Rainy River were completed, the bridge over that river opened, and tracks extended east across an arm of Rainy Lake by 1900. Indeed, the line was in full operation as of New Year's Day 1901. Later tentative interest in the Canadian Atlantic, east from Depot Harbour (near Parry Sound) to Ottawa, with a eye to Montreal, was blocked by the machinations of the Grand Trunk. That company seems also to have bargained in questionable faith with Mackenzie and Mann over possible cooperative east–west track sharing to form a joint transcontinental system. As a result, in 1911 the Canadian Northern, with federal backing, prepared to build eastward to an eventual Atlantic terminus. The route followed the CPR but went northward up the side of Lake Nipigon, then east via modern Geraldton, Longlac, and Sudbury. The line was open from Port Arthur to Toronto in late 1914, but daily transcontinental service by way of Ottawa did not come for two more years.

The Grand Trunk's dream of passage to the Pacific dated back to the seventies, when its proposed Canada/U.S. route avoiding the Shield had been refused.[15] The decision to renew its efforts was made in 1902 and the route chosen was basically the most northerly alternative once proposed by Sir Sandford Fleming for the CPR. The subsequent incorporation and joint arrangement with Ottawa, achieved in 1903, included a firm commitment to a Superior Branch. It was to run south from Superior Junction (near Sioux Lookout) to a Fort William terminus on Mission Island at the mouth of the Kaministiquia River. Under this agreement, the federal government agreed to build, as the National Transcontinental, the section north of Lake Nipigon to Winnipeg, to complete the line via Quebec and the Clay Belt. This trackage the GTR was to lease for ninety-nine years. It was the responsibility of the latter, under the title of the Grand Trunk Pacific, to continue this line to Prince Rupert on the Pacific. Across Ontario and Quebec the concept was a straight and level route for use by long trains behind powerful locomotives at high speeds for intense, cheap freight movement, particularly during winter months.

However, the importance of a Superior Branch for the navigation season was underlined in 1904 when the first sod for the entire venture was turned at Fort William.[16] Indeed, government promised a rail link, by 1907, from Winnipeg to join with this branch north from Fort William. However, muskeg problems as well as shortages of labour and rails frustrated this timetable, and the Superior outlet was not in full use until 1911. By then combined grain storage capacity at the Lakehead totalled 75 million bushels, and technical and organizational improvements were rapidly increasing the rate of grain handling.[17] Yet two years would pass before tracks eastward were 'operable,' and regular service came only in wartime. Ironically, the financial condition of the GTR never allowed it to assume control of the government's share of this railway, and Ottawa operated all trackage east of Winnipeg until the creation of the CNR.

These years were also ones of expanding provincial control over territory in the northwest and of increasing commitment to administration of Native affairs there. Most such matters needing adjustment had origins that either pre-dated, or sprang from, the settlement in 1889 of the last details of the federal–provincial boundary dispute in the northwest. In the wake of the latter had come long, complicated court wrangles. These worked out Ontario's share of Native costs, such as the increased annuity arrangements earlier instituted by the federal administration for the Natives under the Robinson and other treaties. They also involved Ontario's claims of unpaid restitution for timber dues owing from the CPR construction era in the former disputed territory and of unjustifiably large provisions of reserved Native lands there under Treaty No. 3.[18] Such thorny arguments between government levels culminated in a long debate leading up to the further arrangement of a new northern agreement, Treaty No. 9. This James Bay Treaty, as it is also known, was only ratified in the autumn of 1905 but covered all remaining aboriginals within the then-northern Albany-English boundary of the province. Because Native people here sometimes lived or hunted across this northern riparian limit, that boundary was but loosely interpreted in this arrangement.[19] However with federal blessing in 1912, Ontario's northern provincial limits were expanded to those applicable today. All this newly acquired provincial territory north of the Albany was formally added to Treaty No. 9 by the end of that decade. That addition also embraced a small area in the extreme west, which had been initially treatied in 1873 under the old federal District of Keewatin.[20] On Ontario's part, this new treaty probably reflected interest in the economic potential of the new northern gold strike at Red Lake more than any concern for either the Native people or federal concerns for their proper administration. These last events tidied territorial issues of provincial right and responsibility. However, the huge area to which they applied has never attracted much modern resource development beyond its southern fringes. It remains today as an area of taiga to tundra and home to a scattering of Native communities. A land unknown to the bulk of the provincial population, it serves as a favoured area for fly-in hunters and fishermen.

Dangerous Levels of Fishing

Coming on the heels of the western boundary dispute, heated altercations in these decades over resource management and jurisdiction added to already strained federal–provincial relations. Tensions had been gathering through the eighties over the Great Lakes fisheries. Matters centred about Ottawa's ineffective policing and inadequate protection of the provincial industry from U.S. exploitation. Feelings in Ontario ran particularly high after the Conservation Congresses of the early eighties in Washington and Montreal raised public interest in resources management. Indeed, in 1885, Ontario passed its own Fisheries Act parallel to the federal one, although responsibility for this and other resources rested with Ottawa under the terms of the British North America Act. Two years later the province appointed its first fisheries overseers under the Department of Crown Lands but limited their roles to non-contentious matters.[21]

Real action, however, came with the next decade. In 1890, a Royal Commission was struck to inquire into fishing operations on the Great Lakes. The resulting evidence of wholesale over-exploitation, monopolistic tendencies, and dismal working conditions was appended in 1892 to a scathing indictment of the prevailing situation.[22] Meanwhile, the U.S. McKinley Tariffs of 1891 put additional duties on Canadian fish, unless caught with American-owned equipment. This promoted further U.S. control of the provincial industry and encouraged increasingly heavy harvests of this resource in Ontario waters. In 1894–5, an irate province pushed the issue of fisheries jurisdiction to the

Supreme Court, from which it passed to the Privy Council. In 1898 that body confirmed federal responsibility for protection. However, it ruled in favour of a provincial right to license and manage the resource, as in the colonial years before Confederation.[23]

Friction was to continue over the issue of closed seasons and catch limits. But the following spring saw federal authorities turn over licensing and enforcement responsibility to the new provincial Bureau of Fisheries.[24] Unfortunately, the province's lack of experience with the management and policing of this industry permitted excessive levels of harvesting and blatant American monopoly to continue. Indeed in 1897, the plethora of American-controlled firms were amalgamated, with their U.S. counterparts, into the Fisheries Trust under the ultimate control of the Booth Fish Company of Chicago.[25] Its near total control of licences, supplies, prices to producers, and markets soon became evident. The Trust's influence in the Canadian waters of the Great Lakes and elsewhere across the country was further confirmed by the legal creation of the Dominion Fish Company. This wholly owned subsidiary and front for the Trust in Canada was a firm reality by the opening of this century.[26]

Lake Superior

The resultant trends on Superior, which was ecologically the least productive lake in this chain, were the first indications of devastation of the fish stocks to come. The number of steam tugs (taken from the annual reports as a rough surrogate for increased capitalization and technical advance) grew there from eight to twenty between 1891 and 1911. The catch was doubled aggressively to reach beyond four million pounds on the Canadian side (see Table 3.1), while sinking dramatically in already ravaged American waters. Much of this increase along Ontario's shores was achieved through the growing harvest of species other than the preferred whitefish and trout to satisfy the wider demands of the ethnic community of lower lake states. Indeed, it rose from 6 per cent to one-third of this escalating total by 1911, a clear indication of the broad exploitive thrust fostered by the monopoly.

On the Algoma shore, total catches showed a particularly sharp rise after the nineties. While the take of whitefish registered no recognizable trend, that of trout pushed upward to nearly three times the 1891 figure. More critical was the appearance of the first real harvesting of pike, pickerel, perch, and even tuillibee, catfish, and carp to satisfy high market goals. The senior member of Booth's monopoly here was Ainsworth and Ganley, a firm that had already developed a warehousing/shipping facility at Sault Ste Marie and had a history of intensive use of Canadian grounds.[27] Their numerous modern stations (and

TABLE 3.1 Commercial Fisheries Catch (in pounds), 1891–1911

	1891	1901	1911
Lake Superior			
Algoma Shore			
Whitefish	326,200	193,389	356,196
Lake trout	351,400	777,661	964,457
Other		41,120	783,212
Subtotal	677,600	1,012,170	2,103,865
*North Shore**			
Whitefish	939,000	433,677	496,196
Lake trout	447,000	661,062	1,090,457
Other	139,000	434,921	631,980
Subtotal	1,525,000	1,529,660	2,218,633
Total	2,202,600	2,541,830	4,322,498
Inland Waters			
Rainy Lake/Lake of the Woods			
Whitefish		123,553	663,346
Lake trout		22,365	18,375
Other		282,396	879,837
Subtotal		428,314	1,561,558
Other Western Lakes			
Whitefish		111,311	101,141
Lake trout		28,410	62,010
Other		111,476	418,497
Subtotal		251,197	581,648
Grand Total	2,220,600	3,221,341	6,465,704

* This designation also includes inland lakes immediate to the Lakehead.
Source: Compiled from tables accompanying the Reports of the Federal Department of Marine and Fisheries and the Provincial Reports of the Fish and Game Commission, 1892 to 1912.

those of affiliated Clark Brothers) stretched northward to Michipicoten Island and about the Pukaskwa Peninsula. They were serviced by their steamer *Telegram* in the nineties, on its regular schedule north from the St Marys River. Later, these waters were visited with similar regularity by the *Caribou* and *Manitou*, built for Dominion Transport (a sub-element in the Dominion Fish Company) in 1904–5, for the carriage of freight, fish, and passengers.[28] In effect, this long and isolated shoreline had become the Trust's exclusive fishery.

However, their wholesale harvesting as well as the U.S.-destined sale of the whitefish and, more particularly, lake trout from this area came to meet increasing public opposition by the turn of the century. Justifiable claims were made that only culls were retained for local consumption, that independents were not being given a chance, and that broader Canadian markets were being ignored. In 1905, the Lizard Islands was designated a closed area to promote future breeding.[29] Through the rest of that decade loud complaint from public groups pushed for closure of all southerly Superior grounds and cancellation of all Dominion fishery licences north to the Montreal River area. A suspiciously conciliatory Dominion Fish Company, claiming itself blameless of fishery violations, agreed to the surrender of licences south of the Montreal River in 1905, Ironically, by 1912, it was again legally harvesting the grounds of the supposed Lizards' reserve and the adjacent waters.[30] This is but one example of the political as well as economic muscle the Trust could marshal for its own ends on either side of the lakes.

West of the Pukaskwa, conditions were little better (see Table 3.1). While the catch of whitefish declined most sharply by 1900, the biggest decline was that of lake trout, which most authors agree was the more plentiful species in this lake. Offshore gill netting and the more moderate use of inshore pound nets continued to be the main fishing techniques. Strong centres of operation remained at Peninsula Harbour/Heron Bay, Port Coldwell, Rossport, Nipigon, Hurkett (Dorion), and the upper reaches of Thunder Bay.[31] However, dredging in the Kam estuary, breakwater construction off Port Arthur harbour, deepening of that harbour, and the sporadic dumping of elevator screenings off these ports greatly reduced fishing activity. The only exception at the Lakehead was the November herring harvest, which continued unhindered.[32] As in Algoma, however, an increasingly substantial element of the entire catch on this coast was made up of less-valuable species to maximize the companies' financial return.

About 1890 the Port Arthur Fish Company, with its predominantly American exports, had been taken over by Booth of Chicago. It became the key to later control by Booth of most of the fisheries along northern Superior. Despite occasional competition, the Trust's steamer *Hiram Dixon*, with others later, served this terminus, carrying fish as well as passengers and freight to Duluth for many years.[33] A variety of tugs and vessels served points east of Thunder Bay, but railways, principally the Canadian Pacific, provided an immediate demand to supply their dining cars and any markets in Central Canada.

At the turn of the century, the north shore of Superior was plagued by demands for additional licences. These were tendered to federal authorities on behalf of lower-lake fishermen through their political representatives.[34] Emanating principally from Erie, Huron, and Georgian Bay, these demands probably reflected the ravages of earlier over-fishing on those waters. Despite strong local resistance to such increases in intensity, some of these requests were granted, most frequently around Nipigon and eastward, usually to staunch members of the Trust.[35] Yet stations and centres of fishing here were more diverse in their allegiance than on the Ganley-dominated Algoma shore. Strong firms such as the Nipigon Fish Company or the Bowman Fish Company of Rossport did not always cooperate willingly in the emerging monopoly. Through rail access to wholesale markets in Toronto and Montreal, they could escape the Trust's control. So could those small operations from both sides of the Lake Superior that came to fish places far offshore, such as lonely Caribou Island, and to coordinate their shipments to certain U.S. wholesalers.[36]

Whether part of the monopoly or not, members of the fishing community on this shore were very successful. Fishermen from Nipigon, Rossport, Jackfish, and Coldwell held large licences in their immediate waters. They also were the traditional licensees as far east as Peninsula Harbour. On the latter grounds, they sometimes found themselves in fierce conflict with the Sault-based crews of Ainsworth and Ganley, creeping north and west along the shores of the Pukaskwa.[37] Indeed, as in other competitive resource industries, this peninsula came to stand as a rough watershed between operations focused at Sault Ste Marie and others centred largely around Fort William or Port Arthur.

Underlying Misconceptions

However, the catch statistics and information summarized above masked deeper underlying events and issues that coloured operations in the industry on Lake Superior. Two fisheries officers had been considered sufficient to police Huron's north shore and the Canadian littoral of Superior in the early nineties. While more effective surveillance by fishery vessels was adopted when the fisheries were under Ontario's control, the number of overseers grew to only three. There can be little doubt that the gross over-fishing here, documented in the nineties, continued in the new century and became even more blatant under such continuingly inadequate protection. In fact, the records of the overseers report frequent, serious shortfalls in local fish supply, and even temporary abandonment of important stations. Such events were openly attributed to continuous over-fishing.[38] Indeed, recognition of depleted stocks on the north shore and the need for closed breeding areas there resulted in the creation of a reserve, similar to that in Algoma at the Lizards. This reserve was located about Pic River, and on its establishment there was a call for another off Jackfish at the Slates. In the latter case, this demand was strengthened by support from the islands' owner, the lieutenant-governor of Manitoba. He wished to turn the ravaged surrounding waters into a fish sanctuary to match a planned islands game preserve.[39] Yet, in spite of publicly expressed concern about the devastating intensity of the attack on fish stocks west of the Pukaskwa Peninsula, official reaction was minimal. The resource-destructive processes, under which market shortfalls among the prime species were being augmented by growing emphasis on other less profitable elements, continued. Disastrous inroads into total fish supplies, even local breeding stocks, were developing quietly on Superior by 1914.[40]

The causes behind the unchecked nature of such development, here and more generally on the Canadian Great Lakes, were not limited to inadequate official action. They also stemmed from the mix of inadequate science and unsubstantiated belief that made up current precepts in fisheries biology. Central to the matter was the general acceptance of an agricultural model for sustaining the fisheries. Fish farming, initiated by Samuel Wilmot and strongly supported by Dominion authorities after Confederation, was still fully accepted by many laymen and scientists as an eventual panacea for current over-fishing.[41] Behind this championing of pisciculture lay the notion that badly depleted fishing grounds could be restocked with appropriate fingerlings, just as grain fields can be reseeded after harvest. In the same light, the creation of temporary breeding reserves in less-devastated waters was viewed as the equivalent of farmers resting or fallowing their fields in the rotational cycle of agriculture. Faith in a future of sustained yield through such implementations may help explain Ontario's honest, but less-than-adequate, moves to police and prevent the ravage of its fisheries. Unfortunately, much of this faith was eventually to prove misplaced. These fisheries would have been better served by the stronger regulatory measures for which certain elements of the public had continued to press.[42]

This confusion of conservational concepts and agricultural analogies also coloured the approach to the commercial exploitation of inland lakes. As early as 1891 that most knowledgeable Ontario northerner, E.B. Borron, stated:

> With regard to larger inland lakes ... [they are] capable of affording employment to many fishermen and yielding heavily for a time before propagation is required. Later, when fish breeding is better understood, they will provide excellent opportunities for pisciculture.[43]

This observation, using Lake Nipigon as its prime example, within a year of publication drew numerous applications for commercial licences there. However, all such requests were denied. The lake was held to be both a major food source for the Natives around its shores and the principal breeding grounds for the famous sport fishery on the river of the same name. Such immunity from all but Native fishermen also was wisely granted to neighbouring Long Lake. However, part of the catch on both, as on many larger northern lakes like Seul and St Joseph, still went to supply local Hudson's Bay Company posts.[44]

In the new century commercial interest in Lake Nipigon returned upon the publication of conflicting reports of its potential by the local fishery overseers. The federally appointed officer, in 1901, pointed to the poverty of the Native population, their lack of game, and their resultant subsistence on fish when he recommended that the lake be leased to some reliable person who would either operate a commercial fishery there, using Native people, or pay cash for all fish the Indians caught. His provincial counterpart opposed this move in his report for the same year. He reiterated the importance of this lake as a breeding ground for the sport fishery on the Nipigon River. He went on to claim that commercial use would reduce the size of the trophies available to the anglers there.[45] However, Ontario, already very interested in both sport and commercial revenue from leasing inland lakes, seems to have sided with the federal point of view and to have opened contractual negotiations in 1902.[46] This move appears to have been officially envisioned in the long term as an experiment in the kind of pisciculture first enunciated for the lake by Borron a decade before. Under his concept, which was quite in tune with the theorizing of the era, all trash fish and predators would be systematically removed from these waters, creating a huge aquarium and promoting increased food harvest.[47] Toward this end, the Canada Fish Company was licensed and erected a dock and permanent facilities on the southern shore at South Bay, at the upper end of an old trail from the CPR at Nipigon. Unfortunately, their harvest that winter was unexpectedly small, and the road, which proved unsatisfactory in the snowy season, was judged impossible for summer access to market.[48] Interest in a commercial fishery here was not revived until the war years when transcontinental rail came to touch the lake on both its north and east sides.

Western Inland Waters

In the immediate Thunder Bay area and west, pressure to open inland lakes for commercial use was much more intense and problematic. Here too the early issues often focused on Native welfare in areas where the heritage of the fur trade still left many bands unusually dependent on their fisheries. The Lake of the Woods, Rainy River, and Rainy Lake watershed was the first to feel the commercial attack, which was difficult to regulate because of its international flavour. On the Minnesota side of these waters uncontrolled fishing had begun in the late eighties, once market access was available by rail at Rat Portage (later Kenora). On this watershed, by the end of that decade, firms from as far away as Baltimore, Philadelphia, Sandusky, and Chicago had wharves, warehouses, and even freezer plants.[49] At that time, the Canadian situation stood in strong contrast. Pressure to preserve these waters for Native use had been mounting, and a federal covenant, struck between Fisheries and Indian Affairs, commendably had turned this into law.[50] No commercial fishing was to be allowed.

However, this regulation of August 1890 proved unenforceable in the current international mêlée in the area. American companies had already begun to collect a spectacular supply of sturgeon roe on the Minnesota side of the lakes from which they were also procuring large tonnages of whitefish and trout. The highly lucrative harvest of caviar was shipped over the CPR in ever-increasing volume to wholesalers in Germany. The accompanying flow of fish used the same railway to western markets.[51] Both the regulation against fishing by Canadians and the use of Canadian access raised the ire of equally avaricious business interests on the Ontario side. Their outcry focused principally on one theme: open Canadian waters here to commercial pursuits because they currently serve only as a reservoir and breeding ground for the American harvest.[52] However, criticism also pointed to American poaching on the Canadian side. Until mid-decade, there was no overseer here, and an appropriate surveillance vessel was only a matter of discussion.[53] This situation encouraged certain local elements to fish illegally, using equipment that American owners were only too willing to supply. Yet the wholesale slaughter on the Minnesota side, where neither closed seasons nor net regulations seem to have been in force, really focused the broader public reaction on the situation. Such popular concern, both regional and provincial, was in no way abated by a communication in 1894 of the International Fisheries Commission, which, in its typically ineffective manner, declared that there were plenty of fish on these watersheds for all.[54]

So impossible had the trans-boundary reality become by this time and so adamant the local demands for a more 'equitable' solution that Ottawa felt compelled to soften its declaration on behalf of the Indians. It came to permit the use of gill nets by legitimate settlers here and on certain other inland lakes.[55] The rush that followed for such licences was overwhelming, and the result was almost impossible to police. Illegal fishing on lonely lakes became an increasing problem through the rest of the nineties. Meanwhile, a frugal number of pound net licences were granted to interested parties on Rainy Lake and Lake of the Woods. In 1895 some fourteen were being operated on the Ontario side, as opposed to a minimum of 250 across the border.[56] Although the legal Canadian total would be allowed to rise to forty in later years, their harvest and that of hoop or gill nets never approached a third of the American scale. As early as 1895, a wry article in the local press could point out that there were now ten American and ten 'supposedly' Canadian firms fishing on the Lake of the Woods. This gives an indication of the rate at which U.S. control of licences came to smother purely Canadian enterprise on these waters.

After the arrival of the Trust in 1897, such matters ceased to be of realistic concern.[57] At the end of the nineties, the combined international fish catch (still shipped through Rat Portage) from Lake of the Woods and Rainy Lake drainage was reported as about 2,500 tons annually. However, by then, the caviar harvest, which had reached its peak around 100,000 pounds in 1896, was in sharp decline under falling world prices.[58] After 1900, this outrageously wasteful quest, in which the sturgeon flesh was held of little value on removal of the roe and bladders, came to a protracted end.

Despite this international débâcle of the nineties, catches of whitefish, but not trout, in these Canadian waters appear to have increased by the time of the War (see Table 3.1). This reflects the very active fishing on both Rainy Lake and Lake of the Woods through the first decade of the century.[59] Yet, by 1901, the more limited fish populations of these modest water bodies had already encouraged heavy reliance on other stocks to fill available markets. Indeed, even at that date the tonnage of such other species more than equalled that of whitefish and trout combined. This reflected an advanced exploitive stage here that had yet to be reached on Superior.

In contrast to these extreme western watersheds, the management of other inland fisheries west of Thunder Bay seems to have been under much more local control or regional direction. Licences for gill nets (summer or winter) were often assumed by local inhabitants, under the legal guise of colonial settlers. Sometimes in mining areas, as along the Seine River, the catch found immediate sale.[60] However, with the passage of time and the loosening of regulations after 1895, control of the increasingly numerous lakes opened to commercial enterprise shifted quickly to established fishermen. These were sometimes moderately large operators on northern Lake Superior but, more often, smaller independents from those same waters. Such licensees were limited largely to lakes directly along the route of the CPR, for obvious market reasons. However, some prospered, at least seasonally, on less accessible waters such as the Manitou River system. Along the course of the Canadian Pacific, the most important fisheries were those on Eagle and Wabigoon, the lakes about Ignace, and at Savanne on Lac des Mille Lacs.[61] On the route of the Port Arthur, Duluth and Western the earliest lake licences were at Whitefish and neighbouring Arrow.[62] In the case of the smaller among such waters, operations followed a cycle of over-fishing then dormancy.[63] There is surprisingly little evidence to suggest that the construction of the Canadian Northern east toward Port Arthur promoted new fisheries at this time. It did facilitate Minnesota-oriented shipment from the Lake of the Woods and Rainy Lake over a link south from Fort Frances to Duluth. Alternately, the National Transcontinental east from Winnipeg and its branch south from Superior Junction to Fort William opened Lac Seul and Sturgeon Lake to exploitation.[64] However, many inland waters west of the Lakehead saw no commercial use before World War I.

This thrust on lesser lakes, so much more pronounced in western rather than eastern portions of the region, added to the harvest very substantially in the nineties and spectacularly so by 1911 (see Table 3.1). Here the troubled story repeated itself. At the turn of the century, total production was more than half made up of whitefish and trout, although the total catch was comparatively small. A decade later, coarser species were overwhelmingly dominant and the total now equalled that of the whole Algoma shore of Superior. In modern hindsight, this situation with inland licences in 1911 was the most prophetic indicator of the future. However, here as elsewhere, experts of the day, with their faith in hatchery propagation and in pisciculture, apparently saw no cause for concern.

New Directions in Mining

During the 1890s events in the northwestern Ontario mining sector were overshadowed by the successful utilization of Sudbury's complex nickel-copper deposits, as well as by gold production first about Rossland, B.C., then in the Klondike. After the turn of the century, the spectacular silver finds about Cobalt and rich gold discoveries in the Porcupine of northeastern Ontario also caused mining developments west of Sault Ste Marie to pale in public interest and investors' minds.

In 1888, a Royal Commission on Mining was established to seek ways to encourage mineral development on the Shield, which then still meant principally northwestern Ontario. After an exhaustive tour and rigorous investigation, its report recommended publicity aimed at the investment community and a mining school for professional training and ancillary practical education for local prospectors. As well, it suggested a Bureau of Mines to direct development and to publish scientific assessments of mineral finds.[65] The revised Mining Act of 1892 also reinstituted a policy of royalty payments on extracted minerals, despite forceful opposition from the industry. By so doing, it returned mining to the status of fishing and forest use, where exacting of a public share from any profit on Crown resource had a long provincial tradition.[66]

These trends affected different minerals and areas at various times. East along Superior's north shore, general mineral activity subsided quickly. However, sporadic gold interest at the Empire Mine behind Jackfish and exploratory zinc efforts near Schreiber would punctuate the pages of the press through the nineties and later.[67] Much more disconcerting was the sudden collapse in 1892 of long-inflated silver prices in the United States as the gold standard reasserted its official status. With this came an end to the intense activity around Silver Mountain, Rabbit Mountain, and elsewhere in the Thunder Bay area. This, coupled with the collapse of Algoma's copper excitement a decade earlier, brought the image of Superior's shores as 'a major mining area' to a tarnished state.[68]

Gold

Mineral excitement west of the lakes continued to the century's end but with a focus on gold. Here hopes of major capital infusions for mining were promoted through a wide range of glowing accounts. Quickest to appear were excited reports in the *Winnipeg Free Press*, joined over the years by the blatant boosterism of the *Rat Portage Miner* (now *Kenora Miner*) and *Wabigoon Star* (now *Dryden Observer*). Unfortunately, such articles could muster only sceptical and occasional aid from the Toronto or Montreal papers. However, the Ontario Mining Association stepped in to fill that gap with enthusiastic promotional literature for potential investors in central Canada, the United States, and Great Britain. In addition, such mining endeavours were now lavishly covered in the annual reports of the Bureau of Mines, to which passed responsibility for the provision of roads from railway to mineral discoveries.[69] In the end, however, these wide-ranging efforts at support and promotion of gold mining in the Kenora and Rainy River area proved unsuccessful.

About the Lake of the Woods, where the issue of gold had a long if highly speculative past, the nineties were years of modest success, but only at a handful of sites with established names like Sultana, Mikado, or Regina. Energetic attempts at the founding of a local mining exchange were short-lived. Promotional train trips and tours of the area for important interests and speculators from Toronto, Chicago, and other American financial centres did little to attract additional financial attention. New exploratory activity, like significant outside interest, dwindled away about 1900, and the last significant mine of this era, the Sultana, closed when it filled with water in 1906.[70]

After their discovery in the early eighties until the mid-nineties, no real interest was shown in more easterly gold fields. These, including the Manitou,

New Klondyke, and Saw Bill neighboured the CPR's south side between Dryden and Ignace. While some U.S. investment was attracted here, most of the development capital was from Toronto, Hamilton, and Winnipeg, probably encouraged by the concurrent emergence of the first Ontario mining exchange in Toronto.[71] Also of likely importance were provincial outlays on mining roads and on control dams for water levels to facilitate wagon and steamer access.

The first real prospecting and staking rush in all three cases came in 1896. Exploratory work followed immediately, but the commercial results were generally disappointing. Although lavish facilities were erected at the Saw Bill and neighbouring Hammond Reef mines, including hydroelectrical generation, neither came close to returning their investment costs and both were closed permanently by 1900. In the New Klondyke, only the Golden Whale (later Sakoose), which gained a spur from the CPR, earned its keep.[72] At the third field south of Dryden, with its system of steamers from Wabigoon and Dinorwic and its stage road from there to further vessels on Lake Manitou, none but the Neepawa and Independence were even sporadically productive. However, several around the new mining camp of Gold Rock on upper Manitou would be added to this list of inconsistently active mines in the next decade. Few, if any, of these were to prove significantly profitable in this pre-war era. By then, the first finds north of the CPR, made between 1898 and 1901, were gaining significant attention. These included ones accessible by water from Dinorwic or only by pack train north from Ignace to Sturgeon Lake. This last area, particularly the St Anthony's Mine, was to become a focus of gold activity in the new century.[73]

South of these disparate and often disappointing fields lay the Seine River gold country at the eastern end of Rainy Lake. Discoveries in the general area began on the American side in 1893. They quickly spawned the Minnesota town of Rainy Lake City, to the south and east of Fort Frances. During the subsequent winter, the first promising Canadian claims were staked along the navigable section of the Seine below the Sturgeon Rapids. Claims far above this obstacle to direct transport soon followed, amid a rush of heavy prospecting.[74] Official reaction was to initiate work on the extension to the Seine of the mining road south from Savanne to certain iron finds of the Atikokan area; a road from Bonheur via the Saw Bill country to Atikokan on the south; and another from Ignace to the heart of the gold field and the wagon/steamer route from Dryden via Gold Rock through the Manitou system to Fort Frances.[75] However, all supplies and much passenger movement continued to be by steamer from Kenora to Fort Frances and from the latter to the gold camps. This would change only when the Canadian Northern Railway was built through the area about the turn of the century.

The usual pattern of exploration was well under way by the mid-nineties. Investment in stamp mills and serious underground endeavours, largely from U.S. and British sources, was soon in modest evidence. By 1896 the local supply communities of Mine Centre and neighbouring Bell City were becoming established, with stores, hotels, and daily steamer service to their wharves.[76] Indeed, a few aspiring properties turned out their first bricks. However, the Foley was the only substantive money-maker and was considered a success comparable to the Sultana on the Lake of the Woods. It was joined by the Golden Star, Alice A, and Olive, each in profitable overlap with the one before. Of these, only the last seems likely to have paid its owners an acceptable return before closing, as the first flush of interest in this field dwindled in about 1900.[77]

But while most gold activity in the nineties was concentrated in this distant west, one other field, more central to the province, made a likewise brief appearance near the end of the decade. In late August 1897, Ainsworth and Ganley's fish steamer *Telegram* reached Sault Ste Marie with the first news of an exciting gold find near the modern Michipicoten Harbour and Wawa Lake. The effect about the Great Lakes was electric. Here was a potential Eldorado within three days by steamer from either Toronto or Detroit. By the end of September, the townsite of Wawa City on the lake was laid out and buildings were rising. In addition, the old tote road from CPR building days was reactivated from the Michipicoten River estuary. The Bureau of Mines created its first provincial mining district with an appropriate registry officer installed in the then-abandoned Hudson's Bay Company post there. More indicative of the excitement was the arrival of several hundred prospectors and amateur gold seekers, along with the usual band of speculators.[78] A month later, a second town site at the Mission on the lower end of the tote road was under survey and there were calls to dredge the river mouth for an appropriate harbour. Over 250 prospecting licences were granted, but cold weather drove out the greenhorns and only the hardy professionals were settling in for a winter of prospecting and exploration.[79]

The following spring was marked by a second flood of prospects and stakings, and also the first appearance of stamp mills and other primary machinery. Several mines gained sufficient finance to start underground work, and one, the Grace, actually became a tentative producer. In this it was followed by the Jubilee, McKay, Minto, and others by 1899, although the Grace appears unique in having turned an encouraging profit.[80] Several ventures here continued to develop and produce moderately until about 1908, by which time most were served with electrical power from a private hydro installation on the Michipicoten

River.[81] However, like those farther west, these Ontario mines suffered from a chronic shortage of both speculative and developmental capital. Such funds, both national and international, had increasingly been attracted first to rich finds of precious metals in British Columbia in 1891, then to the spectacular Klondike field of 1896, and now to Cobalt and the Porcupine camps.[82]

Iron

Yet such disappointing experience with copper, silver, and now gold was not the total story of mining in Ontario's northwest before World War I. These decades also saw the region's first extraction and smelting of iron ore. Private interest in such Canadian mining and production, which had been lost at mid-century, was revived by national, then provincial, incentives and protectionist legislation by 1890. This ultimately resulted in the rise of blast furnaces in Port Arthur and at Sault Ste Marie as well as in a range of towns in southern Ontario.[83] The existence of good iron deposits just west of the Lakehead at Matawin, Gunflint Lake, Shebandowan, and much farther west around modern Atikokan was well known by 1890. Indeed, at that date Belgian interests attempted unsuccessfully to generate a company for the mining of the Atikokan deposits. However, the concept of smelting these ores on Thunder Bay, using coal shipped up from Lake Erie ports, attracted only passing attention until the end of the decade.[84] After the offer of a handsome municipal bonus and interest in a smelter project by the railway magnates Mackenzie and Mann, a blast furnace to handle Atikokan iron was finally raised in 1907. However, the ore proved disappointing in its character and production was discontinued in 1911.[85]

Similar but more spectacular developments in Algoma were but one of the results of the imaginative mind and colourful actions of Francis Clergue, who arrived at the St Marys Rapids in March 1894. Over the next nine years this American financial genius and promoter initiated a hydroelectric supply for town and industry, a paper plant, and a sawmill complex. In addition, he started an iron and steel works with accompanying mine and the necessary rail and water transport to link mines to blast furnaces and forests to mills. The financial collapse of his integrated industrial pyramid in 1903, complete with strikes and riots, is famous in Canadian business history.[86]

Clergue's turbulent entry into iron mining began in the early days of the Michipicoten gold rush when Alvin Goetz brought to his attention certain adjacent surface deposits of rich hematite north of this gold field. After a quick visit in early 1898, Clergue purchased these claims as well as the siderite deposits on the neighbouring Magpie River. Next came the incorporation of the Algoma Central Railway (ACR), first to link them to water at Michipicoten

Harbour, then later to tap these finds from Sault Ste Marie. This trackage by 1915 also reached north to the National Transcontinental at Hearst, crossing the CPR at Franz and the Canadian Northern at Oba.

As was Clergue's style, all was now haste. Rapid track-laying linked the mines to newly constructed ore docks at the harbour and necessary car shops at neighbouring Brient by the spring of 1900. Delivery of Clergue's first steamer from the Clyde enabled initial summer ore shipments for processing at Midland until the first blast furnace could be completed at the rising Sault Ste Marie smelter in 1901. Two years later the British-financed and U.S.-chartered Lake Superior Corporation was able to mine 200,000 tons annually near modern Wawa. A third of this was shipped to Sault Ste Marie with the remainder going to Ohio ports in return for coking coal. By the outbreak of war, a fleet of modern iron steamers plied from Michipicoten Harbour, and trains were running over the main north–south line, which was joined by a branch to the mines at Hawk Junction. Several hundred permanent employees and their families were resident at the Helen and Magpie mines, and the saga of a future Algoma Steel had well and truly begun.[87]

After several false starts in mineral activity northwestern Ontario seemed to have found a winner in iron. Public excitement over this spectacular development was soon overshadowed during the ten years before the war by finds of precious metals in the northeast. Yet the mining and processing of iron here in Algoma in those same years was being carried out at a scale unimaginable to Ontario's citizens only a few years before.

Forest Demands in Transition

The rising resource conservation movement in the early eighties was bolstered by major conferences in both Canada and the United States. These coloured future public and political outlook, not only on fish harvesting, but also on forest use. To the latter in particular these conferences introduced to North American thinking notions of sustained yield.[88] However, as with fisheries, inadequate science and blind belief limited and delayed the successful application of this laudable theory to provincial forest resources for many years.

In response to the Montreal Congress, Ontario appointed a Clerk of Forestry to its Department of Agriculture in 1883, where his work focused on better woodlot management in Old Ontario. However, the post was transferred to Crown Lands two years later, and its holder, Thomas Southwick, was encouraged to direct his efforts at more northerly issues. In 1898, Southwick's office fostered a Bureau of Forestry as a much more adequate vehicle for the promotion of a sound woodland future.[89]

A Royal Commission on Forestry had been struck the year before, and its report in 1899 did much to support and strengthen Southwick's position and his own beliefs. The membership, including persons from the industry and from the conservation community, made strong recommendations in two areas. It wished to see northern fire protection, which had been tentatively initiated in 1885, improved and extended to cover all remaining pineries. The Commission also strongly recommended programs for the large-scale renewal of cut-over pine lands through 'natural regeneration.' Both principles were part of Southwick's conservation plans. However, while the former was an entirely practical and achievable goal, the latter demonstrated a general lack of understanding of the basic tenets of forest renewal. It ignored both European experience and current literature and flew in the face of reality. The harvesting process was altering the composition of the province's northern forests and would continue to do so under 'natural regeneration' because pine was far from a primary species in the normal sequence of forest regrowth. Like others in the industry and within Crown Lands (the Department of Lands and Forests after 1905), Southwick refused to accept that replanting programs were required for the attainment of sustained pine yields. They also balked at the heavy reliance on professional foresters in future woodland management.[90]

However, Southwick's term in office was not without its positive side. In 1898, Ontario enacted legislation to promote the founding of Forest Reserves. These were envisioned as a selection of large areas where rich pine reserves were to be held against future need or where natural regeneration was to be encouraged. In no way were they to be opened to northern colonization. A resident staff of rangers was to protect these against fires or to promote renewal of mature stands that could be returned to the harvesting cycle.[91] In northwestern Ontario such reserves came to consist of a modest cut-over tract, set aside on the Sibley Peninsula in 1900, a huge fire-torn parcel of 7,300 square miles around Lake Nipigon, laid out before 1905, and a very large wilderness reserve at Quetico, delineated in 1909.[92] Unfortunately, further significant additions to such lands were not forthcoming as both public and political interests returned to an older focus on northern settlement. Indeed, the Bureau was transferred back to the Department of Agriculture in 1905 and was gradually submerged in the rising Colonization Branch, with which its original principles had very little in common.[93]

Lumbering

Such early attempts at salvation and preservation found little sympathy or even understanding among commercial forest interests in the northwest. These were not the now comfortably wealth lumber barons of the Ottawa Valley, whose timber was running out and whose market share dropped to less than one-third of the total by the mid-nineties. Most northwestern interests were still financially insecure in the highly uncertain timber economy. Many only recently had transferred their interests up the lakes from Georgian Bay or from elsewhere in eastern Canada. Most also retained that grasping colonial mind-set that never let tomorrow's need stand in the way of today's profits.[94] Because of their reliance on western markets, the prior U.S. tariffs against Canadian lumber (but not saw logs) had caused them little discomfort. However, they were faced in 1894 with virtual free-trade arrangements between Ottawa and Washington, for lumber and saw logs. Unlike producers on upper Huron, they were not troubled by the sudden escalation of log rafting to American mills. Instead, they were forced to cope with lumber from neighbouring American sources, which began immediately to disturb prairie markets and prices.

Northern lumbermen's unhappiness with the situation boiled over in 1897 when the Americans reinstituted their lumber duties under the Dingley Tariff. Ontario, reacting to the lumbermen's anger, initiated yet one more successful skirmish in federal–provincial litigation by passing its Saw Log Act. This prevented the export of unmanufactured timber from Crown lands after April 30, 1898.[95] American producers, handicapped by shortages of suitable resources in their home states, came quickly to move their massive mills to their Ontario limits, located principally between the French and the Rainy rivers. An accelerating boom of harvesting and milling followed to about 1914. During this era more and more red pine as well as white pine was cut to satisfy the demands of a growing urban Canada, prairie expansion, and American consumers.[96]

The lumbering tradition of the Rainy River/Lake of the Woods watershed was to mature and prosper over these two-and-a-half decades before World War I. In 1891 the three saw communities of Keewatin, Norman, and Rat Portage (an acronym of these names, *Kenora,* was to evolve by 1905) were still home to six large mills, capable of supplying fifty cars of lumber to Winnipeg per day.[97] However, amalgamations were quick to follow. In the mid-eighties, the Minnesota-Ontario Lumber Company had been incorporated in the United States. This firm had established financial links with the old Keewatin Lumber Company under W.J. Macauley. The purpose was to harvest certain pineries on the Minnesota side of the border, which territory had no American market access, and to mill the logs at Norman for shipment over the CPR. Despite some embarrassment suffered during the later Minnesota Timber Inquiry around 1890, this firm, which included the wealthy American Edward W. Backus, established a much closer financial relationship with Keewatin by 1893.[98]

The quality American timber that this axis continued to handle found markets in Winnipeg and would soon benefit from lucrative shipment via the Lakehead to Chicago. While the latter market would die with certain clauses in the McKinley Tariff, the Saw Log Act placed no restriction on rising sales, because of its Canadian manufacture. As a result, Keewatin Lumber enjoyed its most productive years, with this growing infusion of supply to add to the substantial harvests from its own Ontario limits. The peak came between 1904 and 1911 when this output competed easily on western markets with the lower-quality spruce lumber of northern Manitoba and Saskatchewan.[99]

A similar search for more efficient size and financial stability in the early nineties led the other five milling interests of the area to unite as the Ontario-Western Lumber Company. This quickly evolved into Rat Portage Lumber. Through gradual reorganization over the next decade, that firm updated and consolidated its operation into one large establishment here with another big steam mill on the south end of the lake at Beaver Mills (now Rainy River). Unfortunately, this association suffered the loss of both these facilities to separate fires in 1910. The former mill was quickly rebuilt, and in 1911 it and the competing Keewatin Lumber at Kenora turned out a combined total of 38 million board feet of lumber, exclusive of huge quantities of lath and shingles.[100]

These endeavours were not the only large Ontario sawyeries to emerge on this western watershed by 1914. At Beaver Mills, the Rat Portage mill was joined in 1906 by an even larger one, erected by Wisconsin-based Shevlin-Clark, as a sister to an older one in Spooner/Baudette, Minnesota. At the close of the decade, the two on the Canadian side were producing annually in excess of 28 million feet per year. The unfortunate Rat Portage Lumber property at Beaver Mills was lost in the same Minnesota forest fire of late 1910 that destroyed all other mills here on both sides of the river.[101] Because of Shevlin-Clark's American timber losses to this fire and the inadequacy of the log slide at the new power dam upstream at Kouchiching Rapids, Shevlin-Clark moved operations to Fort Frances in 1912, purchasing the physical assets and limits of the Fort Frances Lumber Company. To this Shevlin-Clark added new cutting rights about Rainy Lake and east to the Quetico area, along the course of the Canadian Northern Railway. With the completion of a second large mill here in 1914, Shevlin-Clark had the capacity to saw up to 800,000 feet of lumber per day.[102]

The annual commercial cut of pine that passed through these and other Ontario saws along the waterways to the west of the arctic divide totalled an astounding 100 million board feet per month just before the war. This came largely from a mosaic of discrete timber berths, principally south of the CPR and often on small interior lakes and rivers. Its log transport required complex measures with dams, slides, and artificial water levels as well as the use of the alligator boat to aid in the spring river drives. As the pine limits were abandoned or turned to other timbering ends, new ones were added through regular survey and auction under provincial auspices. While they were always less accessible and farther from the mills, they were still profitable to harvest.[103]

This huge pine cut also included lumber for more domestic purposes. This came from at least a dozen small mills operating modest limits in the Rainy River settlements, in the rising farm community around Dryden, and from larger contributors along the railways. On the CPR, harvests focused on continuing mid-sized mills such as those at Vermilion Bay, at Indian Lake Lumber of Osaquan (near Ignace), or Beck and Sphon at Savanne. Here also, as along both other transcontinental lines, were located the voracious camps and mills of numerous contractors. They were dedicated to making tamarack pilings for port and harbour improvements at the Lakehead and ties, posts, poles, and railway timber from a range of other forest species. Sometimes such operations were but a branch of the activities of firms like Keewatin or Rat Portage Lumber. Yet often they bore names like Shear, Vigar, Graham and Horne, Whalen, Northern Construction, or Greer Brothers, all well-known dealers in the twin cities on Thunder Bay.[104] However, along the northerly course of the National Transcontinental in particular, mill operators were cutting the infrequent, sparse, and most northerly pine, but were largely reliant on the best of the rich native spruce of the taiga. Most noteworthy was George Farlinger, who by 1910 had limits with sawyeries at both Allan Water and McDougall Mills east and west of Savant Lake on the National Transcontinental but had erected a particularly large outfit at Sioux Lookout. He was the most established name in such less valuable lumber north and west of Thunder Bay.[105]

Closer to Port Arthur/Fort William and within Superior drainage, pine supplies were more limited and now less lavish in supply. A cataclysmic forest fire in 1889 had raged north from Grand Marais in Minnesota, often scorching, partly burning, or totally decimating the Superior pineries northward into Ontario, as far as the Cloud River area. The most valuable tracts of pine missed by this fire were in the border country, principally in the Pigeon River and tributary watersheds, such as the Arrow, and about Whitefish Lake. Most berths here were successfully sold in 1890 and became the property of two major American lumbering interests: Alger and Smith Limited of Detroit and D.J. Arpin and Associates of Wisconsin Rapids. Neither was in immediate need of these resources.[106]

Like most rivers in the Superior watershed, those here were short, prone to rapids or falls, and very difficult for lumbermen to drive. While rumour in May 1894 suggested that R.A. Alger and his company would begin their Canadian harvest here that year, no such action occurred until the 1897 season. However, at the time of its timber purchase, this company had extracted a promise from the province to aid in the provision of certain driving improvements. This joint project was pursued in the interim and ultimately spawned long-lived slide and boom companies on both the Pigeon and Arrow rivers.[107] Later, in consideration of the date of the purchase of the Pigeon Limit and of a substantial permanent contribution toward these improvements, this firm was granted certain unusual favours. These included permission to boom its logs to Duluth, after the inauguration of Ontario's embargo on such unsawn exports. Such towing to American mills was commenced from the mouth of the Pigeon in 1898. It continued unabated until the company sold its remaining timber rights, soon after the turn of the century, to Arpin and his Pigeon River Lumber Company. The latter then was already active on the Arrow/Whitefish watershed.[108]

Aided by the now-established slide and boom arrangements on this river, Arpin purchased the existing mill of Graham and Horne at Fort William in 1901. The next year Arpin's Pigeon River Lumber moved to erect a much larger facility on the Port Arthur waterfront. To this operation it quickly added a fleet of five tugs to tow its cut from the mouth of the Pigeon. Its modern mill, run electrically and enlarged to huge daily capacity, became the prime employer in Port Arthur by mid-decade. At the onset of war, its annual output stood in excess of 34 million board feet of lumber each year and its cutting camps employed over 600 persons for the winter harvest.[109] Its yearly production was augmented by local mills in the developing agricultural neighbourhoods in back of Thunder Bay. This was bolstered further by more than a dozen small commercial producers among the villages and sidings of the PAD&W Railway. Unfortunately, little information has been preserved on these lesser operations or on the piling, tie, and railway timber enterprises that were undeniably active here and along rail lines to the east of Thunder Bay.

The story of lumbering north from Sault Ste Marie over these decades is similarly masked by fragmented information. The ACR, chartered in 1899, was given dominion and provincial land grants, including timber and mineral rights, of 7,400 acres per mile. To aid in its selection, Ontario withdrew from the market for a year all unfettered Crown lands in a wide corridor from Goulais in the south to between White River and Missanabie in the north. In November of that year, the cabinet confirmed the company's right to take even pine, without penalty, for ten years, from its ultimate selection of over 1.6 million acres. This selection being confirmed, railway construction quickly commenced. However, while track reached modern Searchmont in 1901 and mile 68 (Pangis) by the time of Clergue's financial collapse two years later, little progress followed until a major refinancing in 1909 promoted rapid completion as previously described.[110]

Timber from its grants was assumed to be a major revenue source from the railroad's inception, as well as a necessary commodity for construction and maintenance. During 1902 therefore, an idle sawmill capable of 130,000 feet per shift was dismantled in Saginaw, Michigan, and reassembled in the rising industrial part of Sault Ste Marie. Along with a rail spur and river frontage, it was also supplied with two veneering machines to handle hardwood. This complex went into production with 200 men the following year. The output from five camps up the line, between Wabos and Pangis, by the next spring made up fifty shiploads for export.[111] A large parallel venture to saw certain types of hardwood and to supply raw blocks for early charcoal experiments in Sault Ste Marie was opened at Searchmont in 1903.[112] Although passage into receivership caused both mills some unease, their operations and those of related cutting camps along the railway appear to have continued uninterrupted. No suitable figures are available for the Searchmount mill, but at Sault Ste Marie production stood at 20 million board feet per month in 1908 and over 26 million four years later.[113] However, given the limited geographical range of pine and good hardwoods northward along this shore and the fact that any pine on these rail grants was reserved only until 1911, such cut levels were unlikely to have been sustained much longer.

Demands for forest products other than pulpwood were far more mixed along eastern Superior's shore, where prime harvesting had occurred in earlier decades. Any expanded lumbering activity here was now quite circumscribed by the surrounding pattern of the ACR reserve. Through the nineties, small limits of pine continued to be sold and modest mills erected, most frequently in the townships and part-townships behind Goulais and Batchawana bays, outside those of the old surveys of retreatied land.[114] Sometimes this interest centred on valuable hardwood, as much as two million feet at a time being arranged through local settlers of that area. Around the turn of the century a jobber for furniture companies in the Berlin (Kitchener) and Strathroy (near London) areas held considerable acreage here. However, he was unable to make a profit and was in deep financial trouble by 1908. Yet flooring firms, cedar dealers, and even those seeking white birch for the manufacture of baskets came and went from this local scene by wartime. Closer about Sault Ste Marie, small mills and limits continued to serve domestic needs. These provided everything from posts and barn boards to finished lumber, sash work, and doors, in a pattern analogous to that followed in other agricultural pockets.[115]

Pulp and Paper

Such lumbering and milling of northwestern Ontario's Great Lakes forest resources continued voraciously into the war years. Yet with the nineties came growing recognition of the value of the taiga species to the north. Technological advances in paper making after 1875 brought the abundant spruce of the latter forest into great demand by the neighbouring U.S. before the end of the century. By then, tariffs against Canadian paper, but not pulpwood, entrenched in both the McKinley and later the Dingly trade enactments, had caused serious pricing disputes between American newspaper publishers and paper milling interests. By 1898, Canadian manufacturers also were showing displeasure and unsuccessfully pressed Ottawa to control American pulpwood supplies. Two years later, Ontario paper interests were rewarded. A provincial Order in Council required all such wood cut on Crown lands to be manufactured at least into wet pulp before export, or face stiff duty. Quebec's refusal to follow suit as well as supplies remaining in American forests until about 1910 combined to limit the effectiveness of this embargo. High U.S. tariff walls against Canadian paper remained in force until 1913.[116]

At the same time, Ontario's government, seeing a further source of resource revenue and northern development, attempted to entice foreign capital into this new pulp and paper phase of forest harvesting and processing. The capital requirements for the necessary plant were far greater than those of the largest sawmilling complex and the incentives had to be of comparable scale. Unlike the old timber policy administered by the Crown Lands Department, any agreements were negotiated, therefore, between the provincial cabinet and private interests. Such arrangements involved much larger blocks of woodland and longer lease periods, compared with lumbering limits. In addition, each required the inclusion of a hydroelectric power source. As experience was gained, these contracts came to include specified mill sizes, employment levels, and other important refinements. Nevertheless, while such incentives promoted numerous early agreements, the tariff situation with the United States caused most capital interests to seek ways to delay subsequent investment. This frustrating situation was only beginning to find its solution with the coming of war.[117]

The first agreement of this type was signed with Francis Clergue in 1894, following his purchase of the huge hydro potential of the St Marys Rapids and the disastrous municipal attempt to harness them. (Only several years later did the province recall E.B. Borron's old advice to lease rather than sell power rights to private parties.) The initially vague arrangement was to encourage Clergue to erect a mill of unspecified size and to provide it 'with a suitable supply of pulpwood.' The limit was actually confirmed, however, as fifty square miles 'from land on either or both sides of one or more rivers flowing into Lake Superior.'[118] This lackadaisical approach to spatial definition of this pulpwood concession was to cost dearly. In 1917, having no records of any subsequent detailed settlement, Queen's Park finally agreed to accept the company's long-standing claim of 'traditional' control over a huge tract on watersheds draining west into Superior.[119]

Work at Sault Ste Marie on a ground wood pulp mill capable of 150 tons per day was completed in 1895 and incorporated a drying procedure that saved much weight in subsequent shipment. At the end of the century, this sulphate mill had grown to employ some 700 men, including bushworkers. Work on its sulphite partner began in 1899 and opened three years later, complete with bleaching processes using chlorine and sulphur by-products from related Sudbury nickel operations.[120] After a brief closure with Clergue's financial collapse in 1903 and low production following in 1904, both were back to full capacity (75,000 cords) the next year as Lake Superior Corporation (LSC). Bad mill fires in the last half of the decade caused shut-downs, but these operations continued profitable and in 1910 were joined by a newsprint mill with four machines capable of 200 tons a day.[121] Separated by that time from the other Clergue holdings and called Lake Superior Paper, it was sold in 1913 to the Spanish River Pulp and Paper Company and so became part of the Mead Corporation of Dayton, Ohio.[122]

Records of the pulpwood sources for this large and successful operation are as vague and incomplete as those for the limit itself. From the inception of the ACR and during its beleaguered progress northward, very considerable amounts of pulpwood were purchased off the railway grant, but also taken from other areas along the right of way.[123] Most of the cutting here and elsewhere on the company's vaguely defined pulp limit was done through contractors and involved the watersheds of such rivers as the Goulais, Chippewa, and Batchawana. Driving the difficult lower reaches of these waterways to the lake required costly preparatory work to minimize loss of stranded pulpwood along their courses. In contrast, drives on their upper reaches to the railway were probably simple. At the outbreak of war, some 37,000 cords were estimated to be derived annually from such sources. However, roughly twice that figure was being supplied by other means.[124] Clergue had been quick to gain control of the harvest off the now high-graded pine limits (Numbers 34 and 61). These covered much of the retreatied townships and were held by a Quebec contracting firm. Later sources also included at least some of the large settler cut from private lands, in bush lots acquired near farmable properties. These were numerous behind Sault Ste Marie and on the associated uplands, as well as in the retreatied townships. They also were to be found inland around Searchmont and the adjacent settlement of Wabos.[125]

During the nineties, James Whalen of Port Arthur, with prominent American paper interests, also obtained a vague forest agreement with the province. Their first arrangement was for an unspecified limit, probably the lower Black and related Pic rivers on the north shore of Superior, in return for the manufacture of pulp and 'other woodenware.' Subsequently, these interests, with additional Canadian backers, shifted their contract to a limit extending back five miles from the shores of Lake Nipigon and the Nipigon River. With this agreement was the promise of a pulp mill on the most southerly hydraulic site on the latter system. As in the case of several northern Ontario deals negotiated in these years, this one remained only a dream and was cancelled in 1906. However, the concession was re-offered the next year with a specification of a 150-ton-per-day pulp mill, to employ 250 men for at least ten months of the year; all was to be in operation within thirty-six months.[126] This more firmly defined proposition prompted no future response among capitalists for more than a decade. Indeed, nowhere on northern Superior, even in the Lakehead cities, was any further interest generated in formal limits and mills during pre-war years.

The same was not true to the west of the Great Lakes country, where in the new Rainy River District talk of pulp and paper at Fort Frances using the Kouchiching Falls had been under discussion since 1897. Finally, an agreement was reached here in 1902 between Ontario and a private group from Winnipeg. This involved a limit of 275 square miles on eastern Rainy Lake, with plans for a mill at the last rapids on the Seine River.[127] An impatient provincial government cancelled this, like other contracts, in 1905 and early the next year retendered the limit with the usual proviso of minimum pulp mill capacity, employment level, and time-frame for completion. Over subsequent years this limit was held dormantly by local interests from Mine Centre, then by the rail-building team of Mackenzie and Mann before its sale in 1909 for active exploitation.[128] Meanwhile the American E.W. Backus, already involved financially in the evolving Keewatin Lumber Company, obtained international permission to begin construction of a power dam and plant at the Fort Frances site in 1906. However, his initial strategy was for pulp and paper production only on the American side, at International Falls that gave free access to American buyers. This was probably realistic since the western Canadian markets for newsprint were still too small to be very profitable. Backus' Ontario-Minnesota Power Company, therefore, refused to commit itself to any formal Ontario limit. However, it seems to have purchased heavily from Rainy River farmers and local dealers with non-Crown sources for export. Not until 1912 did Backus judge prairie opportunities and future American markets sufficient to justify both an Ontario agreement for some 800 square miles north of Rainy Lake and a modest 50-ton pulp mill on the Canadian side at Fort Frances. When this mill was nearing completion after war was declared the pulpwood cut from Backus' Crown lease in this area reached 28,000 cords. Over 16,500 more still were being derived from the settlers of the Rainy River Valley.[129]

At Rat Portage, soon to be called Kenora, interest in pulp and paper emerged in the late nineties, with the promotion of the large and yet unutilized hydro power resources of the Keewatin dam at Tunnel Island. A strongly Canadian consortium promised a mill of 400 tons per day, employing 500 men, in return for a large pulpwood limit, principally down the east side of the Lake of the Woods. However, the intended central Canadian markets were discovered to be too expensive to reach and, as elsewhere, a disappointed province cancelled this agreement in 1906.[130] A subsequent offer of this limit was made in return for a scaled-down mill of 100-ton capacity and 200 jobs, with the added municipal incentive of relief from local taxes for ten years. Not until 1912, when Backus took up this set of options through his Keewatin Lumber interests, did this proposition show promise. By 1914, negotiations were underway for the limit, with a mill to follow when western Canadian demand reached higher levels (see Map 3.1).[131]

Only at Dryden – also in the District of Kenora, which was carved in 1909 from the huge Rainy River jurisdiction – was any similar activity evident before the outbreak of war. This jackpine limit with few resources of spruce or balsam was advertised in earlier years. However, it attracted no attention until the retendering of numerous properties in early 1906, when it was taken up tentatively by a mix of small-town Ontario interests. The Gordon Pulp and Paper Company initially planned a small 40-ton sulphite, 20-ton groundwood, and 50-ton kraft paper operation. It began construction in early 1909 on potential power from the adjacent Wabigoon Falls. After British refinancing in 1910 and a name change to the Dryden Timber and Power Company, its sulphate (kraft) plant was producing 40 tons of pulp per day in 1913, from a strongly settler-based cut.[132] Technical problems with jackpine, coupled with other financial ones, would delay erection of other once-planned facilities for many years. Nevertheless, while production at Fort Frances was imminent and a mill at Kenora was likely, only this small and wavering operation and the larger one at Sault Ste Marie were in regional operation when war was declared.

Countering the impetus behind such promising but tentative development was the continuing export of raw pulpwood, even after the provincial moves to curb this activity in 1900. This leakage to American markets was significant in northwestern Ontario in readily accessible territory about Lake Superior and Fort Frances. Sometimes the harvest was organized directly by contractors, on lands previously alienated from Crown control, such as the ACR grants. Often, however, it came off settler holdings, either as a result of agricultural land clearance and legal cuts on additional purchased bush properties or from questionable free grant acquisition through subsequent timber scalping or from other properties in illegal fashion.

On Superior's northern shore, these pulpwood operations began as early as 1890. At that date, J. Nesbit, a contractor up from Sarnia, was active on several old gold properties about the mouth and lower reaches of the Pic for the Port Huron Sulphite Company mills in southern Michigan. Two years later James Whalen and his associates, presumably under the guise of their first provincial pulpwood agreement, took over this operation. They also added more and more old mining property west along the Superior shore, from which they continued to harvest pulpwood for Michigan shipment till 1898.[133] By that date, Whalen and friends had supposed rights, under their second provincial agreement, to cut pulp from a five-mile band about Lake Nipigon and along the river of the same name. They therefore shifted some of their interest there, running the entire operation under a new label, the North Shore Timber Company. Through these early years, they generated a large towing fleet to serve such production along this northern as well as adjoining northwestern reach of Superior. After the 1900 pulpwood embargo, these interests, through political favour, continued to be the exclusive exporters from Crown territory. North Shore Timber continued to plunder the resources along the Nipigon River until cancellation of their supposed pulpwood agreement in 1905–6 and the subsequent conversion of much of the area to the Nipigon Forest Reserve.[134]

West of Black Bay, as early as 1895, other prominent Port Arthur entrepreneurs were actively harvesting pulp in conjunction with Michigan interests. Their take came from the large and still-uncancelled holdings here of the Ontario Land and Mining Company (originally held by the old Montreal Mining Company). These Lakehead businessmen, on behalf of Detroit Sulphite, also worked similar claims on major peninsulas and islands and on the mainland east to the Slate Islands.[135] They were taken over in 1906 by the Northern Island Pulpwood Company, which, under the local management of W.H. Russell, prospered until its dissolution in 1912. The huge cuts of this consortium of American firms, like those that preceded, went south to U.S. mills in a fleet of old wooden steamers at 20,000 cords a load.[136]

To the east, much of the pulp cut in Algoma was under contract to a range of firms and was destined for pulp and papers operations at Sault Ste Marie. However, Perry Lumber was also an active contributor to the American export of raw pulpwood, seeking supplies from among the settlers and other private property holders along the east side of Superior. Working for the mills at Sault Ste Marie or directly for American consumption, T.J. Everett and others were active on the lower reaches of rivers in the Pukaskwa. Such contractors were also at work on the Magpie and Michipicoten rivers in these years. However, distance made towing costs and risks a limiting factor for the more northerly of these operators. Through most of the period, the transport of this and other pulpwood along the Algoma shore to the St Marys River was provided by six powerful tugs of Ganley Towing, an offshoot of the Ainsworth and Ganley Fish Company.[137] Closer to the border, the Michigan Pulpwood Company, through the nineties, had provided a lucrative alternative to Clergue for settlers with local Crown-cut pulpwood for sale. The provincial embargo on its export in 1900 drew loud complaint in the local press from these farmers.[138] These rural inhabitants soon found ways, however, of using free grants and bush lot purchases to regain their export income.

In the Thunder Bay area, where little interest in the erection of pulp mills appeared by the outbreak of war, the situation was much the same. Through the nineties, while both contractors and settlers continued to rely heavily on the post, pole, and tie markets for forest income, pulpwood climbed steadily in importance. In 1895, contracted cuts of 25,000 cords were shipped to American mills. Locally, lumbermen like W.H. Carpenter at Cloud and Prince bays were highly involved in this industry, as were the settlers and contractors along the PAD&W Railway. To these must be added both the farmers and newer colonists of the Slate and Whitefish valleys, as well as in other townships both inland and to the east of the Lakehead. Contractor cuts of pulpwood, often in conjunction with other forest products, seem to have spread some distance west along the major railways. They also were active about Black Bay and the Black Sturgeon towards Nipigon wherever non-Crown property was available or some form of rights could be procured.[139] In contrast to the Michigan orientation of most exports from Nipigon eastward to Algoma, pulpwood gathered here was usually boomed across Superior to the Ashland, Wisconsin, railhead for transfer to mills on Lake Michigan. Such risky booming over this huge body of water, which became increasingly common after 1900, involved tows in excess of 14,000 cords using four tugs and taking a minimum of 100 hours.[140] In the future, such affiliation with Wisconsin-based interests would strengthen and ultimately broaden to supply local paper producers, as it would about Fort Frances and Kenora. For the most part, such domestic production would find growing western and midwestern U.S. newsprint markets.

Advances in Rural Settlement

In the twenty years following 1890, the rural population of the northwest increased more than two-and-a-half times but still stood at only about 24,000 on the declaration of war. The agricultural (rural) component, given the inevitable inclusion of railway section hands, occasional bushworkers, fishermen, and small businessmen amid tiny rural nodes, was probably no more than four-fifths of that figure. However, this small number of farmers north and west of the lakes, like its new northwestern counterpart, now came to command a disproportionate level of public and political interest. Responsibility for guiding these strong northern thrusts in settlement and road building passed from the old Colonization Branch of Crown Lands, via the Bureau of Forestry, to the Department of Agriculture by 1906.[141]

Ontario had never willingly countenanced developing its northern settlement schemes primarily on the basis of its own rural youth. However, until the mid-nineties it had had little success in attracting colonists from American or European sources.[142] Frustrated by federal preoccupation with prairie immigration and by this lack of provincial success, northwestern leaders increasingly tried their own promotional strategies. Earlier local attempts in the Thunder Bay District were now renewed, particularly by the Lakehead cities where boosterism was on the rise. In the Sault Ste Marie area, a modest booklet called 'Algoma Farmers Testify' was issued and reissued in the 1890s. Both the *Globe* and *Winnipeg Free Press* sometimes took up the task for various urban communities, large or small. They also produced periodic supplements or articles on the Lake of the Woods resources and the potential of the Rainy River Valley and on the advances in Algoma and rural progress at the Lakehead. The local press too came increasingly to boost individual centres and their environs, although the intent was as much advertisement for industrial capital as promotion of rural population.[143]

Feeling the political reaction to its neglect, Ottawa now produced a flow of slick promotional publications, often in the languages of Baltic, Slavic, or Mediterranean countries. Recognizing the implications of the closing of the American frontier in 1896, Ontario vigorously followed suit. Through Crown Lands, it enlarged its cohort of publicity outlets on both continents, subsidized travel to specific northern opportunities, and created a cadre of personnel in each district to aid and direct colonial arrivals.[144] Surprisingly, the province moved even further to encourage young people from the south to settle in rural northern communities, using exhibits in railway cars that annually toured the smaller centres of Old Ontario. Both levels of government also added to funding programs, encouraging northern participation at events like the Canadian National Exhibition and other international fairs.[145]

All these endeavours resulted in an increase in regional population, although the collective extent of their impact is difficult to assess, given the complex world of international migration in that day. However, statistical measures can supply certain general insights into the results beyond the simple population trend. While the constraints of the physical environment had limited the increase in total townships subdivided for agriculture from 57 in 1891 to only 89 by 1911, the number of those touched by free grant legislation had climbed from 24 to 74 (see Table 3.2a). This expansion was most evident in the new or less advanced colonial lands of the Kenora and Rainy River districts. Yet the only townships without some free grant lots by 1911 were the retreatied ones of Algoma and a few behind Thunder Bay that had been surveyed initially for mining.

The general literature treats Ontario's free grant policy as a disastrous scheme for northern settlement that promoted forest theft. This view seems overly

TABLE 3.2a Free Grant as Share of Total Agricultural Townships, 1891–1911

	1891	1901	1911
Algoma West			
Agricultural townships	15	15	15
Free grant townships	4	4	4
Thunder Bay District			
Agricultural townships	20	21	22
Free grant townships	5	14	18
Rainy River District			
Agricultural townships	22	29	37
Free grant townships	15	22	37
Kenora District			
Agricultural townships		9	15
Free grant townships			15
Total Northwest			
Agricultural townships	57	74	89
Free grant townships	24	40	74

Source: Compiled from the Reports of the Department of Crown Lands/Lands and Forests, 1892 to 1912.

TABLE 3.2b Evolution of Free Grant Holdings, 1891–1911

	1891	1901	1911
Cumulative locations	1,212	3,153	9,065
Locations currently held	671	1,264	3,926
Patented current holdings	165	549	2,685

Source: Compiled and aggregated from the Reports of the Department of Crown Lands, 1892 to 1912.

reactive for the northwest, at least in this era (see Table 3.2b). After 1891, but particularly with the new century, cumulative grants rose quickly, reaching about 9,000 by 1911. Over the same period the rate of land abandonment, reflected in the proportion of that figure given as current holdings, did not rise significantly. The region, therefore, appears free of the inordinate increase in the level of timber scalping, so often decried elsewhere in these decades. Indeed, patenting of such properties followed the same rough curve upward as the other two categories, presumably indicating a steady accumulation of successful free grant farms. Much of the reason for this deviation from the apparent provincial norm lies in the surprisingly firm regional treatment of bogus settlement. This firm supervision had always applied across these districts. It probably resulted from the disastrous experience with the problem on earlier free grants, particularly in Muskoka, Parry Sound, and south Nipissing districts. However, this is not to suggest that such activity did not persist here at unfortunate levels, although only on one later occasion, in the Thunder Bay District, did it become briefly scandalous.

The actual jump in colonial activity and its agricultural nature is more accurately reflected in the farm acreage figures for the region (see Table 3.3); unfortunately, these statistics are not satisfactory for a more detailed break-

TABLE 3.3 Agricultural Development (in acres), 1891 and 1911*

	1891	1911
Improved Acreage		
Cropland		
Cereals and legumes	7,160	20,932
Roots	2,830	5,901
Hay	7,080	29,525
Other	830	1,060
Total	17,900	57,418
Pasture	12,231	13,216
Total Improved	30,130	70,634
Unimproved Acreage		
Pasture	111,560	64,477
Woodland and waste		383,479
Total Unimproved	111,560	447,956
Grand Total	141,690	518,590

* Suitable intermediate figures are not available for 1901.
Source: Compiled from Census of Canada, Agricultural tables, 1891 and 1911.

down in this period. The total area acknowledged to be within agrarian boundaries rose more than three times to some 500,000 acres, although the improved portion climbed only from 30,000 to 70,000. This indicates the high levels of bush that still characterized most operations at the time of the war. Among the improved categories, crop land continued to dominate, with hay its largest component, followed by cereals and legumes, both of which were also principally for fodder. With improved pasture, the burgeoning potential of the unimproved coverage (often including slash and waste land) for grazing further underlines the emphasis on livestock in the emerging farm economy. This thrust, for which these lands were best suited, was encouraged by rising domestic demands. It also reflected continuing seasonal pressure from railway contractors and forest operators for everything from fodder and food to heavy draft horses for their camps.

Algoma West

Yet below this level of numerical indicators were developments pointing to other changes in the personalities of these various northwestern communities. In Algoma, canal building on the Canadian side of the St Marys Rapids, by the early nineties, had come to cause most immediate land of cultivable potential to be taken up. Some years passed, however, before the limited rural population in the proximal townships (about 2,000 in 1911) became temporarily unable to satisfy the whole of the resultant demand for the range of items it could produce. This intense need for agricultural supplies was now further heightened by the construction and operation of Francis Clergue's numerous industrial ventures in a rapidly rising Sault Ste Marie. The most immediate result was the addition of a minimum of sixty new families to the farm community here. Over and above these numbers were those who now took up the old remaining veterans' lots, dating back to the Boer War period, in the Township of Korah.[146] Such market opportunities also stimulated population growth and agricultural development in the retreatied Townships to the north. This area now had access to these market developments by road (most frequently used in winter) and by twice-weekly boat during the season of navigation. As a result, most of the remaining farmable land behind Goulais Bay was quickly acquired. However, much of the more marginal acreage here was probably taken up with an eye to pulpwood cutting as much as to any long-term agricultural use.[147]

Few other attempts at colonial expansion back from this eastern shore of Superior seem to have been made. Among the clauses of the Algoma Central Railway charter, however, had been a politically wise but practically questionable requirement that active attempts be made to settle the lands along its right of way. In 1903, the railway negotiated a deal with a Roman Catholic colonization society from Quebec to establish a farm community of 200 French-Canadian families inland from Michipicoten Harbour. However, this venture, in return for a school and church, fell through. Indeed, the only known success that may have come under this regulatory clause was the settlement of numerous Finns in the Wabos and Searchmont area about this time.[148]

These years of growth and relative agricultural prosperity in western Algoma, which came to cover some 43,000 farm acres, resulted in frequent ancillary advances in rural life. Seasonal bushwork remained an important economic drive among newer colonists or those on poorer farm properties. Yet some behind Sault Ste Marie were now able to turn themselves gradually to full-time farming and to erect the substantial frame home that was the common monument to agricultural success. Press comments indicate better and more extensive patterns of rural roads, more schools, new churches, and community halls of more durable materials. In addition, the regional agricultural society flourished. This organization not only continued its now-large annual fair for the district but also was an energetic backer of promotional immigration literature. With the new century, it became strongly involved in the formation of local chapters of the Farmer's Institute as well as in the encouragement of simple township fairs. Finally, its aid was fundamental to the success of a formal market in Sault Ste Marie by 1910 and to a campaign for proper indoor space, which the city fathers arranged some three years later.[149]

As in the other maturing or newly rising agricultural pockets, these efforts at social and economic improvement came to be strongly abetted by further provincial efforts beginning late in the period. Key to this support was the northern extension of the Agricultural Representative system to supply professional advice and help to farm families. In Algoma, the first temporary summer appointee arrived in 1909. He took up an office at Sault Ste Marie. Progress followed quickly with a program of tile drainage for seven farms immediately around the city on low-lying lands in 1910. Experiments were begun with new crops, including hard fruits and a range of different vegetables, in an attempt to broaden the farm base from its heavy reliance on hay and feed grains. Improvements also were started in the livestock sector with the successful encouragement of the first veterinary practice at Sault Ste Marie and continued with the promotion of several breeding clubs by 1913. The latter, with chapters as distant as Goulais Bay, concentrated on cattle, including dairy animals, sheep, and lambs. It also covered heavy horses, many of which were used in regional logging and pulpwood camps. Among these tentative efforts, however, the most important was probably the organization of the first short courses in farming. Unfortunately these would become well attended only after the appointment of a permanent representative in 1913. They then could be scheduled in the late fall to accommodate the many farmers who still went into the bush camps for the winter.[150]

Thunder Bay Townships

While growth of rural numbers in western Algoma tended to slacken with the new century, behind Thunder Bay they more than tripled between 1901 and the war, when they came to exceed 10,000. The new arrivals poured in principally to take up the now-large number of free grants available. Occasionally they qualified for some of the old veterans' acreage here from years before. After 1908, many new arrivals also occupied cancelled speculative properties, including 10,000 acres of former mining patents in townships adjacent to Fort William and Port Arthur.[151] This rural influx, which was already rising in the nineties, had a strong European component, including many Scandinavians and an overwhelming number of Finns. Yet only a few from Great Britain, Mediterranean countries, and Eastern Europe appear in these rural records.[152] Despite a heavy shift in provincial settlement interest to the newly opened Clay Belts of the northeast, a modest component of Ontario youth also continued to arrive. In addition, the flow now included a surprising number of Americans, often coming by boat from the midwest states via Duluth. Some of these may have initially been immigrants to the United States, now moving again with the decline of the forest industry there or after some failed attempt at woodland colonization. However, a considerable number from the eastern seaboard and such states as Pennsylvania, Ohio, Illinois, and Michigan were brought here through the promotional tours of a new provincially appointed settlement agent, R.A. Burriss. This amorphous migration quickly filled the remaining farmland of the Slate and Whitefish river country and more distant acres west of the Kaministiquia. It then spread east among the scattered patches of farmable soil around Pearl and Dorion, into the Township of Nipigon. In 1913 alone the reported result was occupation of 485 new homesteads across this area. These properties for the most part would witness modest clearance and at least some subsistent farm activity, although part of this expansion was more in name than firm reality.[153]

Such rapid rural development through immigration was not the sole impetus for boosting the farm economy of this most populous area of agriculture in the northwest. Certain outside factors were also involved. After 1892, the local press was repeatedly asking, 'Why do we import large quantities of hay, potatoes, barley and oats which our own farmers should supply?' The return of this old imbalance of mining camp days made the cost of urban living here extremely high. It resulted this time from rapid industrial expansion in the Lakehead cities. After the opening of the CPR the need for farm produce had come to outrun agriculture's immediate ability to accommodate the demand.[154] About the time that this returning problem was first noted, however, the same local press observed that 'closure of the silver mines will start more rapid farm development because settlers will no longer be tempted by high wages there to delay the working of their lands.'[155] Had the press been fully cognizant of the evolving situation, it might have noted the rising American call for settler-cut pulpwood in the nineties, a practice that would provide the farmer with an unexpected reward for increasing his efforts at land clearance at and after the turn of the century.

In the older-established agricultural communities of Neebing, Oliver, and Paipoonge, farmers were equally tired of the import competition about which the press complained, but pointed to a need for formal marketplaces in Port Arthur and Fort William through which to deal effectively with the urban clientele. Both towns eventually complied, but with crude outdoor spaces. Even as late as 1912, the facility at Port Arthur was much less adequate than the market house now provided by its competitive sister.[156] Increasing contributions to the produce pool off newer but maturing farms of the Slate and Whitefish valleys came to augment long-standing supply areas to better accommodate the demand. Other farmers, moving later from subsistence towards cash economies, would strengthen this now-growing market equilibrium as they would the inventory of new frame dwellings and improved out-buildings in the local landscape.

By wartime, the older agricultural holdings were beginning to assume a mature appearance, and contemporary newspaper descriptions reflect a growing stability. Comments on the more recent but progressing townships of the surrounding area also suggest solid advances towards agricultural sufficiency. As at Sault Ste Marie, at least one dairy served each Lakehead town, along with the traditional individual suppliers.[157] Wealthy merchants from the twin cities, such as W.S. Piper and Thomas Marks, developed large stock farms or crop acreages in the surrounding countryside, in the mode of landed gentry.[158] Churches, schools, and other rural amenities came to grace farm life and soften rural existence. After decades of hopeful dreams and disappointing achievements, agriculture in this now-sprawling pocket of 350,000 acres was coming of age.

Yet, ironically, this maturing rural economy had yet to attain the same mutual understanding and co-existence with its urban partners that had come to link western Algoma with Sault Ste Marie. The problem principally was an urban one, with roots in the bitter infighting that continued to prevail between Fort William and Port Arthur. For example, since each believed it should host the office of the Agricultural Representative, no appointment was immediately forthcoming. The recently created agricultural society continued to hold its well-attended fairs in either town each fall, but in such inadequate facilities as an immigrant shed. After prolonged controversy and lack of co-operation, a permanent site near the shore and between the communities was accepted by all parties in 1908. Nevertheless, a year later the society was forced to threaten that 'no title to the grounds and no successful approach for provincially funded future buildings would result in no fair.[159]

This openly abrasive urban–rural situation stood in strong contrast to the harmony prevailing among farm communities. By this time they could boast active township fairs among both their maturing members and in such newer areas as around Hymers to the west of Thunder Bay. Similarly, they could demonstrate social cooperation as well as the productive formation of numerous chapters of the Farmer's Institute and related local farm clubs by 1913.[160]

Rainy River Country

Farther west in the Rainy River Valley, where rural numbers reached beyond 6,300 by 1911, a history of protracted delay in land development came to a gradual end. At the opening of the nineties, Alex Locking (a well-educated, thoughtful, and former southwestern Ontario farmer), portrayed the valley in his letters to the *Globe* as a frontier area still only beginning to awaken economically to its potential. Although he could boost its crop and livestock opportunities and its suitability for hard fruits and vegetables, he was forced to admit to continuing winter isolation and otherwise expensive water connections with Kenora. His letters also reflect limited market outlets in the lumbering and mining camps of the area, although in them farmers and their sons were also able to find seasonal wage employment. There were at the time no churches and few schools, although there was hope for a grist and domestic sawmill in his proposed mid-valley village of Lockington.[161] While previous years had seen the settlement of several hundred people, they were still clustered along the river-front. (On the American side, settlement had been highly recommended but did not begin until after 1900.)[162]

As the nineties progressed, the Canadian community grew at an increasingly encouraging rate, the sources of new settlers paralleling those behind Thunder Bay. Lavish overseas publicity, organized from Ottawa and Toronto, now joined Locking and the press in provincial praise of the Rainy River Valley's agricultural opportunities. Positive letters back to hometown weeklies from new settlers after their arrival in the valley also did much to promote this more youthful migration, particularly from Old Ontario's western counties.[163] This continuing flow from previous decades was supplemented by a rising tide of Americans from the mid-west. These were both second-generation settlers seeking a new forested homeland and unsuccessful western grassland colonists retreating to within the tree-line to try again.[164] However, others from more eastern and southern U.S. states were recruited by R.A. Burriss, a former American who came to the northwest via Bowmanville, and who was mentioned above in connection with the Lakehead. He brought several hundred persons to the valley after mid-decade, some to form an unsuccessful religious commune called Christiana.[165]

In contrast, despite every effort, there appears to have been limited overseas interest in the rural opportunities of the Rainy River country. A few families from England were recruited by Locking in the nineties but became dissatisfied and left. At the turn of the century, they were followed by a colony of Galacians, who seem to have remained. Only on the arrival of the Canadian Northern Railway was this situation to alter, with the frequent appearance of Finns in the heightened flow of North Americans.[166] The building of this railway through the valley had much broader implications for rural development than in simply demographic terms. From the announcement of its construction in 1897, the railway's cheaper and much easier access to Winnipeg and other outside markets greatly accelerated the demand for valley land. The railway's route passed inland from the Rainy River causing heavy speculative buying and free grant application among the inland townships. Once constructed, its stations and sidings became the focus of new commercial centres back from the river-front landings, altering the nodal pattern of the valley and promoting further colonization of the back-country. Acreage claimed to be within farm boundaries by 1911, therefore, increased to over 200,000. However, a big percentage of this still remained covered in bush.[167]

While as many as 800 persons a year were purported to be taking up new holdings and while the base of the agricultural economy was much strengthened, these railway years were not without their problems in land management. From their onset, the district agent for both the huge free grant area generated here and for another 70,000 acres of old veterans' lands faced a difficult situation. Incoming settlers in the late nineties and later quite correctly complained of the amount of held undeveloped property dotting their neighbourhoods. Such acreages made comprehensive social organization as well as economic improvement in back-townships difficult. The result was even more rigorous policies for the assessment and inspection of grant lands. These were directed towards prompt completion of current settlement duties and towards uncompromising cancellation of any older unjustified grants. However, many agriculturally inadequate properties and the bulk of the veterans' ones were to remain unclaimed or undeveloped and problematic in local communities for years to come.[168]

Nevertheless, the influx of new colonists, the rising land interest, the spread of settlement inland, and the opening of easier market access combined after 1891 to encourage much related rural improvement. Older settlers, finding release from their previous subsistence and now ensconced in new frame homes reminiscent of southern Ontario architecture, made rapid advances in this stimulating period. As a result, the first threshing machines and binders made their appearance, as did expensive implements like hay presses, along with the first big bank barns, so prized for stablage and hay storage across Ontario at that time. By late decade, when as many as a dozen new homestead agreements were registered on peak days, these more advanced settlers had already organized the Rainy River Agricultural Society, as well as several local chapters of the Farmer's Institute. They also arranged displays of valley produce for the fair at the Lakehead and were promoting an exhibition of their own, at Fort Frances. Small mills, both to handle grain and more often to supply local lumber, were established at several locations by century's end.[169] A decade later, Emo, a new and thriving agricultural town at mid-river, held its own annual fair and the valley was preparing for the arrival of its first temporary Agricultural Representative.[170] As on the margins of the older farming areas of the northwest in 1914, newer arrivals in the valley (the majority of the population) remained subsistence farmers. As such, they were heavily dependent on local colonization road work and seasonal forest employment to augment limited farm income. Because of the valley's short history of rapid advance, even older settlers often remained contributors of ties and posts to railway contractors.[171] The most progressive among the latter now shared in the benefits of full-time farming, wealth, and economic stability as enjoyed by people at the Lakehead or immediately about Sault Ste Marie.

Kenora/Dryden Area

Land in the remaining sizeable pockets of the Kenora District was the last to enter the northwestern Ontario market. After about 1895, the first of the three suitable townships about Kenora and of the twelve near Dryden were considered for subdivision. In the former block, early French-speaking families along the Winnipeg River had been joined quickly in the eighties by Old Ontario youths. The latter came to mine but stayed to help provide the agricultural basics for this growing complex of isolated industries. While Jaffray was the original sub-surveyed township, it was joined by further free grant lands in Melick and Pellatt after the turn of the century. Consistent with a now-familiar tale, a complement of Ontario migrants were soon interspersed with American and European settlers returning from colonial attempts in Manitoba and elsewhere on the grassland west.[172]

About Dryden, Ontario-born settlement began in 1895 around the CPR's Barclay Tank, often on broad expanses of land cleared by fires associated with rail building a decade earlier. It was encouraged by the immediate founding of a government experimental farm for the northwest, adjacent to a town named for the Honourable John Dryden, then minister of agriculture. By 1899, the populations in the immediate townships were rising rapidly, again with a particularly strong thrust from southwestern Ontario.[173] However, this pocket was not yet converted from cash sale at fifty cents per acre. Free grant designation, increasing coverage in immigrant literature, and subsidized rail travel for settlers followed in the new century. Such incentives ultimately led to a scattering of Finns in most townships and a substantial enclave of British settlers around Minitaki. They also generated a further thrust from Old Ontario to west of Oxdrift, a community of Germans at Waldhof, and, about 1911, certain Scandinavians and former grassland colonists in the area of Quibell.[174]

These immigrants to the Kenora District by 1911 numbered 4,600 souls. The bulk of these farm families were bent on moving as quickly as possible away from a subsistence colonial economy. However, some found the production of pulpwood for the local mill, the cutting of ties for railway contracts, and the shipment of firewood to Winnipeg an appealing source of income.[175] As a result, subsistence farming was still the prevalent feature of this countryside in 1914 and homesteaders totally supported by their agricultural activity were the least common element among the settlers of northwestern Ontario.

Tourism Firms Its Base

The number of recreational visitors to northwestern Ontario became increasingly significant in this period and augured well for tourism's future importance in this economy. Such visitors usually had more than moderate income and often, but not always, were American. Those of wealth often brought their servants on their genteel search for guided sporting pleasures and scenic exposure in a benignly natural landscape.[176] Others, within the then-circumscribed upper middle class, could indulge in lake excursions, rough camping, or resort vacations. Still others found day trips the only respite from their usual employment.

The demands for tourism in northwestern Ontario came from two directions: west/southwest and southeast. Vacationers attracted to the Rainy Lake and Lake of the Woods areas continued to come from the west, but a more southerly component was added after 1900. Until the turn of the century, this watershed drew few Americans and remained highly focused on Rat Portage and the CPR. Here, tourists from Winnipeg continued to dominate after 1890, its pleasure-seekers categorized by the three tiers of income set out above. Most basic was the day excursion, epitomized by the annual visit of the Brotherhood of Firemen and Engineers, who arrived with their families for an outing, picnic, and possible steamer trip on the lake. Next came the weekly campers, who for the most part tented at formal grounds on the local Coney Island off Kenora or were involved in group or youth camps run by organizations like the YMCA. Total numbers of these two groups of visitors often exceeded 2,500 in busy summer months. However, this figure also included those who stayed briefly at the new Kenrica Hotel in which the municipality had a financial stake.[177]

Finally, this north half of the Lake of the Woods was an increasing favourite location for Winnipeg's nouveau riche. From the early nineties onward a growing number of these bought islands immediate to Kenora and built summer places on them. With the appearance of the gasoline launch at the turn of the century, these island homes could be as much as ten miles from the railway without significant inconvenience.[178] Summer train service on weekends provided separate cars for husbands commuting to their resident families. With few exceptions, accessible islands were all in western Canadian hands by 1914. Equally important, few structures on these properties had not been built as, or transformed into, palatial modern residences by that time.[179]

Such fine summer vacations included locally organized routs and balls, excursions, parties, and events in the grand manner. Most important among these was the regatta, which grew over the years into a major international event. What began as an invitational rowing competition in the nineties went on to attract clubs from Winnipeg and subsequently from across the American midwest each year. The Lipton Cup competitions drew several thousand spectators and excursionists as well. From these events, Kenora also benefited through lodging and provision of other services.[180] The regatta's status reached a peak in the summer of 1914, with a visit from the Duke and Duchess of Connaught, which was reported in the press in all its late Imperial glitter. However, just a week later, the *Kenora Miner and News* announced the onset of World War I.[181] A genteel era here had come to an end.

Recreational development on the more southerly shores of the Lake of the Woods as well as along Rainy River and about Rainy Lake came about more slowly. Until the Canadian Northern provided railway access in late 1901, it remained largely an excursional appendage to the trade of Rat Portage. Excellent steamers, both scheduled and chartered, served the lower Lake of the Woods, with similar connections up the river to the Kouchiching Falls and on up Rainy Lake. Parties or individuals who had enjoyed the colonial scene along the valley could find overnight accommodation in the small hotel at Fort Frances. From there they could press on to visit the active mining camps of the Seine, spending a day or two in a then-thriving Mine Centre.[182]

With rail access in 1900 and later connections by train between Duluth and Fort Frances, other forms of tourism began to grow. Midwestern Americans found their way to islands and shore properties on the lower Lake of the Woods between Warroad and Baudette, Minnesota. Yet they were also quick to purchase land and summer homes over the Canadian border. The same was true on Rainy Lake where one Minneapolis businessman was said to have accumulated control of 700 islands for cottage development. Fort Frances, like Rainy River, became a mecca for midwest fishermen and hunters, who flocked to the first isolated lodges and rough camps as they appeared on both the large lakes and on other waters as far east as the Quetico area.[183]

Such strongly western and American midwestern interests contrasted sharply with the sources and patterns of tourism demands east across the Great Lakes divide. But local tourists from the growing centres of Port Arthur, Fort William, and Sault Ste Marie also availed themselves of the area's recreational opportunities during the period. These locals often indulged in rough summer camping, hunting, and fishing in the immediate countryside and along neighbouring shorelines. This is particularly well documented in the vicinity of Thunder Bay where, from the early nineties, tent communities were common at several points along the Sibley Peninsula and on Loon Lake.[184] With the passage of years summer occupation spread along the closer shores of Superior to the east of the twin cities, around such old mining centres as Amythest and Silver harbours. As with Loon Lake, access to railway led eventually to patterns of commuting here by family breadwinners from the urban centres. As might be expected, all these summer communities of families began to spawn more permanent structures by the outbreak of war.[185] Commuting to the Sibley Peninsula, and most particularly to the old mainland townsite for Silver Islet, came slowly into the vacation pattern. Here by 1896, numerous families were visited only twice weekly by the tug *Siskwit*. Several years later, when they began to occupy and renovate the old miners' houses as summer dwellings, a daily boat service to Port Arthur was in operation.[186]

However, these same urban areas and their environs, like the thousands of square miles of shore and river drainage between, were also increasingly the haunt of more distant recreational visitors. Many were Americans from adjacent states about the lower or middle lakes, whose usual connection with the Canadian lake-transport system came at the St Marys River. Other such travellers, including many Canadians, came up from southern lake ports, arriving aboard the large lake liners of the CPR, of the amalgamated fleet of the Northern Transportation Company, or on the steamers *Ossifragi* and *King Edward* in the service of the Algoma Central Railway. Carrying as many as 500 passengers and running full through most of the summer period, the first two lines provided a daily service to the Lakehead by way of the new lock at the Canadian Sault. Since all such vessels were coordinated with passenger rail service at both ends of their route, this lake passage for some was merely a pleasant interlude on a longer journey. For many, however, the recreational trip to Sault Ste Marie or to Thunder Bay, with a visit to nearby sights, was a holiday in itself. Large luxury hotels, such as the newly completed International at Sault Ste Marie and others at the Lakehead, came to serve this clientele, along with the usual array of more modest accommodations.[187] The pattern of such holidays, involving brief lake excursions, guided tours, and visits to scenic spots or Native reserves, were sometimes augmented by fishing expeditions and usually by shopping. They differed little in format from those before but now accommodated increased levels of demand.

Summer facilities of varying size and luxury outside these centres were also becoming available for the increasing number of visitors who desired a more rural or sporting retreat, often in the company of Native guides. Those along the north shore of Superior were usually accessible by rail. Here the still-famous trout fishing on the Nipigon River had drawn hundreds of international sportsmen to rough camp over the years. At wartime, such campgrounds were joined by a good summer hotel in Nipigon and a Canadian Northern bungalow lodge along its trackage near southern Lake Nipigon's Orient Bay.[188] Other favourite locations for wealthy American and Canadian sportsmen and photographers included rough facilities at Jackfish and the old hotel at Rossport. From here, as well as Port Coldwell, such visitors found excellent fishing, usually available through local commercial fishermen. A much wider range of river-oriented canoeing and sporting activity along this picturesque shore seems likely but goes largely undocumented in available records.[189]

North from Sault Ste Marie such facilities were accessible from Superior's littoral only by local steamers, including those engaged in the connection of commercial fish as well as the scheduled service of the *Minnie M* to Clergue's mining operations behind Michipicoten Harbour. Destinations for the adventurous sportsmen or vacationing families ranged from the new Algoma Inn at the latter and a brief scatter of more primitive accommodations at commercial fishing camps south to Goulais Bay. Closer to Sault Ste Marie was the large lodge at Pointe aux Pins, which offered luxurious living until a fire about 1910, and at least one complex of cottages with central dining-room down river from the town.[190]

In the interior, access for recreation went hand in hand with the protracted construction of the Algoma Central Railway. Even in 1902 when the tracks extended only a few miles, queries from as far away as Toledo and Detroit prompted the company to run the *Ossifragi* and *King Edward* up from Lake Erie cities. At Sault Ste Marie, special trains awaited the passengers bound for the railhead and points north.[191] This American market came to include many canoeing, fishing, and hunting expeditions, which began and ended at remote points along the right of way. These often used equipment or complete outfits supplied by the railway. By 1912, the demand was such that the ACR commenced a program of cabin building along the route for the accommodation of sportsmen. Soon afterwards, other parties began converting some former construction camps and logging bunkhouses into the first simple tourist lodges.[192] However here, as along the rest of Superior's shore and west of the divide, the scale of pre-war demand for tourism and the segment of the population able to indulge in such broad-ranging recreation can readily be over-estimated.

Urban, Connective, and Hierarchical Growth

As might be anticipated, this also was a period of marked expansion in the nodal and urban sectors of this now rapidly advancing region. This multifaceted development was reflected in a proliferation of small nodal places, permanent and transient, evident on pre-war railway maps, in post office lists, and in business directories. Some arose to serve mining camps on the Shield; others were fishing stations on Superior; still others were in agricultural areas. These latter commonly counted a general store and blacksmith's shop, often a lumber and gristing facility, plus at least one church and hotel. However, many along railways were only the lonely domiciles of section crews or the temporary site of a bunkhouse for a small tie or lumber mill.

Larger but less frequent were the still-unincorporated divisional points. Older CPR ones like Ignace, Schreiber, and White River were home to considerable populations and complete in their rail-related facilities, which now often included a water system and even electric light. Others, like Sioux Lookout on the National Transcontinental, Hornepayne on the Canadian Northern, and Hawk Junction on the ACR, were still socially rough, commercially new, and functionally incomplete. Only by chance was their base likely to be broadened by surrounding agriculture or other resource-related development.

Growth among more populous and long-lived centres by 1914 was industrially startling and commercially prophetic. In 1911 such incorporated urban places accounted for almost two-thirds of the regional population (see Table 3.4). The districts west of Superior were far less implicated in this trend than

TABLE 3.4 Population Profile (percentage urban), 1891–1911

	1891		1901		1911	
	Total Pop.	% urban	Total Pop.	% urban	Total Pop.	% urban
Algoma West	4,435	54	9,747	73	21,158	71
Thunder Bay District	8,000	61	11,219	63	39,496	70
Rainy River District	2,210	–	6,568	18	10,429	30
Kenora District	4,984	36	10,369	63	15,490	56
Total	19,629	46	37,903	57	86,573	62

Note: Native people on reserves are included in all figures.
Source: Compiled from Census of Canada Population tables, 1891 to 1911.

those around Superior. The Rainy River Valley seemingly was touched least of all, although a quickly rising but unincorporated Emo, the market centre for the mid-valley, goes ignored in the figures. Fort Frances, the district seat, home to huge sawmills, a developing pulp and paper complex, and an increasing ethnic mix, had yet to reach the economic status it shortly would attain.[193] In contrast, Rainy River (once called Beaver Mills), while remaining a divisional point and westward market town, had lost its sawmills and was soon to be divested of its log-booming functions.[194]

To the north, the Kenora District had reached but retreated from a more than 60 per cent urban level of 1901 because of the subsequent concerted inflow of rural settlers. Kenora, with the neighbouring village of Keewatin, remained the largest centre. While it retained some sawmilling and expected a future pulp plant, its manufacturing stimulus now centred on the milling of western grain for eastern sale. Other sides to its economy relied on the CPR and its lucrative tourism industry. Like Fort Frances, it also enjoyed electric lighting from a local supply.[195] Other serious contributions to regional urban activity were limited to very new rail and sawmill functions at Sioux Lookout and the tiny kraft paper enterprise at Dryden.[196]

In 1914, as now, the northwestern hierarchy of nodes and urban places had no mid-sized centres, but skipped from the small to the very large. As a result, the shift to urban predominance involved only the three key centres on Superior: Sault Ste Marie, Fort William, and Port Arthur. Each had become a distinct example of the new hydro-based industrialism of the day. The kaleidoscope of industrial activity unleashed by Clergue at Sault Ste Marie around the turn of the century resulted in that small town, with its adjunct 'company town,' Steelton, comprising 71 per cent of western Algoma's population (see Table 3.4). The twin centres at the Lakehead, already dominant in their district in 1891, made up 70 per cent of the population there, despite the heavy influx of rural settlers in the immediately previous decades. Sharing such functions as grain handling and trans-shipment, each had built up a substantial mix of large and small plants and manufacturers. By 1914, all three centres had attained city status and stood among the top fourteen of Ontario's urban communities.

All three also shared a distinct and developing ethnic mosaic. This mix, so different from the relatively staid personality of Old Ontario cities, resulted in often-militant social and political views. A pot-pourri of eastern Europeans, Finns, and Italians changed the Lakehead cities, particularly Port Arthur, from an Anglo-Saxon monochrome to a rich blend of languages, cultures, and religions. Sault Ste Marie also continued to add to its diverse European flavour since the canal-building days in the nineties, but here Italians came to be particularly prominent.[197]

Sault Ste Marie

At the outbreak of World War I, Sault Ste Marie was a vibrantly active and optimistically youthful community that, at the same time, was dirty, smoke-ridden and noisy, as was any centre of heavy industry of the time. As previously related, Clergue's legacy made it home to a pulp and paper plant, large saw and veneering facilities, as well as blast furnaces, coke ovens, and related steel mills. Affiliated operations now included chemical works producing items from creosote and tar to wood preservatives and roofing felt.[198] The newly incorporated Steelton, to the west of the old town plot, continued to be home to much of the community's ethnically mixed labour force. In the wake of the canal construction in the mid-nineties, the waterfront below the rapids now housed huge steamer wharves. With the new century, the major Canadian passenger liners came to use these, as opposed to wharfage on the U.S. side, on their busy upper-lakes schedules. Above the rapids, the shore had been modified for harbourage near the mills and extended with coaling facilities for the Algoma ore fleet. Here and elsewhere, the ACR and CPR had come to establish yards and other facilities. The ACR railway was completing its long-promised line north from Hawk Junction to Hearst. The CPR had been one of the early signs of urban awakening when it arrived from Sudbury in the late eighties. However, the CPR was more interested in a bridge over the St Marys River to tap into certain agricultural markets in the American midwest.

The city itself already hosted an extensive brick business district along Queen Street, as well as water mains, sewers, electric lights, and telephones. It also boasted a much-used street railway system between its industrial, commercial, and residential areas. Continuing development had brought a modest real-estate rush, but with memories of surplus housing after an over-optimistic building boom a decade before, its scope was kept within conservative bounds. Nevertheless, its effects by 1914 had filled several subdivisions with middle-class homes, east along the river, and more lavish residences north on the crest of abrupt slopes overlooking the old riverside community. Public interest in parks and in treed thoroughfares was beginning to soften the scene.[199] Indeed, it was now considerably larger and wealthier than its Michigan partner, with which it had been unfavourably compared for so long. While its near-complete industrial control by the distant British/American interests of the Lake Superior Corporation, may not have been totally agreeable to the citizenry, the resultant buoyant economy undoubtedly was. Interestingly, while the violent events surrounding the collapse of Clergue's empire in 1903 and the brief military intervention that followed was not a popular town topic, Clergue himself remained a very fond public figure.

The Lakehead Cities

At the Lakehead, the fierce rivalry for urban primacy continued. Indeed, the period opened with a sharp squabble over a street railway, aggressively pushed by Port Arthur down its sister's main street and onto the CPR headquarters at Westfort by late 1891. Curiously sanctioned by the legislature, this railway was bitterly opposed by the newly incorporated town of Fort William. However, it did provide a struggling Port Arthur with access to railway-related jobs that its partner considered its own.[200]

Through much of the nineties, the economic advantage in this competition lay with Fort William. Most of the railway payroll and local purchases remained with that community. Indeed, friction between Port Arthur and the CPR over taxes caused the latter to move all its earlier facilities from there to Fort William. Along the Kam this consolidation was accompanied by the addition of new dockage, the erection of large coaling facilities, and a substantial increase in company elevator space. In conjunction with these advances went a continuing migration of the business focus to land near the mouth of the river and east to the now-track-covered site of the old Hudson's Bay Company post. Wealthier elements of the town continued to congregate in the adjacent McKellar Ward, while the less affluent located on lots up the river or in subdivisions otherwise adjacent to this new downtown. Collectively, these developments largely isolated Fort William from the chilling effects of recurrent business recessions that continued to dog Canadian growth until the later nineties.[201]

In contrast, the vulnerable economy of Port Arthur, which had a more working-class population, was stoutly punished over this short period. Declining markets brought an abrupt end to silver mining employment and related spending in its shops. The CPR's departure and the dredging of the Kam brought fewer visitors to the town, less freight to its docks, and tight times to its waterfront. With falling grain prices, these transport shifts combined to curtail any private intentions to erect elevators here after the first locally financed one. (It was later to become the first 'hospital' elevator, used to dry grain and thereby improve its quality.) Declining domestic construction in a community that had momentarily stopped growing further contributed to rising unemployment. Many people drifted away in search of work, causing the population to drop further. Homes were left empty and numerous businesses were boarded up. Bankruptcies mounted and the municipality itself was on the brink of financial disaster by 1897.[202]

Recovery, when it came near the century's end, was rapid. It was spearheaded by the announcement by the Canadian Northern Railway of plans not only to build to the Lakehead but also to use Port Arthur as its terminus there. It arrived in 1901, in the midst of a sequence of mammoth western wheat harvests that fortuitously matched rising demands in overseas markets. This new railway company, with its growing complement of yards, shops, offices, coaling docks, elevators, and ultimate plans for a blast furnace, became as fundamental to Port Arthur's booming economy as the CPR was to Fort William's. Among the side effects of these events was the appearance of large blocks of labour-related housing in back of the harbour area. Here, strong Finnish and Italian neighbourhoods were quick to develop among a new and larger immigrant population. Meanwhile, the business section, which these developments flanked, consolidated itself in a crescent about the lower end of the former Dawson Road (present Red River Road).

By 1913, the two centres at the Lakehead, now cities, were about equal in their race for urban dominance on Thunder Bay, although the arrival of the Grand Trunk at its terminus on Mission Island around 1910 helped Fort William retain a slight edge. The rising scale of prairie harvests since the turn of the century brought to both communities, by 1914, a heavy demand for added elevator space. Such requirements provided thousands of hours of wages, hosted enormous demands for building materials, and resulted in numerous new permanent jobs, including many in grain handling and dock work. So pervasive was the labour demand for such construction that it often interfered with the necessary supply of tradesmen to serve the renewed domestic building requirements of these two booming centres on Thunder Bay. While the over-all impact of these developments on profits in the wholesale/retail sector can be readily imagined, other small fortunes came to be made in real estate. At the outset, the major participants were local, then provincial; when the bubble of over-supply finally burst in 1913, however, the big losers were three large speculative syndicates from England.[203]

These landward developments after 1900 were paralleled by a huge infusion of federal money for the extension of existing breakwalls and the improvement of harbour facilities. Such expenditures also initiated some deepening of the Kam and its deltaic distributors to 25 feet. On the front, the resultant work made protection continuous from the Current River area of Port Arthur to the water off the Kaministiquia estuary. Dredging behind this massive barrier produced an enormous harbour of more than 25 feet in depth. It also opened much shoreline in and between the two communities for future elevator development and promoted the location of the short-lived blast furnace complex and its extensive docks.[204] However, while justified by the burgeoning grain trade and stimulating to both urban economies, such public works engendered few continuing jobs, and short-term prosperity was not what either city sought.

Indeed, both communities were willing to boost their dramatic harbour and its grain trade but neither was satisfied with the rewards of the simple entrepôt role they served where the water met the land. While their port function provided them with very substantial revenues, entrepreneurial returns from the trade accrued to the railways, shipping lines, and Winnipeg-centred grain interests. Grain rehabilitation through hospital elevators was one of several early attempts by local businessmen to share more directly in the profits of the trade. Any success, small or marginal, was sought. The hydro required for the operation of the elevators and other facilities at the port was supplied from local private and public sources and provided some return to the communities.[205] In the short term the same was true with the supply of lumber and other building materials for the construction and periodic maintenance of port structure. Unfortunately, much of the potential tax base had been bargained away as financial enticements to obtain these grain-handling facilities.

By the turn of the century, press editorials expressed frustration at the pace of community development, as did local business and municipal figures. Lacking the huge capital requirements themselves, Lakehead officials watched Winnipeg grain companies and other western firms erect a wave of new elevators along their waterfront. Indeed, after a series of disastrous fires at both its Fort William and Owen Sound terminals, the CPR now began to pass control of its elevating facilities to prairie parties. It had already moved its fleet from grain carriage to exclusive freight and passenger service early in the decade. Both railways encouraged a Winnipeg-based scheme to determine and schedule its daily grain distribution and delivery among Lakehead elevators.[206]

In a final attempt to earn a significant role in the trade, Lakehead businessmen in 1913 constructed a six-storey building in Fort William to serve as a grain exchange, potentially the future centre for the trade in Canada. The exchange never opened its doors, having failed to attract the interest of the major grain dealers, who preferred to continue their operations from Winnipeg.[207] The building, which remains today, became home, in part, to the Canadian Grain Commission and a large department store. All major decisions and most profits from grain handling through this port would always be made in the 'prairie gate' to the west.

The other industries established in these centres before 1890 had been related to the region's mineral, forest, and fishery resources. Unlike Algoma, where such resource-related endeavours formed a new industrial base at Sault Ste Marie, the Lakehead counterparts comprised only a part of the pre-war economy. Most important among them were the huge mills of the Pigeon River Lumber Company, principal employer in Port Arthur in these years. They also included the briefly active blast furnace of the Dominion Bessimer Company. Less spectacular, but also important, were fishing firms and the rising pulpwood export trade.

Even with the new century, the manufacture of pulp and paper failed to appear in either centre. Yet, the further acquisition of such regionally based resource endeavours was not foremost in the expansive dreams of either of these communities. Instead, they focused on success in a broader world of manufacturing and on membership in the rapidly rising urban industrial community of Old Ontario. To this end, each adopted booster campaigns and municipal bonusing programs, perhaps the most energetic in Canada and certainly in Ontario.[208] (Evidence of similar opportunities for industrial expansion appear in the *Sault Star* of the period, but city fathers there seemed much less convinced of the need for such economic diversification.) These expensive attempts to attract industry took two forms: subsidy and guarantees, or property rights and municipal tax relief. Between the late 1880s and 1914, such arrangements, in different combinations, came to cover dozens of cases. These were most numerous in Fort William and most frequently after 1900 in both cities. Such programs required over $2.5 million and involved years of future municipal indebtedness. They sponsored diversely sized companies, from foundries, nail factories, smelters, and shipyards to sawmills, flour mills, starch factories, and rail car manufacture. Some succeeded, others did not, and it is questionable whether either or both communities benefited in the end from such public incentives.

While unable to achieve their more far-reaching goals, both cities entered the war period with strong images of urban dynamism and industrial achievement. Like Sault Ste Marie, they had attained a remarkable level of prosperity in a surprisingly short period of time. They too had increasingly well-built business districts and expanding residential areas as well as basic electric lighting and telephone, sewage and water systems, along with an effective street railway. Very different in social and economic personality, Fort William and Port Arthur were learning, however grudgingly, to live together. Yet, as at Sault Ste Marie, the guiding forces for future development at the Lakehead were still principally in outside hands.

Regional Interlinkage

These three large centres were linked in 1914 by the three transcontinental railways with all the smaller nodes across the northwest. Yet the region was still poorly served for urban/rural-oriented trade at all but the lowest level. The old interconnective problem between trans-regionally designed rail corridors and sub-regionally oriented road nets had lessened, with increasing nodal frequency along the tracks. However, the practical limits on road travel had increased with distance, as agricultural colonization and resource activity expanded in area and farther into the hinterland.[209] The combined result was continuingly weak intra-regional transport and communication. This was one main obstacle hampering the rise of any satisfactory semblance of urban hierarchy. Recognition of this growing situation had brought several decades of intensive provincial programs directed at northern road- and water-related improvements. These efforts and the rural employment they engendered were laudable and appreciated, yet for a variety of reasons, at the outbreak of war, they had brought only limited resolution to the problems they had been addressing.

Away from these major rail corridors as well as the lesser ones of the ACR and the PAD&W, travel remained highly seasonal, often circumscribed, usually arduous, and always costly. Water movement, even over the Great Lakes, was limited to ice-free months, a shortened period in these northern climes. Intensive transport otherwise was normally confined to the dry months of summer or the depths of winter. At these times roads were readily passable for wagon or sleigh and inland waters were negotiable by sledge or steamboat. These limitations still applied in milder form in the more continuously occupied Old Ontario, but harsh environmental and technological problems made their impact in the north much more economically acute.

Cheap, flexible, and stimulating to the local economy, colonization road building remained a principal tool in Ontario's strategy for northward settlement. Related provincial expenditure in the northwest was never as lavish as elsewhere, briefly reaching 20 per cent of the provincial figure at the turn of the century. After the transfer of responsibility for construction from Crown

Lands to Public Works, important new means of implementation came about. The 'by-law road' after 1907 enabled northern municipalities (and later some unorganized townships) to gain very liberal matching grants for work on major thoroughfares if they were completed to a defined standard. By 1911, more than half of all northwestern road expenditure fell into this category, although older modes of provincial finance continued in new, opening areas.

The result was considerable advancement in immediate access, where upgrading and minor extension improved communication in and between maturing farm neighbourhoods. Such programs also created better conditions, at least seasonally, over longer distances within each agricultural pocket. On early completion of the River Road down the length of the Rainy River Valley, numerous other roads were driven inland from steamer landings to encourage interior settlement. In the vicinity of Dryden, a major route was improved several miles west and east, from the Wabigoon River to the rising community of Dinorwic. At the Lakehead, while the route from Fort William to the Minnesota boundary remained only a winter road over its rugged southern stretches, the same was not true of the one east, through more active colonial environs to Nipigon. North of Sault Ste Marie, the old road to Batchawana was altered in its course and much improved late in the period to promote market access. Such advances were of great importance in the eyes of local inhabitants, as these routes tied their rural communities together and improved their access to the nearest market centres. However, they did nothing to knit together the larger region as a well-integrated, commercial whole.

Other government attempts along related lines were enthusiastic but not notably successful. Most were in aid of the mining industry. Such seasonal routes and portage roads were sometimes supplemented by steamer travel. They were most commonly tributary to transcontinental trackage west of the drainage divide and most frequent between the CPR and Canadian Northern. However, along Superior such jointly financed routes linked Michipicoten to Wawa Lake and tied Jackfish to Long Lake from which a Hudson's Bay Company steamer carried on to Longlac Post. An early route north from Red Rock to promote mining about Lake Nipigon later came to host a narrow-gauge tramway to docks on South Bay. From here, in the railway building years, northbound steamers supplied the contractors of the National Transcontinental through Ombabika Bay. In most cases, these well intended efforts were too specific in purpose, too temporary, and too difficult to use to accomplish their laudable aims.

However, certain privately developed water transport was much more successful in this cause. On Rainy Lake, Rainy River, and Lake of the Woods, primitive steamer service dated back to the days of the Dawson Road. It had come to flourish when the railhead at Rat Portage opened these waterways more effectively to mining and logging enterprises, augmented by early colonial needs in the Rainy River Valley. By the pre-war decade separate fleets of small packets and tugs were operating both above and below the Kouchiching Falls at Fort Frances. Indeed, by the new century, one set of moderately large vessels covered the Lake of the Woods, and another, using smaller and shallower boats, negotiated the river with its still-unimproved stretches at the Long Sault and Manitou Rapids.[210] Similarly, on Superior, weakly developed coasting service prevailed along the north shore. It was matched against a much stronger one on the otherwise isolated coast between Sault Ste Marie and the railway docks at Michipicoten Harbour. By wartime, the latter had frequent service to intervening points by three packets connected with the fish trade and the iron mines behind Wawa Lake.[211]

This seasonal array of scattered and tenuous land and water routes lying beyond the discrete and immediate patterns of colonization roads in agricultural pockets completed this weakly developed side of regional linkage. Yet over varied distances, these slow and often difficult passages were the only way to transport supplies, people, products, and even mail to or from railway stations or isolated sidings. While far better than nothing, in this expanding world of resources, the arduous and costly nature of these routes placed severe limits on what could be developed successfully and at what distance beyond rail corridors. This in turn constrained commercial growth in the urban centres at the top of the hierarchy. It limited both their effective capital penetration and their efficient downward market ties to highly localized areas. In the future, such economic symbiosis between urban centres and regional resources, would expand and become much stronger, abetted by improvements in transport access and technology. However, for many years to come, passage across the vast expanse of land and water between Winnipeg and Sault Ste Marie or more distant centres would remain easier than penetration into many vibrantly active parts of the region itself.

Exploitive Expansion under Weakening Direction, 1914–1930

These were the late and uncertain years in a wheat-oriented era of national export trade. In Ontario's northwest, the period was characterized by unsettling events and periodic uncertainties in the production of resources other than wheat for the marketplace. As early as 1912, European financial interests, which here as elsewhere had supported previous rail building and industrial growth, fell sharply. Immediate reductions in commodity demands and rising unemployment followed across the region. These conditions were aggravated by war, with its initial chaos related to the redirection of production and redistribution of labour towards military goals. However, by 1915, completed adjustments brought on rapid wartime and post-war growth. This propelled development to the early twenties, but under an increasing shift to U.S. capital sources. After a second disconcerting lull, the regional economy swept forward again. However, this renewed wave, marred by speculative over-confidence, was destined for brutal termination with the 'crash of 1929' and the crush of the early Depression.[212]

Previous years, with their patriotic demands, exciting thrusts, and periods of uncertainty, nevertheless were ones of dramatic growth. They were witness to a continuing rise in total population, ethnic diversification, and urban concentration. Despite the tragic loss of youth to the war, northwestern numbers increased respectably to 135,000 by 1931, yet this figure was then but half that of the northeast.[213] The twenties in particular saw northern agricultural directions more realistically adapted to natural conditions, to heavier emphasis on livestock, and to higher-quality production and significantly improved economic conditions on the farm.[214] Over these same years, more and more significant regional shifts in power for resource processing occurred, from coal and steam to the hydroelectric energy of the new industrialism.[215] After 1918, activity also came to rely increasingly on transport technology developed during the war, as well as on the experience of veterans with aircraft, tracked vehicles, and trucks.[216] In addition, post-war provincial society sought means to recast old political and economic ideas. Indeed, the sometimes naïve coalition of farmers and labourers under the Drury government of 1919 to 1923 were to become socially prophetic.[217]

Yet not all aspects of this decade-and-a-half were so economically progressive or socially leavening. The period sponsored the first real growth in labour organization for the resource sector. Yet labour's initiatives to combat the harsh living and employment conditions of northern workers saw results only in the forest industry.[218] Be they northern or southern, the problems of working people remained of limited social concern to the majority of Ontario's growing middle class. At the same time, the politically powerful middle class focused quickly on the scandalous results of new inquiries and royal commissions into resource-exploitive activities. Such reports pointed to irresponsible harvesting activity and sly private-sector business practices, which sullied heroic southern images of northern development. They also revealed questionable levels of political patronage, undesirable party favouritism, and inadequate government direction or control, which ran counter to expected public practices of resource stewardship. While such proven shortcomings were largely centred on the forest industry, suspicions were raised of similar excesses in other sectors, such as the fishery, where indeed they had long prevailed. However, the expedient demands of the Depression counteracted any serious pressures towards firm programs of reform.

Alternatives to Railway

While the post-war years witnessed the first appearance of air transport in the northwest, aviation's truly substantial contribution here belongs to our discussion of later decades. Regional applications of aviation in the twenties and thirties remained largely experimental, although auguring exciting possibilities in mining and tourism as well as forest mapping and protection.[219]

The real promise of these years lay in road construction and related transport technology. Strong support for the rural, secondary networks continued under new legislation for northern advancement. Combined with the resulting improvements were the first popular applications of the internal combustion engine to sub-regional transport and the hint of solutions to the earlier problems plaguing the effectiveness of those networks.

However, by 1914, most popular attention to transportation had already shifted from such secondary considerations to the much larger creation of a trunk road system.[220] Initiated as a provincial idea in 1902, the concept of trunk roads became a legislative reality in 1909 and gained quick recognition in the northwest as an effective alternative to the railway's seemingly disinterested approach to regional resource transport and to commercial intra-regional linkage. By 1910, Fort William's Board of Trade was urging a wagon route to Winnipeg and local motorists were pressing for an all-weather surface to Pigeon River. By 1911, Sault Ste Marie was calling for an improved tie to Sudbury, and Fort Frances for a good gravel surface west to Rainy River. A year later, such communities united in a renewed petition for a trunk route from the Lakehead to the Manitoba border.

Such a grandiose concept as the trunk route was, of course, the product of a larger imagination. Since 1910, the western provinces had pressed for a highway linking the Great Lakes to the Pacific. Unfortunately, supportive federal financing, voted in the House, was rejected in the Senate, and Ottawa would not figure in the matter until after World War I.

In contrast, Ontario entered this interprovincial fray quickly and with panache. It immediately located and began construction of a highway between Sault Ste Marie and Subdury. As a westward gesture, it undertook to build a road from Kenora to meet one at the boundary from Winnipeg. It joined Minnesota in discussions of a bridging point on the Pigeon River. It supplied funds to bring the Rainy River Road to reasonable standard and promised proper surfaces from the Lakehead to both Minnesota and Nipigon. It also build short trunk roads – Kenora to Redditt, Dryden to Richan, and Vermilion Bay to Quibell – all points on the new National Transcontinental. However, as an internal memo of May 1912 reveals, Ontario would not even contemplate road construction across the rough and largely empty stretch between Sault Ste Marie and Nipigon. Steamer links here and coasting service along this shore would suffice.

The war years witnessed little further progress, but war's end witnessed the gradual proliferation of car, truck, and bus traffic on the roads of the region, as across the rest of Ontario. Returning popular enthusiasm for motoring was also boosted in 1919 by Ottawa's promise of $20 million over five years for the national trunk road scheme. This infusion was to be the first of many through later decades. Ontario also pledged continuing support, but neither level of government seems to have been in a hurry to begin work. As a result, northwestern regional interests hosted the Dryden Conference, which drew many outside delegates. It initiated the Central Canada Highway Association to promote the immediate linkage of the Great Lakes to the Pacific. While this organization became a prominent Toronto lobby, the Canadian Good Roads Association pressed Ottawa for a national highway from Halifax to Victoria.

Ontario's official reaction, released in 1924, was careful, considered, and conservative. Among other things, it promised upgrading of the Sault Ste Marie to Sudbury road, already in use. It reiterated an old goal of a gravel road from Thunder Bay to Manitoba but avoided any commitment east from Nipigon and moved only slowly on any of its pledges (see Map 3.2). As a result by 1930, the long awaited trunk to Nipigon was open but one from Kenora to Manitoba was only nearing completion. A Fort Frances to Kenora route was usable part way but the Lake Superior Road north from Sault Ste Marie was still managing cars only to Batchawana. Although the route south from Fort William to the Pigeon River crossing (the modern International Highway) was a satisfactory summer thoroughfare, the one west from the Lakehead toward Kenora was gravelled for only 30 miles. Popular interest groups were not amused with the laggardly progress on the national scheme or with the still frustratingly disjointed state of the proposed regional system.

The Peak for Agriculture

Continuing improvement of local roads and road access in the agricultural pockets, the product of the new Northern and Northwestern Ontario Development Acts, introduced a few tractors, even cars, to rural sheds and frequent trucks to rural gates. It also went hand in hand with steady advancements on

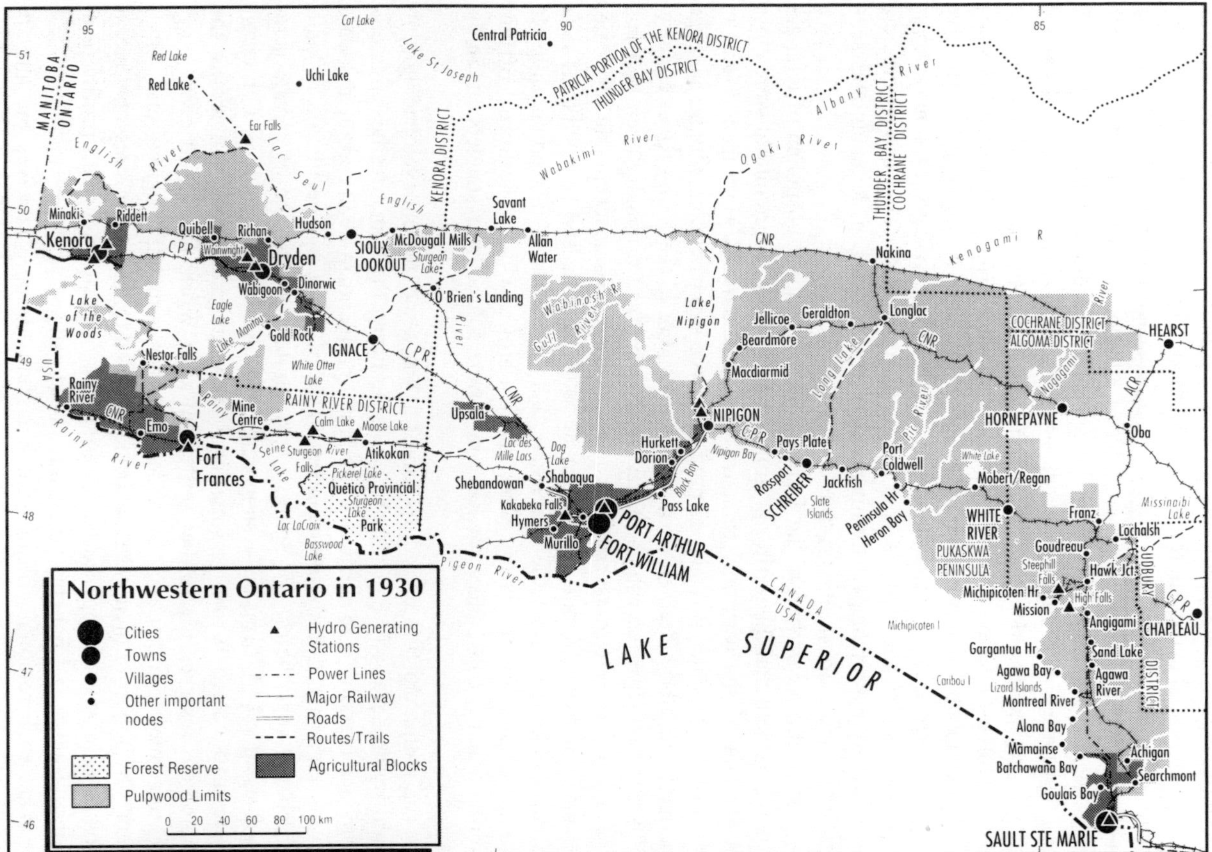
Northwestern Ontario in 1930
Cities
Towns
Villages
Other important nodes
Hydro Generating Stations
Power Lines
Major Railway
Roads
Routes/Trails
Forest Reserve
Pulpwood Limits
Agricultural Blocks
0 20 40 60 80 100 km
LAKE SUPERIOR
CANADA
USA
MANITOBA
ONTARIO
KENORA DISTRICT
PATRICIA PORTION OF THE KENORA DISTRICT
THUNDER BAY DISTRICT
COCHRANE DISTRICT
ALGOMA DISTRICT
RAINY RIVER DISTRICT
SUDBURY DISTRICT
PORT ARTHUR
FORT WILLIAM
SAULT STE MARIE
Kenora
Dryden
Fort Frances
SIOUX LOOKOUT
IGNACE
NIPIGON
SCHREIBER
WHITE RIVER
HORNEPAYNE
HEARST
CHAPLEAU
Red Lake
Uchi Lake
Central Patricia
Ear Falls
Minaki
Riddett
Quibell
Richan
Hudson
McDougall Mills
Savant Lake
Allan Water
Wabigoon
Dinorwic
Gold Rock
O'Brien's Landing
Nestor Falls
Rainy River
Emo
Mine Centre
Atikokan
Upsala
Shebandowan
Shabaqua
Kakabeka Falls
Hymers
Murillo
Pass Lake
Hurkett
Dorion
Macdiarmid
Beardmore
Jellicoe
Geraldton
Longlac
Nakina
Pays Plate
Rossport
Jackfish
Port Coldwell
Peninsula Hr
Heron Bay
Mobert/Regan
Franz
Oba
Lochalsh
Goudreau
Hawk Jct
Michipicoten Hr
Mission
Angigami
Sand Lake
Agawa River
Gargantua Hr
Agawa Bay
Montreal River
Alona Bay
Mamainse
Batchawana Bay
Goulais Bay
Achigan
Searchmont
Quetico Provincial Park
PUKASKWA PENINSULA
Lake of the Woods
Lac Seul
Lake Nipigon
CPR
CNR
ACR

MAP 3.2

the farm and in rural society. Once isolated communities came closer through sports and social events, in the process promoting broader intermarriage. Where church and school had been the foci of older neighbourhoods, the community hall and the ball diamond became added attractions. In ethnic pockets, such halls were often places for political debate and cultural events, particularly among rural Finns.[221] Previous clusters of substantial farmhouses now expanded rapidly, replacing older log homes. Painted white with shake roofs and built in the common Ontario style of the previous century, these houses proclaimed their occupants' rising economic success. In many municipalities primitive telephone services grew to link homes, and in a few privileged rural neighbourhoods electricity eased life in both barn and farmhouse.[222] This also was the era in which transport helped farming satisfy regional urban demands and seek outside markets for modest surpluses.

The twenty years before the Depression also brought unspoken official acknowledgment that the territorial limits of northwestern agricultural were close at hand. After the war, only four new free grant surveys were opened (two in each of the Thunder Bay and Kenora districts). Elsewhere, no suitable acreage remained unsubdivided, either in Algoma West or in the Rainy River country. While twenty-five townships in the Dryden area had originally been laid out, the final eight were re-assessed by that time and found unacceptable for settlement.[223] However, about 1920, a small patch of good soil was sold off near Sioux Lookout to meet the immediate dairying needs of that community. In addition, nine new townships were laid out around Upsala, northwest of Fort William on the CPR, and some lands here were sold to homesteaders late in the decade.[224]

Yet, within existing settled townships at war's end, the undeveloped agricultural acreage was still considerable. Indeed, during the numerous hearings of a provincial inquiry into northern agricultural problems in 1922 certain awkward truths came out. Committee members heard of annoying speculation in lands purchased years before, of aging, empty military grants, and of private acreages assumed by firms in a supposed 'land and lumber' trade.[225] Criticisms were also voiced in the sessions at Port Arthur and Dryden regarding the inordinate reserves for soldier settlement after World War I. At every stop, hearings met with demands for added efforts in completing agricultural settlement. In support of their case, advocates pointed to this sector's regional retention of earnings, as opposed to the migration of bush wages and profits from mines, forests, and fisheries to outside investors.[226]

What such regional boosters did not seem to appreciate was the already startling rate of a recent and continuing advance in agricultural maturity. Free grant locations, by far the largest source of available land in the northwest, nearly doubled before 1930, increasing by some 8,600 (see Table 3.5). Moreover, the number of these grants, old and new, under active occupation rose to over 6,100. Both rates were more rapid before, rather than after, 1921, except for Algoma West. Here the small cluster of free grant townships about Sault Ste Marie seems already to have reached its capacity by 1911. Elsewhere much of the surprising growth had occurred before the constraints of war reversed this trend.[227] Returning rates of demand in post-war years were more modest, probably because good-quality land was in increasingly short supply. However, the all-important process of patenting of the very numerous and proven agricultural holdings continued steadily. It came now to cover a satisfying 96 per cent of all current grants.

As might be anticipated, the recorded number of farms and their populations followed similar general trends, both regionally and in the individual soil pockets. By 1931, a total of 5,200 active farmsteads were on record (see Table 3.6).

TABLE 3.5 Evolution of Free Grant Holdings, 1911–1931

	1911	1921	1931
Algoma West			
Cumulative locations	402	423	425
Locations currently held	202	203	198
Patented current holdings	156	190	194
Thunder Bay District			
Cumulative locations	3,414	5,592	6,695
Locations currently held	1,050	1,636	2,132
Patented current holdings	864	1,488	2,004
Rainy River District			
Cumulative locations	4,507	6,229	7,481
Locations currently held	2,233	2,512	2,653
Patented current holdings	1,409	2,280	2,590
Kenora District			
Cumulative locations	723	1,924	3,043
Locations currently held	429	819	1,125
Patented current holdings	256	691	1,081
Total Northwest			
Cumulative locations	9,046	14,168	17,644
Locations currently held	3,926	5,170	6,108
Patented current holdings	2,685	4,649	5,869

Source: Compiled and aggregated from the Reports of the Department of Lands and Forests, 1913 to 1932.

TABLE 3.6 Rural Profiles, 1911–1931

	1911	1921	1931
Algoma West			
No. of farms	374	379	352
Farm population	–	–	1,675
Rural population	4,608	4,670	3,127
Thunder Bay District			
No. of farms	904	1,590	2,173
Farm population	–	–	8,654
Rural population	10,602	12,483	17,611
Rainy River District			
No. of farms	1,275	1,644	1,728
Farm population	–	–	6,538
Rural population	6,390	8,081	9,619
Kenora District			
No. of farms	297	717	945
Farm population	–	–	3,289
Rural population	4,490	5,609	7,937
Total Northwest			
No. of farms	2,850	4,330	5,198
Farm population	–	–	20,156
Rural population	26,090	30,843	38,294

Source: Compiled from Census of Canada, Agricultural tables, 1911 to 1931.

Solid growth was registered in the large pockets at the Lakehead and in the Rainy River Valley, but none seems to have occurred in the three municipalities next the burgeoning centre of Sault Ste Marie.[228] In contrast, the comparatively youthful townships about Dryden tripled their numbers, coming to vie with Thunder Bay, at almost a thousand farms. Absolute numbers in rural residency followed similarly encouraging upward tendencies, being surprisingly steep in the Thunder Bay and Kenora districts. However, statistics designating farm as opposed to total rural population, available for the first time at the end of the period, reveal that these latter rapid advances were largely a non-agricultural aberration.

The people who took up new homesteads in the northwest over these years continued to be principally from the same varied origins as before. Small numbers of Finns entered lands in the back concessions of many townships, along with a moderate flow of families from southern Ontario. In the Thunder Bay District, however, the second generation of farm populations also became a source of new homesteaders.[229] To lands in Rainy River and Kenora/Dryden came a renewed flow of Canadians and Europeans as well as disenchanted settlers returning from the dry belts of Alberta and Saskatchewan. Other unsuccessful prairie farmers, with original homes from Michigan to Minnestoa, re-entered farming at the Lakehead.[230] Here also in the wake of the war, considerable numbers of Danes took up agricultural holdings from Pass Lake on the Sibley Peninsula to the new western townships of the Upsala area. In addition, a colonization committee set up by the Fort William Board of Trade to advance agriculture in that area played an active role in encouraging other settlement on locally abandoned grants and tax-sale properties.[231] While all pockets came to host some returning veterans, their numbers were disappointing, varying from a meagre five at the Lakehead to sixty along the Rainy River.[232] Across the region the agricultural role of immigrants direct from Europe (generally composed of Scandinavians) remained as modest after 1914 as it had been before.

Over the period, this population came to count almost 805,000 acres within their farm holdings, a healthy increase over the 520,000 acres in 1911 (see Table 3.7). The arable proportion rose from 11 to 18 per cent of this growing total, and the area cleared (pasture plus crop) moved from 26 to 32 per cent or to about 50 acres on the average farm. In the now mature landscape about Sault Ste Marie, almost half the recorded area was in an open agricultural state by 1931. However, the census returns for these years fail to report in any interpretable manner on the townships of the Batchawana/Goulais area. In the recently colonized farmlands of the Kenora District, by contrast, only a little more than a quarter of the area was yet cleared for improved or unimproved farm purposes.

Because of the circumscribed marketing sphere, the limiting climate, and the highly varied soil and drainage conditions prevalent on the average northwestern farm, general patterns of use had changed little with time. According to more detailed measures than tabulated here, about four-fifths of all arable acreage was commonly devoted to hay, feed grains, and legumes. Such roots as potatoes made up much of the rest, save for certain market garden and orchard crops. Similarly, improved and unimproved pasture hosted the normal range of livestock: driving and draft horses as well as varying concentrations of cattle, sheep, and hogs. The relative balance among the latter depended on subregional persuasions or market opportunity, local or otherwise.

The increase in total agricultural area after 1911 raised the uncleared portion of total holdings from about 383,000 to 560,000 acres. However, the energetic progress of the farm community reduced this untamed part of the average farm from slightly less than three-quarters to something just above two-thirds. This amorphous combination of marsh and waste, of sterile sand and gravel or rock

TABLE 3.7 Agricultural Development, 1911–1931

	1911		1921		1931	
	Acres	% of total	Acres	% of total	Acres	% of total
Algoma West						
Cropland	8,459	20	8,660	24	7,233	22
Pasture*	8,007	19	8,759	24	8,305	25
Other†	26,306	61	18,627	52	17,576	53
Total held	42,772		36,046		33,114	
Thunder Bay District						
Cropland	21,507	11	37,907	16	53,749	18
Pasture	24,110	12	26,013	11	36,534	12
Other	154,336	77	168,112	73	208,284	70
Total held	199,953		232,032		298,567	
Rainy River District						
Cropland	22,413	10	43,804	16	56,650	18
Pasture	32,241	14	38,445	14	45,001	15
Other	172,305	76	190,501	70	208,412	67
Total held	226,959		272,750		310,063	
Kenora District						
Cropland	5,039	10	12,739	11	24,092	14
Pasture	13,335	27	23,728	20	23,449	14
Other	30,532	63	81,309	69	121,526	72
Total held	48,906		117,776		169,067	
Total Northwest						
Cropland	57,418	11	103,110	15	141,724	17
Pasture	77,693	15	96,945	14	113,289	14
Other	383,479	74	485,549	71	555,798	69
Total held	518,590		685,604		810,811	

* Includes both improved and unimproved pasturage.
† Includes woodland, slash, and waste, some of which probably served as pasturage.
Source: Compiled from the Census of Canada Agricultural tables, 1911 and 1931, in the appropriate volumes of the Census of Canada.

outcrop, and of forest and slashed-over acreage was part of the heritage of northern agriculture. Whether cedar swamp, poplar ridge, or spruce and balsam stand, such lands had played, and sometimes continued to play, a role in the homesteaders's economy. They were a source of income from ties, posts, poles, and pulpwood, beyond the fence rails and other domestic needs of the farm. Such acreage stood with neighbouring Crown land, now often leased under pulp-cutting licences, and additional farm-owned bush properties as a seasonal source of cash applicable to agricultural ends. This forest-oriented side of northern agriculture, which had persisted from previous decades, was a very necessary element on the colonial farm. However, by 1931, it was becoming less and less prevalent (or even possible) in older townships, as both the individual homestead and the local community expanded and matured.

Resultant Land Use

Examples of the complex imprint left on the rural landscape by 1930 are presented on Maps 3.3a and 3.3b. These maps are compiled from information on ownership and clearance found in old assessment records, preserved in local municipal offices. They cover parts of both larger agricultural pockets of the region: the eastern half of the Rainy River Valley and the urban-centred core of the farmlands back of Thunder Bay. They provide an interesting illustration of agricultural use.

Several features of these maps stand in sharp contrast to the stereotyped images of northern rural conditions in 1930. With the exception of a large preserve about Loch Lomand, now the source of Fort William's water, a surprisingly limited and scattered acreage remained in the public domain. In the Rainy River example, substantial continguous Crown blocks logically were limited to the most northerly and inaccessible surveys. Privately owned but uncleared land was no more common, and that with less than 10 per cent clearance was principally in newer townships away from the river. In contrast, the Thunder Bay example reveals very heavy concentrations of such uncleared bush or cut-over in those rugged surveys towards the Minnesota boundary, where forest harvesting far outweighed agricultural endeavour. Elsewhere, high levels of patented but speculative holdings prevailed, as they had for many years, in the oldest townships immediately inland from Fort William.

Other aspects of these maps also stand at variance with common historical ideas about northern farming that draw heavily on Clay Belt information and experience. Excessively low levels of clearance were not a pronounced feature on these northwestern maps. Where such conditions occurred in these areas, they reflected either recent colonial beginnings or laggardly effort by poor farmers. At the same time, lands of more than average clearance (cited above as 32 per cent) occurred only with modest frequency and in clusters of uneven prominence. The largest area of active agriculture stood between this average and 10 per cent clearance. A comparison of these patterns of clearance and modern land capability maps reveals a reasonable association between well-cleared farm acreage and better land (particularly Class III and IV soils) in

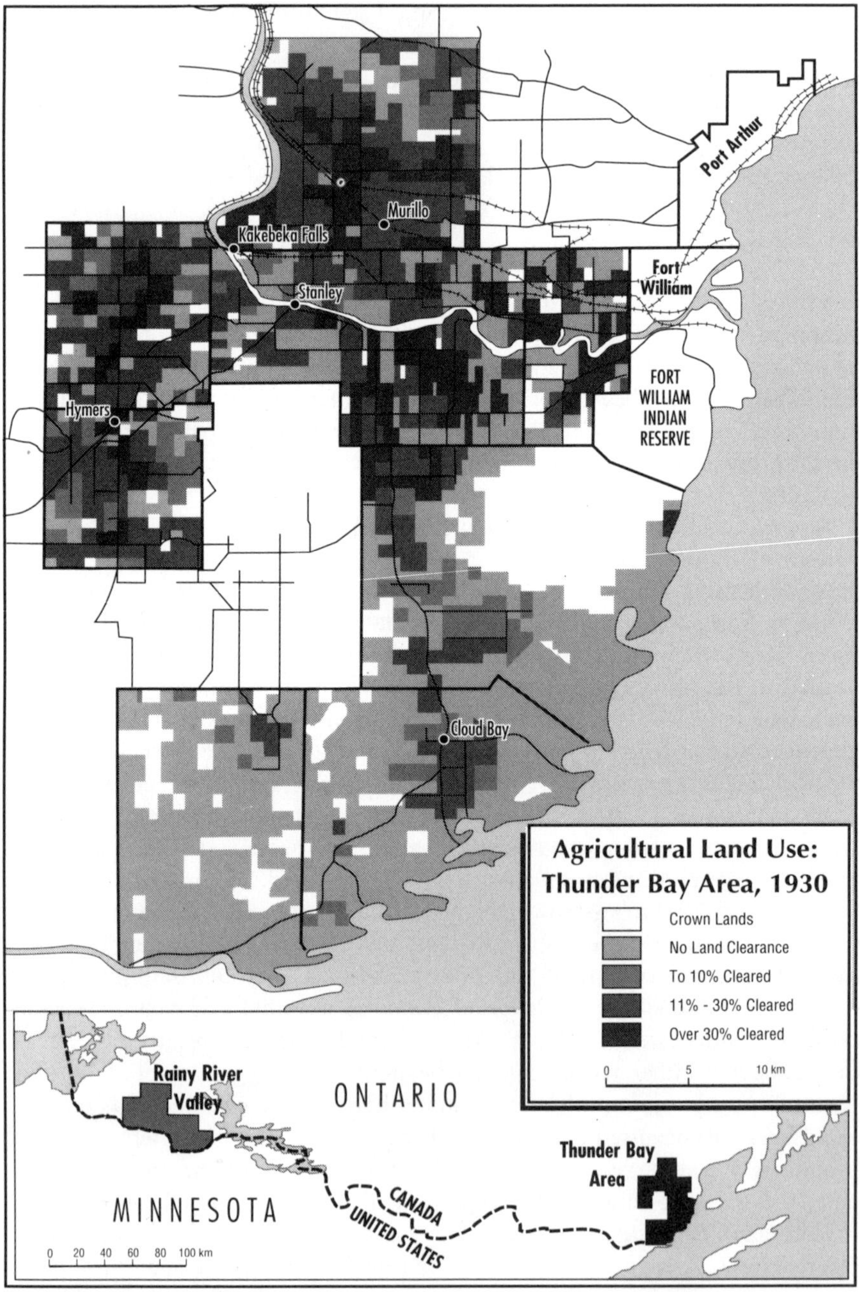
Port Arthur
Murillo
Kakebeka Falls
Fort William
Stanley
FORT WILLIAM INDIAN RESERVE
Hymers
Cloud Bay
Agricultural Land Use: Thunder Bay Area, 1930
Crown Lands
No Land Clearance
To 10% Cleared
11% - 30% Cleared
Over 30% Cleared
0
5
10 km
Rainy River Valley
ONTARIO
Thunder Bay Area
MINNESOTA
CANADA
UNITED STATES
0
20
40
60
80
100 km

MAP 3.3a

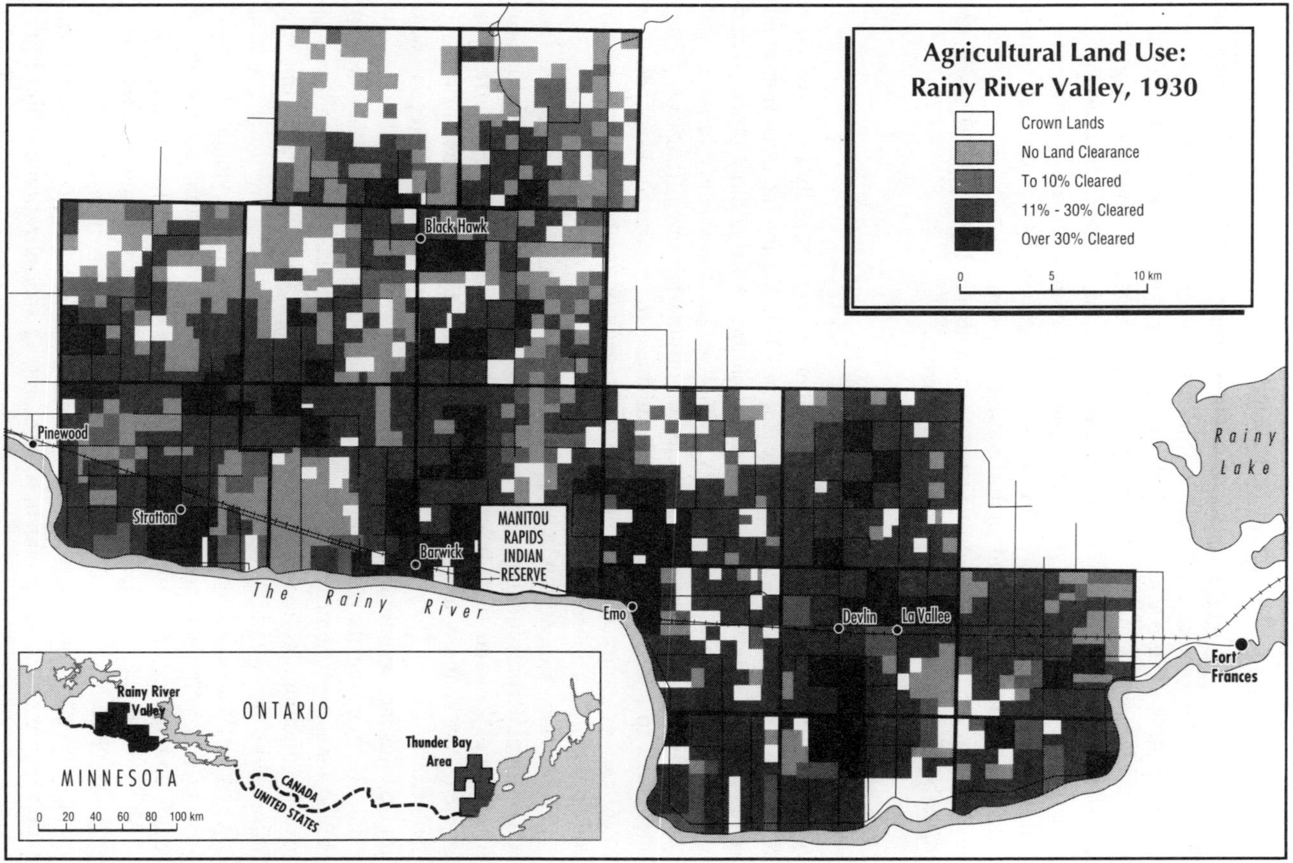
Agricultural Land Use:
Rainy River Valley, 1930
Crown Lands
No Land Clearance
To 10% Cleared
11% - 30% Cleared
Over 30% Cleared
0
5
10 km
Black Hawk
Pinewood
Stratton
Barwick
MANITOU
RAPIDS
INDIAN
RESERVE
The Rainy River
Emo
Devlin
La Vallee
Rainy
Lake
Fort
Frances
Rainy River
Valley
ONTARIO
MINNESOTA
Thunder Bay
Area
CANADA
UNITED STATES
0 20 40 60 80 100 km

MAP 3.3b

both examples. However, moderate clearance levels covered much land of lower agricultural capability. This suggests that the process of land sorting for farm use was still continuing and that other factors, from on-farm pulpwood cutting to late examples of family or kin clustering, were still blurring land use rationalization. These conditions of clearance and use combined to create a rural landscape that was a far cry from the manicured openness displayed across Old Ontario. However, the appearance of this northern land accurately reflected the still-maturing state of farming and the rough reality of the varied soil and drainage conditions with which the settler had to deal. Last, as the pattern of roads, minor and major commercial centres, and railways would suggest, access to market, post office, or neighbours had by 1930 eased remarkably for those who lived in such rural areas.

Contributing Forces

A number of factors contributed to this pattern of determinedly expanding use across the northwest, many of them recent in 1914. Among the most important were emerging government policies and programs aimed at more practical and realizable rural goals. These quietly acknowledged the distinct limits to but capitalized on the recognized potentials of northern farming. Their over-riding intent was to speed the homesteader's advance from initial subsistence to a cash-based economy and to counteract the tragedy of unrelenting rural poverty and related forest abuse.

The province's most important contribution here was through its agents, the Agricultural Representatives. By war's end, these graduates of the Ontario Agricultural College (OAC) at Guelph had come to occupy new offices in Dryden, Fort William, and Port Arthur, in addition to older stands in Emo and Sault Ste Marie.[233] They were the leaders, the innovators and strategists who advised the farm communities and steered northwestern agricultural development. Recognizing the need for field drainage, they promoted tiling and arranged for government traction machines to provide the necessary adjunct of roadside ditching. In the western townships of the Rainy River Valley this was followed in the twenties by further massive projects back from the shore of Lake of the Woods, using ditchers in coordination with a provincial dredge.[234] Such efforts improved the agricultural potential of much rural acreage in the region and opened some of the finest land in this valley to colonial settlement.

By the outbreak of war, all regional centres were fully served with the basic crop and livestock commodities that surrounding farms then produced. As a result, the Agricultural Representatives sought new domestic opportunities and export markets for farm production, encouraging specialization and local processing in their search. In crop agriculture, they fought for the adoption of nutritious and high-yielding alfalfa as a component with clover in the hay crop. This raised the quality of the winter feed as well as its availability for cash sale off the farm.[235] The representatives also were behind the introduction of the first silos on dairy farms. The use of sunflowers with clover for ensilage further enriched winter fodder and added to the potential for year-round milk production.[236] In addition, with an eye to valuable markets in southern Ontario, they promoted the widespread growth of seed potatoes that could be produced here without serious fear of either insects or disease. They also backed clover cultivation, both for hay and for commercial seed production.[237] Much less successful was their encouragement of sugar beets and later of corn fodder. These, with other ideas, were often initiated at a new Government Experimental Station near the Lakehead and distributed to demonstration facilities from the Sault Ste Marie area to Dryden and Rainy River.[238]

In animal husbandry, the provincial agents joined with the Dominion Livestock Branch to promote an aggressive program directed at the more efficient use of the region's rich pastoral potential. In 1914, there was virtually no well-bred stock on northwestern farms, the only exceptions being the recent introduction of a few good stallions at Sault Ste Marie and of six selected bulls across the other three pockets.[239] Indeed, on many farms at that time, existing numbers of even indifferently bred animals were quite low. As a result, the representatives came to encourage local farmers in every locale to band together in livestock improvement associations. Such groups usually selected one breed of cattle or sheep on which to concentrate. Each club could then order through the Livestock Branch carload lots of well-bred animals at very advantageous prices. Such purchases of bulls and cows, ewes and rams, continued through the war and over the years to follow. Their arrival at local railway sidings was annually reported in the local press.[240] As a result, by 1931, northwestern flocks and herds were both much increased in size and greatly improved in quality.

Some of the quick success of these officially directed strategies came through programs of practical education, which also were principally the responsibility of the representatives. These men used the short courses that they ran in fall or winter at local schools or community halls about each territory to promote their progressive ideas. Their sessions were usually well attended and their ideas thoughtfully considered.[241] For those homesteaders new to the area or to their own holding, the representatives helped form Young Farmers groups, which also encouraged discussion and innovative experimentation.[242] In addition, with the help of the Department of Education, they promoted agricultural training and fairs in the rural schools of their jurisdictions.[243] Finally, as qualified judges and acknowledged organizers, they were important supporters of the increasing number of agricultural fairs that came to be held in these years. In addition to the old Central Algoma Exhibition with its new grounds and buildings at Sault Ste Marie, the Lakehead Exhibition (formerly the West Algoma Fair), with an annual draw of 20,000 people or more, ranked as the largest. Another of lesser size grew quickly at Emo and one or two day events were added at Rainy River, in Kenora and Dryden, and at Hymers and Murillo in the Thunder Bay area. The agriculturally competitive and educational side of these events was still their most pronounced feature. However, horse racing before a 2,000-seat grandstand became an important feature at Emo each August.[244]

In addition to such official thrusts were ones generated more directly by the farm communities themselves or by interested private entrepreneurs. One influential catalyst here was the United Farmers Organization with its collective philosophy and chapters covering most farmable townships by the post-war era. By 1920 its trademark, the cooperative, had become the region's most important internal and external vehicle for the marketing plans of the representatives.[245]

The oldest cooperatives were focused on potatoes and clover. One created around the tiny Rainy River centre of La Vallee in 1912 attempted to market an over-supply of local potatoes in Manitoba and southern Ontario. Its success brought pressure for similar operations, which came quickly at Dryden and the Lakehead.[246] The move to cooperatives for seed potato sales in central Canada followed before 1918. These organizations prospered in these centres as well as at Goulais Bay and in Korah and Tarentorus townships of West Algoma. Since average yields ran as high as 200 bushels to the acre, no large area commitment was needed by the individual farmer to participate profitably.[247] While export sales were not always up to expectations, these organizations, which each came to concentrate on one of several varieties, were quite successful through the years. They usually drew enthusiastic support, so much so that in 1931 collective discussions were directed at founding a central warehouse in Fort William for grading, preparing, storing, and shipping the crop.[248] Other early successes were less wide-ranging, but involved measures like the opening of the Oxdrift Seed Growers Co-operative in 1915, with cleaning and grading facilities near Dryden. This proved a highly remunerative enterprise, supplying good cash income to surrounding farmers for many years and encouraging the founding of a less-long-lived counterpart at Emo about 1920.[249]

Also in the realm of crop processing under cooperative mode and again in the Rainy River Valley, where such activity was most strongly supported, was the canning of vegetables. Rainy River Co-operative Canners was incorporated in 1921 with 300 acres under contract. Its plant at Emo, employing about forty people in season, was completed the next spring. It shipped its product so successfully into Winnipeg for the next two years that the operation was bought out by Canadian Canners. That old Ontario firm increased the capacity and escalated its now-substantial contracted acreage of peas across the east half of the valley. This highly profitable effort in cash cropping, which the farmers of the Dryden area attempted unsuccessfully to copy, was in full production at the outset of the Depression.[250]

Other principal areas of cooperative endeavour came in response to problems of milk supplies beyond farm needs. All major centres had a formal dairy of some scale at the outbreak of war, the one at Sault Ste Marie being of considerable size with the most modern equipment.[251] However, much milk was still supplied to these and lesser communities by a scattering of small farmers who, in the twenties, came to form cooperatives to compete more effectively with larger and more-established dairymen. Except in Port Arthur, their long-term success was rare. They suffered chronically from seasonal problems with fluid volume, which rarely could be maintained on general farms with a few cattle and no ensilage to enrich winter feed. Most frequently these individuals lost out to a few large dairy operators or urban enterprises using truck pick-up over extensive milk routes. [252]

In the creamery business, four milk-oriented cooperatives fared better, three being west of Superior. The other, at Stanley, behind Thunder Bay, later encountered stiff competition from a large Burns and Company operation in Fort William, which utilized that area's very considerable supply.[253] The first more westerly endeavour was opened at La Vallee after the end of the war, and another followed at neighbouring Devlin in the same Rainy River country. While the latter was soon taken over by Crescent Creameries of Winnipeg, the Producers' Creamery of La Vallee continued for years to compete successfully for milk poundage and to sell a large production of butter to prairie consumers. Its returns to farm investors and suppliers over time must have been quite considerable. In the late twenties, this operation moved to larger quarters in Fort Frances and added a dairying enterprise. By then its Devlin competition was dissolved, but a new cooperative creamery had opened down the valley at Rainy River.[254] Similar attempts by the farmers of the Dryden area, combining a dairy and creamery, were a less spectacular success. They battled against still-limited local supply and stern competition for this milk from creameries, which paid high prices for rail delivery to their Winnipeg operations from as far away as 300 miles. However, the Dryden plant, founded in 1924, struggled on with increasing success, although dividends to its shareholders and returns to local farmers may have been thin for much of the period.[255]

While co-op cheese factories were frequently discussed and sometimes promoted here as elsewhere in northern regions, only one at Emo was maintained in successful operation. It was constructed in 1915 and, with twenty-five suppliers, went into production the next year, shipping 24,000 pounds to Winnipeg for maturation. The standard was high enough to attract a substantial contract from Swift Canada Limited there. Despite later problems with quality, the plant was still in substantial production and most profitable operation at the Depression.[256] Although the success of such adventures in collectivism can be over-estimated, they were spirited attempts at economic advance that spoke well of the regional farm community.

In the developing livestock sector, however, not all farm groups were attracted to cooperative modes. The beef industry was a notable example, although some form of stimulation was clearly needed by 1914 to bolster local interest in the industry and in herd quality. Indeed, many of the better stockers and feeders on the Dryden and Rainy River Valley pastures were railed in by Winnipeg drovers to be fattened, then sold domestically or remarketed in the west.[257] In dry years, ranchers in southern Alberta and Saskatchewan also leased much pasture here and behind the Lakehead to preserve and fatten numerous beef animals before their eastern sale.[258] Little real local income was derived from such land use, and this realization brought some farmers of the region to see the advantage of beef operations. Using the help of the Dominion Livestock Branch, such emerging stockmen gained supplies of well-bred beef animals with which to build their herds. However, not all agricultural pockets took to the industry. At Sault Ste Marie, beef production remained weakly organized beyond domestic supply. It was not a large export component of Lakehead farm income either, because of distance to eastern markets. However, the numerous rail-side stockpens of the Dryden pocket and Rainy River country became increasingly busy each fall with cattle moving to Winnipeg for profitable sale.[259]

Sheep too were of rising importance in the northwest. Again, eastward transfers by prairie producers served to stir serious local involvement, particularly in the Rainy River country. There and in West Algoma, both about Sault Ste Marie and in the Goulais settlement, local sheepmen were frequent buyers of carload lots of federally selected breeding stock, usually Leisters or Oxfords. Government also provided community dipping tanks across these areas to further encourage a high-quality clip. In addition, the baled fleeces were shipped east, graded, and collectively marketed through a federal agency to the financial advantage of the individual producer.[260] In both areas, lamb clubs appeared about 1920, with growing subsequent shipment each spring from Algoma to Toronto and from Rainy River to Winnipeg. While the industry was plagued over the years by animal predators, the returns were most rewarding for the participants, either as general farmers or major producers. Only late in the twenties, after success could be demonstrated in the above agricultural areas, were substantial numbers of sheep introduced around the Lakehead or Dryden. At the end of the period flocks were growing numerous only in the latter pocket.[261]

Finally, a number of specializations, which in many cases remained adjunct to other farming pursuits, emerged on this buoyant agricultural scene. Encouraged by the large indoor markets now available in Sault Ste Marie and at each of the twin Lakehead cities, important attention was directed at orchard production and the market garden trade.[262] While soft fruits were climatically out of the question, a full range of apples, pears, and plums were produced here for urban consumption. Also grown were a broad spectrum of bush fruits, from currants to raspberries, as well as strawberry crops. While tomatoes were, and remain, only a marginal possibility in gardens at Thunder Bay, most popular varieties of vegetables could be produced about both areas and, like the hard fruits, could be stored for marketing out of season.[263] Along with meat, poultry, and eggs, suppliers in the area of Sault Ste Marie produced maple syrup and honey. The latter was also exported in large quantities westward from apiaries of the Dryden area, where there was a rich growth of wild and cultivated clover. Across the entire region each August, thousands of baskets of wild blueberries also moved east, west, and south by rail and steamer. Although the bulk of this crop came from Native bands, considerable contributions sold on consignment through local merchants were a lucrative addition to normal farm income.[264]

Northwestern Ontario at the end of the twenties certainly was no agricultural Eden or even a maturing twin to the polished acres of southern Ontario. However, advances on the farm, particularly since the war, were modestly satisfying and encouraging. Indeed, the strides made in social and economic conditions seemed to guarantee a secure future on the family farm, contrary to popular thought in southern Ontario.

New Thrusts for the Forest Industry

By the outbreak of war, the era of big pine lumbering in Ontario was drawing to a close. In the Maritimes, Quebec, and along the Ottawa River, that colourful trade was already history, but farther west supplies dwindled only slowly, persisting for three more decades in the Rainy River country.[265] Even here, however, severe wartime dislocation caused high unemployment among mill hands and bushworkers from 1914 to 1916. This was followed by a countertrend that was interrupted briefly in 1921. Recovery through the twenties was hampered by stiffening B.C. competition for western markets and an increasing tendency for Americans to turn to domestic alternatives.[266] As one regional editor expressed it in 1923, 'the pulpwood trade and the post, pole and tie business are back to pre-war levels, but for our lumber industry those days are gone.'[267]

In lumbering, as in the rest of the industry, old management practices faced new labour problems. Despite recruitment ads as far away as New Brunswick, it became increasingly difficult to find skilled personnel to work at the wages that operators were willing to pay.[268] The old, uneducated work force, which migrated with the season from prairie to woodland, from Quebec to Ontario, and from farm or fishery to forest, had just lived through the war. Its membership was much less acquiescent to the foul living conditions that camp owners traditionally provided and more willing to react collectively through walk-outs, demonstrations, and strikes. This growing militancy found acceptance among immigrant workers and strong leadership from socialist elements such as the Finns. Managers and owners reacted bitterly to the new attitude, but were forced to absorb the rising costs of labour in these years of increasing market difficulties.[269]

Conditions of growing competition and declining availability were felt across the region. In Algoma West, the massive sawmill erected by Clergue at Sault Ste Marie cut vigorously only until 1914. Only its much smaller cousin at nearby Searchmont found sufficient logs to survive.[270] At the Lakehead, the huge mills of the Pigeon River Lumber Company cleaned up their pine supply and ceased operation in 1919.[271] While the mills of the Rat Portage and the Keewatin Lumber companies, with up to a thousand mill hands, opened the era with a combined cut at Kenora of almost 45 million board feet, neither lasted the race. Keewatin bought out the competition in 1917–18 but subsequently ran only one of these two plants. Even that firm gradually closed out after 1924, as it shifted to become the forest arm of Backus' rising Kenora Paper Company.[272] As a result, only the huge pair of mills under Shevlin-Clark at Fort Frances, Ontario's largest producers after 1916, and the adjacent capability of J.A. Mathieu Lumber Company, were significantly active in pine at the Depression. Despite less and less accessible limits in the Seine River–Quetico area, their saws worked at near-capacity through the twenties.[273]

The potential of spruce from more northerly taiga sources to add significantly to this sawyery trade can be easily over-emphasized. Such less-valued wood was readily available in both eastern and western lumber markets from more local sources and its supply for dimension lumber in the northwest was limited. 'There [were] many areas north of the Transcontinental in which the timber [even for pulpwood was] so sparsely scattered that it would hardly be considered merchantable.'[274] As a result, while numerous portable mills harvested any suitable spruce along more northerly railway lines, only a few permanent operations persisted. These included ones at Richan, Allan Water, McDougall Mills, Hudson, and, in particular, both the Farlinger mills at Sioux Lookout on the National Transcontinental and those of Indian Lake Lumber, near Ignace on the CPR (see Map 3.2).[275] Here, as elsewhere throughout the region, such activity merged vaguely into the less-discriminating post, pole, and tie industry, where jackpine was now becoming one of the most prominent sources of timber. These largely undocumented endeavours in turn combined with the general contractor or dealer systems, which also used settlers as an effective source of these basic products around farmable areas. Much more than pine lumbering, this mundane and wide-ranging harvest of inferior trees competed with pulp-cutting as the focus of the forest industry in 1930.

Pulpwood and Its Export

The revolutionary rise of the pulp and paper sector resulted from two sets of conditions. In a pragmatic sense, it was stimulated by the final termination of U.S. tariffs on Canadian pulp and paper in 1913, after years of in-fighting between American publishers and paper makers. In this context, it also reflected recognition of declining U.S. pulpwood stocks and severe shortages there in the highly desirable spruce component. In more strategic terms, it was a response to the entrepreneurial realization that the enormous and growing demand for paper across North America could only be satisfied in the future by full utilization of continental pulpwood supplies.[276]

The immediate result of this rise in the international demand for pulp and paper was a jump in recorded pulp cutting across Ontario's north. In the northwest, this leap was from 112,000 cords in 1914–15, or 17 per cent of the provincial total, to 217,000, or 41 per cent, just four years later. This accelerating trend, which continued to the end of the period, reached 523,000 cords, or 49 per cent of Ontario's cut, in 1923 (see Table 3.8). Of this rapidly rising total, the proportion legally generated from freehold acreage increasingly exceeded that harvested from Crown limits through the war years, but the two differed only marginally by 1923. Other indicators reveal a strengthening shift in favour of supplies from Crown limits through the late twenties (see Table 3.9).

Such cut levels for the most part were attained within the law, which, in line with the established policy of home manufacture, continued a stiff duty on pulpwood exported in a raw condition. Only poplar and fire-scorched softwoods cut on Crown lands, settler production in agricultural clearance, and pulpwood taken from patented lands and railway grants were exported free of this penalty.[277] However, from 1914 to the end of the decade, this law was

TABLE 3.8 Pulpwood Production (in cords), 1914–1923

	1914–15	1918–19	1922–3
Total Northwest			
Crown land cut	50,445	90,493	263,343
Freehold cut	61,770	126,658	259,734
Total cut	112,215	217,151	523,077
Percentage of Ontario cut	(17)	(41)	(49)

Source: National Archives of Canada, RG 33/13, vol. 2, G5.

abused in the northwest by a small but politically well-connected group. Known as 'the Old Tory Timber Ring' and abetted by certain Lands and Forests personnel, it manipulated timber licences and used a permit system meant only for posts, poles, or firewood to export pulpwood to the financial advantage of certain dealers, contractors, and large woodland operators. Under this scheme, these entrepreneurs exported under permit and without duty innumerable cords of so-called 'firewood' with origins on Crown limits, free grants, veterans' lands, and mining claims annually to American buyers at high U.S. prices.[278]

This surreptitious trade was corrected only after the Riddell-Latchford Inquiry was set up in March 1920 to look into other laxities in forest management.[279] These hearings probably missed many smaller offenders who were nevertheless scared away from the game. Yet they resulted in a provincial airing of the facts and some legal convictions for major culprits in this export conspiracy. Other related testimony about fraudulent forest practices revealed that a few American firms hired prospectors to take out rights for them on spruce-covered mining claims, even former quarries, with an eye to bogus clearance. Certain regional dealers grub-staked such prospectors on similar claims, old veterans' lots, or tax lands to the same end. District agents for timber and land were found in neglect of their duties of inspection of forest leases and permit lands about both Rainy River and Thunder Bay. Such laxity also involved free grants and their patenting in outlying areas of the latter district. Here certain settlers in one excessively rough township near Nipigon designated themselves as 'The Fourteen Thieves'![280] Local contractors on upper Superior, such as Horrigan Brothers, with its falsely acquired limits, were let off with minor fines, as were smaller mill operators such as the Fort Frances Lumber Company. However, major firms like Russell Timber were sued for repayment of duties and dues on several thousand cords.[281] Shevlin-Clark, like G.E. Farlinger, was prosecuted for receipt of forest grants under patronage. In

TABLE 3.9 Pulp and Paper Production, 1928

	Source		Mill	Production			
	Pulpwood (cords)	Crown Cut (%)	Capacity (T/Day)	Chemical	Mechanical (T/Annum)	Newsprint	Paper
Algoma West							
Sault Ste Marie							
Abitibi Paper	108,820	54	250	26,833	44,845	52,325	7,627
Thunder Bay District							
Port Arthur							
Provincial Paper	94,485	60	235	18,661	17,530	–19,197	
Thunder Bay Paper	86,940	75	250	–	5,332	45,913	–
Fort William							
Abitibi Paper	28,529	16	165	4,171	17,884	20,777	–
Great Lakes Paper	4,769	78	350	–	4,679	6,583	–
Nipigon							
Nipigon Corporation	–	–	–	–	–	–	–
Rainy River District							
Fort Frances							
Fort Frances Paper	56,109	67	325	–	59,927	62,126	–
Kenora District							
Kenora							
Kenora Paper	116,601	62	250	90,024	49,051	62,126	–
Dryden							
Dryden Paper	53,653	42	80	13,619	–	–	8,228
Total Northwest	549,906	57	1,905	153,308	199,248	248,925	35,052

Source: Archives of Ontario, RG 1, E-5, vol. 19, Reports on Pulp and Paper Production.

the search for proof of pulpwood violations, each was found to have falsified books on its lumber cuts over past years. (Such rigging of records was shown to result from a dubious procedure in which scalers were appointed by Lands and Forests but paid partly by the lumbering companies). Farlinger's transgressions were reasonably small, but Shevlin-Clark was legally assessed to owe Ontario $1.5 million. After long arguments, cries for appeal, and threats by the company to close out its mills, matters were settled much less punitively.[282] Ironically, cases were never successfully made against other likely suspects, including both Backus-Brooks at Fort Frances and Spanish River Pulp and Paper at Sault Ste Marie.[283] Subsequent political bluster and counter-claims dulled public concern over this scandal. However, changes in the mining law and tightened forest regulations followed quietly, as did reforms and retirements in the Department of Lands and Forests.[284]

Too much can be made of this political pork barrel and its economic impact on the forest industry. More significant was the transfer of a growing number of bushworkers to commercial pulp camps and the introduction of the steel-framed swede saw, to increase the speed of the harvest.[285] By 1920, over a thousand pulpmen were reported in the shanties behind Thunder Bay. To the west, a small army of woodsmen, some of them farmers from neighbouring agricultural pockets, were employed each winter on Backus' now large pulpwood holdings and on the Dryden area limit.[286] Along the north shore of Superior, earlier pulpwood harvesting continued through the twenties as far east as Heron Bay. It witnessed the first serious cut on such intermediate watersheds as the Steel and Pays Plat rivers.[287] North of Sault Ste Marie, large camps generated by jobbers spent heavily, improving and driving pulpwood down difficult rivers as far north as the Pukaskwa area. From this coast the harvest was boomed south behind tugs or barged away to American mills. Inland cuts continued to come out over the ACR, although harvesting below mile 60 was now reduced to hardwood, largely under American lease.[288] Some firms across the region hired large contractors to conduct their bush operations, while others, like Backus-Brooks in the extreme west, set up subordinate firms for that task or relied on numerous small teams of seasonal labour to fill their needs, from predetermined areas on their limits.[289]

Rising Paper Milling

Over the early years, continental demands for paper forced Ottawa by 1918 to regulate the disposal of the Canadian supply, to cover essential domestic needs.[290] This prodded American capitalists to reflect more seriously on future investment in more Canadian pulp and paper manufacture. In northwestern Ontario, few changes yet had occurred on that side of the industry. The substantial mills at Sault Ste Marie were now under the control of Mead Investments of Dayton, Ohio, along with the rest of Spanish River's holdings. These mills on the St Marys were busy producing an annual 64,000 tons of newsprint, 30,000 of dried sulphite, and 38,000 of similar groundwood pulp, most of it for export. In contrast, the tiny Dryden kraft paper plant was again under reorganization and at Fort Frances only the small groundwood operation of Backus-Brooks continued to ship its wet product across the river to paper machines in International Falls.[291] There was certainly room for expansion.

However, while post-war investors could see the exciting potential, to the frustration of Ontario's dreams of now rapid northern development, they chose to wait until the early twenties before committing their money to such schemes. As a result, they continued to be more than willing to enter upon lavish provincial agreements for limits and power supplies, but still dragged their heels on the erection of promised mills, with the resultant creation of regional employment.[292] E.W. Backus, who held the Lake of the Woods Limit (1,860 square miles) since 1913, now lobbied for the adjoining and much richer English River concession (25,000 square miles), which after much heated debate he obtained in 1921 (see Map 3.4). Work had yet to start on his long-promised pulp and paper mills at Kenora. Here delays were only summarily tolerated because of wartime conditions and later hydro problems arising from new lake level regulations under the International Joint Commission. With war over, the project proceeded quickly. However, in subsequent years, his once-proposed development of power at Whitedog Rapids for his English River concession was quietly forgotten by weary officials.[293] Meanwhile, on Superior, J.J. Carrick of the 'Tory Ring' had landed control of the newly created Pic River Limit in 1916. To this he added the Black Sturgeon next spring, to give a total of 2,300 square miles of valuable pulpwood. The following year, he sold a 30 per cent interest to each of two American financiers (L.L. Alstead of Appleton, Wisconsin, and R.L. Seaman of Chicago) for the capital to build a mill at the Lakehead. However, this facility was a long time coming.[294] Indeed, the only early success in northwestern mill building was Port Arthur Pulp and Paper. This firm was formed in 1916 and completed a small 40 T/day plant for the export of sulphite pulp just two years later. Ironically, the firm was based on Canadian capital and remained so, being assumed by Provincial Paper in 1920. In contrast was Kam Pulp and Paper, in which Toronto backers were forced into liquidation and American sale before their mill was completed in the early twenties.[295]

Meanwhile, the rate of pulpwood production rose after 1918. Much of this increase in initial years, however, was either in freehold cut or in dutiable

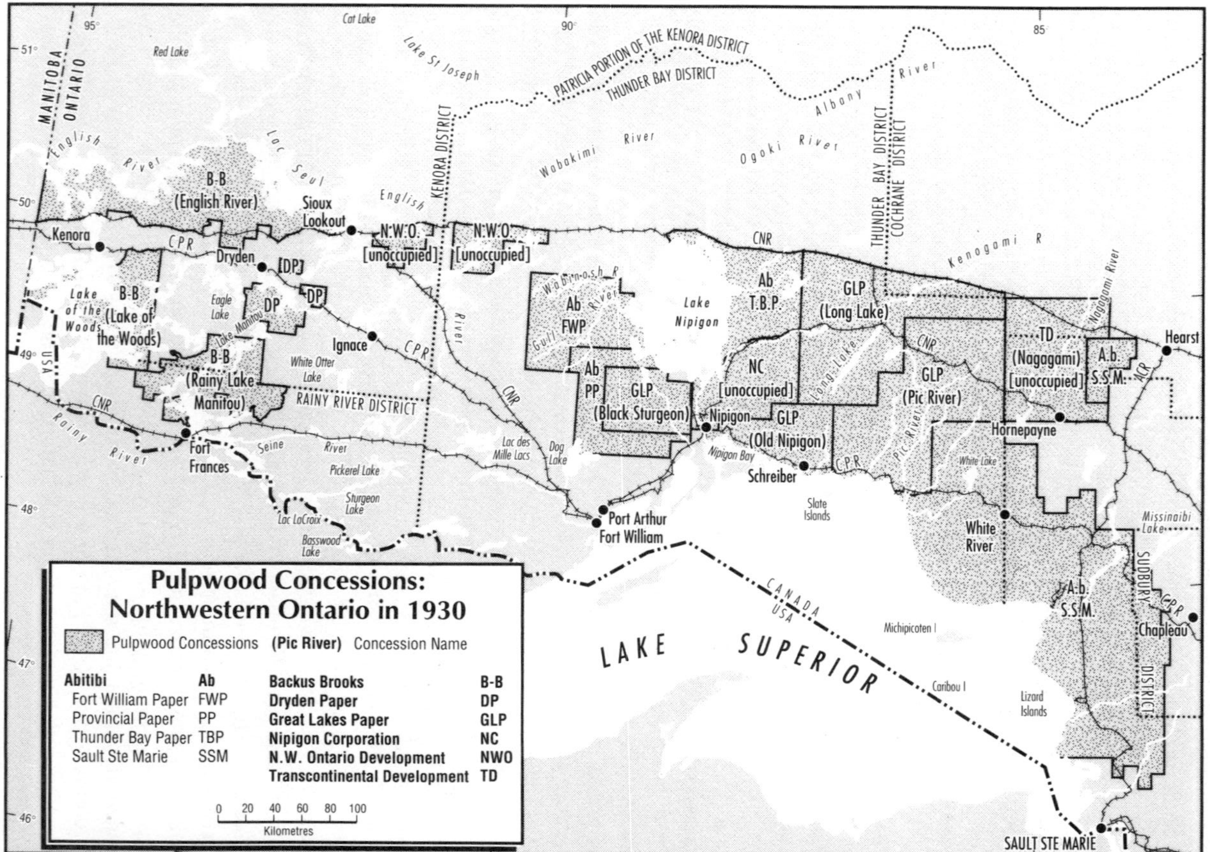
Pulpwood Concessions:
Northwestern Ontario in 1930
Pulpwood Concessions (Pic River) Concession Name
Abitibi Ab
Fort William Paper FWP
Provincial Paper PP
Thunder Bay Paper TBP
Sault Ste Marie SSM
Backus Brooks B-B
Dryden Paper DP
Great Lakes Paper GLP
Nipigon Corporation NC
N.W. Ontario Development NWO
Transcontinental Development TD
0 20 40 60 80 100
Kilometres
MANITOBA
ONTARIO
PATRICIA PORTION OF THE KENORA DISTRICT
THUNDER BAY DISTRICT
KENORA DISTRICT
COCHRANE DISTRICT
RAINY RIVER DISTRICT
SUDBURY DISTRICT
LAKE SUPERIOR
CANADA
USA
Kenora
Dryden
Sioux Lookout
Ignace
Fort Frances
Port Arthur
Fort William
Nipigon
Schreiber
Hornepayne
White River
Hearst
Chapleau
SAULT STE MARIE
B-B (English River)
B-B (Lake of the Woods)
B-B (Rainy Lake Manitou)
N.W.O. [unoccupied]
Ab FWP
Ab PP
GLP (Black Sturgeon)
Ab T.B.P.
NC [unoccupied]
GLP (Old Nipigon)
GLP (Long Lake)
GLP (Pic River)
TD (Nagagami) [unoccupied]
A.b. S.S.M.
Lake Nipigon
Lake of the Woods
Lac Seul
Red Lake
Cat Lake
Lake St Joseph
Eagle Lake
White Otter Lake
Lac des Mille Lacs
Dog Lake
Pickerel Lake
Sturgeon Lake
Lac LaCroix
Basswood Lake
Nipigon Bay
Slate Islands
Michipicoten I
Caribou I
Lizard Islands
Missinaibi Lake
CPR
CNR
ACR

MAP 3.4

spruce, shipped to U.S. consumers at places like Erie, Detroit, Port Huron, and the Appleton vicinity of Wisconsin. Such production came from all areas that had ready access to the American border. Some was railed south from Rainy River or Fort Frances, while large quantities flowed out from the ACR lands or adjacent townships of Algoma West, via Michipicoten Harbour.[296] However, the lion's share, 81,500 cords in 1923, continued to be derived from the north shore of Superior and the peripheral townships of the Thunder Bay area. As earlier, it was watered directly onto steamers along the coast or over the docks of Port Arthur and Fort William, where U.S. paper companies, like Hammermill or the jointly owned Wisconsin subsidiary, Newago, had peeling and loading facilities.[297] However, as the twenties progressed, such shipments, while growing, were a less and less significant element in the total production.

The industry's post-war problems across Canada caused a federal Royal Commission on Pulpwood to be struck in 1923. In northwestern Ontario, as elsewhere, the commissioners were quick to discover that a proposed embargo on all forms of pulpwood export, to promote more domestic manufacture, received a divided response. Private landholders, principally settlers, were strongly opposed, pointing to the price monopoly such an imposition would give the manufacturers (as it did in the isolated one-mill districts) over the current competitive system. Management argued less convincingly that the higher pulpwood prices paid by Americans drove up their costs and made products less saleable in the United States. They claimed that such exports created local shortages, although the Commission's final report determined this complaint to be hollow. In fact, to preserve their own supplies against long-term need, most firms in the early twenties still took as much or more pulpwood from private sources as from their own limits.[298]

Rapid growth in Ontario's pulpwood production and related domestic manufacture over the remaining years before the Depression quickly corrected this situation. Overt American interest and official provincial promotion, combined with rising western markets for newsprint in both Canada and the United States, stimulated energetic mill construction and new rounds of pulpwood agreements.[299] Backus' empire continued along its course, bucking provincial dictums, defying fair-trade regulations, and fighting with both municipal neighbours and the labour force. His Fort Frances Pulp and Paper Company had, by 1925, increased its wet pulp production to 250 T/day. It also began construction of a 300 T/day newsprint mill on the Canadian end of its dam across the Rainy River. On completion in 1927, hydro from three new stations on the Seine watershed fulfilled the additional power requirements, and enlarged limits were acquired for more pulpwood capacity.[300] However, Backus' Kenora Paper Company did not begin construction of a small (80 T/day) groundwood mill until 1923, completing its related hydro facility at the Norman dam only in 1924. Under continuing government threats, the first of two newsprint machines was installed that year and a full paper mill of 250 T/day went into production at mid-decade, along with added sulphite pulp capacity.[301]

In comparison with these large operations west of the height of land, the much smaller Dryden Paper Company stood as a distinctly poor relative, despite its addition of more power from a new dam at nearby Wainwright. After recurrent financial problems from 1918 to 1924, the new Montreal backers of this 80 T/day operation sold their kraft production as wrapping paper for prairie consumption. To this market they added the fabrication of heavy bags for cement and gypsum as a highly successful line.[302] In this most westerly area new operations were contemplated in these years only at Sioux Lookout. Preliminary interest here from Spanish River Pulp and Paper was followed by attempts under George Farlinger and associates to come up with the capital for a mill, but no construction occurred. However, a curiously worded woodland agreement was signed between the North West Ontario Development Company and the province in 1927. It covered Farlinger's existing limits about Allan Water and McDougall Mills and suggested that the idea of a pulp operation here was not dead.[303]

About the Lakehead new capital investment proceeded more rapidly and with better result. On its purchase by Provincial in 1920, the initial Port Arthur Pulp and Paper plant underwent a $2.5 million expansion. This doubled its sulphite capacity to 80 T/day and added both a 50 T/day groundwood facility and its first paper machine by 1923. The latter capacity of this satellite of Abitibi Power and Paper was increased from 35 to 105 T/day capacity in 1929.[304] Here also Kam Pulp and Paper of Toronto, forced into liquidation with a partly completed mill in early 1921, was taken over by Consolidated Power and Paper of Wisconsin Rapids the following year. As the Thunder Bay Paper Company, the mill in Port Arthur was quickly finished and its groundwood capacity for export was soon doubled to 120 T/day. After mid-decade it added a newsprint mill capable of 250 T/day and digester capacity for sulphite pulp production. However, in late 1928, this operation returned to Canadian control when it too was purchased by Abitibi Power and Paper from a financial troubled U.S. parent.[305]

Although rumours of a mill at Squaw Bay had begun in 1916, no pulp and paper activity occurred around Fort William until the end of that decade. At that date an American consortium led by Mead Investments founded the Fort William Paper Company.[306] This firm proceeded immediately to erect a 120 T/day groundwood mill next the lands of the National Transcontinental on Mission Island. To this export operation, it added newsprint manufacture the next year, which grew to 165 T/day capacity after 1925 and again was supplemented by the addition of sulphite facilities.[307] The appearance of a second such operation, however, was much delayed. Great Lakes Paper, involving Alstead, Seaman, and Backus, who took over Carrick's original share in the control of the Black Sturgeon and Pic River pulpwood agreements, was incorporated in 1919.[308] Typically for Backus, the next four years were spent in a complex battle with the province over hydro supplies and legal details, as well as with the municipality over land and taxes.[309] Finally, under Cabinet threat of outright cancellation of arrangements, a substantial groundwood pulp mill appeared in 1924. Exports to Appleton, Wisconsin, were begun immediately, which shipments would be joined by sulphite ones at the end of the period. Meanwhile, after further threats, sluggish construction began on the paper mill, which the initial agreements also required. However, the first newsprint from this still-unfinished facility passed off the machines only in 1928. By that time Alstead and Seaman had sold their controlling interest to International Paper of Canada, with head offices in New York, and Backus had been thrust into the background.[310]

The provision of power to these four Lakehead companies is a complex story in itself. By 1910 Fort William's domestic hydro was being supplied by the Kaministiquia Power Company using Kakabeka Falls as its generating site. In contrast, Port Arthur had erected two municipal dams and stations on the Current River. However, in 1910 Ontario's Hydro Electric Power Commission (HEPC) opened a short transmission line to Port Arthur for added power at the low 'public rate' it applied elsewhere in the province. This hydro it bought from Kam Power. That deal triggered a dispute between Fort William and Kam Power leading to a revised contract at reduced rates, but that city too moved to public power in the twenties. By that time HEPC had erected its first major power facility in northern Ontario at Cameron Falls on the Nipigon River. From here it had strung 105 miles of transmission line to serve the Lakehead, including the rising pulp and paper industry. While Kam Power lost its municipal contract with Fort William, its total capacity remained divided between the Commission and Provincial Paper, by which it was controlled. With Cameron's existing capacity pressed to the limit and two-thirds of its production serving pulp and paper interests, the HEPC opened a second and larger generating facility on the Nipigon at Alexander Falls in 1930.

Such publicly sponsored electrical provision was accompanied by a substantial increase in pulpwood concessions. However, in the quickening pace of mill construction the latter agreements for concessions were often finalized after the fact. So Port Arthur Pulp and Paper (later Provincial) started its mill on a contracted settler cut. In 1918, it was awarded quietly, if surprisingly, the 88 square miles of the Sibley Forest Reserve. To this was added the 1,240 square miles of the 'old Nipigon Limit' in 1920 and an adjunct of 70 square miles in 1924.[311] Similarly caught off guard, the province let 52 square miles of the Black Bay Peninsula in 1920 to the emerging Thunder Bay Paper Company as its initial limit. It followed this with a guarantee of up to five million cords from settler lands until a more adequate accommodation could be made.[312] Finally, hasty early arrangements had to suffice for Fort William Paper. They covered the 993 square miles of National Transcontinental Railway grants in ten scattered blocks across the Thunder Bay and Kenora Districts. This move, however, brought voluble resistance from Ottawa, to whom that railway and, therefore, these lands actually belonged.[313] In contrast, Great Lakes Paper, with its earlier reserves of pulpwood in the Pic and Black Sturgeon drainage, had no immediate needs in the early twenties. It nevertheless arranged the transfer of the Long Lake Limit from a Toronto owner in 1921, but Backus' obstructive behaviour caused Ontario to delay the actual award until 1928.[314]

The three more compliant firms here were more positively treated by the province as this decade progressed. In 1925, in return for promised collective expansion to 1,840 T/day of pulp and 1,525 T of newsprint, each was granted a large new block of pulpwood in the Nipigon Forest Reserve, as well as an advantageous share of the new power to be generated at the Alexander dam.[315] To this agreement was added the Nipigon Corporation, which had taken over the tiny and defunct pulp mill of the Nipigon Fibre and Paper Company. This firm had operated only briefly on local pulpwood and power in 1920 and 1921. However, the corporation's participation remained strictly promissory.[316] Nevertheless, the construction involved in this huge joint venture in paper production and power provision, costing an estimated $41.5 million, was fully implemented by 1926, and was nearing its finish on the era's close.

In Algoma West, progress in the area of mills and limits was much less dramatic. Under the Mead Corporation, Spanish River expanded its production quickly at Sault Ste Marie. Even before 1926, when it sold its holdings here and at Fort William to Abitibi, it employed 650 people in mills producing almost 130,000 tons of pulp and paper a year. Of this, 60 per cent was newsprint, and 40 per cent was groundwood or sulphite pulp; most was exported to the eastern United States.[317] To the huge limits that this old operation had acquired, no additions were made. However, its northern and western boundaries were more specifically defined by the Pic River Agreement. Indeed the only significant change in the district had come in 1921 with the creation of the Nagagami River property of 2,300 square miles, granted to the Transcontinental Development Company of Toronto.[318] While the spruce pulpwood of this area warranted the creation of this large concession, no suitable hydro power site existed in or near its remote location and no harvesting occurred by 1930.

In 1928, the eight active mills of the northwest hit their peak for the period (see Table 3.9), mirroring events elsewhere across the nation. Their scale varied enormously from the large undertaking at Sault Ste Marie or the huge Great Lakes facility at the Lakehead, which was only partly complete, to the tiny one at Dryden. They collectively consumed 550,000 cords of pulpwood annually. (This closing figure would have been even higher had Abitibi at Fort William not been in the midst of installing new machinery.) Of this cut, 87 per cent was spruce and the balance largely jackpine with some balsam fir. With few exceptions the supply now came predominantly from the companies' Crown limits rather than private land.

While figures reported in the press are vague and scattered, these mills employed about 2,500 shift workers and supported an equally large seasonal work force in the bush. Their total productive capacity topped 1,900 T/day of pulp and paper, most firms being capable of more than 200 tons over three shifts. Their actual production of pulp included over 150,000 tons per year from chemical digestion. Of this only the kraft production at Dryden, with a heavy reliance on jackpine, used a sulphate as opposed to sulphite process. In contrast, almost 200,000 tons were mechanically generated as groundwood. In addition to the pulp that was dried and exported, much was converted into some 284,000 tons of paper, 88 per cent of which was newsprint. Only Dryden and Provincial Paper were not involved in such production. Of this newsprint, some was sold in eastern and western Canada, but the largest market was American, particularly the urban presses of the midwest.

The war years and the early twenties had been active and progressive ones for pulp and paper production across the northwest. However, problems of over-expansion, momentarily troublesome in 1921, appeared again on the regional economic horizon in 1926, and then again at the end of the decade, when production glutted North American markets.[319] By late 1928, mills at Kenora and Fort Frances were operating on reduced hours. They ran only sporadically the following year before locking their doors for lack of orders.[320] Despite closure of some of its other mills, Abitibi kept partial shifts at both Sault Ste Marie and Fort William until mid-1930.[321] While Dryden faltered early, Great Lakes stubbornly proceeded with the completion of its facilities, and other mills at the Lakehead struggled to keep running at least briefly through 1929. The onset of the Depression delivered the final knock-out blow.[322]

The first three decades of the twentieth century closed with ominous signs for the industry, reflecting a growing mismanagement of northwestern forest resources. The post-war years had witnessed a decline in good forestry practices by the rising pulp and paper community as well as by the remaining lumbermen. The period also saw a growing willingness by government and northerners in general to accommodate this unhealthy attitude.[323] This outlook is typified by the tawdry behaviour of the 'Tory Timber Ring' or the easy acquiescence of Lands and Forests in schemes to return the recently created Forest Reserves to harvesting. While a few token foresters were hired by companies or the government, they were more often used as woodland engineers or fire-fighters than as environmental managers. Few new trees were being planted in the north over these years, although cutting rates and mill capacities were rising quickly with up-to-date machinery.[324] According to one authority, 'from 1905 to 1942 ... uncontrolled exploitation of forest resources came to be emphasized as the engine for general economic growth.'[325]

Mining in Northeastern Ontario's Shadow

From 1890 to 1940, northern Ontario became the nation's leading metal producer, its mines reaching a prosperous maturity despite the Depression.[326] Yet, as in the years before the war, those to 1930 witnessed no such trends in the northwest. Indeed, the success of Ontario's mining industry was largely focused on the spectacular developments in the northeastern centres of Subdury, Cobalt, the Porcupine, and Kirkland Lake.[327]

In the war years iron was the northwest's major contribution to northern mineral and industrial advance. Lake Superior Corporation's capacity, underused in the rolling of rails for new transcontinentals, was quickly turned to the wartime supply of British munitions and, with the armistice, sought markets for a broader range of products.[328] Meanwhile, its mines in the Michipicoten area were among the most active in Canada. With the initial hematite deposits of the Helen Mine running short, the development of a huge store of siderite on the neighbouring Magpie River followed in 1909. This resulted in the immediate start on a shaft and surface facilities there as well as a rail spur two years later. Experiments were conducted to remove high sulphur content of this ore, employing rotary kilns or roasters with powdered coal as fuel. These successful endeavours resulted in six such sintering machines operating on the Magpie by 1916.[329] Power for this now-large mining effort had been developed at Steep Hill Falls on the Magpie River starting in 1911. Later it was joined by generation from High Falls on the Michipicoten River to power the Helen. At this time, sulphurous ore from the Helen increasingly supplanted the old hematite operation, which closed at war's end, after shipping over 2.7 million tons of ore. Through the slow times at the close of the decade, the Magpie continued to sinter and ship about 100,000 tons annually to Sault Ste Marie and American lower-lake consumers. However, in 1922, production costs and market competition forced its closure.[330] In spite of the sale of Atikokan Mines to Duluth interests in 1921 and rumoured reopening of these in conjunction with the Port Arthur furnace, iron ore production in Ontario stopped until the mid-thirties.[331]

Desultory efforts in other fields covered certain base-metal and some novel demands. Zinc and lead continued to be pursued near Rossport during the war and were mined east of Nipigon and near Dorion over later years.[332] Shortages of sulphur, just before and during the European conflict, generated a short-term market when Japanese, American, and Sicilian sources were lost. Northern Pyrite opened two large mines, one at Goudreau near Wawa and another at Northpines near Sioux Lookout in 1915, to supply munitions needs. The former then closed in 1920, but the latter continued at reduced production until 1928, in the face of returning supplies from Texas and Louisiana.[333]

Gold production trundled on in older fields, with its appeal to local interests and utopian hopes of outside capital. About the Lake of the Woods, such activity was minimal. Along the Seine in the Rainy River District, only famous old mines like the Foley saw further speculative financing.[334] The same indeterminate fate awaited former enterprises at Gold Rock and elsewhere about Dryden as well as the old Empress Mine, north of Jackfish on Superior.[335] At Sturgeon Lake, earlier development, particularly at the St Anthony Mine, continued to stumble along. Accessible now by a rail spur from the National Transcontinental to O'Brien's Landing and a 40-horsepower steamer up the lake, it was in almost constant operation to 1930.[336]

Revived interest in Michipicoten gold came suddenly about 1920, probably in response to Canada's retreat from the gold standard's regulated price of roughly $20.50 an ounce. Higher floating values would persist, with later exception, into the thirties.[337] By 1925, the former Grace Mine (later Darwin) and the old Minto were pumped out and operating, while the local steamers again ran from Sault Ste Marie, packed with new prospectors. With power from the Michipicoten's High Falls and the addition of activity at Jubilee and Parkhill (once the Mariposa), mining and milling here reached an appreciable level by the Depression.[338] Inland a few miles, about Goudreau and east to the CPR at Lochalsh, a few mines, principally the Cline and Goudreau, developed uncertainly on the same electrical supply after 1918.[339] However, none of these old gold fields of the northwest could compete with the modern technology and immense wealth of mines about Timmins and Kirkland Lake.

Yet significant new strikes in the mid-twenties raised hopes of a more lucrative future for northwestern gold and attracted both attention and mining money from the established northeastern centres.[340] Foremost was the Red Lake discovery by the Howey brothers in late 1925 (see Map 3.2). Over the months to follow, this find sponsored a rush north from the nearest rail siding at Hudson of a scale not seen since the days of the Porcupine strike.[341] Howey Red Lake, incorporated in 1926, pushed down a shaft to 500 feet; its early machinery was supplied that next winter by the first sleigh trains up from the Hudson railhead.[342] Early trenching and stripping followed on adjoining properties such as the Madsen and Couchenour-Willans. Regular air service arrived, using the newly invented ski and primitive versions of the pontoon. Rudimentary summer transport over lake and river was eased by marine railways north from Ear Falls in 1929. This promoted erection of a 1,000-ton mill at the Howey on the arrival of hydro from the first Ear Falls generators at the end of the period.[343] By that time other surrounding finds at Uchi Lake and ones even further north in the Berens River country were gathering interest. More important were discoveries in 1928 and subsequent developments just north of Lake St Joseph in Central Patricia, which was discovered from the air by NAME (Northern Aerial Mineral Explorations). In 1930, nascent mines here were joined by plane to Sioux Lookout and by winter road and tractor trains to railway at Savant Lake, 90 miles south.[344]

The second area of rising interest was in the still-lonely territory along the Canadian Northern, east from Lake Nipigon to Longlac. Its capability was harder to prove, but, like Red Lake, its existence had been known many years before.[345] The first rush occurred in 1915 and was followed by a positive Bureau of Mines assessment but little staking. Gold again drew prospectors here to the Jellicoe and Beardmore areas in 1925, when numerous claims were registered but only one mining company was formed. This Toronto-owned Beardmore operation carried out intensive surface exploration, diamond drilling, and underground work before a mill with amalgamation and floatation equipment was built at the end of the decade.[346] As was the case at Red Lake and Central Patricia, the ores of this budding Beardmore/Geraldton gold field were of a lower grade than those of northeastern Ontario. Canada's brief return to the gold standard and a related price slump by 1929, therefore, hampered their development until the early thirties.[347]

Fisheries Past Their Peak

The years of continuing mismanagement in the commercial fishery left stronger and stronger warnings of serious problems for the future, which warnings went ignored by the industry. Indeed, on Superior itself, the peak in gross catch came in 1915, then ebbed.[348] Yet across the northwest as a whole, the total harvest remained around six million pounds a year through the period (see Tables 3.10a and 3.10b). Such figures, however, came to mask a 74 per cent component of species less valued than whitefish and trout, a jump from the already large proportion (42 per cent) prevailing in 1911. Across the region, the fishing-up process was clearly at an advanced stage by the Depression.

Certain technical advances in equipment encouraged the increasing intensity of these operations. In previous decades the traditional fleets of sailboats (mackinaws) had served inshore stations, while tugs with steam lifters expanded onto the offshore grounds with miles more netting. Between 1911 and 1931, as tugs

TABLE 3.10a Commercial Fisheries Catch (in pounds), 1911–1921

	1911	1921
Lake Superior		
Algoma Shore		
Whitefish	356,196	133,453
Lake trout	964,457	577,698
Other	783,212	48,874
Subtotal	2,103,865	760,025
North Shore		
Whitefish	412,635	172,437
Lake trout	1,066,341	521,900
Other	627,230	184,939
Subtotal	2,106,206	879,276
Other lakes		
Whitefish	83,561	1,171,524
Lake trout	24,116	661,371
Other	4,750	134,599
Subtotal	112,427	1,967,494
Total	4,322,498	3,606,795
Western Waters		
Rainy Lake/Lake of the Woods		
Whitefish	663,346	125,500
Lake trout	18,375	7,071
Other	879,837	990,053
Subtotal	1,561,558	1,122,624
Other Lakes		
Whitefish	101,141	259,164
Lake trout	62,101	74,258
Other	418,497	784,701
Subtotal	581,648	1,118,123
Total	2,143,206	2,240,747
Grand Total	6,465,704	5,847,524

Source: Tables accompanying the Reports of the Federal Department of Marine and Fisheries and the Provincial Department of Game and Fisheries, 1912 to 1923.

TABLE 3.10b Commercial Fisheries Catch (in pounds), 1921–1931

	1921	1931
Lake Superior		
Whitefish	1,477,414	255,970
Lake trout	1,760,969	1,328,423
Other	368,412	1,284,305
Subtotal	3,606,795	2,868,698
Western Waters		
Whitefish	384,664	717,270
Lake trout	81,329	113,853
Other	1,774,754	2,126,842
Subtotal	2,240,749	2,957,965
Grand Total	5,847,524	5,826,663

Source: Tables accompanying the Reports of the Federal Department of Marine and Fisheries or the Provincial Department of Game and Fisheries, 1922 to 1932.

grew larger but fewer, the total labour force more than doubled to 700 men across the region, and the mackinaw boat was generally replaced by over 200 gasboats. These versatile vessels greatly intensified the harvest from inshore grounds or inland lakes. Larger vessels with more powerful engines came to work more distant offshore fisheries.[349] Similarly, in the twenties the ice house was combined with the central freezing facility on many operations, an innovation that also encouraged larger catches, whenever those could be obtained. Spoilage or market gluts and low prices could now be avoided, and demand in closed seasons could be served profitably with a frozen and stored product.[350] Nevertheless, the overwhelming cause of the erosion of fish stocks was the continuing immoderate level of harvest each year by an industry, like its forest counterpart, without environmental scruples.

Superior

On the Algoma shore, Booth interests, in the guise of the Dominion Fish Company, continued destructive behaviour and monopolistic operations.[351] Their efforts to strangle any competition and to control all small operators, combined with the export of all the best fish to U.S. consumers, raised public ire in Sault Ste Marie. In 1922, that city's Council petitioned for the confiscation of all the Company's licences up this shore, where the firm had already lost all those south of Batchawana during the war. The upshot was the cancellation of several more net licences north to Alona Bay as well as an important tug licence for the Gargantua Harbour area.[352] However, the next year, Dominion announced that, due to the resultant fall in its profits, its *Caribou* and *Manitou* could no longer maintain a twice-weekly passenger and freight schedule on this shore. That service was essential to the area's residents and tourists, who had no road north of Batchawana. Government was forced to submit to Dominion's tactics, leaving the Gargantua as well as the Michipicoten tug licences in Booth's hands.[353] But the recently confiscated net licences were not returned, and a rising number of small gasboat operators was now to become a thorn in the Company's side, as far north as Montreal River and Agawa Bay. These men totally escaped from the Booth monopoly, selling their catches over the docks at Batchawana to independent fish dealers, who trucked them south to Sault Ste Marie down a gravel highway.[354]

Yet these independent catches must have grown slender by 1931, as must those of the Dominion Fish Company on this shore. Since a decade earlier, the harvest of whitefish and trout here had plummeted to half its pre-war figure. Indeed, coupled with an inexplicable decline in other species, the Algoma total had fallen to a third of earlier catches (see Tables 3.10a and b). While statistics after the early twenties are available only in more aggregated form for both the Canadian side of the lake and adjacent inland waters, there is no reason to believe that this sharp decline did not continue.

Events on the north shore also indicated tightening times for the local members of the fishing community. Again the catch of lesser species along these shores fell sharply and inexplicably after 1911, although their often ethnically based demand continued to grow. Indeed, by far the largest poundage recorded in this category now came from a late fall herring fishery at Thunder Bay and in neighbouring Black Bay, which grew to great importance after 1915.[355] Declines in whitefish and trout along this coast were as steep as in Algoma by 1921 and were followed by a similarly shocking aggregate drop on this lake in the next decade. Under these conditions Booth's monopolistic influence declined early.[356] Several independent companies emerged or persisted at the end of the war, including Nichol Brothers at Port Coldwell, the Nipigon Bay Fish Company at Rossport, as well as a fishermen's cooperative out of these same centres. Yet Thomas Craigie's Fort William Fish Company, Nuttall Fisheries at Hurkett, and Bowman and Company on this shore retained at least marketing ties with the Booth organization.[357] As in years past, Booth's collective harvesting efforts here covered the entire coast north and east from the Pigeon River, as far as Otter Head on the Pukaskwa Peninsula.

Inland Waters

The real changes came not along this shore but in the opening to commercial use of numerous inland lakes in back of it. A few had been so licensed in the vicinity of the Lakehead as early as 1911, but a decade later numerous ones as far east as Hawk Junction and Oba appeared in the records. Collectively these never seem to have provided more than about 150,000 pounds a year.

A large contributor was Lake Nipigon, which previously had remained closed to all but the Native community, except for one brief interval. However, in the late war years the need to supply the troops overseas with 'beef and bacon' caused food shortages at home. These waters and those of other northern lakes, including Long Lake and Nipissing were, therefore, added to the provincial fishery. This solved the problem without cutting into the supplies from the Great Lakes, which were traditionally destined for American markets.[358] After a careful study of Nipigon's potential in the summer of 1917, four firms were contracted to carry out a fall fishery and successfully netted over 100,000 pounds of whitefish and trout in about two months.[359] To the displeasure of the fishing community, who coveted the profits, the newly created Ontario Fish Supply Branch built its own $400,000 plant and wharf at Macdiarmid on the Canadian Northern.[360] Here it erected accommodations, net sheds, and freezing and packing facilities, adding two steam tugs (the *Ombabika* and the *Pytawabek* that had been laid up here since railway-building days. These it leased to the fishermen, whom it continued to contract annually for the lake, while shipping the catch by rail to urban dealers in Montreal and Toronto.[361] By 1919, the harvest in these previously reserved waters reached over two million pounds, a colossal 42 per cent of the entire catch for the Superior area. Of this, the largest proportion was of valuable whitefish. Something approaching this figure was still being taken annually in 1921, greatly enhancing the figures on Table 3.10a for inland lakes of the Superior area. Steady lobbying and complaints by the Dominion Fish Company appear to have pressured the province into selling the project to private enterprise in 1922.[322] However, no single large operator was allowed to monopolize this rich fishery, and the catch continued to be restricted to sale in Canadian rather than U.S. markets.[363] Of the composite figure given for Superior in 1931, something approaching or exceeding one-third probably still came from this one lake. However, its component of lesser species had likely climbed sharply by that time. As on Lake Superior in earlier days, 'commercial fishermen on Lake Nipigon [came in the twenties to] fish three and four times the amount of gill nets they were supposed to ... and there was nobody checking up on them too thoroughly.'[364] The disastrous future of the industry here, as elsewhere, therefore, was assured.

On more westerly waters, the trends of the era followed a different and more complex course. On Lake of the Woods and Rainy Lake, the harvest of whitefish and trout fell sharply in 1915 and never recovered.[365] By 1921 only about 20 per cent of the 1911 catch was being taken, but the tonnage of lesser species (here including large numbers of carp, catfish, and tillibee with the usual pike, pickerel, perch, and mixed coarse fish) had held up (see Table 3.10a). Ironically, local Boards of Trade, which had once fought so loudly for commercial operations, now battled to exclude the industry from the parts of these waters now desired by sport fishermen. Yet the companies doggedly fought back and survived, partly because their fish packets also carried profitable freight and passengers between Kenora, Warroad, and Baudette in Minnesota. These vessels continued to be important on Lake of the Woods in the late twenties and probably ran east from Fort Frances as well.[366]

On the other westerly inland lakes, these fishery trends were reversed. About twenty such bodies of water had appeared in the record for 1911, principally ones accessible from the CPR. Ten years later the number had more than doubled, covering many south towards the Canadian Northern and huge ones north, like Lac Seul on the National Transcontinental. Certain of these are said to have been added in the same drive for additional wartime food supplies as caused the opening of Lake Nipigon.[367] While some were operated by larger companies such as Bowman or Craigie from Superior, many licences were more directly in the hands of numerous gasboat operators.

It was in these increasing inland operations that much of the rapid regional growth in total manpower had been absorbed. Such fisheries, often pursued both winter and summer on larger and deeper lakes, usually had relatively short lives on lesser ones.[368] In 1921 their added use accounted for a doubling of the western whitefish catch and some increase in the take of trout (see Table 3.10a). In addition, as might be predicted from such waters, their harvest increased substantially the poundage of other species caught. Indeed, it more than made up for total losses suffered on Rainy Lake and Lake of the Woods over that decade. The aggregate figures for all western provincial waters in 1931 would indicate that they continued to do so (see Table 3.10b). Thanks largely to their contribution, with that of Nipigon, an official statistical myth of sustained harvest was publicly maintained. However, no one in the industry or in related government research was likely so misled.

Indeed, by 1930, the latter were coming to recognize that farmer Wilmot's long-trusted model for the replenishing of fish stocks through hatcheries and the 'reseeding' of over-harvested areas was wrong.[369] This old technique for renewing nature's bounty had been introduced in the region with the first federal hatchery at Port Arthur, built in 1911 and in operation in 1912.[370] It valiantly attempted both to serve commercial recovery with whitefish, and to renew supplies of speckled trout for the sport fishery. This effort was followed by a second facility, erected by Ottawa at Kenora on donated land. This hatchery also attempted to satisfy the demands of both the commercial and sport fishermen, although each group desired that more than half the capacity of the hatchery be devoted to raising the species it preferred.[371] Ontario entered the field in 1919 with a hatchery dedicated to sport fish on the government plot at Fort Frances and followed it in 1921 with another at Sault Ste Marie for both commercial and sport purposes. A request for a similar dual-purpose facility at Sioux Lookout was never filled, but, in hindsight, there is no modern evidence that had one been built it would have served its designed purpose.[372] Nevertheless, in 1926, wanting to be responsible only for tidal waters, the Department of Marine and Fisheries discontinued its involvement on the Great Lakes, turning over the federal hatcheries to the province.[373] As a result, all responsibility for management of this fishery and for maintenance of its stocks lay firmly with Ontario.

Tourism's Quiet Advance

The economic potential of northern tourism was recognized only vaguely by both government and the general public at the outbreak of war but was in clearer focus by the Depression. Indeed, only in 1922 was a legislative committee struck in Toronto to assess the nature and demand for such recreational activity and the state of the related facilities.[374] One result was the institution of a licensing system to ensure minimum standards of accommodation; another was the initiation of clearer regulations for the survey and disposal of Crown lands for recreational use. As the decade passed, more thorough and consistent rules followed to control the rising levels of sport fishing and hunting, but neither these moves nor the earlier ones gathered much public attention. At the close of the period, therefore, the Minister of Lands and Forests could announce with a semblance of surprise: 'At no point in its history has Ontario been visited by so many tourists. Great demands have come to be placed on hunting and fishing facilities ... and on cottage lots surveyed along lakes suitably near rail or auto access.'[375]

Except in the context of local urban social clubs and fraternal societies, the industry remained almost exclusively middle and upper class and heavily American in its clientele. As far as the Lakehead, participants continued to come overwhelmingly from lower-lake states and more proximal ones. Beyond Superior drainage the prevalent source of tourists remained the U.S. midwest and also Winnipeg. All areas now advertised extensively in attractive brochures including accommodation lists and pictures. They set up displays at major

American exhibitions and sportsman shows; the Lake of the Woods was featured in a movie produced and widely distributed by the CPR.[376] While the automobile enhanced family vacations, the male-oriented hunting or fishing trip remained a very strong element, particularly among the wealthy.[377]

Around Superior

At Sault Ste Marie, the large and popular International Hotel had burned down in 1916, leaving a distinct shortage of tourist accommodation. The return of interest in lake cruise vacations at war's end caused the city some short-term embarrassment in providing rooms for passengers who wished to stop over and sightsee.[378] In the twenties, local people came more frequently to take up cottages and form tent communities along the river, both upstream and downstream of the city, from Bell Point to Pointe aux Pins. In addition, children's camps were established locally near Searchmont, Island Lake, and Gros Cap.[379] To serve the increasing number of Michigan tourists who ferried their cars across to Ontario, rental cabins were established in the area and public camping facilities added in several places, but with particular success at Belleview Park.[380]

Up the Algoma shore, pre-war development continued more slowly for lack of road access beyond Batchawana Bay. There and at Goulais River to the south, cottages became numerous; these were owned by families in Ohio and Michigan who could reach them by car. By 1930 their number was supplemented by visitors to a new resort and more frequent rental properties here.[381] Besides rough camping and fishing by sportsmen along the shore to the north, good lodgings were increasingly available among the scatter of residents at places like Mamainse, Agawa Bay, and the Michipicoten Mission. Like the flourishing hotel at Michipicoten Harbour, the last were accessible twice a week by steamer. Others were reached by motor launch from the head of the road.[382] Such launches were also used along this coast for charter fishing, which was becoming increasingly popular in the twenties.[383]

Up the ACR, recreational development regained its initial momentum quickly after 1918. The beauty of the route – the Agawa Canyon and the Montreal River area, for example – inspired members of the Group of Seven on their first boxcar painting ventures. The railway retained at least some of the rental cabins it had built by 1915 at Anjigami, Agawa River, and Sand Lake. However, it now promoted the private erection of others on lakes with boat access to the line, and left its early outfitter's role to others.[384] Such new outfitting operations, as well as a growing number of elegant lodges with guides and outcamps, quickly appeared as far north as Goudreau and Hawk Junction. By the twenties, they were used by fishing and hunting parties from as far away as Maine, Kentucky, and Indiana.[385] Finally, from the war years the Prairie Club of Chicago came north each summer, chartering a Pullman coach and dining car from the Railway to be pulled in at a siding next to their chosen locale. They were outdone in opulent splendour only by a group of hunters from Grand Rapids who brought their own specially designed railcars as well as their servants and three cooks.[386] Luxury camping had certainly arrived in western Algoma.

At the Lakehead after 1918, local residents continued to expand their tenting and cottaging habits eastward along the railway and on the lower Sibley Peninsula. With the gravelling of the first stretch of the Winnipeg trunk road, those with cars developed similar properties as far west as the shores of Lake Shebandowan.[387] However, nothing in the record suggests that access was yet sufficient to other lakes, like Dog, for such local utilization.

Eastward from Sibley, the Nipigon River continued to attract sport fishermen but its days as a world-famous speckled trout fishery were numbered. Years of trophy fishing had drawn heavily on the stocks and populations of trash fish were growing, despite official efforts at removal or control.[388] The hydro dams, built here by the HEPC in the twenties, also deterred the sportsman, flooding the most valued stretches of rapid water. These projects also deterred spawning because they remained unequipped with migratory fishways until the end of this period.[389] Equally important, large amounts of now-rotting pulpwood from old drives still hampered both the course of the river and the aims of the fisherman.[390] Nevertheless, the new sportsman's lodging, built at Orient Bay by the Canadian Northern, was enlarged in the early twenties and all other local facilities with their Indian guides remained busy up to the Depression.[391] Still farther east, the industry remained more disparate and grew modestly. The old hotel at Rossport increased in popularity with American sportsmen, and the rivers of this shore came into steadier use by adventure-seeking canoeists. The spirit of this majestically lonely landscape (as up the ACR some years earlier) was being transferred to canvass by the Group of Seven.

Within the twin cities themselves changes and additions to past patterns came quickly and lucratively for local businesspeople. The luxury vessels of the CPR and of the newly assembled Canada Steamship Line continued to bring full loads of travellers, excursionists, and vacationers to their docks each summer, as before the war. Such persons helped flood local hotels and other accommodations and generated important tourist dollars for the surrounding area.[392] However, the real jolt to the recreational sector in these years came in 1920 with the opening of a continuous trunk road or highway from Duluth to the Canadian Lakehead. The next summer a rising tide of automobiles negotiated its rough gravels northward, bringing a startling 40,000 visitors annually to the shores of Thunder Bay by 1928.[393] While many came simply for the trip, stayed the night, and returned, an increasing number remained to explore for several days.[394] Both Fort William and Port Arthur created tourist bureaus to serve their need for information. The frequently over-crowded hotels of each came to be augmented, as at Sault Ste Marie, with rental cabins and good camping facilities in public parks.[395] The belated development of northwestern roads, however, prevented motorists from travelling much beyond the limits of the local agricultural pocket. This frustrating situation for those in the isolated communities between here and either the Rainy River country or the northern environs of the Lake of the Woods would be resolved only in the thirties.

West of the Arctic Divide

In the latter area around Kenora, tourism slowed until the armistice, despite attempts to interest Americans in vacations here prior to U.S. involvement in the European conflict.[396] The Winnipeg demand was back to normal by 1919. The world of elegant island estates, rental accommodation in Kenora, and camping communities on nearby Coney Island and elsewhere returned to seasonal prominence. Excursionists regularly raised the already-substantial summer weekend population by three thousand or more.[397] A few miles to the north, Minaki Lodge, built by the Grand Trunk at the war, was also crowded annually with wealthy western visitors. Although burned in 1925, it was soon back in operation. Two years before this fire, the rival CPR had countered with luxury bungalow accommodations on the Lake of the Woods at Devil's Gap (next to Kenora), which it enlarged to thirty units by the end of the decade.[398] While this north end of the lake never drew particular American interest, despite its very fine sport fishing, it came in these years to boast eight busy hotels and lodges in addition to its basic summer cottage trade.[399]

In continuing contrast, the lower reaches of the Lake of the Woods, as well as the territory east across Rainy River and up the Seine, remained a growing American vacation playground. Only the central agricultural townships remained largely uninvolved, except about certain small lakes on their northern fringe. With the opening of the railway north from Duluth to Fort Frances in 1909 and the completion of a bridge at International Falls in 1912, people from Chicago, Duluth, and Minneapolis-St Paul joined the growing numbers from such states as Iowa, Oklahoma, and Nebraska who were attracted here. Most came to hunt and fish.[400]

One population of such sporting devotees continued to use the services of the outfitters of Fort Frances, enjoying the adjacent lake and penetrating as far east as the accommodations of the Mine Centre area. Soon after the war, such visitors also became frequent yearly guests at new lodges and their outcamps at the Cascades and other points north of Rainy Lake on the Manitou waterway.[401] A second large group still preferred the numerous but sometimes older facilities on Sabaskong Bay on southern Lake of the Woods, particularly at or behind Nestor Falls. At least five large businesses had developed here by 1928, at the head of the road north from the Rainy River Trunk. The most famous was the oldest, owned and operated by a local druggist named Calvert. By the early twenties this gentleman was advertising in the best American sports magazines, and his reputation for trophy fish had attracted to his camps an élite U.S. clientele. Indeed, by 1930, his name was becoming a sportsman's watchword among the wealthy membership of men's clubs as far away as Chicago. By that time his operation, capable of 200 visitors a week, employed seventy guides and bore its guests to and from the Rainy River railway station in a commodious new omnibus.[402]

This broad northwestern region was also home to the wilderness recreational potential of Quetico Park. Along its northern boundaries a few straggling fish and hunt camps had developed in the twenties, with access from the Canadian Northern Railway.[403] Created as a game and forest preserve in the earlier era of conservational enthusiasm, it had been designated as a provincial park in 1913. This was no more than a half-hearted attempt to counter the intensive activities of trophy seekers from Minnesota and Canadian hunters, hired to provide game to lumbering operations there. Quetico's southern boundary was the Minnesota border, beyond which lay a considerable band of fresh pine stumps between it and the Superior National Forest. Because of Quetico's growing fame as a wilderness canoe country and its easier access from the American side of the border, the first plan for the conservation of the boundary area here was created by Arthur Carhart of the American Parks Service in 1922.[404] While never acted upon, this management proposal drew much positive interest among ardent Canadian and American conservationists. These same individuals and groups later would form the Quetico-Superior Council in 1928. In their drive for wilderness experiences they became increasingly upset with Shevlin-Clark's continued lumbering activities here and with further hydro dams being considered by Edward W. Backus for this area.[405] These latter schemes, which would alter water levels in boundary lakes and rivers, also drew serious concern from the International Joint Commission beginning in 1925. They also caused the budding Quetico-Superior Council to unveil a grandiose countering plan in 1927, which ignored the international boundary to cover the whole of the huge Rainy Lake watershed. Ontario was most interested in the plan's concepts of forest and wildlife management as well as recreational use. However, it refused to consider the required treaty for this area or the international commission to administer the territory, since both would replace provincial with federal jurisdiction. As a result, while the plan was enthusiastically received by conservationists and later by the U.S. Congress, many years would pass before a compromise acceptable to the province was to appear.[406] In the meantime, friendly cooperation promised by Ontario produced a quiet but modestly positive result for wilderness recreationists and conservationists alike. To the luxuriant and highly contrived vacation patterns prevalent elsewhere in the Rainy Lake country, Quetico came to offer an increasingly popular, important alternative after 1930.

Urban-Oriented Progress

The lethargic official efforts here to complete a trunk road system over these years promoted, by 1930, little improvement in intra-regional transportation beyond the modest level of the agricultural pocket. Rail still dominated in the general collection and distribution system of the northwest. This was also true, along with shipping, in the much larger trans-regional flow of freight and passengers between western and central Canada. The creation of the Canadian National Railway (CNR) in the twenties united the trackage of the Canadian Northern and National Transcontinental, but produced only a few immediate changes.[407] A former plan for a hugely enlarged Grand Trunk terminal at the Lakehead on Mission Island was scrapped in favour of increased use of the well-established Canadian Northern facility in neighbouring Port Arthur. Farther to the north and east, a new stretch of track was laid between Nakina and Longlac, joining the two former systems and promoting more flexible freight routing.[408] However, fears of employment cuts in the existing rail-oriented towns – with their economies built about jobs in roundhouses, at watertowers, coaling depots, and freight yards – proved unfounded.

Smaller Centres

At its most basic level, the pre-war pattern of nodes remained largely unchanged. Only a few small lumbering communities finished their timber, dismantled their equipment, and disappeared, as in the case of McDougall Mills near Sioux Lookout. Others, like Osaquan next to Ignace, were abandoned in the wake of bush fires.[409] Occasionally a mining community was lost, Northpines near Hudson being a prime example, when demand slackened or the ore gave out. The former gold camp at Wawa Lake was not used at this time by Algoma Steel, which built its own dormitories at both Helen and Magpie mines. When these mines closed, Michipicoten Harbour and the Mission were hard pressed to survive the cessation of the ore traffic here in the twenties. In this respect, they shared their plight of survival with several centres in more westerly and now somnolent gold fields, such as Dinorwic, Wabigoon, Gold Rock, and Mine Centre, but they did not die.[410]

The same general stability reigned in larger communities of up to five hundred people. Oba, Franz, and Hawk Junction on the ACR were all very new in 1914 when that trackage finally reached Hearst. While such rail villages as Rainy River, Atikokan, Ignace, Schreiber, and White River were now well established, Hornepayne was also a newcomer, the product of extensive new CNR car shops constructed there about 1924.[411] At this level also was a scatter of agriculturally based communities like Emo, with numerous smaller companions in the Rainy River Valley, or Murillo and Hymers in the farmlands behind Thunder Bay. However, in the long-suffering mining industry, only very new mine towns like Red Lake and its distant supply centre, Hudson on the base of Lac Seul, joined this group before 1930.[412]

More important centres remained sparse and scattered. By the mid-twenties, most were growing pulp and paper towns. Even the smallest and least stable, Dryden, could count a bank, hydro, telephone, water, and sewage among its services. While Kenora and adjacent Keewatin had lost the last vestiges of their sawmills, Backus' pulp and paper endeavours were still accompanied by two large flouring establishments here, as well as the seasonally remunerative tourist industry. His pulp and paper operation at Fort Frances was teamed with the large new lumber mills of Shevlin-Clark and of J.A. Mathieu to the benefit of that town's economy.[413] Only Sioux Lookout, the provisional centre of the recently contemplated Patricia District, rose quickly to a level of urban importance comparable with the above on the basis of sawmills and its railway functions. Indeed, it did so in spite of a fire in 1918 that left few buildings standing and initiated trainloads of relief from outside. Like Kenora and Ignace, it became home to that peculiar northern institution, a railway YMCA, and in common with a much larger range of places, also played host to a Red Cross hospital or outpost facility.[414] After 1927 it would gradually become the administrative and service centre for much of that Patricia portion of the now-huge Kenora District beyond the English and Albany rivers. Nipigon, with its disappointingly brief involvement in pulp manufacture about 1920, was the only community of much importance between the Lakehead, Hearst, and Sault Ste Marie, across what was still the roughest and loneliest part of the region.

By 1930, the population in such incorporated or unincorporated centres and nodes joined that of the three cities of the region to make up most of the 85 per cent that was urban or non-farm. This proportion was well in advance of southern Ontario. Such percentages were still highest in Algoma West and lowest in the strongly agricultural lands of the Rainy River Valley (see Table 3.11). In the Kenora District and behind Thunder Bay, the urban levels remained much closer to the regional average, as they would appear to have done in 1911.

Sault Ste Marie

The reasons behind the Algoma figures are easily discovered. By 1914, the old town plot of Sault Ste Marie and the newer one at adjacent Steelton were both full to overflowing. The rise of suburbs followed, before and after their amal-

TABLE 3.11 Population Profile (percentage urban and rural non-farm), 1911–1931

	1911		1921		1931	
	Pop.	% of total	Pop.	% of total	Pop.	% of total
Algoma West						
Rural non-farm					2,970	11
Urban	14,920	76	21,092	82	23,082	84
Total population	19,528		25,762		27,530	
Thunder Bay District						
Rural non-farm					8,995	14
Urban	27,719	72	35,427	74	46,095	72
Total population	38,321		47,910		63,706	
Rainy River District						
Rural non-farm					3,218	20
Urban	3,189	33	4,553	36	6,872	42
Total population	9,579		12,634		16,491	
Kenora District						
Rural non-farm					4,648	24
Urban	8,665	65	8,880	61	11,602	59
Total population	13,155		14,489		19,539	
Total Northwest						
Rural non-farm					19,831	16
Urban	54,493	67	70,673	70	87,651	69
Total population	80,583		100,795		127,266	

Source: Compiled from the Population tables of the Canada Census, 1911 to 1931.

gamation four years later, and was accompanied by much spill-over into the neighbouring townships.[415] This last development was exacerbated by an increasing number of marginal farmers there. These, during the war, found wage employment in urban industry but kept their rural residences. This trend, now involving farm people from more outlying townships, continued to load this urban fringe through the twenties.[416] At the same time, the population of the urban municipality itself grew only slowly – from 18,000 in 1914 to 23,000 in 1930 – as a result of two inseparable factors. First, the Lake Superior Corporation (LSC), which thrived on rolling rails before the war and regained its momentum in munitions by 1916, maintained employment levels of 2,500 until about 1921. After that date its labour demands varied constantly and inconsistently. Resulting unemployment rates, interacting with the high mobility of immigrant workers, acted as a continuing check on the rate of neighbourhood growth.[417]

Second, attempts to broaden the industrial base here were very largely unsuccessful. Indeed, during the period at least one significant employer, Standard Chemical, disappeared, as did the previously defunct large sawmill that had once supplied wages to a substantial number in the community.[418] Hopes of a shipbuilding and drydock complex, first appearing in 1909, were revived with municipal and federal incentives in 1912–13, then were delayed by the war, and finally came to nothing.[419] Algoma Steel here, by the early twenties, faced declining demand in a dislocated and highly circumscribed marketplace, which defeated most efforts to diversify and modernize. Nevertheless, it remained by far Sault Ste Marie's largest employer, despite its erratic labour needs. Supported in this role by Abitibi, which faltered only late in the twenties, the LSC's iron and steel division was the community's economic bellwether. After the closure of the Corporation's mines at Michipicoten and subsequent reliance on American ore, the corporation wrestled successfully with its financial problems. It resumed real strides in plant improvement in 1926 and in profitability by the late years of the decade. Yet, at the Depression, while it counted more active furnaces and hearths than any other Canadian firm, its location so far from Ontario's industrial heartland made its financial success difficult for investors to understand.[420]

Thunder Bay Centres

At the Lakehead, the twin cities grew encouragingly both during and after the war. Fort William remained the larger, climbing from about 16,500 to over 26,000, while Port Arthur rose from 11,000 to almost 20,000 people. Together they came to number slightly more than 46,000 by 1930, a population exceeding that of most county seats and other cities in southern Ontario. As at Sault Ste Marie, where Italians remained particularly numerous, this urban complex retained a mosaic of growing ethnic neighbourhoods. These often had their own churches and schools as well as continuing hopes for retention of both language and culture. While both cities were homes to people from most European, particularly Slavic, countries by 1930, in Port Arthur the Finns remained the most prominent and numerous group.[421]

In the meantime, final work on Fort William harbour had been completed. This involved only small additions to the massive system of breakwaters that now protected the waterfront of both cities, concentrating instead on finishing an intensive program of deepening on the Kaministiquia and its estuaries and of dredging the last of three large turning basins along its course. This one was at the head of modern freighter navigation near the site of the original town plot (Westfort).[422] Many years would pass before these still-sparring cities would grow to utilize the full capacity of this mammoth Lakehead harbour project begun by Ottawa in 1903. However, as early as 1920, the councils of each city were cautiously looking over a plan for the industrial development of the large frontage that lay between their respective jurisdictions.[423]

The grain trade through these ports grew startlingly over these years. Reports on new elevators, additions to old ones, and related improvements in docks and rail facilities were a common feature in the local press. By the early thirties, each city could count sixteen elevator complexes, those at Fort William storing more than 40 million bushels and those at Port Arthur capable of 52.5 million more.[424] Indeed, between 1913 and 1933, these two ports elevated and shipped over four billion bushels to outside markets.[425] Yet the failure of the business community's dream of a major grain exchange here continued to underline the Lakehead's embarrassingly peripheral position in the management of this, its most famous, function.[426]

In both centres, certain among the industries induced by earlier municipal bonuses to locate here blossomed at least briefly. On the outbreak of war, the Port Arthur Shipyards, with up to 1,200 men, had begun on its first bulk freighter. This, with repair and refit work, tided that firm over the confused months of 1914 when unemployment at the Lakehead ran in the thousands.[427] Through the years to 1920 this yard built forty vessels, mostly lake and ocean freighters, before slow times forced frequent lay-offs and infrequent orders. In the decade to follow it laid only seven more, shorter keels, mostly before 1927. However, it augmented this business with the construction of pulp and paper machinery, which it sold locally as well as from coast to coast.[428]

In Fort William, Canada Car of Montreal, a major manufacturer of railway rolling stock, completed a promised plant in early 1917. Its operation was immediately turned to the construction of mine-sweepers for the French navy and later to vessels for other purchasers.[429] With Great Lake Dredge, which similarly was converted to shipbuilding, its demands quickly drained the city's labour pool. This also put much stress on housing supply, as additional workers migrated from the surrounding rural area.[430] At war's end, Canada Car resumed its intended production of railway rolling stock but, after an initially heavy demand, the financial ills of both Canadian Northern and the Grand Trunk severely reduced orders. By the early twenties this large operation, with a labour capacity of a thousand jobs, was working only spasmodically and in 1924 closed its doors for the rest of the period.[431]

Port Arthur, losing a primary employer with the liquidation of its Pigeon River mills in 1919, and all hope for any revival of its iron smelting dreams after 1921, was hardest hit by post-war unemployment and related labour strife.[432] However, both cities would have suffered even more job losses had a sizeable segment of their labour force not been working in grain handling and the construction that continued on new elevator space. Equally important across these centres were the many new jobs created through the decade, with the appearance of their four pulp and paper mills, as already discussed. Indeed, wages from construction in these fast-growing plants would continue at Great Lakes Paper's large and fast-rising operation to the end of the decade. However, employment in all these mills would dip briefly with slower demand in 1926 and would become less and less regular or available two years later. This principal thrust in pulp and paper introduced a returning focus on regional resources. The substantial wages from the pulp and paper industry, with the addition of the smaller incomes from grain handling and the few successful bonus-based industries, fuelled the economy. Unfortunately, here too, both ownership and decision-making were to remain external and beyond local control. As at Sault Ste Marie and the smaller communities that also suffered from this lack of autonomy, this was a doubtful legacy to carry into the depression years to follow.

Native Reactions

Through the nineties and the three decades after, a pattern of uneven material progress marked the scattered aboriginal communities of the northwest. Echoing earlier, more general assessments, one experienced observer wrote of Treaty 3: 'It may have shorted the Indian in some ways, but they now have twice the food, the clothing and necessities of family life ... as their ancestors ever had.'[433] Such views of established reserve life were amplified with time through steady improvement in housing and in the growing appearance of stoves or ranges, sewing machines, and other domestic amenities or appliances.[434] Surprisingly, however, the Native population climbed from 5,500 in the mid-nineties to only 6,200 in 1931, if the available statistics are to be trusted.[435]

The rate of material advancement no doubt was least in the newer northern communities, where the posts of the Hudson's Bay Company or its sometime rival, Revillon Frères, remained an important focus of barter in fish and fur. However, even on the southern fringes of that vastness beyond the Albany, covered only belatedly by Treaty 9, white activity increasingly touched traditional ways by the onset of the Depression. In the English River watershed, around posts like Osnaburgh House or missions elsewhere, the surveyor gained sporadic employment laying out new reserves.[436] Yet the creation of such tracts as at Eagle Lake, Wabaskang, Grassy Narrows, or Long Lake was not necessarily followed by immediate residency. Until a permanent community appeared, authorities were hard pressed to provide even rudimentary medical attention, and churches found their spiritual cause difficult to address. Accompanying this shift to a sedentary existence on such northerly reserves was a tepid and temporary interest in agriculture. However, this development was more often prompted by the proximal appearance of wage employment, generated by rail development or resource exploitation.[437]

Contrary to these moves to more permanency, shifts and migrations among longer-established reserve populations were common, although most such mobile tendencies had ceased by 1930. For example, the band members who had returned to take up properties at the Goulias and Batchawana missions, after the Pennefather Treaty, had their permanent numbers swollen in the nineties by families returning from the now-damaged fisheries about Whitefish Island in the St Marys River.[438] To this were added those who had resided about the Agawa outpost, closed by the Hudson's Bay Company in 1906, and for whom additional lands had to be acquired by the government.[439] The Gros Cap Reserve at Michipicoten Harbour, once abandoned for points east and inland, now regained much of its former population, only to lose heavily again to the vicinity of the Michipicoten River post. On the closure of this post and the collapse of adjacent gold mining activity, most band members again migrated inland to new homes at Missanabie and near Chapleau.[440] Similarly, the Pic River Reserve lost about half its population to the environs of Mobert in the Pukaskwa Peninsula. Meanwhile, after an internal dispute, splinter elements from the Gull Bay Reserve on Lake Nipigon dispersed to Jackfish Island and Wabinosh House about those waters. Within that same drainage area, some of the Red Rock band moved to local missions at Grand Bay and Lake Helen by the turn of the century, but later relocated in the vicinity of Macdiarmid.[441] Most such adjustments pre-dated 1920 and reflected the shifting wage opportunities for those in older parts of the region.

However, an improving employment picture, quite broadly based, was characteristic across all northwestern districts. Many families from reserves, new and old, came to contribute the lion's share of the thousands of baskets of blueberries now annually shipped east, west, and south.[442] Through the building phase of both the Canadian Northern and National Transcontinental, Natives frequently found wages as guides for survey parties. They also were important as bushworkers along the right of way, as members of construction crews and as labourers in the transport of materials or supplies to contractors along the line.[443] Later they were often employees on section gangs or hired to patrol the tracks as fire rangers.[444] Over the period they were also found in rising numbers in the camps of the forest industry. This kind of work was behind the inland migrations of the Gros Cap band to Chapleau and drew the Pic River membership to Mobert for the harvest of the White River country.[445] Along the Rainy River, settlers commonly employed Natives to help clear new agricultural land, and like those about Superior, the latter found frequent income supplying tug wood and sometimes domestic fuel.[446] Many also continued as commercial fishermen on stations such as Goulais, the Lizards, Michipicoten Island, or at Pays Plat, as well as at Macdiarmid on Lake Nipigon and on the Lake of the Woods. To similar summer and often winter work on inland lakes and rivers they added employment as sportsmen's guides, from Sault Ste Marie to Kenora.[447] By the late twenties Native people were again a prominent element in the work force on the new gold fields, as they had been in the mining efforts of the Seine River, Sturgeon Lake, and Michipicoten areas in earlier years.[448]

On such large and urban-adjacent reserves as Garden River on the St Marys River and Mission Island at the Lakehead, even broader income opportunities were explored. Sometimes the Indians' own timber continued to be a modest source of profit, as did any agricultural production, beyond their own needs, from the acreages they now tilled and herds some now maintained.[449] More importantly, persons from both these bands came to hold jobs in local pulp mills and sawyeries. Some worked the docks of neighbouring ports, served on lake freighters and in the towing trade, or gained experience in construction trades.[450] At the Lakehead, they also earned their way erecting grain elevators, handling grain, and, near the close of the period, helping with the harvest in Manitoba and Saskatchewan.[451] Like the bulk of the work force they joined, Native workers found such employment to be seasonal and sometimes migratory. However, in a strictly material sense, these years were probably the most prosperous Native people had ever enjoyed.

The cultural and social aspects of Native life in the region are much less well documented and some can be only surmised. Working mostly as general labourers, they faced the same bigotry, abuse, and cruelty as did any other minority group. Cultural unfamiliarity with time clocks, schedules, and shifts, as well as a preoccupation with present welfare rather than future security, caused many to be stereotyped as unreliable and unpredictable employees.[452] Their apparent weakness for alcohol and their often trusting approach to those around them left them open to arbitrary treatment and wage discrimination. Even on their reserves they found the rights they believed by treaty to be their own were now open to frequent abuse by corporations and even government agencies, for which redress was far from universal. While fair negotiation with remunerative payment to the Fort William band gained the Grand Trunk its right of way, docks, and harbour property on Mission Island, such Native treatment was a rarity.[453] When, for example, Ontario's HEPC decided to alter conditions on the Nipigon River and the level of the lake above, its last concern was Native property or fishery concerns, although these were loudly expressed. The same was true on Lac Seul with the construction of the first power stations at Ear Falls and the later raising of lake levels.[454] Such arrogantly unjustified action had been paralleled elsewhere in the private community, when power dams were built at Fort Frances and Kenora. However, because these affected white property interests as well, they resulted in corrective legislation after hearings before the International Joint Commission.[455] By 1930, Natives, band by band, had come to recognize what it was really like to be a ward in a white world that they were being trained to enter as equals.

The unfair or ambiguous position of regional Indians in this era is exemplified by events in the Rainy River Valley. Here Ottawa, under Treaty 3 in 1873, had assigned 64,000 agricultural acres in thirteen parcels of varied size to 850 local aboriginals of the Disputed Territory. This had been carried out without consultation with an irate Ontario, which held the grant to be excessive.[456] Its anger was not quenched until the end of negotiations 1907–15, at which time Ottawa and Toronto finally agreed that the province would resume 44,000 acres here, after appropriate joint restitution to and re-accommodation of the Native population. Such procedures, which took place over the decade before 1916, moved 250 people to the one large remaining reserve at Manitou Rapids. The following year the resumed lands were put up to auction for surrounding settlers and, after some problems of pricing, passed into private hands.[457] Yet one must wonder what the bands of the valley thought of these federal–provincial arrangements, which wandered so far from the treaty they had signed and which were made without consulting them.

Officially sponsored religious and educational thrusts into Native life in the region also continued over these decades. Some form of mission aid and training was attempted on most reserves and about ancillary centres. At least in the short term, such efforts gained a dedicated following. Secular education was promoted on all substantial reserves where requested, although its success was questionable, even in the white society around, where schooling came far behind the needs of family farming. The churches continued to promote boarding schools for talented Native youth, seven to seventeen years of age, from across the region. These schools were dedicated to preparation for secondary education as well as to practical trades and domestic arts. Long-existent institutions for boys and now girls at Sault Ste Marie and at the Lakehead were followed by one near Kenora in 1894 and later would include ones north of Dryden and near Sioux Lookout.[458] From these, by 1930, came a modest flow of Native graduates, one not to be disparaged when compared with the proportion of successes in the much larger white rural student population in the rest of the provincial north or south.

However, the attainments of these few must be seen in the context of the accomplishments and more varied drives of the many. Throughout these years achievements towards broader ends were hampered by an ageing Indian Act that treated Native people as adolescents before the law. This out-of-date act continued to direct them towards acculturation which many found unappealing. Indeed, by the 1920s, substantial elements of this regional population were stubbornly trying to retain their Native identity. Increasingly, they resisted the paternal recipe of secular education, religious acceptance, and agricultural support that was forced on them by the Act. Unfortunately, these stirrings towards self-determination struck no sympathetic chords with the public, who were more preoccupied with the exciting possibilities of northern development, or with government officials, for whom the Department of Indian Affairs had, by the 1920s, become a low priority.[459] This lack of leadership in the face of growing calls for Native self-determination was to continue until 1947.

The Vibrant Hinterland

By the Depression the northwest had undergone remarkable growth and change on all fronts. Its territorial limits, jurisdiction, and responsibility, had extended northward in the wake of federal and provincial exploration. So had Ontario's public awareness of its inherent natural wealth. Along with the completion of the regionally oriented Algoma Central Railway, two more sets of transcontinental tracks came to span this vast territory between eastern heartland and prairie west. Its forest industry continued to boom on U.S. and western Canadian demands. Large lumber mills had devoured most of its rich pine and suitable spruce by 1914, while in the post-war decade-and-a-half the pulp and paper economy skyrocketed. By 1929, eight pulp and paper operations held enormous limits, harvested half the provincial pulp cut, and employed the largest segment of the region's population in their woodland operations and mills. Before wartime disruptions, agriculture had remained closely tied to colonial policies of expansion. Yet later developments freed farming from marked seasonal dependence on forest employment. They also helped many farmers progress from colonial subsistence to a moderate cash economy based on both domestic and outside markets. Despite a renewed influx of Scandinavians, the rural population maintained its strong Old Ontario flavour, augmented by others who retreated here from life beyond the western tree-line. Vacationing in the northwest had retained its Edwardian and generally upper-class trappings until the post-war decade. Except for certain local tent or cottage clusters and the élite Winnipeg enclave about Kenora, summer visitors were principally wealthy Americans, usually in search of sporting vacations. The upsurge of middle-class car campers in the twenties further accentuated the U.S. component of the trade but brought with it a strong, family-oriented thrust. Meanwhile, commercial fishing was marred by managerial error, extravagant harvesting, and irresponsible marketing. Mining too began encouragingly in these decades, but silver prices then foundered and gold investment became preoccupied elsewhere, to reappear only near the period's close. In addition, iron, mined briefly at Atikokan and much longer in Michipicoten, ceased by the early twenties because of cheaply available American hematite. As a result of these advances and declines, this growing resource-based economy again witnessed major changes in emphasis.

In conjunction with these changes were improvements to the supportive infrastructure. The first was the expansion of rail routes and the maturation of related nodal facilities as well as an increasing frequency of local sidings. These came to link rural pockets or resource harvesting areas more adequately to urban markets and sources. The gradual rural replacement of the horse by the truck over the twenties also helped to improve this fundamental interaction. However, disappointingly fragmented progress on the national trunk road system still left convenient inter-linkage of the region's scattered parts and pockets far from complete. Second, by 1930, the region's urban side had matured considerably, become more demographically dominant, and added substantially to the rural non-farm element. The three senior members of its hierarchy had come to stand within the twenty largest cities of the province. All three also were now much more involved in the resource-processing side of the regional economy, although the Lakehead centres had first sought a manufacturing base akin to southern Ontario cities through costly municipal bonusing. The now-supportive smaller centres increased considerably in number through the appearance of new rail, mine, mill, and agricultural market centres. However, the peculiar gap between large and small and between functionally varied cities and single-industry towns became more evident. The larger urban centres and many of the lesser ones also grew ethnically varied with substantial infusions of Finns, Italians, and a mix of other European immigrants in the rising work force. Collectively, these improvements in infrastructure, changes in population distribution and composition, and selective advances among resource industries had helped northwestern Ontario advance from awkward economic and social adolescence towards the early stages of developmental maturity. However, by the end of the twenties, the region was already facing the first blows of the hard times that were to test its metal and collective will to survive over the immediate years to come.

4

The Malaise of Depression, Then War, 1930–1950

With the Crash of 1929, Canada and its provincial components entered upon a period of agonizing hardship followed by one of tragic but re-energizing war. The initial U.S. reaction to the dramatic slump in world trade was its protectionist Hawley-Smoot Tariffs of 1930, which prevented profitable entry of a broad span of Canadian imports, from lumber to livestock. However, arrangements finalized with Great Britain in 1932 generated modest preferential markets within the Commonwealth which briefly restored Britain's share in Canadian export trade to 38 per cent. Yet with the bleakest days of the Depression past, reciprocal trade with the United States reached previously unknown levels. War tested Canada's social and economic fibre, broadening and enhancing its industrial cores, while encouraging regulated growth in resource harvesting and processing. As a result, the nation emerged from the reversals of this twenty-year period with a startlingly altered social and economic personality.

Nowhere in Canada were the extreme impacts of these reversals more strongly reflected than in Ontario, which by 1930 had already emerged as a principal focus of economic growth. In the short term, this province would pay dearly for its particularly close trade and investment ties to the Unites States. However in the longer run, these links would strongly further its urban/industrial rise and the much-expanded resource-oriented thrusts that were initiated in wartime.[1]

A Decade of Dislocation, 1930–1940

At the end of the twenties, Ontario's southern counties and northern districts stood in a distinct heartland–hinterland relationship. A young northeast had risen to overshadow, in some ways, an older northwest in a developing New Ontario that now covered almost 90 per cent of provincial territory but made up little more than 10 per cent of the total population. Like similarly vast and under-populated districts in adjoining jurisdictions, northern infrastructure remained weak, communications systems limited, and urban centres narrow in economic function. Given the continuing push for new settlers and new farms, the intensive reliance on resources and resource processing, as well as the heavy dependence on export markets and external investment, New Ontario's reaction to the Great Depression was assuredly distinct from that of Old Ontario.[2]

Yet the impact of the depression decade on the economy and society of the northwest does not always fit well with Ontario's northern historiography. This is particularly true with certain settlement themes, where broad provincial generalizations about rural development are coloured by the final failure of agricultural schemes that had been developed in the Great Clay Belt of northeastern Ontario over these years.[3] Such historical discussions of development do not refer to rapidly rising northwestern tourism, for which there seems little eastern parallel beyond the Huron shore, except on Nipissing and certain lakes like Temagami. On topics like commercial fishing, little has been published, as is the case with transportation. As a result, few comparisons of conditions in the fishing economy can be drawn between the two northern regions.[4] Only in topical areas like mining and forest harvesting, urban industrial impacts, and labour reactions do Depression patterns seem to have been measurably similar across Ontario's north.

A Haven in Farming

The province entered this complex decade with a firm intent to promote further colonization, to encourage better rates of actual settlement, and to facilitate broader advances in agricultural self-sufficiency in New Ontario. With cooperation from other ministries, its now fully fledged Department of Northern Development, under a strong mandate to provide access and promote seasonal employment, was commissioned to manage the task.[5] Most of these goals were weakly pursued in the economic confusion that followed the Crash of 1929. Indeed, deepening depression from 1930 to 1934 and latent but growing public dissatisfaction with northern resource management and exploitive tactics brought sharp reversals to northern policies after mid-decade.[6]

The leading stroke here came in 1935 when, under a new political administration, Premier Hepburn announced that the province was going out of the business of colonization. This ended an era of frontierism that had extended back for a century-and-a-half.[7] However, any deleterious impact stemming from this decision in the rural northwest seems to have been surprisingly small. The related embargo on further township surveys meant little in a region where any serious activity of this type had ceased in the previous decade, as had the related designation of further lands as free grants. What remained open after 1930 was a large residue of old abandoned lots, in which some persons might again see value, and certain marginal ones, which might now warrant speculative possession. In the Thunder Bay District, a few such properties were further subdivided for urban, unemployed families who had been brought north to farm subsistently under a dubious federal–provincial program called Relief Land Settlement.[8] This scheme, which began in 1932, was finally cancelled four years later, but, in the interim, some 143 families were established in areas west of Nipigon. Of these, only 79 remained on their small plots in 1940, a much higher proportion than in other districts where this program had been applied.[9] A few more abandoned or marginal parcels were cancelled from the grant list at the request of local municipalities, who openly labelled them unfit for agriculture.[10] The very large remainder was resumed by the Crown in 1941, with remarkably little local outcry.[11] With this move, another long-standing colonial tradition, the free grant, passed out of existence except for a scatter of veteran lots that were reinstated at federal request in 1946.[12]

The Statistical Evidence

Like the Depression itself, these changes in land policy and practice did little to alter trends in land trading that had been established over prior years (see Table 4.1). A net figure of 1,350 lots was added to the cumulative bank of past locations by 1941. However, this raised the proportion of current private holdings only from 33 to 35 per cent of the total ever held in the region. Ignoring Algoma West, which continued to follow its peculiarly urban-related trends, such proportions were highest in Rainy River (36 per cent) and Kenora (38 per cent) and lowest at the Lakehead (33 per cent). Meanwhile, the level of patenting among these holdings climbed to 98 per cent and would reach 100 per cent by the forties. As a result, the legislation of 1941 removed from the pattern only a few lots that were conceived locally not to have sufficient agricultural merit to be worth patenting, paying taxes on, or retaining.

While the early depression years exacted their toll from all members of the rural northwestern community, the situation appears to have been much less severe for the self-sufficient or subsistent agriculturalist than for the farming bushworker or bogus settler/farmer. The former two categories faced belt-tightening measures, but life for such people had never been easy and the very nature of their principal occupation guaranteed food, shelter, and heat. As elsewhere across the province, their continuing welfare also had much to do with the flexible pattern of general agriculture these farmers followed. By comparison, the now-destitute bush farmer quickly resorted to community charity or government schemes for rural relief. Until the gradual, then quickening,

TABLE 4.1 Evolution of Free Grant Holdings, 1931–1941

	1931	1941
Algoma West		
Cumulative locations	425	427
Locations currently held	198	196
Patented current holdings	194	196
Thunder Bay District		
Cumulative locations	6,695	7,005
Locations currently held	2,132	2,311
Patented current holdings	2,004	2,293
Rainy River District		
Cumulative locations	7,481	8,017
Locations currently held	2,653	2,953
Patented current holdings	3,590	2,922
Kenora District		
Cumulative locations	3,043	3,540
Locations currently held	1,125	1,367
Patented current holdings	1,081	1,236
Total Northwest		
Cumulative locations	17,644	18,992
Locations currently held	6,108	6,827
Patented current holdings	5,896	6,667

Source: Compiled from the Reports of the Department of Lands and Forests, 1932 to 1942.

pace of economic recovery after mid-decade, the majority of these farmers remained trapped on the land and were left to their own devices.[13] Those in the far larger first group found their farms a haven in the most stressful years and then a basis on which to rebuild and progress by the end of the period.

Unfortunately, the available statistics are decennial and do not permit an interim measure of the state of agriculture in 1935. Taken as a whole, these figures reveal that the northwestern population of self-designated farmers in 1931 and 1941 remained around 21,000, although several districts showed a minor decline (see Table 4.2). However, by the close of the thirties, many non-farm people (some of whom were former bush farmers) had been added to the rural community and had reduced the agricultural component to about 40 per cent. This shift was particularly marked around Sault Ste Marie and behind the twin cities on Thunder Bay, but was evident in other pockets where only the Rainy River Valley had added significantly to its total farm population.

TABLE 4.2 Rural Profile, 1931–1941

	1931	1941	
Algoma West			
No. of farms	352	297	(47%)*
Farm population	1,675	1,998	
Rural population	3,127	5,533	
Thunder Bay District			
No. of farms	2,173	2,389	(48%)
Farm population	8,654	8,564	
Rural population	17,611	25,476	
Rainy River District			
No. of farms	1,728	1,858	(53%)
Farm population	6,538	6,981	
Rural population	9,619	11,183	
Kenora District			
No. of farms	945	931	(58%)
Farm population	3,289	3,247	
Rural population	7,937	9,308	
Total Northwest			
No. of farms	5,198	5,475	(51%)
Farm population	21,156	20,790	
Rural population	38,294	51,500	

* Percentage of total farms between 51 and 200 acres in declared farm acreage.
Source: Compiled from Census of Canada, 1931 and 1941.

Actually the number of self-styled farmers had increased slightly over the decade. Both other pockets except Kenora and Algoma were involved, and the total number of farms in the region came to almost 5,500. If the tabulated statistics for 1941 were broken down more fully, they would reveal that 80 per cent of all such units continued to encompass in excess of fifty acres, a situation comparable to that of some southern counties of the day. Indeed, from one-half to four-fifths of all farms in individual districts claimed a minimum of 100 acres, the largest proportions being in the Rainy River Valley and Dryden areas. However, almost half of all units remained, to varying degrees, part-time operations. These included all smaller units as well as others sufficiently close to urban centres for industrial employment. Those farms across each district where bush work remained an important source of added income were still the most numerous. More significantly, almost 40 per cent of all farms were now classed as agriculturally self-sufficient, cash-based units, and most of these must have counted at least 100 acres within their limits.

Figures for agricultural acreage over this Depression decade show surprising improvements by its close, whatever the situation in the harsh early years (see Table 4.3). In all pockets the area under root crops and particularly hay had

TABLE 4.3 Agricultural Development, 1931–1941

	1931		1941	
	Acres	% of total	Acres	% of total
Algoma West				
Cropland	7,233	22	7,196	24
Pasture*	8,305	25	6,154	20
Other†	17,576	53	16,794	56
Total held	33,114		30,144	
Thunder Bay District				
Cropland	53,749	18	59,489	19
Pasture	36,534	12	70,275	22
Other	208,284	70	186,426	59
Total held	298,567		316,190	
Rainy River District				
Cropland	56,650	18	69,646	20
Pasture	45,001	15	90,591	27
Other	208,412	67	180,773	53
Total held	310,063		341,010	
Kenora District				
Cropland	24,092	14	26,776	16
Pasture	23,449	14	45,199	27
Other	121,526	72	95,873	57
Total held	169,067		167,848	
Total Northwest				
Cropland	141,724	17	163,107	19
Pasture	113,289	14	212,219	25
Other	555,798	69	479,866	56
Total held	810,811		855,192	

* Includes both improved and unimproved pasturage.

† Includes woodland, slash, and waste, some of which probably served as pasturage.

Source: Compiled from Agricultural tables, Census of Canada, 1931 and 1941.

grown not only in acreage but also in its proportion of farm area. Except in Algoma West, much more pronounced increases in both these dimensions had occurred in pasturage, while the unused area of woodland and waste on the average farm had declined reciprocally. On this increased pastoral acreage flocks of sheep had almost doubled to 20,000 or more, while cattle numbers climbed about 25 per cent along with horses.

Support from Other Sources

All such tabulations indicate that, by the forties, northwestern farming had left its Depression problems behind, an impression supported by other documentation. These records are brief in their treatment of agricultural hardships in the early thirties. On only one early occasion was an annual fair cancelled 'because of the hard times.'[14] Calls for relief appear only from certain marginal townships near Nipigon, northwest of the Lakehead around Upsala, and about Quibell in the Dryden pocket.[15] Other farm-related references to government aid were limited to notes in the local press intended to alert the needy in any district. Happily, by 1935, comments on improving agricultural prospects and prices were coming to the fore in such sources.[16]

Meanwhile, the rhythm of annual rural events like local ploughing matches and crop or livestock competitions continued from the twenties in surprisingly steady fashion. Each year the traditional two-week short-course was announced for some point in every pocket and was well attended by the men for its agricultural sessions and by the women for its home economy programs. Those held for the few townships about Kenora continued to be sponsored by the Rotarians and staffed from the University of Manitoba.[17] Every autumn was marked by major exhibitions of as long as six days at the Lakehead and Sault Ste Marie. These were attended by several thousand on opening day and came to include midways, grandstand shows, and horse racing by the early thirties.[18] Such features as midways were also added to the agricultural side of the fairs at Emo and Rainy River but were rare among the more modest ones at Kenora, Dryden, Hymers, and nearby Murillo, Upsala, Dorion, and Schreiber (see Map 4.1).[19] Indoor markets continued weekly in all three major urban centres, and one was added at Fort Frances by 1933. In these, as in all other centres with surrounding farm acreages, much civic emphasis during the thirties was placed on local purchasing to protect future agricultural availability.[20]

The importance of the Agricultural Representative in guiding farm development continued over the Depression years and after. Through their support, production of seed potatoes for cooperative, export sale continued quietly and involved a small acreage on many farms.[21] Under such encouragement, over a

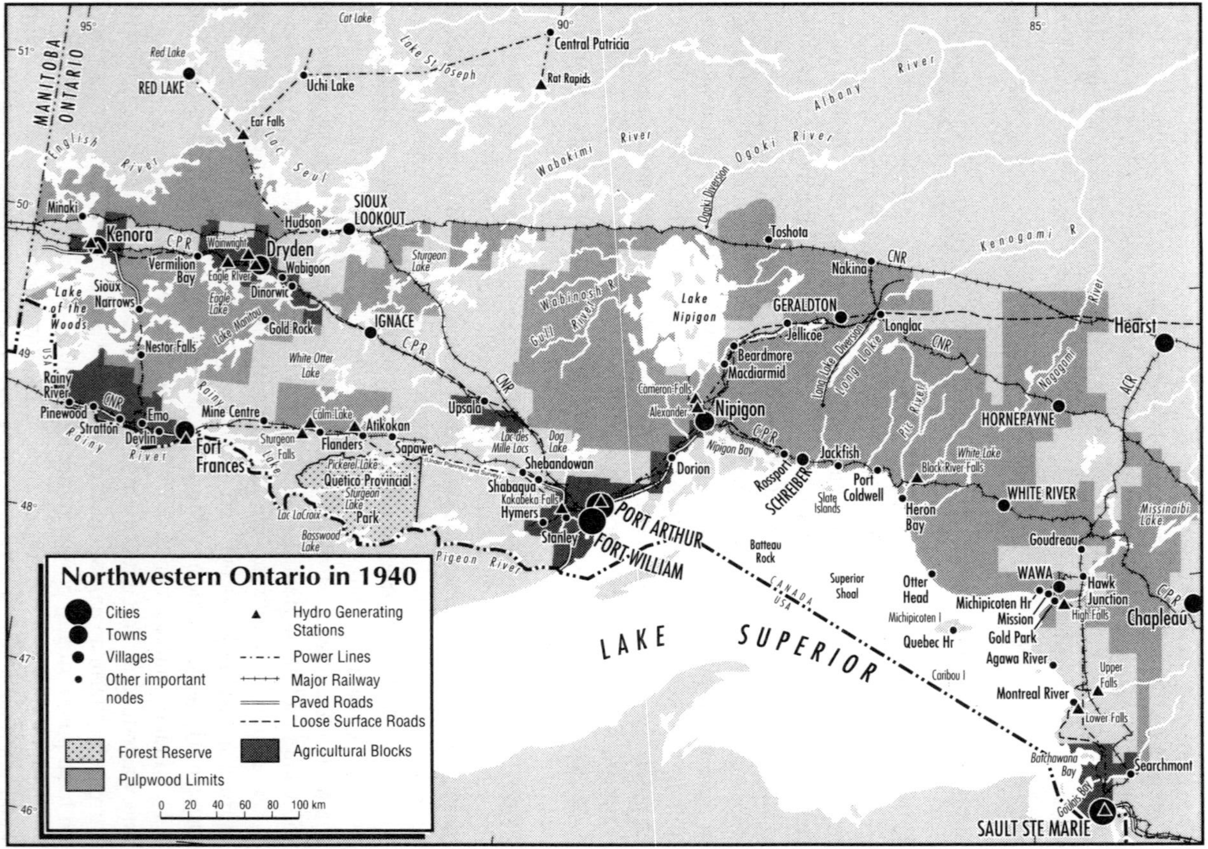
Northwestern Ontario in 1940
Cities
Towns
Villages
Other important nodes
Hydro Generating Stations
Power Lines
Major Railway
Paved Roads
Loose Surface Roads
Forest Reserve
Agricultural Blocks
Pulpwood Limits
0 20 40 60 80 100 km
MANITOBA
ONTARIO
RED LAKE
Red Lake
Cat Lake
Uchi Lake
Central Patricia
Rat Rapids
Lake St Joseph
Ear Falls
Lac Seul
English River
Albany River
Wabokimi River
Ogoki River
Ogoki Diversion
Kenogami R
SIOUX LOOKOUT
Hudson
Minaki
Kenora
CPR
CNR
Vermilion Bay
Wainwright
Eagle River
Eagle Lake
Dryden
Wabigoon
Dinorwic
Sioux Narrows
Lake of the Woods
Lake Manitou
Gold Rock
IGNACE
Sturgeon Lake
White Otter Lake
Nestor Falls
Rainy River
Pinewood
Stratton
Emo
Devlin
Fort Frances
Rainy Lake
Mine Centre
Calm Lake
Atikokan
Sturgeon Falls
Flanders
Sapawe
Pickerel Lake
Quetico Provincial Park
Sturgeon Lake
Lac LaCroix
Basswood Lake
Pigeon River
Upsala
Lac des Mille Lacs
Dog Lake
Shebandowan
Shabaqua
Kakabeka Falls
Hymers
Stanley
PORT ARTHUR
FORT WILLIAM
Wabinosh R
Gull River
Lake Nipigon
Toshota
Nakina
GERALDTON
Jellicoe
Longlac
Long Lake
Long Lake Diversion
Beardmore
Macdiarmid
Cameron Falls
Alexander
Nipigon
Nipigon Bay
Dorion
Rossport
SCHREIBER
Jackfish
Slate Islands
Port Coldwell
Pic River
Black River Falls
White Lake
Heron Bay
HORNEPAYNE
Nagagami River
Hearst
ACR
WHITE RIVER
Missinaibi Lake
Goudreau
WAWA
Hawk Junction
Michipicoten Hr
Mission
High Falls
Chapleau
Gold Park
Agawa River
Upper Falls
Montreal River
Lower Falls
Batchawana Bay
Goulais Bay
Searchmont
SAULT STE MARIE
Batteau Rock
Superior Shoal
Otter Head
Michipicoten I
Quebec Hr
Caribou I
CANADA
USA
LAKE SUPERIOR
95°
90°
85°
51°
50°
49°
48°
47°
46°

MAP 4.1

hundred farmers in Rainy River also began again to experiment with sugar beets as a possible source of cash.[22] Hay was still a principal source of such income, being sold in local urban and bush camp markets, but large tonnages were also railed from the Dryden pocket and Rainy River Valley to Winnipeg each fall. Such western shipments grew truly huge during the prairie droughts of 1935 and 1937.[23] Another important crop dollar on many farms in these last two areas came from the raising of agricultural seed. Under the guidance of the representatives here, initial developments in red clover, begun in the twenties, were broadened by mid-decade to include alsike clover, alfalfa, and timothy; even oats were discussed at one point.[24] Of a thousand farmers in the valley with suitable acreage, over half devoted a field to one or more of these crops by 1934. During that fall they cleaned, bagged, and shipped more than 100,000 pounds of timothy and 70,000 pounds of the others to southern Ontario buyers.[25] Also of importance in this last area was the rising production of hard wheat on land in the lower valley, which a representative in the late twenties had arranged to start draining at government expense. This huge area, which undoubtedly accounted for much of the inordinate jump in crop acreage here by 1941 (see Table 4.3), fostered the construction of substantial grain elevators at both Stratton and Rainy River after 1935.[26]

Livestock advances by the end of the thirties also reflected improving times, the enthusiastic support of the representatives, and the ambitious work of the farmers. In the growing sheep industry, neither Dryden nor Algoma West continued to foster the increases of earlier years. In the outlying areas, where these hardy animals had previously prospered, there were now severe problems with wolves.[27] Despite such predators, sheep became a modest farm element about the Lakehead after their introduction around 1930. On local farms flocks reached about 3,000 head in 1941, although sheep raisers do not seem to have created any significant breeders' association or marketing system for the outside sale of wool or lambs.[28] By contrast, during the early Depression and after, thousands of sheep came to be shipped from Alberta ranches to Mission Island at Fort William. Here they were wintered in shelters and fed on elevator screenings before movement to packers in central Canada.[29]

As in other aspects of agriculture, the real strides were made in the Rainy River Valley. Here the sheep industry was firmly established in the twenties and came to count flocks totalling 17,000 by the opening of the forties. Although prices were undoubtedly low, sheep raising persisted through the harsh years of the early Depression. In 1931, farmers in the valley shipped 2,100 lambs to Winnipeg, and a year later that number reached over 3,000. By 1937 it stood at 4,100, topping 5,000 in 1940.[30] Over a hundred farmers here, coached in breeds and breeding by the local representative, included major flocks as part of their operations at mid-decade. They belonged to the Rainy River Sheep Breeders Co-operative, which at that time baled its annual spring clip at Emo.[31] Subsequently, such preparation was carried out at Devlin and Stratton for the upper and the lower valley respectively. This combined clip, railed south to the Canadian Co-operative Wool Growers for grading and sale, rose from 26,000 pounds in 1935 to over 50,000 pounds by 1940.[32]

With cattle, of which about half were dairy breeds, growth in existing herds was more evenly balanced, if less spectacular, reaching 31,000 head by 1941. Dairymen's associations persisted from the twenties in all areas and through the representatives continued to receive carloads of new breeding stock from government sources on a frequent basis. The representatives used such groups to organize the tubercular testing of all herds, which was now required for milk sale. This program, using local veterinarians, began in 1934 but finished only in spring of 1938.[33] By October of that year, legislation required pasteurization of all milk sold to the public. As elsewhere in the province, this costly requirement proved to be the downfall of independent 'milkmen' who had competed for urban routes with the established dairies.[34] The expense of the equipment bothered few of the latter, a surprising number of which already had pasteurizers in operation. Such enterprises came to be established in mining towns like Geraldton, to which plant all raw milk for its use was brought in by train. They also appeared in mill towns like Sioux Lookout, which developed its own dairy farm in neighbouring Drayton Township.[35] Such operations, along with the remaining co-ops, continued to absorb production from the small farmer, collecting both milk and cream by truck on a daily basis. Around fifty farmers in the Kenora pocket and fifty in Algoma West made up or added to existing dairy supplies. Another 100 at the Lakehead and 130 in the Rainy River Valley followed suit or remained contribution members of co-op creameries. The latter, of which two modest ones remained active around Thunder Bay and three larger operations prevailed in the valley, produced and sold well in excess of 35,000 pounds of butter to major packing houses in 1939.[36] However, attempts to revive cooperative cheese manufacture at Stanley on the Kaministiquia or Pinewood on the lower Rainy River do not seem to have been successful.[37] The same lack of success applied to the once-large cooperative shipments of Christmas turkeys from these areas to both Toronto and Winnipeg stores.[38] In both instances the era of collectivised production was over or was at least coming to an end.

While beef cattle were moderately numerous in this era, they attracted less attention among general farmers than did sheep, for reasons that are not altogether clear. Each pocket had some gainful domestic demand that, in most cases, seems to have absorbed all or most of its beef production. Hence at the

Lakehead, the urban centres provided a substantial market, sometimes served through a local abattoir in Port Arthur but more often through on-farm or in-store butchering.[39] About Sault Ste Marie, cattle were probably much more numerous on the larger farm acreages down the St Marys River, which this study does not cover. The domestic focus, however, was much the same. Neither of these urban-centred areas seems to have been able to compete in Old Ontario markets, for reasons of distance.[40] Production in the Dryden pocket also declined to serve only the immediate demand, even after a successful collective trucking venture forced reduced rail rates for cattle shipped to Winnipeg.[41] However, in the Rainy River Valley, where breeders' clubs remained common, although no cooperative organization ever flourished, exports dominated beef production at least as early as the middle of the thirties. With the help of the representative, well-bred herds were replenished with carloads of new stock obtained from the Livestock Branch. By 1938, several thousand head from small producers moved from local rail sidings down the valley each fall to good prices in Winnipeg stockyards. Indeed, the Agricultural Representatives suggested that more farmers should enter the field.[42]

By the end of the thirties, this regional mosaic of mixed farms across the region had advanced beyond its state in 1929, in spite of the intervening years of hardship. This recovery and improvement on the farm was accompanied by certain other advances in the rural community. All the evidence suggests that horses were still far more common than tractors at the outbreak of war in 1939. However, a rather surprising range and amount of machinery had come to grace the sheds of many farms in the region.[43] A vehicle of some sort – car or truck – was not uncommon on farms. Road building but more often upgrading, through the addition of proper ditches and surfaces more suited to the automobile, continued to offer extra income for the subsistent farmer and to make rural transportation easier. Snowploughing, a service just initiated on the main roads of Old Ontario, began to make its appearance here in the early thirties. Initially, local storekeepers, some farmers, and most pulpwood contractors banded together to keep major secondary roads open in the winter.[44] By 1934, the Department of Northern Development began to purchase suitable machinery for this job. By 1936, when that ministry was absorbed by the Department of Highways, powerful trucks and ploughs maintained at least the principal routes across each pocket.[45] At the close of the decade several hundred miles of roads in most districts were maintained throughout the year, but some of these were more arterial than the major secondaries that farm communities could boast.[46]

Other improvements that made rural life easier also spread slowly during the Depression and after. Commercial radio made its first appearance in this period, even in towns as small as Kenora.[47] Rural telephone, available in all pockets in the twenties, now became universal among rural homes and was accompanied by interlinkage of local systems and connection to long-distance lines. While most rural areas continued to rely on kerosene for lighting, some urban-adjacent expansion in electrical service occurred. About Sault Ste Marie, an earlier power grid in East Korah spread down the remaining concessions of that township by 1936 and added wire through neighbouring Tarentorus by 1939.[48] Behind Fort William, requests for electrical supply began with a petition by seventy-five local farmers in 1928. By 1932 a rural hydro district was formed to manage service for the adjacent townships of Neebing, Paipoonge, and Oliver.[49] However, while plans were made for later extensions here and for rural service in other districts, no further developments were to occur until after 1945. Despite the economic hardships experienced by other sectors, agriculture in the northwest weathered the depressional storm of the early decade with surprising ease. It also returned to its progressive course with an alacrity that northern provincial history rarely acknowledges.

A Failing Fishery

The thirties were tough years for commercial fishing. The industry suffered steep declines in prices during the depression years to mid-decade, with the result that tugs and crews were forced to travel farther and fish harder, against dwindling stocks, to make a living. In Minnesota waters in these years, estimates suggest that harvest outran the rate of replenishment in a ratio of four to one, and no reason exists to believe that over-fishing was any less blatant in northwestern Ontario.[50] The fishing-up process, whereby an increasingly broad range of species had been taken over past decades to fill market demands, now became a fishing-out process, in which basic breeding stocks were being severely reduced. This situation did not go unnoticed in the scientific community or by concerned groups. In 1932, the American Fisheries Society passed resolutions towards legislation to control and conserve fish stocks on Huron, Michigan, and Superior and to protect the sturgeon in the Great Lakes.[51] This was a well-intended gesture, if a little late, but it produced no more effective results than earlier resolutions. Jurisdiction over such matters on the U.S. side belonged to the individual states. They could not agree upon a single policy on which to negotiate an international agreement with Canada. Indeed, a total of twenty-two international conferences at the federal or state/provincial level had been held on such matters over the years to 1936, without any solution. While most states had never legislated closed seasons for whitefish and trout, Ontario's abandonment of such regulations by 1938 did nothing to improve the situation on the lakes.[52] However, conditions became so bad in the thirties that an International Board of Inquiry into the Great Lakes Fishery was struck. At its first meetings in Sault Ste Marie it heard, among others, a plea for cutting the rate of commercial catches 'if it is not already too late.'[53] The issue had become crucial, since the additional ravages of the sea lamprey were already being felt on Michigan and upper Huron, although that eel had not yet appeared above the St Marys Rapids.[54]

As in the case of U.S. statistics for the period, those for northwestern Ontario waters mask much of the problem of over-fishing. Their analysis is made no easier by the level of aggregation at which these provincial statistics were published from the mid-twenties onward (see Table 4.4). During the 1930s, the total regional catch climbed from 6 to over 8 million pounds, the figure for species other than whitefish and trout rising to 60 per cent. The total increase, as well as the increase in such lesser species, came principally from what was now designated 'Northern Inland Waters.' This huge rise in the whitefish catch probably reflects the heavy harvests on Lac Seul, where at least three substantial operations, including Bowman from Nipigon and Superior, were operating from the railhead at Hudson.[55] Like the increases in tonnage of lesser species, it may also reflect growing commercial use of lakes and rivers of the Albany

TABLE 4.4 Commercial Fisheries Catch (in pounds), 1931–1941

	1931	1941
Lake Superior/Related Lakes		
Whitefish	255,970	385,024
Lake trout	1,328,423	1,261,211
Other	1,284,305	1,672,670*
Total	2,868,698	3,318,905
Western Waters		
Whitefish	717,270	1,339,237†
Lake trout	113,853	163,702
Other	2,216,842	3,231,101
Total	2,957,965	4,734,040
Grand Total	5,826,663	8,052,945

* 1.2 million lbs. of this was now herring, very largely from Thunder and Black bays.
† This figure is for 'northern inland waters,' but no clear definition of same is given in the source.
Source: Calculated from tables accompanying the Reports of the Game and Fisheries Department, Ontario, for 1931 and 1941.

watershed, including huge Lake St Joseph. From here the catch was now being flown out to towns like Kenora and Sioux Lookout for freezing and shipment. This expansion of the commercial fishery and the use of aircraft were strongly resented by sportsmen and loudly denounced by groups like the Northern Ontario Tourist Association.[56] In more traditional northwestern areas of commercial harvest, use of Rainy Lake and Lake of the Woods continued, but at decreased catch levels. Hatcheries were largely turned to the production of sport fish, and certain areas and bays were now totally limited to tourist use. Indeed, Minnesota suggested the joint closure of all commercial operations on Rainy Lake, but Ontario did not comply.[57]

The big change on Superior was the demise of Booth Fisheries on the Great Lakes in 1932. Its former Canadian subsidiary, the Dominion Fish Company, retreated from Superior to stations closer to its headquarters at Wiarton on Georgian Bay. The final financial blow for that old trust had been a 40 per cent drop in catch at the same time the fish price plummeted to five cents a pound. Lesser operators, like Bowman, Nichol Brothers, and Royal, now rose to greater prominence.[58] On the Algoma shore, Purvis Fisheries, from upper Huron, bought all Booth's remaining licences, the company fleet, and the facilities at Quebec Harbour on Michipicoten Island in 1933. However, small operators continued to fish from Michipicoten Harbour and all stations south from Agawa and Montreal River. Most of them shipped their catch to Sault Ste Marie by truck from Batchawana and Goulais Bay docks. By 1939, extension of the road north made such shipments possible from Montreal River as well (see Map 4.1).[59]

On the Superior north shore, stations like Heron Bay and ports like Coldwell, Rossport, Jackfish, Nipigon, and Port Arthur were all active. However, their boats were forced to fish extensively on distant grounds. These were as far east as Otter Head, even Michipicoten River, and far out on the lake at Bateau Rock and the recently popular Superior Shoal.[60] Their catch, as was true of Purvis's, came to include large quantities of deepwater species, collectively called chub, which they smoked before marketing, and siscowet (alternatively, siskwit), prized mainly for their oil.[61] As on the Algoma shore, times here were far from easy, even when prices recovered in the later decade. With home waters depleted, catches of trout and whitefish remained modest at best in these communities. So did the harvest of other species, of which by 1941 two-thirds were herring taken exclusively in Thunder Bay each autumn (see Table 4.4). More importantly, the figures over the decade continue to include such inland lakes as Nipigon, which remained moderately bountiful. Here eleven small fishing concerns shipped over a million pounds annually from Macdiarmid near Beardmore to markets in Toronto, Montreal, and Windsor in the late thirties, much of it trout.[62] However, catches, even before that date, were already noted to be in decline as a result of over-exploitation. Clearly, the extravagant days in the northwestern fisheries were over and stringent conditions were coming to prevail.

Troubled Forest Industries

Lumbering

The shrinking lumber industry of New Ontario was hard hit by the events after 1929. Even in the northwest, pine supplies were dwindling, while the best of the sizeable spruce were gone from most easily accessible sites.[63] A U.S. retreat into protectionism in 1930 brought a prohibitive $4.00/thousand feet duty on Canadian lumber, which killed exports, except for the best remaining pine. Even with the 10 per cent Commonwealth preference of 1932, an industry still worth four million to the provincial treasury in 1930 dropped to a quarter of that value over the next three years.[64] To help stumbling operators, government permitted longer periods for interest-free dues payments, then reduced these charges by 60 per cent and finally by an average of 80 per cent.[65] Even so, lumbering remained in difficulty through the decade, its equipment ageing and most of its remaining large mills in want of both timber and markets. While by 1941 the region could still count 190 sawmills with a potential capacity of 1.3 million feet per day, only fourteen were capable of a modest 10,000 feet per day (see Table 4.5). Six accounted for over half the output figure, and the remainder, running on anything from water and steam to gasoline and electricity, were largely part-time operations. Justifiable interest in large and sophisticated mills would not return to Ontario for thirty years.[66]

In Algoma West, a dozen small sawyeries prevailed, principally working the now-tired hardwood stands. Algoma Hardwood, for some years, drove birch down the Carp River to a small mill on Batchawana Bay, from an inland limit of 12,800 acres. Similarly, the Goderich Manufacturing Company took maple, birch, and elm behind Mamainse, using trucks to haul the logs to its booms.[67] The only continuing pine harvest was centred near Glendale, where early tracked vehicles (Lynn Loggers) were introduced with trucks for the haul to the ACR.

TABLE 4.5 Lumber Mills, 1941

Total mills	190
Total capacity/day in bfm*	1,349,500
Total mills +10,000 bf/day	14
Total mills +100,000 bf/day	6

* board foot measure (1 foot x 1 foot x 1 inch)
Source: Archives of Ontario, RG 1, E-12, Lumber Mill Returns 1941.

When this limited supply ran out, the last substantial sawmill at Searchmont closed and was dismantled in 1938.[68]

In the Thunder Bay District, some ninety-eight small operators managed to survive on the second-grade timber remaining to the southwest of the twin cities and up various rail corridors to the north and west. However, no large sawyery again appeared here until E.E. Johnson put a modern plant on Mission Island for his new Great Lakes Lumber Company in 1939. It had an initial capacity of 140,000 feet per day (soon raised to 155,000 feet) and employed 200 hands. Its logs were to be taken from those sections of existing pulpwood limits where sizeable timber was still to be discovered in scattered groves.[69]

To the north and west, where spruce was now the unique source of suitable wood, large saw complexes operated at two points in Patricia, and smaller mills were located at nine rail-oriented sites. The huge but dated machinery from the former Rat Portage Lumber Company near Kenora was moved to Hudson where it sawed logs from the endless sequence of small limits. Farlinger also had a large operation here, along with his facility at Sioux Lookout, but all appear to have been in decline by 1940.[70] At Kenora, Keewatin lumber surrendered its charter in 1932. However, a large replacement, built to utilize over-sized trees from adjacent pulp limits, was working at the period's end. Interestingly, its stock, like that of mills elsewhere, was often located during contemporary aerial forest cruising.[71]

The real heart of northwestern lumber milling remained at Fort Frances, supplied from the Quetico Park, Flanders, and Sapawe areas much farther east. Both Mathieu's Border Lumber (250,000 feet per day) and Shevlin-Clark (800,000 feet per day) ran through the worst Depression years, sometimes on part shifts or shortened seasons for lack of orders. However, by 1934, both companies were up to capacity for at least part of the summer season.[72] Two years later they were experimenting for the first time with winter shifts and adapting trucks and caterpillar tractors to their bush needs. Huge fires in the area of their limits in the late thirties added much salvage work to their existing harvest and round-the-clock operation became common in the mills.[73] However, while Border Lumber negotiated one final limit, Shevlin-Clark closed its doors in 1940 and sold its mills the next year. It had manufactured in its history at Fort Frances over 1.6 billion feet of lumber. The larger of the two sets of machinery, along with its huge building, was dismantled and shipped to Pembroke for re-erection in 1942.[74]

Pulp and Paper

In contrast to the ageing conditions in lumbering, pulp and paper had undergone youthful growth in the twenties, but this development was arrested painfully by the Depression. Only at the close of the thirties would its productive capacity again be on the increase. In the meantime, a total of 6.3 million acres in the Thunder Bay area was apportioned among only four fitfully active mills at the Lakehead. A similar imbalance between harvest potential and productive needs was common to Backus' enormous holdings to the west and Abitibi's situation in Algoma West.[75] The industry's financial dislocation was equally severe. In an attempt to control prices and cut-throat competition, major pulp and paper companies, beginning in the late twenties, had unsuccessfully tried first cartels and then amalgamations. As a result, in 1931, 80 per cent of Canadian operations were under the control of the Backus group, Canadian International Pulp and Paper, the St Lawrence Corporation, and Abitibi Power and Paper.[76] A year later, the first and last were already passing into receivership, and none had the funds either to carry through all the terms of lease agreements or to pay the dues on pulpwood needed from these limits for their continued operation. In order to retain the industry's huge investment against the future and to promote a return of desperately needed employment, the province became a benevolent patron through the disastrous early years of the decade and later.

At Sault Ste Marie, November 1930 witnessed both mill closure and cancellation of all winter cutting plans. The next spring, the receivers acceded to a provincial request to reopen the mill at least slowly, but required a 5 per cent wage reduction in the process.[77] Partial operations over coming months grew to full shifts on five machines by 1934. This gained a penalty-free renewal of the limit for the mill and another 100,000 cords of wood, without dues, for its continued function. By the next spring the facility was up to capacity and would run at that level with increasing regularity to the end of the period, although Abitibi remained in receivership.[78]

Recovery in the Thunder Bay District was more irregular and protracted. All four mills at the Lakehead, three of which were Abitibi affiliates, closed at least briefly at the end of 1930, and Fort William Paper at Mission Island would not successfully reopen until May 1938.[79] The larger Great Lakes Paper plant in Fort William and Abitibi's Thunder Bay Pulp and Paper in Port Arthur were again operating part-time by the spring of 1931. All were making pulp and newsprint for U.S. export from dues-free wood. Along with Abitibi's satellite, Provincial Paper, these mills returned to moderately continuous production by 1936, but even at the end of the decade capacity runs in any one of them were highly unpredictable.[80] By then, the small pulp mill at Nipigon, reopened briefly under Canadian International (Nipigon Corporation) in 1934, was again running.[81]

In Kenora–Rainy River, as elsewhere, initial closure brought local cries for a forced reopening, but these calls were ignored by a province convinced that 'the companies [were] doing their best.'[82] At government request, mill operations under the receivers in Kenora and Fort Frances resumed at partial capacity, with a wage reduction, in 1933. At Dryden, where a similar start-up had been arranged, capacity was reached in 1936. The former Backus mills followed suit, although they would re-emerge from receivership as units in the new Ontario and Minnesota Pulp and Paper Company only in 1941.[83] With this financial resolution, related to an earlier one at Great Lakes and a pending reorganization for Abitibi, the region's pulp and paper industry returned to reasonable health.

Meanwhile, a beneficent Ontario, forgiving dues and ignoring concessional obligations in return for continuing investment and needed employment, acquired considerable leverage in guiding the companies toward recovery. As a result, mills reopened in the early decade and later the various arrangements ending receiverships produced clauses protecting public and provincial interests. In the interim, the province's proration scheme, instituted to assure an equitable distribution of orders, employment, and financial return among the firms, was introduced in 1935. Subsequent refusal by Great Lakes two years later to comply with the rules was countered by a quiet but firm provincial reaction. A later show of open beligerance from Ontario and Minnesota at Fort Frances brought a sudden fivefold increase in its pulpwood dues, which ended the problem.[84]

Ontario's Forest Resources Regulation Act of 1936 followed a review of the unquestionably lavish allocations of northern pulpwood concessions, about which the government had been badgered earlier in the House of Commons. This Act was an aggressive provincial step towards the industry's reconstruction.[85] Armed with this legislation, Ontario set out in 1937 to tailor concession size more closely to the realistic requirements of existing firms and to create new limits from the surplus. Having accepted the province's considerable generosity and still being in a weak financial condition, the corporations were in no position to resist the arbitrary and sometimes ruthless side of the process.

In the extreme west, the former Backus holdings suffered modest trimming north and east of Rainy Lake, but the real losses occurred on the huge English River concession. Some 4,815 square miles from its western end were transferred to the English River Pulp and Paper Company, which promised to add a second mill to Kenora's economy (see Map 4.2). From the eastern portion, a concession of 1,900 square miles was created for Vermillion Lake Pulp and Paper, which planned manufacture of the wood in the Sioux Lookout area. In addition, the rather nebulous agreement in Patricia, once signed with the North West Ontario Development Company, was replaced by one with Western Pulp,

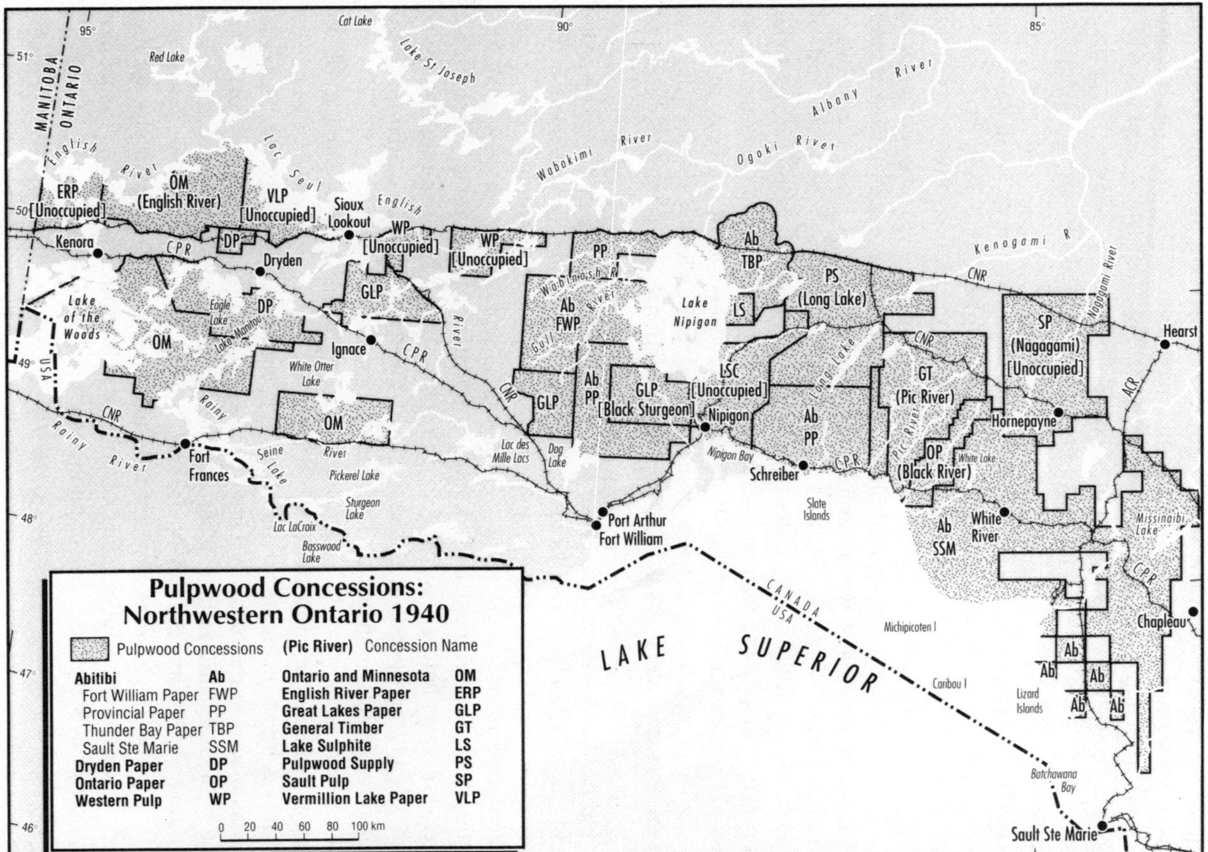
Pulpwood Concessions:
Northwestern Ontario 1940
Pulpwood Concessions
(Pic River) Concession Name
Abitibi Ab
Fort William Paper FWP
Provincial Paper PP
Thunder Bay Paper TBP
Sault Ste Marie SSM
Dryden Paper DP
Ontario Paper OP
Western Pulp WP
Ontario and Minnesota OM
English River Paper ERP
Great Lakes Paper GLP
General Timber GT
Lake Sulphite LS
Pulpwood Supply PS
Sault Pulp SP
Vermillion Lake Paper VLP
0 20 40 60 80 100 km
LAKE SUPERIOR
CANADA
USA
MANITOBA
ONTARIO
Kenora
Dryden
Sioux Lookout
Ignace
Fort Frances
Port Arthur
Fort William
Nipigon
Schreiber
Hornepayne
Hearst
White River
Chapleau
Sault Ste Marie
ERP [Unoccupied]
OM (English River)
VLP [Unoccupied]
WP [Unoccupied]
GLP
DP
OM
PP
Ab FWP
Ab PP
GLP [Black Sturgeon]
LSC [Unoccupied]
Ab TBP
LS
PS (Long Lake)
GT (Pic River)
OP (Black River)
SP (Nagagami) [Unoccupied]
Ab SSM
Lake Nipigon
Lake of the Woods
Lac Seul
Red Lake
Cat Lake
Lake St Joseph
Albany River
Ogoki River
Wabakimi River
English River
Kenogami R
Nagagami River
Rainy River
Rainy Lake
Seine River
Eagle Lake
Lake Manitou
White Otter Lake
Pickerel Lake
Sturgeon Lake
Lac LaCroix
Basswood Lake
Lac des Mille Lacs
Dog Lake
Gull River
Nipigon Bay
Slate Islands
Michipicoten I
Caribou I
Lizard Islands
Batchawana Bay
Missinaibi Lake
White Lake
Pic River
Long Lake
CPR
CNR
ACR
95°
90°
85°
51°
50°
49°
48°
47°
46°

MAP 4.2

which was granted the same tracts near Allan Water and McDougall Mills, in return for a promise of production from a new plant at Fort William. In compensation for land lost to agriculture, Dryden Pulp and Paper received additional acreage to the west of its initial concession. Finally, Backus was permitted to trade parts of his Rainy Lake limit for certain townships east along the Seine.[86]

Such changes were mild in comparison with those exacted in the Lake Nipigon basin and east. The huge accumulation of holdings assembled under Great Lakes Paper was reduced at a stroke by the repossession of its more distant ones: the Long Lake, Pic River, and Nagagami. That firm was left with the Black Sturgeon, was granted pieces of other existing concessions also west of Lake Nipigon, and was awarded certain new holdings along the railways north and west of Lac des Milles Lacs.[87] Lake Sulphite, in return for a mill at Red Rock, got 1,981 square miles carved from the remaining limits about Lake Nipigon.[88] Among the resultant adjustments, Abitibi's Thunder Bay mills lost one old concession but not the Onaman and Ombabika areas northeast of Lake Nipigon. In replacement, it was granted a northern extension to cover the rest of these latter watersheds beyond the former National Transcontinental right of way, as well as a former Great Lakes holding west of Lake Nipigon.[89]

Farther eastward, changes were less radical but resulted in more new concessions and holders. The Long Lake limit, now modestly redefined in the above changes about Lake Nipigon, was taken over by a group of U.S. paper manufacturers under the name of Pulpwood Supply. This arrangement was unusual since it granted the company an export licence for a considerable period of years before it was required to erect a mill.[90] Neighbouring Pic River was slightly expanded, at the expense of the huge old concession of 6,600 square miles once claimed by Abitibi for its mills at Sault Ste Marie. The Pic then passed to another U.S. paper consortium called General Timber, which was granted a lease similar to that of Pulpwood Supply.[91] However, part of this limit was hived off in the arrangement to become the Black River concession. It was placed in the hands of Ontario Paper, yet another U.S.-owned firm, but one with established mills at Thorold, Ontario, that had need of new pulpwood resources.[92] Finally, the old Nagagami limit (2,300 square miles), when resumed from Great Lakes Paper, was turned over to Sault Pulp Products Limited, a subsidiary of Butler Paper of Chicago. This firm promised an immediate mill either at Sault Ste Marie or on the Michipicoten River.[93]

These changes and additions drastically altered the map of forest holdings across the northwest in less than twelve months, anticipating the more effective use of forest resources under returning prosperity. However, by 1940, only the intent had been fulfilled. Neither of the two firms added to the English River country had moved toward mill construction. The same was true of Western Pulp and Paper, which had inherited the older limit in that general area and of Sault Pulp Products on the Nagagami concession.[94] In 1937, Lake Sulphite took up cutting on the limit and operation of the small pulp mill that formerly had been worked by the Nipigon Corporation, while starting work at neighbouring Red Rock on a much larger plant and new town. However, all again came to a halt the next spring with a sudden bankruptcy.[95] Lingering public suspicion of the managerial effectiveness of Lands and Forests was rekindled by these problems. Such suspicions were further fanned by Opposition manoeuvring, forcing a House Committee of Inquiry into departmental operations in 1939. However, subsequent hearings produced neither fruitful corrective suggestions nor conclusively critical proofs.[96]

In fact, given increasingly confused wartime demands which would become more distorted, the industry, under government's persuasive benevolence, was in an enviable stage of recovery. True, only the small and ageing mill at Nipigon had been added even briefly to the eight producers of a decade before.[97] However, overhaul and more intense use of existing machinery had raised total output for the region by 25 per cent over the figure for 1928, with only mechanical pulp manufacture showing decline. Equally important, more than half of the much-increased pulpwood consumption still came from Crown-controlled lands rather than private properties, as it had come to be by 1930.

Throughout the troubled years before 1940, private contractors remained the most common purveyors of pulpwood supplies to these mills, since few manufacturers at this time operated their own camps. As the Depression receded, such suppliers worked more and more frequently, both on company-held Crown limits and on patented or otherwise private lands they controlled.

After Abitibi recommenced cutting in Algoma West in 1932, small contractors still tendered supplies from along the lower ACR. However, real emphasis on Abitibi's limit had shifted to northern areas and camps tributary to the Pukaskwa Depot on the White River or in the area back of Michipicoten.[98] Each was under one large contractor, as was a third area on the upper reaches and interior tributaries of the Michipicoten River itself. This was now worked for Abitibi by Austin and Nicholson, better known for lumber and ties than for pulpwood. Its cut too was driven by water to Superior and towed south to Sault Ste Marie.[99] By 1934, the number of men in Abitibi camps topped a thousand and rose to twice that figure by 1940. At that date, drives again were proceeding on rivers like the Montreal and Agawa, but would have a brief and final history.[100]

North of Superior, the operations of such contractors were more complex, since pulpwood was but one element in a broad harvest that continued to include posts, poles, ties, and pilings. Some contracted large quantities of pulpwood to one mill, but most supplied several or different ones from year to year. The best-known included Campbell-Holmes, D.A. Clark, C.W. Cox, Thomas Falls, C.H. Greer, and the Pigeon River Timber Company.[101] While much of their Lakehead cut came from the limits around Lake Nipigon, some continued to be harvested from other properties as far apart as the upper reaches of the Pigeon-Arrow watersheds and the lower courses of the Black River and the Little Pic.[102] Some of these firms were again capable of 50,000 cords a year by late in the decade, when their collective labour force stood at better than six times the thousand they had employed in 1933.[103]

However, these same operators continued to organize the cut and to deal in the pulpwood produced by settlers, as this source of supply regained substantial markets with domestic mills. Yet, despite its revival and subsequent guarantees of fair in-province prices under the Settler Pulpwood Protection Act of 1937,[104] the availability of this harvest to regional mills was highly varied. About the Lakehead, therefore, mills found themselves heavily dependent upon increasing cuts from their Crown limits through the late thirties. Although such supplies through dealers remained considerable at the Abitibi mills on the St Marys River, much of this cut came south from the retreatied townships or was trucked from areas to the east, as opposed to being from the country behind the city.[105] Interestingly enough, such proximal wood for the Kenora mill was being supplemented by the contractors, before the end of the period, from southeastern areas of Manitoba. About Dryden and Fort Frances mills, however, all or most requirements for manufacture were still provided by local settlers.[106]

Some of this variant pattern in settler production for domestic ends stemmed from government work-creation schemes, begun in the early thirties and based on renewal of such pulpwood exports to the United States. These schemes were experiments, at first unique to the Thunder Bay District, and were intended not only to supplement subsistent farm incomes, but also to solve severe unemployment among bushworkers. Beginning in 1931, contractors here were permitted to clear for U.S. sale as much pulpwood from specified Crown lands – cut, hauled, and peeled by local labour – as they purchased from settlers or hired bushmen to cut on other acreage. These agreements, as of the next year, carried dues lowered from $1.40 to $1.00 a cord for Crown-cut spruce, but specifically excluded any sale to U.S. newsprint manufacturers and retained an old twenty-five-cents-a-cord export duty.[107] They were arranged by individual Order in Council and proved modestly popular, given the prevailing market conditions. After mid-decade, operators in other districts easily accessible to the United States, like Algoma and Rainy River, were encouraged to enter similar arrangements. Some did, but less enthusiastically (see Table 4.6).

By that time, all export charges had been dropped. Ontario was moving increasingly on every front to use its forest resources to stimulate job markets and reduce relief costs, rather than to bolster its public coffers.[108] Later in the decade, the province even signed previously mentioned export agreements with American firms like Pulpwood Supply and General Timber to promote further bush employment. To the same end, they placed the Black River under Ontario and Quebec Paper, although its mills were in southern Ontario. Two other concessional agreements of 1937 permitted U.S. sales of pulpwood. The amount was to be equivalent to a third of the total harvest from the newly hived-off parts of the old English River Limit, but only when the requisite mills were in production. Along with these promotions went the continuing export of thousands of cords through Michipicoten Harbour, by Newyago and other firms with U.S. affiliation. This wood came from old railway leases up the ACR and from settlers in Clay Belt townships around Hearst.[109]

The northwest was pre-eminent in this export market. Of a provincial total of 1.9 million cords for the decade, 85 per cent came from the territory west of the St Marys River. For reasons given above, such pulpwood export was exclusive to the Thunder Bay District until mid-decade, when it came to include some contributions from other areas. At the Lakehead, at least, this market offered a viable alternative to domestic sale for settler-cut pulp, and the impact

TABLE 4.6 Pulpwood Exports (in cords), 1931–1941

	Kenora	Ft Frances	Sioux L.	Lakehead	Sault	Total
1931				860		860
1932				35,407		35,407
1933				26,240		26,240
1934				84,042		84,042
1935				40,005		40,005
1936				111,922		111,922
1937		388		201,151		201,539
1938	111	33,143		238,589		271,843
1939		6,411		212,542	2,072	221,025
1940		9,115		298,774	1,257	309,146
1941		4,987	138	292,611	1,655	299,382
Total	111	54,044	138	1,542,143	4,984	1,601,411

Source: Archives of Ontario, RG 1, E-5, vol. 18, Pulpwood Exports.

is evident in the heavy reliance of mills there on Crown-land harvesting. Its sudden success in 1936 no doubt reflects in part the removal of all export duties on pulpwood, as well as the improving economic conditions. However, one suspects that the peak exports of 1940, which were roughly comparable to half the domestic demand for the region (compare Tables 4.6 and 4.7), were proportionally high for the later years of the period.

Recovery and Labour Strife

By 1940, the general mechanics of the industry had returned to a most encouraging state across the region (see Table 4.7). The home demand for pulpwood stood again in excess of 600,000 cords, slightly more than half of which now came from company Crown concessions. The proportion of Crown-cut wood and settler cut in the supply of these provincial mills, however, was varied with the level of access the settler had to the now-much-expanded export market. Because of the harsh economic realities of the past decade, mill capacity, like equipment and technology, had not changed significantly since the late twenties. While over-all plant capability remained almost 2,000T/day, chemical pulp production stayed at less than half that of mechanical (groundwood), and newsprint output was roughly ten times that of other paper. In terms of capacity and production, however, each mill was different from every other. These tabulated measures underline the nature of Canadian industry, in which the level and nature of activity continued to be influenced by American finance, products, and markets.

The combined domestic and export cut for 1940, of more than 900,000 cords from the region, was certainly a mammoth increase over the slender harvests of the early thirties when woodland unemployment ran rampant. In those deepest years of economic dislocation, bushworkers who could find work at all faced declining wages and deteriorating camp conditions, as falling pulpwood prices pared profits for the operators.[110] Serious labour reaction was quick to appear. Indeed, the first strike in the northwest centred on the Lakehead in 1930, prompted by the unexplained deaths of two union organizers attempting entry to camps near Shabaqua the previous winter.[111] Severe unrest in the same district in 1933 focused partially on wages, but also on food and housing conditions in some camps. This bitter dispute with the Lakehead Lumberman's Association, involving labour violence and strike-breaking tactics, raged from June until December, when a fragile truce was finally arranged.[112] The same year saw a revolt and ugly attempts at strike-breaking in some of the lumber camps of the Rainy River District. The next year similar actions occurred north

TABLE 4.7 Pulp and Paper Production, 1940

	Source		Mill	Production			
	Pulpwood (cords)	Crown Cut (%)	Capacity (T/Day)	Chemical	Mechanical (T/Annum)	Newsprint	Paper
Algoma West							
Sault Ste Marie							
Abitibi Paper	114,271	43	306	25,702	65,733	74,449	5,989
Thunder Bay District							
Port Arthur							
Provincial Paper	62,248	91	100	22,069	15,498	–	27,196
Thunder Bay Paper	68,825	91	276	10,838	52,027	61,526–	
Fort William							
Abitibi Paper	42,994	91	184	6,083	33,254	38,671	–
Great Lakes Paper	91,915	58	368	7,868	323	97,397	–
Red Rock							
Lake Sulphite	–	–	–	–	–	–	–
English River Pulp	10,706	93	36	–	12,046	–	–
Rainy River District							
Fort Frances							
Fort Frances Paper	69,374	24	290	–	71,033	66,987	–
Kenora District							
Kenora							
Kenora Paper	100,497	34	280	19,082	70,883	84,046	–
Dryden							
Dryden Paper	53,653	42	80	13,585	34	–	8,228
Total Northwest	614,483	63	1,920	105,227	320,781	423,076	41,413

Source: Archives of Ontario, RG 1, E-5, vol. 19, Reports on Pulp and Paper Production.

of Sault Ste Marie.[113] Labour disputes flared up along Superior's north shore through the spring and early summer of 1935 in camps of the Nipigon area and east to those of the Pukaskwa. By the end of the year, the most recalcitrant among the association of fourteen operators at the Lakehead were forced to agree to labour's demands. However, the short-term settlement came only after weeks of heated negotiation at Port Arthur.[114]

Meanwhile, Ontario, reacting to these disruptive events and concerned with their cause, initiated an inquiry into the situation here and elsewhere in troubled northern lumber camps. The result was the Woodsman's Employment Inquiry Act, which laid down firm and realistic conditions of employment for the industry. The stage was finally set for one moderate collective agreement, covering all bush operations from the Black River to the Manitoba border. This binding agreement for the northwest was concluded in the spring of 1936.[115] Returning good times and calmer labour conditions were both important stimulants in the renewed vigour and positive outlook that marked pulp and paper production at the beginning of the forties.

Unfortunately, one important aspect of our modern forest industry – stewardship, or conservation – had received little firm or energetic support from either government or industry in the twenties. The tough economic times of the thirties promoted continuing inaction, even deterioration, in these important areas of forest management. Provincial legislation of the pre-Depression days had never been put into practice, with the result that pest protection, reforestation measures, and policies to assure sustained yield remained little more than theoretical.[116] Even the unique efforts of Abitibi in the twenties to establish an experimental tree-planting program in Algoma West were not continued or reintroduced in the thirties.[117] Quiet work by government foresters and forestry students over the years, however, produced Ontario's first forest inventory in 1930. Unfortunately, a purge of such professional personnel by other elements in Lands and Forests followed, under the guise of cost cutting. This crippled the early effective use of this remarkable set of maps and reduced the overall professional field staff in the northwest from 120 to 46.[118] These moves produced no counter-reaction from the public. People were dulled by hard times and momentarily forced by expediency to ignore the long-term impact of rising forest exploitation in favour of short-term employment and economic renewal.

Surprises with Metals

In the autumn of 1930, the *Northern Miner* announced: 'industry is flat and unemployment runs high, but not in Northern Ontario's mining camps.' The following July it published a lead article entitled 'North West Ontario Awakens to a New Dawn and Fair Outlook.'[119] The first pronouncement referred to an unexpected bonanza in mineral production, which would continue through the decade, and the second to the revitalization that such success helped bring to mining in the northwest. The region's bad reputation in foreign money markets, earned before 1900, had dissipated at last. New gold discoveries of the later twenties had also started a broad regional revival of investment in exploration and development.[120] This was aided in 1934 by two events: the foremost was an increase in the price of gold from $20 to $35 an ounce; the other was the merger of the Standard Stock and Mining Exchange, with its sullied past, and the Toronto Stock Exchange, with its impeccable reputation.[121] Investors might look askance at new taxes, once applied only to nickel and now levied on all metals, but they came to accept these charges because of otherwise sympathetic government mining regulations.[122]

Gold

The initial interest in gold, of which Ontario was now the largest Canadian producer, was felt in every old gold field across the northwestern districts as local men, for want of work in other vocations, went mining. Many old shafts and tips were reopened or re-examined early in the decade, and the press was full of rumoured reactivations or reported re-capitalizations. In addition, each mining district across the region announced sharp increases in registered claims and declining rates of later cancellations, as prospecting increased and more exploration ensued.[123]

After the hike in the gold price, most old fields witnessed at least speculative reactivation of former producers. On the Lake of the Woods, the most successful was the Wendego, which went into serious operation in 1935, but others, like the Kenricia, also operated profitably.[124] The Little Klondike south of Dinorwic, the Sakoose north-east of White Otter Lake and on eastward to the Straw Lake Beach and Moss shortly followed suit. At Gold Rock near Dryden, to which the government had now opened a good road, several old mines, including the Laurentian and Big Master on Lake Manitou, gathered considerable new investment and plant.[125] Of those around Mine Centre, the Foley, Olive, and Upper Seine all ran busily for at least a short time. East of the Lakehead, the North Shore and Empress in the Schreiber area saw similar revival. Few were more than marginally successful at the bank.[126]

Indeed, the four most substantial mines of the region (Wendego, Kenricia, Straw Lake Beach, and Upper Seine) in 1940 had a combined output of only about $600,000 (see Table 4.8). Around Sturgeon Lake, north of Ignace, the St Anthony mine, with renewed American financing, installed a new plant,

TABLE 4.8 Gold Production Value (in dollars), 1940

Red Lake Field	8,642,271
Pickle Lake Field	4,709,585
Beardmore/Geraldton Field	9,620,330
Kenora/Rainy River Field	609,739
Total*	23,581,925

* Ignores lingering output from Sturgeon Lake and Michipicoten areas.
Source: *Northern Miner*, March 16, 1941.

including a hydro station, in 1932. It was soon joined by several other active properties, at least one of which became a producing mine. Despite lulls in rich ore supplies over the years, in 1940 the St Anthony was still a profitable operation, with an annual output of almost half a million dollars.[127]

In the larger Michipicoten field, activity continued and grew from the late twenties, both around Goudreau-Lochalsh and adjacent to the rising Gold Park townsite south of Wawa Lake. In the former patch of claims, the Krezmar, Goudreau, and Cline were reassessed, but only the Cline was eventually returned to operation. After 1939, its ore grade fell steeply, and this, with other complications, caused closure in the early forties.[128] Elsewhere near Gold Park, the Parkhill, with its up-to-date machinery, operated through the early thirties but was rejoined by the refinanced Minto/Jubilee in 1933 and the Grace (renamed Darwin) the following season.[129] After 1934, around Gold Park, both the Darwin and Parkhill were driven to new depths, each producing steady profits of $20,000 to $40,000 a month. However, a sudden depletion of rich ore closed the first in 1938 and the second in 1940.[130]

But it was now the big new mines, with their substantial financing and modern equipment, that spelled real success in northwestern gold. These developments were based on the transplant of previous northeastern experience, skills, innovations, and finances and were concentrated in the recently discovered fields of Red Lake/Central Patricia as well as Beardmore/Geraldton. With their lower-grade ores, however, neither area grew particularly active until gold reached $36 an ounce.[131]

At Red Lake, only the Howey (judged Ontario's most efficient mine) kept operating through the early thirties, when it retired its final debts. Other properties here carried out surface exploration, but only the McKenzie erected machinery and sank a shaft before 1934.[132] By then, the first mine at the related discoveries on Woman Lake had begun.[133] In 1940, the number of producing mines about Red Lake had risen to a dozen, including more isolated ones at Berens River and Uchi Lake.[134] Collectively that year, Red Lake mines produced over $8.5 million of gold (see Table 4.8). To the east about Pickle Lake, near Central Patricia, north of Lake St Joseph, only two large producers developed. The Central Patricia came first with a shaft and mill by 1930. However, lower-than-predicted grades of ore combined with the depressed economy to force reorganization, and a fire delayed resumption of operation until 1933.[135] It was followed into production that year by the nearby Pickle Crow, and both were reported in very good ore by 1934.[136] Intense large-scale production then raised their combined output to astonishing levels of as much as $4.7 million in 1940.

Across the 'Seventy Miles of Gold,' as the stretch east of Lake Nipigon from Beardmore to Geraldton came to be known, developments followed a similar pattern but at a slower pace. However, much prospecting and exploration in this area east of Lake Nipigon had yet to occur as the decade opened.[137] The initial mine at Beardmore continued operation through the early thirties, passing to U.S. backers as the Northern Empire in 1933. The first serious finds in the Geraldton area were reported in late 1931 and test drilling there started the next year, with underground work at the Little Long Lac begun in 1933. Meanwhile, rumours of gold around Jellicoe appeared in the press,[138] yet skilled prospecting must have been proceeding silently along the entire corridor. When the popular rush began in 1934, the major speculators and well-known members of the mining community had already carved their places. Some had quietly located their private Pullman cars at nearby sidings. Others who worked through third parties remained behind the financial scene in Toronto.[139] By the end of 1936, nine substantial mines were being worked between the rising towns of Geraldton and Beardmore, each of which could claim three in their immediate area, with the Sturgeon River, Tombill, and Bankfield between. Many more properties, from Long Lac and Caramat in the east to distant Toshota to the north, were being worked at least speculatively. Most important, total production had already reached $7.1 million by 1937.[140] At the end of the decade the number of producers rose to eleven, and annual output hit $9.6 million (see Table 4.8). By that date gold production across the northwest was said to be almost 100 per cent greater than in the late twenties.[141]

Iron

Iron was second in regional importance, despite its late reappearance in the decade. Government bonuses, offered in the late twenties to encourage iron mining in Ontario, failed to motivate the Lake Superior Corporation to reopen either the Magpie Mine or the Helen closer to Wawa Lake.[142] By that time, American steel producers were beginning to recognize the finite future of their own hematite supplies about Superior and to look speculatively at these siderite deposits previously worked early in the century. Indeed, in 1930, the huge Bethlehem Corporation gained permission to drill the Ruth claim in the Goetz Range here. It later abandoned this exploration due to unacceptably high arsenic levels in the ore.[143] Research at the University of Michigan capitalized on practical experience gained at the Magpie to devise larger and more efficient sintering machines with which to remove more of the sulphur from such siderite ores.[144] The Lake Superior Corporation itself undertook an assessment of the potential of these deposits in the Goetz Range in 1934. This evaluation suggested profitable operation, if a government bounty were forthcoming and if some exchange of siderite for American hematite could be arranged for a usable mix in the furnaces at Sault Ste Marie. Nevertheless, in 1935, with mill activity starting to recover at Sault Ste Marie, the company's fleet was still importing U.S. ore from about Superior and coal from Lake Erie ports.[145]

In the spring of that year, Sir James Dunn, after years of trying, gained control of the Lake Superior Corporation with its Michipicoten Mines and mills at Sault Ste Marie, now called Algoma Steel, replacing the old conservative management style with a new, vital, and aggressive approach.[146] Reopening the mines and diversifying the mills were assigned high priorities. Under the newly created Algoma Ore Properties, assessments, evaluation, and plans for redevelopment of the Helen proceeded rapidly. For these projects, Dunn himself raised the capital in the United States and negotiated a substantial bonus with government for the first ten years of production.[147]

By early 1937, with all arrangements in place, the task of reopening was begun, taking until the autumn of 1939 to complete. A fire after closure in the early twenties had completely destroyed any plant, so that work began from scratch. Even the loading docks at Michipicoten Harbour were very dilapidated after years of disuse.[148] At the pits, a long, diagonal shaft and skip system was developed to carry the ore to a large and modern sintering plant.[149] On the nearby plot of the long-abandoned mining town of Wawa City rose the new company community of Wawa.[150] When production began in July 1939, the sintering plant was turning out 1,200 tons of 54 per cent iron each day, but with experience this output rose to 1,600 tons. Any output that exceeded Algoma's own requirements was shipped to Hanna Steel in Cleveland in exchange for hematite.[151] In contrast to earlier operations, the mine and beneficiating plant worked through the year, stockpiling in winter for shipment later by the company's fleet. This return to production marked the first iron mining in Canada since 1922.[152]

Meanwhile, rumours of a huge iron discovery near Atikokan, west of the Lakehead, hit the press in early 1938.[153] As previously noted, knowledge of rich deposits in this area dates back to 1866 or before, and one location had been worked briefly before 1911 by the Atikokan Iron Company for the furnace at Port Arthur. Later, glacially strewn boulders of pure hematite had been identified, but the lode remained hidden until the winter of 1930–1. At that date, test drilling through the ice suggested that it lay under Steep Rock Lake.[154] Delayed by the Depression, more extensive drilling began again in late 1937 and proved successful the next spring.[155] Development plans followed on the heels of further assessments, which established the existence of a hundred million tons of ore.[156] However, these plans faced huge engineering problems and staggering costs associated with the dewatering and dredging of this large body of water. Combined with early wartime trouble in raising funds, these problems delayed the real start of this enormous task until 1943.[157]

Roads and Hydro Systems

Ironically, rapid progress on the long-awaited trunk road system, which had seen so many delays and broken promises since its inception, finally came with the socioeconomic upheaval of the thirties.[158] Under the depressed conditions that opened that decade, this national road-building scheme was rapidly converted into a massive employment project, jointly funded by Ottawa and the provinces, in the northwest as elsewhere. By the summer of 1931, 3,500 men using 300 teams of horses were at work in some thirty-five road camps in the Thunder Bay District alone. Twenty-eight more tent communities were set up west towards Kenora, with an equivalent number in the Rainy River country, as well as a number along the Lake Superior Road north of Sault Ste Marie. This level of seasonal activity, involving from eight to ten thousand men, was typical across the region until 1936. By then much of the northwestern effort was complete and the federal–provincial alliance was entering a troubled interlude.[159]

Some of these road workers were local settlers or unemployed men from the forest industry. About half were men from Old Ontario's urban industrial centres where the situation was most desperate. Such import of workers was sometimes questioned heatedly within the region where it was felt that priority should be given to the local labour force.[160] Living arrangements in these camps varied. Workers were paid 30 cents an hour for an eight-hour day, with 75 cents reserved for board and lodging, no princely arrangement even in those hard times. Under good camp foremen, the drudgery of the work was relieved by sports, sometimes including competitions or ball tournaments with other local people in surrounding communities. Under less able or considerate leadership, however, the experience could be grinding and embittering.[161]

These untrained and often unmotivated pick-and-shovel crews may not have generated the best results. Nevertheless, they produced several hundred miles of passable gravel road in the northwest during the most arduous years of the Depression and later. A good road was opened from Fort William, by way of Dryden, to Kenora and on to the Manitoba border by 1934. Two years later, the route from Kenora to Fort Frances was completed, with a bridge at Sioux Narrows. At the close of 1937, the much-improved trunk road from Port Arthur was opened across the Nipigon River, west to Schreiber, and work was well advanced on the route from Nipigon, north and east towards Kapuskasing. The last was open to Geraldton in 1940, and on to Hearst with a final link there by 1943. As a result, the region finally had the semblance of a highway system and Ontario could be said to have acquired its first interprovincial linkage.

However, with these final moves, the province had placed itself in an embarrassing position from which it could not immediately extricate itself. Long adhering to its 1912 decision against any road between the Lakehead and Sault Ste Marie for reasons of exorbitant costs, it had bowed to federal pressure for an exploratory survey from Nipigon to Schreiber in 1928. From the formal announcement of this survey, Queen's Park was battered by lobbies, petitions, and pleas from both the northeast and northwest. The former demanded a route from Schreiber to White River, north to Hearst, and east across the Great Clay Belt to Kapuskasing, then south to North Bay. The latter fought for a road from White River to Michipicoten and hence to North Bay, by way of Sault Ste Marie and Sudbury. In July 1931 the two northern factions met at the North Bay Conference and a vote of the delegates approved the Sault Ste Marie route, or so northwest interests continued to claim. Ontario, however, knowing this course to be the more expensive, refused to be drawn into a decision. However, it continued healthy support to the Lake Superior Road and initiated aerial exploration of the White River to Michipicoten route. Again responding to heavy federal pressure in 1934, it agreed to an eventual extension of the jointly funded road east from Schreiber to White River. But a year later Toronto announced it was still considering three routes from the latter: White River to Sault Ste Marie, White River to Hearst, and Nipigon to Hearst by way of the new Geraldton gold field. It added coyly that it would approve any two on which Ottawa agreed to share the costs, although it knew that such lavish support was beyond the capacity of hard-pressed federal coffers at the time.

Because of cooling relations between Ottawa and Toronto and the advent of war in 1939, there matters would stand for a decade. However, a statement by the premier of Ontario on the opening of the road to Geraldton in 1940 made it very clear that the current trunk road would reach east across the Clay Belt rather than down the side of Superior. By 1940, the Northern Development

Department, which had been emasculated by Hepburn in 1936, had its road-building responsibilities removed to the Department of Highways. This ended over eighty years of separate northern and southern road administration in the province. Equally important, northwestern Ontario now had a reasonably developed intra-regional transport system and the means to improve those commercial urban linkages that had remained so weak for so many decades.

Coincident with these developments in road linkage, hydro sources and transmission fields were expanded among the industrial cities, resource towns, and mining communities of the region.[162] In 1930, the first Ontario Hydro Electric Power Commission (HEPC) generators at Ear Falls began to supply the gold field around Red Lake, over private lines established by the Howey Mine there. On the Nipigon, the Cameron station was joined by the spectacular generation at Alexander Falls, from water stored behind the then-largest control dam in the world. To the west, private stations at Kouchiching Falls and up the Seine, on the head of the Winnipeg River, and on the Wabigoon powered industry at Fort Frances, Kenora, and Dryden. To the east, these were joined by the old generators at Sault Ste Marie and a reactivated plant at High Falls on the Michipicoten under Great Lakes Power, as well as several private generators at the Lakehead. Collectively, these advances had a respectable capacity of over 218,000 kilowatts by 1930.

Through the thirties, Dryden Paper added a small station on the Eagle River. The HEPC added capacity at Ear Falls to meet Red Lake's growing needs and erected a small generator at Rat Rapids to satisfy the mines at Pickle Lake. In this process it fostered higher water levels on Lac Seul, which generated much relief work in an attempt to salvage timber from the area to be flooded. It also added another sequence of marine railways on the route to Lake St Joseph, paralleling those from Ear Falls to Red Lake.[163] With large additional supplies on the Montreal River by Great Lakes Power and small ones both at a mine on Berens River and by Ontario Paper on the Black River, the total capacity was raised modestly to 294,000 kilowatts by 1940.

The most ambitious projects, however, arose from certain HEPC surveys of the interlaced stream pattern along the James Bay divide in 1925. The first proposal was either for the capture of much Albany drainage as a sixth Great Lake or for similar diversion of only some of this vast potential to southerly generators. In either case, redirection was to be from the Ogoki River into Lake Nipigon. While the second alternative was quite plausible, no immediate action followed. Ten years later a parallel plan was advanced to divert Kenogami–Long Lake flow into Superior. It called for prior forest clearance from the storage area behind the proposed Kenogami dam and about Long Lake, where levels were to rise six feet, forcing flow south to the Aguasabon River and

Lake Superior.[164] This scheme initiated cutting by Pulpwood Supply on the Long Lake Limit in the later thirties. Because of official concern over interbasin transfers for hydro generation, the short man-made channel between Long Lake and the Aguasabon headwaters remained only a shallow pulp canal into the next decade. However, the Ogoki diversion south from a principal dam at Waboose Rapids was permitted by a joint Canada–U.S. agreement to add its significant flow through the turbines on the Nipigon River. The immediate electrical contribution of such arctic waters to generation down the lakes was estimated at 270,000 kilowatts, of which 7,500 were taken at the Canadian Sault Ste Marie.

Hand in hand with increased production went broadening northwestern transmission. As noted previously, short-distance movement from power site to market had begun by 1910 between Kakabeka and Thunder Bay soon after the perfection of alternating current. About 1920 had come a longer line between Cameron Falls and Thunder Bay. By 1930, Great Lakes Power was building a 112-mile line south to Sault Ste Marie from its enlarged Michipicoten plant, pioneering the use of an aluminum conductor. Within three years it had extended this line north to the reactivated iron deposits at Wawa and mines at Goudreau, the former becoming a key part of Sir James Dunn's Algoma empire. Similarly, hydro from the new stations on the Seine River was being transmitted to Fort Frances and International Falls by 1930, while that from Ear Falls was flowing north to Red Lake. By World War II, HEPC power from Ear Falls also served mines and communities about Sioux Lookout and Uchi Lake (with an extension to Casumit Lake). In addition, it reached Crow River, where these lines joined those from Rat Rapids. In 1941 Ear Falls power also came south to augment the mill supply at Dryden. By that time, Nipigon stations had been providing energy to eleven rising gold mines around Beardmore, Geraldton, and Longlac for several years. A line also supplied some Manitoba hydro to the Ontario-Minnesota paper plant in Kenora. By wartime, the urban, industrial, and mineral foci of the region were well supplied, and public power had come to the fore over private production.

Tourism under Adverse Conditions

Recognizing tourism's lucrative potential, Ontario now began to aggressively promote that industry during this period. In 1931 it initiated the first official tourist literature for the U.S. market and appropriated funding for information booths to handle local questions and arrangements.[165] The impact of this move is impossible to measure, given the period's high unemployment. Indeed, this adolescent industry frequently gave conflicting signals during the early decade. Despite the Depression, the sport trade of the Rainy River country witnessed a substantial increase in American participation in 1931 and after.[166] The luxurious CPR lodge near Kenora continued, between 1930 and 1934, to be booked full as many as three years in advance, while the competitive CNR facility at Minaki sank into the red and suspended operations in 1933.[167] Minnesota's highway rebuilding north to Pigeon River by 1931 was expected to attract more tourists to the Canadian Lakehead than the 46,000 of the previous year, yet the numbers actually fell by about 25 per cent over the next two summers.[168] In contrast, at Sault Ste Marie, 1931 saw an increase of 13,000 travellers over 1930, this largely American influx reaching nearly 80,000 by 1933. However, this figure included travellers destined for the Huron north shore as well as Algoma West.[169]

Such conflicting trends began to subside by about 1934. Automobile traffic over the new road from Winnipeg joined the railway in transporting a tide of returning visitors. These flooded facilities at Kenora most weekends, and the old regatta reappeared as a significant summer event.[170] Striking increases in bridge traffic at Fort Frances broke all records by 1935, the preponderance of these visitors still originating from homes in the U.S. midwest.[171] At the Lakehead, visitors by car, principally from Minnesota and Wisconsin, reached 50,000 at mid-decade, in addition to excursionists and cruise participants from lower-lake ports.[172] Over 90,000 visitors to Canada brought cars across the St Marys River by ferry in 1935, when all the old-established tourist areas could be said to have returned to or surpassed their pre-Depression popularity.[173]

Tourist operators here, now employing a range of advertisements, from films and radio ads to glossy brochures and booths at major exhibitions, moved quickly to increase their share of the U.S. market. At the close of the period, about sixty commercial camps and lodges served the Lake of the Woods, now with a trunk route down its east side. A sizeable number of such facilities could also be found about Rainy lake and on the northern and western fringes of the adjacent valley.[174] Road touring was now increasing the popularity of old sporting retreats like Nipigon and Rossport on Superior's north shore. The Silver Islet community had come to include a hundred cottages, while 700 more lined Thunder Bay, with more on inland lakes as far as Whitefish, to the south of the twin cities, and Shebandowan, to the northwest.[175] Most of these areas were home to increasing local demands for vacation properties. In addition to a major cottage complex near Sault Ste Marie at Pointe aux Pins were well-established facilities in that city itself. A steady increase in cottaging was apparent from Goulais Bay north to Batchawana. Equally important, some twenty-four major lodge complexes now dotted Algoma West, up the Superior shore, accessible by launch as well as along the route of the ACR, being reached by boat from rail.[176]

In this sturdy if mixed growth, the automobile and its now frequently middle-class owner continued to play an important role in shaping the nature of current vacationing.[177] However, the key to the industry's expansion into new regional areas was the rapidly completed trunk road system that provided automobile access. Completion of the route from Fort William to Kenora and beyond in 1935 created the first simple lodgings and camps at Quibell, Eagle River, Eagle Lake, Dryden, nearby Waldhof, and Ignace. The additions of a few campgrounds along the route and further cottage complexes at Vermilion Bay and Dinorwic by 1940 were modest but positive strides, as was the first advertising south of the border.[178] Similarly, tourist accommodations, served earlier by rail at Sioux Lookout, increased in number when a road north from Dinorwic opened the waters and shores of Lac Seul to sporting opportunities.[179] Likewise, the completion of the trunk route north from Nipigon, to Beardmore and then Geraldton, opened part of Lake Nipigon and the surrounding area to auto access and tourist dollars.[180] From such terminal points both here and in older-established areas, fly-in operations using small planes to convey parties to wilderness areas began to appear, serving the demands of the more adventurous hunter, fisherman, or canoeist by 1940.[181] While the number seems suspiciously high, approximately 500 outfitters and tourist operators were said to have been licensed by Ontario in the northwest at the outbreak of war.[182]

Urban Travail

Like those in the rest of Ontario, the cities and towns of the northwest suffered in the Depression. Yet little in the census of 1931 indicates the depth and complexities of these urban difficulties to mid-decade or hints at the trends in recovery that marked the rest of the period. However, the figures do give some clues (see Table 4.9). For example, while the population of the northwest rose by roughly 42,500 from 1931 to 1941, the urban component climbed by only a third of that amount. Indeed, if annual municipal statistics for Sault Ste Marie are any indication, urban numbers stagnated or fell slowly to 1936, recovered modestly by 1940, then leapt ahead with the impetus of war.[183]

Yet, over the same ten years, the census reflects a healthy increase in the rural non-farm proportion, sometimes quite spectacular in the city-centred districts of Thunder Bay and Algoma West. Some of this rebalancing reflects early wartime pressure on urban industrial housing, which caused an immediate spill-over of residency into neighbouring townships. However, much of this trend was due to back-to-the-land migration during the earlier thirties.[184] Nev-

TABLE 4.9 Population Profile (percentage urban and rural non-farm), 1931–1941

	1931		1941	
	Pop.	% of total	Pop.	% of total
Algoma West				
Rural non-farm	2,970	11	3,540	11
Urban	23,082	84	25,794	80
Total population	27,530		32,215	
Thunder Bay District				
Rural non-farm	8,995	14	16,912	20
Urban	46,095	72	57,990	68
Total population	63,706		85,200	
Rainy River District				
Rural non-farm	3,218	20	4,202	22
Urban	6,872	42	7,102	37
Total population	16,491		19,132	
Kenora District				
Rural non-farm	4,648	24	6,061	18
Urban	11,602	59	12,623	38
Total population	19,539		33,372	
Total Northwest				
Rural non-farm	19,831	16	30,710	18
Urban	87,651	6	103,509	61
Total population	127,266		169,919	

Source: Compiled from the Census of Canada, 1931 and 1941.

ertheless, the severity of industrial disruption in the decade caused the long-dominant, urban/rural, non-farm total to register a proportional fall across the region, except in the Thunder Bay District.

Other, more detailed, records reveal that the urban work force, with its heavy industrial dependence, was shockingly vulnerable to the tough reverses in the economy. Unemployment, already a regional problem in pulp and paper communities, steepened abruptly in early 1930, as mills closed, other industries cut back drastically, and businesses failed in a continuing spiral of urban decline. Simultaneously, relief costs for municipalities and government agencies escalated, while tax revenues and other sources of public finance plummeted. In Sault Ste Marie, the city fathers faced serious tax arrears by the steel mills and were forced finally to sue the Algoma companies for sufficient sums to cover the city's operating costs. Sioux Lookout, able to collect only half of its tax bill at mid-decade, was forced for a time to operate without any municipal administration.[185] After the Ontario election of 1934, the political slogan 'put the men back to work' became an operating maxim in the battle to reduce relief costs.[186]

Within urban communities of any size, unemployment affected both transient and resident workers. In the first category fell the army of single men who, in their seasonal migration from job to job, gathered each fall in centres like Thunder Bay and Sault Ste Marie, waiting for winter work in the bush camps. However, as of the autumn of 1930, little such employment was available and their destitution plagued both cities and towns.[187] This unwelcomed addition to heavy domestic relief rolls kept local aid basic and brief in duration. Yet not all these unfortunates could be employed in make-work projects such as building airstrips for National Defence or roads for the province. Not even special projects such as the clearance of pulpwood about Lac Seul, ahead of the rising waters now storing behind the enlarged dam at Ear Falls, could keep everyone working.[188] Those unable to be accommodated in such ways joined the wave of unemployed who flocked anywhere that work was rumoured. For these men, many of whom had limited English and fought resultant prejudice as well, the early thirties must have left dreadful memories.[189]

Residential unemployment was generally more prevalent and usually weighed more heavily on the municipal conscience. However, single men were treated the same as the transients, unless local dependents were involved.[190] Married men with families usually could gain access to garden plots on municipal land to grow food, or to Crown lands to cut fuel for domestic consumption.[191] In most communities, authorities rationed employment among such family heads for what capital works they could muster, from drainage and sewer extensions to street repairs and park creation. Such relief work came and went as industries reopened even briefly or the railways sponsored a flurry of periodic activity on tracks in various divisional units. Rather than bear the stigma of unemployment, most of the labour force accepted pay cuts, if jobs could be retained even temporarily or part-time, except where the offered working conditions were absurd.[192] The burden on the families of steel workers at Sault Ste Marie, or elevator personnel at the Lakehead, or rail or mill workers elsewhere, was often crushing. Those unable to support themselves often retreated to the homes of rural parents or subsisted as rural squatters.[193]

Yet these conditions did not touch all urban communities in the same way, to the same extent, or even for the same length of time. At Sault Ste Marie, the decline was steep but recovery was rapid, as has already been noted in pulp and paper manufacture there. The steel mills, which had planned to broaden their range of products before severe financial problems struck, were progressively reorganized after Dunn's take-over in 1935.[194] Diversification into channels and I-beam manufacture, plate, and tin-plate brought growing sales, expanding plants, and high employment by the beginning of wartime demand.[195] With the rapid development of the new Chromium Mining and Smelting Company and the firm return of Abitibi to healthy employment, the combined work force of these major industries ran over 3,000 before 1940.[196] As a result, the municipal corporation re-entered upon a solid fiscal position, having retired its depression debts and returned its relief budget to normalcy.[197]

Around the Lakehead, the revival of both shore-based and dock-side industry was slightly more protracted. While most recovery among pulp and paper mills came early, the return of Abitibi's Mission mill was very tardy. In grain handling, poverty prices followed by periodic prairie drought delayed any rebound to even modest levels of employment until 1937. Nevertheless, Canada Car, inactive for fifteen years, was by that date beginning to produce military aircraft for small powers like Turkey and its work force would climb by 1940, in response to orders for bombers to serve in Europe.[198] Similarly, Port Arthur Shipbuilding, idle for a decade, reopened its yard in 1939 to build corvettes and later minesweepers for the Canadian navy, using a labour force of 500 by 1941.[199] By that time, a long-abandoned starch works, also a product of the earlier era of industrial bonusing at the Lakehead, had been converted to shell manufacture, adding to war-related employment.[200] These belated increments to the wage bill provided a final lift to the more lethargic recovery of the twin cities. This revival also gained impetus through new employment from the large sawmills of the Great Lakes Lumber Company as of 1940.[201]

Elsewhere, forest, railway, and a few mining communities followed different and often less-fortunate patterns. At Fort Frances, hard times in both mills and camps of the forest industry were followed by years of slowly returning employment, before the closure of Shevlin-Clark's huge plant in 1940. Similarly, Kenora retained its pulp and paper operations but lost permanently the newer of its two large flour mills (the Robin Hood) to fire in 1939.[202] Both centres, however, continued to benefit from the seasonal cushion of tourism, a growing source of regional income in which the older paper town of Dryden and the newer centre of Sioux Lookout had come to share. The latter, holding despairing hopes of more participation in the pulp industry, was recovering from the loss of Farlinger's large saw operations to fire. It was also disturbed by recurrent bouts of railway unemployment and was among the region's most troubled centres throughout the decade.[203] Such rail-related problems were shared by Ignace, Schreiber, Hornepayne, and White River, which also rode the economic roller-coaster of single-industry communities over these years. However, such communities ended the decade less dismally than Nipigon, where construction jobs on the new Red Rock paper facility and future work in that mill evaporated in the 1938 collapse of Lake Sulphite. That fiasco left the town with some railway jobs, a scatter of seasonal sources, but only sixty permanent positions in its antiquated pulp plant.[204] This community came close to sharing the fate of Goudreau and Gold Park, which fell silent and largely empty by 1940 on the closure of the last mines of the Michipicoten gold field (see Table 4.8).[205]

In contrast, other mine towns or villages, like Red Lake, Pickle Lake, Beardmore, Geraldton, and Wawa, were flourishing on the outbreak of war. The first four were the new foci of specialized services, from the professions, banks, and businesses, to newspapers, dairies, and continuation schools. Each served a surrounding cluster of mine dormitories of varied number, which had few amenities beyond the company store and sometimes a public school.[206] Like the gold industry that spawned them, these places developed during the thirties and were little touched by the Depression. Wawa was specifically constructed at the end of the thirties for Algoma Steel and its Helen iron mine. The idea of a service centre with satellite mining villages was a direct transplant from northeastern Ontario, of an older laissez-faire approach to mine development. The centralized community of Wawa pointed the way to an increasingly planned model for mining as well as for other single-industry towns of the northwest.[207] For the moment, however, the most significant developments within the overall urban pattern were growing intra-regional linkage by trunk road and rising service by public or private hydro from local generation or more distant sources.

Engines of War, New Prospects with Peace, 1940–1950

When Canada declared war in September 1939, it was confronted by a complex logistical task that was to be hampered at every level by a still-uncoordinated recovery from the Depression. Only a year later was the country readying a master plan for full mobilization, resource allocation, industrial priorities, and domestic regulation. By the spring of 1941 this plan was in place. As already indicated for northwestern Ontario, the wartime stimulation of the economy, along with rising rates of military enlistment, was rapidly eliminating lingering unemployment.[208]

With peace after mid-decade, the national, provincial, and regional patterns of life and work had again to adjust to buoyant post-war times. While some restrictions and controls were to be retained or even reinstituted over months of demobilization, many official and private plans for the future were cast, even before the fighting stopped. In Ontario, legislation promoting the now-predominant urban industrial society was passed in 1944 and implemented with the creation of the Department of Planning and Development the next year.[209] Similarly, key industries that were encouraged by Ottawa to expand during the war were now planning to convert their production to peaceful ends. Others were mapping out schedules for future modernization and development when victory was assured.[210] Just as some understandable delays had preceded mobilization, so demobilization was plagued by awkward problems, including fierce labour disputes, after hostilities ceased. Some of these troubles lingered till the latter part of the decade. Events, developments, and emerging patterns of resource exploitation in the northwest clearly illustrate this war-related double adjustment that pervaded the social and economic climate of the forties.

The Rebalance in Mining

Northern Ontario entered World War II as the nation's leading producer of precious metals, with rising hopes of international importance in iron ore. Wartime demands decidedly changed this situation, emphasizing the regional mining and related processing of the latter metal.[211] These changes and events altered the complexion of mining and primary manufacture in both the northeast and northwest by the beginning of the fifties.

Gold

Ontario's northern gold production declined steeply as the war progressed, and its revival was tentative during the immediate post-war years. In 1939, the province had promised measures to encourage even higher records of gold production than already achieved and so fund the import of U.S. war materials. A year later, this plan to give the industry a high priority for wartime growth was adopted by Ottawa for the nation as a whole and created a flutter of interest. However, as the inevitable entry of the Americans into the battle became clear, this priority was cancelled, with devastating effect on all but the richest mines.[212] After the war, gold mining was caught between rising costs and an officially fixed price, causing investors to shy away from the industry, particularly its exploration and development side. The industry was also encumbered by many old mines, dated in technology, inefficient, and running low on commercial ore. When early post-war attempts to subsidize this sagging industry failed to gain public acceptance, Ottawa initiated the Emergency Gold Mine Assistance Act in 1948, which is said to have assisted weaker companies.[213]

The impact of wartime stresses was first felt in the oldest gold fields of northwestern Ontario. On the removal of the high priority for gold production mentioned above, the last mine in the Wawa/Goudreau area was abandoned, to fill with water in 1942, and that same year the St Anthony finally folded on Sturgeon Lake.[214] Within twelve months, the Wendego closed on Lake of the Woods, and ones of the Seine River, east of Rainy Lake, went into liquidation. Others about Gold Rock, near Dryden, and to the southeast as far as the Shabaqua area, west of the Lakehead, also seem to have petered out by 1943.[215] None of these would attract further attention for at least a decade.

The war's effect on newer and richer fields was less disastrous but not less pronounced. In the Geraldton/Beardmore area, five large producers cleaned up their ore stocks and closed by the end of 1943 for the duration of the war.[216] The few that remained limped on with drastically curtailed operations, and only the Leitch added to its capital equipment.[217] Most revived quickly, if briefly, on war's end. About Red Lake and Pickle Lake in the Patricia, production was severely cut by 1943, although only three significant pre-war producers closed out their operations. Indeed, at Red Lake, several mines remained in very solid financial condition through the rest of the war.[218] During the rest of the forties, these fields demonstrated their resilience by their quick return to full production. By 1946, output from both was again climbing, and two years later the Central Patricia and the Pickle Crow in the Pickle Lake field were enjoying production and sales not seen since the beginning of the decade. Before 1950, they were energetically involved in shaft deepening and other indications of expansion.[219] At Red Lake, the Cochenour-Willans, McKenzie, Hasaga, Madsen, Campbell, Dickenson, and Staratt-Olsen, several of which were new, also were in highly profitable production by the end of the forties.[220] By that date, the combined output of these, with the Geraldton/Beardmore field, far surpassed their previous record production of $7.7 million, set only in 1947 (see Map 4.3).[221]

The truly controlling issue in both old and new gold fields during the war was labour availability. Indeed, labour shortage was the first cause listed in most wartime clean-ups and closings. Once the industry lost its high-priority status in 1942, its ability to shelter the work force from other wartime needs became very limited. By September of that year, up to 30 per cent of the labour required on these fields had been lost. A year later, 15,000 skilled miners and other personnel had been redirected to the forces or other priority jobs, a situation that would worsen until 1945.[222] Not surprisingly, when operations like Uchi Lake, an adjunct to Red Lake, went bankrupt in 1943, the whole of the labour force was taken up quickly by other short-handed mines.[223] Because the losses to the industry were skilled men, replacement with general labourers was not feasible. Most companies that remained active did so by concentrating their depleted manpower on key parts of their total operation, sometimes in

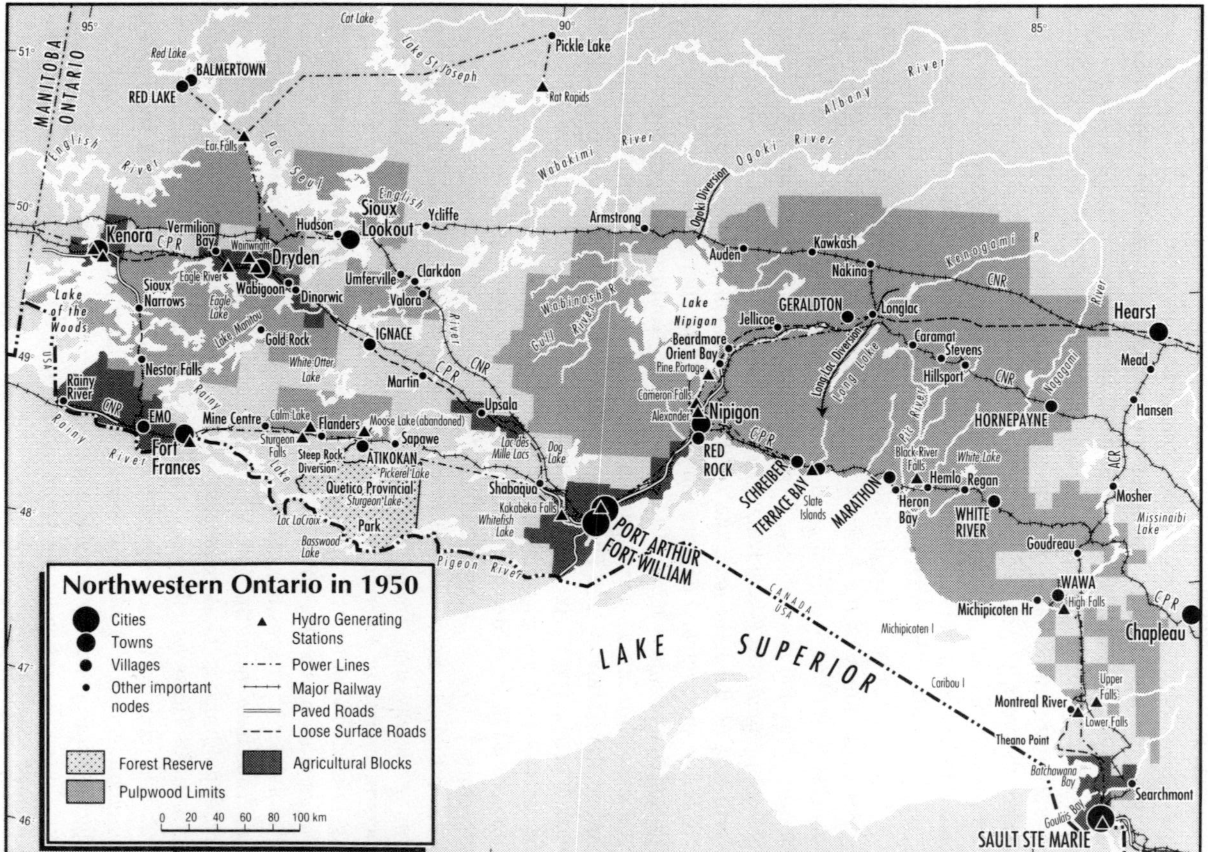
Northwestern Ontario in 1950
Cities
Towns
Villages
Other important nodes
Hydro Generating Stations
Power Lines
Major Railway
Paved Roads
Loose Surface Roads
Forest Reserve
Pulpwood Limits
Agricultural Blocks
0 20 40 60 80 100 km
MANITOBA
ONTARIO
RED LAKE
BALMERTOWN
Red Lake
Cat Lake
Pickle Lake
Rat Rapids
Lake St. Joseph
Ear Falls
Lac Seul
English River
Albany River
Ogoki River
Ogoki Diversion
Wabakimi River
Kenora
Vermilion Bay
Wainwright
Dryden
Eagle River
Wabigoon
Dinorwic
Hudson
Sioux Lookout
Ycliffe
Armstrong
Auden
Kawkash
Nakina
Umfreville
Clarkdon
Valora
Sioux Narrows
Lake of the Woods
Eagle Lake
Lake Manitou
Gold Rock
White Otter Lake
IGNACE
Martin
Nestor Falls
Rainy River
EMO
Fort Frances
Mine Centre
Calm Lake
Sturgeon Falls
Flanders
Steep Rock Diversion
Moose Lake (abandoned)
ATIKOKAN
Sapawe
Pickerel Lake
Quetico Provincial Park
Sturgeon Lake
Lac LaCroix
Basswood Lake
Upsala
Lac des Mille Lacs
Dog Lake
Shabaqua
Kakabeka Falls
Whitefish Lake
Pigeon River
PORT ARTHUR
FORT WILLIAM
Wabinosh R
Gull River
Lake Nipigon
Beardmore
Orient Bay
Pine Portage
Cameron Falls
Alexander
Nipigon
RED ROCK
Jellicoe
GERALDTON
Longlac
Long Lac Diversion
Long Lake
Caramat
Stevens
Hillsport
Kenogami R
SCHREIBER
TERRACE BAY
Slate Islands
MARATHON
Pic River
Black River Falls
White Lake
Hemlo
Regan
Heron Bay
WHITE RIVER
HORNEPAYNE
Nagagami
Hearst
Mead
Hansen
ACR
Mosher
Missinaibi Lake
Goudreau
WAWA
High Falls
Michipicoten Hr
Chapleau
Michipicoten I
Caribou I
Montreal River
Upper Falls
Lower Falls
Theano Point
Batchawana Bay
Goulais Bay
Searchmont
SAULT STE MARIE
LAKE SUPERIOR
CANADA
USA
CPR
CNR
95°
90°
85°
51°
50°
49°
48°
47°
46°
MAP 4.3

sequence, to keep their mines running. Because these mines were all comparatively new, their men were young and more vulnerable to conscription than many in the ageing gold towns of the northeast. In one year, the youthful community of Geraldton lost a third of its population to this process and related family out-migration.[224] However, at war's end, high rates of returning workers were immediately reflected in the recovering and reopening process. Within the year, those firms that had weathered this era of regulated dislocation were often back to full production. The communities that served them 'had ceased to have that run-down and partly empty appearance of the war years.'[225]

But while their apparent courses of recovery might follow similar stages, these gold fields were left in distinctly different conditions by the end of the forties. The mines of the Beardmore/Geraldton group, which would produce about $100 million worth of gold by 1955, were rapidly reaching the end of their reserves and profitability. Here, the major centres were already adjusting their employment to take advantage of increasing jobs in the forest industry.[226] Northwest of the Lakehead, the smaller Pickle Lake cluster would return to prosperity, but renewed exploration would add no more producers to the slender number of mines there.[227] Only Red Lake would reflect prolonged future prosperity, hosting a remarkable number of new or expanded operations, including the Campbell and Dickenson, which still stand among the richest Canadian producers.[228] As a result of these counter-trends and developments, the precious-metals picture of the northwest in 1950 was much more circumscribed than a decade earlier, in both spatial pattern and productive expectation.

Nevertheless, these war and post-war years witnessed a plethora of minor mining endeavours. Those left over from the thirties now had little official encouragement, in a period when only the final years were marked by returning interest in exploration and development.[229] Such activities ran from the brief operation of a chromium mine northeast of Lake Nipigon to the discovery of molybdenum deposits next Michipicoten Harbour. They also encompassed numerous base metal finds in Algoma West, the active reassessment of the old pyrite holdings at Goudreau, and a flurry of gold seeking south of Sioux Lookout.[230] However, the only exciting rush came with the rediscovery of uranium, reported first on the east Superior shore a century before in the early publications of the Geological Survey of the Canadas. Theano Point and West Algoma more generally became a mecca for prospectors as of 1948. The area then hosted the energetic but short-lived Camray Mines, as well as other exploratory ventures among the many claims staked here, before attention was refocused eastward about Elliot Lake.[231]

Iron

In contrast to these largely desultory attempts, iron mining prospered in the northwest through the forties. Indeed, it reversed its importance relative to gold's from the prior decade, so becoming the senior member of the region's mineral industries. This resulted from the high wartime priority granted to steel manufacture. Although Ottawa's original intent had been to encourage only adaptation of plant and maximum use of existing capacity, almost immediately it was forced to recognize that expansion also would be necessary. However, the government found major corporations quite reticent to answer its demands because of lingering memories of decades of over-capacity, generated by their enthusiastic compliance in such efforts during World War I. To attain its ends over the steel crisis of the early forties, therefore, Ottawa was forced into generous policies of financial support and other investment incentives. At Sault Ste Marie, these efforts engendered a much-needed early increase in rolling mill facilities and a new and modern fifth blast furnace to boost output. Yet president Dunn refused to allow his Algoma Steel to buy capital equipment that would not find sound post-war employment for domestic and overseas markets.[232]

Given this development on the St Marys River by 1942 and the protection of most of the labour force under the control of Algoma Ore Properties at Wawa, increased mine production was bound to follow. Indeed, that year, and for the duration of the war, the sintering plant ran a third over capacity. It annually processed about 550,000 tons of siderite, two-thirds of which was shipped to American ports in return for hematite delivered to Sault Ste Marie.[233] Also in 1942, Algoma leased the Josephine deposit near Wawa to Sherrett-Frobisher, which later formed the Michipicoten Iron Mining Company to work this and the adjacent Ruth ores under a seven-year contract, signed in 1944. For this venture Algoma took on all beneficiating.[234] By 1944, a second open pit was under development at the Helen, but even this mine was now feeling a belated labour pinch that would continue to war's end.[235]

Meanwhile, Canada–U.S. wartime cooperation finally produced all-out action on the huge Steep Rock project because of U.S. fear of an iron ore shortage if the conflict was prolonged.[236] Much of the colossal investment required came from public agencies in that country, while Canada provided tax concessions as well as all infrastructure arrangements and facilities. In the first month of 1943, the Steep Rock Iron Ore Development Act was ratified and work began.[237] At the site this involved the diversion of the Seine River and draining of the lake through a system of canals and dams. With this went six months of continuous pumping to remove the first 188 billion gallons of water. That was followed by high-pressure sluicing of bottom sediments and their removal by powerful suction dredges. In September 1944, the first truckload of ore left the initial pit at orebody B, but full production there came only the next May.[238] While this early work was progressing, the CNR erected a modern high-pocket ore dock at the Lakehead, and Ontario's Hydro Electric Power Commission began work to supply the energy this enormous project would ultimately require. To this end, it added generating capacity at Nipigon, while extending its high-voltage line 130 miles west from Fort William to Atikokan and the mine. It also arranged to make up the power losses to Ontario and Minnesota Pulp and Paper at Fort Frances, when a generating station at Moose Lake became inactive on the completion of the Seine River/Steep Rock Lake diversion.[239]

When completed, the first phase of Steep Rock development was already contracted to supply ten U.S. and Canadian corporations with its high-grade hematite. However, by this time, the war that had precipitated its undertaking was now drawing to a close.[240] The development's first full year of operation, which fell prior to the final defeat of Japan, was marked by logistical problems in transport. During the summer and fall of 1945, a lack of sufficient ships to carry the carloads of ore arriving at the docks caused frequent bottlenecks. These problems reappeared the next year due to an unexpected fuel shortage among lake freighters, complicated spasmodically by a shortage of rail cars.[241] Not until 1947, therefore, did production from orebody B come to reflect its true capacity.

The fuel shortage on the lakes in 1946 was but one sign of much larger disorders in this highly international industry. A prolonged coal miners' strike in the United States cut off sure supplies of coal for transportation and coke for smelting. Even at Algoma, which had long owned the Cannelton Coal Company in Pennsylvania, the problem was acute. In Canada, that year was also marked by a bitter dispute between the major companies and the Steel Workers Union, which was battling to become the industry's collective-bargaining unit. So disruptive was this last strike to the process of post-war reconstruction and peacetime steel production, that government reassumed its regulatory role for the industry. Despite the official encouragement of growth that began again in 1947, big steel in Canada did not return to steady expansion and serious international competition until 1949.[242]

This disorderly sequence of events and delays in the steel industry's return to peaceful progress was not mirrored in related mining activity. At Steep Rock, near Atikokan, seasonal production rested at about one-half million tons in 1945, a figure similar to that of the Michipicoten Range about Wawa. In spite of continuing problems with transport, the Steep Rock shipments almost doubled in the next year. By 1947, forecasts were for three million tons annually, when further progress in draining would make possible the opening of orebody A, then in the discussion stage.[243] Indeed, by 1949, even property C was under a negotiated lease for eventual utilization by the Caland Ore Company, a subsidiary of Inland Steel of Chicago.[244]

At Wawa, despite the collapse and abandonment of the Josephine as unprofitable, Michipicoten Iron continued to work the ores of the Ruth. However, in 1948, its holding company, Sherrett-Gordon, arranged the transfer of rights here and for the untapped Lucy to a third party for further development. Through the period these operations came to add another half-million tons of ore annually to the sintering plant.[245] Over this same five-year period, Algoma Ore Properties, after deep drilling the Helen, moved from open pit to underground mining in 1949. In the process it greatly altered a spectacularly long surface skip to transfer the ore for sintering and to the latter plant added over 3,000 tons daily capacity with a fourth machine. It also moved to year-round mining as well as beneficiation, which had proved unsuccessful with the open pit. In addition, by late in the decade, it was busy exploring locally, both the Bartlett property and Siderite Hill, as well as drilling the Britannia block of magnetite ore located behind the Goulais/Batchawana area.[246]

As a result of these activities in the northwest, the combined production of the Michipicoten and Steep Rock iron ranges, which stood at 1.1 million tons in 1945, climbed to 1.9 million in 1947 and reached 2.4 million tons in 1950.[247] Given the state of the Canadian iron and steel industry until the final years of the period, most of this mounting output found markets in the United States. Indeed, a U.S. strategy for the conservation of home supplies against future military and domestic requirements was clearly at work here. The result was not only a willingness to stimulate the wartime initiation of Steep Rock but also the desire to barter for Superior and Ungava ore production later.

Redirection and Restructuring in Forest Activity

Wartime Complications

These were difficult years for the forest industry which found its post-Depression needs curtailed and its traditional practices opposed on several fronts, during war and peacetime. Loggers and pulp cutters were prized by the army for their skills and had proven to be an enthusiastic membership in the first wave of volunteers for military service in 1940. As a result, severe shortages in bush labour were evident by 1941, from the Manitoba border to the north shore camps of Superior, although the problem was not acute in Algoma West until the following year.[248]

Available statistics for the region suggest that this situation reached its nadir in December 1943 (see Table 4.10). This occurred in the wake of an associated flurry of labour unrest over work and living conditions, which was quickly muzzled by Wartime Prices and Wages legislation.[249] Under a modest wartime manpower priority assigned to the industry by Ottawa, numbers of bushworkers moved upward encouragingly in the Geraldton area of the Thunder Bay District, where new companies opened yet unexploited limits. The number of bushworkers increased near Sioux Lookout in Patricia, where Great Lakes now initiated full harvesting on limits granted in the thirties. Even in 1946, growth was slow in Rainy River and Kenora because of an unusually high reliance on the settler cut, which continued to prevail down the valley and around Dryden. In Algoma, since most camps were now north of Michipicoten and Superior, high transportation costs would appear to have limited harvests destined both for domestic use and for export consumption and thus labour demands through the war.

Meanwhile, by 1943, increasingly beleaguered employers were in search of alternate sources from which to hire for their woodland operations. Among early suggestions in the northwest was the use of Japanese Canadians from the several internment camps in the region. Another was a call to employ German prisoners of war (POWs) to help in the bush.[250] After 1940, three large prison facilities were established, at Red Rock as well as at Ney and Anglers near modern Marathon on the Superior north shore. Now a total of thirty-nine smaller branch camps were located for woods work west of Sault Ste Marie. Only one of these, at Flanders near Quetico in the limit of the Border Lumber Company of Fort Frances, was to serve other than for the harvest of pulpwood.[251] By early 1945, some 9,000 POWs were incarcerated in the region, most of whom had served at least one season on these cutting projects. Opinions vary on the actual utility of these men to the industry, given their initial

TABLE 4.10 Supply of Bushworkers, 1943–1946

	1943	1944	1945	1946
Algoma West	2,463	2,346	2,693	3,088
Thunder Bay	4,066	5,982	8,708	10,786
Rainy River	709	600	754	1,056
Kenora	925	1,600	1,701	1,788
Patricia	913	1,300	1,520	1,920
Total	9,076	11,828	15,376	18,638

Source: Sessional Papers of Ontario, 1943–1947, no. 3, 'Reports of the Department of Lands and Forests, 1943–1946.'

inexperience and their understandable reluctance to serve the Allied cause. All that is certain is that they were a convenient stopgap under the pressure of the times.[252]

But while labour shortages posed one set of problems, official controls and directives for marketing rankled much more among managerial minds still attuned to laissez-faire business principles. For the handful of lumber mill operators remaining in the northwest, their lot was simple. As of September 1942, their civilian markets were sharply curtailed and their output reassigned to fields as diverse as aircraft manufacture and wartime housing.[253] These restrictions would not be lifted until 1945.

For pulp and paper companies and related woodland operators such wartime measures were more complex, invasive, and financially irksome. Most manufacturers found their mills still operating at less than capacity, with one or more of their expensive paper machines moth-balled for the duration.[254] Across the region, even in the brightening months of 1945 but before the federal wartime measures were removed, many mills were still running at no more than 75 per cent capacity.[255]

On the provincial front, matters were equally unpalatable to management, although by the end of the decade certain major pulpwood holdings significantly increased. The new provincial cabinet of 1943 was unhappy with both the forest policies and regulatory muscle applied by its predecessor. It moved quickly to announce a withdrawal from all pulpwood export agreements of the pre-war era, with a return to a manufacturing requirement as of December 31, 1946.[256] To prove its determination, Queen's Park also moved quickly to cancel the old concessional agreements with English River Pulp and Paper, Vermillion Lake Pulp, and Western Pulp and Paper in Kenora/Patricia and Soo Pulp Products in Algoma West for non-fulfilment of contract. That same year it reopened negotiations with General Timber on the Pic and Nagagami limits and Pulpwood Supply on the Pic watershed for new and diminishing levels of pulpwood exports. At the same time it activated firm dates, as was allowed in their contracts, for pulp mill construction (see Map 4.4).[257] The province also proved it was willing to confront violators of existing pulpwood export arrangements. It found Ontario and Minnesota, for example, quietly transferring pulp from its Rainy River holdings and plant at Fort Frances to sister mills at International Falls so as to benefit from higher U.S. paper prices. The government's blunt threat to terminate that company's lavish provincial supplies brought swift, if grudging, compliance.[258] Such firm measures tended to exacerbate already cool relations between government and the industry.

This wartime contest of wills was not helped by a conflict between paper and lumber interests over wood supply and Ontario's stance on that issue. For

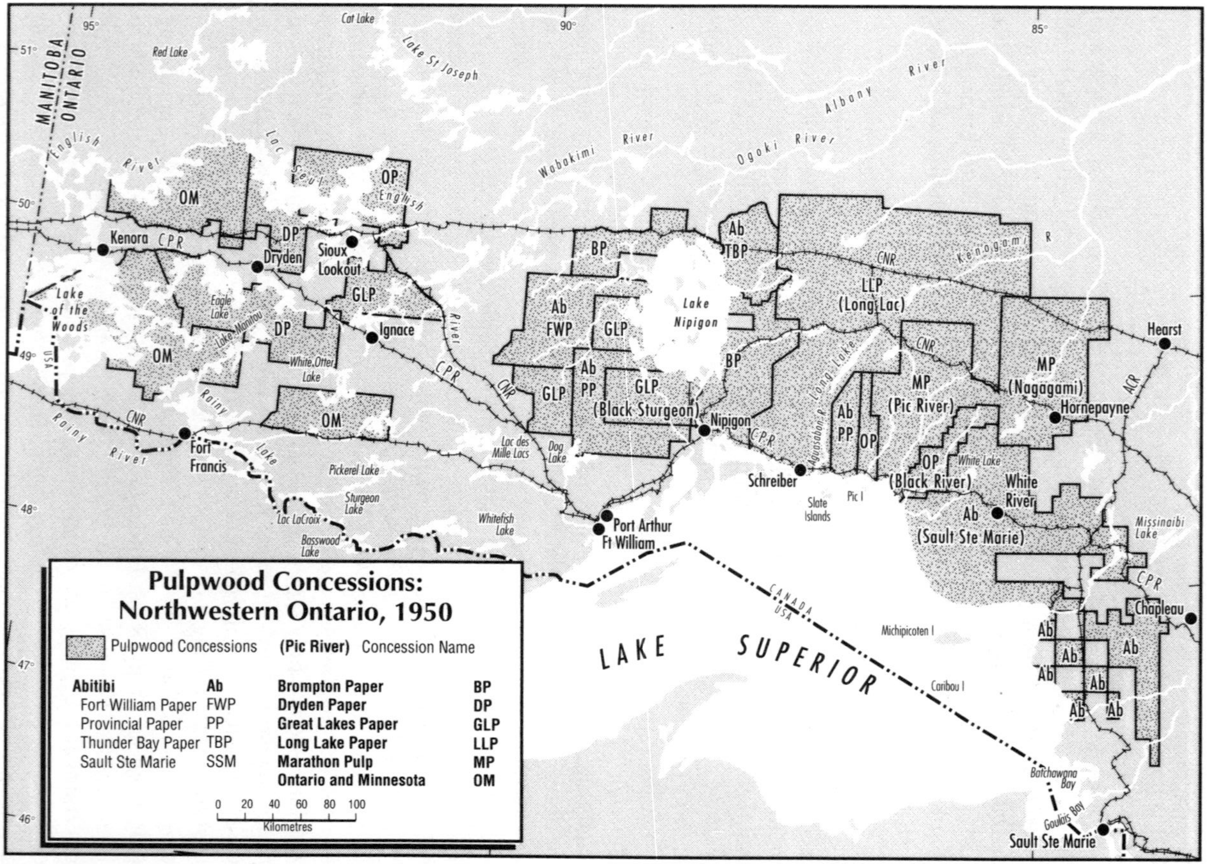

Pulpwood Concessions:
Northwestern Ontario, 1950
Pulpwood Concessions
(Pic River) Concession Name
Abitibi Ab
Fort William Paper FWP
Provincial Paper PP
Thunder Bay Paper TBP
Sault Ste Marie SSM
Brompton Paper BP
Dryden Paper DP
Great Lakes Paper GLP
Long Lake Paper LLP
Marathon Pulp MP
Ontario and Minnesota OM
0 20 40 60 80 100
Kilometres
MANITOBA
ONTARIO
USA
CANADA
LAKE SUPERIOR
Kenora
Dryden
Sioux Lookout
Ignace
Fort Francis
Port Arthur
Ft William
Nipigon
Schreiber
White River
Hornepayne
Hearst
Chapleau
Sault Ste Marie
Lake Nipigon
Lake of the Woods
Red Lake
Cat Lake
Lake St Joseph
Lac Seul
Albany River
Ogoki River
Wabakimi River
English River
Rainy River
Rainy Lake
Eagle Lake
Lake Manitou
White Otter Lake
Pickerel Lake
Sturgeon Lake
Lac LaCroix
Basswood Lake
Whitefish Lake
Lac des Mille Lacs
Dog Lake
Long Lake
Aguasabon R
Kenogami R
White Lake
Missinaibi Lake
Slate Islands
Pic I
Michipicoten I
Caribou I
Batchawana Bay
Goulais Bay
CPR
CNR
ACR
(Long Lac)
(Black Sturgeon)
(Pic River)
(Nagagami)
(Black River)
(Sault Ste Marie)

MAP 4.4

a number of years, in all contracts covering pulp limits, a clause had been inserted ensuring access to appropriate saw logs for lumbering companies. This regulation, intended to promote wise use of the resource, had never been firmly enforced and was rarely complied with. Among certain lumber contractors, this non-compliance was a sore point. The issue came to a head with the rights and requirements stated in the provincial agreement of the new Great Lakes Lumber Company. In 1940, this firm had been encouraged, by a province still dedicated to 'putting the men back to work' and an Ottawa busy on wartime plans, to erect a large and modern sawmill at the Lakehead to harvest supplies of saw logs from pulpwood concessions. While the unrelated Great Lakes Pulp and Paper Company complied in permitting access to such larger timber on their concessions, other firms in the area refused. They claimed that if they were expected to plan the most efficient harvest of their limits (a vacuous issue at this time), they should control all harvesting. In 1943, Ontario demanded compliance with the regulation, but the industry sullenly refused. With the situation rapidly getting out of hand, Toronto let matters stand for the moment, since E.E. Johnson, owner of Great Lakes Lumber, admitted he had adequate supplies to 1949.[259] Nevertheless, the recalcitrant companies, in addition to looming post-war labour problems and curtailed pulpwood exports, now faced the problem of sharing forest rights with lumber companies at peacetime.

To no one's surprise, the removal of Ottawa's wartime regulation of pulp, paper, and lumber in 1945 was followed within a year by a provincial Royal Commission on Forestry. Its results reflected important changes in Ontario's relations with the industry and set the whole issue of woodland use on a more modern, conservational course.[260] Under the experienced and sometimes visionary chairmanship of Howard Kennedy, the commissioners took to the field to view the situation and to hold public hearings across the province. The final report was lengthy and insightful and contained seventy-two recommendations, chief among them being the promotion of strong forestry principles, including sustained yield and rigorous reforestation. Different clauses stressed the need for the appropriate use of all woodland resources for the most efficient production of paper and lumber. One recommendation was for the cessation of pulpwood exports. Here it pointed to the related economic advantage of value added through home manufacture. The report strongly criticized hydro authorities for their ineffective harvest of timber from areas to be dammed and flooded, as well as contractors for rapacious high-grading and wasteful cutting practices. It pointed to the loss caused by the indiscriminate bulldozing of tress in the construction of bush roads and even highways. It also championed better living conditions for bushworkers. Through its pages were numerous, bluntly chosen photographs illustrating the iniquitous results of each issue it addressed.

Because of the still illogical and uneven distribution of forest resources among the companies, the report recommended that all concessions be cancelled, reorganized on a watershed basis, and reassigned in a more rational and equitable way.[261] Such revolutionary ideas and wide-ranging criticism shocked the more conservative in the industry into stubborn resistance. However, progressive thinkers in both the industry and the Department of Lands and Forests were much more enthusiastic about the report's far-reaching recommendations and gave it their approval. More important, the public, on whom the photos had a strong effect, gave the report its approval. As a result, implementation of certain recommendations followed quickly, and, over the next two decades, 80 per cent of the Commission's suggestions would be applied.[262]

One of the province's immediate moves was in the area of pulpwood exports. Ontario's wartime announcement of the termination of all pulpwood exports from Crown limits by 1946 had not been acted upon. In 1947 the province passed formal legislation to reduce such exports to zero within ten years. Despite loud complaints from contractors and companies, the province stuck to its plan.[263] Indeed, concession agreements of 1942 with the Ontario and Quebec Paper Company on behalf of the *Chicago Tribune* and of 1944 with Marathon Pulp regarding that firm's acquisition of the Nagagami limit had set the precedent for this regulation. Subsequent negotiations followed with the latter company as it emerged from the membership of General Timber to take over the Pic limit and erect its mill. The province's firm stance on the matter was underlined further by the enforced agreement with the Long Lake Pulp Company (Kimberly-Clark), as it similarly evolved out of Pulpwood Supply on the Long Lake limit.[264] These were important measures in Ontario's recovery from expedient and sometimes unwise forest policies, invoked under conditions of depression and war. However, neither the first nor last of these agreements required manufacture of anything more than pulp at these new Canadian plants.

As these corrective events unfolded, the post-war absence of alternate European paper sources, as well as the extreme proximity and reliability of Canadian pulp and paper supplies for U.S. needs, helped create a boom in demand. Plans for mill modernization in the northwest, which had been delayed by other wartime priorities, were now quickly implemented. In 1945, Ontario and Minnesota set out to spend $6 million on refurbishing their facilities at Fort Frances and Kenora, while the kraft mill at Dryden also entered upon heavy expenditures on plant.[265] A year later, Abitibi, now emerging from fourteen years in receivership and complex legal battles, undertook mechanical upgrading in its mills at both the Lakehead and Sault Ste Marie. Great Lakes Paper soon followed suit.[266] Brompton Pulp and Paper, a Quebec firm, had taken over the assets at Red Rock and the Nipigon Limit of bankrupt Lake Sulphite in 1941. However, it had been compelled to wait out much of the war before completing the already partially built mill and company town there by the fall of 1945.[267] Like Dryden, this was a kraft operation intended to capitalize on the container revolution in the United States, which greatly increased the kraft need for linerboard, paper boxes, brown bags, and wrapping paper.[268]

That same year the large bleached kraft mill and company town at Peninsula Harbour (Marathon) was opened by Marathon Pulp. The last huge tow of raw pulpwood from its Pic River limit had been hauled directly to its parent company at Rothchild, Wisconsin, only that spring.[269] However, the pulpwood that Marathon cut on its Nagagami holdings briefly continued to pass south over the ACR to Sault Ste Marie and on to an associated company, Rhinelander Paper, also in Wisconsin.[270] In 1946, construction also began on the mill, HEPC power dam and station, as well as the company town of Terrace Bay, near the mouth of the Aguasabon River. All initial work for Long Lake Pulp and Paper there was completed within two years.[271] Before the power installation was finished in 1947, the last big cut from this Long Lake limit was driven over the Aguasabon Falls to Superior. Like so many huge booms before, it was marshalled in the sheltered waters between the Slate Islands, for export by ship or rafting to American mills.[272] Not surprisingly, by 1949, the eleven mills now operating across the northwest were running profitably at record levels and were preparing for a new wave of expansion.

These immediate post-war developments went hand in hand with a revolution in the bush. Here operators in 1945 still anticipated the restoration of 'normal' wage levels and earlier styles of camp operation. However, they found the returning labour force unwilling to work under these conditions. The situation exploded in a bitter and intense strike across northern Ontario at the beginning of October 1946. That dispute was most widespread around Port Arthur and in camps as far west as Sioux Lookout, as well as those east from Beardmore to Geraldton. This labour disturbance coincided with ones in other industries like iron and steel, and was timed to correspond with the departure of the last German POW pulp cutter. Workers demanded higher wages and better living conditions. Management wanted to reduce labour costs, which they considered to have been inflated by late wartime manpower shortages. For labour, it was a fight for union recognition and collective bargaining. For Queen's Park, it was an intolerable obstacle to economic recovery that required quick intervention. A solution, under a binding agreement, was engineered within the month.[273]

Post-War Issues

This resolution, however, only papered over deep-seated labour-related issues that arose with peace. The war had altered the old sequential rhythm of seasonal work. For decades, this pattern had carried men from the camps to the river drive, on to a summer in mills or in construction, into the fall with the prairie harvest, and through winter again in the bush. Now pulp cutting was a summer as well as a winter occupation, a situation that in the northwest had become increasingly common after the mid-thirties and had already had its impact on this annual cycle. In addition, many skilled woodworkers had found permanent jobs in urban industries during the war. Others left the military with new qualifications for other occupations, finding less arduous and better-paying employment elsewhere in the quickening post-war economy. Camp recruiting was now a tough and frustrating task for employers, often requiring the use of inexperienced workers whose productivity was limited and whose stay was often brief.[274]

The result of these developments brought petitions from groups like the Thunder Bay Timber Operators for the revival of selective European immigration, which gained a sympathetic response from Ottawa in early 1947. Over the following weeks a flood of applications for such employees were processed by the Department of Labour. By October, allotments of foreign workers were reported in the press across the northwest, as they arrived in the camps. Unfortunately, this solution to the labour problem proved only marginally successful. These immigrants were inexperienced, often unhappy with the physical side of the work, and occasionally shocked by the living conditions. Often experiencing social or political discrimination as well, they were prone to jump their contracts and head for urban employment. In addition, company applications for workers sometimes proved to be far more than were needed and, combined with an unexpected influx of prairie labour in 1948, required the reassignment of many in the northwest to jobs in mining.[275] This over-supply of labour was not aided by an early spring thaw in 1949, when camps closed and wages were curtailed by March, leaving many new-comers destitute on the streets of the Lakehead and Sault Ste Marie, until summer work became available. In fact, by that time, the burst of pulpwood demand that had begun at mid-decade was tapering off, now that mill stocks on both sides of the border had been returned to pre-war levels and production had reached full stride.[276]

Other attempts to solve the labour problem took more traditional courses. In agriculturally centred areas of the northwest, settler cutting seems to have continued at limited levels in the early forties but was again frequently reported in these early post-war years. Indeed, as early as 1945, in the still-substantial pulpwood stands of the western Rainy River Valley, farmers and contractors were already negotiating cuts and prices for large wood delivered at Fort Frances or in dumps for booming to Kenora. Here, as at Dryden, settlers remained an important labour source for local mills.[277] In the townships from Nipigon to the Minnesota boundary settler cut also regained momentum, with thousands of exportable cords being driven down the Kaministiquia and lesser rivers in the late forties.[278] In the Batchawana/Goulais River area during these same years, local settlers and dealers were trucking pulp to Sault Ste Marie or delivering it to the shore to be hauled south by Abitibi's tugs.[279] However, on much of the private lands in all these agricultural areas, good pulpwood stands must have been becoming rare and the quality and species available more and more circumscribed.

By the late forties, woodland contractors either became large operators or faded from the scene. Some of these now-substantial firms found all their employment cutting on major limits for the pulp and paper companies that held them. Some combined such harvesting with exporting pulpwood from other holdings, while a few concentrated on forest products other than pulpwood. For example, D.A. Clark employed 1,700 men in his operations by 1947. He was then a major supplier of hydro poles from properties between Beardmore and Longlac. In addition, he was the principal in the newly formed Nipigon Lake Timber Company there. As well, the Alexander Clark Timber Company, out of Sturgeon Lake and Sioux Lookout, was using a series of small limits in both areas for the production of export pulpwood. Also at the Lakehead, the Pigeon River Timber Company, which had its own towing and rafting service, was similarly harvesting and shipping from a small limit on the Little Pic to U.S. mills but was also a major contractor on the Black Sturgeon limit for the Great Lakes Pulp and Paper Company. At the same time, Northern Wood Preservers was now one of two large tie companies in the province. For its mills and creosoting and storage facilities at the mouth of the Kaministiquia, it took much of its cut from a 185-square-mile limit in the Nipigon country.[280] Oscar Styffe was another substantial contractor at Port Arthur. There was one large firm on the Rainy River and several smaller contractors served Abitibi in Algoma. In contrast an increasing number of pulp and paper companies in the northwest were coming to carry out at least a major part of their own expanding woodland operations.

Such emerging attempts at economies of scale were not the only approaches to cost-cutting that made a serious appearance in the region's forest operations by 1950. Trucks and powerful tracked vehicles for bush hauling with which to reduce the labour requirements had seen limited service before the war. Wages, which by 1948 were 11 per cent above those of 1941 in a continuingly tight labour market,[281] now induced numerous experiments to raise individual efficiency and reduce manpower requirements. This was particularly true in young, flexible, and innovative firms like Marathon and Long Lake Pulp and Paper (Kimberly-Clark), which pioneered the use of power saws by 1947 and by 1949 were doing much of their hauling to dumps or siding with specially designed diesel trucks.[282] In 1945, on the Nagagami Limit, Marathon was preparing to use specially built wagons and caterpillar tractors in the bush and trucks over their roads to Hornepayne, where an early power slasher at the railyard quickly reduced the logs to eight-food wood for shipment.[283] By 1947, operations there and on the Pic limit needed 30 per cent less labour for twice the normal production, through such mechanical innovations.[284] At the close of the decade, Marathon abandoned its tracked vehicles in the bush in favour of yarding techniques. Under this system all timber was skidded from the stump by powerful winches and cables to a proximal, central point to be put through mobile slashers before truck haulage. At the time this was termed 'the first integrated harvesting system in Canada.'[285]

Both Marathon and Long Lake were among the first to adopt other cost-conscious measures in a quickening industry. Even during the war, responsible members of the timbering community had become increasingly aware that, for a variety of reasons, the old camp system of permanent log structures was no longer suitable. Construction costs were now too high for their periodic abandonment and replacement on new sites. Experiments with structures on skids that could be dragged behind trucks or tractors to new locations were not the solution either, because of the number of such smaller buildings needed and the damage incurred on each journey.[286]

While cost was the major driving force in post-war innovation, social issues also played a role. The conditions of camp life were a key point in the strike settlement of 1946, which set firm minimum amenity levels, similar to those recommended in the Kennedy Commission Report a year later.[287] Most small operators and certain recalcitrant contractors in the northwest refused to consider anything more than the brutally basic accommodation that had sufficed earlier. Others saw improved working conditions as an advantage in attracting and retaining a more skilled and experienced labour force. Such firms attempted to achieve these goals in a number of ways. Experiments were carried out with prefabricated units, complete with plumbing, hot water, furnaces, cafeteria dining, recreational facilities, and pleasant dormitory conditions. However, by the end of the decade, such 'panel camps' had generally been found to be prohibitively expensive to knock down, transport, and reassemble.

In the meantime, a new approach to mobility had been found. This involved the establishment of one or more depots on any limit, within a planned context of bush roads, log dumps, and cut areas. These depots could comfortably house all the crews, with their families, as well as the facilities for equipment maintenance and repair.[288] By 1948 such communities were established by Marathon or Long Lake Pulp and Paper at Stevens, Caramat, and Longlac, with plans for ones at Hillsport and Nakina. Variations, which added depots in the form of residential subdivisions along with equipment and repair yards to existing communities, were extant under Abitibi at Orient Bay as well as under Brompton at Beardmore, Jellico, and Geraldton.[289] On this important issue of housing, as on other economic and social fronts, these moves were encouragingly positive for future improvement and change.

Accompanying trends in the fields of conservation, protection, and renewal of northern forest resources were less fruitful through the forties. The reorganization of Lands and Forests, both in its district structure and central redefinition, was a good beginning that augured the return of the forester to a central role.[290] Fire control was already aided by watch towers, radio networks, and rudimentary air support systems. Beginning in 1945, these were expanded and new technologies were introduced. The future importance of this service was underlined by the costly losses of the Mississauga/Chapleau fire, which, late in the decade, destroyed or damaged much fine timber in and on the fringe of Algoma West.[291] A new aerial forest inventory, superseding that of the thirties, and covering the province to the most northerly CNR right of way and beyond, was initiated in 1946. While work on this long-term planning tool was progressing well by 1950, it too had only limited impact on the northwest of the post-war decades.[292]

Similarly, these were important formative years for pest control, particularly in spruce budworm research across northern Ontario. Infestations of this insect were an old problem that gained prominence in the thirties, as the impact on pulpable forests came into perspective. Serious outbreaks had been reported in all districts of the northwest by 1940 and grew in intensity through the next decade. As of 1944, the first experiments with aerial spraying began, using the new chemical DDT, a move that only later was discovered to be ecologically hazardous.[293] In 1945, some 64,000 acres in the Black Sturgeon limit, next to Lake Nipigon, were so treated; because of mounting insect problems from the Long Lake to Nagagami limits to the east, spraying followed there in 1946.[294] Subsequent assessments of these experiments were carried out by both provincial and U.S. scientists. They were concerned with the effect of spraying on flora and fauna, while foresters were interested in its success among spruce and balsam forest elements. The outcome of the provincial studies seems to have gone unreported, but the results of the U.S. ones were expressed without any cautions about expanding the use of this insecticide, although recommending much salvage cutting as a supportive procedure.[295] Despite these efforts, 3.5 million acres in the Superior watershed were estimated to be infected by 1949. As a result, the spruce budworm quickly became the focus of research at the new federal–provincial entomological laboratory at Sault Ste Marie.[296]

Very real fears of future shortages in pulpwood resources, similar to those in lumber, were voiced during the forties. The crucial areas of planning, management, and replenishment of future forest resources preoccupied the public, government, and industry.[297] Clauses with terms like 'sustained yield,' 'planning,' and 'management' had crept into concessional agreements before the opening of the decade. But the supposed requirements for regular harvesting plans and related woodland inventories were ignored by most of the companies, who regarded them as an unacceptable interference in their private business. Government rarely was either willing or in a sufficient position of strength to force the issue. In short, through the early years of the decade this issue of government supervision, together with policies on pulpwood exports and saw-log supplies, generated strained relations between officials and operators.[298]

While the issue of saw-logs on pulpwood limits would not be solved in the period,[299] matters of forest management, like wood exports, were on the road to resolution at the war's close. The precedent leading to this desirable situation came in 1945, when Abitibi Power and Paper, struggling back from receivership, agreed to submit, within five years, estimates of species, ages, and size-classes for each of its concessions. These were to be accompanied by maps and plans of the company's annual and long-range harvesting, for government study and approval. Abitibi also agreed to bear future responsibility for the appropriate management of its assigned forest resources and to incorporate into its plans any changes required by the Department of Lands and Forests.[300] Two years later, the province incorporated these measures into its Forest Management Act, which, among its reforms, also set a reasonable renewal date on concessional agreements.[301] In northwestern Ontario all firms with mills and limits came slowly to conform with these regulations. Such a move was made more palatable for some by the concurrent return of very profitable conditions and the firm but tactful encouragement of the province. Not all such plans were completed or were intended to be in place by 1950. However, both sides now boasted a complete complement of trained foresters to deal with this task and with the ongoing drive for proper woodland management. Nevertheless, few seed orchards or nurseries had yet been initiated and few firms were reported to be about to start even small or tentative replanting programs, which were needed to attain some rudimentary move toward sustained yield.[302] Despite its proven inadequacy, natural regeneration was still the method most relied upon across the region to provide the forest of the future.

Tourism's Youthful Trials

Wartime Preparation

These were exciting years of administrative developments, changing tastes, and innovations for the budding vacation trade in Ontario's northwest. The province's growing awareness of tourism's potential was encouraged by Ottawa's tactful encouragement of provincial participation over the late thirties. A provincial Bureau of Tourism was established in 1941 as part of the Premier's Office. Its task was not only to promote the industry but also to coordinate related activities then shared by the departments of Game and Fisheries and of Lands and Forests.[303] However, the Bureau's promotional role was quickly curtailed when the war moved into more critical phases.

Only a few figures are available to assess the general performance of tourism in the northwest to 1945 (see Table 4.11). However, these statistics for outfitters probably reflect trends faced by others who also dealt with recreational travellers. Such facilities tended to increase slowly in number as overcapacity from the thirties was replaced by near-capacity booking through an increase in American demand before Pearl Harbour and before Canada's full wartime mobilization of late 1942. This growing tourism was valuable to Ottawa in its scramble for new sources of dollars to sponsor its growing military commitments. More important, the subsequent decline after late 1942 in the number of licensed establishments reflected problems much less severe than those experienced by mining or forest harvesting in these years.

TABLE 4.11 Licensed Tourist Outfitters, 1941–1945

	1941	1942	1943	1944	1945
Algoma*	95	92	87	76	77
Thunder Bay District	30	32	22	21	17
Rainy River District	32	37	42	31	28
Kenora District	157	158	144	127	137
Patricia Provisional	2	2	2	1	1
Total	316	321	297	265	260

* Figures include all of Algoma, not just Algoma West, no doubt inflating the total figures.
Source: Sessional Papers of Ontario, 1940–1946, no. 9, 'Reports of the Departments of Game and Fisheries for 1940–1945.'

Some authors have suggested that 'the War interrupted our affair with the automobile.'[304] This may be true in part, but Ottawa, needing American tourism's contribution to its war chest, applied special measures to encourage U.S. auto travel in Canada.[305] While gasoline was rationed in 1942, severely limiting the recreational horizons of Ontarians, touring Americans received coupons for eighty gallons at customs, and at resorts additional fuel and rationed provisions were supplied.[306] Although benefiting only operators near the border, such measures kept the tourists coming to Rainy River–Lake of the Woods, the Lakehead, and Algoma West.[307]

Ontario added two other incentives to the federal support of the tourism industry, the effects of which were felt only later. The first of these involved a rethinking of northern land-use policies, related to the old requirement that recreational tenure on public land be limited to lease agreements.[308] In 1941, a committee of the Department of Lands and Forests reported in favour of a move to land sales. Resultant revisions in the Public Land Act established both a clear definition of recreational property and the procedures for purchase from the Crown. Meanwhile, an appropriate division was created to manage the outcome, during a full reorganization of Lands and Forests.[309] These changes were welcomed in the northwest, as elsewhere, but their impact would be delayed by regulations suspending domestic construction for the duration of the war.

The second provincial incentive involved a surprisingly early move to prepare for the return of peacetime recreational demands. In 1944, the budget of the Bureau of Tourism and Recreation was doubled towards this end. That same year, the appropriate division of Lands and Forests started detailed preparations for the expected rush to obtain new cottage lots on Crown lands.[310] Late the following year, a new Department of Travel and Publicity was organized, replacing the efforts of the former Bureau in 1946. This much more adequate agency was quick off the mark, with early spring advertising in the United States and strong liaison with neighbouring states, which also anticipated rising traffic. The Department combined such efforts with U.S. distribution of newly designed regional publications as well as four new travel films. It also arranged a publicity tour for U.S. newspaper editors, the first since 1942, and the construction of northwestern tourist reception centres at Sault Ste Marie, Fort Frances, Pigeon River, and Keewatin/Kenora.[311] Also in 1946, the old Department of Game and Fisheries was folded into Lands and Forests to streamline tourism's administrative structure. A special Tourist Camp Regulations Act now provided for an immediate inspection of all facilities across the province to raise the minimum standard of accommodation and service to more desirable levels. Such inspections proceeded through 1947 and became a requirement for a licence to operate the next season.[312] In the northwest, the latter move gained wide praise in the press, which sometimes pushed for even more rigour in the inspection process.[313]

Peacetime Advances

These extensive official preparations turned out to be fully justified. The flow of summer visitors began to climb again in border areas of the region on the termination of travel restrictions in 1945, and traffic was back to pre-war levels across the region in 1946. This was particularly welcome in the environs of Dryden, Ignace, Sioux Lookout, Beardmore, Geraldton, and Longlac, which had been located beyond the range of visitors' gasoline allowances during the war.[314]

It is impossible, however, to determine further details of post-war growth from the enthusiastic representations of the local press or from the general and ill-defined figures cited in government reports.[315] Suffice it to say that the data suggest a record advance in every phase of the industry by the end of the decade. Such marked trends also promoted the updating of facilities in older locations and witnessed the first real push of both tourists and operators into less accessible and more northerly areas.

At the close of the forties, the northwest's expanding tourism trade was even more overwhelmingly American in clientele than in earlier years and, as before, each part of the region drew most of its tourists from a specific area. Like upper Huron, Algoma West drew tourists mostly from Michigan, Ohio, and Pennsylvania, while Wisconsin and Minnesota were prime markets for operators about the Lakehead and east along the new pre-war trunk road system.[316] However, the whole of the Rainy River, Kenora, and its Patricia extension was a principal vacation land for the midwest states. Except for local residents with recreational property nearby, the only true Canadian enclave continued to belong to the Winnipegers at northern Lake of the Woods. In 1950, Canadians still had neither the wealth nor leisure time to participate as fully as Americans in recreational pursuits. Moreover, southern Ontario still lacked a convenient auto route west of Sault Ste Marie with which to replace the disappearing cruise ships that had once coursed north to the Lakehead from Sarnia or Georgian Bay ports.[317]

While northwestern Ontario's recreational facilities continued to grow along traditional lines, they also now branched out into new fields. The most common form of vacation pattern remained the male-dominated fishing/hunting lodge, often with an array of wilderness out-camps reached by canoe, boat, or now sometimes by float plane. These remained most common up the ACR in

Algoma or in the Rainy Lake and southern Lake of the Woods watershed, although some now were added farther north.[318] An emerging variant was the fly-in fishing operation, which now appeared in older tourist districts, and which was sometimes troubled by questionable flights into the back country from the American side.[319] However, real progress in fly-in operations came in centres like Red Lake, Hudson, Sioux Lookout, and Nakina, with their ready access to the untouched sporting potential of the Patricia country.[320] Fishing remained the specialty of both lodges and fly-in operators. However, an unexpected rise in the number of non-residents who came north for moose season swamped the 2,000 available guides in the autumn of 1946, to the embarrassment of the operators.[321] These sport-oriented facilities were also coming under increasing pressure from the growing population of family vacationers, who sought a much broader range of amenities, children's activities, and the opportunity for their own house-keeping cabin.[322] Owners, new and old, were facing some hard decisions about which of these clienteles would be the most profitable in the future.

Their decision was made no easier by two vacation alternatives that first appeared at war's end. The first was the middle-class family cottage. These multiplied quickly with the new opportunity to purchase rather than lease Crown holdings. So heavy and immediate was this demand that available surveyors could not keep up with it. Many of those who participated in the rush for lots after 1945 were Americans who had been long-time lodge visitors to the same area.[323]

The second was the family-oriented rental cabin, with boat and swimming beach, either as a vacation alternative or a source of simple overnight accommodation for those travelling with children, in these years before the motel. For such mixed purposes, Crown land was frequently purchased at this time by local business interests. Like cottage properties, the supply of such sites was highly circumscribed by the trunk road system, which remained in its pre-war infancy. The result was the emergence of the first cabin complexes along all routes, often at picturesque points, but sometimes in mixed clusters at major key highway junctions or about urban centres.[324]

Some of these commercial operations also quickly adapted to include sites for another vacation alternative, car camping and trailering. This trend arose from a desire to spurn still-crowded city parks like Bellevue at Sault Ste Marie or Chippewa and Current River at the Lakehead in favour of more rural environs.[325] Although the number of car camper sites cannot be determined, some thirty-nine facilities of this type were available across the northwest by the early fifties (see Table 4.12). Most were in the huge districts of Thunder Bay and Kenora, along the trunk route from Winnipeg via Nipigon to Kapuskasing.

TABLE 4.12 Car Camper Sites, c. 1950

	Provincial Parks	Provincial Roadside Parks	Commercial Tent/Trailer Camps
Algoma West	1	3 (80)	2
Thunder Bay District	1	14 (117)	16
Rainy River District	1	3 (40)	5
Kenora/Patricia	0	8 (61)	16
Total	3	28 (298)	39

Source: George Wells and Iris Wells, *Auto Camper's Guide to Canada* (New York: Harper and Brothers, 1955), 126–53.

They were much less common in the road-starved environs of southern Patricia. This was true also both in Algoma, where cars could reach only a few miles north of the Montreal River, and in the Rainy River country, where a preference for the pre-war style of vacation seems to have stalled their appearance.

A second modest contribution to car camper accommodation was Ontario itself, imitating programs initiated in Michigan, among other states. In 1944, provincial parks at Sibley (near Nipigon) and a much larger one called lake Superior had reached the drawing-board for future addition in the northwest to Quetico. But except for eight sites at the road's end on Lake Superior's southern boundary, in 1950 all use was still by canoe or backpack in these loose preserves of public land.[326] However, at war's end, the Department of Highways had begun the provision of basic roadside sites in a total of twenty-eight regional locations. Only five – Goulais Bay on the Algoma shores, Middle Falls on the Pigeon River, Shuniah near Thunder Bay, Rushing River south of Kenora, and One Sided Lake in the Rainy River District – had more than twenty-five sites. The rest had fewer than seven.[327] Combining all car camping sites (government ones counted about 300), a total of no more than perhaps 600 car camping families seem likely to have been able to find accommodation on any summer night across the northwest. This figure, while astonishingly low in modern terms, was nonetheless promising in the years of immediate post-war adjustment.

Agriculture in Transition

Conflicting Thrusts

For Ontario's farmers, the forties represented an uncertain high point between a modest but proud and stable past and an insecure, under-valued, and less profitable future. This, perhaps, was inevitable in a province preoccupied with the goal of a predominantly urban, industrial economy.[328] Nowhere was this truer than in the northwest, where agriculture had coped so well with the problems of the previous decade, compared with most other sectors of the community. In rural records of the decade, one gets a sense of a conflict between old thrusts and new trends, a situation that did not bode well for the future.

Young people on the farm were not immune to the demands of the war and many from the rural population of these districts left home as volunteers or military conscripts. Others moved to wartime employment in the nearest city. Not all came back. After the war, many rural residents abandoned the farm altogether.[329] In the northwest, these events were reflected in a net loss of 1,500 farms by 1951 (see Table 4.13).

TABLE 4.13 Rural Profile, 1941–1951

	1941	1951
Algoma West		
No. of farms	297	204*
Farm population	1,998	977
Rural population	5,533	8,325
Thunder Bay District		
No. of farms	2,389	1,863
Farm population	8,564	8,793
Rural population	25,476	37,180
Rainy River District		
No. of farms	1,858	1,371
Farm population	6,981	6,068
Rural population	11,183	11,649
Kenora District		
No. of farms	931	551
Farm population	3,247	3,781
Rural population	9,308	9,428
Total Northwest		
No. of farms	5,475	3,989
Farm population	20,790	19,619
Rural population	51,500	66,582

* Because of altered divisions in farm size classes between the two census years, no comparable percentage of dominant size range can be calculated here.
Source: Compiled from Census of Canada, 1941 and 1951.

Countering this process were the newcomers who settled among the soil pockets in the later years of the decade. As early as the spring of 1946, regional authorities were in correspondence with officials in Ottawa, seeking future immigrants to refurbish and strengthen regional farm populations. Over the following years, upward of a hundred families, many from the Netherlands, took land in the Rainy River Valley, and others are known to have joined the rural communities behind the Lakehead.[330] Such immigrants also visited Algoma and Dryden in their search for new homes, but none seem to have chosen land near Sault Ste Marie and few were tempted by farms in the Kenora pocket.[331] To this modest post-war flow were added the war veterans, for whose possible arrival preparations had begun in 1944.[332] As many as 190 of these returnees and their families found farm lots in the Rainy River country by 1950. In contrast, around Dryden and the major urban centres of the northwest, such persons most frequently selected small rural holdings and took jobs in industry.[333]

Although farm numbers fell considerably in every district, the result of these departures and additions was only a small net loss in farm population. However, the size of the latter varied considerably across the region (see Table 4.13). In the Kenora–Dryden pocket and about Thunder Bay the farm population remained slightly above pre-war levels, despite a decline in actual farms. Elsewhere, both figures fell, the drop in Algoma West being linked to the impact of urban sprawl. In Rainy River, however, even given the healthy inflow of veterans and immigrants, a decline of almost a thousand had followed frequent abandonment of marginal endeavours on the northern fringe of the better valley lands. In townships like Morson, McCrossen, Spohn, Fleming, and Potts, the derelict log cabins, rotting outbuildings, and reverting fields from this era can still be found in considerable number today. However, in other pockets, such relicts of past patterns of rural endeavour have survived less frequently in outlying townships. In all cases, they stand in sharp contrast to the well-built homes, substantial barns, and related structures that reflect comfort and continuing well-being over these years of stress and change. Yet, in all pockets, other residences are indicative of the increasing rural non-farm numbers that continued to infiltrate the farm community and to do so at particularly high rates in environs adjacent to urban, industrial areas.[334]

The uncertainty of agricultural's northern role, exemplified here by these statistics and field observations, had been recognized in the thirties, across province and nation, by authorities already concerned about farm income levels. Yet their experiments in market management and commodity control of that day would find significant application only in the fifties.[335] In an attempt to come to grips with its post-war, rural obligations as well as its urban, industrial strategies, Ontario appointed an Agricultural Commission in early 1944. The results of its hearings across the northwest revealed a surprisingly conservative, even unimaginative outlook among regional farmers. Their requests and suggestions included more help with drainage, more attention to hydro, more encouragement to settlement, more support for livestock breeding, more provision of clearing equipment, and lower freight rates.[336] Yet all these ideas had been voiced before; they simply supported pre-war aims for developmental ends that were now in doubt under new post-war conditions.

Faced with this paucity of new or modified regional initiatives, Toronto continued the traditional approach. This the farmers appeared to hold operable, even crucial for the future of their calling. Efforts were mounted to encourage both immigrants and veterans to locate among these pockets. By 1947, the still badly drained lands in the southwestern Rainy River Valley were being opened by another 115 miles of deep ditches and more would follow.[337] In addition, government bulldozers and grubbers were hard at work clearing additional acreage for settlers, new and old.[338] Considerable help with livestock continued, while hydro lines, by the end of the decade, were again beginning to creep along rural road allowances.[339]

These officially encouraged activities, along with others, had their inevitable mix of short-term success and failure after the war. Indeed, even before war's end, former urban markets for pressed hay had faltered with the advent of the automobile. They would continue to decline as woodland operations gave up the horse and farmers themselves more widely adopted the tractor.[340] In the Rainy River country, heavy cooperative shipments of wool to Toronto and lambs and sheep to Winnipeg continued. However, wool exports faced price uncertainties with the introduction of synthetic fibres, and other commodities met rising international competition.[341] By 1951, only 6,500 sheep remained in flocks, once containing three times that figure in the valley. Meanwhile, an important, if less substantial, sheep industry behind the Lakehead declined even earlier under added problems of predators. Sheep raising came to a near standstill in other pockets as well.[342] Cattle exports to Winnipeg packing houses from the valley returned to normal levels with peace and encouraged considerable growth in beef raising there. Behind Thunder Bay, however, this trade was only marginally profitable because of the rising cost of feed grain, which could not be home grown effectively; around Dryden beef cattle levels fell sharply because of marketing problems late in the decade.[343]

Cooperative creameries, cheese factories, and commercial milk production all persisted after 1945, although milk producers sometimes complained of low prices.[344] At decade's end the first appearance of margarine and declines in dairy exports to Britain began to depress the price of both butter and cheese in the region.[345] Such cooperative production, while found elsewhere, remained most predominant along the Rainy River, which, in the raising of potatoes and quality clover seed, also shared major importance with areas around Dryden and Thunder Bay.[346] In the forties all these cooperatives merged under the original Producers' Co-op, which also came to operate four retail outlets between Rainy River and Fort Frances.[347] Such commercial organization, for both purchasing and marketing, had by that time become one of the pillars of Ontario's post-war strategies for countering sagging farm income.[348]

Against this background of mixed progress and impending problems, the basic social institutions that focused on the church and community hall continued undisturbed. Although the aging exhibition at Sault Ste Marie lost its momentum with the war and later folded, its partner at the Lakehead prospered, improving its facilities for what had become a highly urban audience.[349] Nevertheless, healthy fall fairs, of varied size and duration, continued to attract rural attention in Emo, Rainy River, Kenora, and Dryden.[350] While a few Guelph agricultural graduates could be counted among the region's youth, the annual spring short-courses, still held in every district but Algoma West, were popular among both farmers and their wives. Similarly, the clubs dedicated to improvement in various fields of farming continued their regular operations. The weekly farmers' market in the urban centres might sometimes have declined because of advances in commercial retailing, but the general temper of agricultural life was still very reminiscent of the past.

Resulting Land Use Conditions

The above characteristics of the rural society found their parallel in the appearance of the rural countryside with its substantial and well-tended farmsteads. These same characteristics were exemplified again by the pattern of land clearance, taken this time from assessment rolls at the end of the forties, for the same sample townships previously portrayed for 1930 (see Maps 4.5a and b). The more distant townships south of the Lakehead centres showed an increased scatter of lots on which limited farm clearance had occurred. This very modest change, however, resulted in little increase in the sparse pattern of property on which such marginal endeavours had produced more than 30 per cent clearance, and many of these lots probably now lay dormant. On the richer, varied, and more suitable lands behind the twin cities, a large increase was registered in the over-30-per-cent category, with many lots now more than half cleared of their trees. At the same time, some adjoining lots of less potential bore some new clearing, although others had been allowed to revert to bush or to return to the Crown for unpaid taxes.

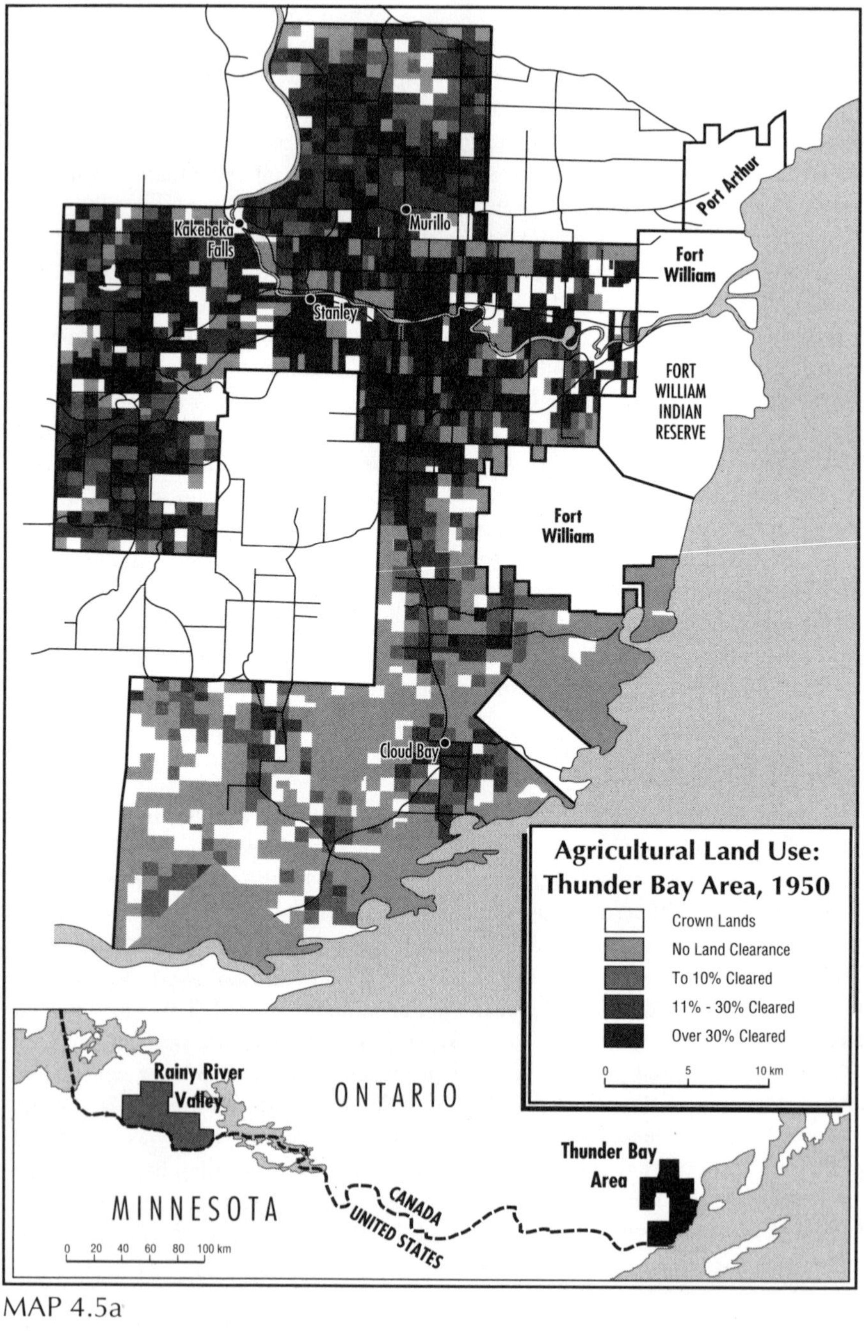
Port Arthur
Murillo
Kakebeka Falls
Fort William
Stanley
FORT WILLIAM INDIAN RESERVE
Fort William
Cloud Bay
Agricultural Land Use: Thunder Bay Area, 1950
Crown Lands
No Land Clearance
To 10% Cleared
11% - 30% Cleared
Over 30% Cleared
0
5
10 km
Rainy River Valley
ONTARIO
Thunder Bay Area
MINNESOTA
CANADA
UNITED STATES
0
20
40
60
80
100 km

MAP 4.5a

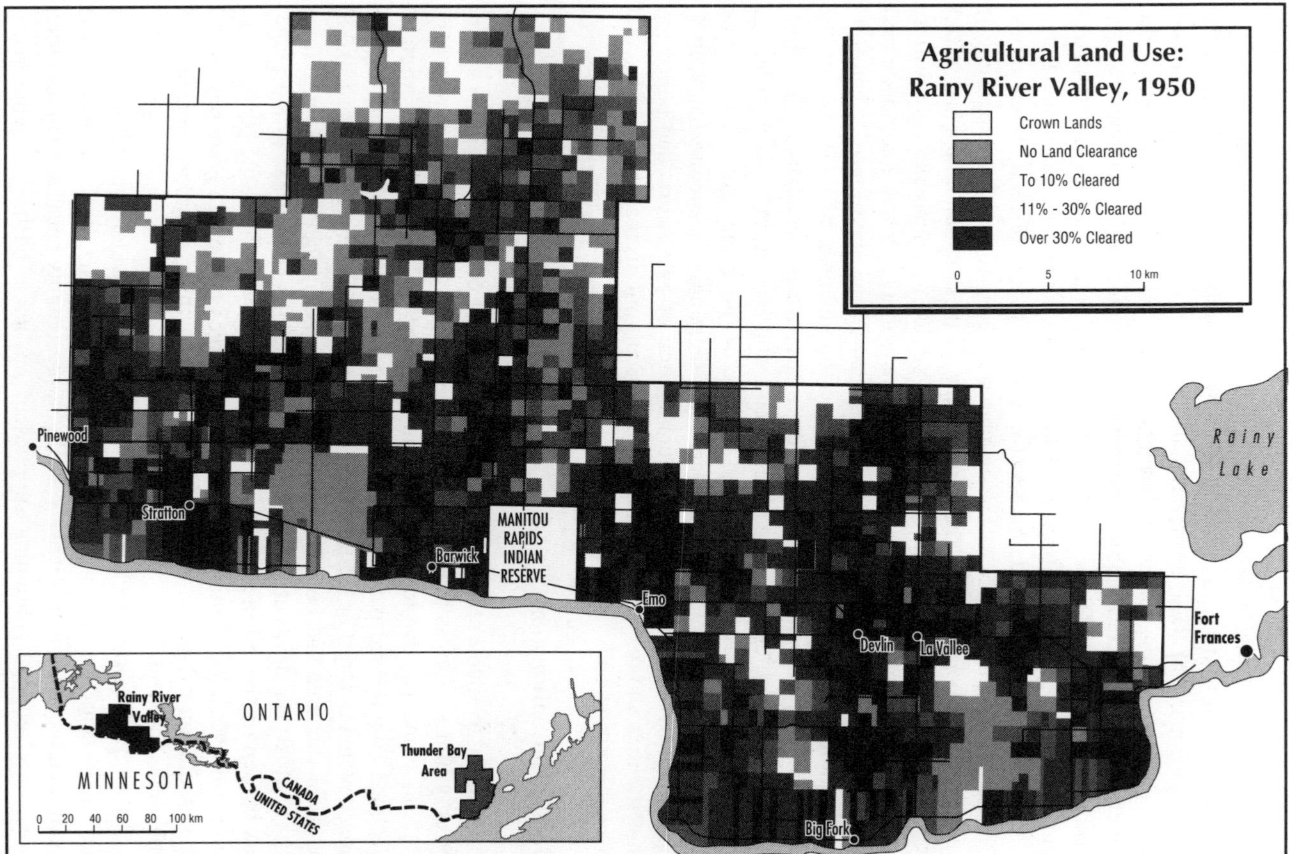
Agricultural Land Use:
Rainy River Valley, 1950
Crown Lands
No Land Clearance
To 10% Cleared
11% - 30% Cleared
Over 30% Cleared
0
5
10 km
Rainy Lake
Fort Frances
Pinewood
Stratton
Barwick
MANITOU RAPIDS INDIAN RESERVE
Emo
Devlin
La Vallee
Big Fork
Rainy River Valley
ONTARIO
MINNESOTA
Thunder Bay Area
CANADA
UNITED STATES
0 20 40 60 80 100 km

MAP 4.5b

Except for two substantial tracts in the Rainy River example, most Crown lots and undeveloped private acreage continued to lie in the back townships more proximal to the Shield. As in the case of similar properties south of the Lakehead, many of these in private hands were in varying stages of regrowth after pulp harvesting either by farmers or contractors, who had reaped the benefits of the relaxed cutting and marketing regulations of previous years. While farm clearance levels above 30 per cent seem less marked in both extent and contiguity than those back of Thunder Bay, such acreage, concentrated close to the river-front, had come to form major blocks of rural communities. On the intervening matrix of less-valued soil, very substantial expansion of lesser clearance appeared as the membership of these communities had added land about the fringe. Other townships here, stretching inland along the valley, with their now well-developed road systems suitable to the automobile and their networks of tidy commercial centres, had all the appearance of comfortably maturing northern agriculture. General comparison of these patterns of clearance with the modern land capability maps reveals a much higher relationship between well-cleared acreage and better soil classes, in a larger pattern in which clearance has now ceased to occupy or move onto most lots of low capacity. These now moderately cleared and seemingly prosperous landscapes, however, were the product of the accumulation of past efforts and belied the uncertainties and the rising conditions of agricultural distress that now loomed over the northwest.

Statistical Confirmation

Indeed, the available statistics indicate changes that other records either ignore or only hint at. Across the region a quiet decline in total land held for agriculture accompanied dwindling farm numbers over the forties. While cropland declined slightly and pasture advanced, the real focus of change was in farm area devoted to forest or slashed-over woodland (see Table 4.14). Some 150,000 acres of this area had been dropped from declared agricultural holdings since 1941. Most was now cut over and, in tightening times, was seen as a growing tax burden or beyond the wooded acreage necessary for domestic purposes. In some instances, the termination of the last vestiges of the free grant policy and the institution of stricter regulations on settler cutting may have encouraged such abandonment.[351]

The impact of this decline in farm holdings was widely varied among the soil pockets of the region. In the districts of Thunder Bay and Kenora the decline in forest-related acreage was slight, presumably because some outlying townships retained continuing supplies of profitable bush.[352] Algoma West,

TABLE 4.14 Agricultural Development, 1941–1951

	1941		1951	
	Acres	% of total	Acres	% of total
Algoma West				
Cropland	7,196	24	5,630	41
Pasture	6,154	20	4,694	35
Other	16,794	56	3,318	24
Total held	30,144		13,642	
Thunder Bay District				
Cropland	59,489	19	60,622	22
Pasture	70,275	22	69,453	25
Other	186,426	59	148,081	53
Total held	316,190		278,156	
Rainy River District				
Cropland	69,646	20	70,247	23
Pasture	90,591	27	129,579	41
Other	180,773	53	112,873	36
Total held	341,010		312,699	
Kenora District				
Cropland	26,776	16	22,344	19
Pasture	45,199	27	30,510	26
Other	95,873	57	64,566	55
Total held	167,848		117,420	
Total Northwest				
Cropland	163,107	19	158,843	22
Pasture	212,219	25	234,236	32
Other	479,866	56	328,838	46
Total held	855,192		721,917	

Source: Compiled from Agricultural tables, Census of Canada, 1941 and 1951.

which was no longer a large producer of settler cut, witnessed very high levels of abandonment, reducing its proportion of total farm acreage to a third. In the much larger Rainy River pocket, where settler pulp production also had a marked history, the proportional decline was similar, but the amount abandoned approached 68,000 acres. Much of this huge sum lay in the back townships where farm development was most recent, where agricultural clearance was shown to be most limited, and where previous dependence on forest income was most pronounced. However, in this process of declining total acreage and farm numbers, the result was not only the abandonment of worthless acreage but, except at Sault Ste Marie, a substantial increase in average farm size from about 155 to over 180 acres (compare Tables 4.13 and 4.14).

Variant adjustments in cropland and pastoral levels also occurred in these rural pockets of agriculture. Cultivation in the two largest pockets rose, but in very limited amounts, even behind Thunder Bay, despite the growing demand of rising urban population on the bay. The market there had presumably begun to find competitive supplies of basic items elsewhere. In the remaining pockets, the component of farm acreage fell noticeably, squeezed at Sault Ste Marie by urbanization. However, about Kenora and Dryden, these declines were dictated by the loss of former western outlets and the resultant reliance on more limited local demand. In the Dryden pocket, pastoral acreage followed a similar course for the same reason, further underlining a growing agricultural problem that was also indicated by plummeting farm numbers.[353] Around the Lakehead, the decline in flocks and beef herds of the thirties and forties had yet to register significantly in falling pasturage figures.

These northwestern trends in the livestock sector, along with the apparent static state of urban demands for local cash crops (fresh fruit, vegetables, etc.) pointed to future troubles for the farmer in the fifties. However, in the Rainy River Valley, the addition of new settlers, the return of the Manitoba market for beef and dairy products, and the success of cooperatives stimulated some new crop acreage but much more unimproved pasturage. This unimproved status merely reflected the current stage in the ongoing process of land drainage and clearance towards improved status and perhaps arable use that was continuing in the western valley. In any case, at the beginning of the fifties, the Rainy River country was the healthiest and most productive of northwestern Ontario's agricultural areas, as it had been since early in the century.

Urban Trends and Developments

While the peculiar demands of this decade interrupted or delayed all infrastructural projects in transport, except certain hydro-related ones, their impact on regional population was to promote mobility and growth. As in the rest of Ontario,[354] the non-agricultural component gained further dominance (see Table 4.15), covering, by 1950, 87 per cent of a total 207,500 people in the region, although the increase in urban numbers was less than that in rural, non-farm residents.

Large Centres

Among long-established centres, growth was predictable, under the industrial exigencies of war or the immediate adjustments to peace. In the three major

TABLE 4.15 Population Profile (percentage urban and rural non-farm), 1941–1951

	1941		1951	
	Population	% of total	Population	% of total
Algoma West				
Rural non-farm	3,540	11	7,348	18
Urban	25,794	82	32,452	80
Total population	32,215		40,777	
Thunder Bay District				
Rural non-farm	16,476	19	28,387	27
Urban	59,990	70	75,462*	72
Total population	85,200		105,367	
Rainy River District				
Rural non-farm	4,202	22	5,581	25
Urban	7,102	37	9,386	42
Total population	19,132		22,132	
Kenora District				
Rural non-farm	6,061	18	5,647	14
Urban	12,623	38	15,328	39
Total population	33,372		39,212	
Total Northwest				
Rural non-farm	30,274	18	46,963	23
Urban	104,793	62	132,628	64
Total population	169,919		207,488	

* Of this total, 6,127 were in the new centres of Marathon, Red Rock, and Terrace Bay.

centres, the population climbed significantly but not alarmingly, each adding something slightly over 5,000 people. As might be inferred from earlier comments, one major factor affecting change was probably Ottawa's wartime labour priorities for industry. Another was the differential rate at which individual industries adjusted to post-war market and labour demands.[355] In the twin cities at the Lakehead, where such priorities for pulp and paper manufacture were modest, real wartime growth was slow but post-war expansion came rapidly. Given government's high priority for steel-making during the war and the prolonged labour strife in that industry in the late forties, a reversal of these trends applied at Sault Ste Marie. However, rising wartime demand before 1940 had already converted numerous ancillary industries in these cities – foundries, forges, shipyards, and metal fabricators – to military production, as in 1914. These conversions, with their related labour needs, undoubtedly had a modifying impact since much of the labour force needed in the war years either arrived and left between census years or arrived before 1941 and left before 1951.

In all three centres, many young workers were lost to the war but their wives and families still lived at home. Therefore, those newcomers who were ineligible for military duty but helped fill this labour gap, along with others migrating to new war work in these cities, found housing in short supply as early as 1940. Every effort was made to provide for this continuing inflow, of which an increasing proportion was female. Indeed, in Fort William where many young women were employed at Canada Car in the manufacture of military aircraft, the construction of special dormitories was authorized to solve an immediate problem. Yet as the local press made clear, the accommodation crisis continued here, as elsewhere, for many months. While a belated national program of wartime housing came at mid-decade, only a post-war boom solved this urban situation. However, as Table 4.15 reveals, a large number of those who faced housing shortages in the interim chose or were forced to find homes in the surrounding townships and to commute to work from there.[356]

Small Towns and Single-Industry Towns

In smaller towns, population changes were of a less predictable nature. In both the Kenora and Rainy River districts, urban figures grew. However, in the former, the rural, non-farm population actually fell, and in the latter, the urban growth rate of Fort Frances exceeded that of the non-farm component. Such centres suffered mildly from housing shortages during the conflict and most reported much immediate post-war construction, even annexation, which may temper these 1951 statistics.[357] Interestingly enough, pulp and paper communities here, recipients of the first flow of European immigrants by 1950, sometimes included Germans returning to the bush or mill where they had worked as POWs.[358] Most centres came to have at least a Red Cross hospital over the decade. Many with established high schools or continuation schools came to receive students from the surrounding countryside as school bussing made its first tentative appearance.[359] Some centres that had remained unincorporated, now became improvement districts, a stage initiated by the province in 1943, which was preparatory to the granting of full municipal status.[360] However, events had tended again to increase the gap between these smaller communities and the cities at the top of the hierarchy, in terms of size, function, and regional importance.

More important in this decade was the addition of certain small single-industry towns. Unlike their earlier regional counterparts, Marathon, Red Rock, and Terrace Bay were laid out professionally, under very sophisticated planning principles. They were intended to be aesthetically attractive, socially effective, and municipally efficient in their provision of utilities, education, health care, and recreation. Such model towns represented not the beginning but a maturing stage in official thought and experience regarding northern resource communities, their problems, and their always uncertain futures.

Experiments in such planning went back to Thomas Adams, who, during his term of employment with the Federal Commission of Conservation from 1909 to 1921, had laid out both Iroquois Falls and Kapuskasing in northeastern Ontario.[361] However, in the years before his arrival and in much of the two decades after his departure, the birth and growth of such single-enterprise towns was often haphazard. The result was usually an ugly sprawl, in and beyond an unimaginative grid of rectangular lots and road allowances, with homes and businesses serviced by inadequate utilities and uncertain water supply.[362] Northern resource towns at that time were considered as nothing more than impermanent creations, worthy of little thought or expenditures. By the late thirties, the public, the government, and labour were beginning to demand reform of this aging industrial view of urban development.[363] However, by 1950, what emerged was still only an uneasy amalgam of philosophies, ideas, and pragmatic concepts.

In the northwest, the earliest single-enterprise centres to reflect something of Adam's ideals were hydro villages. These were erected by both Ontario's HEPC and Lake Superior Power (Great Lakes Power) at all isolated generating stations to house the families of personnel required to operate and maintain each facility. Examples included ones at Rat Rapids and Ear Falls, at Cameron and Alexander stations on the Nipigon, at High Falls on the Michipicoten, and both upper and lower generators on the Montreal River. Most of these caretaker villages have disappeared in this age of remote automation. However, pictures and remaining buildings reveal basic but comfortable company homes and the simple provision of recreational, commercial, educational, and religious needs considered adequate in their day.[364]

Other significant urban developments in the early forties centred on the mining industry. Unlike such disastrously unplanned places as Red Lake or Geraldton, with their jumble of satellite pit villages,[365] Algoma's community of Wawa had key improvements woven into its fabric. While it inherited the unimaginative rectangular survey of the old gold town (Wawa City) of the late nineties, it was provided with excellent, modern sewage, water, and power systems. As the town's modern business district attests, private enterprise received strong encouragement, but the Algoma Ore Division of Algoma Steel was careful to provide initial housing and essential facilities for health, education, and recreation.[366] Indeed, it had little choice if it were to attract and keep the necessary skilled workers under the then extreme conditions of isolation.

The community development for the Steep Rock iron project, which followed in 1943, rapidly transformed Atikokan from a small rail village of 250 into a centre of 2,500 by 1950.[367] In the interim, a fully modern construction camp served all the needs of those employed on early drainage and diversion work. This enabled province, company, and inhabitants to design and build an appropriately planned town of segregated uses, curvilinear streets, and full utilities and facilities.[368] Atikokan quickly came to be administered under improvement district status to ensure appropriate management of fire and police, as well as maintenance of water and sewer services.[369] Success here with this form of administration led to its application at Red Lake and Geraldton to confront the myriad problems attending their unplanned rise. Next Red Lake an improvement district was also initiated at Balmertown, which was a new community built to house and serve the now-rising Campbell Red Lake and Dickenson Mines.[370]

In this drive for improved social conditions and planned communities, the forest industry made a particularly innovative contribution during the later war years.[371] With its origins in that industry's search for reduced costs and stable labour conditions, this new plan was the idea of A.J. Auden, a senior forester with Abitibi at the Lakehead. In late 1943, he submitted to the newly formed Lakehead Rehabilitation and Post-War Reconstruction Commission an experimental plan to develop 'forest villages.'[372] The first of these he proposed to create in Purdom Township on the south shore of Lake Nipigon.[373] Concepts of permanent settlement, sustained resource use, and cooperative organization formed the basis of his plan. His aim was to create new communities, each consisting of twenty-five veterans or post-war immigrant families, which might be permitted later to grow to 100 households. Each family head was to be granted a small lot in the village and a large block of neighbouring woodland. A professional forester would annually mark all trees in each block that were ready to harvest and would define all areas of each property suitable for agricultural clearance. Communally organized industries in the village would transport, process, and market these resources and manage a sustained harvest of fish from specified lakes and fur from local trap lines or fur farms. In addition, income would be gained from seasonal labour, such as river driving and work in the tourist industry. The latter would be derived through the establishment of sporting lodges in the village with adjunct out-camps. Related income as fishing or hunting guides could also be earned. Local access roads would be built under initial provincial grants and highway links to the outside world would continue to be a government responsibility.[374] Although idealistic, the plan caught the attention of the new Ontario Department of Planning and Development, which, in 1944–5, funded a full-scale study and five-year plan for such a community. There is no evidence, however, that Auden's Purdom experiment or any other such forest village ever resulted.[375]

However, Auden's idea immediately caught the attention of regional pulpwood operators and paper companies. Some were attracted by Auden's concept of complete use of area resources to sustain each community, and could see how his model, in variant form, could address their needs. With its emphasis on sustenance of family communities on a mixed base of resource income, the concept of the forest village became bonded to the emerging idea of depots in place of scattered cutting camps. By 1947, officials at the Lakehead, where most of these notions were under consideration, had come even to conceive of villages with both an agricultural and supportive tourist side to their forest economy. More often they were envisioned to be residential family communities with facilities for transporting the work force to and from the expanding area of cutting sites and for maintaining or repairing harvesting equipment.[376]

By the close of the decade, the term 'forest community' in place of depot had come into popular usage for such centres among the members of the Lakehead Timberman's Association.[377] A growing number of these small, important nodes from Vermilion Bay, west of Dryden, to Heron Bay, east of Marathon, and up the ACR, now bore that loose designation.[378]

Some, like Caramat or Valora, were planned villages, complete with homes, bunkhouses, recreational and health facilities, as well as a store. Many amounted only to simply machinery workshops and company-built subdivisions added to existing centres, such as Beardmore. All, however, were privately planned enterprises with provincial encouragement. A few had even been designed with an eye to conversion to tourist or vacation resorts, if or when local forest endeavours declined.[379]

Planned Additions

Related to, yet distinct from, such developments was the rise, in the 1940s, of the three new paper towns – Red Rock, Marathon, and Terrace Bay – on Superior's north shore, referred to earlier. Like the modern mills that sponsored their appearance, these were the creation of individual companies, and their design and dramatic births collected much public attention.[380] The oldest among these projects was at Red Rock, where a town survey and mill plot were laid out in 1936 by Lake Sulphite, which, on its bankruptcy in 1938, left twenty unfinished homes, other buildings, and a partly completed plant. After use as a POW camp in the early forties, these structures were completed by

Brompton Pulp and Paper in 1944. That firm also modified the original plan to make more aesthetic use of the landscape and added another 185 houses and facilities for education, health, and shopping as well as the appropriate public utilities the province now required.[381] The other two communities, Marathon (formerly Peninsula), initiated in 1944, and Terrace Bay, set out in 1946, were also conceived for immediate populations of 1,000 to 1,500 and reached that target by the end of the decade.[382] All were provided with the same range of facilities, functions, and utilities, and all quickly assumed improvement district status, in which organization, however, each company (Marathon Pulp at Marathon and Long Lake Pulp, later Kimberly-Clark, at Terrace Bay) retained a very firm position.[383] The layout of each town shows an increasingly holistic approach to planning, reflected in the level of harmony achieved between road patterns, functional requirements, and physical environs. Indeed, Terrace Bay is probably the most aesthetically pleasing example of a post-war town in northwestern Ontario.[384] Here, as elsewhere, much of the motive behind such planned development stemmed from the forest industry's recognition that such northern expenditures were now key to a stable and satisfactory labour force. At the same time, the new members of the nodal pattern of 1950 are the most obvious monuments to the increasing public interest in socially responsible actions on the part of industry. Finally, they stand as visual reminders of the rising importance of planning in the provincial approach to northern resources management.[385]

Tried, Tested, and Found True

After the crucible of depression and the exigencies of war, the northwest had returned by 1950 to a more predictable course of development. However, having scrambled to survive Booth's early collapse and having endured subsequent years of struggle under inadequate prices, the regional fisheries were in further weakened condition. Agriculture, which had proudly surmounted the uncertainties of the thirties and continued the sorting of its lands in the forties, was a healthy, if much leaner, industry. The thirties had separated good farmers from bad. The forties had offered many farm youths an escape to military service or urban war work from which few returned to the land. After a complex of detours in the early depression, tourism had returned to earlier levels. Continuing its American thrust and its increasing emphasis on family car camping, the industry rose to major regional economic importance before the end of the period. In the thirties, gold mining had prospered and expanded in new areas but, with wartime, had faded in favour of a huge revitalization of steel and iron ore production. The forest industry, already prey to uncertainties by 1929, had been troubled by Depression markets then by war restrictions on production in pulp and paper. It also had suffered a steep decline in suitable timber resources for lumber manufacture. With war's end the move to new fabrication methods for construction materials and a resurgence in pulp and paper, involving the erection of new mills and mill towns, had returned this sector to its former economic prominence.

In conjunction with these developments went progress in related infrastructure. The Depression had turned trunk road construction into a mammoth employment project that resulted in a gravelled route across northern Ontario by 1950. This, with well-tended rural road systems and the advent of the snow plough, provided the first rudimentary, year-round interconnection of the region by truck, car, and bus. While hydro here was not new to the urban scene, surprising long-distance expansion of transmission systems occurred in the thirties and in selective cases even survived much-reduced general priority in wartime. However, at the period's close most local developments in rural, residential power had yet to begin, while much older and more ubiquitous telephone service remained most primitive by modern standards.

Over the thirties, the urban sector faced severe financial and social dislocation. With the exception of gold mining towns, the heavy burden of unemployment taxed the resources of the communities to the extreme. Recovery came to different centres at different rates and times, depending on the nature of their economic base. Yet the forties opened with growing, if differential, urban demands for industrial production and the accommodation of the work force to promote that end. These demands, combined with those for military service, stripped the labour supply in some single-industry towns but had less impact on others, which had activities of higher wartime value. Inevitably, these demands hit the large regional centres, with their complex manufacturing capabilities, hardest. The effect on both the twin cities at the Lakehead and Sault Ste Marie was an enormous surge in productive effort and the sprawl of non-farm, residential use into adjacent townships. The most obvious result of these and related events across the hierarchy was the elevation of urban and rural non-farm population from regional dominance to predominance in both the economy and the society.

Yet, after all the countering trends of these trying years, the mid- and late forties introduced others indicative of returning peace-time ideals and preparations for a fresh start. On the side of resource harvesting, these changes brought a growing reliance on mechanization and economies of scale. In resource processing, they were epitomized by the appearance of planned communities and a push for improved living conditions in older, single-industry, resource towns. Both reflected recognition of changing labour demands, characteristics, and requirements. All were harbingers of the boisterously progressive, yet increasingly conservationist thinking that would characterize the era ahead.

5

Modern Complications in the Northwest, 1950–1994

Across Canada, the twenty-five years following 1950 were ones of unprecedented advance in both living standards and levels of social service. These improvements were fostered under a booming economy, although this buoyancy has since faltered, even in central Canada. In a thriving Ontario, the population almost doubled to over eight million in 1976, due not only to the baby boom and post-war immigration but also to increasing life expectancy. With a maturing industrial complex with close American ties and a mushrooming service sector, over three-quarters of this population was concentrated in Metro Toronto and other urban centres. Farm numbers declined sharply in spite of increased agricultural productivity. Meanwhile, an effective highway network and modern air transport system combined to link Ontario internally and externally. These developments were supplemented by early pipelines and long-distance electrical transmission lines as well as an expanding net of communication systems. As in the other provinces and at the federal level, government increasingly entered the lives of post-war Ontarians, planning their economic course, ensuring their social well-being, and regulating their impact on the environment.

Into the nineties, this elaborate bureaucratic pattern continued to evolve, its infrastructure to improve, its social safety net to broaden, and its immigration policies to increase the urban dominance. This has come about despite rising problems of service-related public indebtedness, coupled with shifting global trade patterns, market alignments, and financial structuring, capped by stultifying economic recession. Save for brief difficulties during the energy crisis in the late seventies and early eighties, Old Ontario was able to escape serious economic problems until recent years. With the rest of hinterland Canada, the northern districts of the province, however, have been less fortunate, suffering in the economic doldrums for much of the last two decades.[1]

Rapid but Unbalanced Development, 1950–1980

In the northwest of 1950, as elsewhere above the Great Lakes, post-war progress was already a reality, which fact Queen's Park was careful to bring to the public's attention. In Ontario's populous southern counties, this carefully orchestrated publicity was intended to renew images of vast northern resources, new strides in their development, and innovative drives towards stewardly management. In northern regions and among the financial/industrial community that sponsored these advances, such publicity was intended to convey confidence and enthusiasm, both towards what was already being accomplished and in what could be responsibly expected.[2] This official campaign was a bold, clever, and sincere attempt to renew a dynamic northern heritage lost in the bitter expediencies of past decades. It was to prove remarkably successful in its intent and responsive to changing times in its approach to emerging problems. However, by the seventies, the over-consumption of resources forced both the public and political leaders to recognize the potential for neglect and the excessive use of the northern environment.[3]

Developments under government aegis in the northwest, as in the rest of the provincial mid-north, stood at odds with more southerly changes in these years. Over 80 per cent of northwestern trade in 1950 was already in direct exports of finished, semi-finished, and even some raw resources to the United States (mainly beneficiated minerals, pulp, paper, and construction-grade lumber). Old Ontario's exports to the U.S. still hovered around 50 per cent of its total exports at that date, although it would rise over the following years.[4] At the opening of the period, U.S. vacation dollars were noticeably important, but by 1980, tourism would vie with the forest and mining industry for supremacy in the regional economy.[5] The rising service sector may have transformed the functional personality of major and minor urban centres in the northwest, but its impact was never to compare with that in southern cities, particularly Metro Toronto. Yet burgeoning communications and general mobility had an effect on the northwest perhaps more fundamental to its human and economic development than in more advanced parts of the province. At the same time, the continuing primary nature and limited diversity of the region's industrial base caused decades of buoyant times to quickly give way to stumbling uncertainty, with the energy crisis and related recession of the late seventies. Assured growth did not eventually return to this resource-oriented region in the same way it did to the broader, more confident, and credit-driven economy of southern Ontario.[6] While agriculture shrank and rural, non-farm use expanded in reflection of southern trends, the impact of these changes in northern rural organization was tellingly different. Although total population grew, the rate of growth declined after 1970. As a result, falling labour requirements in the modern workplace and the attraction of other regions decreased immigration and began to promote growing youthful out-migration. Such factors, combined with the fear of an impending bust, after yet another boom in the cyclical history of the region, were coming to permeate business outlook, to dog public thinking, and to foreshadow personal decisions as the seventies closed.

Strides in Communication and Transport

Land Transport

Changes and improvements in one or more of these fields touched every aspect of development across the northwest over these decades. In 1950, the rural pockets, with their urban centres, had been linked only recently with the national system of gravelled trunk roads. Winnipeg and the Lakehead were now tied tenuously across the Clay Belt to Kapuskasing, then via North Bay to Toronto and Montreal. However, in 1949 Ottawa passed the Trans-Canada Highway Act, in which it would share equally with the provinces in upgrading this system to all-weather status, with uniform engineering standards from coast to coast. Ontario joined energetically in this program over the existing route. However, it continued to procrastinate over the enormously expensive alternate down the rugged side of Superior, between Terrace Bay and the Montreal River. For six years it waffled over the issue, to the frustration of both Ottawa and regional voters, while it nudged ahead with the proposed route sporadically and suggested alternates unacceptable to either party. Fed up with this and parallel behaviour in other provinces, Ottawa renegotiated its contracts in 1956, assuming 90 per cent of the cost here for the remaining 165 difficult miles. Four years later, an energized Ontario completed the route, with formal opening ceremonies at Wawa in the autumn of 1960 (see Map 5.1).[7]

Ontario's commitment to further road and highway expansion in the northwest was much more edifying. Its tradition of funding rural road improvements was soon only a small part in the aggressive schemes to promote full intra-regional interconnection with this national system. In 1965 a long-sought highway was opened from the Thunder Bay area to the Rainy River Valley, completed by a spectacular bridge over the narrows of Rainy Lake. This augmented the earlier construction of the final bridge linking the latter area to Kenora and was followed in the seventies by an additional direct route from Dryden south to Fort Frances. To meet mining needs, a number of lesser projects were also undertaken. Under an earlier agreement, roads replaced marine railways linking Red Lake to the future Trans-Canada Highway and Pickle Lake would

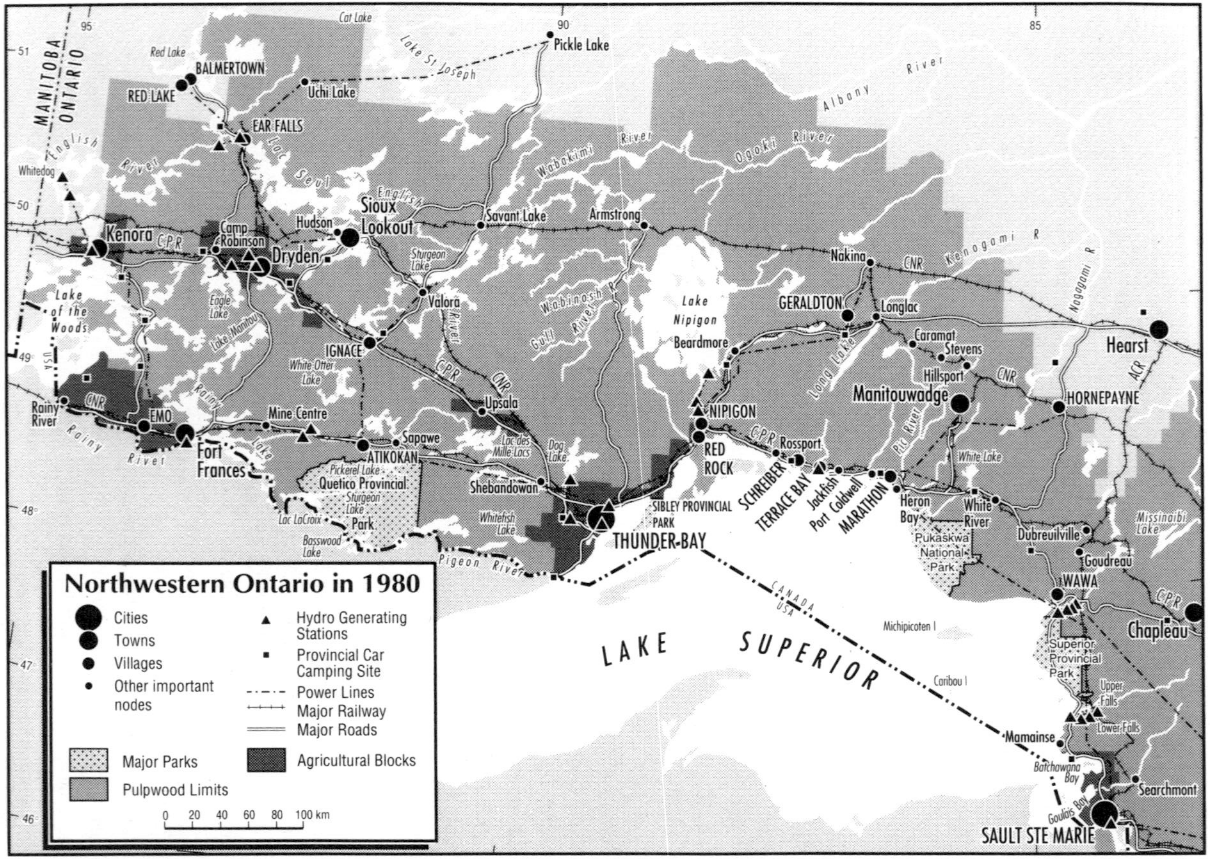
Northwestern Ontario in 1980
Cities
Towns
Villages
Other important nodes
Hydro Generating Stations
Provincial Car Camping Site
Power Lines
Major Railway
Major Roads
Major Parks
Pulpwood Limits
Agricultural Blocks
0 20 40 60 80 100 km
MANITOBA
ONTARIO
LAKE SUPERIOR
CANADA
USA
Kenora
Dryden
Sioux Lookout
Fort Frances
THUNDER BAY
SAULT STE MARIE
Hearst
Chapleau
Manitouwadge
RED LAKE
BALMERTOWN
EAR FALLS
IGNACE
ATIKOKAN
EMO
NIPIGON
RED ROCK
GERALDTON
SCHREIBER
TERRACE BAY
MARATHON
HORNEPAYNE
WAWA
Pickle Lake
Uchi Lake
Savant Lake
Armstrong
Nakina
Longlac
Caramat
Stevens
Hillsport
Beardmore
Rossport
Jackfish
Port Coldwell
Heron Bay
White River
Dubreuilville
Goudreau
Mamainse
Searchmont
Hudson
Camp Robinson
Valora
Upsala
Sapawe
Mine Centre
Shebandowan
Rainy River
Whitedog
Quetico Provincial Park
Pukaskwa National Park
Superior Provincial Park
SIBLEY PROVINCIAL PARK
Lake Nipigon
Lake of the Woods
Lac Seul
Michipicoten I
Caribou I
CPR
CNR
ACR

MAP 5.1

receive similar attention by 1960.[8] With joint private/public financing, roads were completed from Sioux Lookout to Valora, from Hemlo siding to Manitouwadge, from Geraldton to Nakina, and from Hornepayne north to the highway east to Hearst. After 1958, such construction often involved federal funds as well, under the Roads to Resources program of the Diefenbaker years. The results included major links to White Dog from Kenora, from Ignace north to Pickle Lake, White River to Hornepayne, and the Lakehead to Armstrong by 1966.[9] Some of these and many others, sometimes called industrial roads, were built in conjunction with pulp and paper firms seeking help to open new parts of their huge concessions. Indeed, by the late seventies, it became common for contractual clauses governing roads to be written into the evolving Forest Management Agreements. In only thirty years, ground access to resources and interconnection of communities had moved from being difficult and seasonal to easy and year round through government promotional policies.[10]

For railways in this era retooling, reorganization, and reduction were the watch-words of an increasingly competitive world. In 1950 the CNR and CPR were at a crossroads, requiring firm leadership and decisive action. Both were burdened with aging rolling stock, outmoded equipment and plant, and archaic managerial thinking – the result of two decades of lean times. More importantly, both faced steeply increasing operating costs and labour troubles as well as federal regulative measures intended to force equitable service, rates, and employment levels for a nation of unusual regional economies. Regulation of the railways' rising competitors – buses, and, more important, trucks – like the expanding highway net they used, was a provincial matter. From the twenties, when it introduced licenses for all three classes of vehicles, the province's stance had been one of encouraging road transport as an alternative to rail. Indeed, delayed action on the recommendation of a Royal Commission report of 1935, was instituted in the fifties by the Ontario Highway Transport Board to monitor commercial vehicles while promoting the rights and needs of the travelling public.[11]

In the early fifties, the railways faced increasing competition not only from buses and cars, but also from airplanes. Luxury train service, like CP's *Canadian* and CN's *Super Continental*, was introduced to win back long-distance travellers.[12] In the northwest, previously a modest source of domestic travellers and always a generator of tourist interests, change came quickly in shorter-range travel. Between Sudbury and Sault Ste Marie, for example, daily passenger service became tri-weekly in 1956, was reduced to a Budd car in 1963 and disappeared for want of ridership in 1977.[13] However, while ACR service to Wawa and Michipicoten Harbour died with the arrival of the Trans-Canada

Highway, primitive scheduling north to Hearst continued serving other isolated places along the line and the growing tourist demands north of Sault Ste Marie.[14] The reduction in service in the fifties and sixties characterized these once well-travelled routes, as the more versatile bus and the increasingly common family car entered the picture. Finally, the remaining passenger services of both railways were united to become VIA Rail in 1978.[15]

Railway freight fared much better, although it too was subjected to severe rethinking and rationalization. Not surprisingly, both national railways failed to compete in the short-haul end of the business where trucks had the same flexible advantage as horse-drawn drovers' wagons had once exerted. Increased trailer size, tractor power, and engine efficiency, as well as the improved surfaces they travelled, made the truck able to invade the mid-range market by the sixties and even the long-range one a decade later.[16] Nevertheless, the railways were able to keep over two-thirds of the total freight tonnage to the end of the period, although not always the most remunerative cargoes.[17]

Rail's success stemmed from basic changes contemplated in the later forties, initiated with the fifties, and completed a decade later. These changes involved massive improvements in road-bed and trackage, signalling and communication, repair shops, and yard facilities, as well as the creation of specialized rolling stock for the transport of items as diverse as automobiles and grain. Most important, however, was the move from steam to diesel electric power.[18] Despite their initial high price, diesel locomotives paid high returns in speed, traction, and the length of trains, as well as in reduced shop-time and much longer distances between fuel stops. Diesels also required lower track maintenance cost and resulted in more efficient winter operation.[19] In northwestern Ontario, the ACR completed its conversion to diesel by 1953, but its much larger cousins were fully equipped with such new engines only about five years later.[20]

The railways felt the benefits immediately, resulting in a wave of new imaginative thinking and aggressive action in marketing and service. In the northwest, where the original rights of way had been chosen with an eye to minimum cost and shortest passage across the Shield rather than to regional freight generation, the transport of raw resources was regarded as a field of minimal profit, including the grain that flowed out through the Lakehead.[21] Now, however, such bulky cargoes as pulpwood and ore were being energetically sought after. Forest industries were wooed to truck their harvest only to the nearest siding, rather than on to the mill. The new beneficiated iron pellets as well as refined and separated base metals came to be carried in special hopper cars, designed not only for easy loading and unloading but also with covers to prevent loss in transit. Both major railways also participated in the provision of spurs and sidings as required. The CPR built only one substantial branch from its main line to the spectacular new mines at Manitouwadge. However, the CNR duplicated this move and added many miles of new track north from near Savant Lake to the new iron deposits of the Ear Falls area.[22]

Yet the move to diesel and the related campaign for the retention of market share had its ugly side, which brought much economic and social stress to rail-dependent communities. The demise of steam locomotion spelled the end of those clusters of ash pits, water towers, and coaling stations at regular intervals along the right of way, as well as the jobs that had gone with them for decades. It also resulted in the closure of certain round-houses and repair facilities among divisional points, because of reduced maintenance requirements, and in the discontinuation of some crew-change centres, because increased speed permitted longer distances between them. All rail towns, villages, and lesser places in the northwest were affected. However, the blow was less severe for places like Kenora, Fort Frances, Sioux Lookout, Schreiber and Hornepayne, than for others such as Rainy River or White River. At Rainy River, during the fifties, the repair depot was closed and sold for its brick, while the community's remaining role as a crew-change centre was in danger of being moved to Fort Frances.[23] White River suffered equally, being reduced from a full divisional point, complete with livestock resting pens, to little more than a re-icing station for passenger cars and fish cargoes.[24] At lower levels in the system, the effects on employment were no less harsh. Because of reduced track maintenance required under diesel power, some twenty-six sectional crews lodged at eight-mile intervals between Hawk Junction behind Wawa and Hearst in 1950 were reduced to only five by 1970. Evidence suggests similar attrition across the region.[25] The benefits of railway modernization and increased efficiency notwithstanding, it was a high price to pay for a generation of railway workers who had once believed their traditional world was secure.[26]

Water and Air Travel

Lake shipping was also buffeted by post-war change, but it too responded resiliently. Passenger traffic dwindled with the emergence of alternate vacation patterns and travel forms. The appeal of liners was reduced due to their age and declining maintenance as well as to deadly fires, which destroyed their former image.[27] In freight, the Lakehead was home to more than two dozen elevators at the opening of this period. These were capable of 300 million bushels a year in storage and transfer to the large fleet of old canalers that seasonally hauled grain down the Lakes.[28] After the opening of the large locks of the St Lawrence Seaway in 1958, the pressure on the dockside system increased considerably.

From that time, the rising international demand from numerous foreign vessels and the increased capacity of the new Canadian fleet of large diesel bulk carriers competed intensely for elevator space each fall.[29] Indeed, the latter worked the harbour of the twin cities increasingly through the navigation season, bearing away huge cargoes of western coal and potash as well as regionally manufactured paper to the ports on the lower Lakes. Such vessels also dealt in beneficiated iron ore from Steep Rock and from the new mines north of Ear Falls, as did others serving Wawa through Michipicoten Harbour.[30] As early as the sixties the Port of Thunder Bay was visited on average by 2,000 ships each year, making it Canada's busiest after Montreal and Vancouver.[31] However, the much wider range of freight over this waterfront, promised by the Seaway and resulting in the huge modern 'roll on' Keefer Terminal, was to remain an unfulfilled dream.[32]

Commercial aviation in Ontario was still in its adolescence in 1950, after a prolonged childhood in which the provincial north, with its problems of distance and access, played a pre-eminent role. Early experimental aviation began in the twenties in connection with the forest industry. Pulp and paper companies sporadically used air reconnaissance as a means of timber assessment, and the government used aircraft seasonally, as of 1921, to aid its provincial forest mapping program.[33] The success of the latter application resulted in the creation of the Ontario Provincial Air Service in 1924, with hangars and repair facilities in Sault Ste Marie. By the thirties, the Service graduated from air photography to forest fire protection. At that time it had twenty planes, and twice that number in the early fifties.[34]

Meanwhile, the value of air access to the mining industry in areas away from existing means of ground transport was first demonstrated during the Red Lake gold strike of 1925 and after. By 1930 the ski and the pontoon enabled year-round service and the first attempts at aerial prospecting by a company called Northern Aerial Mineral Exploration (NAME).[35] In the following two decades numerous small charter firms served prospectors, trappers, commercial fishermen, and even wealthy sportsmen; their major clients, however, remained mining companies and isolated northern communities. Only a few graduated to the ranks of the truly regional carriers that evolved by the thirties in western Canada.[36]

Dreams of an airline to provide passenger service from coast to coast were realized in April 1937 with the creation of Trans-Canada Airlines (Air Canada after 1965).[37] Two years later it initiated its first service from Winnipeg to Toronto, avoiding the Great Lakes by a route involving Armstrong and Kapuskasing. Only in 1947 was regular service considered by way of the pre-war airstrip at Fort William. This landing field was already handling daily flights from U.S. points, as was a small Michigan one on behalf of Sault Ste Marie.[38] By 1955, the over-the-lakes route between west and east was served by Viscounts but graduated first to turbo-prop then to jet aircraft a decade later. A modern airport was completed at Sault Ste Marie in 1964, facilities at Fort William were upgraded, and a new airport at Dryden was opened in 1969. The basic corridor for trans-Canadian flights by an increasing range of companies was firmly established.[39]

In the aftermath of the war, an earlier federal program that had created air strips principally in southern Ontario was resumed among northern settlements, particularly more isolated ones. In the fifties, this engendered an active lobby in Queen's Park for the establishment of effective northern regional air service. An inquiry reported in 1963 that the area's basic facilities were adequate, but raised doubts about sufficient demand.[40] A three-year experimental contract was arranged between the province and White River Air to provide scheduled service between Sault Ste Marie, Sudbury, Earlton, and Timmins. At the end of the three years, Ontario Northland was ordered to create such a service to cover all northern regions by 1977. Under the title norOntair, and with money added to speed up the program of air strip movement, flights were begun in 1968.[41] On commencement of full service in 1980, this regional carrier covered some sixteen communities in the northwest, including junctures with major airlines at Dryden, Thunder Bay, and Sault Ste Marie.[42]

Electrical Generation and Transmission

In electrical transmission, these thirty years were equally progressive. The period opened with efforts by both Great Lakes Power (GLP) in Algoma and the HEPC (soon to become Ontario Hydro) to expand rural electrification from the limited cores then served. Under this provincially subsidized drive, hydro lines came to cover even the back townships in agricultural pockets, to serve many tourist areas, and to extend to distant resource towns.[43] Even some old municipal systems, once served from other sources, were converted to public power. In addition, during these years, certain changes occurred in trunk service. In the early fifties the main line west from Nipigon via Thunder Bay to Atikokan was extended to Ignace, then on to Kenora; a similar line east to Beardmore and Geraldton pressed onward to both Nakina and Longlac. Meanwhile, power from the Aguasabon came to serve communities to the west and linked eastward through Marathon and Manitouwadge, although it was not pushed on to White River and Hornepayne for some time.

To accommodate this new demand, as well as the steep rise in both industrial and urban domestic need, new generating capacity was required. To this end, Ontario Hydro opened its Aguasabon station, having obtained federal and U.S. permission to utilize the Long Lake diversion of arctic water. It also completed the Pine Portage project on the Nipigon, raising the level of that lake considerably in the process, just as it did the waters of Lac Seul at its dam and station at Ear Falls. Downstream on the English River from this station, it opened radio-controlled stations, first at Manitou Rapids near Ear Falls and later at the White Dog and Caribou near its entry to the Winnipeg system. In 1959 Ontario Hydro constructed generators at Silver Falls, behind the Lakehead, to which it added a 100,000 kilowatt thermal station on Thunder Bay in 1963, having exhausted all economic hydro sites yet feeling the need for additional contingent capacity.

GLP followed a similar course of expansion in Algoma. It was slower to develop new sources, raising its existing dams on both the Michipicoten and Montreal Rivers and adding generating units to existing stations there in the early fifties. In the decades after 1953, GLP constructed the new Scott Falls, McPhail, and Hollingsworth stations on the Michipicoten and both the Gartshore and Hogg on the Montreal. Of the 1,471,000 kilowatts of hydro power available in 1980 from northwestern Ontario rivers, (over a third having been added in this short span of time), 80 per cent was created by Ontario Hydro.

These developments were also accompanied first by interconnection of the old regional transmission systems focused on Ear Falls, Thunder Bay, and Sault Ste Marie. In the early seventies this united system came to be linked to a provincial grid and then to the continental one. By that time the overwhelming demands of Algoma Steel's mills and Ore Division had forced GLP to seek additional power from Ontario Hydro's Mississaugi station to the east. To ensure continuity of supply, the two utility systems were fully interconnected at Anjigami (near Wawa). At the same time, Ontario Hydro's Eastern and Western divisions were tied together here by a line from White River. In 1972, the last international gap about the Great Lakes was closed, and a more adequate trunk interchange was instituted between Ontario and the prairie provinces to the west.

Unlike hydroelectricity, developments in petroleum transmission in Canada were unique to the post-war years. In the late forties, access to growing American transmission technology and Alberta's first big gush of oil combined to promote a pipeline east to Duluth by 1950. Here tankers loaded the oil for transport to Sarnia refineries.[44] The success of this venture, sponsored by Imperial Oil but constructed by Interprovincial Pipelines, spawned a plan by Trans-

Canada to build a similar line for gas to eastern communities by an all-Canadian route. To promote this project, a Crown corporation, the Northern Ontario Pipeline Company, was formed to handle that portion of the route across the Shield. This company then altered the pipeline's course to run east from Thunder Bay, following the course of the CNR across the Great Clay Belt, and south to North Bay, rather than directly to Sault Ste Marie.[45] On the completion of the line, and its numerous pumping stations and links to towns along the route, plans were afoot to supply Sault Ste Marie from the trunk at North Bay and to service the communities between.[46] However, while the capacity of the main line has been greatly enlarged, this convenient source of domestic heat and energy has rarely sponsored the new industrial growth that was envisioned at its inception.[47]

Telecommunications

Telecommunications is the most difficult sector to assess as far as its impact on the northwestern Ontario economy is concerned. The Depression witnessed the collapse of some of the province's rural telephone companies, and the shortages of the forties exacerbated problems with old and inadequate equipment. In 1948, the province began to encourage amalgamation or sale of the companies to better-financed organizations. About 80 per cent of them would be acquired by Bell Telephone by 1972, which company had the financial resources for the massive modernization, expansion, and upgrading required.[48] While crude long-distance service had bridged the Shield in 1932, only by 1965 in established regional communities was high-quality long-distance reception becoming a reality. Such improvements were strongly supported by the emergence of the first microwave towers, which by the late fifties, marched along the northern skyline on a predictable route: from Winnipeg to the Lakehead, then via the Clay Belt to Timmins and North Bay, where, joined by a branch from Sault Ste Marie and Sudbury, they proceeded to both Toronto and Montreal.[49] By the mid-sixties, wireless telephone connections to separate systems in isolated resource towns and Native reserves were making their appearance.[50]

Advances in radio and television were rapid but varied by region. The local radio reception of the forties was soon supplemented in both east and west by CBC broadcasts from Winnipeg and Sault Ste Marie, as well as by U.S. signals in border areas. The creation of CBC, Thunder Bay, in 1954 was a significant addition that, with the later rise of repeaters in communities across the region, promoted an alternative to local private broadcasting, both AM and FM. Television, both private and public, first appeared in major centres during the mid-fifties, then spread to smaller urban communities, particularly with the advent of cable. With the late seventies, the arrival of the satellite dish introduced broader coverage to remote areas, from varied stations or networks.[51]

Mining Expansion and Change

The mining industry entered this period with optimism and energy. Ontario's annual mineral production climbed from about $200 million to almost five times that level over this thirty-year period. While the pace slowed to more manageable proportions and Ontario's lead over the other provinces narrowed, confidence only began to falter late in the seventies.[52] At the opening of the period, post-war labour costs were rising quickly, and mechanization, which had already altered the forest industry, was producing enormous changes in the scope and scale of mine technology and machinery, both above and below ground. These changes included the appearance of trackless operation and a huge increase in electrical demand.[53] Such changes were accompanied by expenditures in exploration and development, abetted, as of the late fifties, by federal–provincial aerial programs of geophysical survey over large and promising new tracts and by cost-sharing arrangements for subsequent access roads.[54] However, while these policies persisted for some time, the old issue of public share in Crown resources reasserted itself after 1960. The result was much harsher taxation of the industry by the early seventies.[55] As 1980 approached, the industry faltered as a result of the disruption of world markets with the OPEC crisis, shifting demands, the exhaustion of certain deposits, high costs of production, and over-reliance on the U.S. industrial base.[56]

Iron

Iron ore, in 1950, was Ontario's chief mineral and its potential continued to expand with exploration. The deposits of siderite at Wawa were now dwarfed by the first phase of development of the hematite at Steep Rock Lake near Atikokan. At the latter, the Errington (ore body B) was already shipping 1.2 million tons from its seasonal operation and would be joined by the Hogarth Pit (ore body A) within three years. A combined annual output of 5.5 million tons was eventually anticipated.[57] Caland Ore, a division of Inland Steel of Chicago, having contracted for ore body C, commenced its dredging in 1953 and shipped its first product in 1960. Canadian Charleston, which had taken up the short-term extraction of iron from certain glacial gravels of the area, shipped about 180,000 tons of enriched ore annually, for the six-year period ending in 1965.[58] By the beginning of the sixties, all aspects of this mammoth operation were up and running, with concentrating facilities being used on the lower-quality ores.[59]

While Caland thrived through the sixties and most of the following decade on 2 million tons a year, the late fifties and early sixties was a period of less stable conditions for Steep Rock Mining Co. itself.[60] The company's main problem was highly variable market demands from U.S. steel manufacturers with alternate sources about the Great Lakes and in Ungava. This caused Steep Rock Mines to run sometimes at capacity but often on limited shifts and hours.[61] Only with the addition of full beneficiation to iron pellets between 1964 and 1967 was this problem solved. Firm markets followed in Detroit and Chicago and a major financial share in the company was acquired by Algoma Steel, in return for 250,000 tons of pellets annually.[62] Like Caland, these pits ran regularly from the mid-sixties to the late-seventies, the final section of the deposit being dredged and opened in 1971. However, both mining and pelletizing were terminated in 1979, although shipping would continue into the early eighties.[63] What had once seemed an endless source of riches had been mined out in less than forty years and, while new deposits existed some forty miles north at Bending Lake, they were not economical to exploit.[64]

At Algoma Steel's older enterprise at Wawa, the firm and increasing demand anticipated at war's end was being realized. Some 70 per cent of one million tons of annual sinter continued to flow by the company's fleet to mills on the U.S. side of the lower lakes. As previously, these vessels returned with coking coal from Algoma's mines in West Virginia.[65] Indeed, the Algoma Ore Division (AOD) was in the midst of devising a twenty-year plan to produce 30 million tons of sinter, with U.S. markets in mind. To this end it had recently explored Siderite Hill in the immediate neighbourhood and carried out a preliminary drill evaluation of its magnetite holding in the Britannia block behind Goulais/Batchawana.[66] It had also recently converted the old open-pit Helen Mine to underground operation. In so doing it promoted more year-round operation, requiring the winter use of the ACR to supply the furnaces on the St Marys River.[67]

No sooner was this plan put into operation in 1953 than the U.S. demand for ore dropped sharply the following spring.[68] The cause of this drop was not hard to find. For some years, metallurgical institutes from Ohio to Minnesota had been seeking a means to beneficiate to pellet form the low-grade taconite that remained in huge quantities in the old iron ranges about Superior. Success at the Batelle Memorial Institution in Ohio produced the first primitive supplies with which these steel companies, often the owners of such taconite sources, were now experimenting.[69] However, most found their furnaces unable to deal satisfactorily with the high manganese values encountered. Hence these former

U.S. customers were back on sinter in 1955 and would remain loyal to Algoma's siderite until the early sixties when improved smelting and pelletizing techniques were firmly in place.[70] Such setbacks did not alter AOD's plan for long-term production; it merely changed the orientation of the market, as Algoma came to appreciate the rising Canadian steel opportunities to be served in this fast-paced, consumer-oriented, and urban-directed era.[71]

As a result, the key word at both Wawa and Sault Ste Marie became production. At the former, the plan to use Siderite Hill went ahead in 1956, with the new Sir James open pit opened two years later and the underground George W. MacLeod set in operation in 1960. These replaced the Helen, which staggered to the end of its production in 1962.[72] In 1967 the Ruth and Lucy were reactivated to help the Sir James pick up extra load while the MacLeod, now covering 85 per cent of total output, was modified to take up all production. As might be expected, these changes resulted in additions and improvements in sintering capacity, capped in 1979 by the completion of a spectacular, long incline-tunnel and conveyor belt from the crusher in the bottom of the MacLeod, to this sintering plant for beneficiating.[73] Meanwhile, output reached 1.85 million tons of sinter in 1960, which figure remained steady through the seventies. Booming Canadian demand for steel required a flow of the new hematite pellets from Steep Rock combined with the sinter to satisfy demands at Sault Ste Marie. However, Wawa continued to supply over half of the growing needs of Algoma Steel furnaces and by the mid-sixties was only a minor participant in sales to the U.S. ore market.[74]

But the demand for iron ore, first from U.S. interests until the taconite revolution, then from major Canadian steel producers facing booming requirements, did not stop here. From 1950 until markets fell stagnant in the late seventies, indications of a rising tide of exploration and acquisitions were reported in the northwestern press and the columns of the *Northern Miner.* Always in the background of the descriptions of these large but low-grade surface deposits was the promise of concentration and beneficiation, which could make their distant locations economically viable. By the mid-fifties, those deposits of real significance in the region had been discovered or rediscovered.[75]

The first of these was around and under Iron Bay, on Bruce Lake, a few miles north of Ear Falls, which community later became the dormitory for the neighbouring Griffith Mine developed on Iron Bay. The Griffith deposits were initially described as 260 million tons of hematite that could be pelletized to 64 per cent, but later proven estimates were much larger.[76] Between 1955 and 1965, it was evaluated by several companies and groups but held by a consortium called the Iron Bay Trust. That syndicate eventually leased the property to

Stelco, with promises of gas by a branch of the Trans-Canada Pipeline to run the pelletizer and a line from the CNR to transport the product to the ore docks at the Lakehead.[77] Production began in 1968, with the pits later enlarged twice in the seventies. Considerable changes to the Griffith's beneficiating facility for sponge iron production occurred about 1975, and the mine remained a highly productive source for the furnaces at Hamilton and Nanticoke in 1980.[78] Among these low-grade projects, only the Griffith became a producing mine.

The second prospect was the huge Skibi Lake find, some thirty miles north of Nakina, which Anaconda Canada assumed from its speculative holders in 1956. Drilling followed over three years before development began in 1961 on a road and pilot beneficiating plant, which was later closed out.[79] However, Anaconda retained the property with plans to have concentrated ore pumped as slurry to a beneficiating plant on Lake Superior, before final transport.[80] Dofasco took over this multi-million dollar project in 1975 but abandoned the deposit as uneconomical two years later.[81]

Between these two, but farther north, lay the third, involving property around and the islands in Lake St Joseph. Estimated to be capable of producing 220 to 250 million tons of ore at different local sites and explored after 1956 by several parties, this deposit, capable of producing 60 per cent iron with beneficiation, was snatched up by Steep Rock Lake in 1960.[82] Algoma Steel later negotiated its control through Steep Rock in 1967, beating both Dofasco and Stelco to this position. Estimates suggested fifty years' supply at four million tons of beneficiate a year. This project, also involving possible pipeline transmission south to the railway, hung in the balance from 1972 to 1976 but was shelved when uncertain markets loomed.[83] Subsequent events would prove this move a wise one.

Base Metals and Nickel

While iron ore played a major role in the rise of mining after 1950, its importance came to be rivalled by the scale of base metal extraction, which resulted in a major shift in northern mineral emphasis.[84] However, such a move was really a return to the roots of the northwest's mining history, specifically, the Superior copper boom of the mid-nineteenth century. Indeed, copper in association with other elements continued to be found right up to the modern era.[85] In addition, rich lead works at the Omega near Sibley and zinc ones at the Zenith site behind Schreiber had operated sporadically for decades and were again under use around 1950.[86]

At that date base metal exploration was also proceeding in several other areas of long-known occurrence: near Mine Centre on the Seine, about Savant

Lake north of Ignace, behind the Lakehead around Kashabowie, east of Heron Bay in the Pukaskwa, and inland from Pancake Bay in Algoma.[87] Luck, however, was with three weekend prospectors from Geraldton, who in late 1953 discovered the spectacular copper–zinc deposits around Manitouwadge in the bush between Longlac and White River (see Map 5.1).[88] When the post-Christmas rush of prospectors began, two exploration firms, General Engineering Co. (Geco) and Lun Echo, already had control of the key claims. Indeed, the former, as operator for Noranda, and the latter, as foster parent for the Willroy consortium (eventually taken over by Lake Shore Mines), were preparing to drill.[89] By March, 1954 both holders were in consultation with the province over roads, railways, townsites, and power and telephone supply, all of which passed under initial development that summer. A year later, with town construction well advanced, branches from both CN and CP arrived, as did a road north from the Trans-Canada and hydro lines with power from Aguasabon near Terrace Bay.[90] Both these low-cost, high-grade mines were shipping concentrates by late 1957: the Geco to Noranda, Quebec, and the Willroy (formerly controlled by Lun Echo) to smelters in Illinois.[91] While the former was still a major producer in 1980, the latter, followed on the same ore body by the Willecho and finally the Big Nama, ceased operation for lack of productive ore three years earlier.[92]

Such spectacular activity was accompanied until the late sixties by limited success elsewhere in the region. The Coldstream deposits of the early fifties, west of Thunder Bay, were made a commercial producer by Noranda in 1957 but, after a chequered career, this mine cleaned up its last good copper ore and closed a decade later.[93] Similar modest deposits drilled behind Batchawana and Mamainse in Algoma struggled into production as the Tribag and the Copper Corp. property in 1965. The Tribag mill and other equipment were trucked down from the old Pickle Crow in Patricia. Both folded in the early seventies.[94] Finally, persistent exploration in the Schreiber area opened mining at Duck Lake, with a concentrator at Selim Siding on the CPR and shipment to the United States for smelting. This operation too foundered in the early seventies.[95]

Although good copper prices persisted through the sixties and found increasing support from allied elements later, more spectacular finds in the region appeared only after 1965.[96] Such finds, like Manitouwadge, were again in new areas to the north of the established ones where base metals had a long history. The first strike was made in 1968 by a British exploration firm participating in a staking campaign near the former Uchi Lake gold field, fifty miles north of Ear Falls. By 1971, its small but very rich Silco mine was shipping copper and zinc concentrate by truck to the new CN railhead near the latter community and would continue to do so through the decade.[97]

The other two significant finds were further east. One at Sturgeon Lake near Valora had been staked and drilled, with modest results, by several firms during the fifties.[98] However, the really exciting finds began in 1969 on nearby Block 7 of the old National Transcontinental Railway grant, now held, with its mineral rights, by Abitibi as a pulpwood concession.[99] The result was a joint venture with Mattagami Mines (Noranda) to open the large Mattabi pit in 1972. The copper and related metals were shipped via CN to Noranda, Quebec, after milling and concentrating on site, using hydro delivered north from the Atikokan-Ignace power corridor.[100] This operation was joined two years later by another joint venture on a continuation of the same ore body, with Falconbridge as a senior partner. This latter was exhausted by the close of the period. However, a move by Noranda at Mattabi to new underground reserves and its opening of adjacent Lyon Lake enabled that company to continue producing and milling into the eighties.[101]

A more northerly large base-metal strike, the last to date in the region, was made by the Union Minière Exploration and Mining Company (Umex), a Belgian-based multinational. Its 1970 drill program generated a staking rush to the Pickle Lake area and resulted in Umex's giant surface and underground operation, the Thierry Mine, by 1975.[102] From its mills, specifically designed containers of concentrate were transported south by flat-bed truck to railway for transfer to Noranda's smelter. However, this mine opened to increasingly variable market prices and often worked through the rest of the decade at less than capacity.[103]

Like most base-metal prices, those for nickel were strong in the fifties but, unlike some others, continued to move unsteadily upward into the seventies.[104] Reports of nickel in association with other minerals in drill-cores were common only west of the Lakehead. In the Rainy River Valley a sudden flurry of staking and major interest by Falconbridge and Noranda occurred in 1952 and the following year, but was peripheral to older interest to the north and north-east.[105] Earlier efforts by Inco had produced intensive prospecting over a fifty-mile radius about Kenora and now witnessed much specific exploration at Eagle Lake near Dryden and on sites in the Manitou back-country.[106] This was followed by expensive underground work at Populus Lake, to no profitable end, by Noranda and Falconbridge in 1956.[107] However, further nickel/copper prospecting to the northwest of Kenora ultimately produced a mine at Gordon Lake in 1962, but with the access from Manitoba.[108]

Elsewhere by 1960, nickel had long been reported in both the Shebandowan area behind Thunder Bay and southwest of the twin cities in the Minnesota border townships. Nevertheless, developmental interest came only at mid-decade. Inco, after an intensive copper/nickel drill program, completed an exploratory shaft on Lake Shebandowan in 1967 and began immediately on a mine. This double-shaft endeavour opened in 1972 and into the eighties shipped sufficient ore annually to Copper Cliff to create as much as 10,000 tons of nickel.[109] Meanwhile, large, low-grade deposits in Pardee Township to the south had also been assessed by Great Lakes Nickel as of 1965. A U.S.–Belgian consortium (Amax) bought heavily into this venture in 1968, bringing much-needed financing for a drilling program. This was followed through the seventies by further capital to finish this work and to create a careful feasibility study. In 1980, however, the mining project was still on hold while the viability of the project received yet further study.[110]

Gold

In contrast to such base-metal activity, gold, the hallmark of Ontario mining, continued after 1950 along the lethargic course it had assumed under wartime regulation and amid later problems of archaic method, old technology, and rising hourly wages.[111] Ottawa's Emergency Gold Mining Assistance Act tried to bridge the gap between the regulated price per ounce of $35 U.S. and actual production costs over the next twenty thin years. However, such help attracted few new investors or exploratory dollars.[112] Even after the United States withdrew from its expensive attempts from 1968 to 1971 to regulate the price of gold and allowed it to seek its free-market value, Ontario's mines were slow to respond.[113] In fact, provincial output sank to a record low by 1975 while the world price per ounce rocketed to $850 U.S. by 1980.[114]

There were no new strikes of significance in the northwest over these years. Although local prospecting activity continued and occasional speculative flurries followed, it was always in old, well-tried areas. Until well into the seventies, substantial funds for truly wide-ranging exploration were focused elsewhere in the industry. In the old Sapawe area near Atikokan, such local efforts generated one short-lived gold mine in the sixties, while about the Lake of the Woods the old Duport and the Mayburn had seen brief revival during the decade before.[115] The aging fields of the Manitou, south of Dryden, and the Seine River drew some attention. South-east of Sioux Lookout, yet another attempt was made to revive the once active St Anthony's mine on Sturgeon Lake. Two finds in the Minnitaki area north-east of Dryden produced a modest rush in 1950, but resulted in only one real exploratory venture at the Newlund location, briefly optioned by Noranda. In the late sixties another staking campaign involved lands near Savant Lake, but this too came to nothing.[116] On the north shore of Superior, and on the mainland west of Marathon (later site of Hemlo) exploration for gold was as unsuccessful as elsewhere.[117]

As previously indicated, in the larger and more active fields the late forties and early fifties saw quick regeneration. East of Lake Nipigon, around Pickle Lake, however, such recovery was brief as the simple reality of ore exhaustion played out its hand. Along the former 'seventy miles of gold,' mines with famous names like the Northern Empire, Mosher, Bankfield, Tombill, Magnet, Little Long Lac, and Hard Rock fell like dominoes. By 1955, in this area, only the Leitch near Beardmore and the MacLeod-Cockshutt next Geraldton remained in operation. Of these, the former closed its doors in 1964 and the latter cleaned up its last ore in 1970, while the Theresa at Longlac, founded in 1951, had come and gone.[118] Farther to the north and west around Pickle Lake, the Central Patricia Mine, after valiantly renewed exploratory efforts, gave up in the early fifties. Its partner, the Pickle Crow, found new ore, sank a second shaft, and continued operations until 1965, finally closing out in the following year.[119]

Only in the other two gold fields of pre-war eminence – the modest one in the Michipicoten vicinity and its more spectacular partner in the distant Red Lake area – did this story of decline not apply. In the former field, the renewal of interest in the Goudreau near Wawa at the Ego mine and revival of the old Cline generated much speculative interest and prospecting activity. Yet the reopening of the former Minto south of Wawa as the Surluga was to pay longer dividends.[120] The latter was initially opened and operated by Cominco in the early sixties. After a short spell of inactivity, it was pushed determinedly forward with other backing and poured its first brick in 1968. Again in financial problems but now armed with the old head-frame of Algoma's Helen Mine and good cyanide processing, it was resurrected in the early seventies as the Pursides, to continue its chequered career.[121]

However, the really aggressive survivor among old gold fields was the one about Red Lake and the new companion community, Balmertown. In 1950 it was still host to eight functioning mines, three of which – the Starratt-Olsen, Dickenson, and Campbell Red Lake – were new.[122] By 1960, the latter two, along with the older Madsen and Cochenour-Willans – known as the 'big four' – still employed 1,500 miners and had an annual production value of $15 million.[123] Through the sixties, mine numbers shrank, despite the successful attempts of both the Madsen and Cochenour-Willans to remain open under escalated gold prices. However, the Dickenson and Campbell kept this field the northwest's model for bullion production into the early eighties.[124]

While the industry was slow in its reaction to the new free gold market, it was not totally remiss in recognizing this profitable change of the seventies. Across most old gold fields dating back to the nineteenth century and after, a wave of mine re-examination gathered momentum. Such exploration sometimes passed underground but, in these preliminary phases, more often focused on the reworking of old tip heaps, the product of much more primitive modes of mineral extraction. In the Seine River Valley, those around Mine Centre were fully involved by 1974, and others including the Goldlund (once Newlund) south from Sioux Lookout followed suit.[125] Early reconsideration and similar efforts were developing quickly after 1975, from Beardmore to Geraldton, and gained rapid momentum there.[126] So were others at Goudreau and Wawa, about the Lake of the Woods, around Dryden, even behind Jackfish on Lake Superior, east of Terrace Bay.[127] By 1980, both local and corporate energies were set for larger-scale development. However, what was needed was not a program of reworking or re-expanding but a new strike.

A Knot of Forest Problems

Across Ontario's woodland domain these were decades of particular dynamism in pulp and paper making. However, the period was also marred by growing contention, even contradiction, between the evolving elements of policy and practice. These problems stemmed from uneven rates of development and uneasy interaction between such variants as technical innovation, perception of forest use, market demands, conservation pressures, and environmental strictures. For example, while total wood harvest levels for the period vacillated around a mean of 575 million cubic feet per annum, the volume of pulp and paper produced rose significantly, as did the prices. This apparent conundrum resulted from the replacement of firewood by electricity, propane, and petroleum for domestic heat, which increased the proportion of the total available for pulping. Meanwhile, new technology increased the rate of fibre recovery in the manufacturing process by as much as 50 per cent.[128] Although the provincial industry thrived on these developments, its share of a rising, continental demand for paper actually shrank in the sixties as new American sources appeared in southern Appalachia. However, operations in northwestern Ontario, with their traditional ties to markets in the U.S. cities of the Mississippi Valley, were little affected in this way.[129] Finally, influenced by the above factors, the companies invested heavily in modern plant as well as labour-saving equipment and evinced slowly growing interest in such matters as sustained yield and waste abatement. At the period's close, roughly 70 per cent of all the northwest's manufacturing employment remained related to this huge and dominant industry. However, air and water pollution from its mills, increasingly a focus of public concern, became a serious regulatory problem for government.

Cut levels on many forest concessions were also criticized as exceeding sustainable limits.[130]

Woodland Mechanization

The earlier move to mechanize woodland operations across the northwest now gained impetus as the pool of unskilled, seasonal workers shifted from rural to urban areas. The period also witnessed the declining importance of settler cutting and the eclipse of the small contractor.[131] At the end of the forties, the former, often working under agreement with the latter, still took 75,000 to 100,000 cords from the Rainy River country and a similar amount from lands about Dryden. By the sixties such contributions were shrinking in absolute size, as they had earlier elsewhere, and were falling sharply in relative importance to the total harvest.[132]

The decades after 1950 were ones of experiment, invention, and innovation in the regional industry. Earlier attempts to popularize the chain-saw and trucking and tractor hauling came to real fruition with the fifties. During that decade, the 45-pound saw of 1951 lost over half its weight, and a large cadre of skilled operators came to serve each company.[133] Meanwhile, the opening of forest roads, often with government help, and the appearance of the first post-war highways spurred the intensive use of trucks in wood transport. This promoted the opening of new limits or parts of limits previously inaccessible by railway or inconvenient for water driving. The result was particularly evident in the Kenora District and its Patricia portion. Here, harvesting spread northward by truck roads from water-based log dumps at places around Dryden, Eagle Lake, and Vermilion Bay as well as from rail sidings near Redditt, Camp Robinson, Sioux Lookout, Ignace, and east at Taché, and Martin.[134] As highways spread out through the region and road systems sprawled deeper into the back-country, river driving declined and, by the early seventies, remained on only the Pic and Aguasabon.[135] Trucking and railing proved to be faster, cheaper, convenient year round, and delivered wood to the mill in better condition.

These important advances contributed little to reducing the costs of felling, skidding, and processing for transport, which comprised 75 per cent of woodland expenses.[136] Attempts by the Canadian Pulp and Paper Association to create an ordered and cooperative approach to these problems failed, despite its eventual formation of the Logging Research Association in 1962. Most of the country's pulp and paper firms chose to find their own solutions, in cooperation with budding equipment suppliers.[137] The drive to replace the horse in skidding had brought early experimentation with winching systems as well as tractors and crawlers modified from their agricultural purposes. However, real success came only with the rise of prototype mechanical skidders in the mid-fifties.[138] These powerful diesel units were articulated for forest handling, had four-wheel drive to accommodate seasonal conditions, and were equipped for winching, pushing, and dragging from the stump. They were in common use by the sixties and became central to a team of three to four cutters who received hourly wages with production incentives, as opposed to the former piece-work system.[139]

These developments were paralleled by more prolonged periods of experimentation and innovation in wood processing equipment, such as improved mobile slashers to reduce trees to wood of desired length for trucking. Such machinery was in commercial production by the sixties, as were moderately good bunchers. Satisfactory de-limbing equipment appeared in the northwest in the seventies, but a satisfactory tree harvester had yet to be designed.[140] By this time, three systems coordinating these various pieces of machinery had been introduced to replace the old cut-and-stack routine of Swede saw days. The first of these completed the processing in wood yards near the stump; the second did so after the trees were skidded to the road for easier trucking; and the third reduced the entire tree to chipwood on site.[141] While all systems were used in northwestern Ontario, as elsewhere, the second was the most popular.[142]

Such mechanizing trends transformed most facets of forest operations, leaving few jobs or activities the same. The seasonal and largely unskilled work force – once over 25,500 in the region at the outset – was reduced to 6,000 full-time woods specialists by 1970.[143] These workers were often trained by the company for a specific task, bussed from home to work-site daily, and frequently employed on shift. They were accompanied by teams of skilled mechanics and technicians who were required to maintain and repair the complex equipment. Wage levels for such personnel were equal to those in the more comfortable, urban, industrial centres in southern Ontario.[144] The machinery on which both groups worked represented a huge corporate capital investment. To earn its keep it had to function year-round, twenty-four hours a day, whenever market demands were sufficiently high. As a result, clear-cutting, as opposed to more selective harvesting, became an everyday reality, drawing public criticism for its effect on the environment.

Pulp and Paper Making

Such mechanization of harvesting and hauling, with its wide range of social, economic, and environmental ramifications, was accompanied by equally important changes on the manufacturing side of the industry. In 1980 Ontario produced 4.3 million tons of pulp and paper, of which 73 per cent came from mills in the northwest. This represented a near doubling of provincial output over the previous thirty years, but a three-and-a-half-fold increase from forests north and west of Sault Ste Marie. This growth in output was accompanied by a set of countering trends.[145] Despite substantial increases in tonnage over these years, regional generation of newsprint dropped from three-quarters of all production to slightly over a third (see Table 5.1). Meanwhile, pulp, principally for bleached and unbleached kraft, had come to assume about half of all out-

TABLE 5.1 Pulp and Paper Production (in thousands of short tons), 1950–1980

	1950		1960		1970		1980	
Newsprint:								
Fort Frances	80		82		63		–	
Kenora	105		215		262		230	
Red Rock	70		60		73		72	
Sault Ste Marie	97		100		71		95	
Thunder Bay	302		659		724		690	
Total	654	73%	1,116	68%	1,193	58%	1,087	35%
Kraft Pulp (wet):								
Dryden	30		56		118		195	
Fort Frances	–		–		–		161	
Marathon	90		140		140		155	
Red Rock	78		146		200		239*	
Terrace Bay	–		93		127		388	
Thunder Bay	–		–		186		408	
Total	198	22%	435	26%	771	37%	1,546	49%
Other Paper:								
Dryden	—		50		50		64	
Fort Frances	—		—		—		195	
Sault Ste Marie	—		—		—		135	
Thunder Bay	40		45		48		108	
Total	40	5%	95	6%	98	5%	502	16%
Grand Total	892		1,646		2,062		3,135	

* 85% turned immediately into liner board

Sources: Government of Ontario, *The Economic Future of the Forest Products Industry: A Study for the Royal Commission on the Northern Environment* (Toronto, 1981) with additions and alterations based on the appropriate years of the *Pulp and Paper Manual of Canada* (Gardenvale, Quebec: National Business Publications) as well as *Pulp and Paper Canada: Manual and Directory, 1980* (Westmount, Quebec: Southam Business Publications).

put, and other paper products had risen to absorb 16 per cent of the market. However, while employment in such manufacturing continued to rise from the late forties into the seventies, its rate of increase in this age of modern technology was far from commensurate with that of productivity. More importantly, the size of the work force tended to stabilize after 1977, as U.S. midwest markets, which consumed 80 per cent of regional newsprint and 50 per cent of its kraft production, softened.[146]

These broad trends in output and changes in emphasis reflected deeper shifts in modern pulp and paper manufacture. The appearance of new mills and early moves to update and refurbish old plants of the twenties continued to colour development in the fifties. At Kenora, one new paper machine was added and two others were reworked for more speed in a continuing modernization program that touched Ontario-Minnesota's other mill at Fort Frances as well.[147] The kraft operation at Dryden was upgraded in two stages to double production by 1960 and the old bag-making plant was replaced by a much larger one.[148] In Fort William, expansion at Great Lakes Paper made it the fourth-largest manufacturer of newsprint in Canada. Abitibi's capacity to create that same product in two Lakehead mills was augmented and improved,[149] and its Provincial Paper division there was upgraded to increase the quality of fine and coated paper it generated.[150] In the new facilities at Red Rock, Terrace Bay, and Marathon, work proceeded through the sixties to bring these state-of-the-art sulphate mills to peak efficiency and their bleached and unbleached kraft production to full capacity.[151] Finally, at Sault Ste Marie, the region's oldest newsprint operation was upgraded and pushed to the limit of its otherwise ageing machinery.[152]

Over the subsequent twenty years to 1980, expansion among these eleven mills followed one of two courses, sometimes both. One of these involved increasing and improving output along established product lines. In the kraft sector, this was very common in mills at Dryden and Terrace Bay, where plant expansion was most marked.[153] There was also a general move to dry wafer pulp, for easy market shipment or transfer to sister mills. In newsprint, this process involved the addition of considerable sulphite and groundwood pulp capacity, as well as further high-speed paper-making machinery.[154] The second course involved diversification or change in the final product. Abitibi, at Sault Ste Marie, moved slowly from newsprint to specialty items including offset and directory paper, as well as bleached groundwood pulp.[155] As a variant, at Fort Frances, a plant producing 125,000 tons of newsprint and mechanical pulp was converted in 1960 to copy paper and kraft pulp, the latter shipped to International Falls and Kenora for further manufacture.[156] The addition of such kraft capacity to existing output also occurred at Great Lakes in Thunder Bay and mills elsewhere.[157] In contrast, the kraft mill at Red Rock not only began to convert its pulp to linerboard, as did the plant at Dryden to paperboard, but it also entered in a small way on newsprint manufacture.[158] Finally, Provincial, with its new grades and types of fine paper, raised its annual productive capacity over the seventies from 48,000 to 108,000 tons.[159]

The results of these changes by 1980 are shown in Table 5.2. The table also reveals a related facet of this buoyantly profitable but capital-consumptive industry over these years: the restructuring of many old firms or their outright take-over by larger corporate enterprises. In the fifties, Brompton Pulp and Paper operations at Red Rock were sold to the St Lawrence Corporation and later became a division of its Dominion Tar and Chemical (Domtar) affiliate.[160] In 1957, Long Lake Pulp and Paper formally took the name of its sometime U.S.

TABLE 5.2 Pulp and Paper Industry, 1980

	Process	Produce
Algoma West		
Sault Ste Marie		
Abitibi	groundwood	specialty papers
Thunder Bay District		
Thunder Bay		
Abitibi	groundwood, sulphite	newsprint
Great Lakes	sulphite	newsprint
Provincial	sulphite	fine papers
Marathon		
American Can	sulphate	kraft pulp
Red Rock		
Domtar	groundwood, sulphate	newsprint, linerboard
Terrace Bay		
Kimberly-Clark	sulphate	kraft pulp
Rainy River District		
Fort Frances		
Boise-Cascade	groundwood, sulphate	offset, kraft pulp
Kenora District		
Kenora		
Boise-Cascade	groundwood, sulphate	newsprint, paper
Dryden		
Reed Paper	sulphate	kraft pulp, paper, paperboard

Source: *Pulp and Paper Canada: Manual and Directory, 1980* (Westmount, Quebec: Southam Business Publications).

owner, Kimberly-Clark, while neighbouring Marathon became part of American Can.[161] As of 1964, Anglo-Canadian, with mills at Quebec City, purchased Dryden Paper as part of a much larger regional scheme. Four years later it transferred these holdings to the Canadian arm of Reed Paper International of London, England.[162] That same year Ontario-Minnesota became a division of the large U.S. producer, Boise Cascade, but later these mills at Kenora and Fort Frances were reorganized as Boise Cascade Canada Ltd.[163] Finally, in 1978, what had become Great Lakes Forest Products fell to the control of the CPR, while Abitibi merged with Price before being taken over by Toronto-based Olympia and York.[164]

The now highly developed manufacturing systems that these large firms had helped to create and now controlled were also much more efficient in their total use of forest resources and of the wood fibre they sought. Since the fifties, with the successful addition of sawmill waste and sawdust to non-mechanical pulp generation,[165] the drive for more stewardly use of all wood harvested had been gathering gradual momentum. By 1960, such materials were joined by a much larger component gleaned from wood chips, trucked or railed to the mills from other suppliers or generated from roundwood already delivered to their storage yards.[166] At that time, eight northern consumers, including Marathon, St. Lawrence Corp. (Red Rock) and Abitibi in Fort William, were using 200,000 tons (bone dry) a year. A decade later, 260,000 tons were being supplied from thirteen sources across the northwest, but the four major consumers there were utilizing an additional 100,000 tons from further east.[167] Indeed, by that date, Ontario's largest user, American Can at Marathon, was responsible for 40 per cent of the regional total. Over the following years it would move to much heavier reliance on such production from sources as far away as the Michipicoten area.[168] In the seventies, even the ever-present bark around most mills came to be used for heating, to reduce the enormous energy costs tied to pulp and paper making.

Not unrelated to these drives for economy were ones aimed at more efficient fibre recovery, again centring on chemical processing of the wood supply. Such endeavours, involving the rise of complex, high-yield wood digesters, added increasingly to both sulphite and sulphate facilities. With improved recovery methods, these digesters increased resultant fibre tonnage, sometimes startlingly.[169] When these digesters were added experimentally to sulphate plants, it was found they gave good fibre recovery from an increasing range of unused species found in the forest. By so doing, they initiated the first industrial steps in breaking the traditional reliance on spruce. However, while these desirable, if profit-driven, trends towards forest conservation were laudable, they represented correction of only one area of the complicated woodland management problems accumulating over these decades.

Accompanying such forest management concerns were those related to pollution generated by the mills themselves. Poor air quality was the more noticeable, because of the unpleasant odour associated with pulp making, but the industry's deleterious effect on water was far more destructive to the environment. Neither of these problems had been regarded as unusual before 1950; their recognition about that time was part of a growing public reaction to all forms of pollution everywhere. This awareness subsequently was intensified with the rapid increase in plant size and the growing complexity of pulping technology. Formal recognition of such environmental issues came with the creation of the Ontario Water Resources Commission (OWRC) in 1956, later dissolved into the new Ministry of the Environment in 1972. In the latter year, Canada and the United States signed the Great Lakes Water Quality Agreement, which was added to the regulative efforts of the International Joint Commission (IJC) over boundary waters.[170]

The IJC, in the late forties, had begun detailed studies of water quality in the St Marys River in order to isolate sources of pollution. Early in the following decade it also forced creation of large settling ponds by Steep Rock Mines to correct both aesthetic and biological problems the operation was creating in the Seine River and Rainy Lake.[171] Meanwhile, after years of complaints by residents on both sides of the Rainy River, the first primitive attempt was made in 1948 to correct fibrous emissions from the groundwood plants at Fort Frances and International Falls. The inadequacy of this effort resulted in legal proceedings by a group from the Rainy River Valley in 1953. This generated an offer by Ontario-Minnesota to remove 80 per cent of the physical waste from its emissions but a request to leave the chemical aspects of the problem until later. This arrangement was refused and the wrangling continued through the decade.[172] Similarly, historic complaints by commercial fishermen about mill pollution brought the first efforts, in 1950 at the Lakehead, to experiment with alternates to dumping pulp waste liquors into local rivers.[173] Complaints of the same nature in Nipigon Bay and along Lake Superior, as well as ones related to the old problem of bark in commercial nets, however, went unresolved. So did a 1954 report of high levels of chemical pollution in the Wabigoon River below Dryden, which problem would later have startling consequences.[174]

Only with the sixties and seventies did the pace of correction and control quicken, in response to more concentrated government regulation and awakening recognition by most pulp and paper firms of the rising environmentally protective role the public expected of them. In boundary waters, the IJC moved on the Rainy River problem, forcing Ontario-Minnesota (later Boise Cascade) to spend over $5 million on the abatement of physical pollution by 1969 and much more over the next decade to reduce chemical emissions.[175] Acting with the cooperation of the OWRC, the IJC also negotiated heavy spending by Abitibi on its air and water problems at Sault Ste Marie in the late sixties. Abitibi was later required to spend $3 million more to reduce that mill's fibrous contamination of the St Mary's River by 90 per cent.[176]

Elsewhere across the northwest, the OWRC brought significant improvements in both the physical emissions from mechanical pulping and chemical ones related to sulphate and sulphite processing. At the Lakehead, its efforts resulted in heavy expenditure over time by Abitibi at its groundwood plants and by Great Lakes on its more complex problems with liquid compounds.[177] Among kraft producers, particularly east of Thunder Bay, the OWRC's work was made easier by the early formation of a Kraft Mill Effluent Improvement Committee, which met annually for many years from 1961 to discuss water pollution problems and to compare corrective ideas.[178] However, even here occasional enforcement of the regulations was necessary. In 1970 the mill at Red Rock was fined for neglect after a serious pollution spill. About the same time, Kimberly-Clark won an award for its efforts from the Canadian Institute of Pollution Control. Yet that firm later found itself under a government order to have all the pollution devices at its enlarged mill upgraded for full operation by 1980. This same order also initiated the first drive to rehabilitate the release area for Kimberly-Clark emissions in Moberly Bay on Lake Superior. Only Marathon appears to have remained free of punitive treatment through these years, when improvements and expansion of facilities in the sulphate sector required frequent change and updates to control pollution.[179]

But the ugly situation that developed at Dryden dwarfed all other pulp-related pollution problems of the period. In 1959, the long-established kraft mill, which had for decades poured its effluent into the Wabigoon, had installed its first air pollution controls and equipment towards the reduction of river contamination. Under its new owners, Reed Paper, these rudimentary provisions for environmental preservation were upgraded unenthusiastically, as required.[180] Finally, in 1970, with four other mills across the province, this one was ordered to stop using mercury as an anti-slime measure in its bleaching process. In the midst of a world-wide mercury poisoning scare, Reed complied only slowly with this demand, delaying its absolute cessation until 1975. This was well beyond the deadline it had been given. It also was two years after the highly publicized discovery that fish being consumed by Native communities downstream contained as much as thirty times the acceptable mercury level.[181] Further infractions followed in 1976. As a result, the company was charged, tried, and convicted on ten other counts in 1977, despite a belated attempt by Reed at mitigation through the announcement of a $10 million anti-pollution program.[182] The firm was given until 1982 to clean up its air and water problems under this plan, but later claimed it could meet that deadline only with government financial help. This Queen's Park refused to consider, as it did any delay in the established deadline for this work as suggested by its own standing Committee on Resources. Instead, Ontario demanded that the company spend $13 million by the agreed deadline. This resulted in the sale of all Reed's holdings here to Great Lakes in November 1979.[183] 'Reed simply walked away from its financial responsibilities after two decades of abuse' was the summation given by the *Sault Star*.[184] Reed's behaviour stood in contrast to the sometimes hard-nosed but more compliant stance that other pulp and paper firms in the region assumed on such publicly sensitive environmental issues.

Lumber and Building Products

Not all of the problems in the forestry sector, however, centred exclusively on pulp and paper production. Some were shared with or were exclusive to the lumbering or building side of the industry. The numbers of sawmills across northern Ontario continued to fall until the seventies, despite the continent-wide construction boom of the post-war decades.[185] This was caused, in small part, by the declining availability of preferred species like pine and spruce, in tired, mill-related forest holdings; but largely by the tendency for existing reserves, even of jackpine, to be inaccessibly locked away by the holders of pulpwood concessions.[186] This situation around the Lakehead was publicized by the colourful behaviour of E.E. Johnson, owner of Great Lakes Lumber, before the opening of the period. Ministerial intervention in this case took the form of a very specific 1951 directive in which all pulp and paper companies in the province were ordered to supply lumber firms with logs in their forest harvest that were suited to sawmill operations. This demand gained only grudging compliance from some firms in the northwest.[187] Indeed, although the issue was dealt with in the revised Crown Timber Act of 1958, no harmonious and uniform solution would appear before the eighties. Instead, a rash of individual agreements between the two sides of the industry were struck.

By 1980, the issue of sharing the forest resource for its most efficient utilization also applied to provincial plywood mills, veneering companies, and manufacturers of both chip and particle board.[188] In the meantime, sawmilling experienced a revival in the seventies, with the erection of new plants and the refurbishing of old ones. In some instances these changes were instigated by former sawmill owners but more usually by a pulp and paper company for the integrated use of its limits. Such super mills were 'small log' operations, using high-strain, small-kerf bandsaws, full-tree harvesting by high-speed chippers, advanced levels of automation to save on labour, and every economy of scale.

They were directed principally at the enormous demand for studs in the United States. By 1979, the volume of their provincial production was claimed to be higher than in the peak years in the great pine lumbering era of decades earlier.[189]

Of the twenty modern saw facilities that appeared in northern Ontario by the eighties, twelve were in the northwest.[190] While three decades earlier these would have been accompanied by a number of smaller ones, such lesser producers had become rare by 1970. Even before then, regional sources indicated that automation in woodland and mill on this side of the forest industry had cut employment to 44 per cent of the 12,300 workers of 1956. At the same time that production rose, U.S. tariffs on Canadian lumber fell in the sixties.[191] During these shifts and changes, certain famous old mills were lost. The aging Farlinger mill of the Patricia Lumber Co. at Sioux Lookout was taken over by Great Lakes in 1952 and operated for five years before being dismantled. Its parallel at Fort Frances, operated for over thirty years by the Mathieu family, cut its last lumber in 1954. The final blow was its loss of water access to its pine limits, with alterations made to the Seine River to correct pollution problems at Steep Rock Mines.[192] With its demise, the last of the old, once-steam-driven giants disappeared.

To counteract their loss at Fort Frances, Mathieu and Co., by 1961, refurbished and enlarged a mill at Sapawe, near Atikokan and more proximal to forest leases in Quetico Provincial Park. The latter it inherited from the old firm of Shevlin-Clark. This new electrical operation, complete with chipper, came to handle 300,000 cords of saw-logs annually, some 40,000 yearly cords of pulpwood from these limits being railed east to Domtar at Red Rock. The Sapawe mill burned in 1953, to be replaced by one capable of 25 million board feet per annum and designed as a small log facility. After a bankruptcy in 1967, the entire enterprise passed to Domtar. With Ontario-Minnesota Paper, Domtar in 1971 lost its share of 400 square miles of limits in Quetico, being assigned instead a new tract, with suitable access, to the north of Sapawe. This state-of-the-art operation remained in active use by Domtar through the decade.[193]

In addition to modest independents at Red Lake and Kenora, Boise Cascade also erected a modern plant at the latter, to take care of its dimensional lumber.[194] Other important developments, from the Lakehead west, came to be associated with major pulp and paper companies in Dryden and Thunder Bay. Colenso Lumber of Steinback, Manitoba, by 1951 established a mill capable of 4 million feet a year behind Vermilion Bay, with a forest lease accessible by logging road from the new Red Lake highway. Another modest endeavour in this area was Chukuni Lumber, which incorporated at Snake Falls in 1945 but moved to Ear Falls a decade later. In spite of an addition to its forest resources at that time, Chukini closed for lack of wood supplies in the late sixties. Its plant was purchased by the Colenso which had recently sustained a destructive mill fire. Soon after, Colenso replaced its first sawyery with a modern one capable of 10 million board feet per year, then sold the whole to Reed Paper of Dryden in 1969. However, this soon passed, with the rest of Reed's woodland leases and other operations, to Great Lakes Forest Products. This mill served Great Lakes' western needs into the eighties, with an earlier subsidiary sawmill near Sturgeon Lake.[195]

About Sioux Lookout, which had been economically distressed by the closure of the Farlinger mill in 1957, spasmodic redevelopment of sawmill and related woods employment at nearby Hudson marked the next two decades. First came the small Lac Seul Equipment Company's mill enterprise there, then in 1967 the larger Lac Seul Land and Lumber effort. This included booming logs across the lake from more distant limits, and, under a provincial grant, the addition of the first kiln driers.[196] In the early seventies, a further infusion of government capital brought full small-tree harvesting and chipping machinery with a commensurate rise in productive capacity. This attracted Oregon interests, who sold the chips to Great Lakes at the Lakehead but marketed the lumber through U.S. dealers.[197] Unfortunately, their attempt proved only marginally profitable, even with advantageous wood allowances arranged by the province. As a result, Mackenzie Forest Products, a member of the Buchanan Group, which had earlier purchased the extensive mills and kilns of Great West Lumber in Port Arthur, took up the challenge. It shipped the chips from this Hudson plant to Abitibi at the Lakehead. Meanwhile, it tendered the lumber output, in combination with the even larger flow from its Lakehead mills, for American consumption.[198] Abitibi in contrast, with forest leases east of this area, continued to truck its own dimension timber to the Lakehead, where it had purchased the large and varied milling assets of Northern Wood Preservers in 1949.[199]

East of the twin cities on Thunder Bay, the efforts of Buchanan continued to remove from certain paper companies the need to handle their dimensional timber harvest. Domtar, with mills at Red Rock, was a case in point. Meanwhile, near Hornepayne, about 1970 the Haavalsrud Lumber Company contracted with Ontario and Quebec Paper (OQP) to harvest and convert to lumber all suitable trees on OQP's limits using its huge new mill. From this plant it shipped all lumber for U.S. sale but sent all chips and mill waste to OQP's Thorold pulp and paper operation.[200] In contrast, at Longlac, Kimberly-Clark built a more modest mill between 1950 and 1952. This steam-driven producer of rough lumber burned down two years later, was rebuilt and improved, but declared unprofitable in 1968. In its place, the company erected a modern chip and sawmill capable of 20 million feet of dimensional lumber a year, or over three times the former capacity. To this it added a smaller stud mill at Terrace Bay in 1973. Near the end of the seventies, these combined facilities were shipping remarkable quantities of lumber annually into the United States.[201] Meanwhile, in the late fifties, Marathon, later American Can, had taken over a sawyery, erected by Nipigon Lake Lumber, to accommodate this side of its harvest, which operation was later assumed on behalf of the firm by Buchanan.[202] Abitibi of Sault Ste Marie did not enter the picture on its lease in the Pukaskwa until 1975, at which time it completed a huge, highly automated operation at White River, capable of 70 million board feet a year, with kiln drying. This installation poured life back into that sagging town later in the decade, after the decline of intense pulpwood harvesting in this area and the loss of the district headquarters for the Ministry of Natural Resources to Wawa.[203]

Western Algoma was foreign territory to such large-scale softwood milling in these years, with one very notable exception: in 1951, Dubreuil Brothers Ltd. moved their small, French-speaking community and mill north to the Magpie valley, near Wawa, from Island Lake, behind Thessalon and northeast of Sault Ste Marie. Here they lumbered and sawed for a decade, as pioneers in the serious use of jackpine and in the chipping of refuse for the pulp industry. In 1962 they moved to their present site, creating the town of Dubreuiville and constructing a modern mill with kiln facilities. Their energetic expansion made this one of the largest sawmill complexes in northern Ontario by the mid-seventies, with a capacity of 60 million board feet a year.[204]

Elsewhere along eastern Superior, commercial forest interests focused on veneering as well as the manufacture of wallboard and flooring. Use here was made of the remaining yellow birch, maple, and poplar resources on the upland north of Sault Ste Marie and in Superior Provincial Park. Such efforts started, at the opening of the fifties, under Roddis Lumber, with modest mills near Sault Ste Marie. By mid-decade this firm was utilizing about 10 million cubic feet of logs each year. After a buy-out by Weyerhauser Canada Limited in 1961, these woodland demands expanded rapidly and the plant became Sault Ste Marie's third-largest employer. Long before 1980 its output annually had reached 140 million square feet of veneer and a smaller volume of maple flooring.[205] Hay and Co. began the manufacture of wallboard at Searchmont in 1955, selling those operations in 1962 to Weldwood, who continued to make specialized panelling. Although it never appears to have had a mill closer than Mattawa, Guelph Plywood also harvested veneer logs in this part of Algoma, until it transferred its woodland right in Superior Park to Roddis in 1960.[206]

Related endeavours elsewhere within the taiga forest zone of the northwest were slower to appear. West of the twin cities, a particleboard operation at Atikokan was built by Oshkosh, Wisconsin, interests in the late seventies.[207] In 1957, local capital sources founded the Norply plant at Nipigon, near the tiny, ancient, and only recently abandoned pulp mill. This operation, aimed at the growing market for low-grade aspenite from local hardwoods, passed to Buchanan's control in the late sixties and was then sold to MacMillan-Bloedel in 1973. That firm was in the midst of constructing a huge, modern, aspenite mill on the Kaministiquia near Thunder Bay. It converted the small plant to the manufacture of a variety of laminated specialty products, for which some of the outer veneers were obtained from other regions.[208] In 1966, the Nipigon endeavour was joined by a Weldwood plant at Longlac, using similar poplar resources to manufacture underflooring, with cheap sheathing supplementing this product at the end of the decade. In the early seventies, a waferboard mill was added, and laminated production moved to poplar-cored quality wallboarding when the mill was again enlarged in 1978.[209] As in the case of all modern sawmills of the region, these operations were seeking markets in the building industry and were fully involved in the sale of chips and wood waste to the pulp industry, often to the companies from whose limits they gained their logs under various individual arrangements.[210]

Government's Directive Role

These examples of cooperation for mutual benefit and public advantage unfortunately were but one side of forest practices in these years when progress and problem generation were the touchstones of change. Measures like the 1947 Kennedy Enquiry into forest use and the decentralization of Lands and Forests administration substantially promoted more efficient forest use and more potentially effective resource management. Also important were the Forest Management Act of 1947, the grandparent of subsequent legislation, and the related forest resources inventory (FRI) which, along with subsequent measures, was basic to the later strategic design in forest policy.

The Forest Management Act and Abitibi's aforementioned acquiescence with its requirements began the final breakdown of united industrial resistance to the serious application of principles of sustained yield and planning. This in turn ushered in the beginnings of more efficient and appropriate utilization of the public resources that forest companies held in trust. The Act of 1947 required that the huge woodland concessions held by such firms, as well as any more for which they chose to apply against future need, were now to be operated as forest management units (FMUs). Each was to be held for terms of only twenty years, renewable on evidence of wise use. Each was to be covered by a suitable long-term plan for access, harvesting, and regeneration, submitted within five years. These plans were to be subject to departmental alteration and were to be followed, every five years, by a short-term plan, equally open to official change, or refusal if initial goals were being abused. Acceptance of these requirements came cautiously, sometimes very tardily from an industry that regarded the legislation as regulatory meddling and was in no hurry to comply. All other suitably forested public lands were cast as Crown management units (CMUs), for which similar plans were required to be submitted by district foresters; all short- or medium-term lessees were required to comply with such arrangements.[211] Some firms were tardy in their compliance and in the submission of their initial plans. Nevertheless, the emerging pattern of an enormous core of company units, surrounded by a belt of Crown-managed tracts was apparent across the northwest by the early fifties.[212]

One of the specifications of the Forest Management Act of 1947 was the generation of a full forest inventory of commercial timber in the province and its regular update, since the current crude tool on which decisions still had to rely was the old forest mapping exercise of the twenties.[213] This new endeavour began in 1947 and, with extensive use of air photography as well as frequent ground checks, was finished in 1954 for the then-accessible north, beyond the most distant railway line. Work then began on the inaccessible area beyond, toward the absolute boundary of the Albany River in northeastern Ontario and a limit slightly above the fifty-first parallel across much of the northwest to the Manitoba border.[214] However, this ultimate limit to northern expansion was questioned at the time and subsequently by both white and Native interests as being dangerously optimistic in environmental terms.[215]

A third measure, added only in 1953, also was intended to promote the ordered and responsible drive for maximum future forest productivity. A revision of the Crown Timber Act replaced the slow and complicated method formerly used to arrange forest licences with the simple and flexible use of the Order in Council, within a clearly specified set of conditions.[216] Such a move was important to the companies that were busy sorting and sometimes altering the bounds of existing holdings with an eye to encompassing the maximum high-quality woodland in their holdings under the new forest management system. It was equally important to the government, anxious to facilitate the opening of all accessible forest property and to push the forest frontier northward into the inaccessible area now being inventoried.[217] Interestingly enough, these same revisions to the timber legislation also included the first specification of penalties to be imposed on firms that persisted in wasteful or otherwise undesirable harvesting practices.[218] As Ontario Premier Leslie Frost underlined in 1950, the new provincial policy was to stress regulations to 'protect, sustain, regenerate and use the forest resources wisely.'[219]

Over the next quarter-century of broad change in the northwestern Ontario forest industry, these early official moves were to play an important role. Even a cursory comparison of Maps 4.4 and 5.2 graphically reveals their impact on the distribution of woodland activity and on the pattern of operators across the Crown and company management units by 1980. Most companies had made serious adjustments to the boundaries of their former holdings and many had taken on additional territory in the interim. At the same time, the industry had been compelled to give up or had been prevented from assuming certain lesser tracts. These had been withheld in order to satisfy new demands for alternate use, principally recreation. The aggregate area of such vacation lands now, for the first time, exceeded all earlier withdrawals for rural settlement.

Boise Cascade had retained the bulk of its former concessions, giving up some to satisfy the vacation trade, but had taken up a large new unit to the north of the English River near the Manitoba border. Brompton Paper, now Domtar, and Abitibi (later Abitibi-Price) with its affiliate, Provincial Paper, had undergone limited changes in their leases behind Thunder Bay. Yet Abitibi had reduced its aging woodland leases dramatically in Algoma West. Some of these holdings were lost with the creation of both Pukaskwa and Superior parks. Others were abandoned about 1970, in old ACR townships, and still others on the lower White River watershed were harvested intensely for Abitibi's Sault Ste Marie mills, before being excluded from future operations.[220] Certain additional northern blocks passed wholly or in part to other pulp producers like Ontario and Quebec Paper or to lesser firms such as Dubreuil Brothers Lumber. Those holdings, which Abitibi retained on this side of the region, focused exclusively on the upper White River. Its neighbours here, American Can and Ontario and Quebec Paper, while trading or giving up various tracts in the old Nagagami concession, remained otherwise little changed. However, OQP had moved the centre of its operations inland from Heron Bay to Manitouwadge.[221]

Big gains in territory went to only two companies: Kimberly-Clark and Great Lakes Forest Products. As part of the plan for a multimillion-dollar expansion at Terrace Bay in 1974, the former was granted an additional 4,500-square-mile tract north of Nakina, extending to the Albany River.[222] With the company's other extensive leases, this made it by far the largest regional forest operator east of Nipigon. Yet its size was dwarfed in 1980 by the combined area of Crown and company management units assembled by Great Lakes between there and Manitoba. That empire in the west had begun in the wake of

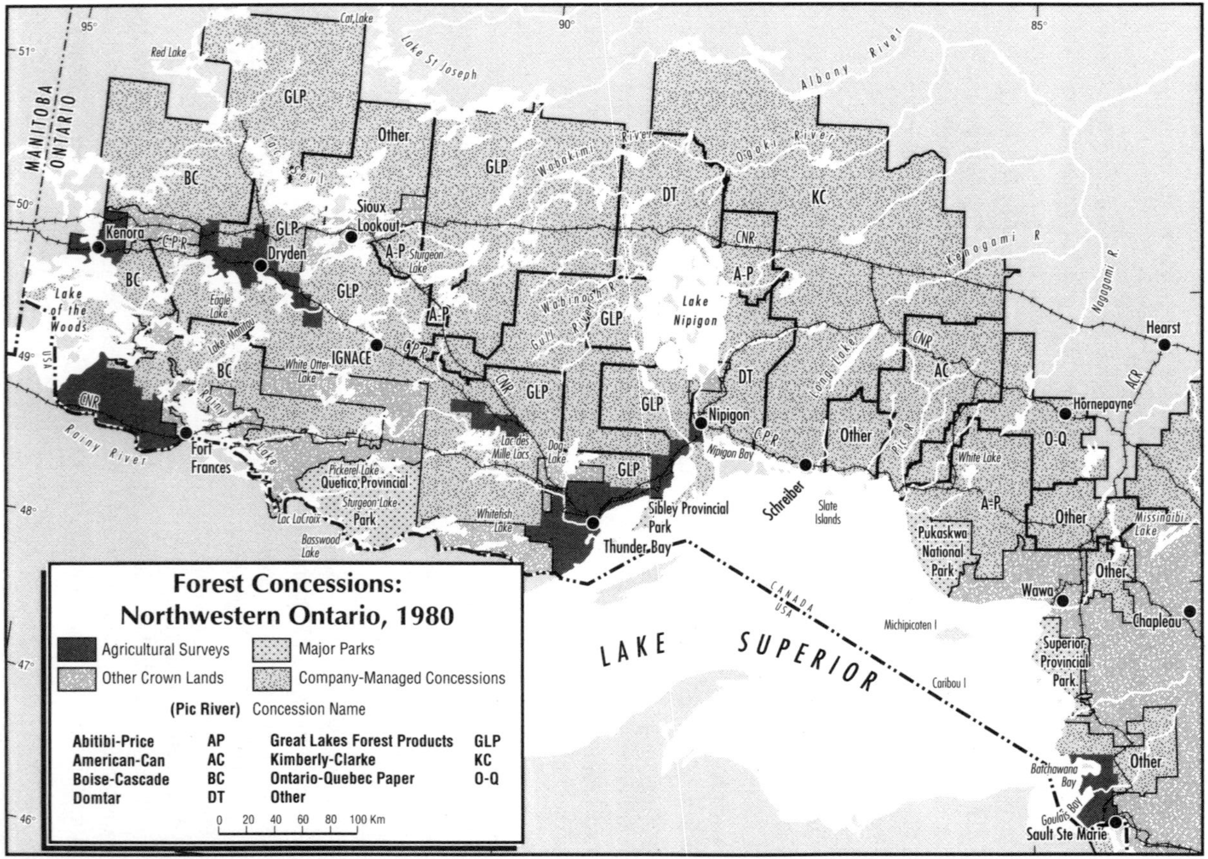
Forest Concessions:
Northwestern Ontario, 1980
Agricultural Surveys
Major Parks
Other Crown Lands
Company-Managed Concessions
(Pic River) Concession Name
Abitibi-Price AP
American-Can AC
Boise-Cascade BC
Domtar DT
Great Lakes Forest Products GLP
Kimberly-Clarke KC
Ontario-Quebec Paper O-Q
Other
0 20 40 60 80 100 Km
MANITOBA
ONTARIO
Kenora
Dryden
Sioux Lookout
IGNACE
Fort Frances
Thunder Bay
Nipigon
Schreiber
Hearst
Hornepayne
Wawa
Chapleau
Sault Ste Marie
Lake of the Woods
Lake Nipigon
LAKE SUPERIOR
Sibley Provincial Park
Quetico Provincial Park
Pukaskwa National Park
Superior Provincial Park
Albany River
Ogoki River
Wabakimi River
Kenogami R
Nagagami R
Rainy River
Rainy Lake
Lake St Joseph
Lac Seul
Red Lake
Cat Lake
Slate Islands
Michipicoten I
Caribou I
CANADA
USA

MAP 5.2

the Kennedy recommendations about a reorganizational consolidation of existing limits, with losses east of the Nipigon River being replaced by a substantial block near Ignace. In response to an energetic program of mill expansion at the Lakehead, Great Lakes came to hold other units in western Thunder Bay and eastern Kenora districts by the mid-sixties. By then these efforts were advancing into southern Patricia culminating in the early seventies with a large licence to the northeast of Sioux Lookout.[223]

Meanwhile, in the early fifties, Anglo-Canadian had indicated an interest in the tract of then inaccessible forest north of Lac Seul and the English River. It was granted this reserve while company studies of potential timber volume and possible sites for a large chemical pulp mill here were underway.[224] Also planning a western empire, its successor, Reed Paper, had taken over the assets and woodland leases of the Dryden mill in 1953. Reed followed this move with a tentative northern agreement for the 7,500-square-mile Pakwash Management Unit in 1955. For this, it suggested mills near Sioux Lookout in four years, if Ontario Hydro would develop the Maynard Rapids and if Ontario would dredge a tow canal from Lac Seul.[225] But despite official consent and an extension to 1964 for completion of the project, the company backed out of the arrangement.[226] By 1979 part of this unit passed to Boise Cascade, but the bulk was assigned to Great Lakes when it acquired Reed's Dryden operation and undertook ambitious mill rehabilitation and expansion there.[227] With this last event, the modern forest frontier in northwestern Ontario had reached its maximum northern extension.

By the early 1980s, such territorial expansion and adjustment were reflected in an increase of about 10 million acres in the northwest's forest covered under agreements (see Table 5.3). However, only 60 per cent was a net addition to productive forest acreage, given regional subtractions for recreation, newly patented lands and Native reserves, as well as tracts burned or otherwise barren of timber. The northward sweep of much of this increase brought important alterations to the composition of the growing stock (see Table 5.4). Principally, it generated an absolute increase in the volume of mature and immature jackpine and doubled the inventory of spruce, the two most popular pulping species.[228] The contribution of other forest elements seems to have changed little, although pine, for reason of both its limited northern range and its continued harvest, was even further reduced in availability.

Yet the most significant change signalled by this expansion was a 37 per cent rise in harvest levels across the northwest by 1980, something in which the rest of northern Ontario did not share[229] but which had been the fundamental intent of government policy in the region since the forties. As recognized in 1950, the forest concessions were much larger than contemporary harvesting

TABLE 5.3 Northwestern Exploitable Area (in thousands of square miles), c. 1950–1985

	c. 1950		1985	
	Area	% of total	Area	% of total
Productive forest				
Crown	56,650	87	62,128	83
Patented and other	1,995	3	2,949	4
Total	58,645	90	65,077	87
Unproductive area	6,164	10	10,061	13
Total area	64,809	100	75,138	100

Source: Government of Ontario, *Forest Resources Inventory; Summary District Reports*, 5, 6, 9, 14, 15, 16 (Toronto: Dept. of Lands and Forests, 1953) and Government of Ontario, *The Forest Resources of Ontario* (Toronto: Ministry of Natural Resources, 1986).

TABLE 5.4 Northwestern Productive Forest (volume of growing stock in millions of cubic feet), c. 1950–1985

	c. 1950		1985	
	Area	% of total	Area	% of total
Conifers				
Pine (red/white)	764	1	410	–
Jackpine	11,617	20	15,088	18
Spruce	20,796	36	42,805	51
Balsam fir	4,307	8	4,050	5
Other	546	1	508	1
Total	38,030	66	62,861	75
Hardwoods				
Poplar/birch	19,262	34	20,475	25
Other	42	–	94	–
Total	19,304	34	20,569	25
Grand Total	57,334	100	83,430	100

Source: See Table 5.3. Both sets of statistics omit Algoma West, and those for 1985 include additional northern parts of Patricia and slightly different boundaries elsewhere.

levels required.[230] Only 23 per cent of the mature timber was being cut at its appropriate maturity, which was deemed inefficient by foresters and resulted in over-aged stands, with their own peculiar problems for future stewardly management. Even among coniferous species, only 43 per cent were being taken at the appropriate time, although among the traditionally preferred spruce the cut ran as high as three-quarters of that suitable supply.[231]

Sustainability

In 1980 the gross total for harvesting still lingered at less than 45 per cent, but the coniferous cut across the limits averaged 80 per cent of the allowable limit for sustained yield. On older limits, such as those most southerly ones in Rainy River/Kenora and east from Thunder Bay, harvesting rates for spruce and now jackpine seem to have reached, or exceeded, acceptable long-term figures.[232] Equally important, although hardwood utilization had risen from the minimum level of 1950, serious under-harvesting continued among white birch and the many varieties of poplar or aspen. In addition, in old cut-over tracts, birch and poplar rapidly were increasing their number and size on a preponderance of naturally regenerating sites.

Other aspects of the evolving woodland side of the industry also came to prove problematic, initiating much heated conflict among the companies, the public, government, and official agencies over the years. Problems cannot be laid at the feet of any single party; indeed, what had been launched by the province with public support and industrial acquiescence was an enormous experiment towards the more appropriate management of a mammoth resource. This experiment was firmly grounded in theory and driven by sound intentions as well as high expectations. However, the participants had, as yet, little practical knowledge or experience of how to proceed.

In some sectors of this experimental plan, such as forest protection, the outcome was quite positive. Long-time efforts at fire control reached levels of expenditure that promoted a maturing approach to and effective coverage of both commercial leases and the accessible forest as a whole.[233] Final additions were made to the former pattern of radio-linked watch towers in the fifties and early sixties. A decade later, air surveillance was added across the forest districts of the northwest.[234] Such use of aircraft came to supplement their earlier role in the transport of fire-fighting crews. Indeed, the importance of the Provincial Air Service in this regard resulted in its integration into the Forest Protection wing of Lands and Forests in 1957.[235] By that time, attempts at the aerial water bombing of problem fires had proved successful and, with improvements in technique, would usher in huge aircraft specially designed for the purpose.[236] There were still losses of as much as a million acres of timber in dry years like 1961, 1974, and 1980, yet efforts at protection reduced the average annual loss levels of previous decades and the occurrence of large holocausts.[237]

The same kind of control and moderating efforts were also achieved as a result of entomological studies and work in forest pathology carried out in the new laboratories in Sault Ste Marie. These had been opened under federal–provincial funding in the forties.[238] While the migratory infestations of the budworm remained particularly ravaging from 1970 to 1974 and generated large salvage cuts, their destructive effects were much less severe than had been common previously. This was the direct result of aerial DDT spray programs, which were curtailed in the late sixties, when that insecticides's deleterious effect on birds and animals was finally recognized. More acceptable substitutes like fenetrothean (an organic phosphate compound) were employed, but more judiciously, through the seventies.[239]

Real conundrums within the area of sustained yield were to appear in these decades and would reach worrying levels by 1980. A principal concern was in the area of regeneration, which in prior decades had been ill-understood and left almost totally to the vagaries of nature and a regrowth of 'weed trees' like poplar. Although recognition of the problem had been growing after World War II, its implications were first bluntly expressed in the 1954 White Paper *Suggestions for a Programme of Renewable Resource Development*. This document stated that at current rates of cutting, remaining commercial stands of white and red pine, which had never seen significant reforestation in the north, would be gone in seventeen years. The pulp and paper industry was projected to be but twenty years away from the harvesting of immature stands, particularly spruce. The White Paper also predicted that a wood shortage would prevail until 1990 when suitable regrowth would become available.[240] This document reiterated what the forestry community had been stressing for more than a decade and supported the intent of certain clauses in the Forest Management Act of 1947 and sections in the revised Crown Timber Act of 1953. It also was a strong force for the massive northern expansion of the area within forest lease.

This White Paper led directly to Project Regeneration, mounted in 1957 as an energetic attempt to devise and pursue better measures of regeneration and thereby assure more suitable forest resources in the mid- to long-range future.[241] With its introduction, each major forest firm was required to initiate an active reforestation program under the direction of the firm's own professional foresters. Such programs planted as many as 350,000 seedlings annually, obtained from government tree farms.[242] These provincial nurseries increased quickly in size and number to include ones near Thessalon, White River, the Lakehead, at Dryden, and in the Rainy River country. Some companies, like Kimberly-Clark, even created seed orchards and tree farms of their own.[243] Firms controlling freehold lands often replanted these along with their cut-over

Crown tracts. Meanwhile, the province encouraged the reforestation efforts of farmers on lots reverting to bush or of community groups on abandoned rural lands in their environs.[244] Because of continuing problems with white pine blister rust, introduced to Canada in 1914, much of the stock was not of prime lumbering species, except for red pine. Instead, it concentrated on spruce and jackpine for pulpwood.[245] Such planting went in tandem with aggressive experiments in scarification and other aspects of site preparation. By the end of the fifties the total annual plant across the north had climbed to over 35 million seedlings, considerably more than half of which were placed in sites west of Sault Ste Marie.[246] Much effort was expended in this process and much of a practical nature was learned about this novel field of silviculture. Yet a general lack of coordination was one major reason why the province took back all responsibility for regeneration in 1962.[247]

Over the rest of the period, however, intensive efforts continued to climb. Manual planting of prepared sites came to involve the experimental use of fertilizers and herbicides and was supplemented with early attempts at aerial seeding.[248] Under shared federal–provincial funding, joint programs with industry promoted the harvesting of old blocks of over-mature timber and their replanting with appropriate stock. With similar finance under the Agricultural Rehabilitation and Development Act (ARDA), much regenerative work was carried out on dormant or abandoned agricultural acreage across the region.[249] However, in spite of the intensified and expanded results, the escalating costs involved caused much official soul-searching. The result was a call for a sequence of studies to determine the value of the endeavour and to evaluate its expense.

The Brodie Study Unit Report of 1967 was the first of these assessments. It concentrated on the state of the industry and the efficiency and appropriateness of its use of provincial forest resources under current managerial methods. In 1970 the Department of Treasury and Economics made several minor policy recommendations for the northwest in its *Design for Development.* It was followed in 1972 by a long-range supply and market appraisal, using the existing managerial philosophy to tender a series of alternative balances between harvest and regeneration for Ontario to consider, and placing a price tag on each.[250] However, none of these studies got to the root of the problem.

Finally, in 1976, a report by K.A. Anson addressed the issue bluntly. He stated that cut rates continued to out-run the regenerative process, despite lavish financial infusions, because forest management for sustained yield was simply not working. The principal obstacle to its success, he suggested, lay in conflicting perceptions of the forest: the public was concerned with forest protection, not its managed use; the industry with short-term wood allocation instead of long-term management supply; and the government understood regulation but not management.[251]

Other observers addressed the issues from inside rather than outside the regional context, at about the same date. They put the case in more practical terms: the forest operators had the men and equipment but no inherent incentive; government had the incentive but not the tools; and the local woodsworkers would rather cut than plant.[252]

In 1980 a long-standing complex of outmoded and narrow impressions still haunted woodland use. Such attitudes had brought the forests of the region to a state for which there could be no quick or painless remedy.

The Fisheries in Crisis

Strong indications of the bleak future of the fisheries were present in the thirties. Over the forties and into the fifties, the very low fish prices of the Depression continued to prevail.[253] Some small producers in the northwest had been driven from the industry or had left for armed service, never to return. Increasing numbers were forced gradually to go part-time, finding supplemental employment in other fields. On Superior, where total catches had declined by 25 per cent to 2.6 million pounds by 1951, large operators were already issuing stern warnings about the inevitable economic effects of these shortfalls.[254] Indeed, all such producers – three on the Algoma shore and four more to the north and west – were struggling financially to find fish on the one hand and to discover market returns worthy of that search on the other. Several would disappear during the financial troubles to follow. Purvis closed the station at Michipicoten Island in 1957. These grounds were then assumed by a new interest up from Lake Erie, Ferro-Clad, which shifted the headquarters to Mamainse Harbour. Also during the fifties, other firms operating from traditional ports between Nipigon and Heron Bay either folded or merged into the operations of Kemp Fisheries at the Lakehead.[255] On the region's inland lakes, especially the larger ones, the lot of commercial interests, both Native and white, was certainly cursed by similar problems of harvest and price. Although their contribution may have continued to exceed that of Superior, an unfortunate official lumping together of all inland catch statistics across the provincial north makes it impossible to examine the situation more exactly.[256]

On Superior, commercial fishing was nearly wiped out in the fifties by the arrival of the lamprey, an oceanic eel that preyed on lake trout in particular and that was well established in the lower lakes by the twenties. Its devastation of fish stocks swept slowly northward, contributing to the near-collapse of the industry on northern Huron two decades later.[257] First sightings on Lake Superior occurred off the entrance to the St Marys River in 1945 and north off the Pukaskwa Peninsula in another three years. After that, it was only a matter of time before there was a steep decline in lake trout populations.[258] It came dramatically in the mid-fifties, when the trout catch plummeted by 56 per cent in one year, to about 527,000 pounds, before reaching a scant 48,000 pounds in 1961 (see Table 5.5). In regional fishery lore, the lamprey is held to be the scapegoat for this crisis and the depleted conditions of subsequent decades. Yet scholarly opinion interprets it as only the final straw for stocks long and inexcusably eroded by human abuse before the forties even began.[259]

The catastrophe brought rapid political response. By 1946, Ontario had inaugurated research into Huron's lamprey problem at South Bay on the Manitoulin Island, and in this venture it was quickly joined by Ottawa. In the same year, the International Sea Lamprey Committee was formed as the precursor to the Great Lakes Fishery Commission of 1955 and was responsible for concerted Canada–U.S. action on the problem.[260] The first reaction on Superior was the placing of nets and some electrical weirs across the lower reaches of more than forty Ontario rivers and streams used by the lamprey to spawn.[261] This effort was augmented or often replaced by use of a chemical lampricide (TFM). This treatment over several years, beginning in 1958, was successful in curbing the problem and bringing it under control by the mid-sixties.[262]

This eradicative approach, however, was accompanied after 1961 by energetic attempts to re-establish the basic breeding stocks. In the absence of other alternatives, this involved the expensive seeding of the lake with millions of trout fry.[263] Because of its enormous scale, this hatchery-based project was modestly successful. However, this was true only in conjunction with stiff

TABLE 5.5 Lake Superior Commercial Fisheries Catch (in pounds), 1951–1981

	Lake Trout		Whitefish		Herring			
	Lbs.	% of total	Lbs.	% of total	Lbs.	% of total	Aggregate of Total	Total Catch
1951	1,506,365	57	340,758	13	504,673	19	89	2,654,618
1956	527,288	25	302,504	14	821,331	38	77	2,144,985
1961	48,263	2	118,551	5	1,777,180	76	83	2,353,036
1966	102,016	4	134,737	6	1,553,375	68	79	2,269,864
1971	150,384	4	253,011	8	2,577,222	77	89	3,367,420
1981	176,387	9	172,506	8	1,327,191	64	81	2,060,279

Source: Calculated from tables accompanying the *Reports of the Department of Game and Fisheries*, later a branch in Lands and Forests, then in Natural Resources.

quotas that Ontario imposed on its trout fishery here in the spring of 1962. Under these new regulations, commercial operators at the Lakehead were allowed 11,000 pounds annually, on the north shore, 6,000 pounds, and on the Algoma side, 23,000 pounds. To this slim total was added another 4,000 pounds under licences to the sports fishery.[264] Loud complaints followed from the commercial producers because these changes involved the cancellation of all licences not actively used for more than two years. Government also drew much heated reaction in the early sixties when fishermen had collectively expended the quota by summer and were forced to rely on hard-pressed whitefish supplies and low-value catch until the fall herring season.[265] Indeed, the latter fishery, which was principally about Thunder Bay, rose sharply from 20 per cent of the total catch by weight in 1951 to 65–75 per cent through the sixties (see Table 5.5). So heavy was the deprivation among all available stocks that in 1973 herring too were put under quota, forcing even more reliance on the growing harvest of lesser species.[266]

Other attempts were made in these years to aid and stabilize this now much-reduced commercial fishery. Intense programs of seeding these waters with whitefish fry were mounted at the opening of the sixties and directed at bolstering short-term future harvests.[267] This was a heroic, fruitless venture. Hatcheries were by then recognized as useful to the commercial industry only in special situations, like the introduction of new species or the replenishment of fundamental breeding numbers, as in the case of the lake trout. More important, by the end of the decade Ontario's longstanding but questionable tradition of whitefish breeding for commercial ends was quietly terminated. Many hatcheries closed, and the remainder were reduced and reoriented to the promotion of sport fishing. Not surprisingly, by 1980, the annual level of fry planting here (as across the province) stood at less than 1 per cent of its peak between 1920 and 1940.[268]

Even before the inception of quotas in 1962, innovative means of raising the market value of lesser grades of fish were actively sought by regional interests and government agencies. The first experiments were with smoked fish, chub in particular, an idea successfully introduced by Ivan Purvis at Michipicoten Island and widely adopted on the upper lakes.[269] This was followed by official attempts to discover new approaches to packaging and marketing such as canning, pickling, and fast-freezing, only the last of which was successful. Subsidized central freezer plants slowly appeared by 1970, for the use of producer groups under the management of Ferro-Clad Fisheries in Algoma and Kemp Fisheries in Fort William. Earlier attempts at freezing had already occurred in the mid-fifties in Port Arthur, where the Diamond Fish Co. had experimented with the technique for herring (to be sold in Duluth) and much larger quantities of trash fish for a general market in animal food.[270] Considerable impetus to this whole movement was supplied by a federal Royal Commission examining the health of the Great Lakes fisheries and those in the western provincial interiors. This official body held hearings across the region in 1965. However, its related push for a system of cooperative processing facilities and marketing boards found only tepid response in northwestern Ontario.[271] At the end of the seventies, therefore, frozen products were an important element of the market, but fresh fish, trucked to Montreal, Winnipeg, New York, or cities of the American midwest, was still far more important to regional producers.

Over this period, the seeds were sown for a more technically efficient and environmentally aware industry. During the fifties, cotton gill nets, so prone to rot and wear, were slowly replaced by much lighter and more durable nylon ones. These were prevalent on Superior before the end of that decade. However, the pound net, with its requirement for strength, moved only to heavy synthetic twines. Its modification, the trap net, because it did away with the pile-driving of support poles, greatly reduced the labour in seasonal placement.[272] Where and when money was available, strides were also made in tug design and more efficient diesel engines, as well as in hydraulics and power winching, to reduce manpower requirements.

At the opening of the period the fishing industry was still struggling to correct old pollution problems, such as spawning beds bark-littered from years of log or pulpwood booming, floating litter from sawmills and log transport, as well as effluent and fibre discharge from pulp and paper processing.[273] By 1965, the particulate pollution from sawmills and booms was slowly becoming a thing of the past, but chemical pollution from sulphate and sulphite pulp processes and fibrous discharge from groundwood mills was increasing rapidly. Rising public anger over such environmental irresponsibility was joined with weak, but encouraging, corrective legislation to help these rather inarticulate fishermen obtain some moderate satisfaction through improved water quality.[274] Subsequently, popular awareness and concern about such environmental issues increased rapidly through the seventies, initiating changes in a broad range of northern resource-exploitive fields.

On the inland lakes of the northwest, fisheries information is less available. Here, the lamprey eel was never an issue to be contended with. Although commercial operations on Rainy Lake and specified areas of the Lake of the Woods continued, on-going friction between the tourist community and the commercial fishermen produced periodic heat, as in decades past. Nevertheless, intermittent attempts by the appropriate provincial agency to mediate continued to the late seventies.[275]

Similar confrontational situations marked most inland waters that lay within the northerly expanding, tourism range. On smaller lakes, productive capacity was often limited and unable to sustain commercial harvesting of real intensity, even when limited to the winter season.[276] Many were ruined for the sportsman in the process. On larger water bodies like Seul, St Joseph, Lac des Mille Lacs, Nipigon, Oniman, and Long Lake, shared use was not necessarily a problem, and active fisheries by substantial firms (often subsidiary to Lake Superior companies like Kemp) were prevalent.[277]

In the northern or Patricia portion of the Kenora District, as in the Rainy River-Lake of the Woods watershed, elaborate Ontario surveys of capacity and use marked these years.[278] Such efforts were coordinated with federal studies and incentive programs as far north as the Albany/English River systems.[279] These were intended to promote and stabilize Native commercial participation in the sixties and seventies, replacing income often still related to the Hudson's Bay Company in the forties.[280] However, mercury contaminants closed out such endeavours on the Winnipeg River below Kenora in May of 1970, as well as on a range of lakes and river stretches below Dryden on the Wabigoon and lower English River watershed. After nine years, this ban was partially lifted to allow Native groups to fish commercially, but only for the production of highly processed plant fertilizers.[281] Nevertheless, in other parts of Patricia and elsewhere, commercial fishing, which was often cooperatively organized, had a strong aboriginal component, and links to Winnipeg outlets, prevailed into the eighties.[282] By that time, a battered and ravaged industry had finally come to accept a more responsible, if much less colourful and central, place in the regional pattern.

Farming in Decline

As across the rest of the province and the nation, Ontario's northern districts faced a rising complex of changes in their agricultural sector, which problems grew to prominence in the fifties. On the one hand, these difficulties reflected sharp post-war competition for butter and wool from such new products as margarine and synthetic fibres, causing a decline in farm exports to traditional trading partners like Great Britain and the appearance of cheap agricultural products from the United States on Canadian dining tables. On the other hand, such problems mirrored the lingering effects of depression on farm income levels. Although domestic demand for food in an increasingly urban society was climbing rapidly, many farm youths left agriculture for better pay elsewhere, promoting some ageing in the rural population. While the number of farmers shrank, farm size grew, as did specialization under rapid mechanization and advancing agricultural technology, which collectively induced climbing productivity from declining acreage.[283]

Causal Factors

Northern Ontario farming was particularly punished by these developments because of its peripheral position in the province and the constraints of temperature and growing season that reduced its competitive ability.[284] Although farm size here finally reached the provincial mean, farm numbers and populations fell drastically, particularly before the early sixties. Across the northwest over the next thirty years, the frequency of farm units would drop to one-quarter and their population to one-fifth of the 1951 figures. All agricultural pockets were markedly affected. Ironically, expansion in the rural, non-farm component more than made up for the shortfall in the Kenora District, grew commensurately around Sault Ste Marie, dropped modestly in the Rainy River Valley, and was adversely affected by urban amalgamation at the Lakehead in 1970 (see Table 5.6). Part of this shift in occupational balance reflected the simple transition of family income from farming to more remunerative, industrial employment. Part arose from a continuing trend among urbanites for rural habitations. Either of these drives might involve the retention or abandonment of the agricultural holding. Another element in this process, in every region but Algoma, was the replacement of some previous families by Swiss, Dutch, or Mennonite populations of varying sizes.[285]

Agrarian causes behind such disruptive change in community life were numerous and varied in importance. Some farmers were simply unable to finance the capital costs of remaining competitive in extra-regional markets. Some in specialized supply of produce to regional consumers were forced out by the supermarket chains. Others could no longer make ends meet because of the narrow range of products open to them, the limited yields they could attain, and the intense competition their offerings now faced (potatoes or roots for example).[286] By the sixties, except in highly specialized fields like the irrigated raising of strawberries or other seasonal fruit on a part-time basis, these farms were rapidly disappearing, even on properties close to the urban centres.

Much of the rural reduction or rationalization was alternately related to two other facts of rural life. Of these, the earlier, more complex, and less understood one was tied to the traditional role of the settler in the pursuit of seasonal forest income, which was coming to its end.[287] 'Pulp farming' even as an infrequent way of life among the inhabitants of soil pockets had drawn to its close with the hardships of the thirties. However, many farmers on poorer or more limited holdings were still producing seasonal pulpwood in the fifties, from their own holdings or for wages elsewhere. This fortuitous source of extra cash was now endangered by the increasingly large-scale, mechanized, and year-round operation of the modern forest industry.[288] Settler cutting was gone

TABLE 5.6 Rural Profile, 1951–1981

	1951	1961	1971	1981*
Algoma West				
No. of farms	204	72	47	11
Farm population	977	934	666	210
Rural population	8,325	16,157	7,365†	8,365
Thunder Bay District				
No. of farms	1,863	850	419	358
Farm population	8,793	3,966	2,202	1,120
Rural population	37,180	27,598	19,235†	26,218
Rainy River District				
No. of farms	1,371	781	496	456
Farm population	6,068	3,382	2,278	2,190
Rural population	11,649	9,208	8,625	8,492
Kenora District				
No. of farms	551	238	135	130
Farm population	3,781	1,012	647	510
Rural population	9,428	26,720	26,815	32,797
Total Northwest				
No. of farms	3,989	1,941	1,097	955
Farm population	19,619	9,294	5,793	4,030
Rural population	66,582	79,683	62,040	75,872

* Figures for 1981 reflect a somewhat more stringent definition of 'farm' and 'farmer' than that which applied earlier.

† Figures subsequent to major urban boundary expansion.

Source: Compiled from Census of Canada 1951, 1961, 1971, 1981.

from Algoma West and largely so behind Thunder Bay by 1960. But with other forms of woods work, pulpwood would continue for over a decade more to contribute substantially to farm incomes further west, particularly in the back townships of the Rainy River country.[289] However, those bush lots that persisted made up a decreased proportion of total holdings, especially in relation to crop and pasture, as Tables 5.7 and 5.8 attest.

The second important factor was linked to Ottawa's tardy formulation of a policy for a national action program to correct major social and economic inequities in Canadian agriculture. This began to occupy federal thinking only in 1961 and attracted Ontario's enthusiastic attention. Since Ontario Premier

TABLE 5.7 Agricultural Land Use Adjustments (change by decade as percentage of total change), 1951–1981

	1951–61	1961–71	1971–81	Actual Loss 1951–81 (acres)
Cropland	–54.5%	–50.0%	+4.5%	54,549
Pasture	–46.4	–31.3	–22.3	125,869
Cropland and Pasture	–49.9	–40.0	–10.1	180,418
Other	–67.3	–20.8	–11.9	248,615
Total agricultural change	–58.2	–27.0	–14.8	439,034

Source: Census of Canada for the appropriate intervals.

Mitchell Hepburn's decision in the thirties to opt out of 'the business of colonization,'[290] the province had developed no clear guidelines for northern agriculture. Over the fifties, it continued to honour old doctrines through a largely uncoordinated mix of dated programs. Finally, in 1961, this aimless approach was challenged in the final report of the Commission of Inquiry into Ontario Agriculture. Here the province's policy was described as a 'futile rear-guard action' in the pursuit of unrealistic goals. The document went on to promote new thrusts for modern agricultural progress in northern rural communities.[291]

The ARDA Solution

The report's blunt thinking formed the basis for Ontario's participation with federal agencies to resolve the mounting problems of ageing, poverty, dislocation, and marginality in agriculture across Canada.[292] The initiation of Ottawa's Agricultural Rehabilitation and Development Act (ARDA) in 1961 was followed in 1963 by the more useful tool of the Canada Land Inventory. This program, using concepts of multiple-use planning, ranked the country's soil resources in seven descending classes of value for agriculture.[293] This procedure confirmed that no soils in the northwest ranked higher than class three and confirmed their most appropriate use to be for intensive livestock raising and supportive activity.[294] At the same time the cartographic results of the inventory underlined the truth that much land, turned to farming in the past, would be better suited to forest or recreational use.

The real push for reform, however, began only after a major nation-wide conference in Ottawa in 1966. It encouraged measures to promote farm enlargement through the buyout of elderly or inadequate owners. Release or resale of the appropriate portions to surrounding farmers followed, as did the

TABLE 5.8 Agricultural Balances, 1951–1981

	1951		1961		1971		1981	
	Acres	% of total	Acres	% of total	Acres	% of total	Acres	% of total
*Algoma West**								
Cropland	5,630	41	2,724	35	1,370	29	209	20
Pasture	4,694	34	2,946	38	2,315	49	642	60
Other	3,318	24	2,103	27	1,067	22	215	20
Total held	13,642		7,773		4,752		1,066	
Thunder Bay District								
Cropland	60,622	22	45,969	28	37,692	35	37,922	44
Pasture	69,453	25	48,240	30	33,935	32	26,383	31
Other	148,081	53	68,514	42	35,222	33	21,411	25
Total held	278,156		162,723		106,849		85,716	
Rainy River District								
Cropland	70,247	22	60,930	27	48,745	27	51,173	32
Pasture	129,579	41	103,359	47	79,637	43	62,344	40
Other	112,873	36	57,537	26	54,797	30	44,231	28
Total held	312,699		221,826		183,179		157,748	
Kenora District								
Cropland	22,344	19	19,462	26	13,994	26	14,989	31
Pasture	30,510	26	21,262	29	20,491	39	18,998	39
Other	64,566	55	33,438	45	18,707	35	14,365	30
Total held	117,420		74,162		53,192		48,352	
Total Northwest								
Cropland	158,843	22	129,085	28	101,801	29	104,293	36
Pasture	234,236	32	175,807	38	136,378	39	108,367	37
Other	328,838	46	161,592	35	109,793	32	80,222	27
Total held	721,917		466,484		347,972		292,882	

* Figures are approximations only.
Source: Census of Canada for the relevant years.

conversion of less-valuable acres to community pastures and transfer of the remainder to other uses under the provincial Crown.[295] Such nation-wide procedures persisted through the sixties and, despite reductions in federal participation, remained active in Ontario until 1979, when ARDA activity was formally terminated.[296]

Federal–provincial expenditure across the northwest under the ARDA agreements from 1962–1979 ran to over $4 million, which was a generous outlay for so limited a northern population. Roughly $800,000 was distributed across Algoma and in Kenora; $1 million was supplied to Rainy River, and twice that sum served the problems around Thunder Bay.[297] However, expenditures were negligible about Sault Ste Marie and small on the repossession of certain submarginal properties in the retreatied townships to the north.[298] Surprisingly few purchases occurred in the Kenora District and all seem to have been reallocated for future forest use. In contrast, down the Rainy River Valley, some 105 retirees gave up their acreage, of which 68 per cent was released, with another 15 per cent resold to neighbours.[299] Much of the balance was formed into community pastures, the largest being in the west end of this pocket.[300] Similarly, of 170 properties of varied size resumed under ARDA between the Nipigon and Pigeon rivers, almost three-quarters were also transferred to more active members of the neighbouring farm community. Again, a portion of the remainder was converted to community pastoral use.[301] Certainly as an agent of farm rationalization and enlargement, ARDA's endeavours would appear to have succeeded admirably in their intent.

The government program's ancillary aid to help major groups in most agricultural communities also was commendable. These endeavoured to promote both beef and dairy options for farms in both Kenora and Dryden area townships, the dairy option being more successful in farm communities around the Lakehead. However, the most exemplary results were achieved in the Rainy River country.[302] Valley farmers, having suffered under declining wool demands and devastating predator problems, had abandoned their once-strong emphasis on sheep and lambs in favour of near total reliance on cattle. They retained the dairying needed for their strong and diverse co-op operations in buying, marketing, and retailing dairy products, but greatly expanded their expenditure on beef raising. Using the model of Manitoulin enterprise, they started an annual auction sale of feeders at Stratton. This, from its inception in 1960, drew mid-western as well as Manitoba bidders, after a strenuous attempt at full brucellosis vaccination.[303] After the valley became a Rural Development Area in 1963, ARDA support was utilized to encourage the creation of a pool of well-bred cows and performance-tested bulls. This was followed in 1967 with funds for a proper show ring and seating at Stratton, which facility was fully enclosed at the decade's close and augmented by an abattoir in 1976.[304] Aid of this kind during these years of disconcerting change was very important to the survival of those dedicated cores of farmers among the agricultural pockets of the region.

Yet here as elsewhere, ARDA has been accused, in hindsight, of placing too much emphasis on land rationalization, as well as on projects to further develop already sustainable agriculture among farmers. Some critics claim that too little was spent on the rehabilitation of those trapped by poverty or circumstance on submarginal holdings.[305] This may be true, although there is little concrete evidence in the northwest to support such a claim. However, the agricultural statistics would seem to disprove any serious negligence under ARDA in this regard (see Table 5.7). Of the nearly half-million acres given up for taxes over the thirty years after 1950, nearly 60 per cent were abandoned by 1961, before ARDA was enacted. Of the 60 per cent of the total loss that was woodland and waste (termed 'other' on the table), more than two-thirds were also given up in this initial decade. Less spectacular but similar trends for cropland and pasture also occurred. Apparently, at least the bulk of the truly marginal and submarginal operators had been forced from their rural homes while the very policy to help them was being devised.

These same agricultural statistics also indicate several other trends in rural activity (see Table 5.8). Among farmers more successful in their struggle to maintain an agricultural way of life, there was a move to shed cut-over bush lots, which could no longer be expected to contribute to the future farm economy.[306] While this tendency was strongest at the opening of the period, its continuance also contributed to a radical rebalancing in the shrinking agricultural pattern across the region. This brought much more intensive land uses to a dominant position on the average farm. Where at the outset only 54 per cent of the normal farm was under crop and designated pastoral use, nearly three-quarters was so defined in 1981. More important, this enlarged proportion had undergone stringent reassessment over previous decades and only the best of such acreage of 1951 had been retained. In this re-evaluative process, considerably more than twice as much pastoral as opposed to crop acreage was discarded. Much of this loss was grazed woodland or unimproved cut-over, which now added little to anything but the tax bill.

Interestingly enough, after a like pattern of reduction to 1970, cropland acreage increased again slightly in every important farming area. However, this upturn was of little significance among the now-constricted number of agricultural townships behind Thunder Bay. Dairying was the most prevalent specialization there, while dairy with some beef was notable around Dryden. However, beef was the more important market commodity of the Rainy River

Valley by 1981. Only in the Dryden and Rainy River areas did pastoral acreage continue to exceed cropland. In all three, the major field crop was now hay or hay ensilage, the prohibitively expensive growing of feed grains being replaced by western imports under subsidy.[307] The unusually high proportion of cropland at the Lakehead seems to have had little to do with the prevalent livestock interests of the region. Instead, it reflected the continuance or growth of urban-related uses: fruit growing, market gardening, nurseries, and sod farms.[308]

Trimmed to 40 per cent of its previous capacity, northwestern Ontario's agriculture in 1980 was a much leaner industry than thirty years before, and its trials were not entirely over. However, along with farming elsewhere across the province, it had graduated from a simple way of life to a complex business operation, demanding the utmost in efficiency.

Tourism Comes of Age

Over this period, tourism became a major contributor to the northwestern Ontario economy. By the mid-sixties, nearly a million people each summer visited the region on vacation, joining an increasing proportion of the local population able to enjoy the out of doors.[309] The number of visitors would continue to rise into the seventies, then stabilize at about a million and a half, before dipping with the energy crisis of the late decade.[310] At its peak, estimates placed tourism third in regional economic importance, behind forest and mining industries. By the mid-seventies it generated $12.5 million about Rainy Lake and River, $40.4 million in the Lake of the Woods area, $39 million across the Thunder Bay District, and $37.4 million in Algoma West.[311] Some towns gained as much as 60 per cent of their gross revenues from this seasonal trade; in many that figure was above 40 per cent. In Sault Ste Marie tourism ranked first after steel in dollar value to the community.[312]

This growth reflected a continuation of official encouragement and expenditure on advertising, information services, and regulation. Ontario spent heavily on U.S. media coverage of its various regions, as did the industry itself, and in the seventies organized successful advertising tours in Europe.[313] The government also completed its location of major information centres at northwest border-crossing points. The province also helped finance appropriate subregional literature to accompany private brochures at local outlets and included all accommodations in its provincial guides for those planning a trip. It persevered as well in the inspection and licensing of all private facilities that were to be rented to visitors. With the passage of time, these regulations came to cover sewage disposal and water supply.[314] All such moves were aimed at helping the industry remain competitive in the challenging world of commercial recreation.

However, the most important government contribution to the northwest's tourist economy was the expansion of the regional highway system and road network, which greatly enhanced regional appeal and opportunity. Upgrading the trunk system to Trans-Canada Highway standards was primary to this end, as was the opening of its Lake Superior route in 1960. The latter was roughly coordinated with the opening of the international bridge at Sault Ste Marie, with Michigan's spectacular linkage across the Straits of Mackinac, and with completion of the interstate highway system north from Ohio to the St Marys River.[315] Even before the Superior route was complete, American visitors flooded the accommodations at Sault Ste Marie. Campers, on the northward heels of the Trans-Canada contractors, were creating temporary grounds at the annual 'end of the road.'[316] Once this highway was open, accommodation and fuel supplies were similarly overtaxed at Wawa, White River, and even in Marathon. This was the final stretch in the Lake Superior circle route that both countries had been anxious to add to similar circle routes around each of the other Great Lakes.[317] Also in the early sixties, the major new highway from the Lakehead area to the Rainy River Valley was completed, as were roads northward from the Trans-Canada, like the one to Red Lake, all of which presented many new travel opportunities. Another route was soon added about Lake of the Woods, with the cooperation of both Manitoba and Minnesota.[318] Meanwhile, construction was completed on a new link from near Fort Frances north to Dryden. It enabled the development of a road loop from there, via Kenora, and south to a new bridge at Fort Frances. This was designated as the head of the Great River Parkway along the Mississippi from New Orleans.[319] These latter moves greatly expanded potential travel experience and vacation use in the Northwest beyond Thunder Bay.

Commercial Accommodations

Along these major routes, this was the era of the one-floor motel, which, like the two-storey motor hotel, made its rapid appearance in any sizeable community or at any other suitable location, and largely replaced that previous generation of overnight facilities, the cabin complex. The motel came to serve those people who crossed the region for vacation destinations elsewhere, who came to tour the northwest, or who were tracing parkway or circle routes through some part of the region.[320]

These travellers rarely stayed in any place for more than one night, thus, motels were not competitive with older forms of lodge accommodation intended for extended vacationing. In cores around the lower Lake of the Woods, about Rainy Lake, at Orient Bay on Lake Nipigon, and at points accessible from the ACR in Algoma, such lodges were long-established enterprises. These lodges traditionally catered to an American clientele and were frequently owned by Americans in this post-war period.[321] To accommodate the increasing trend to family vacationers, most provided recreational facilities, central dining rooms, and housekeeping opportunities. Some still catered to fishermen in the spring and hunters in the autumn.

Generally, the old male-dominated sporting vacation was now facilitated by the many new fly-in operators, many of whom were small charter companies. For them, the transport of fishermen or hunters with their canoes and camping gear was but one source of seasonal income. Others were heavily involved in the vacation trade through established bases at places like Sault St. Marie, White River, Nakina, Sioux Lookout, Kenora, Fort Frances, and Atikokan. Like their predecessors, they complained bitterly, into the seventies, about the charter licences Ottawa granted U.S. competition in the border areas.[322] Many of these operations remained of moderate size; however, some came to operate as many as nine aircraft to fifty private outpost camps supplied with as many as three boats per unit. Like the lodges, such operators were heavily dependent upon American clients, and their return rate was similarly very high from year to year: about 70 per cent.[323]

As in earlier periods, those who came to vacation west of Superior were generally urban and from states like Illinois, Iowa, Nebraska, and Oklahoma as well as Wisconsin and Minnesota. In contrast, those who came to Algoma were principally from Michigan and the lower-lake states.

This was also the period when private cottaging became a major contender in the vacation pattern among a much broader range of income groups. As in other parts of Ontario, cottaging was very popular among Canadians, who made up more than half of the owners. Although cottagers about Kenora continued to be mainly from Manitoba, elsewhere the majority were locals from urban centres or people resident in the northwest.[324] However, the region attracted few vacationers from heavily populated southern Ontario, which found its vacation properties in more immediate northern locations.

Tight curbs were placed on where and how many surveyed cottage lots were made available each year, and other measures were instituted to ensure desirable patterns and preserve public shoreline. Cottage use quickly increased in density about old cores of earlier eras. These included the upper reaches of the Lake of the Woods, the Superior shore about the Lakehead and certain inland lakes there, the region above Schreiber, and all accessible shores from the St Marys to the Montreal River.[325] By the early sixties, some 10,000 cottages dotted regional shores. A decade later this number had climbed to over 15,000, not counting the large number now in Algoma West north of Sault Ste Marie, which probably added another 4,000. More than half of those counted in 1972 were in the immediate area of Kenora and Thunder Bay, while more moderate numbers were found elsewhere, with very few in the Patricia.[326] However, by 1980, even here most towns across the region had a cottage area commensurate in size with the needs of its own local population.

Car Camping

The real explosion in vacation travel came in the form of car camping, which appealed mostly to young people and families. Car camping represented an inexpensive alternative to either motels or resort holidays, and cut sharply into anticipated growth rates for other forms of commercial accommodation.[327] While available camping sites across the northwest numbered only a few hundred in 1950, by the late sixties the number of public and private ones exceeded 2,000 and would increase by more than half before 1975.[328]

With the sixties, car camping facilities were provided either by private or municipal grounds or by the province. The former went heavily for comfort, with electricity, water, and sometimes sewage facilities on site. Many had such amenities as laundromats and hot showers easily available. Their clientele was usually older and owned trailers or, later, full recreational vehicles. Privately owned campgrounds had often been an expedient addition to an older cabin complex and frequently came with convenient boat and motor rentals. Such commercial or municipal properties stood in strong contrast to the large, wooded, and highly planned government facilities. These camping grounds, sometimes providing only basic sanitary and water supplies, emphasized simple living, tenting, hiking, and sometimes outdoor education facilities.[329]

Rising recreational demands in the early fifties and the early lack of sites led to an increase in unorganized roadside camping. This occurred often on Crown land, but sometimes on private property or within the limits of forest concessions where such intrusion was not appreciated. The result was not simply loud complaint from the citizenry and tourist interests, but a growing litter and garbage problem along public highways. By-laws, fines, police action, and an experimental permit system for rough camping on designated Crown tracts did not eradicate the problem, in this age of vagabond truck campers, vans, and motor homes.[330]

The most successful corrective measure was the provision of attractive camping parks, capable of absorbing the demand for a more natural setting than most private or municipal grounds could normally supply. Official efforts in this direction commenced in 1953, with an extensive tour of U.S. facilities and a study of their policies. This resulted in provincial legislative action and the creation of a Parks Division in Lands and Forests to seek, examine, select, and develop suitable locations across Ontario. In the north, where most land was Crown held, acquisition was simple, as were the basic rules that all such properties should cover a minimum of 500 acres, should be no more than 150 miles apart, and should be established first along the busiest highways.[331]

Such parks across the northwest, with their emphasis on the car, were under rapid preparation in the late fifties. Some thirteen, including enclaves in all three older and more traditional forest reserves, were in at least rudimentary operation by 1960 and were found in all districts but the huge Patricia territory (see Table 5.9). These included ones north from Sault Ste Marie and west from Thunder Bay to Kenora along the Trans-Canada. Others were located along the alternate Trans-Canada Highway, from Hearst to its terminus west of Quetico, as well as along the Lake of the Woods. In the sixties more were added, the majority of which were along the new Lake Superior route, principally west of Wawa, with others near Red Lake, Sioux Lookout, and Hornepayne on lesser roads.[332] In the seventies two older ones were closed but several among the more popular and established parks like Pancake Bay, near Sault Ste Marie, and White Lake, east of Marathon, saw substantial enlargement.[333]

Almost as soon as a suitable balance was struck between demand and supply across the region, evidence was appearing to suggest that Canadians, who were now in a slight majority as users, were beginning to change their vacation tastes. Those who had been most often attracted to northern recreation were losing interest in or were shifting away from the former car-oriented pattern. These were primarily a new generation of young adults, increasing rapidly in number over the seventies, who sought a rougher, more physical vacation style and a closer commune with nature. These traits allied them with an older

TABLE 5.9 Provincial Parks, 1950–1980

	1950†	1960	1970	1980
Algoma West	1	2	5	5
Thunder Bay District	1	5	11	13
Rainy River District	1	3	3	3
Kenora District	0	4	5	6
Patricia Portion	0	0	2	3
Total	3	14	26	30

* Limited to those intended for overnight use.

† These early parks in 1950 had only the simplest of camping provisions.

Source: Department of Lands and Forests/Ministry of Natural Resources annual reports, and provincial road maps from the years in question.

tradition of canoeists, primitive campers, and backpackers who were the backbone of the conservation/environmental movement.

By the fifties, U.S. conservationists, with their Canadian counterparts, finally succeeded in obtaining Ontario's support for the trans-border management of the tract of land called Quetico in Canada and Superior in the United States. In 1961, a joint council was set up to advise both governments on how to utilize, yet reserve, this unique wilderness, which had become popular with tourists from Minnesota and, increasingly, with new highway access, from Ontario. The efforts of this council have resulted in the termination of wood harvesting, mining, and hunting here since the early seventies. Control over access has been strengthened, and the park has been designated as a primitive area, unsuited to the use of outboard motors or snow machines. Finally, the number of people utilizing the area's canoe routes and packing trails at any one time has also been severely curtailed.

These hard-won achievements were eventually mirrored by improvements in the land-use plans of other large preserves at Sibley and, in particular, at Superior in Algoma.[334] A similar approach to concept and management was also entrenched in the plans for Pukaskwa National Park, near Marathon. This huge tract was identified as a good example of boreal lands in the late sixties and secured by a memorandum of agreement between Ottawa and Toronto in 1973. However, its transfer to Parks Canada occurred only in early 1978, with a proviso honouring the aboriginal rights of the Natives covered by the old Superior Robinson Treaty, and its development was to take five more years.[335]

Extending the Season

The major weakness of northern tourism has always been its highly seasonal nature, which for many operators made it a part-time occupation. However, over the post-war decades, several encouraging developments helped to extend the activity pattern to both spring and fall. The increase in sports fishing during May and June, as well as the energetic growth of the autumn hunt for deer, moose, bear, ducks, and other wild fowl, helped lengthen the tourist season. Such growth was also experienced by the owners and employees of fly-in firms, as the sixties progressed and leisure time increased. Motel owners and large-accommodation managers, who at best could look forward to lean off-season earnings, also benefited from the longer tourist season as growing numbers of middle-income retirees came to the region. Such persons often preferred to travel under less crowded conditions, to enjoy the experience of watching spring's return to the region or to seek the aesthetic pleasure of northern fall colours. They came not only in private cars but, as the period progressed, by tour bus from Canadian and U.S. lower-lake centres and cities of the midwest. Together with the predominantly American sportsmen, these seniors were having a notable effect on regional income as 1980 approached.[336]

The period witnessed more conscious efforts to encourage tourism and recreational visits to the northwest during the winter. The best-known example was the Algoma Central with its specialized form of rail service. In 1949, the company resumed its pre-war tradition of providing one-day excursions for local people to enjoy the autumn colours along its right of way from Sault Ste Marie to the spectacular Agawa Canyon. This operation unexpectedly attracted Michigan interests, and the ACR quickly found it remunerative to make the tour daily during the fall then to run its service from May to October.[337] By the early seventies, with much-improved and expanded rolling stock, it was scheduling twin trains daily through this extended season and carrying more than 100,000 people each year, with continually rising demand.[338] Early in that decade, the railroad added 'the tour of the line,' which enabled railway buffs and scenery seekers to enjoy a two-day excursion to Hearst and back. By 1980, a 'snow train' trip into the Agawa country was already under consideration.[339]

Such bold moves to generate visitor revenues in winter came in the wake of other mixed attempts elsewhere. Most winter festivals among the towns and cities of the northwest were aimed at local participation with a range of sports and events. At Sault Ste Marie though, advertisements were directed at potential Michigan interest, and experiments at Kenora tried to attract summer residents from Winnipeg.[340] Much more successful were attempts to promote U.S. interest in winter recreational opportunities in border areas, particularly in Algoma West. Here, snowmobiling proved rewarding, principally with persons who owned summer places, once numerous trails were opened in Superior Provincial Park in 1972.[341] Also lucrative was a ski resort at Searchmont, which opened six slopes with tow facilities and increased that number to eight by the end of the sixties. However, a less-accessible one near Wawa, which opened in 1966, failed to make the grade.[342]

At Thunder Bay, the long-recognized potential of the steep Nor-wester slopes was finally realized. The professionally rated jumps at Big Thunder opened to host the Canadian championships in 1975 and were the scene of the World Cup at the end of the decade.[343] Related downhill resorts, like Candy Mountain, also proved profitable, despite their distance from large urban markets. However, the economic importance of such highly site-specific sporting attractions by 1980 had come to be rivalled by more area-oriented recreational modes. These new sources of income focused on snowmobiling and ice fishing, as well as downhill and cross-country skiing by the region's own people, with their strong bent for year-round outdoor activity.

Urban, Suburban, and Rural Non-Farm Advances

Northwestern Ontario's urban and rural non-farm areas continued to share in this mix of resource-related trends, being equally affected by the gathering uncertainties of the late seventies. Yet urban centres also underwent changes of their own; manufacturing, with its peculiarly northern constraints, was reaching maturity and the rising service industry was broadening the employment spectrum.[344] Urban growth, paralleled by a pattern of farm abandonment, continued from World War II onward; the non-farm component of the total population jumping from 87 per cent in 1951 to beyond 98 per cent at the beginning of the eighties (see Table 5.10).

Sault Ste Marie

While these tendencies were evident across the northwest as a whole, they were most pronounced about Sault Ste Marie and the Lakehead. At the former, the urban population of 30,000 doubled after annexation of the highly suburbanized townships of Korah and Tarrentorus in the mid-sixties, and climbed to 80,000 by 1981.[345] While other firms abetted this rise, particularly Abitibi-Price and Weyerhauser, the basic contributor was the Algoma Steel Corporation (ASC). Algoma not only grew spectacularly but also expanded its product lines over these years. In the mid-fifties, the corporation produced over one million tons of steel in a twelve-month period for the first time. With markets booming, it kicked off an expansion plan by erecting a new bar and strip mill capable of twice its large, rail-rolling capacity. It allowed Mannesmann interests to acquire 25 per cent of the Dunn family corporate holdings and also to build a seamless pipe mill to supply western gas and oil-related construction.[346] In 1959, ASC added a new bloom and plate mill and, two years later, opened Canada's first flanged beam plant, following this with a new wide-strip facility in the sixties. In 1971, the company capped these achievements with a modern wide-plate operation to turn out a product as large as 160 inches wide and 4 inches thick.[347] Although the whole plan proceeded with an eye to labour efficiency, it raised the unionized payroll of the ASC to 10,000 persons by 1981.[348]

By 1960, this rising steel production was creating conflict among the province and the public, under the toughened pollution standards required of post-war industry. At the corporation's Wawa mines, market opportunities had greatly increased sintering capacity. Resultant intensification of sulphur-bearing emissions in the atmosphere threatened 350 square miles of vegetation downwind and the livelihood of numerous tourist operators about Hawk Junction.[349]

TABLE 5.10 Population Profile (percentage urban and rural non-farm), 1951–1981

	1951		1961		1971		1981	
	Pop.	% of total	Pop.	% of total	Pop.	% of total	Pop.	% of total
Algoma West								
Rural non-farm	7,348	18	21,538	33	6,794	8	10,993	12
Urban	32,452	80	43,088	66	80,332	92	82,697	88
Total population	40,777		65,560		87,792		93,900	
Thunder Bay District								
Rural non-farm	28,387	27	23,632	17	17,033	12	25,098	16
Urban	75,462	72	110,920	80	126,155	87	127,779	83
Total population	105,367		138,518		145,390		153,997	
Rainy River District								
Rural non-farm	5,581	25	5,826	22	6,347	25	6,302	28
Urban	9,386	42	17,321	65	17,125	67	14,306	63
Total population	22,132		26,529		25,750		22,798	
Kenora District								
Rural non-farm	5,647	14	25,705	50	26,168	49	32,287	54
Urban	15,328	39	24,754	48	26,415	50	26,624	45
Total population	39,212		51,440		53,230		59,421	
Total Northwest								
Rural non-farm	46,963	23	76,701	27	56,342	18	74,680	23
Urban	132,628	64	196,083	70	250,027	80	251,406	76
Total population	207,488		282,047		312,162		330,116	

Source: Census of Canada for the appropriate years.

Despite continuing local complaints and only minor company measures towards reduction, a firm government demand for suitable stacks on the plant was not made until 1974. By their completion four years later, almost no vegetation remained in a wide swathe for 13 miles northeast of the mines, and severe damage was reported for another broad 22 miles beyond.[350]

At Sault Ste Marie, the IJC, in an early boundary waters study of the sixties, identified the ASC and Abitibi as major users of water and dischargers of pollutants into the St Marys River. Both companies responded with corrective actions, a phenol recovery unit added to the former and bark strainers and white-water filters to the latter's discharge system.[351] At the opening of the seventies, heightened levels of air pollution from Algoma Steel's 250 coke ovens and aging blast furnaces were declared a major nuisance. Ontario threatened closure, unless serious work on abatement of both chemical and particulate levels of discharge was well advanced by December 1972. Despite the enormous and sudden expense, the corporation, by early 1973, was operating its ovens under a new smokeless discharging system and was in the process of converting its furnaces to a modern oxygen-based steel-making process. By mid-decade, replacement of some of its older units by much larger furnaces of a new European design was nearing completion.[352] While these moves greatly reduced the emission of sulphur compounds, they failed to cure the heavy dust fallout that remained at three times the acceptable level. In 1978 this prompted the Ministry of the Environment to request further appropriate action, to be completed by the early eighties.[353]

As in other major centres in the increasingly Toronto-centred, provincial urban hierarchy of these decades, Sault Ste Marie became home to a variety of services. Growth in its population and increasing provincial emphasis on health and education sponsored an increase in new hospital beds and medical facilities. It also sponsored growth in the primary and secondary school capacity, the addition of a community college, and an enhanced role for Algoma University College.[354] The expansion of government into society brought district offices for most provincial ministries and some federal agencies. The office of the Department of Lands and Forests (Ministry of Natural Resources as of 1972) here was elevated to regional status, after the addition of the Forest Insect Laboratory (federally and provincially funded). This was broadened by the later addition of a federal Chemical Control Research Unit.[355] In addition to all the new privately provided services, were new municipal initiatives. These ranged from recreation to welfare services, which programs drew on the city's increased tax base.

These were also years of marked civic programs for urban improvement, many intended to cope with the common phenomena of suburban retreat and peripheral mall development. In 1963, Sault Ste Marie gained official approval for a major waterfront redevelopment project.[356] This plan, in the long term, included the construction along the river of public structures like the city hall, main library, and art gallery, joined by hotel and apartment complexes. A decade later, it was augmented with a parallel move by the Algoma Central to revise its rail facilities and create a riverside mall.[357] With all this activity went an energetic program to revitalize and beautify the city's adjacent core and efforts to encourage and strengthen its long and colourful cultural heritage.[358]

Thunder Bay

The twin cities at the Lakehead were the dominant regional centre in 1950, being better placed within the northwest to serve that purpose. As modern regional transport and communication systems subsequently developed, this role as growth pole or focus increased. Nevertheless, although the scale of development here might sometimes be larger, Thunder Bay, as these places came to be known, shared many of the features of post-war growth already noted in Sault Ste Marie. It too became a centre for government offices of major regional importance, including Ontario Hydro. It also witnessed major growth in both health care and educational facilities, capped by the rise of Lakehead University.[359] As along the St Marys River, these additions were accompanied by a marked increase in population, which climbed from 75,000 in 1951 to approximately 125,000 thirty years later. Over the early decades of this growth, the community's already marked ethnic diversity was further strengthened by heavy immigration from Baltic, Eastern, and Mediterranean Europe.[360]

In other ways, post-war development at the Lakehead was quite different from that at Sault Ste Marie. The industrial personality of the twin cities had long enjoyed a wider base in which the central focus was the processing of forest products. As discussed elsewhere, steady growth in the pulp and paper sector, as well as in lumber and stud manufacture, had occurred over these decades, which also witnessed the addition of a major chipboard plant under MacMillan-Bloedel. Such heavy sources of employment were bolstered by a range of small plants, or product lines in larger industries, that served regional needs. One such operation turned out a range of tree harvesting equipment like slashers and skidders, log-hauling trailers, and mill equipment.[361] These were paralleled by two large multiple manufacturers, each employing over a thousand persons in their operations over much of the period. Canada Car, under a sequence of owners that included both A.V. Roe and Hawker Siddeley, produced various combinations of transport equipment. These ranged from train cars to buses and subway/light-transit rolling stock, and from propeller aircraft to military jets and airplane parts.[362] Its partner was the Port Arthur Shipyards, which had become the property of Canada Steamship Lines in 1946 and which found its basic income in the repair and maintenance of the Great Lakes fleet. That company was also involved into the sixties in the building of both grain carriers and the new tankers supplying Sarnia refineries with western oil, before lake fleets reached capacity. Its engineering division, when not otherwise employed, was a major designer of parts, modifications, and equipment for regional pulp and paper mills. This role declined by the seventies, as mills moved to highly refined equipment, often of European design.[363]

Along the twenty-seven miles of lake and river frontage at the Lakehead, which the Thunder Bay Port Authority claimed as harbourage, these years involved much renovation and updating. Such action was related to the already enormous grain elevator capacity.[364] What changes occurred came early and concentrated on either the processing of western grains into glutens and vegetable oils or the addition of massive drying equipment for the rehabilitation of the crop in bad years.[365] Such harbour-oriented operation continued to contribute very significantly to community employment.

Other harbour developments in this period centred on the introduction of new types of use. The original ore dock to serve Steep Rock was greatly enlarged, after the discovery and development of the Griffith Mine near Ear Falls, from which the beneficiated ore continued to be shipped in 1980.[366] In the mid-fifties, an oil refinery and asphalt operation was opened on an island at the mouth of the Kaministiquia, although in the long run it was not to prove profitable and closed. This was joined in the sixties by a thermal generating station under Ontario Hydro, to which a large state-of-the-art coaling dock was later added.[367] The rise of potash mining in Saskatchewan triggered the appearance of specialized storage and loading facilities elsewhere among the elevators. The huge, but only marginally successful, Keefer Terminal, for varied types of roll-on freight, also found a waterfront home.[368] All these varied additions to harbour use added substantially to the number of jobs available.[369]

Many of these developments in services and manufacturing as well as in entrepôt functions transpired within the frame of municipal amalgamation that created the City of Thunder Bay. Fierce rivalry between Fort William and Port Arthur, persistent since their inception, had long thwarted this step, although with urban growth it had come increasingly necessary. Duplication of urban services, weakly developed inter-urban infrastructure, and archaically complex relations with neighbouring municipalities made the cities' operations unnecessarily costly, ineffective, and inefficient. Since recent attempts had shown that a local resolution of the issue was most unlikely,[370] the province initiated a series of detailed studies that culminated in a review commission in 1965. On the basis of its final report, Queen's Park announced that the twin cities, along with adjacent Neebing, McIntyre, and part of Shuniah, would become a new city. As of 1 January 1970, this new administrative unit would cover 157 square miles and include a population of 108,000 people.[371]

This municipal union smoothed the way for leaner government, improved services, long-term planning, and coordinated urban development. The immediate ramifications were in the rationalization of everything from fire protection to the library system and the interconnection and improvement of sewage and water utilities. They also encompassed energetic encouragement of infilling in the inter-city area. This went with the creation of effective road communication across this belt near the harbour-front, as well as behind the built-up area, in the form of the Trans-Canada bypass. Although the obstructive aspects of the traditional rivalry would pass only slowly by 1980, this regional capital was a more attractive place to live or do business, as well as more responsive in servicing its citizens.

Single-Industry Towns

In the regional hierarchy of 1950 there remained an enormous gap between these major centres and the next tier, which included Kenora or Fort Frances with about 10,000 people, and Wawa or Dryden half this size. Indeed, the bulk of the still largely unincorporated pattern of settlements of that date averaged only about 2,500 and numbered only about twenty-five places of any significance. This configuration would not change. Most of these communities of less than 10,000 would experience at least modest, if irregular, growth into the seventies, yet, the major cities were home to at least 80 per cent of urban residents by 1980.[372]

This substantial cluster of small towns and lesser places was composed of a variety of elements and age groups. Some, like Atikokan, Marathon, Red Rock, and Terrace Bay, were very new in 1950, while others, including Manitouwadge, were products of the period itself. In contrast, some like Ignace, Schreiber, or White River, dated back to the era of railway-building, to agricultural colonization, to early pulp and paper development, or to mining discoveries, as already discussed. Those that had risen as saw or rail towns, like Rainy River, or as fishing communities, like Rossport, survived in some other form or, like Brient (next Wawa), Port Coldwell, Jackfish, and Camp Robinson, gradually disappeared.[373] In short, even in these maturing years, the regional pattern was not immutable.

Only a few communities had been fortunate enough to establish a reasonably broad employment base and to enjoy a resultant degree of economic security. Centres like Kenora and Fort Frances, while closely tied to the forest industry, continued their long tradition of tourism and retained some of their former railway importance. Sioux Lookout, with its more chequered functional past, had become the provincial administrative centre for the huge Patricia area. Indeed, as of 1950, it had become the centre for Native health care for the area between Hudson Bay and Manitoba, north to the eighty-sixth parallel. It became host to a Mid-Canada Line facility in 1960 and the centre of the northern Wawatay Native Communications radio system in 1973.[374]

However, the majority of these scattered places were based on a single economic pursuit, most commonly in the resource sector (see Table 5.11). Such single-industry communities were usually small, grew slowly after their initial appearance, suffered from poor infrastructure, at least in their formative years, and were sometimes isolated. Most important, their economic health was totally at the mercy of exogenous market conditions, corporate decisions, and government policies.[375] Those that were developed to manage and maintain isolated electrical generating stations were the most specialized. While those colonies belonging to Ontario Hydro were dismantled by 1980,[376] one or two others remained under Great Lakes Power in Algoma West but are too small to be considered here.

Prior experience with such towns and their weaknesses led Queen's Park to adopt a firm and imaginative leadership role in their creation and control in the

TABLE 5.11 Designated Single-Industry Towns, 1976

	Population		Population
Atikokan	5,803	Manitouwadge	3,551
Beardmore	605	Marathon	2,283
Dryden	6,799	Nakina	620
Dubreuilville	–*	Nipigon	2,724
Ear Falls	1,982	Pickle Lake	508
Geraldton	3,127	Red Lake/Balmertown	4,893
Hearst	5,195	Red Rock	1,694
Hornepayne	1,694	Schreiber	2,010
Ignace	1,983	Terrace Bay	2,098
Longlac	1,934	Wawa	4,272

* Added by the authors, although still at this time a private company town with no official population.
Source: Oiva Saarinen, "Single sector communities in northern Ontario: The Creation and planning of dependent towns," in *Power and place: Canadian Urban development in the North American context*, edited by Gilbert A. Stelter and Alan F.J. Artibise (Vancouver: University of British Columbia Press, 1986), p. 228, but ignoring his inclusion of Sault Ste Marie.

fifties. The groundwork for this move had been laid in the Planning Act of 1946, which required official approval of plans for any such new community in the province. Atikokan and Balmertown were among the first to be developed under this plan.[377] In 1954, the government formed the Cabinet Committee on Townsites, specifically to formulate and carry out policies to cover the comprehensive planning and satisfactory establishment of new northern communities. The committee's prototype was Manitouwadge, where it attempted to capitalize on the best elements of private plans recently executed at Marathon and Terrace Bay, and to learn from other U.S. examples and experience in Ungava, Quebec.[378] While the full capacity of the three-phase schedule for the addition of neighbourhoods here was never utilized, even though building continued for a decade or more, the concept and the aesthetic use of landscape in the plan was copied to advantage elsewhere.[379]

By 1960, both the woodland side of the forest industry and provincial community planners were anxious to step back and re-examine their work and ideas about bushworkers' accommodations that had begun in the forties. After their adventure with forest communities and variants on that idea, woodland operators preferred to add new depots and subdivisions to existing centres like Longlac, Nakina, or Armstrong. Indeed they were now prepared, with reticence, to abandon their investment in experiments such as Caramat or Heron Bay as they were to later abandon Valora and Camp Robinson.[380] In response to the northward movement of harvesting, these woodland operators came to revive and sustain the use of mobile bachelor camps for isolated areas of cut. However, their real thrust now was to provide commuter service to the cutting site from existing local centres where their employees were free to locate with their families.[381]

Government's approach to single-resource communities in the seventies had to deal with all such towns and their varied resource bases. Ontario adopted two alternate paths to be followed for such places. First, seeing its own advantage in what the forest industry had elected to do with its bushworkers, the province began to encourage new resource-related, residential development to concentrate in existing centres in order to broaden the employment base and make more efficient use of municipal services there. Its attempt to do so with the Anglo-Canadian Pulp and Paper Company and a proposed mill near Sioux Lookout failed, yet its diversion of all incoming Griffith Mine employees to subdivisions in Ear Falls did much to bolster that small settlement through the seventies.[382] Second, for small, isolated communities – for example, individual mining projects north of Salt Ste Marie and west of Thunder Bay, as well as at woods-related ones up the ACR or in the Pukaskwa country – the government required that a simple plan be put forward to its planners for approval and/or change. However, it retreated from its earlier role in northern community development after its deep involvement at Elliot Lake.[383] At the same time, as a result of the rise in new resource developments, Ontario found itself becoming increasingly involved in issues of environmental protection in policies that strongly opposed the founding of new resource towns. An early case, involving both these issues, arose during the seventies out a conflict between vacationers and Inco's proposed nickel venture on Lake Shebandowan.[384] Before mining proceeded here, the company was forced by the government to comply with stiff environmental requirements.[385] Equally important, while Inco was permitted bachelor accommodation on site, all families were to be housed in the neighbouring village.[386] This same dictum was applied later in that decade to the Griffith iron mine north of Ear Falls and the base-metal developments on Sturgeon Lake. At the latter, both Falconbridge and Noranda were required to put in appropriate subdivisions 60 kilometres south at Ignace. Similarly, the Umex copper project near Pickle Lake involved company provision of modern housing units in the neighbouring town.[387] Nevertheless, when faced with a multi-sponsored plan for an iron mining project in this same isolated area, around Lake St Joseph, Ontario agreed to mount jointly financed studies to determine the environmental impact and an appropriate townsite for the scheme. However, this mega-development never reached fruition, due to declining iron ore markets of the late seventies, and provincial involvement ended at the paper stage.[388]

As the period passed, the lot of those living in such resource towns, new or old, as well as in the other lesser communities of the northwest, improved steadily in other ways. Many such places climbed the ladder of municipal status, from improvement district to township, winning more autonomy in their public affairs and in planning control over their immediate environs. Through their own efforts, the citizenry of many of these centres attracted new Red Cross hospitals or financed the enlargement of earlier health facilities. Such medical amenities were more aggressively promoted by the government after its entry into the health care field. As a result, by the seventies, the region was moderately supplied with public ambulance service and coordinated medical programs. Developments in primary and secondary education, under provincial encouragement, brought the bus, centralized schools, and much improved training to university and college entry levels across most districts. Government-sponsored libraries, a regional library system, and company or civically generated sports facilities and community centres also appeared. In older communities, provincial loans and subsidies helped replace archaic sewer and water systems, augmented fire protection, and promoted curbs, gutters, and paved streets. Strikes, shut-downs, rail cut-backs, and other employment-centred issues periodically troubled individual towns or the whole system in this period. However, what communities lost in their fluctuating micro-economies, they usually more than made up for in increasing infrastructural amenity and social security.[389]

Rural Non-Farm Issues

Such improvements also influenced the lives of the large and growing rural, non-farm component, which in 1981 covered nearly a quarter of the regional population (see Table 5.10). Despite the corrective attempts of annexation and amalgamation, the numerical importance of the rural, non-farm populations was again blurring the rural–urban boundary about both major centres of the northwest. Around Thunder Bay and Sault Ste Marie, former farm houses now retained only as residences with no farm acreage were surrounded by subdivisions, hobby properties, and rural estates. However, in these areas the general trend of conversion to non-farm use had come to be controlled by local planning regulations.[390]

The same land use control was true across the extensive tracts of agriculture in all the municipalities down the Rainy River Valley. In this large area, rural, non-farm occupation was limited to the territory around Fort Frances, the only real focus for wage employment for both rural men and women. Here, riverfront property west of the town had had a particular residential appeal. However, at the beginning of the eighties total numbers in this area had not changed significantly for over a decade.

A similar situation existed in the Kenora District, following an enormous leap in the non-farm figure after 1951. With the advent of the sixties, this total, which then stabilized, had come to equal half the population in a district where few had remained in agriculture. The most important cause of this was the heavy rural expansion of forest harvesting into the huge portion of that district in the fifties, which was bolstered in the seventies by mining. While most families supported by such employment resided in nodal communities, not all of these were incorporated and separately listed in the urban census for the period.

Second in importance was the decline of the farm population in the old agricultural pockets, as residents turned to more remunerative jobs in the mills of Dryden and Kenora or from full- to part-time farming. By 1981 such residents were no longer classified by the census as a farmer. Unlike rural Rainy River, few of the numerous townships of the Dryden area had ever become municipally organized. Most now refused even to consider the move because of the lower taxation and the provincially subsidized services that applied to unorganized areas. This status made these townships a cheap haven for many people who had urban, industrial employment but who wished a rural home. However, any financial advantages in such a status were offset by a relatively primitive administration and the lack of regulation or zoning to control residential sprawl.[391]

This last situation, however trivial and parochial, provides a simple example of a fundamental view among some of the regional population, which governed their approach to the use of their natural surroundings as late as 1980. Such people adhered to an outmoded, colonial perception that stressed individual attainment over general advantage and short-term gain over long-term reward. In the much larger context of resource utilization, such thinking, which had a lingering parallel in industrial management, was still sufficiently strong to nudge the region, economically, socially, and thereby environmentally, towards a most difficult future.

A Region in Flux, 1980–1994

The last fifteen years have been difficult and distressing ones both for the people of the northwest and for the broader community with interest or investment in its resources and resource-based manufacturing. In some sectors of manufacturing, problems were already severe and under advisement by 1980. In others, trouble was only looming or had yet to appear. However, world market disturbance during the OPEC crisis had ushered in an era of uncertainty and impending instability for the region, as across the north in general.

At the crux of the situation was the common fear of a severe bust after the post-war boom, which belief was rooted in the prevailing economic model of cyclical northern Ontario development. While this fear would linger through the eighties, the model would prove inapplicable to modern conditions. The broad federal–provincial social safety nets and wide-ranging financial programs for beleaguered municipalities and troubled industries successfully challenged the model's operation, as did supportive factors, such as the mature infrastructural system, the improved education and training level of the work force, and the enormous array of technology that would promote industrial efficiency. Also, the level of both private and public investment in the region, was now too great to consider losing.

Accompanying these lingering fears of disaster was a shift in the attitude of the majority of the region's citizens towards the utilization of the resource base and the preservation of the environment.[392] The resultant more stewardly or conservational perception of regional surroundings and a more tolerant approach to multiple use, still weakly developed by 1980, were strongly evident by the early nineties. This new attitude among the populace appears to have been the result of rethinking the tenets of a long-held exploitive philosophy of resource use, as well as a more realistic reassessment of the impact of such an outlook on a sustainable future. In industry, there has been a concomitant willingness to reconsider operational approaches to and adaptive and innovative measures for resource use.

Traditionally, northerners and northern industry have been much more resistant to government regulation or interference in their affairs by outside interest groups than their Old Ontario counterparts. Yet the regional mood of the nineties is a more conciliatory and compliant one in such fields where regulation and restriction have come increasingly to be the provincial vehicle for correction and management.

The Fisheries in Convalescence

Superior

After decades of abuse, when harvests on some licences were as much as five times the sustainable level, and in the wake of the lamprey ravage, the fisheries on Canadian Lake Superior are in an encouraging state of recovery. This return to health has been patiently pursued by fisheries biologists since the annual restocking program under the International Great Lakes Fisheries Commission in the late fifties. To further encourage the recovery of lake trout breeding populations, this recuperative effort was increased from half a million fingerlings annually to three times that figure by the mid-eighties.[393] Also contributing to the renewal of commercial potential has been the continuing reduction of part-timers among inshore fishermen and some declines among the larger offshore firms. Balanced against these declines was the total conversion of the gill net industry from polyfilament to more effective monofilament use. Other changes in 1984–5 converted the industry from simple quotas, where large operators had the advantage, to the more equitable individual quota by species and zone.[394]

Modern processing by Ferro-Clad at Mamainse, Anderson, at Michipicoten Harbour and Kemp in Thunder Bay served the marketing needs of Superior through the eighties. This system provided efficient truck transfer of fresh and frozen products to Montreal and Toronto, Chicago and St Louis.[395] However, the recent reduction of Kemp's facility to a re-icing depot and the sale of Ferro-Clad to a Lake Erie firm leave questions about the nature and scope of future marketing. Nevertheless, a strategic plan announced in 1986 to increase substantially the lake trout populations as well as harvesting levels by the end of the century would appear to be operating most successfully.

Yet, the surprise of the last decade has been a rocketing increase in whitefish. This species is now dominant in what traditionally was a lake trout water body (see Table 5.12). Another marked change in the harvesting pattern of the eighties has been a sharp decline in the herring catch, which, from the sixties on, had annually made up over 75 per cent of the remaining poundage. The collective result of these developments has been to increase the supply of preferred species available to fishermen, despite a decline in total catch. It also has provided a profitable return on harvest levels well within the sustainable limits of this huge water body.[396]

Inland Fisheries

On Lake Nipigon, the inevitable crash after years of gluttonous harvesting came in 1956 and was followed by the usual decline in the number of participants, many of them Natives from local bands. Kemp Fisheries took over and refurbished the old government processing centre at Macdiarmid about 1960, with marginal early success. Many in this area, under low catch conditions, chose to participate in the Freshwater Fisheries Co-operative out of Winnipeg until 1974. However, local fishermen then found it financially advantageous to leave that organization for the free market via this Kemp outlet.[397] Through these decades of limited and variable use, stock recuperation occurred quickly in the formerly rich whitefish fishery. At least as early as 1980, Nipigon's total catch level again equalled that of the whole Canadian side of a recovering Lake Superior (see Table 5.12). Indeed, its whitefish harvest, vacillating around a million pounds each year to the present, stands considerably above that of its much larger sister. Its lake trout population, always a secondary source of income, also has returned to a healthy level, compared with that same adjacent water body. Meanwhile, an unaccountable rise in the harvest of ling and mullet has boosted the mixed catch of other species to an unexpected level.[398] At present, there are eleven licences on the lake, of which three are held by Natives at Gull Bay and two by the Rocky Bay Reserve. The latter band has recently refurbished the Macdiarmid facility again, on its abandonment by the Kemp organization. Most of the remaining licences on Nipigon are held by white operators with headquarters at Hill Bay near Beardmore or Orient Bay at the base of the lake.[399] As in the case of Superior, this commercial fishery, which is a mainstay for both Native reserves, has returned to a modestly lucrative state in which the current catch is well within the quota levels for sustainability.

TABLE 5.12 Commercial Fisheries Catch (in pounds), 1981–1993

	1981	1993
Lake Superior		
Whitefish	172,506	604,404
Lake trout	176,387	198,139
Other	1,711,386	693,977
Total	2,060,279	1,496,520
Lake Nipigon		
Whitefish	1,184,542	986,121
Lake trout	83,189	133,494
Other	765,692	474,111
Total	2,033,423	1,593,726
Grant Total	4,093,702	3,090,246

Source: Calculated from the *Annual Report of the Ministry of Natural Resources for 1981* and from statistics supplied by Mike Petzold, Lake Superior Fisheries Management Unit, Sault Ste Marie, and Richard Salmon, Lake Nipigon Fisheries Assessment Unit, Nipigon. Suitable statistics for inland lakes were not readily available.

Further afield among the inland lakes of the northwest, the health of the commercial fishery is harder to determine. Among modern planning priorities it stands at the bottom of the list, below residential and sport angling. These also come after the prime two: stock conservation and treaty rights. In more northerly parts of Patricia, all commercial fishermen remain members of the Freshwater Fisheries Co-operatives, which enables them to avoid the normal payment of a provincial royalty on their catch and equalized air transport costs.[400] Most lakes of substantial size, and all that host Native communities in this area, have a history of recent commercial use, but not all are open for licensing every year because of their limited sustainable capacity. The largest of these water bodies, Lac Seul and Lake St Joseph, are the most heavily used by white inhabitants and have together about fifteen full-time and part-time operators. Elsewhere, the predominant licensees are Native people, and many of their operations take place in the winter season, concentrating on pike and wall-eye, with some whitefish and trout. In the Red Lake district, for example, where there are eight bands on five reserves totalling over 4,000 persons, the annual catch for commercial sale stands at 140,000 pounds, well within the capacity of surrounding lakes. Given the spiralling population growth in the Native community across the entire north, however, this commercial demand will more than double by the end of this decade, commensurate with the subsistence requirement for home consumption in the district. To the frustration of the non-Native fishermen, no new licences, therefore, will be opened to them, although the number of Native ones for economic support must now rise rapidly.[401] As part of this same problem are serious questions about the present and future health of the Co-op, which has closed out its processing plant at Red Lake and now relies uniquely on its facility at Pickle Lake to prepare the catch for shipment to Winnipeg.[402]

In the Kenora and Rainy River country, the conflict between the angler and the commercial operator has had a long history. Over the decades, the contribution of the resource to the local economy as a generator of recreational dollars has been proved to be greater than that from its industrial harvest.[403] In 1984 there were still ten commercial licences on the Rainy Lake watershed: half the total were on the lake itself and four of the total were in Native hands. The entire commercial catch was 111,500 pounds, as opposed to 373,500 pounds taken by anglers and 25,350 pounds harvested for Native domestic consumption. As in all other areas, the Native subsistence catch was predicted to rise quickly with an increase in population. While commercial use was anticipated to remain constant, the sport fishery was expected to expand over the next two decades by about 25 per cent.[404]

Ironically, for a variety of reasons, by the early nineties any real commercial fishery on the watershed was a thing of the past.[405] Its counterpart on the Lake of the Woods, however, lives on. Here licences remain numerous, although only two are held by reserves. On the Native fisheries, quotas on wall-eye stand at 57,200 pounds, but on non-Native licences the limit on this highly valued sport fish is less than half that figure. These operators, as members of the Ontario Fish Producers Association, are liable for the provincial catch royalty, while the Native participants are not. Annual harvest levels are respectably high, but well within the capacity of the lake, and in recent years have included increasing amounts of the whitefish that these waters once held in abundance.[406] Statistics on capital investment and employment here, as on other inland lakes and Superior, are not readily available. The fishing industry across the northwest has clearly returned to modest health under conservative approaches to management. However, it is unlikely ever again to hold the regional economic importance it once claimed.

Gold Again to the Fore

In no other resource field have the post-OPEC disruptions and shifts in world markets been felt more strongly in the northwest than in mining. Added to the depressing effects of the crisis, metal markets, except for gold, recently have been confused further by the dumping of raw metals onto global markets by former members of the Soviet Union in a desperate quest for currency. Parallel to these events has gone the inevitable rash of mine closures, as profitable ore, under modern low prices, has run out. An understandable reluctance among investors to sponsor the exploration and development to bring slimly profitable ore bodies to production has compounded the problem.

While both federal and provincial governments were quick to mount incentive programs to promote exploration and development, they have had only limited success. Ottawa initiated a national tax incentive scheme in 1978 with what were known as flow-through shares. Ironically, intense interest in this financial vehicle for investor profit came only after 1980 and focused on gold, where it sponsored the rise of many junior companies that had entered the mining game since 1950. The scheme was a notable failure in the promotion of interest in such exploratory work in any other metals. By 1989, therefore, this tax break was under modification, making it less attractive to the gold community as well.[407]

About the same time, Queen's Park introduced the Ontario Mineral Exploration Program, which, by 1981, had sponsored over ninety projects at a cost of $93 million.[408] Again, however, most of the interest has come from juniors in gold-related endeavours. This initiative and two lesser funds related to prospecting and technical improvement have been curtailed by recent cuts in government spending.[409]

Since 1986, even exploration and development in gold has lost most of its lustre. Values as high as U.S. $800 an ounce in 1980 have dropped slowly to more realistic levels of half that value or less.[410] Equally important, skilled and experienced personnel to operate and maintain the highly technical equipment and systems in the modern mining industry have come to be in short supply. Because of alternate, more attractive job opportunities, they also became more expensive to retain. (Indeed, established firms that commonly had introduced practical employee training programs in the seventies now found these indispensable in their battle to keep a satisfactory work force.) This problem, coupled with steeply rising electrical costs, has forced the gradual closure of an increasing number of marginal mining endeavours. Their plight was intensified on Black Friday (October 17, 1987) on the Toronto Stock Exchange, when plummeting gold stock values severely eroded investor confidence. Only very recently have there been signs that confidence may be returning.[411] Meanwhile, unacceptable environmental conditions left on the abandoned mine sites added to the potential safety hazards remaining on many older ones. As a result, firmer regulations governing operational pollution and conditions of closure were added to the Mining Act in 1992. The Ministry of the Environment now insists that, in addition to other requirements, each company submit and have approved a sound plan of operation before it initiates mining activity. At that time, companies must post a sufficient bond to guarantee safe and satisfactory closure as well as full rehabilitation of the site when mining concludes.[412] While laudable and necessary, these rules will add substantially to the cost of any future mining venture.

Iron

Iron ore was the first to experience the faltering markets that were on the horizon and affecting decisions after the mid-seventies and dropped in the world's industrial lap in 1980.[413] For northwestern producers, this trend took the form of a severe decline in steel demands by the ailing U.S. auto industry. Declining markets also resulted from mounting competition with North American steel by cheaper Asian, South American, and Australian sources. Demand problems, exacerbated by new smelting techniques, some of which used sponge iron beneficiates, and an increasing inclusion of scrap in the steel-making process continued to plague iron ore producers into the nineties.[414]

With the last shipment of stock-piled pellets from Steep Rock in February 1980, only the Griffith Mine and the Algoma Ore Division (AOD) remained productive in what, a decade before, had been Ontario's most promising iron region.[415] Production at the Griffith slackened in 1982 and pelletizing there was much reduced in 1983. Late the next year, Stelco announced the termination of its lease of the Griffith from the Iron Bay Trust. After an extra year to enable adjustments in the surrounding community, the operation was mothballed in early 1986.[416] In the early nineties, the facility was dismantled, the site cleaned up, and even the CNR tracks north from the main line were removed. As would have been the case with similarly distant, low-grade operations contemplated for the region in the seventies, transport costs to water had made the Griffith uneconomic under modern ore price conditions (see Map 5.3).

Production at Wawa also suffered sharp reverses over these years but the timing, cause, and nature of these setbacks were different from those at the Griffith. While peaking in production in 1979, Algoma Steel at Sault Ste Marie faced severe market decline, not in 1980 like many world producers, but after 1982 when Canadian steel had its first disastrous year.[417] During the previous boom there, mills had thrived on all the sinter the AOD plant could process annually. To this was added the final 7 per cent of the total requirement, which initially was hematite from Steep Rock. On its impending closure, this addition came from the Tilden taconite mine at Ishpeming, Michigan on Superior, into which Algoma had bought.[418] As tough times arrived at Algoma Steel, the

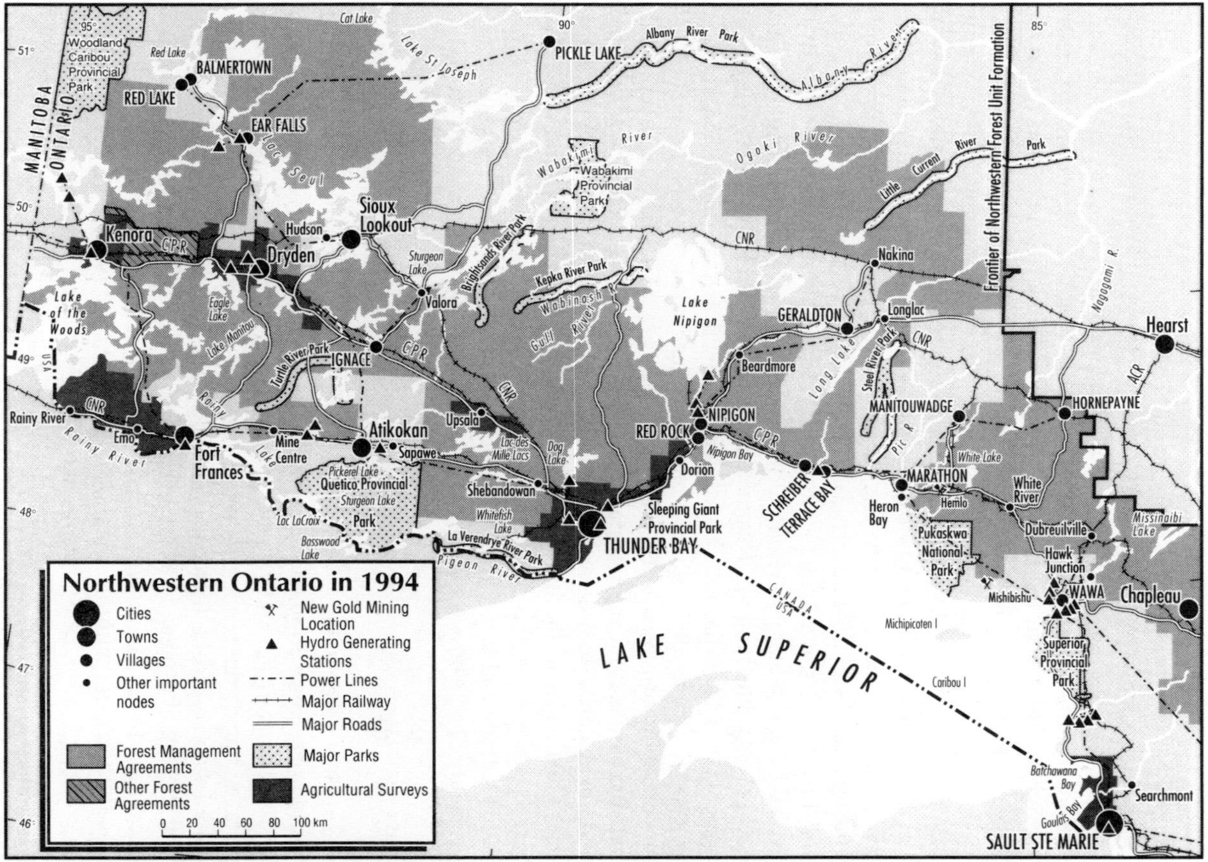
Northwestern Ontario in 1994
Cities
Towns
Villages
Other important nodes
New Gold Mining Location
Hydro Generating Stations
Power Lines
Major Railway
Major Roads
Forest Management Agreements
Other Forest Agreements
Major Parks
Agricultural Surveys
0 20 40 60 80 100 km
MANITOBA
ONTARIO
Woodland Caribou Provincial Park
Red Lake
RED LAKE
BALMERTOWN
EAR FALLS
Lac Seul
Cat Lake
Lake St Joseph
PICKLE LAKE
Albany River Park
Albany River
Wabakimi Provincial Park
Ogoki River
Little Current River
Park
Frontier of Northwestern Forest Unit Formation
Kenora
Dryden
Hudson
Sioux Lookout
Sturgeon Lake
Valora
Brightsands River Park
Kepka River Park
Lake of the Woods
Eagle Lake
Lake Manitou
Turtle River Park
IGNACE
CPR
CNR
Rainy River
Emo
Fort Frances
Mine Centre
Rainy Lake
Atikokan
Sapawe
Upsala
Lac des Mille Lacs
Dog Lake
Pickerel Lake
Quetico Provincial Park
Sturgeon Lake
Lac LaCroix
Basswood Lake
Shebandowan
Whitefish Lake
La Verendrye River Park
Pigeon River
THUNDER BAY
Sleeping Giant Provincial Park
Lake Nipigon
Dorion
RED ROCK
NIPIGON
Nipigon Bay
Beardmore
GERALDTON
Long Lake
Longlac
Nakina
Steel River Park
MANITOUWADGE
Pic R
SCHREIBER
TERRACE BAY
MARATHON
Heron Bay
Hemlo
White Lake
Pukaskwa National Park
White River
Dubreuilville
Hawk Junction
WAWA
Mishibishu
HORNEPAYNE
Hearst
ACR
Nagagami R.
Missinaibi Lake
Chapleau
Superior Provincial Park
Michipicoten I
Caribou I
CANADA
USA
LAKE SUPERIOR
Batchawana Bay
Goulais Bay
Searchmont
SAULT STE MARIE
51°
50°
49°
48°
47°
46°
95°
90°
85°

MAP 5.3

relative cost of 1.7 to 1.9 million tons of railed sinter compared with that of shipped taconite pellets came to figure large in steel pricing. From 1986 on, the tonnage transported by the Algoma Central (ACR) from Wawa decreased slowly to about 800,000 tons in 1993, with a commensurate rise in taconite demand. Indeed, a study commissioned before Dofasco took over the majority interest in Algoma Steel from the CPR in 1989, indicated a very uncertain future for the AOD after 1990. Ultimate closure has been a real threat since 1992.[419]

The recent restructuring of the Algoma Steel Corporation, which is now financially controlled by its employees, has introduced certain innovations in technology. The mills are now experimenting with different ratios of sinter and pellets to determine the proportion that makes the best steel for the least cost. They are also looking at a process by which the Tilden Mine could provide pre-fluxed pellets, reducing the processing required at smelting.[420] Meanwhile, the AOD, in a strategy to regain former production levels, is running tests on a new process called tolling. This method takes and recycles scale and other steel oxide wastes from the mill by introducing them as flux during the sintering process.[421] The results, both environmentally and economically, have attracted moderate interest across the industry. There are also plans to accept such metallic oxides from any integrated steel producer in the Great Lakes Basin, to add this material, to order, in the beneficiating process at Wawa, and to return that tolled sinter to the initial supplier for steel production.[422] Until the broad market viability of this new process is proved and the ratio experiments between siderite and taconite have reached the conclusive stage at Algoma Steel, the future of this only remaining iron mine in Ontario will remain in limbo.[423]

Base Metals

Base-metal production has had a particularly rough ride on the roller-coaster of world prices since 1980. However, zinc, copper, and lead have continued to be profitable and nickel and valuable trace elements have helped support the base-metal sector of the mining industry. However, major mine closures have occurred with surprising frequency. The huge Umex Thierry copper development near Pickle Lake, opening to declining prices in the late seventies, never worked at capacity for any prolonged period, was reduced to maintenance in 1982, and was left to flood, with its equipment up for sale, by 1985.[424] To the south, the Falconbridge effort at Sturgeon Lake closed for lack of ore at the opening of the eighties. The Mattabi continued on new ore until its reserves failed in 1989, and its closure was soon followed by that of its subsidiary at Lyon Lake.[425] The famous Geco at Manitouwadge was destined to become history in 1995, for lack of profitable ore after more than forty years of major production.[426] Nickel too has lost its promise. Plans for the deposits south of Thunder Bay in Pardee Township disappeared in the eighties and Inco's mine at Shebandowan was condemned to run sporadically through the period.[427]

On the brighter side, a partnership between Zenmac and Falconbridge brought the zinc-dominated deposits at Winston Lake near Schreiber through the development stages. Later under exclusive ownership by Falconbridge, a mill was moved from Sturgeon Lake to the site by 1987, when Falconbridge sold Winston Lake Mine to Minova. The mine opened in 1988, with the concentrate being trucked to a loading facility of the CPR. This system of transport was much improved in 1991, with specially designed vehicles and transfer measures to reduce the accompanying air pollution at Schreiber.[428] By that time, an additional dual body of ore at adjacent Pic Lake had been discovered, and soon after this rich mine was sold to a European company seeking concentrate for two German smelters. A tunnel is now being driven to these new deposits, which, it is hoped, will extend the life of Winston Lake into the next century.[429]

Gold at Hemlo

The only real winner since 1980 in the northwest's broad array of minerals has been gold. With its disappointing record in previous decades, gold is now the only one to enjoy high prices and moderately firm demand. These conditions stimulated the Campbell and Dickenson mines at Red Lake to spend heavily on updating, installing pollution controls, and increasing their proven reserves by 1990. However, intensive exploratory work in the surrounding area turned up no new deposits for future development.[430] In contrast, around the old abandoned mines at Pickle Lake, ambitious drill programs by major companies produced numerous finds early in the eighties, three of which have proved of immediate interest. Dome's small Dona Lake Mine, a few miles south, went into production in 1989 at 40,000 ounces a year but may close shortly after a brief but profitable life.[431] The Golden Patricia, a fly-in mine developed by Australian money, lies seventy miles northeast of Pickle Lake and has operated successfully since late 1988.[432] The Musselwaite property, backed in the middle eighties by Dome, Corona, and Inco, was shelved in 1989 for reasons of cost due to its northern site. However, it is currently being reassessed by one of the partners with hopes of production in the near future.[433]

With gold's return to favour, such avenues as the reworking of old mine tailings and the reassessment of former workings by local people and small companies were well under way in the late seventies, across all historic gold fields in the region. In most, such interest was short-lived or tentative in the eighties. However, in the Beardmore area in particular, but also about Sioux

Lookout and Wawa, such exploration and development work continued through most of the decade, involving a surprising array of mining interests, both large and small.[434] Under these wide-ranging efforts, a few old properties were brought to the production stage. Examples include: the Duport (later Consolidated Professor) near Kenora, the Norlund (later Goldlund) near Sioux Lookout, the Theresa south of Longlac, and the Citadel (once Surlaga) near Wawa.[435] None of these, however, have stood the test of time.

Many of these endeavours on old gold fields, which were the work of junior companies, were intended for partial sale to large operators or other juniors for final development. After 1982, this pattern also characterized certain areas where new finds were being made, particularly in the Mishibishu Lake country of the Pukaskwa Peninsula and the territory east to about the line of the ACR. Over the years leading up to the explosive rush after mid-decade, the pages of the *Northern Miner* recorded a lively growing interest in exploratory work here. These efforts sometimes went underground when sufficient money could be found for a shaft. Some properties, like the Krezmar, Magnicon, and Magena, actually enjoyed a brief period of mining and milling before this thriving exploration camp ground to a standstill in 1991.[436] Today plans are afoot to resume development of one such mine, using the Magnicon's mill, now that mild investor confidence seems to be returning. In the meantime, the high value of certain precious metals like platinum and palladium have captured sufficient capital interest to result in some exploration and one successful mine. This successful palladium mine, begun in 1987, north of Thunder Bay at Lac des Iles, was developed by a remarkably unstable and environmentally irresponsible junior company and is now in production under mature U.S. ownership.[437]

However, the spectacular discovery for which Canada will be remembered in the world mining community, also a product of initial exploration by juniors, was that at Hemlo. A hunt for gold in this zone between Marathon and White River had gone on for decades but, while all the indications were present, nature kept the location of the ore body a secret. Only in 1981 did a deep drilling program by a West Coast junior, International Corona, make the strike. Its subsequent agreement with Teck Corporation ushered in plans for the David Bell Mine here.[438] In the same year, an array of other juniors joined the quest to isolate the ore body and to locate others, and by November 1982, Noranda bought heavily into Golden Sceptre and Goliath for the immediate development of the Golden Giant Mine. The wild rush continued over a wide area, but the third producer, the Page-Williams, was developed by the enormous firm of Lac Minerals in 1983. By mid-1985, the mines held by Noranda and Teck-Corona were already producing, while Lac's deposits were nearing that stage.[439]

However, a lawsuit launched by Corona against Lac over the Page-Williams Mine became a prolonged legal struggle that ended only in 1989. The Supreme Court of Canada upheld an earlier provincial ruling awarding the mine to Corona, on payment of $21 million to Lac for its development costs.[440] In 1989, these three mines, which stand together along the side of the Trans-Canada Highway, produced over a million ounces of gold. This level of extraction in the unusually soft, friable, and easily mined ore continues today at very low cost. Hemlo will continue to lead Canadian gold production, on current proven reserves, well into the next century.[441] However, in other minerals, particularly base metals and iron, only future discoveries and world market trends will dictate the nature and extent of regional mining activity over coming decades.

Continued Forest Complications

Over most of the last fifteen years, problems in the forest industry and related ones in forest use continued to grow in size and complexity. Unanticipated market reverses disrupted the manufacture of pulp and paper in the early eighties and again in the early nineties. Tariff disputes over softwood exports to the United States have generated an uncertain sequence of lows and highs in regional lumber production. Meanwhile, foresters, academics, and public-interest groups have warned of potential over-harvesting and subsequent under-regeneration. Their concerns have been accompanied by calls for broader approaches to forest management, with more attention to aspects beyond simple wood supply. The forest industry has expressed its need for more consistent, realistically attainable direction or regulation in its management activity and environmental protection requirements. Critical comments from public groups and private sources have been increasingly directed at government agencies, of which the Ministry of Natural Resources has become a common target. Only in the nineties has meaningful debate culminated in hopes for the eventual resolution of such forest issues.

Paper Markets

Pulp and paper making in the northwest began the eighties buoyantly, with all mills running hard, inventories low, and a stream of capital improvements proceeding confidently, to prepare for trends predicted for the region.[442] Two years later, a prolonged but moderate slump slowed newsprint demand as world-wide recession reduced advertising lineage and as alternate news media cut into the readership of U.S. midwest newspapers. Combined with vacillations in demand for market pulp and severe U.S. competition in kraft, this trend for newsprint continued to dampen overall production levels by mid-decade, returning to trouble this sector of the industry more seriously in the opening years of the nineties.[443]

These mixed conditions promoted changes in ownership patterns and even fostered some business failures. In 1983, American Can transferred 80 per cent of its mill interest on Superior's north shore to James River, Marathon, a new Canadian subsidiary of a Virginia-based firm. The balance of plant finance and all woodland responsibilities were taken up by the Buchanan Group of Thunder Bay.[444] A year later, the old Abitibi mill at Sault Ste Marie, which hovered in an equally marginal condition, passed to the St Marys Paper Company under Chicago control.[445] Later in the decade, Great Lakes Forest Products merged with another CPR subsidiary to form the nation-wide Canadian Pacific Forest Products. However, in 1993, after five disastrous years, that firm was dissolved into a public company, and its Dryden and Lakehead holdings ultimately passed to the present owners, Avenor.[446]

This last change came with a number of others stemming from the industry's straitened conditions. St Marys Paper passed into receivership in 1993 but has continued to operate advantageously during the ongoing negotiations for its possible purchase by Belgravia Investments of Vancouver. In the same year, Abitibi-Price permanently closed its Bare Point operation in Thunder Bay. It also sold Provincial Paper to an employee-dominated firm that appears to have returned that endeavour to profitability.[447] In addition, the brutal financial stress of these years resulted in restructuring at Red Rock and Terrace Bay, with sudden and severe reductions in employment levels.[448] Elsewhere, alternate schemes for continued profitability have been found. These have involved the compliance of union locals in wage freezes, more flexible job definitions, early retirement packages, and well-conceived employee–management work-smart programs. Finally, in this restructuring process, much more fiscal responsibility has been transferred by corporations to the management and labour force of individual mills.[449]

Surprisingly, over the same years of doldrums, recovery, then deep stress, corporate expenditure to increase cost efficiency has been huge. Spending to meet the necessities of rising levels of pollution abatement also has been large. Both goals, however, have been encouraged by substantial government incentives and loan guarantees, where justified. At Boise Cascade's mills, the main push toward cost efficiency has been directed at raising total productive capacity by 50 per cent while increasing the fibre yield from 63 to 80 per cent of wood volume.[450] Over the eighties, Great Lakes Paper (now Avenor) spent some $500 million at its two mills, principally on cleaning up, rebuilding, and expanding its recent purchase of Reed's holdings and old mill at Dryden.[451] Abitibi-Price sank nearly $200 million into increased yield from both its newsprint plants at Thunder Bay. About the same time, it refurbished the fine-paper machines at Provincial Paper, where it also replaced the old coating facility in 1984. At Sault Ste Marie it revamped its pulp processing system, a move from which its successor, St Marys Paper, was probably the true beneficiary. That new firm proceeded to convert and replace old machinery for its intended production of super-calendared paper for U.S. mail-order catalogues and advertising inserts.[452] Along the north shore of Superior, Domtar improved its linerboard plant at Red Rock during the early eighties to make it more competitive in U.S. markets. Kimberly-Clark at Terrace Bay greatly expanded its mill to accommodate the larger harvest from its new northern forest units.[453] James River, Marathon, meanwhile, constructed new high-yield pulp digesters early in the decade and followed this with a modernizing program in a move to total reliance on wood chips and a planned increase of 32 per cent in fibre recovery.[454]

With the nineties have come new fields of investment, promoting cost reduction and efficient use of forest resources. To counter the startling increases in hydro costs of the late eighties, several mills from Kenora to Sault Ste Marie have built co-generating plants. These now provide as much as half their energy needs in the form of electricity and steam, using natural gas to ignite bark and yard wastes, termed 'hog fuel.'[455] Three companies, Boise Cascade at Kenora, and Avenor and Abitibi-Price in Thunder Bay, have invested heavily in recycling equipment, using newspaper and magazine waste from the U.S. midwest to produce paper with as much as a 40 per cent reused content.[456] This range of improvement projects across the northwest has been a major contributor to short-term employment and to the whole regional economy in this unsettled period. At the same time, the use of labour-saving devices has reduced the work force in the industry, as have closures and necessary restructuring processes.[457]

Pollution Abatement

In addition to these drives for more profitability have come a broadened range of initiatives to reduce air and water pollution. Federal environmental regulations, initiated in 1973 and made comprehensive in 1977, were still weakly applied at the beginning of the eighties. At that time Ontario's supplemental legislation remained largely focused on particulate matter, despite the mercury problems of the prior decade. However, the eighties brought increasing recognition of chemical pollutants, most strongly associated in the forest industry with mechano-chemical pulping and chlorine bleaching processes. As a result, Ontario's Environmental Protection Act was modified to include the monitoring and regulation of the biochemical oxygen demand (BOD) levels in mill water emissions.[458] This recognition of new chemical dangers was broadened in 1985 when U.S. researchers discovered dangerous dioxin levels in the water below the mills at Fort Frances/International Falls. The upshot was the discovery of a whole range of toxic organochlorides, of which dioxins and furans are the most prevalent. These are now monitored and regulated by the Ministry of the Environment and Energy (MOE).[459]

With this rising wave of government regulations and strong public concern for the environment, the companies of the region have complied in responsible fashion. For example, in the decade beginning in 1981, Boise Cascade spent $57 million at Fort Frances, reducing odour by 92 per cent and particulate emissions by 97 per cent. It also attained a more than acceptable reduction in BOD levels in its waste water and considerable improvement in its discharge of organochlorides. This mill was committed to spend another $25 million on secondary treatment facilities and on chlorine dioxide generators by 1995. This modification of the bleaching system will further cut its dioxins and furans to below the currently required level.[460]

Other companies have committed themselves to similarly encouraging levels of expenditure, according to their size and type of process. Such compliance has forced some, in the wake of the unprofitable early nineties, very close to the wall. James River, Marathon, already encumbered by serious debt problems, faces a $40 million pollution control order. In an attempt to comply, it is seeking the help of its bankers and both the federal and provincial governments. Red Rock, scrambling back from what might have been permanent closure, is similarly encumbered with an approaching deadline. Compliance here will cost $25 million. Even excluding these extreme cases, the effort of the industry to accommodate public opinion and government goals for pollution control deserves more commendation than it has received.[461]

Government employees of the MOE and Environment Canada did not find their increasing role as monitors an easy one. As each new pollutant was added to the danger list, they were required to issue a rash of new control orders and deadlines, while most practical aspects, including decisions on tolerance levels, had yet to be determined. Without such information, their ad hoc decisions on acceptability were sometimes difficult to defend among more militant environmentalists. At the same time, inconsistency in their decisions between individual cases understandably drew sharp questions from the companies.

Partially to alleviate this situation, but mainly to solve larger issues, Ottawa initiated its Municipal and Industrial Strategy for Abatement (MISA) in 1986.

This created nine broadly based committees, each with a defined industrial field of responsibility. These committees were charged with developing guidelines to set realistic goals, achievable standards, and suitable regulations to ensure the protection of land, air, and water quality in their specific sector. Guidelines for the forest industry were the first to be submitted, approved, and put into effect in 1992, with a twelve-month delay in compliance from the end of that year for all mills built before 1971.[462]

Meanwhile, the IJC fostered local participation in the process of rehabilitation. It pin-pointed over forty trouble spots on the Great Lakes where contributions to the formulation of remedial action plans (RAPs) might usefully be made by concerned community members. Those on the Canadian side of Superior were in Thunder Bay, Nipigon Bay, and Moberly Bay, near Terrace Bay, as well as Peninsula Harbour, at Marathon, each the site of long-term pulp mill contaminants. Plans have now been created for each of these, and work at three, with monies from the Great Lakes Clean-up Fund, was begun in 1990.[463]

While encouraging, however, these examples of co-operative solution have not progressed without their rough patches. The most serious of those in the pulp and paper industry has come in the debt-ridden years of the early nineties. In late 1991, Greenpeace put out an ardent call for chlorine-free discharge across the Great Lakes Basin before mid-decade.[464] Most companies ignored this challenge, but some of the most severely troubled reacted the next year to hints that the province was considering such a plan. Kimberly-Clark opined that under present market prices, such a move was out of the question and that the use of chlorine bleaching was not an issue with its clientele. The president of James River, Marathon, put matters more forcibly: if the matter became law, his operation would be out of business by 1995.[465] Quiet support for this latter statement from other hard-pressed mills across the region was clearly evident in the local press.

Nevertheless, in February 1993, Queen's Park announced its intention to reduce the legal emission levels of organochlorides from pulp and paper processes to zero by 2002. The immediate reply from the industry pointed out that 0.8 units per ton of pulp was considered acceptable in the United States as well as Quebec and that only in British Columbia was a zero rate being sought. It went on to note that the proposed test for such levels, which used absorbable organic chlorides (AOX) as its measure, was under question by Environment Canada, the IJC, and major U.S. research laboratories. Subsequently the government backed down, deciding on 0.8 as an acceptable limit by the new century but promising an ultimate achievement of zero discharge.[466] Ironically, the really contentious issue in this debate has been swept aside for the moment: the expensive conversion of Ontario's mills from chlorine to hydrogen peroxide bleaching. The latter is almost universal in Europe and popular in western Canada because of its apparently low pollutant values.[467]

Building Products' Markets

Market analysts of the seventies, so optimistic about the future of pulp and paper, were no more accurate with their gloomy forecasts for lumber. Their predictions failed to take three factors into account: the rise of small-log sawmill technology, the much-improved system of saw-log procurement from pulpwood limits in the eighties, and the rapidly expanding use of former weed species, both for pulpable fibre and for the manufacture of building materials, in the current decade. At the same time, two deterrents have risen to slow unfettered expansion. First, an on-again, off-again Canada–U.S. trade war over softwood lumber during the last decade frequently exacted a 15 per cent duty on this important regional export. That dispute now appears to have been resolved and the flow of such dimension lumber south across the border from mills here has ballooned in the wake of recent disastrous floods in the Mississippi Valley. Second, in both countries, housing starts and, therefore, the demand for all types of building materials, has continued, from the late seventies, to vacillate wildly under uneasy economic times. Nothing suggests that these unpredictable conditions will cease to trouble this aspect of the trade in the near future.

Like pulp and paper, the lumber side of the forest industry has assumed a different organizational personality since 1980. The earlier pattern of corporately integrating stud or dimension mills with pulp and paper operations remains only at Dryden and White River.[468] Such mills, built under Boise Cascade at Kenora and Great Lakes Forest Products at the Lakehead, proved unprofitable and now stand empty.[469] Most others – at Hudson, Sapawe, Longlac, as well as Northern Wood Preservers and Great West Lumber in Thunder Bay – have been gradually acquired by the rising Buchanan Group. This firm recently has also taken over Dubreuil Brothers at Dubreuilville near Wawa and is currently erecting a specialty hardwood mill on property near the Lakehead.[470] The large Haavalsrud plant near Hornepayne – on Ontario and Quebec Paper (now Quno) holdings since 1981 – Buchanan, and a range of small but independent operators west to Kenora now compose the northwestern Ontario contributors to softwood lumber exports. However, this largely de-integrated set of producers have an aggregate capability that continues to dominate the provincial statistics.

Over the eighties variable markets and competitive conditions quietly reshaped the modest list of mills manufacturing other building materials. Both the Weyerhauser plywood and flooring plant at Sault Ste Marie and the Weldwood panelling factory at nearby Searchmont were purchased by G.W. Martin in 1985. While the latter was later closed, the former large and sophisticated facility has continued as a success in the hands of the local LaJambe Forest Products.[471] Despite awkward problems in both plywood and waferboard markets in the eighties, Weldwood's other regional plant at Longlac has not only survived but is planning a $10 million expansion program. This is intended to convert both facilities there, as of 1997, to the joint manufacture of a new laminated board directed at the cabinet-making trade.[472] However, about Thunder Bay, harsh conditions in that decade closed both the Great Lakes and much larger MacMillan-Bloedel waferboard plants.[473] The latter's small plywood affiliate to the east at Nipigon has continued its profitable operation into the present. With a now locally owned particleboard operation to the west of Atikokan, it too is adding to the leaner but still healthy character of this sector in the mid-nineties.

In the first half of 1994, exciting indications of immediate further developments appeared. These are in response to a provincial initiative toward the more complete use of regional forest resources. An Alberta firm, H. Jager Developments, has started work on a $108 million oriented strandboard mill near Wawa, to begin operations in 1996.[474] Another western company, Tolko of Vancouver, is in the last stages of planning for a similar large plant to be located somewhere between Kenora and Ear Falls and to open before the close of 1997.[475] Meanwhile, Georgia-Pacific has recently decided to proceed with a flakeboard operation at Leigh Bay on the St Marys River near Sault Ste Marie. This will have a million board foot capability directed at the U.S. furniture industry.[476] These three projects, with an estimated 800 direct jobs, will almost double the employment potential in this part of the forest industry. With other related mills rumoured to follow, they reflect probable patterns of expansion and regional trends into the new century.

Woodland Issues

In the woodlands division, the same pattern of periodic slump, associated layoffs, and unemployment with actual closures has prevailed. Perhaps the most important reaction to the financial constraints of the period has been the growing acceptance of technological adaptation toward the use of a growing range of species and increasing reliance upon their harvesting. Even into the seventies, there was much resistance to the use of anything but spruce in pulp manufacture, although such a preference was only justified in groundwood mills. By the end of that decade, common acceptance of jackpine and balsam was apparent in chemical pulp processing plants, although spruce was still a preferred component. With the eighties came the addition of tamarac. More recently, poplar, so numerous in its varieties and so prolific across the region, has ceased to be regarded as a weed, and is sometimes used in chipboard and cheap plywood. It is now accepted as a valuable source of pulp chips and of material for quality laminates and sophisticated manufactures like oriented strandboard. The concept of whole tree use, which appeared first in the seventies, has now broadened to whole forest utilization.

Much of the industry's willingness to move in this direction has been dictated by the rising transport costs associated with lengthening distances from virgin stands of black spruce or even high-quality jackpine. Such expenses were already beginning to attract the attention of company accountants in 1980, when the regional average haul for the northwest was estimated at 150 kilometres (96 miles) each way.[477] With the move of harvesting north into the newly opened management units, these rising costs have proved impossible to justify, particularly under the variable low prices that have come to prevail for both lumber and pulp.[478] The situation is most clearly exemplified by the actions of Kimberly-Clark. At the outset of the eighties, with a special road grant from the Ministry of Northern Development and Mines, that firm was opening the Ogoki haul road to its new northern holdings. It has subsequently given up its two most distant management units and abandoned its plan for other harvesting north from Nakina. Indeed, it is finding most of its current supplies on the chip market or in its immediate area, serviced from Longlac.[479]

Other firms have continued to pursue cutting to the terminal points on haul routes of the seventies, but government's increasing unwillingness to sponsor road building and cost constraints of recent years have combined to deter much expansion.[480] Instead, the tendency has been to curtail distance and to take the increasingly broad range of acceptable speciation on those closer holdings from which the spruce had been removed in decades past. As an alternate solution to haul costs, the Buchanan Group experimented in the late eighties with bundling saw logs in groups at Marathon and towing huge booms of these bundles to their mills at the Lakehead. More recently, they have successfully placed a barge on Lac Seul capable of carrying two trucks, to save 160 kilometres (102.4 miles) between cut sites and its Hudson sawmill.[481]

Cost and broader capital constraints have introduced other slow but marked changes to woodland operations. As Boise Cascade had done in the late seventies, despite a bitter resultant strike,[482] more and more harvesting and hauling has been turned over to private contractors, among whom the Buchanan operation is the largest. This move rids the corporation of large wage bills and capital costs for equipment, as well as those related to maintenance. A more exciting innovation has come with the increased entry of chipping into forest harvesting to augment older patterns of such wood processing at the mill or to reduce sawmill wastes for transport to the pulp and paper industry. To this end, Avenor and others are experimenting with mobile chippers, used at the cutting site. Stationary chipping plants, central to transport corridors and prepared to do custom work for groups of contractors in surrounding areas, have also begun to appear. So have fleets of appropriately designed trailers for mill hauling.[483] However, immediate developments have been slowed by problems with adequate debarking prior to processing and with species separation, both in chipping and later on chip delivery at the mill. Until these and other related headaches find solutions, some trucking of roundwood to chemical pulping operations will continue, while that method will remain the mode of transport to those groundwood mills where chips are unusable.[484]

Public Forest Concerns

These woodland-related developments have gone hand in hand with growing public demands for better management of harvesting and regeneration, and for both the industry and the Ministry of Natural Resources (MNR) to recognize other goals and uses than the corporate demand for wood.[485] The company stance on this supply matter and related issues in 1980 is well summarized in the Reed Report on future fibre availability, which was commissioned by ten pulp and paper interests. Reflecting both industry and public fears, it stated bluntly that northern Ontario faced a period of severe softwood shortage. The report went on to recommend that the government quickly intensify its management program, institute better inventory methods, and encourage full utilization of a broader ranger of woodland species, to stretch the available resources. But in keeping with the industry's lingering paranoia over future wood supply and its desire for exclusive control, it strongly suggested a review of the current land use plan, which, it held, had consigned far too much of the total area to other agencies and uses.[486]

The province ignored the latter recommendation, since it was quite aware of public opinion on that matter and since it had been committed from the mid-sixties onward to concepts of multiple and alternate land uses in the north.[487] The other demands Queen's Park found easy to accept, and the MNR was in an advanced stage of preparation for the promotion of these goals. Indeed, it was already creating the first of its Forest Management Agreements (FMAs), which were contractual arrangements, under the Crown Timber Act, between any company on a current management unit and the Ministry. Their intent was to assure a sustainable wood supply under appropriate harvesting and regeneration programs. As under prior arrangements, management plans were to be for twenty years with review every five years. However, these were to be much more demanding of effective company stewardship. The MNR was to share the cost of building forest roads and providing the nursery stock or seed for regeneration. The company assumed full responsibility for planting and tending all reforestable sites, until regenerative success could be assured.[488] Through such agreements, much emphasis was to be placed on Third Party Agreements, under which all wood best destined for uses other than pulping would be harvested, transported, and processed at an appropriate alternate facility. More or less analogous rules for cost sharing of roads and reallocation of saw or veneer logs also were set to apply to volume agreement holders on Crown Management Units (CMUs). However, under Crown Management Agreements (CMAs), planning and management remained the duty of the District Forestry Staff.[489]

Such arrangements were popular in the industry and very successful in promoting their desired ends. The first FMA in the northwest was for the 1,800 square miles of the English River country near Ignace and was put into effect in 1980. It was followed with five more by 1984; today such agreements apply to twenty-two management units across the region, or about 70 per cent of the Crown forest land base. Most of the remainder, in the hands of either large or small operators, is under CMU designation.[490] However, government budget cuts, in a time of rocketing nursery, silvicultural, and road-making costs, have reduced enthusiasm on both sides and have steeply reduced the impetus to carry out regenerative activity and road construction.[491] These contracts have always carried a guarantee of public access and of what are now termed non-timber values and uses. This side of their operation has recently been reviewed in the much larger context of public and community thinking on forest issues. These views are laid out in a Report of the Ontario Forest Policy Panel to the Minister of Natural Resources. However, no action has yet been taken on its suggestions.[492]

The MNR was also preparing to move on the other two issues raised by the 1980 Reed Report. Accepting the criticism of its inventory methods, it initiated a computerized model in 1981 in hopes of more effective update. To this it added a selective air photo program, using infra-red film to more cheaply check on regeneration during and after the tending sequence. Subsequently, it devised what it believed to be a truer mathematical measure of maximum allowable depletion (MAD) under variable physical conditions of regrowth.[493] In 1985, the MNR also invited Dr. G.L. Baskerville, dean of forestry, University of New Brunswick, to carry out an independent audit of Ontario's northern forest. In his report, Baskerville, like every evaluator before him since 1947, pointed to a future gap in the wood supply, because of over-concentration on key species and inadequate silvicultural endeavours over past decades. He forecast a shortfall in supply, in lumber first, but a crucial shortage across the entire industry, from 2010 to 2030. However, he also opined that the problem would be far more severe in the northeast than northwest and suggested a number of moves that might alleviate the blow. In his conclusions, Baskerville reiterated his earlier statement that the problem was related not to present but to past managerial efforts.[494]

His qualified criticisms, along with the results of a recent self-evaluation of managerial success by the MNR and loudly expressed concerns about its responsiveness to public concerns, culminated by the early spring of 1992 in firm government action. Queen's Park ordered the first Class Environmental Assessment by Ontario's Environmental Assessment Board. These public hearings regarding timber management practices on provincial Crown lands lasted more than 400 days in Thunder Bay and Toronto. They wound up in November 1992, with the release of the final report and binding recommendations in early 1994.[495] The report concluded that the forest practices operating under the MNR's guidelines were acceptable and adequately safeguarded those land uses other than for wood supply with which the public had shown concern. At the same time, it made numerous recommendations, with deadlines for action by the Ministry. These made Local Citizens' Committees an integral part of timber management, with an additional vehicle for similar local aboriginal participation. It required the Ministry to develop a policy on roadless wilderness areas by 1997 and was critical of the lack of prior restrictions on forest harvesting, to the exclusion of other uses. After a study of the role of clear-cutting in forest harvesting and habitat retention, the report concluded that areas with an upper limit of 260 hectares (650 acres) will adequately serve the industry and the requirements of a healthy moose population.[496] It showed strong concern over the recent reduction in artificial regeneration and ordered that this matter be reconsidered and that suitable financial commitment to this end be set out in timber production policy. It also approved the use of herbicides in the tending process and the reinstatement of chemical, as opposed to biological, insect control 'as a final resort' during severe infestations. Most important, the assessors concluded that 'no convincing evidence was put before [the hearings] that the Ontario forest industry is facing a timber shortage today or that one is likely in the future.' However, the members specified the need for a clear definition of demand/supply projections and of regeneration needs to fulfil provincial sustained yield objectives.[497] Indeed, one of the most immediate results of the report was legislation to revise the Crown Timber Act to provide for the sustainability of Crown Forests in Ontario. This passed first reading on June 1, 1994.[498] The outcome of these meetings may not have pleased or satisfied all parties concerned. As in the case of any document of its type, holes in its conclusions have already appeared. For example, while its provision for clear-cut size will adequately serve the habitat requirement of moose, in lieu of clearance by the natural offices of fire, it falls far short of the requirement for the more northerly woodland caribou. Yet this inquiry has cleared away many misconceptions and offers a base on which to work towards the resolution of complex forest-related issues.

Several fortuitous outside factors have combined to promote such positive ends. The lull caused by the economic downturn reduced any sense of urgency among participants, which in turn encouraged a thoughtful side to the debate and fact-finding process. The rising thrust of recycling, with the use of large amounts of old with new material for paper, has removed some of the pressure for former high levels of forest harvesting into the foreseeable future. As a result, balanced and considered plans for multiple use will have the necessary time for careful design and an atmosphere conducive to satisfactory implementation. This whole process will be aided in the future by the much fuller utilization of fibre from the prolific but lesser forest species, provided that this drive is accompanied by an adequate program of silvicultural renewal. The outcome could carry Ontario forward to the new world of sustainability, which lies, as yet, beyond current simplistic concepts of conservation and preservation.

Changing Times in Tourism and Recreation

New Parks and Park Policies

By the end of the seventies, changing popular tastes were demanding not only more parks, but also a different provincial mix under a typology introduced in 1967 (for the six relevant categories and their definitions see Table 5.13).[499] Also in the late seventies, falling revenues from car camping and a firm political move to curtail park spending were followed by the first plans for selective privatization across the system. Even schemes for future commercial lodges in certain larger parks, such as Sibley (now Sleeping Giant) near Thunder Bay, were now being entertained.[500] However, many more acceptable means of addressing operating costs came later to prevail over what has proved to be a long financial drought. Along with these stringent measures, more imaginative marketing, an expanded reservation system, and heavier emphasis on amenities seem to have stabilized demand in all but the most northerly regions. As a result, a new cost-conscious equilibrium has been struck for provincial parks on major regional highways, which are reasonably proximal to midwestern or southeastern clienteles. Elsewhere demand has continued to dwindle, then dip

TABLE 5.13 Classes of Provincial Parks

WILDERNESS PARKS are substantial areas where the forces of nature function freely and where visitors travel by non-mechanized means and experience expansive solitude, challenge and personal integration with nature.

NATURE RESERVES are areas selected to represent the distinctive natural habitats and landforms of the province. They are protected for educational purposes and as gene pools for research to benefit present and future generations.

HISTORICAL PARKS are areas selected to represent the distinctive resources of the province in open-space settings. They are protected for interpretive, educational and research purposes.

NATURAL ENVIRONMENT PARKS incorporate outstanding recreational landscapes with representative natural features and historical resources. These parks provide high-quality recreational and educational experiences.

WATERWAY PARKS incorporate outstanding recreational water routes with representative natural features and historical resources. These parks provide high-quality recreational and educational experiences.

RECREATION PARKS support a wide variety of outdoor recreation opportunities for large numbers of people in attractive surroundings.

Source: Government of Ontario, *Ontario Provincial Parks Policy* (Toronto: Ministry of Natural Resources, 1992).

more sharply with the nineties, while revenue losses have mounted. In fact, in 1994, two among these more out-of-the-way parks opened only under cost-sharing agreements with adjacent communities, at least one failed to open at all, and nine more will close five weeks earlier than usual for the first time in the history of the provincial park system.[501]

However, this fifteen-year span has witnessed an explosion among new forms of parks that are inexpensive to create and maintain, yet popular with the public, as well as a revolution in parks policy. Both of these trends have had their strongest impact in the provincial north. The creation of new kinds of parks reflects a desire among baby boomers and their progeny for wilderness adventure as a recreational mode, compatible with their strong environmental concerns. Such vacation patterns trade cars and campers for canoes and kayaks or boots and backpacks while forgoing easy access and amenity for excitement and physical challenge. These baby boomers have energetically joined with the long-standing wilderness preservation/conservation movement since they share recreational goals. This has generated an increasingly powerful and articulate association of interests under a common cause – reform in parks policy and future expansion, particularly in more northerly areas. In addition, this agglomerate group of wilderness seekers and preservationists/conservationists has come to constitute a force in the broader debate over future northern land use, which was echoed recently in the Class Environmental Assessment (EA) for Timber Management on Ontario's Crown lands.

The resultant lobby group could be said to have had its model in the earlier Quetico Council, but its effective role really began with the creation of the Provincial Parks Advisory Council in 1974. This citizens' advisory committee often proffered forceful recommendations on appropriate issues to the Cabinet and the Ministry of Natural Resources (MNR). Between 1976 and 1978 the Council's goals were promoted by a comprehensive program for Strategic Land Use Planning (SLUP) with the MNR. The subsequent integration of park planning into this process resulted, in 1981, in a list of 245 potential park locations of varied size and designated type.[502]

This government list of potential park preserves triggered the outbreak of a long-impending struggle for popular support, between the above lobby and other more traditional interests. The latter, held that the removal of these parklands for narrowly defined recreational use (wilderness) was unnecessary, unjustified, and an unacceptable threat to livelihood. However, these interests were ill-organized and sometimes inarticulate. They included resource industries worried about future territorial constraints on their operations. Support also came from groups such as anglers and hunters, certain tourist operators who anticipated exclusion from park areas, and even Native people to whom parks are a philosophical anathema. The press often portrayed this debate simplistically as a struggle between New and Old Ontario or between working-class needs and middle-class values.

After two years of altercations, the Cabinet, through the Minster of Natural Resources, called a truce. In 1983, it announced its approval of 155 new parks from the original list, some of which, like Wabakimi in the northwest, had been severely reduced in area. It also determined that non-conformal uses, like forest harvesting and hunting, were to be allowed. The government adhered to this policy firmly, in spite of strong opposition, until 1988, the year before the last of these parks were formally put into operation.[503]

Within the more emotionally charged global context of environmental concern in the nineties, such themes of protection have assumed a new political complexion. After Canada signed the United Nations Convention on Biological Diversity in 1992, Ontario released its Natural Heritage Areas Strategy. This committed Queen's Park to the completion, even expansion, of its 1983 plan of new parks/protected areas by the year 2000. In 1994, it launched 'Keep It Wild' to assure this goal of converting more than 7 per cent of the provincial land base to natural heritage designation. In the meantime, recognizing serious public concerns, the MNR, in 1992, announced the first call for popular input towards a proposed Environmental Assessment for Provincial Park Management. If or when completed, this could stand, with the now-finished one on Timber Management, as the second pillar of Ontario's future policy on northern land use.[504]

The impact of this escalation in park numbers, area, and diversity of purpose in the northwest has been most impressive geographically. In 1980, the region could boast at least one of each type of park but the waterway designation. However, it could claim more than ten only in the recreational and natural environment categories, most of which hosted extensive car camping facilities. Collectively, the total number of parks was only twenty-nine and the aggregate area about 700,000 hectares or 1.75 million acres (see Table 5.14). In 1994, even excluding several beyond the northern Albany/English River boundary of this study, the total is much more than twice the 1980 figure (compare Maps 5.1 and 5.3). The total number of provincial parks under study here, counting many very small ones among the nature reserves, has grown to 83, covering about 1.6 million hectares or 4 million acres. That may increase further with the proposed addition of two more large wilderness preserves and the possible expansion of Wabakimi, which is already in the public consultation stage.[505] Such expansion has cost the province very little, most lands involved being already vested in the Crown and requiring little money to operate because of the generally low intensity of intended use. Ironically, the financial return to the government and to the northwestern Ontario economy would seem to be

TABLE 5.14 Provincial Parks System, 1980–1994

Class	1980		1994	
	No.	Area (ha)	No.	Area (ha)
Wilderness	1	475,819	3	1,080,819
Waterway	0	0	7	232,107
Natural environment	11	222,153	17	276,428
Natural reserve	4	1,503	43	66,125
Recreation	12	5,411	12	5,411
Historical	1	289	1	289
Total	29	705,175	83	1,661,179

Source: Government of Ontario, *Ontario's Provincial Parks Class Environmental Assessment for Provincial Park Management*, Special report no. 1, 17–19, and tabulated from information supplied by Ronald LeeKam, Park Planner, Ministry of Natural Resources, Thunder Bay.

commensurately low. The inexcusable part is that, to the region, it always will be so.

Three other park developments were evolving to their current stage as the eighties began. Two of these were the product of Parks Canada, the largest being Pukaskwa, a wilderness operation of nearly 19,000 hectares or about 47,000 acres with one campground for highway-oriented campers. Opened to public use in 1983, this typical example of the Shield and boreal forest has never been gazetted formally as a National Park, due to certain unresolved Native land claims.[506] In contrast stands the Sault Ste Marie Canal, which ceased commercial use because of structural problems and was transferred by the Seaway Authority to Parks Canada in 1979.[507] This small area has since become a delightful Canadian Heritage attraction on the Ontario side of the St Marys River. Much more spectacular, but in a similar historic mode, is Old Fort William at Thunder Bay, a re-creation of former fur-trade days. It was initiated by Ontario in 1977 and opened two years later. This huge complex reached adolescence in the eighties and has now gained full maturity after a total capital investment of over $30 million.[508] It has become a popular tourist attraction for its adjacent city, its theme, like that of the canal at Sault Ste Marie, being sufficiently broad to interest a wide range of Canadian, American, and European visitors.

Broadening Seasonal Interest

Commercial tourism in the northwest, like that in the rest of the province, has been shaken from its former buoyancy of the seventies. The first tremors came when the OPEC crisis raised gasoline prices sharply and curtailed tourist travel to this relatively distant locale, even for regular vacation visitors.[509] After a return to modest profitability in the early decade, widespread problems returned about 1988. Canada, sixth among international travel destinations, had begun its decline to its current position of number ten, in the face of growing world competition for tourist dollars.[510] Coincidentally in North America, at all levels, the pattern of vacationing was disturbed by the 1991 Gulf War, which kept many Americans close to home and, for some, permanently altered their holiday habits. Much more important, the late eighties saw the escalation of winter vacationing as well as changing modes of summer recreation. The former thrust now sent many south for sun or west to ski, while the latter involved a move to luxury resorts and Great Lakes' boating or to rough adventuring on land or water.

In the northwest the cumulative blow of these shifting patterns has been softened by the conservative nature of both clients and operators, the qualified importance of tourism across the regional economy, and the undeniable natural attractiveness of this sprawling landscape. These and other factors have slowed or even mitigated against the need for change. Yet only recently has government abandoned the band-aid approach to problem-solving, as exemplified by its onerous and expensive bailout of Minaki Lodge in the early eighties.[511] Instead, federal and provincial support is now directed at initiatives like harbour improvements for the numerous new marinas that have appeared or sponsorship of much-needed training programs and job-creation efforts in the hospitality trade.[512]

For reasons of distance from major population centres and of uncertain economic times, Ontarians' participation in northwest tourism has declined more significantly than has that of Americans.[513] At the same time, because of relative proximity to targeted markets, certain portal areas – Algoma West as well as Kenora/Rainy River, for example – have been less negatively affected than the hinterlands. The long-established vacation habits in these areas still include the same sport-related or family holiday at a usual resort or lodge, summer home, or cottage. Thunder Bay has been less fortunate, suffering sharply under the decline in visitors from Ontario and other parts of Canada, and only partially able to recover its popularity with Duluth/Superior and adjacent Wisconsin and Minnesota. Declining profits there and among the numerous centres along the major traffic arteries east and west of the Lakehead, from Longlac to Atikokan, Wawa to Dryden, typify the early nineties. The major loss of regional clientele has been among motel-oriented visitors, who have found other places to go or other seasons to go on vacation. Frequently in these places and among communities outside these corridors, the local economic impact is noticeable but not acute, since their participation in the industry has always been peripheral to their other functional strengths. Retired people have continued to add to spring and fall revenues from auto rambling and bus tours. However, their contribution has not sufficed to make up for the overall profit shortfall, and, even with additional revenue occasioned by the annual overflow of fishermen and hunters from more typical quarters, is unlikely ever to do so.[514]

In total dollar amounts, summer tourism across the region, with its established seasonal shoulders, seems not only to be holding its own in the early nineties, but appears to be in the early stages of recovery to former levels.[515] However, no suitable statistics exist with which to test this assertion. What figures there are hold few surprises and reflect little gross alteration over the last decade, although they provide no indication of establishment size, quality, or vacancy rate (see Table 5.15). About 700 establishments, from resorts to motor inns, cabin complexes to outfitters camps, dot the region. Over three-

TABLE 5.15 Tourist Accommodations, 1994

	No. of Establishments	Establishments with Fly-In
Algoma West	87	15
Thunder Bay District	174	21
Rainy River District	75	11
Kenora/Patricia	362	90
Total	698	137

Source: Compiled from *Accommodations '94* and *Fishing Packages '94*, both published by the Ontario Ministry of Culture, Tourism and Recreation.

quarters of these are located in the adjoining districts of Thunder Bay and Kenora (about a third of the figure for the latter lying in the Patricia portion). Except about the upper end of the Lake of the Woods, where Winnipeg visitors prevail, this large area, with the neighbouring Rainy River District, remains a traditional playground for American vacationers. This explains its heavy concentration of fly-in fishing facilities, so popular with U.S. midwestern urbanites. Interestingly, the ratio of such facilities to total establishments is even higher in Algoma West. This would appear to mirror a similar fascination among other American recreationalists, although the total number of outlets is much smaller.

Winter Opportunities

Nevertheless, major new private and public investment has been made and new developmental activity has come to focus on winter possibilities, which were already in an experimental phase by 1980. At Thunder Bay, international ski jumping and excellent downhill facilities on the slopes of the Nor'westers continue to attract steady growth in use from residents, the U.S. plains states, and world competitors. Success in downhill here has stimulated quality ski resorts at Kenora, directed at Winnipeg devotees[516] in particular, and behind the other regional gate of Sault Ste Marie. Here, after the failure of an extravagant plan for King Mountain and after a prolonged financial struggle, the numerous runs and support facilities at Searchmont have become popular with both Michigan and local skiers. Lesser developments elsewhere, as near Marathon, offer excellent local sport but seem to have little hope of standing alone as tourist attractions.[517]

Because of its more universal appeal, cross-country skiing has become an important component of winter recreation. In most centres, local clubs or private operators now offer well-groomed and challenging networks of trails, and some communities are gaining reputations for loppets in the winter season. In Algoma West, for example, about 150 kilometres of excellent trails, some stretches even lighted for evening use, as well as a popular spring loppet at Wabos (near Searchmont) are drawing popular attention. At Thunder Bay, such activities have been under very active development too and will balance that city's hosting of the Nordic Cup Ski Championships in 1995.[518]

However, the most intense and universal developmental efforts continue to be focused around the ubiquitous snowmobile. Participants in this sport now number more than 200,000 regulars, of whom perhaps 40 per cent live north of the French River. Resultant commercial revenue across Ontario from these enthusiasts and other devotees from the United States already accounted for $300 million in 1991 and, in 1993, climbed to $500 million. To promote the health of this growing business, Ontario provided $14 million in 1992, and clubs across the province added $7 million more. These monies have been spent to aid in the completion of the Trans Ontario Provincial Snow-Trail (TOPS) system and to improve extensive local networks linked to it.[519] This huge, aggregate grid of trails across the northwest offers exciting opportunities for scenic travel over ever-increasing distances. Even maps are available, giving not only routes but fuelling points and resort or motel accommodations. However, it will probably develop under the same rules of accessibility as the rest of the recreation industry. Visitor use will fan out from Sault Ste Marie and Kenora/Fort Frances and less intensely from Thunder Bay. Over large intervening tracts, use will be considerable, but more predominately by local residents. When the commercial uncertainties currently dogging regional tourism and recreation resolve themselves, the economic contribution of winter sport will likely have taken up or exceeded any current shortfalls related to the decline in summer motel-oriented travellers.

Agriculture in New Equilibrium

Reshaped to a much leaner form and reduced to a narrower footing, northwestern Ontario farming has retained something of its former momentum over the last decade and a half. A long-time interest in cooperatives and in tile drainage died under provincial austerity in the late eighties.[520] Total farm numbers have fallen about two hundred units over the last decade, to about 750 in 1991, reflecting the loss of more land of now marginal value and of some of the less adaptable farmers (see Table 5.16). In Algoma West and behind Kenora, agriculture of more than casual pursuit has disappeared, and very obvious reductions in both farms and farm populations mark every other agricultural pocket.

TABLE 5.16 Rural Profile, 1981–1991

	1981	1991*
Algoma West		
No. of farms	11	?[†]
Farm population	210	?
Rural population	8,365	9,006
Thunder Bay District		
No. of farms	358	271
Farm population	1,120	930
Rural population	26,218	30,913
Rainy River District		
No. of farms	456	352
Farm population	2,190	1,225
Rural population	8,492	10,197
Kenora District		
No. of farms	130	124
Farm population	510	370
Rural population	32,797	34,696
Total Northwest		
No. of farms	955	747
Farm population	4,030	2,525
Rural population	75,872	84,812

* Figures for 1991 reflect a more stringent definition of 'farm' and 'farmer' than that which applied in 1981.
† Data unavailable.
Source: Census of Canada for the relevant years.

However, these trends are shared with the rest of provincial agriculture. The farm component in the northwest now makes up only about 3 per cent of the rural population. In this farm component, the hobby elements make up 24 per cent, moderate-sized and often part-time operations account for another 40 per cent, and the balance (36 per cent) of dedicated agriculturalists occupy substantial farms in excess of 400 acres.[521]

These large operators and some of medium acreages are the truly significant element, responsible for most active crop and pastoral land today (see Table 5.17). In both these categories, the trend in every district has mirrored that in the rest of Ontario: increased production but on less, but better, acreage. Crop area across the northwest continues to be commonly devoted to quality hay and

TABLE 5.17 Agricultural Balances, 1981–1991

	1981		1991	
	Acres	% of total	Acres	% of total
Algoma West				
Cropland	209	20	–	–
Pasture	642	60	–	–
Other	215	20	–	–
Total held	1,066	?*		
Thunder Bay District				
Cropland	37,922	44	26,675	42
Pasture	26,383	31	15,586	24
Other	21,411	25	21,360	34
Total held	85,716		63,621	
Rainy River District				
Cropland	51,173	32	55,001	32
Pasture	62,344	40	61,092	35
Other	44,231	28	57,969	33
Total held	157,748		174,062	
Kenora District				
Cropland	14,989	31	13,613	27
Pasture	18,998	39	12,129	24
Other	14,365	30	25,114	49
Total held	48,352		50,856	
Total Northwest				
Cropland	104,293	36	95,289	33
Pasture	108,367	37	88,807	31
Other	80,222	27	104,443	36
Total held	292,882		288,539	

* A very low (but indeterminate) level of hobby farming is all that persists.
Source: Census of Canada for the relevant years.

haylage (the northern answer to corn silage). Among hobbyists, to whom only modest amounts of hay and pasture are important, some residual land has been allowed to revert to scrub and semi-forested condition.

Among serious practitioners on 200 acres or more, two patterns have continued to persist in farm operation: beef farming and dairying. Beef farming remains most prominent and profitable in the Rainy River Valley, with roughly 200 producers, and around Dryden, with twenty-five. However, only about a dozen in total are full-time, with an average of considerably over a hundred animals. The remainder have often increased their herd to about 60 head of well-bred stock, which they find they can manage with tight budgeting of their time. Typically these cow-calf operations are based on Charolais-Hertford crosses, for size and quality, with the product ready for market after eighteen months. Until the mid-eighties, the ultimate destination was either western Canada or sometimes southern Ontario. Since 1986, however, the modest Canadian dollar and other factors have caused most to be sold south via Winnipeg or to large Alberta finishing operations for ultimate U.S. transfer. These cattle contribute to families that usually have two other sources of income, and their collective addition to domestic bank accounts as well as the local economy runs into the millions of dollars.

As in prior decades, dairying has remained a second major source of farm income. Adjacent to Thunder Bay, the eighties witnessed a substantial drop in related farm numbers, with a sharp increase in hobby operations, to about a third of the 1991 farm total. Yet milk production, with a fringe of ancillary nurseries, sod farms, and market gardens, continues to make up the commercial side of the industry. Principally in post-war, second-generation Dutch hands, about 60 large and modern dairy farms are now capable of supplying all the milk needs of the surrounding area. To the west, dairy production adds about $5 million to local coffers, four-fifths accruing to producers in the Rainy River Valley. Again this reflects the modern capture of milk quota, often by Low Countries immigrants of the post-war period. Until 1987, production from here was directed by the Milk Marketing Board to Vacationland Dairy at Kenora, while the remainder went for processing to a Beatrice dairy at Dryden. Subsequent to hearings into the movement of the latter's operations, either to Winnipeg or Thunder Bay, the entire supply has passed to Kenora.[522]

As in the case of beef income, dairy dollars would appear to assure a firm future for a small, but lucrative, regional farming industry. However, mixed concerns are being expressed by milk producers about the Milk Marketing Board's introduction of a one-price, one-transport-cost policy for all of Ontario as of the autumn of 1994. One can only hope, with the regional farmers so dedicated to their northern lands and life, that the strong livestock-oriented economy they have fostered will survive the unusual, external stresses it now faces, along with other challenges of the future.

Urban Uncertainties

The mixed troubles and changes of recent years among the resource industries of the northwest have also been felt in the urban-related scene, including the communication network fundamental to its function. Except for the completion of a new road from the Atikokan area to Ignace and a shorter one to Dubreuilville from the Trans-Canada Highway, development since 1980 has been limited to maintaining or upgrading the existing pattern. In electrical generation, too, the eighties witnessed more modest growth. Leading up to the financial troubles it now faces, Ontario Hydro added only a thermal unit at Atikokan (200,000 kilowatts). Great Lakes Power used the last of its hydraulic capacity for a larger replacement station at Sault Ste Marie and two small ones (79,500 kilowatts) on the Magpie River near Wawa.[523] However, Trans-Canada Pipelines has added substantially to its capacity for eastern markets and currently is completing a fourth 42-inch pipe across the region. At the same time, the new system of fibre optic cable, to serve the northwest on its cross-Canada passage, is nearing completion. This will further enhance regional telecommunications. Both projects have provided useful injections of money into the economies of many small communities along their routes.[524]

On the negative side, the region has been shaken recently by announcements that threaten deep cuts in other forms of transportation. While the increasing use of west coast ports in the shipment of grain and other products has made their western trackage thrive, both the CN and CPR have come to face huge losses and gross over-capacity elsewhere. As a result, in the spring of 1994, these railways announced they were negotiating a possible reduction to one main line, from Winnipeg to Sudbury. However, the route has not yet been selected and regulatory approval has yet to be sought, much less granted, by Ottawa.[525] The future impact of such a move on the communities along whichever line is eventually cancelled can readily be imagined, as can the immediate unsettling effect on all centres along either set of tracks.

This impending problem has been accompanied by the resolution of one that has dogged the Algoma Central. It was already troubled financially in 1982, by its mileage north of Hawk Junction, and was put under 80 per cent subsidy to continue service to isolated communities there for the next five years.[526] In 1987, negotiations were begun between the ACR, the Ontario government, and the Wisconsin Central Railroad regarding running rights across the St Marys River. This culminated in July 1994 in the sale of the ACR to Wisconsin Central. While the sale was a sound business arrangement for both Wisconsin and Queen's Park, the price for employees was high: their numbers were reduced from 500 to 217.[527]

In the related field of air transport, future problems also loom, resulting from a recent announcement by Ottawa of its intention to cut financial contributions to airport operations across the nation. By the end of the century, national funding to such facilities will be limited to capital projects, with operating costs being left to the municipalities. Since service levels at most airports in areas such as the northwest result in substantial operating deficits each year, the local reaction has been rapid and angry.[528] Meanwhile, over the troubled eighties, as business travel slowed, regional carriers like norOntair were forced to reduce service or to honour scheduled flights to lesser places on the basis of demand only.[529] While the latter step at least recognized the essential nature of such service among smaller and more isolated communities, the former federal decision ignored this important reality.

Thunder Bay and Sault Ste Marie

Although the personalities of the region's two major centres remain distinct, the patterns in their recent pasts have followed quite similar courses. Both have endured rates of unemployment as high as 30 per cent, as their industries and businesses have grappled with the need for cut-backs, shut-downs, or permanent closures. Like all lesser centres across the northwest, these cities have faced these problems with their own programs, which have been bolstered by federal–provincial work-creation projects. These centres are now enjoying more acceptable unemployment levels and more encouraging futures.[530] Also, both have seen the transfer of government agencies to their domains, waterfront renewal work, major highway improvements in their environs, new airport terminal facilities, and other construction within their bounds. At Sault Ste Marie, the results have even extended to major new sewage and water supply facilities.[531]

Yet no one can deny the financial difficulties and uncertainties that have confronted the citizenry of these communities. At the Lakehead, the convoluted trends in the forest industry periodically caused serious work disruptions in plant, mill, and factory, resulting in permanent closure of Abitibi's Bare Point pulp and paper mill, Canadian Pacific Forest's stud mill and hardboard plant, and MacMillan-Bloedel's large chipboard facility. Most of these losses came after long battles to save them. The only one of these major struggles that was won was at Provincial Paper, through a successful take-over by company employees in 1993.

Tribulation at the Lakehead was increased by difficulties in two other major and long-standing industries. The Port Arthur Shipbuilding Co. (later Portship), long owned by Canadian Shipbuilding and Engineering, a subsidiary of Canada Steamship Lines, had for years been forced to rely largely on repair, maintenance, and inspection work. The near cessation of ship construction on the Great Lakes, which led to the demise of the Collingwood yards, put this ageing facility on the danger list in 1986. In 1993, even the dry-dock operation here at

Portship was ordered to be closed to preserve the parent company's large, modern operation on the Welland Canal. Currently this landmark is inactive, save for the specialized ends of Pascol Engineering.[532] In contrast, Canada Car, its erratic history here going back to 1912, by 1980 was heavily involved, under Hawker Siddeley, in the production of subway and rapid transit cars. Through the decade, this large plant, affected by international competition, was sometimes open, sometimes closed, and sometimes on part-time. Over the same period, the Urban Transportation Development Corporation (a provincial agency), became involved in conjunction with Hawker and later Lavelin Corporation. As its tenders or contracts for rolling stock, from Toronto and California to Hong Kong and Mexico, failed or succeeded, so the work force decreased, or expanded to capacity (1,000 employees).[533] As of January 1992, this operation passed to Bombardier Canada Limited and, with secure orders from as far away as Turkey, is under extensive construction and renovation before its reopening near the end of 1994.[534]

Meanwhile, the very raison d'être of the twin cities – their famous ports – has fallen on difficult times. Total cargo handled here, reaching as high as 23 million tonnes in the early eighties, has since declined (see Table 5.18). Iron ore production at Steep Rock and then Ear Falls, which industry once shipped as much as 4.7 million tonnes (or 5.2 million tons) a year, ended in 1986. In addition, the economic downturn has caused declines of 60 to 80 per cent in potash, as well as in other bulk and general cargo since 1980. Because of its huge volume and the number of jobs dependent on its handling, however, the real loss has been in grain shipments, which have fallen from nearly 15 million to little more than 8 million tonnes (8.8 million tons) over the last thirteen years. The cause here has been the continuing shift in Canadian exports to an

TABLE 5.18 Cargo Statistics, Port of Thunder Bay (in metric tonnes), 1981–1991

	1981	1991
Grain	13,874,632	8,157,168
Coal	2,274,690	2,387,642
Iron Ore	1,220,485	–
Potash	1,445,651	551,830
Bulk	730,339	289,101
General	638,992	102,092
Total	20,184,789	11,487,833

Source: Thunder Bay Harbour Commission, Port Authority, Thunder Bay.

Asian focus and the related western Grain Transportation Act, which facilitates the passage of prairie production to the ports of Vancouver and Prince Rupert.[535] Only the steady shipment of coal remains to brighten the immediate future. Nevertheless, the people of the Lakehead and their businesses, as well as municipal leaders, have come to terms with this situation. They now accept that these events affect not just their city, but the entire Seaway and its once-famous fleet of bulk carriers, many of which have been moth-balled.[536]

At Sault Ste Marie, such industrial troubles have been less widespread but no less difficult to accommodate. As noted for the Lakehead, the major problems here became evident in the earlier eighties but reached crisis stage only a decade later, after firm attempts to counter or resolve them. The uneasy future of the ACR became evident with its subsidy requirement in 1982 and was underlined by the commencement of joint negotiations for its sale in 1987, which led to its very recent transfer to Wisconsin Central. Similarly, at St Marys Paper, its heavy debt load from the purchase of an ageing plant and extensive renovations elicited scepticism regarding its viability as early as 1985, although the company struggled on against deteriorating market prices until its bankruptcy in 1993; an uncertain era in receivership followed. But much more critical for the community after 1982 were the growing troubles at Algoma Steel Corporation, the city's largest employer.

The problems at Algoma Steel towered over those at the two industries discussed above. In addition to the disastrous condition of international and North American steel markets through the eighties, the corporation faced immediate needs for further capital-intensive modernization of its ageing plant. That facility had developed too many product lines and too much related, but unused, capacity over the years.[537] It also faced the expense of complying with further pollution control orders for its air and water emissions.[538] Surmounting these troubles was not helped by the company's transfer, first to the control of the CPR, and later to Dofasco.[539] Mounting indebtedness, stemming from the necessary modernization and from massively unprofitable operation, brought work-sharing and lay-offs among a labour force of 10,000 in 1981. That number fell to 6,500 by 1987 and to 4,000 about the close of the decade.[540] These factors eventually drove the corporation to its knees, forcing a restructuring in 1992, with the help of the province and the unions. This resulted in the creation of Algoma Steel Incorporated, a no-frills concern, 60 per cent of which is employee-owned.[541] Despite rave reviews in the financial press for its rapid return to profitability, company leadership urges caution. It cites as reasons for a cautious outlook the unknown duration of its good fortunes in a reviving North American steel market, its level of indebtedness, and its involvement in the several anti-dumping cases between Canada and the United States.[542] Sault

Ste Marie is not quite over the difficulties of the eighties. Yet with Algoma Steel's revival, the reconstituted ACR, and a possible end to receivership at St Marys Paper, a much leaner community with its shrunken industrial labour force can look with more assurance to its future. However, what is significant in all three instances here, as at Thunder Bay to some lesser degree, was the subsequent level of labour–management cooperation and sacrifice. Wage concessions, administrative cuts, work-smart programs, and a growing cooperative spirit created a model for better industrial relations.

The eighties have also made evident certain northern demographic problems that have been growing quietly since the fifties. These centre on the national birth rate, which has declined steeply in recent decades, and on the rising regional rate of youthful out-migration. They are complicated by the propensity of modern immigrants to Ontario to settle in Toronto or near large southern centres. The resultant slow decline in the rate of population growth in the northwest, relative to that in southern Ontario, has been exacerbated by the confused economic events of the last fifteen years, which have increasingly forced unemployed adults to join their children on the trek to other locations (see Table 5.19). While the two urban foci of the northwest have managed marginal growth, most lesser centres have encountered a worrying net decline and ageing trends, even among some single-industry communities.[543] The overall result in the Algoma West and Thunder Bay districts has been near-stable population since 1981. Yet among more westerly partners and the region as a whole, a slight decline has occurred in urban numbers. At the same time, all but Algoma West have registered a curious and unexpected rise in rural, non-farm residents, sufficient to record a small increase in total regional population.

Lesser Towns

The impact of this adjustment in urban populations has varied noticeably among the communities of the northwest. In subcentres with as many as 10,000 people, the net result of demographic process has been least acute. Tourist dollars, added to the paper-oriented economies of Fort Frances, Kenora, and Dryden, have helped them over rough patches. Modern technology has reduced the labour requirement in the mills at all three, but their size and alternative job opportunities have allowed them to retain many of their young people.[544] Sioux Lookout has recently come to represent not only the focus for health care for the Natives on reserves north of the Albany River, but also the centre of band administration for this huge territory to Hudson Bay. It emerged in the eighties as the dynamic capital and commercial centre for the Natives of Patricia and a growing white and aboriginal community of more than 4,000.[545] At Geraldton,

TABLE 5.19 Population Profile (percentage urban and rural non-farm), 1981–1991

	1981		1991	
	Population	% of total	Population	% of total
Algoma West				
Rural non-farm	10,993	12	10,278	11
Urban	82,697	88	83,991	89
Total population	93,900		94,269	
Thunder Bay District				
Rural non-farm	25,098	16	29,983	19
Urban	127,779	83	127,897	81
Total population	153,997		158,810	
Rainy River District				
Rural non-farm	6,302	28	8,972	39
Urban	14,306	63	12,800	56
Total population	22,798		22,997	
Kenora District				
Rural non-farm	32,287	54	34,326	58
Urban	26,624	45	24,052	41
Total population	59,421		58,748	
Total Northwest				
Rural non-farm	74,680	23	83,559	25
Urban	251,406	76	248,740	74
Total population	330,116		334,824	

Source: Census of Canada for the relevant years.

population has increased, but less noticeably, largely through government programs that have moved nearby Native communities into housing and facilities specifically created for them there, but now encourage Native homes dispersed within the community. At Wawa, however, the situation has been a less happy one because of continuing uncertainty about the AOD's mining and sintering operations. This has caused a sequence of lay-offs through the eighties; the mine continues to be worked, while the company endeavours to reduce the sulphur dioxide levels from beneficiating.[546] To Wawa's industrial problem may be added the demise of the exciting gold interest that pervaded this area in the flush of the eighties. However, new jobs will be added by the new strandboard operation in the neighbourhood and work generated at adjacent Michipicoten Harbour. This was recently sold by Algoma Steel to a new company, Nicholas Technical Services, with aggressive plans for bulk cargo handling through that port. Hopefully, these events will also broaden the town's employment base and help cushion against its uncertain mineral future.[547]

Among single-industry towns of 2,500 people, events generally have proved more tellingly difficult. While mining communities like Red Lake and forest-related ones such as Longlac, Nipigon, Terrace Bay, and White River have managed to retain or regain a status quo in the nineties, most have been less fortunate. Indeed, the era since 1980 has been marked by reduction not only in economic health but in absolute numbers.

Railway-based centres, not seriously affected by events of previous decades, have seen hard times or can anticipate them. Schreiber has survived comfortably due to its diversified job opportunities in tourism, mining at Winston Lake, and Kimberly-Clark's nearby pulp and paper mill. However, at Rainy River, CN is finally about to abandon its crew change arrangements. At Nakina, where such 'run-through' policy was approved in 1988 and Kimberly-Clark's northern woodland aspirations have died, the situation is much more trying.[548] This is even truer at Hornepayne. That old divisional centre was designated a growth point in CN maintenance in the seventies. It also was where railway, provincial, and private capital combined to develop an indoor complex for shopping, as well as service and educational facilities, as an experiment for combating winter conditions in small northern communities. Today its railway maintenance function is a shadow of the past, and its future depends very largely on the choice of the trans-regional route to be negotiated between the railways.[549]

In other functional sectors, conditions have often run distressingly parallel. Red Rock has undergone severe shrinkage and still faces an insecure future with its troubled Domtar linerboard mill.[550] Outright mine closures affecting Atikokan, Ear Falls, Pickle Lake, Ignace, and Manitouwadge have caused serious local distress. With the cessation of work at Steep Rock in 1980, Atikokan set out to survive. It became the site of an Ontario Hydro thermal generating station and attracted a particleboard mill, developed its Quetico-related recreational and tourist potential, and gained much benefit from employment at Buchanan's sawmills at Sapawe.[551] Despite similarly diligent attempts, Ear Falls has been less immediately successful in its quest. The termination of Umex operations near Pickle Lake precipitated a substantial worker relocation project. However, the subsequent appearance of a new gold mine at neighbouring Dona Lake has done something, along with the rise of a major operations centre for Austin Airways (now an Air Canada associate), to rectify the situation.[552] However, the graduated closure of base-metal extraction at Sturgeon Lake has left Ignace with a sharp decline in tax revenues from housing and a major debt for expanded utilities.[553] At Manitouwadge, the closure of the famed

Geco mine was completed November 1994, although as in all other instances cited above, it will not result in community abandonment.[554]

Indeed, Manitouwadge stands as an example of success in government policy. Because of government policy opposing the creation of new single-industry towns, the gold discovery at Hemlo and the resultant labour demands for the mines brought a plan to distribute the new labour force between the adjacent and narrowly based communities of Marathon, Manitouwadge, and White River. Noranda chose to expand its accommodations at Manitouwadge, but Lac Minerals and Teck Corona settled principally at Marathon. This left White River hoping for an influx from the Mishibishu gold field, which possibility remains in the future.[555] While Manitouwadge has been left, thereby, with an all-important option after Geco's closure, Marathon, now a pulp town with a golden future, is the real winner. In 1983, this community of 2,300, with help from Ontario, acquired vacant land in the original town plot from James River, Marathon. It planned and serviced this property before its sale to the mining companies for trailer, apartment, and family dwellings. These in turn were built upon and transferred to employees at highly advantageous mortgage rates.[556] Accompanied by additional expansion of shopping and service facilities, capped by a mall planned in 1989, this town has become a centre for more than 6,000 people.[557] Indeed, in comparison with places like Ear Falls or Ignace, Marathon stands as the model of what can be achieved with appropriate planning and foresight, as well as a full measure of luck.

Meanwhile, during the decade when the northwest's urban troubles were festering, Ontario recognized the seriousness of the symptoms. It struck an advisory committee to examine the state of all such resource-dependent communities across its north. That body's report and recommendations were presented to the minister of Northern Development and Mines in early 1986.[558] In its deliberations, the committee had assumed the broadest possible approach, reviewing the whole gamut of the north's economic and social dilemma from the perspective of these communities. The final document touched lightly on nodal, agricultural effects and dealt more firmly with those related to tourism. However, it spent considerable time on the urban side of mining and forest troubles. It then turned to common concerns such as education and retraining, out-migration and ageing, financial and business weaknesses, as well as the need for community leadership and participation.

While the report stirred limited public interest, later study of its numerous and often refreshing recommendations suggests that its significance was not missed by the pertinent provincial agencies. Indeed, elements in its seventy-odd pages curiously foreshadow much that has developed since in forest, mineral, and even recreational policies. In addition, its call for financial recompense by the province for past profits from northern resource utilization, which monies usually migrated elsewhere, resulted in Ontario's laudable creation of the Northern Heritage Fund in 1991.[559] Under this program, which will see an endowment of $35 million by 2005, northerners with sound business plans may apply for matching development funding. Success carries the proviso that significant profit must result within two years, or such a government grant will become only a loan. Yet despite commendable moves such as this, the province has made no direct attempt to address the most fundamental recommendation of this committee, which pointed to the need for an explicit, long-term policy to direct northern Ontario's future. Statements on timber management and the possibly impending ones on parks are steps in the right direction. Native affairs is largely a federal jurisdiction, requiring cooperative deliberation, as transport increasingly seems to be. But clear decisions on the future role of the northern agricultural community remain to be made. Also needed are well-designed programs to study the role of exploration and development in mining. Equally necessary are imaginative approaches to the unusual problems that face northern urbanization, from the single-industry town to the highly industrialized city.

Native Communities in Transformation

To do more than offer a sketch of modern trends in Native life in northwestern Ontario is beyond the scope of this book. Probably a request for a more comprehensive discussion would daunt most Native leaders as well. They at present are embroiled in ongoing conflicts over aboriginal unity and local autonomy. The individual bands also face the challenge of taking up the self-governance and fiscal responsibilities they now seek. This foment among Canada's Native peoples may be dismissed as confusing, or regarded with suspicious concern, by parties in the rest of the population. However, it is a far healthier reaction to their desires and needs than was their docile acquiescence over much of this past century.

After about 1900, a shift away from Native interest among both federal politicians and the public became increasingly noticeable across this nation. The separate Department of Indian Affairs, newly created in 1902, signified the importance of that Cabinet portfolio of the day. However, much of its strong administrative drive had been lost by 1914, when the focus of most public and political concern was on war. In that European conflict, as in the second one later, Native youth served frequently and valiantly but without fanfare or, perhaps, much public knowledge. Those who came back, like their white comrades, were often mentally, if not physically, scarred. Yet unlike most others, they found it difficult or impossible to readjust to the reserve and to being 'only an Indian.' Two decades later, aboriginal administration had degenerated to no more than a branch of the Department of Mines and Resources. Meanwhile, popular opinion had become preoccupied with the economically uncertain twenties, then with survival in the depression years, only to return to dwell on war again. This is no excuse for the resultant social and material degeneration that increasingly marked the lot of forgotten Native communities. However, along with the generally inarticulate complaints of these long-suffering people, these circumstances explain the cause of this degeneration.[560]

Popular recognition of backward conditions on reserves, of second-rate status for Natives in the community, and of the paternalism that governed their legal rights brought the stirrings of reform after 1945. By the end of that decade, a much-altered Indian Act was taking shape, paving the way for improved social and economic conditions on the reserve. Indeed, by 1966, a reformed Native administration had been returned to importance in the federal Cabinet, as the Department of Indian Affairs and Northern Development, while material improvements were beginning to make their appearance on the reserves. This ministry, after a sequence of reorganizations and internal restructurings, was provided by Parliament in 1985 with the refreshingly liberalized Native legislation it now administers. Yet in today's highly aware society, the ministry's efforts towards improving conditions for Natives generate criticism from both aboriginal and concerned non-Native groups.[561] Some criticism is well deserved. Sometimes however, it appears misdirected, when the specific issues involved in the criticism are not under the purvey of that ministry.

Like the Native population as a whole, northwestern Ontario's aboriginal communities continue to face serious and, sometimes seemingly unresolvable, problems. Among the most disturbing is the shocking level of substance abuse. However, the use of inhalants like gasoline or glue seems less common in this region than among more northerly centres of the Hudson Bay Lowland. Nevertheless, extreme levels of Native alcohol consumption have increasingly troubled northwestern communities. Such problems affected Kenora through the seventies and even more recently turned reserves like Osnaburgh into an area of mostly burned and boarded-up buildings housing only those few who chose to remain. Substance abuse still worries many responsible chiefs and band councils as they attempt to plan and implement positive reforms in the social and economic life of their communities.[562] Such abuse is but one of several related results of underemployment, boredom, and underutilized human capacity, most prevalent on reserves that are distant and isolated from centres of economic activity.

This lack of challenge and opportunity in relatively inaccessible communities has to date found no ready solution. Commercial fishing on isolated reserves, with air shipment to Manitoba for cooperative sale, was a popular project in recent decades. It is now in decline. Certainly, recent provincial dictums for the forest industry and mines to hire Native employees when operating in the vicinity of reserves is a very worthwhile move. However, mines become inactive and forest harvesting moves on, while reserves, like resource towns, do not.[563] Stranded communities, like Aroland near Nakina, or those among the now-struggling mines around Central Patricia, are the result. Even the best intentions of Ottawa or band leaders have found no means by which such situations can be resolved in a positive way.

Some bands with more attractive locations have mounted successful campaigns to counteract the causes and symptoms of unhealthy community conditions. They have encouraged on-reserve activity or income generation, as well as organized entry into the job market outside. Two, for example, have taken on the operation of resorts: one a former CPR bungalow complex next to Kenora, the other a new lodge and conference facility near Dryden.[564] At Rocky Bay on Lake Nipigon, another has revamped an old fishing station and now holds substantial commercial licences for that lake.[565] At Garden River near Sault Ste Marie, a large new bingo hall is now a lucrative source of band income. Even in these instances, the weakness in Native preparedness to operate such enterprises, or even to govern totally their own affairs, is the startling lack of education and experience among community members. For the moment, skilled persons to run resorts, to manage small businesses, to handle band finances, or to master the legal intricacies of reserve administration too often must be hired from the local white community.

Frustration and open irritation are also justifiable reactions to the slow progress that seems to have accompanied the legal and monetary correction of territorial wrongs inflicted on Native peoples over past decades. In the northwest, to date at least, claims against government do not appear to be frequent. Appropriate remuneration for a major highway driven across the Garden River Reserve has recently been paid by Ontario.[566] Garden River's historically affiliated band from Batchawana Bay earlier negotiated adjacent additional land as a reserve of its own in eastern Sault Ste Marie. This it was allowed as recompense for long-promised territory at Garden River and for the destruction of a former fishery in the St Marys River.[567] Negotiations are now underway at the Lakehead to adjust the boundaries of the old Fort William Reserve and to acknowledge certain Native claims of a century and a half ago. However, Ontario's big trial will probably come when its unilateral resumption of the reserves of the Rainy River District early in the twentieth century is put on the table by the Natives of Treaty 3. Meanwhile, the federal impasse over Pukaskwa Park with the Pic River band remains unresolved.[568] Cases against private industry have yet to surface. A prime candidate is Francis Clergue, founder of the iron and steel industry in Algoma, with his high-handed assembly of land for Michipicoten Harbour, which came to cover some of the Native reserve there. Most encouraging are the current on-going attempts by Ontario Hydro to resolve and make restitution for the destructive impact of its power dams, which flooded large Native acreages and damaged or destroyed sacred sites around such lakes as St Joseph, Seul, and Nipigon.[569] Such attempts may ultimately need to include consideration of the deleterious impact of inter-basin transfers on both Albany River flow and that of the Nipigon and Long Lake/Aguasabon into Lake Superior.

Despite this complex intercultural debate, the achievements in the region are both encouraging and substantial. While the exactness of the statistics is suspect, a regional Native population of 6,000 in 1931 and 12,000 in 1951 has reached about 16,000 with the nineties. This is a healthy reminder of the positive side of Native progress. Since the Second World War, however, numbers in West Algoma and Rainy River inexplicably declined, while bands elsewhere remained roughly constant, save on more northern reserves, which grew substantially. As a result of this growth on northern reserves, an increasing amount of fisheries quota has had to be reserved in major lakes of the Albany drainage, for future domestic Native needs.[570] However, the real escalation of numbers is focused north of the Albany line. Unfortunately, it is within this provincial far north that the disastrous impact on the traditional fur economy of the recent European reaction to the use of the leg-hold trap is also most strongly felt. Nevertheless, links from this more northern area to the northwest region are strong, and focus largely on Sioux Lookout, which hosts a hospital complex, the studios of Wawatay (a Native radio and television service), and the administrative offices of many northerly bands.[571]

More important, simple observation across the northwest during the past decade of field study reveals much about the rate, nature, and scale of material and social progress on most reserves. This has been accelerating since the liberalized funding of development programs began in the early seventies.[572] One cannot but be struck by the increase in overt signs among these people of their new pride in being Native, their growing interest in language and culture, and their blossoming self-assurance. Such pride is translated into community dignity, self-discovery, and assurance, gained from the employment of federal monies on projects towards self-determined, rather than officially imposed, goals. It is reflected in rising levels of participation in band politics and interest in band management, and in the active support of self-generated businesses and other revenue-producing schemes. While lawns and hedges, ornamental trees and flowers have little place in Native society, amenity levels among reserves have risen surprisingly. This is especially true where effective leaders and active councils have come to the fore. In such communities, basic modern services, from water and sewers to fire protection and paved streets, are now much in evidence. So are well-kept schools and recreational facilities, as well as modern band offices and even day-care centres. Few homes lack television or telephone, even when as remote as the Gull Bay Reserve on upper Lake Nipigon. Such places are often unrecognizable in appearance when compared with photos from 1960.

There is undeniably a long way to go before Native needs are reconciled, but the immediate efforts required towards this end must come from within both aboriginal and white societies. In the Native community, only major acceleration in the existing drive for cultural definition and self-discovery will foster broader self-assurance. Only strong gains in education and skill-training will join with that assurance to promote a firm base for self-government. The white community must first learn to discard its inaccurate stereotypes and appreciate Native people for who they are. The white community must act realistically and responsibly to encourage the cultural, economic, and political aspirations of this fundamental element of Canadian society. The authors believe, based on ten years of regional observation and broader Canadian travel, that the white and aboriginal communities of northwestern Ontario are as far as or farther along the track to resolving the problem than are most in the rest of the country.

The Present Region and Its Future

Northwestern Ontario's boisterous post-war expansion was replaced by economic and social uncertainty by the 1980s. The region is currently recovering from nation-wide recession and its white community looks forward to what it hopes will be a brighter but probably more subdued economic future. Meanwhile, long ignored Native complaints rose from gentle murmurs to vociferous demands for recognition and resolution. In the northwest, as elsewhere, federal, provincial, and aboriginal authorities have begun serious efforts to resolve numerous Native land claims and to initiate aboriginal self-government. Much remains to be worked out at official levels, and many problems within the greater Native community and on the individual reserve have yet to be resolved. However, the future for aboriginal people here is certain to be economically improved, more self-directed, and culturally accepted by the surrounding white society.

The forest, mine, and tourist industries, the dominant elements in the regional resource economy before the OPEC-triggered downturn, have since coped remarkably with straitened times. Earlier trends toward year-round harvesting and broadening mechanization have resulted in intensive cost-cutting measures. Pulp and paper plants, which had already grown large and complex on increasing chemical pulp production, have made major capital expenditures to increase efficiency to remain competitive. The new small-log lumbering, which, with rising laminate manufacture, had often become integrated with pulp and paper, has now lost that tie. Despite early problems under free trade and frequently limp housing markets, it has expanded by offering innovative products in new markets. In the industry as a whole, the complete utilization of each tree and all forest species has moved from an espoused goal to a necessary economic reality.

Similar themes of mechanization, economies of scale, and innovations in engineering figured in big iron and base-metal mining projects by the seventies. However, a combination of wavering prices, fluctuating markets, and declining regional ore reserves have severely reduced such mineral activity today. Nevertheless, the industry has enjoyed renewed gold interest, which has resulted in continuing production in older mines and the new Hemlo bonanza.

Summer tourism through a continuing rise of American and Canadian car campers reached its regional zenith, before the effects of rising gasoline prices hit resorts and motel owners in the late seventies. New factors such as changes in modes and season of vacationing also sliced deeply into car camping revenues. While resort use has again climbed, campgrounds now stand underused and have sometimes closed. However, the rise of spring and fall touring among older people and energetic attempts to encourage winter recreational visitors would appear to have promoted new stability, even growth. Future developments in these three major, if now leaner and more efficient, sectors will continue to point the way for the northwest's economy.

In the remaining resource areas of farming and fishing, earlier predictions of trouble had become realities even before the recession had begun. The arrival of the lamprey on Superior and the international program of eradication and revival that followed have resulted in a much-reduced commercial industry there. On inland waters, the future appears equally restricted. Attempts at stock rejuvenation and better marketing systems have had only tepid success. Growing Native domestic needs in northern areas will limit much future increase here of white-held licences.

In agriculture, the widening national gap between post-war farm income and urban wage was soon compounded regionally by declining internal and outside markets as well as by fading winter income from forest employment. Under

ARDA's belated accommodation, however, farmers, some aged or disinterested and others on marginal land, were freed to retire or escape to urban jobs, if not urban residency. A still-shrinking farm community has come more and more to utilize only the best regional acreage, principally behind Thunder Bay and in the Rainy River Valley, where it continues to specialize in dairying, or in part-time beef or urban-oriented cash cropping. While such activity will continue and prove lucrative, its contribution to the regional economy will remain limited, as has been increasingly the case since the Depression and World War II.

The collective impact of these changes and reverses has been strongly felt in the regional urban hierarchy, especially among its senior members. Here early growth had engendered a mushrooming service population, supplemented by European immigrants. This was followed by rising unemployment and out-migration as major businesses and industries cut back or worked their way through bankruptcy and closure or receivership and reorganization. In the interim, government offices continued to be transferred to these centres to broaden their bases while major public-improvement projects provided additional short-term employment. Over this same span of years, the numerous single-industry towns, which long had suffered stress as technology altered both jobs and job numbers, now often feared for the industries themselves. However, time has shown the latter fears to have been unfounded and industrial bases in the larger centres of the northwest to be remarkably resilient and adaptive. Meanwhile, revolutionary improvements in transport and communications had been achieved by the late seventies, linking this 'land between' with the rest of Canada and providing a high level of internal connectivity. Unfortunately, subsequent reductions in air service have cut into this network of interlinkage just as a declining St Lawrence Seaway has reduced regional connection to the world beyond its bounds.

The growing government financial support and encouragement to economic development that has marked the last four decades has brought with it increasing regulation and direction. This has been particularly evident in the region's three major resource-oriented sectors. Particularly in forestry and mining, earlier official requirements for conservation, preservation, and restoration quickly came to include controls to curb air and water pollution. These industries have also seen increasing public demands for sustainability and environmental protection. The public has also pushed successfully for more consideration of its recreational needs under the concept of multiple use of northern Crown lands. This has required very heavy capital outlay by companies in tough economic times on an increasing range of complex anti-pollution controls. Equally important is the growing recognition, acceptance, and conviction of the need for these measures among those who live and work in the region. Increasingly, they too have been brought to recognize that their future in northwestern Ontario will rely heavily on the continuing bounty of the region's resource base and on the broad maintenance of its environmental health.

Notes

Abbreviations

Printed Government Sources

JLAC Journal of the Legislative Assembly of the Province of Canada
SPC Sessional Papers of Canada
SPO Sessional Papers of Ontario
SPPC Sessional Papers of the Province of Canada

After the discontinuation of the SPC and SPO series, reports and other departmental publications are listed by title, ministry, and date.

Repositories

NAC National Archives of Canada
- RG 1 Executive Council, 1764–1867
- RG 5 Provincial and Civil Secretaries' Offices, 1760–1867
- RG 10 Indian Affairs, 1677–1978
- RG 11 Public Works, 1821–1967
- RG 15 Interior, 1821–1961
- RG 23 Fisheries and Oceans, 1883–1980
- RG 33 Royal Commissions, 1873–1981
- RG 39 Forestry, 1874–1974
- RG 45 Geological Survey of Canada, 1842–1956
- RG 76 Immigration Branch, 1865–1988
- MG 24 Nineteenth-Century Pre-Conference Papers
- MG 26 Prime Ministers' Papers, 1867–1950

MG 27	Political Figures, 1867–1950
NMC	National Map Collection
	National Library of Canada

AO Archives of Ontario

RG 1	Crown Lands
RG 11	Immigration
RG 14	Transportation and Communication
RG 16	Agriculture and Food
RG 52	Colonization Roads
MU 831	Dawson Family Papers
MU 1319	Peter Heenan Papers
MU 1468–9	The Irving Papers
Map Collection	
Pamphlet Collection	

AOD	Algoma Ore Division, Wawa
APL	Atikokan Public Library
	Beardmore Public Library
BRL	Brodie Resource Library, Thunder Bay
DPL	Dryden Public Library
	Ear Falls Museum
EFPL	Ear Falls Public Library
EPL	Emo Public Library
	Federal Department of Agriculture Library, Ottawa
FFM	Fort Frances Museum
FFPL	Fort Frances Public Library
GPL	Geraldton Public Library
	Hornepayne Municipal Office
HBC Arch	Hudson's Bay Company Archives (notes gratis John Peters)
	Hymers Museum
	Ignace Public Library
	Keewatin Public Library
KPL	Kenora Public Library
LUA	Lakehead University Archives, Thunder Bay
LUPL	Lakehead University Patterson Library, Thunder Bay
LWM	Lake of the Woods Museum, Kenora
	Longlac Public Library
	Map Collection, Robarts Library, University of Toronto
MPL	Marathon Public Library
	Medicine and Science Library, University of Toronto

MTL	Metro Toronto Library
	Mines Branch Library, Department of Northern Affairs and Mines, Toronto
	Ministry of Natural Resources Library, Maple
	Ministry of Natural Resources Main Library, Toronto
NM	Nipigon Museum (burned 1992)
	Nipigon Public Library
	Ontario Hydro Public Reference Centre, Toronto
PM	Paipoonge Museum
	Queen's University Archives, Kingston
	Rainy River Public Library
	Red Lake Museum
	Red Lake Public Library
RRPL	Red Rock Public Library
	Regional Collection, Weldon Library, University of Western Ontario, London
	Schreiber Public Library
	Serge Sauer Map Library, University of Western Ontario, London
	Terrace Bay Municipal Office
TBPL	Terrace Bay Public Library
TBM	Thunder Bay Museum
SSMM	Sault Ste Marie Museum
SSMPL	Sault Ste Marie Public Library
SLPL	Sioux Lookout Public Library
	University of Guelph Archives
WPL	Wawa Public Library
	White River Municipal Office

1: Climates of Northwestern Change, 1800–1850

1 Astor's role on the upper lakes is presented in Fred Landon, *Lake Huron* (New York: Bobbs-Merrill Company, 1944), 68–9, and in Grace L. Nute, *Lake Superior* (New York: Bobbs-Merrill Company, 1944). The broader role of his American Fur Company is reasonably dealt with in David S. Lavender, *The first in the wilderness* (Garden City, NY: Double Day Ltd., 1964).

2 Harold A. Innis, *The fur trade in Canada*, rev. ed. (Toronto: University of Toronto Press, 1962), 200–7; for an interesting summary of the Pacific and trans-Pacific aspects of this expansion, see Barry M. Gough, 'Canada's adventure in China, 1784–1821,' *Canadian Geographic Journal* 93 (Dec. 1977): 28–37.

3 D. Wayne Moodie, 'The trading post settlement of the Canadian Northwest, 1774–1821,' *Journal of Historical Geography* 13 (1987): 360–3.

4 Douglas Hill, *The opening of the Canadian West* (London: William Heinemann Ltd., 1967), 39–41.
5 Elizabeth Arthur, *The Thunder Bay District, 1821–1892* (Toronto: University of Toronto Press, 1973), xx.
6 E. Voorhis, *Historic forts and trading posts of the French regime and of the English fur trading companies* (Ottawa: Department of the Interior, 1930). For further information see Grace L. Nute, 'Posts of the Minnesota fur trade area, 1660–1855,' *Minnesota History* 11 (1930): 353–85.
7 For the most comprehensive map of such information see 'Posts of the Canadian fur trade' in *The National Atlas of Canada*, 4th ed. (Ottawa: Department of Energy, Mines and Resources, 1975), 79–80.
8 Innis, 154–60. An interesting theoretical treatment of such competitive post locationing is given in Donald B. Freeman and Frances L. Dungey, 'A spatial duopoly: Competition in the western Canadian fur trade, 1770–1830,' *Journal of Historical Geography* 7 (1981): 252–70.
9 Carolyn J. Harrington, 'The influence of location on the development of an Indian community at the Rapids of the St. Marys River.' M.A. dissertation, University of Western Ontario, 1979, 124; Graham A. MacDonald, 'The Saulteur-Ojibway fisheries at Sault Ste. Marie, 1740–1920,' M.A. dissertation, University of Waterloo, Waterloo, 1978, 56–7; Arthur J. Ray, 'Periodic shortages, native welfare and the Hudson's Bay Company, 1670–1930,' in *Interpreting Canada's North*, ed. Kenneth S. Coates and William R. Morrison, 96–7 (Toronto: Copp Clark Pitman Ltd., 1989).
10 Arthur J. Ray, 'Some conservation schemes of the Hudson's Bay Company, 1821–1850: An examination of the problems of resources management in the fur trade,' *Journal of Historical Geography* 1 (1975): 50–1; Ute McEachran, 'The reoganization of the fur trade after the merger of the Hudson's Bay Company and North West Company, 1821–1826.' Discussion Paper no. 39 Department of Geography, York University, Toronto, 1988, 6–10.
11 Nute, *Lake Superior*, 42–5; Innis, 167–9; Gordon Charles Davidson, *The North West Company* (San Francisco: University of California Publications in History, 1918), 18–19.
12 Marjorie Wilkins Campbell, *The North West Company* (Toronto: Macmillan Canada, 1973), 107–12.
13 Davidson, 104–7.
14 Campbell, 112–13.
15 Innis, 228–9; and Campbell, 138 and 160–1.
16 Campbell, 113; Innis, 222; and Landon, 192–9.
17 Harrington, 127–9.
18 Innis, 214–16 and 226–8.

19 Davidson, 212–13; Innis, 221–2; and Nute, *Lake Superior*, 117–19.
20 Campbell, 113–14; and Innis, 222. For an interesting description of this lock, and the discovery of its remains many decades later, see James Cooke Mills, 'The gateway to the inland sea: The Sault Ste. Marie canal and its importance to Canada,' *Canadian Magazine of Politics, Science, Arts and Literature* 38 (1912): 31–2.
21 Innis, 223–5, Campbell, 114, and Davidson, 215–16, all mention this route north from York (Toronto) via Lake Simcoe to Penetanguishene. However, P.J. Robinson in 'Yonge Street and the North West Company,' *Canadian Historical Review* 24 (1943): 253–65, makes it quite clear that the actual use made of it can easily be overemphasized.
22 Graham A. MacDonald, 'Commercial civility and old Sault Ste. Marie,' *Beaver* (Autumn 1981): 19–26 and 52–9.
23 For a solid and interesting account of these events and the ultimate merger of the North West Company and Hudson's Bay Company in March 1821, consult Campbell, 198–280.
24 Innis, 159–60, 219–26, and 289.
25 McEachran, 10 and 41–7.
26 Doug Owram, *Promise of Eden: The Canadian expansionist movement and the idea of the West, 1852–1900* (Toronto: University of Toronto Press, 1980), 29–30; Elizabeth Arthur, 'Beyond Superior: Ontario's new-found land,' in *Patterns of the past*, ed. Roger Hall et al. (Toronto: Dundurn Press, 1988), see especially p. 133; Anna Margaret Wright, 'The westward expansion of Upper Canada, 1841–1867,' M.A. dissertation, Queen's University, 1940, 7.
27 Harrington, 151–2; Arthur, *The Thunder Bay District*, xlii–xliii; and Innis, 288.
28 Arthur, *The Thunder Bay District*, xxxvii.
29 Arthur J. Ray, *Indians in the fur trade ... 1660–1870* (Toronto: University of Toronto Press, 1974), 117–24; and Innis, 274.
30 The most important studies here are by Arthur J. Ray, including his *Indians in the fur trade*, as well as 'Some conservation schemes of the Hudson's Bay Company, 1821–50,' 49–67, and 'Periodic shortages, native welfare, and the Hudson's Bay Company, 1670–1930,' 94–111.
31 John S. Galbraith, 'British American competition in the border fur trade of the 1820s,' *Minnesota History* 36 (1959): 245–6; Alvin C. Gluek, *Minnesota and the manifest destiny of the Canadian Northwest* (Toronto: University of Toronto Press, 1965); 40–3; and Innis, 330.
32 Ray, 'Some conservation schemes,' 49.
33 Arthur, *The Thunder Bay District*, xix–xxiii; and Owram, 10–12.
34 Arthur, *The Thunder Bay District*, xxv–xxvi and xxxiv–xxxv; Graham A. MacDonald, 'The Agawa Outpost, Lake Superior,' *Beaver* (Autumn 1978): 38–43;

and John Weiller, *The Michipicoten Hudson's Bay Company post, 1821–1904*, Research Report no. 3 (Toronto: Ministry of Culture and Recreation, Ontario, Historical Sites Branch, 1973), 3–64.

35 No single work deals with all such routes systematically, although Eric W. Morse, *Fur trade canoe routes of Canada / then and now* (Toronto: University of Toronto Press, 1969) is reasonably informative. More specific information can be found in John A. Alwin, 'The uncelebrated boats of the Albany,' *Beaver* (Spring 1975): 47–53, and Michael J. Shchepanek, 'Trade posts of the Mosse-Michipicoten trade route,' *Canadian Geographic Journal* 82 (1971): 66–9, and scattered references in Innis, as well as BRL, Historical files, Nipigon, no. 1, K.C.A. Dawson, 'A report on the Lake Nipigon fur trade posts,' and TBM, Subject files, A.L.K. Switzer, 'The Long Lac Post'.

36 The route and its crude marine railway are described in the *Northern Miner*, Oct. 11, 1878, and Jan. 9, 1936; for a discussion of earlier conditions on this route see Shirlee A. Smith, 'James Sutherland, inland trader,' *Beaver* (Winter 1975): 18–23.

37 Arthur, *The Thunder Bay District*, xix–xxv and xxxiv–xxxv; and Owram, 10–26.

38 Graham A. MacDonald, 'The ancient fisheries at Sault Ste. Marie,' *Canadian Geographic Journal* 94 (1977): 54–8; and Harrington, 108 and 123.

39 John H. Peters, 'Commercial fishing in Lake Huron, 1800 to 1915,' M.A. dissertation, University of Western Ontario, London 1981, 26–7; Marion M. Davis, 'Stories of St. Helena Island,' *Michigan History Magazine* 10 (1926): 419; Joseph Bayliss and Estellle Bayliss, *Historic St. Joseph Island* (Cedar Rapids, IA: The Torch Press, 1938), 99.

40 Thomas F. Waters, *The Superior north shore* (Minneapolis: University of Minnesota Press, 1987): 174–5; Marion M. Davis, 'Three Islands,' *Michigan History Magazine* 12 (1928): 526; and Lynn L. Halverson, 'The commercial fisheries of the Michigan waters of Lake Superior,' *Michigan History* 39 (1955): 4.

41 For a comprehensive treatment of this trade on the American side, see Grace L. Nute, 'The American Fur Company's fishing enterprises on Lake Superior,' *Mississippi Valley Historical Review* 12 (1926): 483–503.

42 McEachran, 9; MacDonald, 'The Saulteur-Ojibway Fishery at Sault Ste. Marie,' 16; and John Van Oosten, 'Michigan's commercial fisheries of the Great Lakes,' *Michigan History Magazine* 22 (1938): 108.

43 J.L. Goodier, 'The nineteenth-century fisheries of the Hudson's Bay Company trading posts on Lake Superior: A biogeographical study,' *Canadian Geographer*, 28 (1984): 324–46; Otto Fowle, *Sault Ste. Marie and its great waterway* (New York: The Knickerbocker Press, 1925): 382; and Weiler, 35–7.

44 Goodier, 'The nineteenth-century fisheries,' 346–56, offers a very detailed analysis of the stations on the Canadian shore in this period; see also Weiler, 19–20 and 29.

45 Thomas E. McKenney, *Sketches of a tour of the lakes ... in 1823*, Reprint (Minneapolis: Ross and Harness, 1959), 193; MacDonald, 'The Agawa Outpost,' 54–6; and Bayliss and Bayliss, 95–9, who cite Samual P. Jarvis on the tons of maple sugar and hundreds of barrels of fish handled here by a local trader.

46 William L. Bancroft, 'Memoirs of Captain Samuel Ward with a sketch of the early commerce of the upper lakes,' *Michigan Pioneer and Historical Collections*, 21 (1912–13): 336–66; and Davis, 'Stories of St. Helena Island,' 419–22.

47 Lewis Beeson, ed., 'Sault Ste. Marie in the 1850s,' *Michigan History* 39 (1955): 294–95; William H.G. Kingston, *Western wanderings or a pleasure tour through the Canadas* (Montreal: Benjamin Dawson, 1856), 231–33; and Weiler, 27–9.

48 Nute, 'The American Fur Company's fishing enterprises,' 501–3; two contemporary assessments of the fishery here and elsewhere on the lakes can be found in the *Bytown Gazette* (April 24, 1845), citing the *Buffalo Commercial Advertiser*, and the [Toronto] *Examiner* (Jan. 6, 1847), citing the *Rochester Recorder*. Additional information on the companies involved can be found in James L. Carter and Ernest H. Rankin, *The journey of Charles W. Penny in 1840* (Marquette, MI: The John M. Longyear Research Library, 1970), 15 and 71, and Bella Hubbard, *Memorials of half a century in Michigan and the Lakes Region* (New York: The Knickerbocker Press, 1888), 581–2.

49 Kingston, 244–5.

50 Nute, *Lake Superior*, 39; James Douglas, 'The native copper mines of Lake Superior,' *Canadian Naturalist* 7 (1875): 318–36; and MTL, Baldwin Room, Manuscripts and booklets, 'Lakes Superior copper and the Indians,' 77–81.

51 For further details on mineral development on the American shore, see Robert J. Hybels, 'Lake Superior copper fever,' *Michigan History* 34 (1950): 97–119, 224–44, and 309–26. For Native implications consult Elizabeth Neumeyer, 'Michigan Indians battle against removal,' *Michigan History* 55 (1971): 275–88, and R.H. Keller, 'An economic history of Indian treaties in the Great Lakes region,' *American Indian Journal* 4 (2) (1978): 2–20.

52 *The Great Lake Saga* (Chicago: Beer and Company, 1898), 188; for an interesting description, see the *Bytown Gazette* (July 3, 1845) citing the *Albany Journal*.

53 JLAC, 1847, appendix T, 'Report on the affairs of the Indians of Canada,' sec. III, app. 23, Evidence of Mr. Superintendent Anderson to questions of the Commissioners of 1840.

54 Frances M. Heath, *Sault Ste. Marie: City by the Rapids* (Burlington: Windsor Press, 1988), 42.

55 AO, RG 1, A-I-2, vol. 32 (Parke to Keating, Nov. 5, 1844).

56 JLAC, 1844–5, appendix W, 'Report of the Geological Survey of the Canadas, Progress in 1843.'

57 Lew Allen Chase, 'Early copper mines in Michigan,' *Michigan History* 29 (1945): 22–30.

58 H.V. Nelles, *The politics of development: Forests, mines and hydro electric power in Ontario, 1849–1941* (Toronto: Macmillan Canada, 1974), 20.

59 NAC, RG 1, E-1, vol. D (Aug. 4, 1845), 476–7.

60 Dianne Newell, *Technology on the frontier: Mining in old Ontario* (Vancouver: University of British Columbia Press, 1986), 58 and 63.

61 NAC, RG 1, E-1, vol. D (Aug. 10, 1845), 482–3, and (Oct. 16, 1845), 604–5. Indeed, this volume is full of applications for locations and actions by the Executive Council for 1845.

62 NAC, RG 1, E-1, vol. E (July 31, 1846), 583.

63 JLAC, 1847, appendix AAA, 'A return of all papers and documents ... relating to grants ... for mining purposes in Lake Huron and Superior.'

64 NAC, RG 1, E-1, vol. E (Apr. 18, 1846), 332.

65 AO, RG 1, Surveyor Instructions, Book 5 (Papineau to McNaughton, May 13, 1846) and NAC, RG 1, E-1, vol. F (Oct. 7, 1846), 5.

66 JLAC, 1847, appendix C, 'Report of the Geological Survey of the Canadas, Progress in 1846–1847.'

67 These figures were compiled from JLAC, 1847, appendix AAA, 'A return of all papers and documents ... relating to grants ... for mining purposes in Lake Huron and Superior,' in 1851, appendix U, 'A return of all people with licenses for opening and working mines on Lake Huron and Superior' (see also the related map accompanying JLAC, 1852–3, appendix ZZZ), and AO, RG 1, G-I, vol. 2, no. 1 (Dec. 30, 1865).

68 Newell, 64–5.

69 For a good example of this rhetoric, see *Globe*, July 7, 1846.

70 The result of this pressure inside and outside the colonial legislature was JLAC, 1847 appendix AAA, cited above.

71 Calculated from tabular mining information in AO, RG 1, G-1, vol. 2, no. 1, and vol. 7, nos. 2 and 17.

72 George I. Quimby, *Indian life in the Upper Lakes region, 11,000 BC to AD 1800* (Chicago: University of Chicago Press, 1960), 147; for a stimulating contrast, see D. Peter MacLeod, 'The Anishinabeg Point of View: The history of the Great Lakes Region in 1800 in nineteenth-century Mississaugi, Odawa and Ojiwa historiography,' *Canadian Historical Review* 73 (1992): 194–210.

73 Ray, 'Periodic shortages, native welfare, and the Hudson's Bay Company,' 94–6, cites other authors stressing the conservational relationship between the natural pattern of Indian use of their surroundings and the short-term ability of these environs to sustain Native requirements before the rise of the fur trade.

74 Ray, *Indians in the fur trade ... 1660–1870*, 117–24, makes this point for lands north and west of Superior, but his comments also apply to the area east of that lake and north of Huron.

75 Paddy C.S. Reid, *The archaeology of Northwestern Ontario: The prehistoric and fur trade period* (Toronto: Ministry of Culture and Recreation, Ontario, Historical Planning and Research Branch, 1980), 117–24. Place names of today, such as Warroad on the Minnesota shore of the Lake of the Woods and Sioux Lookout, reflect this fractious relationship between the two groups that continued from prehistoric into historic times.

76 AO, RG 1, A-I-4, vol. 34 (Price to Anderson, Nov. 25, 1848) and A-I-1, vol. 173 (Anderson to Price, Dec. 2, 1848).

77 Peters, 26–7; and Harrington, 107–8.

78 MacDonald, 'The Saulteur-Ojibway fishery,' 89–90.

79 Innis, 275.

80 Ray, 'Some conservation schemes of the Hudson's Bay Company,' 54.

81 These agricultural endeavours were frequently mentioned by later visitors like Henry Y. Hind and were a major problem for S.J. Dawson when arranging the lands to be reserved for Indian use here after Treaty 3 in 1873. For good accounts of the role of fish and rice in this area, see Tim E. Holzkamm et al., 'Rainy River sturgeon: An Ojibway resource in the fur trade economy,' *Canadian Geographer* 32 (1988): 194–205, and F. Morgan, 'Wild Rice Harvest,' *Beaver* (Autumn 1960): 24–31.

82 McEachran, 9.

83 Innis, 274, made this point, upon which several later researchers have elaborated. MacDonald, 'The Saulteur-Ojibway fishery,' 133–6, suggests increased reliance with time and the formal maintenance of rabbit-raising habitats, at least about eastern Superior. Certainly in the Rainy River Valley there is evidence of prolonged reliance as late as the seventies in SPO 1879, no. 7, 'Report of the Department of the Interior for 1878, Indian Affairs.' Parallel reliance on fish was also said to be true over several decades for many traders in country where large game was exceedingly scarce (*Toronto Mirror*, Sept. 1, 1848).

84 AO, RG 1, A-I-4, vol. 34 (Price to Anderson, Aug. 7, 1849) and NAC, RG 10, vol. 513 (Campbell to Anderson, Aug. 10, 1949).

85 AO, RG 1, A-I-1, vol. 180 (Anderson to Elgin, Dec. 5, 1849). The authors have in their possession a typescript entitled 'Documentary background to the land claims of the Indians of Lake Superior,' of which one 124-page volume deals in detail with the events here to 1850 and a second, of 140 pages, examines the resulting Robinson Treaty. Both cite a wide range of documents transcribed in full or in part from archival sources in Ottawa and Toronto and together provide a most interesting interpretation of events.

86 Arthur, *The Thunder Bay District*, xlii and xlvii; and Harrington, 151–4.
87 Arthur, *The Thunder Bay District*, xlix.
88 Harrington, 147–53.
89 For more details on such policies and the Manitoulin Establishment, see R. Bleasdale, 'Manitowaning, an experiment in Indian settlement,' *Ontario History* 66 (1974): 147–57, or W.R. Wightman, *Forever on the fringe: Six studies in the development of the Manitoulin Island* (Toronto: University of Toronto Press, 1982), 10–19.
90 NAC, RG 1, E-1, vol. C (Petition of Charles O. Ermatinger to the Executive Council, May 8, 1844), 400, and vol. D (Aug. 22, 1845), 509–10.
91 NAC, RG 1, E-1, vol. G, among the Minutes of the Council for 1848 are copies of letters relating to these matters; one (Arthur to Shingwauk, Sept. 19, 1839) and another (Anderson to this Shingwauk, May 4, 1841).
92 Elizabeth Neumeyer, 275–88.
93 NAC, RG 1, E-1, vol. C (Shingwauk and other Chiefs to the Governor-in-Chief of Upper Canada, Aug. 11, 1843), 182.
94 AO, The Irving Papers, box 26, pkg. 31, no. 4.
95 NAC, RG 10, vol. 513 (Campbell to Anderson, July 31, 1848) and vol. 571 (Ironside to Varden, Sept. 17, 1846). A reasonably cogent summary of these petitions and problems is to be found in SSMM, box A, folder 3, Alan Knight, 'Allan Macdonell and the Point of Pines-Mica Bay Affair,' Ph.D. research paper no. 2, n.p.
96 NAC, RG 10, vol. 534 (Anderson to Campbell, Aug. 20, 1848).
97 A fuller treatment of the complicated events of that fall and next year is to be founding Nancy M. Wightman and W. Robert Wightman, 'The Mica Bay Affair: Conflict on the upper-lakes mining frontier, 1840–1850,' *Ontario History* 83 (1991): see especially 200–5.
98 *The Illustrated London News*, July 28 to Aug. 25, 1849.
99 Arthur, *The Thunder Bay District*, xlvi.

2: New Assessments, New Beginnings, 1850–1890

1 Doug Owram, *Promise of Eden: The Canadian expansionist movement and the idea of the West, 1856–1900* (Toronto: University of Toronto Press, 1980) is the key work drawing these themes together; it finds its basis in a much older paper by Arthur G. Doughty, 'The awakening of Canadian interest in the Northwest,' *Canadian Historical Association Reports* (1928): 5–11.
2 A.R.M. Lower, 'The assault on the Laurentian barrier, 1850–1870,' *Canadian Historical Review* 10 (1929): 294–307, remains the classic interpretation to the colonial approach to the Shield in this period.

3 Douglas McCalla, 'The commercial policies of the Toronto Board of Trade, 1850–1860,' *Canadian Historical Review* 50 (1969): 57–8; and Owram, 45–78.
4 Richard S. Lambert and Paul Pross, *Renewing nature's wealth* (Toronto: Hunter Rose Company, 1967), 104–8.
5 R.L. Jones, *A history of agriculture in Ontario, 1613–1800* (Toronto: University of Toronto Press, 1946), 289–303, and G.T. Glazebrook, *Life in Ontario: A social history* (Toronto: University of Toronto Press, 1968), 146–50.
6 Douglas Hill, *The opening of the Canadian West* (London: William Heinemann, 1967), 61–3.
7 Donald Swainson, 'The Northwest Transportation Company: Personalities and attitudes,' *Transactions of the Historical and Scientific Society of Manitoba*, ser. 3, 26 (1969–70): 59–77.
8 Elizabeth Arthur, *The Thunder Bay District, 1821–1892* (Toronto: University of Toronto Press, 1973), xix–xxxiii.
9 E.E. Rich comments on this outlook in the closing chapters of *The history of the Hudson's Bay Company, 1670–1870*, vol. 2 (London: The Hudson's Bay Company Historical Society, 1959).
10 Arthur, xxv.
11 Simpson offered to assume the task at the outset (see NAC, RG 1, E-1, vol. K, 30 [May 23, 1851]), and the Company continued this service for over two decades (see NAC, RG. 10, vol. 353 [Indian Affairs to H.B. Co., Montreal, Feb. 8, 1870]). Arthur J. Ray, 'Periodic shortages, native welfare and the Hudson's Bay Company, 1670–1930,' in *Interpreting Canada's North*, ed. Kenneth S. Coates and William R. Morrison (Toronto: Copp Clark Pitman, 1989), 103, suggests that the Company's inflated prices, given that payment was in goods, made this an ironic disservice to Native welfare.
12 John S. Galbraith, 'The Hudson's Bay land controversy, 1863–1869,' *Mississippi Valley Historical Review* 36 (1949) 462–3.
13 NAC, RG 1, E-1, vol. C, 221–6 (Dec. 27, 1843).
14 Owram, 29–30 and 41–2.
15 AO, RG 1, Surveyor's Instructions, Book 5 (Bouthelier to Salter, June 25, 1847).
16 AO, RG 1, A-I-1, vol. 9 (Simpson to Crown Lands, Mar. 11, 1851), and NAC, RG 1, E-1, vol. L, 614–16 (Feb. 26, 1856).
17 NAC, RG 5, A-1, 141268-9 (June 19, 1856), and AO, RG 1, A-I-2, vol. 39 (Cauchon to Simpson, Sept. 26, 1856).
18 *Globe*, Dec. 15 and 23, 1856; see also the *Sarnia Observer*, Dec. 18, 1856.
19 *Globe*, June 27, July 23, Aug. 28, and Dec. 1, 1857.
20 AO, RG 1, A-I-2, Vol. 35 (Cauchon to Thompson, Jan. 5, 1857).
21 AO, RG 1, Surveyor's Instructions, Book 7 (Scott to Wilson, Apr. 12, 1873) and RG 1, A-I-3, vol. 8 (Wilson to Scott, Oct. 26, 1873).

22 AO, RG 1, A-II-2, vol. 4 (Pardee memos on H.B. Co. claims, May 4, 1880 and May 18, 1881).
23 Graham A. MacDonald, 'The ancient fisheries at Sault Ste. Marie,' *Canadian Geographic Journal* 94 (1977): 58, and Carolyn Harrington, 'The influence of location on the development of an Indian community at the Rapids of the St. Marys River,' M.A. dissertation, University of Western Ontario, London, 1979, 222.
24 Arthur, xxvi.
25 For some insight into this questionable trade and its policing problems at Nipigon, see NAC, RG 10, vol. 525 (Indian Affairs to Dupont, July 15, 1866), and vol. 333 (Dupont to Indian Affairs, July 19, 1867), and at Michipicoten NAC, RG. 10, vol. 574 (Dupont to McKay, Sept. 10 and Nov. 10, 1866).
26 J. Weiler, *The Michipicoten Hudson's Bay post*, Research Report no. 3 (Toronto: Ministry of Natural Resources, Ontario, Historical Sites Branch, 1976), 19–29.
27 See, for example, the *Huron Signal*, Oct. 6, 1853; the *Owen Sound Comet*, Oct. 14, 1853; and the *Oshawa Vindicator*, Oct. 15, 1853.
28 JLAC, 1852–3, 'Report of the Select Committee on ... the western part of this province above Lake Huron. For a popular version, see the *Leader*, Sept. 27, 1853.
29 AO, RG 1, A-I-1, vol. 73 (Robinson to Bruce, Sept. 24, 1850).
30 AO, RG 1, A-I-1, vol. 19 (Keating Report, Oct. 24, 1853).
31 AO, RG 1, A-I-1, vol. 19 (Bridgeland Report, Nov. 10, 1853).
32 JLAC 1857, 'First Report of the Commissioner of Crown Lands, 1856,' Cauchon citing Sir William Logan, 36–7.
33 As quoted in A. Kirkwood and J.J. Murphy, *The undeveloped lands of northern and western Ontario* (Toronto: Hunter Rose Company, 1878), 85.
34 AO, RG 11, B-I, App. R, Box 12, 2-9-1.
35 AO, RG 1, Surveyor's Instructions, Book 5 (Cauchon to Salter, May 29, 1856).
36 JLAC, 1857, 'First Report of the Commissioner of Crown Lands, 1856,' Cauchon citing Salter's Report in app. R, 262-71.
37 AO, RG 1, A-I-7, Box 8 (Letter Palmer to Talford, Nov. 17, 1856, forwarded to Cauchon, Feb. 2, 1857).
38 *Leader*, June 30, 1857; and *Globe*, July 12, 1857. Indeed the *Leader* had been willing to entertain such ideas as early as June 29, 1856.
39 AO, RG 1, A-I-2, vol. 5 (Vankoughnet to Crown Lands, June 22, 1857).
40 JLAC, 1858, 'Report on the exploration of the country between Lake Superior and the Red River Settlement, 1857, Instructions and Communications.'
41 AO, RG 1, Surveyor's Instructions, Book 5 (July 18 and 22, 1857); and NAC, RG 1, E 1, vol. S, 487–9 (Jan. 30, 1858) and 489–91 (Apr. 8, 1858), and vol. T, 581 (Mar. 10, 1859).

42 Hill, 61.
43 JLAC, 1858 and 1859, 'A Report on the exploration of the country between Lake Superior and the Red River Settlement,' H.Y. Hind and S.J. Dawson, respectively. Excellent maps accompany these reports.
44 *Globe*, Aug. 21, 1857 and Oct. 6, 1858, as well as Gibbard's personal account in the *Barrie Northern Advance*, Oct. 15, 1856.
45 AO, RG 1, Surveyor's Instructions, Book 5 (Russell to Herrick, June 19, 1859).
46 SPPC, 1863, 'The Report of the Commissioner of Crown Lands for 1862' appends Herrick's 'Explorations from Sault Ste Marie to Fort William ... in 1859.' An excellent map illustrating Herrick's journey and major features along its route is to be found in NMC, no. 16776/410 Lake Superior.
47 AO, RG 1, vol. 1940, no. 3978 (Aug. 6, 1866), and RG 1, Surveyor's Instructions, Book 7 (Russell to Salter, Sept. 13; to St. Claire, Sept. 18; and to Forest, Sept. 22, 1866).
48 SPO, 1868, 'The Report of the Commissioner of Crown lands for 1867,' xi–xii.
49 AO, RG 1, Surveyor's Instructions, Book 7 (Richards to Beatty, June 4 and 18, 1870 and Hutchensen to Fleming, June 27, 1870). Such exploratory ventures after Salter were also intended to provide the north with a locational grid within which the future factor of mining locations, timber berths, and agricultural subdivisions could be woven precisely.
50 The most convenient summaries of this environmental information are to be found in 'Professor Bell on the Nipigon Territory,' *The Canadian Naturalist and Quarterly Journal of Science*, n.s. 5 (1870): 118–20, and in Kirkwood and Murphy, 185–7.
51 *Globe*, Oct. 31, 1870.
52 AO, RG 1, Surveyor's Instructions, Book 5 (Papineau to Vidal, Dec. 4, 1845, and Bouthelier to Vidal, Apr. 1, 1846).
53 AO, RG 1, A-I-1, vol. 73 (Higginson to Papineau, Oct. 15, 1845).
54 AO, RG 1, A-I-2, vol. 2 (Crown Lands to Wilson, Sept. 18, 1856); AO, RG 1, A-I-4, vol. 30 (Crown Lands to Wilson, Oct. 8, 20, and 23, 1856); and SSMPL, Algoma District, file no. 1.
55 NAC, RG 1, E-1, vol. T, 396 (Dec. 18, 1858) and the *Globe*, Apr. 25, 1859.
56 AO, RG 1, Surveyor's Instructions, Book 5 (Russell to Salter, May 30, 1860).
57 JLAC, 1858, 'The Report of the Commissioner of Crown Lands for 1857,' as well as Kirkwood and Murphy, 41–3 and 171–3.
58 Such surveys were laid out on behalf of the Indian Branch, and the plans for them appear in AO, RG 1, Surveyor's Instructions, Books 5–7. A reasonable summary inventory is presented in NAC, RG 10, vol. 530 (Davidson to Indian Affairs, Oct. 19, 1870).

59 AO, RG 1, Surveyor's Instructions, Book 5 (Vankoughnet to Herrick, June 6 and July 1, 1859). An excellent map covering these subdivisions and the adjoining territory is to be found in LUPL, Map Collection.
60 Nancy M. Wightman and W. Robert Wightman, 'Agricultural settlement in Northwestern Ontario to 1930,' *Thunder Bay Historical Museum Society Papers and Records* 17 (1989): 48–54.
61 See, for example, Joseph Bayliss and Estelle Bayliss, *Historical St. Joseph Island* (Cedar Rapids: Torch Press, 1938), 38–72, and W.R. Wightman, *Forever on the fringe: Six studies in the development of the Manitoulin Island* (Toronto: University of Toronto Press, 1982), 57–93.
62 *Leader*, June 8, 1859; SPPC, 1861, 'The Report of the Commissioner of Crown Lands for 1860,' app. 38; *Barrie Northern Advance*, May 29, 1861; and AO, RG 1, A-I-4, vol. 32 (Russell to Wilson, Apr. 22, 1865 and May 29, 1866).
63 Arthur, liv. For more specific examples see AO, RG 1, A-I-4, vol. 32 (Russell to McVicar, June 7, 1861 and May 27, 1862).
64 SPO, 1873, 'The Report of the Commissioner of Crown Lands for 1872,' Mining inspection reports, E.B. Borron, Oct. 31, 1872, 55.
65 Kirkwood and Murphy, 174.
66 W.R. Wightman, 'The Canadian steam packet service on the Upper Lakes,' *Inland Seas* 46 (1990): 248–50.
67 NAC, RG 5, A 1, 141216 and 14122607 (May 20, 1848); and Edward H. Capp, *The story of Baw-a-ting, being the annals of Sault Ste. Marie* (Sault Ste Marie: Sault Star Press, 1903), 184.
68 NAC, RG 1, E-1, vol. Q (June 28, 1856), vol. S (Apr. 8, 1858), vol. U (Aug. 23, 1859); and SSMM, Ermatinger Papers, Box 41, file X981.21.1 (Sept. 17, 1857 and Oct. 20, 1858).
69 NAC, RG 1, E-1, vol. V (Nov. 20, 1860).
70 John Disturnell, *A trip through the Lakes of North America* (New York: J. Disturnell, 1863), 96.
71 NAC, RG 1, E-1, Vol. B (May 26, 1843); vol. V (Nov. 20, 1860) and SPPC, 1865, 'A Report on the free port of Sault Ste Marie,' 25–49.
72 Capp, 195.
73 AO, RG 1, A-viii, vol. 36 (Order in Council, June 12, 1859); SPO, 1867, 'The Report of the Commissioner of Crown Lands for 1867,' app. 24, 40; and *Sault Star*, May 19, 1973.
74 Frances Heath, *Sault Ste. Marie: The city by the rapids* (Burlington: Windsor Publications, 1988), 78, and SSMPL, Demographic file.
75 As Jesse Edgar Middleton and Fred Landon make clear in *The Province of Ontario: A history, 1615–1927*, vol. 1 (Toronto: Dominion Publishing Company, 1926), 1016, mid-century information about this community is slim, but at least

general descriptions are available in the *Leader*, June 8, 1859 and the *Globe*, Nov. 25, 1859.

76 *Globe*, Aug. 24, 1861.

77 Ibid., July 11, 1860, and SSMPL, scrapbook 31.

78 The writer has encountered records of this same process on the Manitoulin Island about this time. See Wightman, *Forever on the fringe*, 78–88.

79 Capp, 199; *Sault Star*, Apr. 1, 1937, Dec. 24, 1940, and July 29, 31, 1971; and SSMPL, vertical files, no. 023.

80 A.R.M. Lower, *The North American assault on the Canadian forest* (Toronto: The Ryerson Press, 1938), 141–7. For a larger context, see Lambert and Pross, 125–40.

81 NAC, RG 1, E-1, vol. E, 563–74 (July 24 and 29, 1846).

82 *Huron Signal*, Oct. 6, 1853.

83 JLAC, 1858, 'Report of the Special Commission ... on Indian Affairs in the Canadas,' app. 27.

84 AO, RG 1, A-I-1, vol. 19 (Keating Reports, Oct. 24, 1853).

85 NAC, RG 1, E 1, vol. 10, 270 (July 16, 1855).

86 JLAC, 1857 and 1858, 'The Report of the Commissioner of Crown Lands for 1856 and 1857,' app. P and app. B, respectively.

87 A sale of berths on Huron and Superior was advertised in the provincial press for October 1863 (see *Sarnia Observer*, Aug. 21, 1863), but there seem to be no records that it was ever held.

88 See, for example, NAC, RG 10, vol. 254 (Carney to Crown Lands, Mar. 17 and May 29, 1860).

89 NAC, RG 10, vol. 337 (Fuller to Indians, Jan. 9, 1869); vol. 367 (MacDonald to Indian Affairs, Feb. 26, 1869) and vol. 352 (Jones to Indian Affairs, Sept. 10 and Nov. 22, 1869).

90 NAC, RG 10, vol. 397 (Wilson to Indian Affairs, Apr. 13, 1869), vol. 352 (Harris to Indian Affairs, Sept. 10, 1869), vol. 353 (Harris and Jones to Indian Affairs, Sept. 2, 1870) and vol. 355 (Jones to Indian Affairs, Jan. 12, 1871).

91 NAC, RG 10, vol. 1875, no. 896 (Shortis to Howe, Dec. 28, 1869 and Howe to Shortis, Dec. 29, 1869) and vol. 399 (Cooper to Indian Affairs, Sept. 16, 1870).

92 Graham, A. MacDonald, 'The Saulteur-Ojibway fisheries at Sault Ste. Marie, 1640–1920,' M.A. dissertation, University of Waterloo, Waterloo, 1978, 57–76.

93 JLAC, 1858, 'The Report of the Commissioner of Crown Lands for 1857,' app. V (1).

94 William H.G. Kingston, 'Western wanderings or a pleasure tour in the Canadas (Montreal: Benjamin Dawson, 1856), 232 and 245.

95 A.B. McCullough, *The commercial fisheries of the Canadian Great Lakes* (Ottawa: Environment Canada, Parks Service, 1989), 28; John Goodier, 'Fisher-

men and their trade on the Canadian Great Lakes: One hundred years,' *Inland Seas* 45 (1989): 286–7; and Kingston, 320.

96 JLAC, 1858, 'The Report of the Commissioner of Crown Lands for 1857,' app. V (1).

97 Thomas F. Waters, *The Superior North Shore* (Minneapolis: University of Minnesota Press, 1987), 176–7; John Goodier, 'The nineteenth century fisheries of the Hudson's Bay trading posts on Lake Superior: A biogeographical study,' *Canadian Geographer* 28 (1984): 355–6; and *Globe*, July 3, 1852.

98 McCullough, 20; and Lambert and Pross, 113.

99 AO, RG 1, Surveyor's Instructions, Book 5 (Vankoughnet to Gibbard, June 25, 1859); and Lambert and Pross, 153.

100 SPPC, 1860, 'The Report of the Commissioner of Crown Lands for 1859,' app. 31, 84–91.

101 *Globe*, June 20, 1859.

102 Wightman, 'The Canadian steam packet service,' 250–1. This also applies to further shipping information, which follows.

103 SPPC, 1862, 'The Report of the Commissioner of Crown Lands for 1862,' appended being the report of William Gibbard on the fisheries of Lake Huron and Superior, and *Barrie Northern Advance*, June 3, 1863.

104 SPPC, 1862, 'The Report of the Commissioner of Crown Lands for 1861,' app. 11; SPPC, 1863, 'The Report of the Commissioner of Crown Lands for 1862,' app. 42(b); and Goodier, 'Fishermen and their trade,' 296.

105 MTL, Balwin Room, 'Remarks on the Upper Canadian surveys,' 1863, 74.

106 NAC, RG 10, vol. 524 (Indian Affairs to Mansfield, July 1, 1865).

107 *Globe*, Aug. 24, 1864.

108 SPC, 1970, 'The Report of the Department of Marine and Fisheries for 1869,' app. 10, 70–1.

109 SPC, 1869, 'The Report of the Department of Marine and Fisheries for 1868,' app. 8, 98–9.

110 SPC, 1871, 'The Report of the Department of Marine and Fisheries for 1870,' app. K, 278–9, as well as app. L, 280.

111 AO, RG 1, G-1, vol. 7 (Superior mining licences and patents to 1860).

112 See for example *Globe*, May 5, 1856 and July 19, 1859.

113 JLAC, 1857, 'The Report of the Commissioner of Crown Lands for 1856,' app. S, 271.

114 Nancy M. Wightman and W. Robert Wightman, 'A most promising mining country: Northwestern Ontario, 1845–1900, *Thunder Bay Historical Museum Society Papers and Records* 19 (1991): 38–9.

115 W.G. Miller, 'Mines and Mining,' in *Canada and its provinces*, ed. Adam Shortt and A.G. Doughty (Toronto: Publishers Association of Canada, 1914), 18, 618–20.

116 Middleton and Landon, 505–6.
117 *Globe*, July 20, 1852.
118 *Huron Signal*, Aug. 4, 1853, citing *Lake Superior Journal;* and *Leader*, Sept. 1853.
119 AO, RG 1, A-I-1, vol. 19 (Gros Cap Surrender, Apr. 10, 1855).
120 NAC, RG 10, vol. 226 (Wilson to Indian Affairs, July 8, 1856); vol. 614 (Chesley to Ironside, Sept. 16, 1856 and Palmer to Indian Affairs, Sept. 22, 1856.
121 AO, RG 1, Surveyor's Instructions, Book 5 (Russell to Salter, Oct. 6, 1856).
122 AO, RG 1, Surveyor's Instructions, Book 5 (Russell to Herrick, June 16, 1859) and RG 1, G-1, vol. 7, no. 24 (Superior mining licences and patents to 1860).
123 AO, RG 1, A-I-2, vol. 5 (Vankoughnet to the Executive Council, Mar. 14, 1861).
124 *Barrie Northern Advance*, June 24, 1863.
125 During 1863 and 1864, NAC, RG 10 Letterbooks contain frequent correspondence between mining men or their representatives and the Superintendent General of Indian Affairs about obtaining locations here.
126 *Huron Signal*, Nov. 11 and 22, 1864 citing *Lake Superior Journal*; *Leader*, Oct. 19, 1865; and *Globe*, Oct. 28, 1865.
127 *Globe*, Aug. 17, 1866 and Aug. 29, 1869.
128 *Globe*, Feb. 3, 1866, and NAC, MG 24, I-8, vol. 40, 171–2.
129 H.V. Nelles, *The politics of development: Forests, mines and hydro electric power in Ontario, 1849–1941* (Toronto: Macmillan Canada, 1974), 19–20.
130 Middleton and Landon, 504–7.
131 Peter McKellar, 'Early mining,' *Thunder Bay Historical Society* (1918): 15–17.
132 Government of Ontario, 'A brief history of mining and mineral legislation in Ontario,' in *Ontario mines and minerals: A green paper* (Toronto: Ministry of Northern Development and Mines, 1988), App. B.
133 Nelles, 23–30.
134 SPPC, 1863, 'The Report of the Commissioner of Crown Lands for 1862,' app. 43.
135 AO, RG 1, A-4, vol. 19 (Gibbard's Mining Report, Dec. 1862).
136 NAC, MG 24, I-8, vol. 40, 171–2.
137 *Globe*, Oct. 21, 1865.
138 LUA, MG 5, Flatt Collection, f 9.
139 *Leader*, Oct. 28, 1867; and *Sarnia Observer*, Nov. 15, 1867, citing *Lake Superior Mining Journal.*
140 *Sarnia Record*, Oct. 19, 1868, citing *Ontonagon Miner*.
141 *Nor'Wester*, Jan. 19, 1868; and *Sarnia Observer*, July 31, 1868.
142 SPO, 1870–1, 'The Report of the Commissioner of Crown Lands for 1869,' app. 15, 20–1.
143 *Globe*, July 25, 1868; and *Nor'Wester*, Aug. 18, 1868.
144 *Globe*, Aug. 26, 1869 and May 25, 1870.

145 JLAC, 1858, 'The Report of the special commission to investigate Indian affairs in Canada,' part III, Schemes for the management and support of the Indian Department.

146 For a summary of earlier policies, see Wightman, *Forever on the fringe*, 10–12. Later developments are treated in the early chapters of James Douglas Leighton, 'The development of a federal Indian policy in Canada, 1840–1890,' Ph.D. dissertation, University of Toronto, Toronto, 1975.

147 See NAC, RG 10, vol. 515 (Bruce to Robinson, Apr. 26, and May 29, 1852) with reference to the British stance on presents for the Lake Superior Indians.

148 MacDonald, 'The Saulteur-Ojibway fishery,' 79–80; and Harrington, 169–70 and 212.

149 Arthur, xlvi; and R.H. Keller, 'An economic history of the Indian treaties of the Great Lakes region,' *American Indian Journal*, 4 (1978): 2–20.

150 NAC, RG 10, vol. 518 (Pennefather to Crown Lands, Oct. 7 and 30, 1857).

151 AO, RG 1, A-I-4, vol. 34 (Rolph to Prince, Mar. 19, 1852), A-I-1, vol. 19 (Bridgeland to Crown Lands, Aug. 18, 1853 and Keating to Crown Lands, Oct. 14, 1853); and NAC, RG 10, vol. 515 (Bruce to Robinson, May 29, 1852).

152 AO, RG 1, Surveyor's Instructions, Book 5 (Russell to Bridgeland, Sept. 1, 1853).

153 AO, RG 1, A-I-1, vol. 19 (Keating to Crown Lands, Oct. 14, 1853) and vol. 206 (Crown Lands to Keating, Oct. 22, 1853).

154 AO, MU 831, no. 42 (Dawson to Pennefather, July 24, 1860) as well as NAC, RG 10, vol. 520 (Pennefather to the Civil Secretary, July 25, 1860 and Pennefather to the Chiefs, Oct. 29, 1860).

155 AO, RG 1, A-I-1, vol. 73 (Robinson to Bruce, Sept. 24, 1850) and NAC, RG 10, vol. 613 (Bruce to Ironside, July 25, 1851).

156 NAC, RG 10, vol. 621 (Bruce to Ironside, Aug. 7, 1852) and vol. 206 (Keating to Crown Lands, Oct. 22, 1853).

157 JLAC, 1858, 'The Report of the special committee to investigate Indian affairs in Canada' – see all testimony re north shore of Huron and Superior in part II, app. 27 and 28. Note in the introduction to part III of this same document that Britain's cut in Native support is cited as one cause of Indian economic problems here.

158 Government of Canada, *Canadian Indian treaties and surrenders* (Ottawa: King's Printers, 1912), 1, 227–33, as well as NAC, RG 10, vol. 519 (Pennefather to Crown Lands, June 21, 1859), vol. 511 (Chesley to McIntyre, Aug. 10, 1859).

159 NAC, RG 10, vol. 245 (Wilson to the Civil Secretary, Sept. 17, 1858), vol. 252 (Battese to the Civil Secretary, Dec. 10, 1859), vol. 258 (Ironside to the Civil Secretary, Mar. 23, 1861), and vol. 615 (Spragge to Wilson, Nov. 28, 1863).

160 AO, RG 1, Surveyor's Instructions, Book 5 (Vankoughnet to Herrick, June 20 and July 1, 1859).

161 *Leader*, July 30, 1860.

162 *Globe*, Sept. 22, 1859.

163 Morris Zaslow, *The opening of the Canadian north, 1870–1914* (Toronto: McClelland and Stewart, 1971), 15.

164 *Sarnia Observer*, June 16, 1871; *Manitoban*, Sept. 2, 1871; *Globe*, Apr. 29, 1872, and Sept. 2, 1874; and NAC, RG 11, Vol. 658, no. 3823 (Apr. 19 and 26, 1872).

165 *Globe*, Aug. 29, and Sept. 4, 1870.

166 NAC, RG 10, vol. 363 (Pither to Archibald, Apr. 7, 1867); *Globe*, June 27, 1870; and NAC, RG 11, vol. 658, no. 14462, (Dawson to Public Works, Feb. 7, 1871).

167 NAC, RG 11, vol. 267, no. 15780 (Public Works to Dawson, Apr. 25, 1871).

168 *Manitoban*, Aug. 5, 12 and 19, 1871; NAC, RG 11, vol. 3576, 366 (Indian Affairs to Public Works, June 5, 1872); and *Manitoba Liberal*, Aug. 27, 1872.

169 NAC, RG 15, vol. 230, file 543 (Morris to Campbell, Oct. 9, 1873), RG 10, vol. 1918, no. 2790A (Interior to Morris, July 23, 1874); and Canada, *Canadian Indian treaties and surrenders*, 1, 303.

170 The most significant works on this dispute are by Norman L. Nicholson, *The boundaries of Canadian Confederation* (Toronto: Carleton Library Series, 1979) and Morris Zaslow, 'The Ontario Boundary Question,' in *Profiles of a province* (Toronto: Ontario Historical Society, 1967), 107–17.

171 Zaslow, *The opening of the Canadian north*, 149.

172 SPC, 1872, no. 4, 'The Report of the Department of Public Works to June 30 of 1870,' The Pacific Railway survey.

173 SPC, 1872, no. 33, 'The Report of the Department of Public Works since June 30, 1870'; the *Manitoban*, Sept. 2, 1871; and SPC, 1875, no. 7 'The Report of the Department of Public Works for 1874,' The Report on the Pacific Railway explorations to June 30.

174 These three different routes are traced on a contemporary map across northwestern Ontario in NMC, H.2/400, 1874, and the selection of the one via Thunder Bay with the reasons behind its choice are particularly well treated in the *Winnipeg Free Press*, July 7, 1874.

175 *Globe*, Sept. 25, 1865 and Apr. 12, 29, 1873; *Winnipeg Free Press*, Aug. 30, 1875, citing *Rat Portage Northern Star*, Oct. 25, 1879; and *Herald*, July 5, 1890. See also Robert Bell, 'Mineral regions of Lake Superior,' *The Canadian Naturalist Quarterly and Journal of Science* n.s., 7 (1875): 49–51.

176 NAC, RG 15, vol. 234, file 3837 (Dennis to Interior, Nov. 18, 1875).

177 See, for example, *Canada Lumberman,* Apr. 1, 1883; NAC, RG 15, vol. 1218, file 177894 (Bergon to Interior, Sept. 26, 1881); and *Winnipeg Free Press*, June 16, 1882, citing *Rat Portage Progress*.

178 The Nipigon case is well illustrated by a series of ten articles in the *Globe*, July 18 to mid-October 1888, that reminisce about a first visit to that river in 1868. Reference to sport fishing elsewhere appear in John Disturnell, *Lake Superior*

guide (Philadelphia, 1874), 10. Commercial inland references include P.A. Ryan, 'A history of commercial fishing on Lac des Mille Lacs, 1885–1985,' Ministry of Natural Resources, Ontario, Thunder Bay District, 1986, Report no. 1986–2, and BRL, Fisheries History, vertical file no. 19, 'Commercial fishing in the Rainy River District.'

179 Their reports are to be found in the annual summaries of the work of the Geological Survey of Canada and, in the case of E.B. Borron, in the Ontario Sessional Papers for 1881, 1883, and 1884. An excellent summary of this material is to be found in John Peters's historical position paper on northwestern Ontario, done in the 1970s for the Ministry of Culture and Recreation, Ontario, a copy of which the authors have on file.

180 Perhaps the best example of such a stark description is in a series of articles in the *Globe* over the month of September 1880. The alternate tendency to boosterism and bias is equally well exemplified in the same newspaper of November 1, 1870.

181 Nancy M. Wightman and W. Robert Wightman, 'The Mica Bay Affair: Conflict on the upper lakes mining frontier, 1840–1850,' *Ontario History* 83 (1991): 200–1; SSMM, box 3A, folder no. 3; Alan Knight, 'Allan Macdonnell and the Point of Mines/Mica Bay Affair,' Ph.D. research paper no. 2, n.p.

182 Brian S. Osborne and Donald Swainson, *The Sault Ste. Marie Canal: Three centuries of development* (Ottawa: Environment Canada, Parks Branch, 1983), 55–84.

183 Wightman, 'The Canadian steam packet service,' 248–64.

184 *Owen Sound Comet*, Apr. 4, 1862, citing a letter in the *Oshawa Vindicator*. See also Doughty, 'The awakening of Canadian interest in the northwest,' 9–10.

185 *Leader*, Mar. 9, 1864.

186 *Sarnia Observer*, Nov. 15, 1867; *Nor'Wester*, Jan. 19, 1868; and SPC, 1870, no. 2, 'The Report of the Department of Public Works for 1869,' The Lake Superior and Red River Road.

187 SPC, 1871, no. 4, 'The Report of the Department of Public Works for 1870,' The Lake Superior and Red River Road and NAC, RG 11, vol. 652, no. 919274 (Dawson to the Executive Council, Jan. 17, 1870).

188 NAC, RG 11, vol. 652, no. 9835 (Mar. 4), no. 10381 (Apr. 9) and no. 10880 (Apr. 19, 1870); *Barrie Northern Advance*, Feb. 17 and Apr. 21, 1870; *Owen Sound Advertiser*, Mar. 24, and Apr. 17, 1870.

189 *Globe*, June 9, 1870.

190 Jack Manore, 'Mr. Dawson's Road,' *Beaver* (March 1991): 6–11.

191 *Globe*, July 15, 18, Aug. 15, Sept. 8, 10, 19, 28 and Oct. 4, 1870.

192 *Globe*, Sept. 15 and Oct. 1, 1870.

193 Capping the detailed records and reports of the Department of Public Works in both the National Archives and Sessional Papers of Canada, 1870–1878, as well as

the many newspaper columns devoted to the history of the Dawson Road's development, maintenance and use, is a succinct summary description of its maturing state in the *Sentinel*, Sept. 9, 1875.

194 NAC, RG 11, vol. 658, no. 3776 (Public Works to Dawson, Feb. 6 and 8, 1871); *Globe*, Sept. 24, 1872, Aug. 14, 1873, and Aug. 29, 1874; *Manitoban*, Mar. 29, 1873; SPC, 1875, no. 7, 'The Report of the Department of Public Works for 1874,' Northwestern communications; and FFM, Transportation file, no. 1.

195 See pertinent sections of the annual reports of the Department of Public Works for 1875 to 1878 in the Sessional Papers of Canada as well as more detailed commentary in *Winnipeg Free Press*, Mar. 8, 26 and May 28, 1878; *Sentinel*, Apr. 11 and 25, 1878; and *Herald*, Nov. 7, 1888.

196 *Globe*, Oct. 11, 1871, May 3, June 26, Aug. 1, Sept. 24, 1872 and June 5, July 14, 1873; *Manitoban*, June 20, 1874; and *Winnipeg Free Press*, July 13 and 27, 1874.

197 NAC, RG 11, vol. 525, no. 55636 (Grant to Public Works, Dec. 6, 1875) and vol. 526, no. 65244 (Grant to Public Works, Jan. 28, 1877); *Owen Sound Advertiser*, Nov. 3, 1870; *Sarnia Observer*, Mar. 3, 1871, citing *Montreal Witness*; and *Winnipeg Free Press*, July 27, 1874, and June 19, 1875.

198 Charles M. Studness, 'Economic opportunities and the westward migration of Canadians during the late nineteenth century,' *Canadian Journal of Economics and Political Science* 30 (1964): 570–84; and Hill, 145–7.

199 Wightman, 'The Canadian steam packet service,' 225; *Globe*, Mar. 8, May 3, 1876, Apr. 24, 1877, and Oct. 28, 1882; and *Winnipeg Free Press*, Apr. 23, 1877.

200 *Winnipeg Free Press*, Oct. 7, 1874, and May 13, 1878; and *Globe*, June 10, 1875.

201 NAC, RG 11, vol. 525, no. 55636 (Carpenter to Public Works, Feb. 18, 1876) and vol. 697, no. F1-35222 (Public Works to Andrews, May 9, 1876); SPC, 1879, no. 8, 'The Report of the Department of Public Works for 1878,' The Fort Frances Canal; *Winnipeg Free Press*, Apr. 29, 1876, and Oct. 30, 1878; and *Globe*, Mar. 8, 1876.

202 Peter McKellar, 'How Nipigon Bay lost the CPR shipping port on the Great Lakes,' *Thunder Bay Historical Society* (1911–1912): 25–7. See also *The question of the terminus of the branch of the Pacific Railway on the north shore of Lake Superior* (Ottawa: McLean, Rogers and Co., 1874), 1–24; and Robert Crawford, *The answer to the question of the terminus* (Collingwood: The Enterprise Press, 1874), 1–22.

203 *Globe*, Oct. 12, 1880; *Winnipeg Free Press*, Sept. 30, 1881, and Apr. 6, May 4, 1883; *Herald*, June 24, 1882; and *Sentinel*, June 22, 1882.

204 *Sentinel*, Apr. 27, and Oct 11, 1882; *Herald*, Aug. 8, 18, Sept. 26, Nov. 7, 1883, and Jan. 17, 1884.

205 *Algoma News Review*, Feb. 13, 1974.

206 Hill, 202, and *Globe*, Mar. 18, and Apr. 9, 1885. For these events in colourful context and more detail see Pierre Berton, *The last spike: The great railway, 1881–1885* (Toronto: McClelland and Stewart, 1972), 357–79.
207 *Globe*, Oct. 9 and 29, 1885, and *Winnipeg Free Press*, Nov. 2, 1885.
208 *Globe*, Mar. 26, 1887, citing *Algoma Pioneer*; *Sault Michigan Democrat*, May 12, 1887; and *Winnipeg Free Press*, Nov. 15, and 29, 1887.
209 *Winnipeg Free Press*, Aug. 2, 1883; *Sentinel*, Nov. 28, Dec. 5, 1884, Aug. 6, 1886, Jan. 28, Sept. 3, 1887, and Jan. 3, Aug. 11, 1890.
210 It was frequently said of rail construction and timbering gangs that one crew was always coming into camp, another was actually working, and a third was on its way back to civilization. The transience of this population and of those employed in forest and mining industries is obliquely referred to, as is their ethnic diversity, in Elizabeth Arthur, 'Beyond Superior: Ontario's new-found land,' in *Patterns of the past: Interpreting Ontario's history*, ed. Roger Hall et al. (Toronto: Dundurn Press, 1988), 141–2. A more complete picture of the urban implications is presented in Thorald J. Tronrud, 'Frontier social structure: The Canadian Lakehead, 1871 and 1881,' *Ontario History* 79 (1987): 145–65.
211 Nancy M. Wightman and W. Robert Wightman, 'Road and highway development in Northwestern Ontario, 1850 to 1990,' *Canadian Geographer* 36 (1992): 366–80.
212 This point is most effectively made by Elizabeth Arthur in *The Thunder Bay District*, lxxxii.
213 Jones, 289–92.
214 Lambert and Pross, 94–6.
215 Wightman and Wightman, 'Agricultural settlement in Northwestern Ontario,' 50–2.
216 George W. Spragge, 'Colonization roads in Canada West, 1850–1867,' *Ontario History* 49 (1957): 1–17; Keith Parker, 'Colonization roads and commercial policy,' *Ontario History* 67 (1975): 31–8; and Lambert and Pross, 86–91.
217 NAC, RG 10, vol. 371 (Order in Council, Aug. 6, 1866), and Kirkwood and Murphy, 41 and 171.
218 Irma E. Pattison, *An historical chronology of highway legislation in Ontario, 1774–1961* (Toronto: Department of Highways, Ontario, 1964), 60, and Wightman and Wightman, 'Road and highway development,' 366 and 369.
219 A. Margaret Evans, 'The Mowat era,' in *Profiles of a province* (Toronto: Ontario Historical Society, 1967), 308–10, and Jones, 293.
220 Kirkwood and Murphy, and the anonymously authored *North-Western Ontario: Its boundaries, resources and communications* (Toronto: Hunter Rose and Co., 1879).
221 Wightman and Wightman, 'Agricultural settlement,' 48–9.

222 Glazebrook, 148–56.

223 I.G. Davis, 'Agriculture in the northern forest – the case of Northwestern Ontario,' *Lakehead University Review* 1 (1968): 129–53.

224 Wightman and Wightman, 'Agricultural settlement,' 53–4, and 'Road and highway development,' 368–9.

225 *Owen Sound Advertiser*, 20 July 1871; *Farmer's Advocate*, 13 (1878): 62; *Globe*, May 10, 1881; and *Winnipeg Free Press*, June 23, 1883.

226 *Algoma Pioneer*, Dec. 2, 1887; and *Globe*, Apr. 26, 1890.

227 See for example NAC, RG 10, vol. 1975, no. 5721 (Fuller to Howe, Sept. 2, 1870, and Howe to Fuller, Mar. 24, 1871).

228 NAC, RG 10, vol. 389 (Davidson to Simpson, May 10, 1871); SPC, 1874, no. 17, 'The Report of the Department of the Interior for 1873,' Indian Branch; NAC, RG 10, vol. 1916, no. 2704 (Interior to Van Abbott, May 2, 1874); SPO, 1881, no. 4, 'The Report of the Department of Crown Lands for 1880,' Colonization Roads; and AO, RG 52, 1-A, 1882, nos. 1362–4.

229 SSMPL, scrapbook no. 1, 'The settlement of the Goulais Valley'; NAC, RG 10, vol. 2363, no. 73267 (Nov. 20 and Dec. 21, 1886), vol. 2366, no. 73850, pt. 1 (Sept. 26, 1889 and Sept. 16, 1890), which records the history of all limits here to their ultimate incorporation into Licence 61½.

230 Information on free grant townships here was compiled from the annual reports of the Commissioner of Crown Lands in the Sessional Papers of Ontario for the period.

231 Arthur, *The Thunder Bay District*, lxxxii.

232 *Globe*, July 23, 1873; *Sentinel*, Aug. 26, 1875, Sept. 20, 1877, Oct. 2, 1879 and Aug. 27, 1881; and *Herald*, Aug. 1, 1883.

233 AO, RG 52, 1-A, no. 6841 (May 4, 1877), no. 1037 (Aug. 17, 1879) and no. 23 (Nov. 21, 1879) and *Herald*, Feb. 7 and Apr. 11, 1883.

234 AO, RG 14, B-10-5, no. 76 for 1879; SPO, 1880, no. 4, 'The Report of the Commissioner of Crown Lands for 1879,' Colonization Roads.

235 AO, RG 1, Surveyor's Instructions, Book no. 7 (Scott to Fornier, Nov. 2, 1872), RG 52, 1-A, no. 1725 (Oct. 1, 1882) and *Sentinel*, Sept. 7, 1882.

236 *Globe*, Nov. 4, 1870; and *Herald*, Feb. 7, 1883.

237 *Sentinel*, July 16, 1880, and Jan. 14, 1881.

238 *Herald*, Jan. 16, 1885, July 30, Oct. 16, 29, 1887, Jan. 8, 1888, and Feb. 2, Apr. 17, 27, May 18, 1889; and *Sentinel*, Jan. 8, Sept. 3, Oct. 21, 1886, Mar. 25, May 13, 1887, and Oct. 10, 1890.

239 *Sentinel*, May 27, 1884 and May 29, 1885; AO, RG 52, 1-A, no. 299-1885 (Dec. 11, 1884); and PM, Mining file, 'The Silver Mountain Road.'

240 *Globe*, Sept. 2, 1875, *Winnipeg Free Press*, June 19, 1875 and Apr. 21, 1886; and NAC, RG 15, vol. 235, file 4652 (Order in Council, June 20, 1867).

241 NAC, RG 15, vol. 235, file 4652 (Order in Council, June 10, 1876); AO, RG 52, 1-A, no. 2557 (Dec. 9, 1890); and Pattison, 108.

242 *Sentinel*, Sept. 1878, citing *Alberton Star*; and *Winnipeg Free Press*, Aug. 13, Sept. 24, 1879, Aug. 11, 1881, Oct. 6, 1883, and Sept. 2, 1884.

243 *Herald*, July 17, 1886: SPO, 1887, no. 18, 'The Report of the Commissioner of Crown Lands for 1886,' Colonization Roads; and AO, RG 52, 1-A, no. 2227 (Oct. 22, 1887), no. 2138 (Nov. 11, 1889), and no. 2557 (Dec. 9, 1890).

244 *Herald*, Aug. 14, 1886; *Globe*, Nov. 13, 1886; and SPO, 1887, no. 18, 'The Report of the Commissioner of Crown Lands for 1886,' Thomas Bolger's survey report.

245 NAC, RG 15, vol. 235, file 4652, (Dennis Memo, May 18, 1876); and *Globe*, Jan. 15, 1887.

246 *Globe*, Aug. 18, 25, 1886 and June 29, 1887; and *Herald*, May 9, 1889.

247 *Globe*, Aug. 20, 1887 and Aug. 3, 1889.

248 Randal E. Rohe, 'The upper Great Lakes lumber era,' *Inland Seas* 40 (1984): 72–3.

249 Lower, *The North American assault on the Canadian forest*, 15–54.

250 W.G. Rector, *Log transport in the Lake State lumber industry, 1840–1914* (Glendale, CA: The Arthur H. Clark Co., 1953), 167–9; Tom Woodside, *A history of the Sault Ste. Marie Forest District*, District Forest History Series, no. 20 (Toronto: Department of Lands and Forests, Ontario, 1965), 105; and Waters, 112.

251 NAC, RG 10, vol. 329 (Cooper to Indian Affairs, May 30, 1871), vol. 531 (Spragge to Wilson, Aug. 25, 1871), vol. 340 (Scott to Indian Affairs, Oct. 3, 1871), vol. 355 (Jones to Indian Affairs, Jan. 12, 1871), vol. 335 (Davidson to Indian Affairs, June 21, 1871), and vol. 2019, no. 8287 (Interior to Van Abbott, June 19, 1877).

252 NAC, RG 10, vol. 2366, no. 73850 pt. 1, numerous related correspondence on the issue from Nov. 22, 1878 to Sept. 16, 1890.

253 Lambert and Pross, 157–61, covers the background to Ontario's early forest fire protection and contentions that miners and prospectors were major culprits in such timber losses. Other contributors in the northwest are frequently mentioned in the press, as for example *Barrie Northern Advance*, June 2, 1870; *Sarnia Observer*, July 21, 1871; *Globe*, Oct. 9, 1872, June 26, 1875, Aug. 12, 1878, Sept. 3–29, 1880, and June 17, 1883; and *Herald*, June 15, 1889.

254 NAC, RG 10, vol. 358 (Lees to Indian Affairs, Dec. 6, 1871 and Feb. 28, 1872) and vol. 2115, no. 21900 pt. 1 (Oliver to Howe, Mar. 21, 1872 and McDonald to Howe, Dec. 7, 1872); and TBM, Subject files, William Scott, 'Lumbering in the Thunder Bay District.'

255 NAC, RG 1, E-7, vol. Z (Orders in Council, June 9, 1872, May 23, 1873, and Oct. 10, 1876.

256 LUPL, J.P. Bertrand, 'Timber wolves' (unpaginated typescript), Port Arthur, 1960.

257 NAC, RG 39, vol. 417 (Order in Council, Nov. 1, 1881); Zaslow, 'The Ontario boundary question,' 111; and NAC, RG 1, E-7, vol. Z (Order in Council, Nov. 15, 1882).

258 A.A. Anderson, 'The development of the harbours of Port Arthur and Fort William,' *The Thunder Bay Historical Museum Society Papers and Records* 11 (1983): 42–3; Bertrand, chapter 1; and *Herald*, Aug. 20, Sept. 16, 1882, Jan. 10, 1885, and Apr. 21, 1888.

259 *Herald*, June 16, 1881 and Apr. 15, May 16, Aug. 26, Sept. 2, 1882.

260 *Herald*, Oct. 25, 1882; and *Globe*, June 23 and Aug. 26, 1882.

261 *Herald*, Aug. 26, Sept. 16, Nov. 29, 1882 and May 30, June 6, Nov. 14, 1883; and *Winnipeg Free Press*, June 14, 1883.

262 *Herald*, Dec. 18, 1886.

263 *Herald*, Jan. 3, 1883.

264 NAC, RG 1, E-7, vol. Z (Order in Council, Nov. 15, 1882); NAC, RG 10, vol. 2115, no. 219000 pt. 1 (Farigana to Indian Affairs, Oct. 11, 1882); *Herald*, Mar. 14, 21, June 6 and Dec. 27, 1883; and *Sentinel*, July 7, 1883.

265 Bertrand, chapter 1; *Herald*, Oct. 17, 1882, Mar. 6, 1884, and Oct. 12, 1887; *Sentinel*, May 28, June 4, 1886, and Oct. 28, 1887; *Fort William Echo*, Aug. 14, 1886; *Winnipeg Free Press*, June 4, 1887; NAC, RG 39, vol. 417 (Memo, Dec. 17, 1887); and TBM, The Horne Diaries, A4/5/1 977.45.37, (Winter, 1888–9).

266 NAC, RG 15, vol. 229, file 590 (Ginty to Dennis, Mar. 29 and Dennis to Ginty, Apr. 13, 1872) as well as vol. 231, file 55 (Macauley to Interior, Jan. 2, 1874).

267 NAC, RG 15, vol. 232, file 2857 (Macauley to Interior, Feb. 21, 1875, Dennis to Interior, Mar. 5, 1875), vol. 234, file 3837 (Macauley-Fuller Dispute, July 6, to Nov. 18, 1875) and file 3240 (Dennis to Miles, Aug. 31, 1875).

268 NAC, RG 15, vol. 234, file 3837 (Dennis to Interior, Nov. 18, 1875) and vol. 235, file 5229 (Memo, Nov. 30, 1875 and Order in Council, Apr. 14, 1876).

269 Allan Shaw, *The days between 1876–1926* (Kenora: Spoke Press, 1973), 1; LWM, verticle files, Lumbering/Ontario-Minnesota Pulp and Paper Co.; SPC, no. 23, 1882, 'The Report of the Department of the Interior for 1881,' Dominion Lands Branch; and *Winnipeg Free Press*, Oct. 1, 1879 and July 14, 1881.

270 *Winnipeg Free Press*, July 2, 1881; and *Globe*, June 23, 1882.

271 SPC, no. 18, 1881, 'The Report of the Department of the Interior for 1880,' Dominion Lands Branch for 1879; NAC, RG 15, vol. 1222 (McArthur to Interior, Dec. 7, 1883); LUA, Flatt Collection, MU 5, file 224 (State to Mark, May 13, 1884); L. Suomi, *Dryden District forest history, 1882–1940*, District Forest History Series, no. 12 (Toronto: Department of Lands and Forests, Ontario, 1960); and *Sentinel*, Aug. 4, 1883.

272 For information on the scale of over-cutting by railway contractors west of the Great Lakes divide, see LWM, W.D. Lyon Letterbooks (Lyon to Mowat, Feb. 23,

Nov. 11, 1881, Apr. 15, 1882, and Mar. 6, 1883); and NAC, RG 15, file 1943, which amounts to a full volume of forest abuses here for the period, 1880–4.

273 *Canada Lumberman*, May 15, 1883; *Herald*, Mar. 14 and Apr. 11, 1883.

274 NAC, RG 15, vol. 122, file 212933 (Manning, McDonald and McLearer to Interior, July 4, 5, 1883 and May 4, 1884).

275 *Winnipeg Free Press*, May 7, 1883 and Feb. 12, 1884; *Globe*, July 16, 1885.

276 Gertrude Horan, *A history of Rat Portage, Kenora, 1879–1905* (Kenora, 1954); LWM, verticle files, no. 23, Pioneers; and *Sentinel*, May 15, 1885.

277 *Herald*, June 30, 1888. This was but one of the seasonal problems with fluctuating levels on Rainy Lake and Rainy River; stranded logs in low water years (*Herald*, June 22, 1889) and burst bag booms during spring freshets (*Winnipeg Free Press*, June 20, 1890) were two others.

278 NAC, RG 10, vol. 3800, no. 48542 (McQueen to Fisheries, June 28, 1890); *Winnipeg Free Press*, Nov. 22, 1888; and *Herald*, Feb. 8, 1890.

279 The legal or illegal procurement of pine from the American side in this area was first noted in the *Winnipeg Free Press*, Nov. 27, 1880. The first claim of illegality by Americans appeared in the *Canada Lumberman*, July 1, 1882, citing *St. Paul Pioneer*. However, the evidence suggested that much of this questionable cutting was being done by U.S. proprietors who were forwarding their harvest to Rat Portage mills and shipping it over the CPR (*Winnipeg Free Press*, Feb. 12, 1884 and *Sentinel*, Jan. 16, 1891). However, by the end of the period, with the Minnesota border country still unsettled here, theft and questionable American cutting probably did mean, as the Minnesota Timber Expedition claimed, that four of five logs shipped down the Rainy River came from the U.S. side (*Winnipeg Free Press*, Oct. 1, 1890 and Feb. 6, 1891).

280 *Winnipeg Free Press*, Feb. 12, 1884; and *Herald*, June 8, 1886.

281 *Globe*, Aug. 21 and 25, 1883; *Winnipeg Free Press*, Feb. 12, 1884 and June 23, 1886; *Herald*, July 31, 1886.

282 *Winnipeg Free Press*, Oct. 27, 1886, June 9, 1887, Nov. 22, 1888, Apr. 26, 1889 and Apr. 22, 1890.

283 NAC, RG 39, vol. 417 (Order in Council, Nov. 11, 1881); *Canada Lumberman*, Apr. 1, 1882; and *Winnipeg Free Press*, Mar. 16, 1882.

284 The records of the Dominion Lands Branch of the Department of the Interior (NAC, RG 15) between late 1881 and 1884 are filled with requests for such licences and their confirmations.

285 For an interesting re-examination of this precedential case and the underlying legal arguments, see Anthony Hall, 'The St. Catharines Milling and Lumber Company versus the Queen,' in *Aboriginal resource use in Canada*, ed. Kerry Abel and Jean Friesen (Winnipeg: University of Manitoba Press, 1991), 268–86.

286 NAC, RG 15, vol. 1182, file 10955 (Coleman to Interior, June 10, and Oct. 9, 1884) and vol. 1222, file 212933 (Hall to McDonald, Oct. 29, 1884); *Herald*, Aug. 1, 1883, Aug. 3, Sept. 5, 1885, and May 28, 1887.

287 TBM, K. Dennis Collection, Timbering Section; and *Globe*, June 28, July 16, and Oct. 20, 1990.

288 *Winnipeg Free Press*, Aug. 26 and Sept. 15, 1890.

289 *Globe*, Oct. 2, 1890.

290 AO, RG 1, Surveyor's Instructions, Book 16 (White to Gillon, Jan. 1891).

291 Of the numerous works on this spectacular mine the most recent are Elinor Barr, *Silver Islet: Striking it rich in Lake Superior* (Toronto: Natural Heritage/Natural History, 1988), and Dianne Newell, *Technology on the frontier: Mining in Old Ontario* (Vancouver: University of British Columbia Press, 1986), 77–89.

292 Wightman and Wightman, 'A most promising mining country,' 40–5; and Keith Dennis, 'Oliver Dounais ... the Silver King,' *Thunder Bay Historical Museum Society Papers and Records* 2 (1974): 12–21. For transport references here, see NAC, RG 52, 1-A, no. 299 (Conmee to Laird, Dec. 11, 1884); *Herald*, July 31, 1886; and *Sentinel*, Aug. 11, 1890.

293 NAC, RG 15, vol. 227, file 722 and vol. 228, file 731 list all these locations, giving the holders, their surveyor, the date of claim and registration, 1870–1. See also *Globe*, Oct. 20, 1871, and Apr. 29, 1872.

294 *Globe*, Aug. 25, 28, 1875 and Apr. 18, 1876.

295 *Herald*, Jan. 3, 1883; *Winnipeg Free Press*, Apr. 6, 1883; *Globe*, May 4, 1883, and Aug. 27, 1887; and *Sentinel*, May 26, July 7, 1883, and June 13, 1884.

296 *Globe*, Apr. 29, 1873, Apr. 18, 1876, May 7, 1877, and Aug. 27, 1887; and *Herald*, July 5, 1890.

297 *Globe*, July 7, 1871, Mar. 4, 1873, and Apr. 19, 1876; and *Herald*, Nov. 8, 1890.

298 *Herald*, June 10 and 17, 1882; and *Sentinel*, Aug. 8, 1884, and June 4, 1886.

299 *Globe*, Aug. 4, 1881; and TBL, Local History files, 'The Zenith-Prospect Mine.'

300 Peter McKellar, 'The Otter Head tin swindle,' *Thunder Bay Historical Society* (1912–1913): 11–13; and *Huron Signal*, Apr. 13, 1872, citing a letter to *Chatham Planet*.

301 *Sentinel*, Jan. 6, 1882.

302 Ibid., Jan. 29, 1887; *Globe*, Sept. 8, 1888; and *Winnipeg Free Press*, July 2, 1888.

303 SPO, 1891, no. 68, 'The Report of the Mining Inspector for 1890,' Iron in Northwest Ontario; *Herald*, Mar. 22, June 28, and Aug. 18, 1890; and *Winnipeg Free Press*, Aug. 30, 1890.

304 *Globe*, May 10, 1881.

305 For full documentation of these developments, see Wightman and Wightman, 'A most promising mining country,' 43.

306 *Globe*, Sept. 28, 1865; and *Sarnia Observer*, Apr. 29, 1870.

307 *Winnipeg Free Press*, Oct. 22, 1883 and Oct. 20, 24, 1879, citing *Rat Portage North Star*.
308 *Winnipeg Free Press*, Mar. 12, June 7, and Aug. 2, 1880.
309 Ibid., Oct. 12, 1880, and *Globe*, Apr. 11, 1881 mark the first of a long series of editorials on these problems through most of the following decade.
310 Ibid., June 16 and July 14, 1882.
311 Ibid., Apr. 13 and Aug. 9, 1882.
312 Ibid., Mar. 10, 19, 1883, Apr. 22, and May 16, 1883, among numerous other articles on sudden progress here.
313 *Globe*, June 30 and Sept. 25, 1883; *Winnipeg Free Press*, May 18, 1883; and 'Mining on the Lake of the Woods,' *Canadian Mining Review* 3 (3) (1885): 6.
314 'Gold mines of the Lake of the Woods,' *Canadian Mining Review* 3 (5) (1885): 7.
315 *Globe*, Sept. 10, 1888.
316 Ibid., Mar. 6, 1890.
317 *Winnipeg Free Press*, July 24, 1889 and July 8, Sept. 15, 1890. See also Wightman and Wightman, 'A most promising mining country,' 44.
318 P.A. Ryan, 1–2.
319 *Winnipeg Free Press*, Dec. 3, 1883; SPC, 1886, no. 11, 'The Report of the Department of Marine and Fisheries for 1885'; and Val Macins, *The fisheries of Lake of the Woods* (Toronto: Sport Fisheries Branch, Ministry of Natural Resources, 1972), 16.
320 Waters, 176–7.
321 Such changes on Superior began in 1870 according to A.H. Lawrie and J.F. Rahrer, 'Lake Superior: A case study of the lake and its fisheries,' Great Lakes Fisheries Commission, Technical Report no. 9 (Ann Arbor, 1973), 31–2. For an interesting general study of these technical improvements and changes in capital organization on the Canadian side of the lakes, see McCullough, 23–50.
322 *Algoma Pioneer*, Sept. 17, 1875, contains a good summary article on the issues and their operation on Superior.
323 Lambert and Pross, 154; McCullough, 83–86 and 100–1; *Globe*, July 25, 1870, Mar. 21, 1879; and *Herald*, Jan. 19, 1883.
324 *Winnipeg Free Press*, Mar. 28, 1882.
325 For a broader review of this matter, see John H. Peters, 'Commercial fishery in Lake Huron 1800 to 1815,' M.A. dissertation, University of Western Ontario, London, 1981, 80–6; Wightman, *Forever on the fringe*, 96–7; and Goodier, 'Fisherman and their trade,' 298–9.
326 *Herald*, Jan. 19, 1888 and Nov. 15, 1890.
327 *Globe*, May 14, 1874.
328 Goodier, 'Fishermen and their trade,' 286; G.M. Grant, *Ocean to Ocean: Sandford Fleming's expedition through Canada in 1872* (Toronto: J. Campbell, 1873), 74; *Collingwood Enterprise*, Apr. 24, 1874; and Lynn W. Halverson, 'The commercial

fisheries of the Michigan waters of Lake Superior,' *Michigan History* 39 (1955): 1–17.

329 *Globe*, Aug. 21, 1875. The situation here was mirrored on the American shore; see June D. Holmquist, 'Commercial fishing on Lake Superior in the 1890s,' *Minnesota History* 34 (1955): 243–9, and M. Kaups, 'North shore commercial fishing, 1849–1870,' *Minnesota History* 59 (1978): 43–58, where such persons of mixed blood gradually were replaced by Scandinavians.

330 Goodier, 'Fishermen and their trade,' 286–7; and *Sentinel*, June 20, 1884. Another 'coaster' on this shore in the '70s may have been the tug *Bertha Endress* up from Sault, Michigan.

331 G.B. Goode, 'The Report of the Commissioner of Fish and Fisheries for 1887, pt. III: The fisheries of Lake Superior' in *The commercial fisheries and fishery industry of the United States* (Washington: 1891), 67–70.

332 Goodier, 'Fishermen and their trade,' 288.

333 *Herald*, May 8, 1886. She was soon joined by the *Gordon Gauthier*, out of Quebec Harbour and the *Telegram* at Michipicoten (*Globe*, Sept. 9, 1887).

334 Goodier, 'Fishermen and their trade,' 296; and *Sentinel*, Nov. 1, 1877.

335 This statement is gleaned from the names of newcomers sometimes given in Goodier but more frequently from a wide range of community history information in local library files or the regional collections of BRL.

336 Goodier, 'Fishermen and their trade,' 296; and *Sentinel*, Nov. 1, 1875.

337 SPC, 1876, no. 5, 'The Report of the Department of Marine and Fishery for 1875,' Fishery Division, app. 16; and SPC, 1879, no. 3, 'The Report of the Department of Marine and Fishery for 1878,' Fishery Division, app. 19.

338 Goodier, 'Fishermen and their trade,' 293–7.

339 *Sentinel*, Dec. 17, 1880. For more details on this rapidly rising company, see *Herald*, May 6, June 6, July 15, and Sept. 10, 1882; and *Sentinel*, Aug. 10, 1882.

340 A.B. McCullough, 28.

341 *Herald*, Oct. 11, 1882; and *Sentinel*, Oct. 13, 1882.

342 Goodier, 'Fishermen and their trade,' 43–4; and *Herald*, Oct. 11, 25, 1882 and Sept. 19, 1883.

343 TBM, vertical files, *Port Arthur Illustrated*, a supplement from the *Manitoba Colonist*, 1889.

344 *British Colonist*, Sept. 12, 1846, June 3, 1848; and *Globe*, July 24, 1857.

345 *Globe*, Aug. 19, 1857, for example.

346 Wightman, 'The Canadian steam packet service,' 254–5.

347 *Globe*, Sept. 27, 1875 and July 15, 1878; and *Sentinel*, June 6, 1884 and June 19, 1885.

348 *Globe*, May 25, 1877 and Aug. 3, 1878; *Sentinel*, Aug. 31, 1880; *Fort William Echo*, May 28, 1886; *Herald*, Mar. 21, 1885 and Sept. 7, 1889; and AO, Pamphlets, 1887, no. 54.

349 SPC, 1874, no. 4, 'The Report of the Department of Marine and Fishery for 1873,' Fishery Division, app. T.
350 *Sentinel*, Aug. 16, 1877; and *Globe*, June 8, 1880. For some of the descriptions of these years, see AO, Pamphlets, 1887, no. 54, which includes a diary of fishing that summer at Camp Alexander on the Nipigon. See also a series of ten articles remembering fishing trips here from 1868 onward in the *Globe*, July 18, 1888.
351 *Sentinel*, Aug. 4, 1883.
352 One example of this unfortunate situation appears in a comparative description of these communities in the *Globe* for June 21, 1881.
353 John Disturnell, *The Lake Superior guide*, 9–10.
354 *Sault News* (Mich.), June 30, 1888.
355 *Globe*, May 24, 1878, citing *Alberton Star*.
356 *Winnipeg Free Press*, Mar. 17, June 29, 1881, and June 19, 1882; NAC, RG 15, vol. 269, file 40437 (Jan. 17, 1882); and LWM, pamphlet 964.19.1.
357 *Winnipeg Free Press*, Aug. 2, 1884.
358 Ibid., July 12, 1889, and Aug. 26, 1890.
359 Ibid., Aug. 20, 1890.
360 *Globe*, Sept. 2, 1874, gives a good description of this town's rapid birth and early personality.
361 *Sentinel*, Apr. 20, and Aug. 3, 1876; *Winnipeg Free Press*, Oct. 5, 1877 and Oct. 30, 1878; and *Globe*, Sept. 20, 1877 and Sept. 9, 1878.
362 *Winnipeg Free Press*, May 23, 1879 and Sept. 26, 1882; *Globe*, Aug. 23, 1879; and *Canada Lumberman*, Oct. 15, 1883.
363 For an interesting view of the history of this town, its valley and its district, and the settlement of the boundary issue, see Elizabeth Arthur, 'Orientation and Disorientation at Rainy River,' *Ontario History* 72 (1981): 195–218.
364 Horan, 20–2; Shaw, 64 and 80; *Globe*, Mar. 19, 1881; and *Winnipeg Free Press*, July 6, and Sept. 26, 1882.
365 *Globe*, June 27, Aug. 2, 1883; and *Winnipeg Free Press*, Aug. 3, 1883.
366 *Globe*, Oct. 17, 1885; *Winnipeg Free Press*, May 8 and July 30, 1886; and Horan, 22–3.
367 AO, Pamphlets, 1883, no. 46, 14 and RG 52, 1-A, no. 1786 (Sept. 20, 1886); and *Winnipeg Free Press*, Nov. 22, 1887, Feb. 10, Dec. 5, 1888, and Apr. 21, July 17, 1890.
368 *Globe*, June 9, 1870 and Aug. 1, 1872.
369 BRL, Local History files, no. 19; *Globe*, June 10, and Aug. 21, 1875; and Joseph M. Mauro, *Thunder Bay: A history of the Golden Gateway of the great north-west* (Thunder Bay: City of Thunder Bay, 1981), 65 and 104.
370 *Herald*, Mar. 27, 1883, May 2, Nov. 29, and Sept. 4, 1884; *Winnipeg Free Press*, July 14, 1883 and Apr. 11, 1884; *Sentinel*, Mar. 7 and Nov. 28, 1884; Mauro, 116–124; and Anderson, 43.

371 Brent F. Scollie, 'The population of Thunder Bay, 1884–1901,' *Thunder Bay Historical Museum Society Papers and Records* 7 (1979): 21–9; *Winnipeg Free Press*, June 6, 1885 and Sept. 27, 1890; AO, Pamphlets, 1889, no. 63; and *Globe*, Mar. 7, 1889.

372 BRL, History files, no. 19; *Globe*, Aug. 1, 1872 and Mar. 4, 1873; and AO, RG 14, B-10-5, no. 76.

373 For an excellent analysis of the situation, the comparative development of these two communities, and the origin of their long-term rivalry, see Elizabeth Arthur, 'The Landing and the Plot,' *Lakehead University Review* 1 (1986): 1–17.

374 BRL, History files, no. 122; *Sentinel*, Sept. 23, 1875; and *Globe*, Aug. 26, 1875.

375 BRL, History files, nos. 19 and 122; *Globe*, Sept. 10, 1877; and Mauro, 65.

376 Harry Sellers, 'The early history of the handling and transportation of grain in the District of Thunder Bay,' *Thunder Bay Historical Society Papers* (1909–10): 21; and J.J. Wells, 'History of Fort William,' *Thunder Bay Historical Society* (1912–1913): 16.

377 Anderson, 46; and A.L. Russell, 'A brief history of Port Arthur harbour,' *Thunder Bay Historical Society* (1915): 22.

378 Sellers, 21–4; Wells, 16–17; Scollie, 23; *Herald*, Apr. 10, Sept. 4, 1884, and Apr. 3, 23, Aug. 21, 1886; and *Sentinel*, May 6, 1887 and Mar. 30, 1888.

379 Excellent insight into both these issues at the Lakehead is to be found in Thorald J. Tronrud's 'Frontier social structure: The Canadian Lakehead, 1871–1881,' *Ontario History* 79 (1987): 145–65, and the early chapters of his *Guardians of progress: Boosters and boosterism in Thunder Bay, 1870–1914* (Thunder Bay: Thunder Bay Historical Museum Society, 1993).

380 Doreen Rice, 'Sault Ste. Marie Ferries,' *Inland Seas* 20 (1964): 115; SSMPL, Local History binder no. 34; AO, RG 1, A-II-2, vol. 4, Oct. 7, 1876; and *Sault Star*, Dec. 19, 1922 and July 29, 31, 1971.

381 *Sault Star*, Aug. 25, 1979.

382 John Abbott, 'Sault Ste. Marie, explorations in the origins and evolution of municipal government,' *Laurentian University Review* 17 (1985): 62; and *Sault Star*, July 12, 1971.

383 *Herald*, Sept. 29, 1888; *Globe*, Mar. 9, 1889; *Toronto World*, July 19, 1889; *Sault Star*, Apr. 17, 1975; and SSMPL, Local History vertical file, Sault Ste Marie.

384 While George F.G. Stanley points out the expedient forces behind treatying in 'The Indian background of Canadian History,' *Canadian Historical Association Reports* (1952), 14–21, R.J. Surtees in 'The development of an Indian policy in Canada,' *Ontario History* 61 (1969): 87–98, has emphasized the strong religious and moral concerns for Native welfare that produced the concept of the reserve, both in this colony and across the British Empire.

385 See Wightman, *Forever on the fringe*, 7–19 and 40–56, as well as Tony Hall's recent study of the impact of the Robinson and Manitoulin treaties on the aborigi-

nal society, 'Native limited identities and newcomer metropolitanism in Upper Canada, 1814–1867' in *Old Ontario: Essays in honour of J.M.S. Careless*, ed. David Keane and Colin Read (Toronto: Dundurn Press, 1990), 148–73.

386 Comparative text of these treaties is available in *Canadian Indian treaties and surrenders*, 1, 147–51, and 303–4.

387 For example, NAC, RG 10, vol. 2124, no. 23641 (Petition, Fort William band to the Governor General, Oct. 11, 1880).

388 NAC, RG 10, vol. 318 (Chiefs to Indian Affairs, Feb. 18, 1871) and vol. 335 (Davidson to Indian Affairs, May 2, 1871 and Indian Affairs to Davidson, June 21, 1871).

389 NAC, RG 10, vol. 2137, no. 27806 (Pic band to Governor General, July 28, 1880) and NMC, H3/440, Survey map, Pic River Reserve, 1885.

390 NAC, RG 10, vol. 2385, no. 79150 (Abbott to Indian Affairs, Aug. 20, 1884).

391 NAC, RG 10, vol. 2926, no. 190939 (McRae to Indian Affairs, Sept. 20, 1887); and SPC, 1888, no. 15, 'The Report of the Department of Indian Affairs for 1887.'

392 NAC, RG 15, vol. 234, file 3240 (Dumas to Miles, Oct. 5, 1875), vol. 3697, no. 15706 (Pither to Vankoughnet, Aug. 15, 1879) and vol. 3713, no. 20694 (Pither to Vankoughnet, no. 20694, May 26, 1880).

393 NAC, RG 10, vol. 1918, no. 27900 (Dawson to Meredith, Oct. 9, 1874), vol. 3697, no. 15700 (Pither to Vankoughnet, Aug. 15, 1879), vol. 3705, no. 18368 (McIntyre to McCall, Jan. 1, 1885), vol. 37722, no. 24230 (Dubois to Indian Affairs, Sept. 24, 1885), vol. 3815, no. 56761 (McIntyre to McCall, Apr. 3, 1889), and vol. 3564, no. 82, pt. 25 (Panton to Indian Affairs, Oct. 3, 1890).

394 NAC, RG 10, vol. 3830, no. 62509, pt. 1 (Order in Council, Oct. 30, 1875) and vol. 3726, no. 25000 (Order in Council, Nov. 25, 1880); and SPC, 1878, no. 10 'The Report of the Department of the Interior for 1877,' Indian Affairs.

395 SPC, 1889, no. 4, 'The Report of the Department of Indian Affairs for 1885'.

396 Indeed, the final bonus on the second licence alone added $12,000 to the appropriate annuity fund (NAC, RG 10, vol. 2115, no. 21900, pt. 1, [Indian Affairs to Donnelly, Jan. 17, 1884)]; with earlier charges and fees, the estimate of $50,000 may be conservative.

397 NAC, RG 10, vol. 1955 (Chiefs to Indian Affairs, Sept. 25, 1874), vol. 2124, no. 23641 (Vankoughnet to Dawson, Apr. 22, 1881) and most correspondence in vol. 2115, no. 21900 (Nov. 12, 1880 to Dec. 16, 1889).

398 NAC, RG 10, vol. 2926, no. 190939 (McRae to Indian Affairs, Sept. 23, 1887). For a more general statement on Native employment here in this decade, see Thomas W. Dunk, 'Indian participation in the industrial economy on the north shore of Lake Superior, 1869 to 1940,' *Thunder Bay Historical Museum Society Papers and Records* 15 (1987): 3–13.

399 NAC, RG 10, vol. 1949, no. 4354 (Pither to Indian Affairs, Jan. 18, Feb. 25, 1875) and RG 39, vol. 417 (Memo, June 25, 1875).

400 *Sentinel*, May 15, 1885.

401 NAC, RG 10, vol. 3802, no. 50265 (Indian Affairs to Vankoughnet, Jan. 21, and Vankoughnet to White, Jan. 25, 1889) and vol. 3800, no. 48542, which deals with this matter of American trespass, 1886–1890, leading up to this Native take-over of the Reid and Co. fishing station.

402 This most complex of several mining cases is laid out in NAC, RG 10, vol. 3696, no. 15410, vol. 3800, nos. 50358, 50361, 50574, vol. 3805, no. 50855, vol. 3799, no. 48507, vol. 3805, no. 51467 and vol. 3895, no. 97971, covering the period Apr. 12, 1881 to Apr. 16, 1889.

403 NAC, RG 10, vol. 3678, no. 11678 (McCall to Interior, Mar. 22, 1879) and vol. 3733, no. 26763 (Pither to Indian Affairs, Sept. 2, 1880); and *Winnipeg Free Press*, June 4, 1881 and Mar. 14, 1883.

404 J. Donald Wilson, 'A note on the Shingwauk Industrial Home for Indians,' *Journal of the Canadian Church History Soc.* 4 (1974): 66–71; NAC, RG 10, vol. 575 (Plummer to Howe, Feb. 2, 1871), vol. 329 (Choné to Howe, May 15, 1871), vol. 531 (Howe to Choné, June 7, 1871), and vol. 2194, no. 39305 (Martin to Governor General, Aug. 15, 1882).

405 *Sentinel*, Aug. 16, 1877; NAC, RG 10, vol. 2129, no. 25339 (Langvin to Ontario, Dec. 18, 1880 and Jan. 3, 1881), vol. 3623, no. 5067 (McPhair to Morris, July 15, 1875) and vol. 3837, no. 7083 (Provencher to Indian Affairs, Sept. 25, 1876).

406 Such grants were modest but probably adequate; $200 to the school and $125 annually for the teacher, see for example NAC, RG 10, vol. 531 (Howe to Choné, June 7, 1871).

407 The yearly reports of Indian agents in RG 10 are full of such information on the acquisition of agricultural implements, etc., and on subsequent Native attention to farming. See NAC, RG 10, vol. 3623, no. 5067 (McPhair to Morris, July 15, 1875), which also includes comments on inadequate instruction in farming.

408 Again, as noted along the Algoma shore of Superior before 1870, the Rainy River Valley population was heavily reliant on rabbits as well as wild rice at this time (see SPC, 1879, no. 7, 'The Report of the Department of the Interior for 1878,' Indian Affairs). The growth of the latter crop in a formal way had spread north in the eighties from its established regional core about the Lake of the Woods to become very important about Lac Seul (NAC, RG 10, vol. 3807, no. 52443 (McCall to Indian Affairs, Oct. 22, 1888).

409 For an interesting treatment of this fish, its use, and devastating destruction in the western part of northwestern Ontario, see Tim E. Holzkamm et al., 'Rainy River

sturgeon: An Ojibway resource in the fur trade economy,' *Canadian Geographer* 32 (1988): 194–205.

410 SPC, 1888, no. 15, 'The Report of the Department of Indian Affairs for 1887.'

411 See, for example, *Winnipeg Free Press*, Mar. 14, 17 and Apr. 2, 1883.

412 NAC, RG 10, vol. 3830, no. 62509, pt. 2 (Hogg to Indian Affairs, Oct. 9, 1893) and the appropriate tables of the *Census of Canada*, 1871 and 1891.

3: Ontario's Emerging Northern Empire, 1890–1930

1 While revisiting the historical themes of old masters like Creighton, Careless, and Lower, this summary introduction reflects the newer works of Owram and Hill and their treatment of western Canadian perception behind national expansion in this period. However, at its core is the more provincially focused attention of new Ontario scholars such as Nelles, Drummond, Gillis, Swainson, and Lambert and Pross, and the fine northern interpretations of Morris Zaslow.

2 Randall White, *Ontario, 1610–1985: A political and economic history* (Toronto: Dundurn Press, 1985), 193–200; and Ian M. Drummond, 'Ontario's industrial revolution, 1867–1914,' in *Progress without planning*, ed. Ian M. Drummond (Toronto: University of Toronto Press, 1987), 103–33.

3 Morris Zaslow, *The opening of the Canadian north, 1870–1914* (Toronto: McClelland & Stewart, 1971), 163.

4 For a reasonable summary of this issue see Nancy M. Wightman and W. Robert Wightman, 'Road and highway development in northwestern Ontario, 1850–1990,' *Canadian Geographer* 36 (1992): 366–7 and 370–1.

5 The *Globe*, Jan. 18, 1912, offers a sound example.

6 The seminal work here remains to be written, but in addition to volumes of local press, references over the period on useful fact and theory appear in Gordon Brock, *The province of northern Ontario* (Cobalt: Highway Book Shop, 1978); John Martelli, 'Regional protest and alienation: The case of northern Ontario,' M.A. dissertation, University of Western Ontario, London, 1993; S.J.R. Noel, *Patrons, clients, brokers: Ontario society and politics, 1791–1896* (Toronto: University of Toronto Press, 1990); Don Scott, 'Northern alienation,' in *The government and politics of Ontario*, ed. D.C. MacDonald (Toronto: Macmillan Canada, 1975), 236–47; G.R. Weller, 'Algoma and Superior: Prospects for political separations in Northern Ontario and Northern Michigan,' a paper presented at the annual meeting of the Western Social Science Association, Denver, 1982; and W.D. Young, *Democracy and discontent* (Toronto: Ryerson Press, 1969).

7 Morris Zaslow, *Reading the rocks: The story of the Geological Survey of Canada, 1842–1972* (Toronto: Macmillan Canada, 1975), 154–5, 228–9, and 238–9.

8 Richard S. Lambert and Paul Pross, *Renewing nature's wealth* (Toronto: Queen's Printer, 1967), 64–5, provides the best graphic depiction of this expanding survey fabric.

9 SPO, 1901, no. 51, 'Report on the survey and exploration of Northern Ontario during 1901'; see particularly the reports of Party 4 to Party 10.

10 Lambert and Pross, 300–1.

11 I.G. Davis, 'Agriculture in the northern forest: The case of Northwestern Ontario,' *Lakehead University Review* 1 (1968): 132–5.

12 *Fort William Journal*, Aug. 22, 1891; *Rat Portage Miner*, July 21, 1905; SPC, 1906, no. 19(a), 'Report of the Royal Commission on Transport for 1905,' 13.

13 This regional topic is well covered in T.D. Regehr, *The Canadian Northern Railway* (Toronto: Macmillan Canada, 1976), 79–110 and 304–18.

14 *Fort William Journal*, Mar. 1, 1893 and June 12, 1897; and FFM, Transport file, no. 2.

15 Development of this line is covered in A.W. Currie, *The Grand Trunk Railway of Canada* (Toronto: University of Toronto Press, 1957), 394–435.

16 *Fort William Journal*, Sept. 6, 1904.

17 By this date, wooden elevators had been replaced by steel tanks, tile silos, tile, and finally concrete units. See Harry Sellers, 'The early history of handling and transport of grain in the district of Thunder Bay,' *Thunder Bay Historical Society, Papers and Records* 2 (1909–10): 21–6. Electrical power and innovative machinery was now common to their operation. See Nancy M. Wightman and Robert W. Wightman, 'The rise of electric power in Northwestern Ontario: Its impact on regional development, 1890–1990,' in *Geographic perspectives on the provincial norths*, ed. Margaret Johnston (Toronto: Copp Clark Longman, 1994), 39. A special company had been mounted to manage grain transfers between the railways, the elevators, and the vessels (*Port Arthur News*, June 11, 1908). The original fleet of carriers, largely of wooden canalers, was increasingly augmented by iron and steel vessels of 20,000 bu. or more capacity (*Port Arthur News*, Sept. 15, 1908).

18 For background, see *Statutes of Canada 1891*, 54–5 Vic. C. 5; *Statutes of Ontario 1891*, 54 Vic. C. 3; SPC, 1900, no. 58, 'Award of the arbitrators ... provinces of Ontario and Quebec'; SPO, 1905, no. 61, 'Return ... re Indian Claims, Treaty No. 3 to 1904,' and 1909, no. 50, 'Claims against Ontario ... re Treaty No. 3 to 1908.' Much additional background exists in the salient divisions of AO, Irving Papers.

19 J.L. Morris, *Indians of Ontario* (Toronto: Department of Lands and Forests, 1943), 53–4. Further details appear in SPO, 1906, no. 77, 'Return ... Treaty No. 9 as of April 1906,' and SPO, 1908, no. 71, 'Return ... Treaty No. 9.'

20 J.L. Morris, 43 and 54–6; SPO, 1929–31, no. 3, 'Report of the Department of Lands and Forests, Ontario, 1928, 1929, 1930'; and SPC, 1929–30, no. 12, 'Report of the Commissioners ... on the adhesions of Treaty No. 9 for the year 1929.'

21 Lambert and Pross, 449; and A.B. McCullough, *The commercial fishery of the Canadian Great Lakes* (Ottawa: Canadian Parks Service, Environment Canada, 1989), 94.

22 SPC, 1893, no. 10c, 'A review of the report of the Dominion Fisheries Commission on the fisheries in the province of Ontario, 1893–1894.' This large document is bound separately but designated a supplement to vol. 7 of the sessional papers for that year.

23 Lambert and Pross, 449–50; and McCullough, 56 and 95.

24 McCullough, 95–6.

25 John Goodier, 'Fishermen and their trade on Canadian Lake Superior: One hundred years,' *Inland Seas* 45 (1989): 284–306; and McCullough, 56–7. General documentary references include *Winnipeg Free Press*, 17 May 1897, and SPC, 1908, no. 22, 'Report of the Minister of Fisheries for 1906.' More specific ones are frequent in NAC, RG 23, as for example vol. 140, no. 471 (Memo, Port Arthur Fish Co., May 17, 1898) and vol. 323, no. 2753 (Prince Memo on Lake Superior fishery, Aug. 17, 1898).

26 McCullough, 57.

27 *Sault News* (Mich.), Jan. 3, 1894; NAC, RG 23, vol. 121, no. 1194 (1894–8); and RG 10, vol. 121, no. 140 (1897–8).

28 Goodier, 291–3; G.A. MacDonald, 'East of Superior: A history of the Lake Superior Provincial Park Region,' Parks Branch, Ministry of Natural Resources, Ontario, Wawa, 1974, 120–8; and Don Steer, *The Montreal River Harbour area: A history and description from oral and printed sources* (Sault Ste Marie: Sault Ste Marie Museum, 1991). See also *Sault News* (Mich.) in which numerous articles on the increasing presence of Ainsworth and Ganley on this shore begin on Jan. 3, 1894. On the issue of fish transport, see *Owen Sound Advertiser*, April 17, 1896; *Sault Star*, May 12, 1904; *Goderich Signal*, Mar. 16, 1905; and *Rail and Marine World* (1906): 167.

29 NAC, RG 23, vol. 371, no. 3244 (Duncan to Minister of Fisheries, Aug. 13, 1911).

30 *Sault Star*, May 4, June 15, July 6, 1905, Sept. 24, 1908, July 14, 1910, and Apr. 4, 1912; NAC, RG 23, vol. 371, no. 3244 (Petition ... Fish and Game Protection Association, Oct. 2, 1908).

31 Goodier, 293–303; MacDonald, 117; James A. Mountain, 'The inhospitable shore: An historical resource study of Neys Provincial Park,' Parks Branch, Ministry of Natural Resources, Ontario, North Central Region, n.d., 72–83; NAC, RG 23, vol. 157, no. 471 (Overseer's correspondence, April to Sept. 1894, Jan. 3, May 5, and Sept. 14, 1896, and Apr. 20 and Sept. 13, 1897); *Fort William Journal*, Aug. 2, 1890; and *Port Arthur News*, Nov. 28, 1907.

32 Goodier, 301; *Port Arthur News*, Nov. 12, 1915 and Nov. 18, 1916; and *Fort William Times Journal*, Dec. 15, 1917.

33 *Fort William Journal*, Apr. 25 and 28, 1894; and NAC, RG 23, vol. 157, no. 471 (Prince Memo, May 17, 1898).
34 NAC, RG 23, vol. 140, no. 239, pt. 3 (Ministry of Fisheries to Cameron, Jan 21, 1897).
35 NAC, RG 23, vol. 157, no. 471 (Craigie to Cameron, Apr. 16 1895); and *Port Elgin Times*, Mar. 8, 1897.
36 Goodier, 293–303; Mountain, various pages, see particularly 73, 79, 83 and 90. NAC, RG 23, vol. 249, no. 1594 (Overseer's correspondence, June 4 and Dec. 5, 1906) supply good evidence on this point, but many more examples of independence on this shore appear here.
37 NAC, RG 23, vol. 157, no. 471 (Jan. 3, 14, May 5, 1896, and Apr. 20, Sept. 13, 1897); and BRL, North West Ontario, file 43.
38 SPO, 1890, no. 17, 'Report of the Minister of Fisheries for 1889,' 1900, no. 11A, 'Report of the Minister of Fisheries for 1899,' 1908, no. 22, 'Report of the Minister of Fisheries for 1906,' and 1911, no. 13, 'Report of the Minister of Fisheries for 1906'; and NAC, RG 23, vol. 392, no. 3691 (Overseer's correspondence, May 13, 1912).
39 The idea of breeding reserves at the Lizards, Pic Island, and the Slates had its origin in SPO, 1892, no. 11A, 'Report of the Minister of Fisheries for 1891.' In the case of the Slates, additional correspondence is to be found in NAC, RG 23, vol. 157, no. 471 (Interior to Fisheries Ministry, June 30, 1895, Patterson to Costigan, Apr. 7, 1896, Slate Memo, Apr. 20, 1896, and Reed to Fisheries Minister, and Macdonnell to Fisheries Minister, July 4, 1896), and vol. 336, no. 2931 (Patterson to the Minister of Fisheries, June 26, 1902 and Jan. 3, 1903).
40 This unfortunate process has been labelled 'the fishing-up sequence' and has been studied in several articles by A. Rigier, who, with K.H. Loftas, first published a description in their 'Effects of fisheries exploitation on salmonid communities in olagotrophic lakes,' *Journal of the Fisheries Board of Canada* 29 (1972), see particularly their diagrammatic presentation on page 961.
41 Lambert and Pross, 457–9; and McCullough, 83–90.
42 Lambert and Pross, 458–9.
43 SPO, 1892, no. 3, 'Report on the lakes and rivers, water and water-powers of the Province of Ontario by E.B. Borron, 1891,' 5.
44 NAC, RG 23, vol. 199, no. 951, pt. 1 (Marks to Minister of Fisheries, Mar. 3, 1894) as well as numerous others that follow in this year and file, and RG 10, vol. 2752, no. 148313 (Fisheries Minister to Indian Affairs, Apr. 10, 1894, Indian Affairs to Fisheries Minister, Apr. 24, 1894, and Donnelly to Indian Affairs, Apr. 18, 1894).
45 SPC, 1902, no. 22, 'Report of the Minister of Fisheries for 1901'; and SPO, 1902, no. 31, 'Report of the Fish and Game Commission for 1901.'

46 SPO, 1892, no. 3, 'Report on the lakes and rivers, waters and water powers of the Province of Ontario by E.B. Borron, 1901,' 1899, no. 27, 'First report of the Game and Fish Commission of Ontario, 1898,' 1903, no. 75, 'Report of the Minister of Public Works for 1902', 1903, no. 31, 'Report of the Fish and Game Commission for 1902,' and 1904, no. 31, 'Report of the Fish and Game Commission for 1903.'

47 SPO, 1892, no. 3, 'Report on the lakes and rivers, waters and water powers of the Province of Ontario by E.B. Borron, 1901.'

48 SPO, 1904, no. 31, 'Report of the Fish and Game Commission for 1903.'

49 *Winnipeg Free Press*, Jan. 17, 1891, Mar. 27, 1894, May 15, June 3, 1895, and Mar. 29, May 17, 1897; *Rat Portage Record*, Aug. 31, 1894; NAC, RG 23, vol. 140, no. 239, pt. 1 (Memo, Nov. 27, 1894) and pt. 3 (Chadwick to Fisheries Ministry, May 13, Sept. 19, 1896, and Apr. 12, 1897).

50 SPC, 1891, no. 8, 'Report of the Minister of Fisheries for 1890.' For general background on this fishery, see John Dobie, 'Commercial fishing on the Lake of the Woods,' *Minnesota History* 35 (1957): 272–7, and Val Macins, *The fisheries of the Lake of the Woods* (Toronto: Sports Fishing Branch, Ministry of Natural Resources, 1972). See also 'Rainy River historical notes,' ed. W.E. Pearson, found in BRL, Northwestern Ontario Fishing, file no. 19.

51 *Winnipeg Free Press*, Jan. 17, 1891 and June 23, 1893; SPC, 1895, no. 10, 'Report of the Minister of Fisheries for 1894'; FFPL, Local History Files, Commercial Fishing; and LWM, Hunting and Fishing file.

52 *Rat Portage Weekly Record*, Feb. 13, Mar. 26, 1892, Mar. 3, 1893, and Sept. 21, 1894; *Winnipeg Free Press*, June 23, 1893 and Jan. 25, 1894.

53 NAC, RG 23, vol. 223, no. 1224 (Fisheries Ministry to Chadwick, Apr. 2, 1894 and Chadwick to Smith, Apr. 30, 1894).

54 NAC, RG 23, vol. 223, no. 1224 (Hayter-Reed to Smith, Nov. 7, 1894, and Chadwick Memo, Nov. 13, 1894). More general comments on the ineffectiveness of such international bodies with reference to commercial fishing can be found in McCullough, 101–3.

55 NAC, RG 23, vol. 123, no. 164, pt. 1 (Order in Council, Mar. 21, 1894) and vol. 140, no. 239, pt. 1 (Colcleigh to Smith, Apr. 4, 1894).

56 Correspondence regarding licences on lakes east along the CPR as far as Ignace, on certain lakes north of it, and an ever-increasing number south of it and east of the Lake of the Woods fills much of NAC, RG 23, vol. 140, no. 139, pts. 1–3 over the next decade. This comparative issue of pound nets is also addressed in no. 239, pt. 2 (Gauthier to Olds, Apr. 1, 1895).

57 *Rat Portage Record*, Dec. 11, 1895, which also finds support for its claims in NAC, RG 23, vol. 140, no. 239, pt. 1 (Memo, Nov. 27, 1894), vol. 223, no. 1224 (Haskins to Smith, Jan. 26, 1895, Rainy River Board of Trade to Costigan,

Jan. 28, 1895, and Chadwick to Smith, May 29 and 30, 1895), and *Winnipeg Free Press*, Mar. 27, 1895.

58 LWM, Local History, Gertrude Horan, *A History of Rat Portage, 1879–1905* (Kenora, 1956); FFPL, Local History, Fisheries file; *Winnipeg Free Press*, June 30, 1896, and May 22, 1899; and SPC, 1900, no. 1A, 'Report of the Minister of Fisheries for 1899,' and 1904, no. 22, 'Report of the Minister of Fisheries for 1902.'

59 Macins, 16–19.

60 *Winnipeg Free Press*, Mar. 16, 1897; and NAC, RG 23, vol. 140, no. 239, pt. 4 (Shepport Memo, June 24, 1898).

61 For further information on such lakes, see NAC, RG 23, vol. 140, no. 239, pts. 1–3 in particular; *Port Arthur News*, Sept. 18, 1908; and P.A. Ryan, 'A history of commercial fishing in Lac des Mille Lacs, 1885–1985,' Ministry of Natural Resources, Thunder Bay District, 1986, 2–7.

62 NAC, RG 23, vol. 157, no. 471 (Overseer to Fisheries Ministry, July 20 and 23, 1894) and vol. 123, no. 164 (Macdonald to Fisheries Ministry, Apr. 19, 1895).

63 See Ryan, 2, for the cycle's expression on Lac des Mille Lacs.

64 NAC, RG 23, vol. 140, no. 239, pt. 3 (Chadwick to Fisheries, Sept. 19, 1906); *History of the Sioux Lookout Forest District*, District History Series, no. 6 (Toronto: Department of Lands and Forests, 1963), 9; and SPO, 1911, no. 13, 'Report of the Game and Fisheries Commission for 1910.'

65 Peter George, 'Ontario's mining industry, 1870–1940,' in *Progress without planning*, ed. Ian Drummond, 52–7 and 63–74; H.V. Nelles, *The politics of development* (Toronto: Macmillan Canada, 1974), 25–30; and Jessie E. Middleton and Fred Landon, *The Province of Ontario*, vol. 1 (Toronto: The Dominion Publishing Co., 1972), 507–9.

66 Nelles, 27–32.

67 For a general overview of events in these years, see Nancy M. Wightman and W. Robert Wightman, 'A most promising mining country: Northwestern Ontario, 1845 to 1900,' *Thunder Bay Historical Museum Society Papers and Records* 19 (1991): 40–50, and Dianne Newell, 'Silver mining in the Thunder Bay District, 1865–85,' ibid., vol. 13 (1985): 39–43. More specific north shore references would include the *Fort William Herald*, July 15, 1890, July 3, 1897, and Apr. 7, July 1, 1899; *Winnipeg Free Press*, May 30, 1892, Dec. 4, 1895, Aug. 24, Nov. 19, 1896, and Apr. 10, 1899; *Globe*, Apr. 23, 1896, and July 6, 17, Oct. 3, 1899; and SPO, 1897, no. 33, 'Report of the Bureau of Mines for 1896.'

68 Wightman and Wightman, 'A most promising mining country,' 43.

69 So lavish are the early Bureau of Mines Reports that they are often factually overwhelming (see, for example, SPO, 1900, no. 5, in which the northwestern

commentary goes on for 130 pages) and limited explicit use of them is made here. Nelles, 30–2; Dianne Newell, *Technology on the Frontier* (Vancouver: University of British Columbia Press, 1986), 86–7; and *Winnipeg Free Press*, Mar. 11 and 14, 1892.

70 *Winnipeg Free Press*, Dec. 28, 1896, and June 4, 1897; *Rat Portage Miner*, Apr. 20, 1900; and LWM, Local Mining, file 3.

71 J.F. Whiteside, 'The Toronto Stock Exchange ... to 1900,' M.A. dissertation, Trent University, Peterborough, 1979, 31–7 and 202–25. For evidence of rising interest in this area, see *Rat Portage Record*, Aug. 17, 1894; *Winnipeg Free Press*, June 13, Nov. 7, 1896, Feb. 9, Apr. 1897, and Jan. 22, 1898; *Fort William Journal*, Nov. 20 and Dec. 18, 1897; *Globe*, Apr. 12 and Sept. 13, 1897.

72 *Winnipeg Free Press*, Dec. 15, 1897, Mar. 2, Apr. 2, 1897, Aug. 18, 1898, and Jan. 21, 1899; *Fort William Journal*, Aug. 11, 1897, June 3, 10, 16, 17 and Sept. 23, 1899; and *Canadian Mining Review* 20 (June 1901): 159–60.

73 Wightman and Wightman, 'A most promising mining country,' 46–8; *Fort William Herald*, May 18, 1893; *Winnipeg Free Press*, Sept. 7, 1897; and *Fort William Times Journal*, Mar. 26, 1901. For some additional indication of the significant rise of interest at Sturgeon Lake, see *Wabigoon Star*, Apr. 3, 1902, and *Port Arthur News*, Dec. 7, 1907, July 25, Sept. 17, 1908, Mar. 3, 1909, and Nov. 13, 1910.

74 Wightman and Wightman, 'A most promising mining country,' 48; *Rat Portage Record*, Jan. 26 and Apr. 6, 1894; *Winnipeg Free Press*, Feb. 15, Mar. 31, May 4, 1894, June 13, 1895, and Apr. 16, 1898; *Globe*, May 26, 1894; and *Fort William Journal*, Dec. 15, 1894.

75 Wightman and Wightman, 'Road and highway development,' 366–80.

76 *Winnipeg Free Press*, Oct. 24, Nov. 3, 1896, and Aug. 5, 11, 1897; *Globe*, May 7 and June 12, 1897; and *Rainy Lake Herald*, Oct. 6, 1898.

77 *Globe*, June 12 and 19, 1897; *Winnipeg Free Press*, Sept. 20, 1897, Feb. 19, Mar. 4, Apr. 16, Sept. 23, Nov. 5, 1898, and May 10, 1899; *Rat Portage Miner*, Nov. 11, 1898, and Feb. 15, 1901; and *Rainy Lake Herald*, Dec. 22, 1898.

78 *Sault News* (Mich.), Aug. 28 and Sept. 6, 18, 1897; Globe, Sept. 8, 9, and 11, 1897; and AO, Pamphlets, 1899, no. 65.

79 *Globe*, Oct. 6, 23, and Nov. 13, 1897; and SPO, 1898, no. 33, 'First report of the Bureau of Mines, 1897.'

80 *Sault News* (Mich.), Apr. 16, May 14, June 18, Oct. 8, 1898, and Sept. 15, 1899; *Globe*, Apr. 24, 1899; and *Sault Star*, Nov. 14, 1901.

81 *Sault Star*, Dec. 4, 1902, Nov. 19, 1903, Mar. 10, 1904, Aug. 22, 1907, and Feb. 27, 1908.

82 As noted in the *Globe*, Oct. 3, 1895, growing interest in the mines of the Rossland area in the nineties had diverted much national and international capital west to

British Columbia. Despite later financial failure among mines there, 1896–8, interest in the spectacularly exciting finds in the Klondike and their continuing focus in the press further detracted from the more modest gold fields of northwestern Ontario (see the *Globe*, June 27, 28, 1897, and May 27, 1898, to support this view).

83 Middleton and Landon, 504–10; and Kris Inwood, 'The iron and steel industry,' in *Progress without planning*, ed. Ian Drummond, 185–204.

84 SPO, 1901, no. 5, 'Report of the Bureau of Mines, 1901'; *Winnipeg Free Press*, June 20, Sept. 12 and 13, 1891; *Fort William Journal*, Oct. 28, Dec. 16, 1891, Nov. 9, 16, 1892, Dec. 9, 1899, and May 27, 1902; *Port Arthur News*, Jan. 14, 1908; and BRL, History Files, Iron Mining, no. 11, Steep Rock Lake.

85 *Sault Star*, Feb. 23, 1905; *Fort William Journal*, Dec. 2 and 9, 1906; *Port Arthur News*, Jan 14, 1908; BRL, History Files, Iron Mining, no. 11, Steep Rock Lake; and Inwood, 205.

86 So many sources are available on this remarkable man and the history of his projects that only a few need mention. On his adventures in iron and steel, Duncan McDowall, *Steel at the Sault ..., 1901–56* (Toronto: University of Toronto Press, 1984), 1–50, is the most thorough work, while Inwood, 185–204, provides the most recent summary. For his railway exploits, see the work of J. Konarek, 'Algoma Central and Hudson Bay Railway: The beginnings,' *Ontario History* 62 (1970): 73–81, and O.S. Nock, *Algoma Central Railway* (London: Adam & Charles Black, 1975). The latter also covers his shipping enterprises. Other facets of his empire are addressed particularly well in Margaret Van Every, 'Francis Hector Clergue and the rise of Sault Ste. Marie as an industrial centre,' *Ontario History* 56 (1964): 191–202.

87 For a popular review of the shift to the northeast, see Philip Smith, *Harvest from the rock: A history of mining in Ontario* (Toronto: Macmillan Canada, 1968), 115–203.

88 One interesting review of the movement and its leading Canadian figures appears in Donald MacKay, *Heritage lost: The crisis in Canada's forests* (Toronto: Macmillan Canada, 1985), 28–57.

89 Lambert and Pross, 181–4, and R. Peter Gillis and Thomas R. Roach, *Lost initiatives: Canada's forest industries, forest policy and forest conservation* (New York: Greenman Press, 1986), 87.

90 Nelles, 204–5; Lambert and Pross, 185–7; and Gillis and Roach, 87–90.

91 MacKay, 45.

92 Gillis and Roach, 90–7; and Lambert and Pross, 255–6. The extent of these reserves as depicted in Map 3.1 is derived from contemporary maps in the Serge Sauer Map Library, University of Western Ontario, and in the National Map Collection, Ottawa.

93 Gillis and Roach, 97; and Lambert and Pross, 186–7.

94 Gillis and Roach, 84–6; and A.R.M. Lower, *The North American assault on the Canadian forest* (Toronto: Ryerson Press, 1938), 188, whose acute summary statement on attitude is paraphrased here.

95 Peter W. Sinclair, 'The North and North-West: Forestry and agriculture,' in *Progress without planning*, ed. Ian Drummond, 78–9; Lambert and Pross, 144; and Gillis and Roach, 83–6.

96 Lower, 186–7.

97 *Winnipeg Free Press*, June 27 and 30, 1891.

98 *Sentinel*, Jan. 16 and 30, 1891, citing *St. Paul Pioneer Press; Rat Portage Record*, July 23, 1892; *Canada Lumberman*, Oct. 15, 1909; *Kenora Miner*, Dec. 15, 1928 (review article); and *Winnipeg Free Press*, May 12, 1886, and Apr. 27, 1891.

99 *Fort William Journal*, Feb. 13, 1895; *Rat Portage Miner*, Aug. 31, 1899; and A.R.M. Lower, 182.

100 LWM, D.C. Cameron file; *Winnipeg Free Press*, Mar. 27 and May 20, 1893; M. Thompson, *Rainy River, our town, our lives* (Rainy River: n.p., 1979): 10; *Kenora Miner*, July 20, 1910, and Nov. 11, 1911; and *Canada Lumberman*, Feb. 1, 1912.

101 Thompson, 15 and 24–31.

102 *Canada Lumberman*, Nov. 1, 1911; *Fort Frances Times*, July 18, 1912; and FFM, Forest Industry file.

103 Unfortunately, while volumes of records in AO, RG 1 are devoted to the dozens of small limits, their rise, shift, and abandonment, days spent in the map collections of the NMC, the AO, as well as both the University of Toronto and University of Western Ontario fail to supply sufficient locational information for effective mapping here or elsewhere across the region.

104 LUPL, Bertrand, 'Timber wolves' (unpaginated typescript), 1960, Logging operations ... 1887–1920; NAC, RG 15, vol. 1221, file 195613 (Doves to Stephenson, Jan. 3, 1890) and vol. 1222, file 210376 (Sparks to McArthur, Aug. 20, 1904); *Rail and Marine World* (1908): 293; *Fort William Journal*, Feb. 23, 1893, Apr. 8, 1896, July 29, 1899, May 17, 1901, and July 29, Aug. 15, 1902; Elinor Barr and Betty Dyck, *Ignace: A saga of the Shield* (Winnipeg: Prairie Publishing Co., 1979), 57–9; and *Canada Lumberman*, Sept. 15, 1920.

105 *Tracks beside the water – Sioux Lookout* (Sioux Lookout: Sioux Lookout Historical Society, 1967), 48.

106 For general information on operations here, see Elinor Barr, 'Lumbering in the Pigeon River watershed,' *Thunder Bay Historical Museum Society, Papers and Records* 4 (1976): 3–9; Bertrand, Logging operations at the international boundary, n.p.; and TBM, Subject Files, 'Lumbering in the Thunder Bay District' (mimeo), Jan. 26, 1934.

107 AO, RG 52, 1-A', no. 236 (Raney to White, Feb. 8 and White to Raney, Feb. 20, 1894), no. 495 (Raney to Hardy, May 1, 1894), no. 2064 (Walters to White, Nov. 27, 1894), and no. 2227 (Ross to White, May 10, 1895); and *Fort William Journal*, Oct. 10, 1894.

108 AO, RG 1, E-7, vol. 2 (Order in Council, May 23, 1895); *Rainy Lake Herald*, Sept. 1, 1898; *Fort William Journal*, Oct. 21, 1899, and Sept. 2, 1902; *Globe*, Aug. 30, 1898; and LUA, Box xvii, no. 81b, Oct. 16, 1899.

109 *Fort William Times Journal*, Sept. 20, 1900, Jan. 9, 1901, and May 22, 1902; *Port Arthur News*, May 14, June 15, 1907, and May 2, 1908; and *Canada Lumberman*, May 15, 1908.

110 See Konarek, 73–81, and Nock, 39–62, for further construction details (the A.C.R. land grant, shown as part of pulpwood limits on Map 3.1, is derived from maps in the latter work, 175–7). AO, RG 1, E-7, vol. 3 (Orders in Council, Apr. 29 and Nov. 22, 1901). Similar Orders of July 20, 1909, and June 30, 1910, extended the right to cut pine here until 1911.

111 *Sault Star*, Jan. 23, July 31, Nov. 2, 1902, Mar. 26, Aug. 6, 1903, and May 26, 1904.

112 *Sault Star*, Apr. 17, July 10, 1902, Mar. 26, Apr. 30, 1903, and Oct. 20, 1904.

113 *Canada Lumberman*, Feb. 1, 1908, and Feb. 1, 1913.

114 *Sault News* (Mich.), Dec. 30, 1893; AO, RG 1, E-7, vol. 2 (Orders in Council, Apr. 20, June 4, 1895, and Nov. 22, 1899), E-3-A, vol. 19 (Crown Lands to Clergue, Sept. 11, 1895), and E-2, vol. 4 (Crown Lands to Simmons, Sept. 1 and 9, 1897).

115 NAC, RG 10, vol. 2931, no. 212013, pt. 1 (Wilson to Stewart, Apr. 20, 1900, Wilson to MacLean, July 21, 1900 and MacLean to Wilson, July 24, 1900 and June 12, 1901); *Globe*, July 16, 1898; and *Sault Star*, Dec. 22, 1904, Apr. 26, 1906, Oct. 8, 1908, Nov. 4, 1912, June 24, 1913, and May 23, 1914.

116 When poplar pulpwood was first shipped from the Sault, a perceptive local editor noted this as 'the commencement of what one day will become an important industry in this sector of the country' in *Algoma Pioneer*, Mar. 5, 1886. For a summary of the related trade problems this editor did not appreciate, see Nelles, 81, as well as Gillis and Roach, 92–9.

117 Sinclair, 81–2; Lambert and Pross, 250; and Nelles, 36–8.

118 AO, RG 1, E-4-B, vol. 4 (F.C. Clergue ... pulpwood agreement, Nov. 21, 1894); and SPO, 1896, no. 44, 'A return ... further details of ... pulpwood agreement' (not printed).

119 Tom Woodside, *A history of the Sault Ste. Marie Forest District*, District History Series, no. 20 (Toronto: Department of Lands and Forests, 1965), 112–3. The ultimate boundaries shown on Map 3.1 are derived from a map printed in the *Fort William Times Journal*, May 18, 1921.

120 Van Every, 194–5; *Sault News* (Mich.), Apr. 27, 1895, and Oct. 7, 1899; SPO, 1901–1903, 'Reports of the Department of Crown Lands for 1900–1902.'

121 SPO, 1904–1906, 'Reports of the Department of Crown Lands for 1903–1905'; and *Sault Star*, Oct. 25, 1907, and May 21, 1908.

122 *Sault Star*, Aug. 9, 1913, as well as review articles, June 22, 1927, Mar. 16, 1937, and particularly July 29, 1971.

123 *Sault News* (Mich.), May 22 and June 18, 1901; and *Sault Star*, Aug. 6, 1903 and Jan. 24, 1907.

124 NAC, RG 23/13, vol. 2, G-5 (Historical tables created for the Royal Commission on Pulpwood, 1923–24).

125 The complex world of Perry Lumber and its relations via Niagara Pulp and Paper to St Maurice Pulp and Paper is a major theme through NAC, RG 10, vol. 2366, no. 73850, pt. 1 and 2, and vol. 2931, no. 212013, pt. 1 around the turn of the century and later. See also *Sault Star*, Sept. 12, 1901, and June 23, 1904; *Globe*, June 17, 1899, and June 16, 1900; and *Canada Lumberman*, Apr. 15, 1908.

126 AO, RG 1, E-7, vol. 2 (Order in Council, 'Calvert and Whalen ... pulpwood agreement,' Apr. 24, 1895); SPO, 1900, no. 80 and revised reissue, 1902, no. 64, 'Nipigon ... pulpwood agreement,' Apr. 18, 1900, and 'Nipigon,' Feb. 4, 1902; and AO, RG 1, E-7, vol. 3 and E-4-B, vol. 2 (Orders in Council, Feb. 9 and 10, 1906), cancelling the former agreement and readvertising under new terms. See also AO, RG 1, E-7, vol. 3 (July 8, 1910) for later developments.

127 *Rat Portage Miner*, Oct. 2, 1897, and Mar. 11, 1898; and SPO, 1903, no. 68, 'Rainy Lake ... pulpwood agreement,' Jan. 6, 1903.

128 AO, RG 1, E-7, vol. 3 and E-4-B, vol. 2 (Orders in Council, Feb. 9 and 10, 1906), cancelling the former agreement and readvertising under new terms (Rainy Lake ... pulpwood agreement, Apr., 1908); and *Port Arthur News*, Sept. 21, 1909.

129 *Rat Portage Miner*, Apr. 15, 1898, and Feb. 3, 1905; *Port Arthur News*, July 30 and Aug. 21, 1908; *Fort Frances Times*, May 2 and 30, 1912; AO, RG 1, E-7, vol. 3 (Fort Frances ... pulpwood agreement, Jan. 10, 1911); and NAC, MG 26, vol. 63 (Ontario-Minnesota Power to Laurier, May 23, 1910), and RG 33/13, vol. 2, G-5 (Historical tables). (Delineation of these limits on Map 3.1 is taken from NMC, no. 51761 and no. 51762.)

130 SPO, 1901, no. 76, 'Lake of the Woods ... pulpwood agreement, Apr. 4, 1901,' which like its partner at Nipigon delineated a 5-mile band of shoreline and 'adjacent waterways'; SPO, 1902, no. 3, 'Report of the Department of Crown Lands for 1901'; *Rat Portage Miner*, July 12, 1901.

131 AO, RG 1, E-7, vol. 3 and E-4b, vol. 2 (Orders in Council, Feb. 9 and 10, 1906) cancelling the former agreement and readvertising under new terms, and RG 1, E-7, vol. 3 (Orders in Council, May 21, 1913, Jan. 31 and Apr. 29, 1914) surrounding 'Lake of the Woods ... pulpwood agreement.' See also *Kenora Miner*,

Nov. 6, 1912, and May 3, 1913, remembering that Backus, through his involvement with Keewatin Lumber and its hydraulic interest, became owner rather than lessee of the hydro source, as had Clergue at the St Marys Rapids. (Delineation of this limit also depends upon material in the NMC.)

132 AO, RG 1, E-7, vol. 3 and E-4-B, vol. 2 (Orders in Council, Feb. 9 and 10, 1906) cancelling this earlier offer and readvertising the limit under new terms with a clear delineation of the area which is used on Map 3.1. See also *Kenora Miner*, Jan. 20, 1908; *Canada Lumberman*, Feb. 1, 1909; and *Dryden Observer Star*, Jan. 26, 1913.

133 AO, Pamphlets, 1962, no. 4; and BRL, *Port Arthur Centennial, 1857–1957* (n.a. and n.d.), section on Early Logging.

134 Bertrand, chapter on Pioneer Pulpwood Operations; NAC, RG 10, vol. 230, no. 2672 (Goudreau to Indian Affairs, Sept. 28, 1897, Indian Affairs to Goudreau, Feb. 16, 1898, and Fisheries Ministry to Indian Affairs, Mar. 9, 1898); *Nipigon Gazette*, Feb. 9, 1983; and *Sault Star*, Dec. 7, 1901.

135 Bertrand, Pioneer Pulpwood Operations; *Fort William Journal*, Jan. 4, 1896; *Winnipeg Free Press*, Nov. 2, 1896; and BRL, Historical Files, Slate Islands.

136 Bertrand, Pioneer Pulpwood Operations; *Port Arthur News*, June 18, 1907, Sept. 18, 1908, and Apr. 3, 1909; and *Canada Lumberman*, Apr. 1, 1912.

137 NAC, RG 10, vol. 2366, no. 73850, pt. 1 (Perry Lumber to Indian Affairs, Apr. 26, 1897, and Van Abbott to Indian Affairs, May 22, 1897); *Sault News* (Mich.), Oct. 6, 1900, and May 10, 11, 16, June 8, 1901; *Sault Star*, Sept. 12, 1901, and June 12, 1902; G.F. Vosper, 'Logging in Lake Superior Provincial Park,' Ministry of Natural Resources, Wawa District, 1984, 8–28; Donald MacKay, *The lumberjacks* (Toronto: McGraw-Hill Ryerson, 1978), 288; and W.J. Alexander and W.L. Oliphant, 'The Big Tow,' *Inland Seas* 17 (1961): 264–6.

138 *Sault Star*, Sept. 12, 1901.

139 Bertrand, Pioneer Pulpwood Operation. Articles in *Fort William Journal*, June 30, 1894, and May 10, Nov. 27, 1895; Sentinel, May 8, 1895; *Port Arthur News*, Apr. 5, 1901, Mar. 2, 1902, and Apr. 9, 1905 provide good examples of this mixed supply.

140 *Port Arthur News*, Apr. 5, 1909, July 28, 1910, and July 27, 1912.

141 White, 352; A.R.M. Lower, *Settlement and the forest frontier in Eastern Canada* (Toronto: Macmillan, 1936), 61–70; Zaslow, *The opening of the Canadian north*, 173–8; Lambert and Pross, 100; and Peter W. Sinclair, 84–5 and 87.

142 Nancy M. Wightman and W. Robert Wightman, 'Agricultural settlement in Northwestern Ontario to 1930,' *Thunder Bay Historical Museum Society Papers and Records* 17 (1989): 49–50; Margaret A. Evans, 'The Mowat era,' in *Profiles of a province* (Toronto: The Ontario Historical Society, 1967), 308–10; and Lambert and Pross, 308–10 and 424–6.

143 Wightman and Wightman, 'Agricultural settlement,' 52–3; *Sault News* (Mich.), Feb. 10 and Dec. 15, 1894; AO, Pamphlets, 1894, no. 21; *Winnipeg Free Press*, Aug. 24, 1895, Apr. 26, 1897, and July 10, 1908; *Kenora Miner*, July 28, 1909; George R. Pattulo, *Northwestern Ontario ... a brief description* (Port Arthur: Evening Herald Publishing Co., 1883); and Walpole Roland, *Algoma West, its mines, scenery and industrial resources* (Toronto: Warwick and Sons, 1887).

144 The best single collection of such official immigration literature, both federal and provincial, is to be found in the Library of the Federal Department of Agriculture in Ottawa. For a full description of the elaborate organization of agents, local land guides, railway arrangements, shelters, etc., see *Enterprise* (Keewatin), July 26, 1900, and *Globe*, July 12, 1900.

145 Wightman and Wightman, 'Agricultural settlement,' 53; and SPO, 1901–1906, 'Reports of the Director of Colonization 1900–1905.'

146 *Globe*, Apr. 26, 1890, and June 3, 1893; J.J. Kehoe, 'The Sault Ste. Marie Ship Canal,' *Canadian Magazine of Politics, Science, Arts and Literature*, 1893, 589–90; *Ontario Agricultural College Review* 2 (1891): 84–6; and *Sault News* (Mich.), Nov. 10, Dec. 15, 1894, and June 8, 1901.

147 NAC, RG 10, vol. 2366, no. 73850, pt. 1 (Van Abbott to Indian Affairs, Apr. 26, 1897); and Wightman and Wightman, 'Road and highway development,' 372. The *Telegram* and *Minnie M.* were said to offer a boat a day on this shore (*Sault Star*, Sept. 12, 1901) and were later replaced regularly by the *Manitou* and *Caribou* (*Rail and Marine World*, 1906: 167). A chapter of the Farmers' Institute, for example, was also founded at Goulais Bay (*Sault Star*, Mar. 26, Apr. 30, 1903, Mar. 30, 1905, and Sept. 11, 1912).

148 *Sault Star*, Mar. 26, 1903, and Apr. 4, 1961 (reminiscent article).

149 *Ontario Agricultural College Review* 2 (1891): 84–6; *Sault News* (Mich.), Oct. 11, 1890, and Dec. 15, 1894; *Sault Star*, Feb. 11, 1903, Dec. 16, 1909, May 5, 19, June 9, 1910, May 21, 1912, Sept. 7, 1912, and July 12, 30, 1913.

150 AO, RG 16, series 16-66, ms. 597 (Reports of the Agricultural Representatives at Sault Ste. Marie, 1909–14). See also SSMM, Box no. 14, file 985.96.1 and a summary of agricultural progress in *Sault Star*, Jan. 18, 1912, and June 5, Nov. 15, 1913.

151 Wightman and Wightman, 'Agricultural settlement,' 55.

152 For further background on Finnish immigration across northwestern Ontario, see Oiva Saarinen, 'Geographical Perspectives on Finnish-Canadian Immigration and Settlement,' *Polyphony* 3 (1981): 16–22. More details on this and other ethnic communities about Thunder Bay appear in Dallen J. Timothy, 'Ethnic Islands in the Thunder Bay Frontier: A study of four Finnish settlements,' M.A. dissertation,

University of Western Ontario, London, 1993, and *Thunder Bay Mosaic* (Thunder Bay: Thunder Bay Multicultural Association, 1983).

153 *Fort William Journal*, May 1, 1897, Mar. 4, Oct. 14, 1899, and July 26, 1900; *Winnipeg Free Press*, Apr. 23, 1900; and *Port Arthur News*, Aug. 1, 1900, Aug. 28, 1912, and Sept. 9, 1913. See also SPO, 1900–1906, 'Reports of the Director of Colonization, 1898 to 1905.'

154 *Fort William Journal*, Feb. 24, 1892, Mar. 9, Aug. 17, 1894, and Oct. 29, 1898.

155 *Fort William Journal*, Nov. 11, 1891.

156 *Fort William Journal*, July 9, 13, 1892, and Sept. 18, 1893; TBM, Port Arthur Board of Trade Minutes, Sept. 11, 1912; and *The Canadian Dairyman and Farming World*, Oct. 21, 1901, 17.

157 *Fort William Journal*, Feb. 17, 1892; *Rat Portage News*, Sept. 9, 1912; Wightman and Wightman, 'Agricultural settlement,' 61; and *The Canadian Dairyman and Farming World*, Oct. 21, 1908, 17.

158 *Winnipeg Free Press*, Apr. 2, 1897, and Apr. 23, 1900; *Fort William Journal*, Oct. 30, 1897, June 12, 1910, and Aug. 20, 1914; and *Port Arthur News*, Nov. 17, 1911, and Sept. 12, 1913.

159 TBM, Port Arthur Board of Trade Minutes, Feb. 23, 1914; *Sentinel*, Oct. 7 and 14, 1892; *Fort William Journal*, Oct. 8, 1892 and Oct. 6, 1894; and *Port Arthur News*, Mar. 6, Sept. 12, 1908, Aug. 20, 1909, and Jan. 21, 1910.

160 *Fort William Journal*, Oct. 3, 14, 1891, and Feb. 18, 1901; and *Port Arthur News*, Aug. 1, 1908, Sept. 26, 1912, and June 7, 1913.

161 *Globe*, Apr. 19, 26, July 19, Sept. 30, 1890, and Apr. 2, 1892.

162 *Globe*, Aug. 16, 1890, June 5, 1897, and Apr. 30, 1898; *Rat Portage Record*, Oct. 31, Nov. 28, 1891, Nov. 30, 1894, June 10, 1898, and Aug. 30, 1901; *Winnipeg Free Press*, Oct. 11, 1890; and *Rainy Lake Herald*, Oct. 27, 1898.

163 AO, RG 1, D24, vol. 1 (Stephenson to White, Feb. 7, 1898); *Rainy Lake Herald*, Nov. 1, 1890, and June 2, 8, 1899; *Globe*, Aug. 16, 1890, May 24, 1892, Apr. 30, 1898, and July 8, 1899; *Rat Portage Record*, Nov. 30, 1894; and *Port Elgin Times*, Sept. 10, 1896, and Feb. 4, Apr. 8, May 13, 27, 1897.

164 SPO, 1892, no. 20, 'Report of the Department of Crown Lands for 1891'; *Winnipeg Free Press*, Mar. 16, 1894; *Rainy Lake Herald*, June 16 and Sept. 8, 1898; and *Rat Portage Miner*, July 8, 1898.

165 AO, RG 1, D24, vol. 1 (Stephenson to White, Dec. 20, 1897, and Feb. 7, 1898), RG 76, vol. 166, no. 47195, pt. 1 (Correspondence dated Dec. 11, 1897, Mar. 3 and Aug. 17, 1898); *Rat Portage Miner*, Dec. 23, 1897, and Apr. 8, July 8, 1898; and *Rainy Lake Herald*, Sept. 8 and 29, 1898.

166 SPO, 1902, no. 32, 'Report of the Director of Colonization for 1901'; SPC, 1903 and 1905, no. 25 'Reports of the Department of the Interior 1902–1904'; *Winnipeg*

Free Press, July 11, 1891; *Rainy Lake Herald*, Mar. 23, 1899; and *Rat Portage Miner*, May 15, 1903. The Finnish village name Emo here begins to figure in the press by the late nineties, suggesting that the arrival of this ethnic group may be earlier than actual reports would indicate.

167 AO, RG 1, D24, vol. 1 (Stephenson to White, Dec. 20, 1897), vol. 3 (Stephenson to White, Dec. 9, 1899), and vol. 6 (Stephenson to White, Sept. 24, 1904); SPO, 1902, no. 32, 'Report of the Director of Colonization for 1901,' and 1906, no. 3, 'Report of the Department of Crown Lands for 1905'; SPC, 1905, no. 25, 'Report of the Department of the Interior for 1903–1904'; *Globe*, June 5, 1897, and July 28, 1898; *Rainy Lake Herald*, Oct. 27, 1898; and *Fort Frances Times*, Dec. 11, 1911.

168 AO, RG 1, D24, vol. 1 (Stephenson to White, Dec. 20, 1897), vol. 6 (Stephenson to White, Sept. 24, 1904), and A-I-7, Box 11, no. 3 (Memo on Land Problems, Mar. 20, 1900); SPC, 1903 and 1905, no. 25, 'Report of the Department of the Interior for 1902–4'; SPC, 1906, no. 3, 'Report of the Department of Crown Lands for 1905'; *Rainy Lake Herald*, Sept. 29, 1898; *Kenora Miner*, Oct. 12, 1906; and *Port Arthur News*, July 8, 1907.

169 *Rainy Lake Herald*, July 5, 1890, Aug. 11, Sept. 1, 8, 29, Nov. 24, 1898, and July 13, Aug. 10, 1899; *Rat Portage Record*, Oct. 24, Nov. 28, 1891, and Oct. 2, 1894; and *Winnipeg Free Press*, Aug. 7, 1897.

170 *Fort Frances Times*, May 16, Sept. 12 and 19, 1912.

171 Wightman and Wightman, 'Road and highway development,' 366 and 372–3; *Rat Portage Record*, June 26, 1894; *Rainy Lake Herald*, Dec. 1, 1898; *Rat Portage Miner*, Feb. 24, 1899; *Port Arthur News*, Mar, 8, 1912; and Fort Frances Times, Dec. 19, 1912, serve as good examples of settler activity with reference to railway timber.

172 *Rat Portage Miner*, May 8, 1894, and Oct. 6, 1903; and LWM, Historical Files, Agriculture.

173 *Fort William Journal*, May 15, 1895; *Winnipeg Free Press*, June 10, 1895; *Port Elgin Times*, May 28, 1896; and *Rat Portage Miner*, Feb. 24, 1899.

174 Wightman and Wightman, 'Agricultural settlement,' 56–7.

175 SPO, 1902, no. 32, 'Report of the Director of Colonization for 1901'; *Farmer's Advocate* 47 (1912): 426; *Fort Frances Times*, Dec. 21, 1911; *Dryden Observer Star*, June 26, 1913; and *Kenora Miner*, Oct. 14, 1914.

176 Save for certain highly circumscribed works – Geoffrey Wall, 'Recreational land use in Muskoka,' *Ontario Geography* 11 (1977): 11–28; and R.I. Wolfe, 'The summer resorts of Ontario in the nineteenth century,' *Ontario History* 54 (1962): 149–60, and his 'The changing pattern of tourism in Ontario,' in *Profiles of a province*, 173–7 – this fascinating northern topic has seen limited academic treatment.

177 *Winnipeg Free Press*, July 21, 25, 1891, Apr. 8, 1892, and Aug. 7, 1893; *Rat Portage Miner*, Aug. 10, 1900; and *Kenora Miner*, Aug. 31, 1906, Aug. 24, 1907, Aug. 7, 21, Dec. 22, 1909, and Aug. 20, 1910.
178 *Winnipeg Free Press*, June 3, 24, 1891, June 7, 1892, and Aug. 7, 1893; *Rat Portage Miner*, Aug. 24, 1899, and July 6, 1906; and *Kenora Miner*, Aug. 20, 27 and Nov. 1910.
179 *Winnipeg Free Press*, June 18 and Aug. 10, 1894; *Rat Portage Miner*, Aug. 10, 1900; and *Kenora Miner*, June 24, 1911, and June 13, 1914.
180 *Kenora Miner*, Aug. 10, 1910, and June 17, 1914.
181 Ibid., July 20, 1914.
182 *Rat Portage Record*, Aug. 17, 1894; *Winnipeg Free Press*, Aug. 10, 1895, and Aug. 9, 1897; and *Rainy Lake Herald*, Oct. 20, 1898, and Aug. 3, 1899.
183 *Kenora Miner*, Sept. 11, 17, 1907, Dec. 4, 1909, and June 24, 1911; *Rainy Lake Herald*, summer issues, 1903–1908; *Fort Frances Times*, May 16, Aug. 15, 1912, and July 30, 1914; and FFM, History file, Tourism.
184 *Sentinel*, Aug. 14, 1891, and July 26, 1895; and *Fort William Journal*, July 25, 1896.
185 *Port Arthur News*, Jan. 23, 1910; and *Port Arthur Chronicle*, Oct. 12, 1913.
186 *Fort William Journal*, July 25, 1896; and *Port Arthur News*, Feb. 26, June 20, 1910 and Aug. 22, 1913. Further comments and detail about the recreational use of Silver Islet's mainland community are to be found in Elinor Barr, *Silver Islet: Striking it rich in Lake Superior* (Toronto: Natural Heritage History Inc., 1988), 121–8.
187 W.R. Wightman, 'The Canadian steam packet service of the Upper Lakes,' *Inland Seas* 46 (1990): 259–62; *Fort William Journal*, Aug. 26, 1899; *Port Arthur News*, Aug. 23, 1909, and Mar. 14, July 20, 1910; and *Sault Star*, Mar. 16, 1962 (reminiscent article).
188 *Globe*, July 1, 1899; AO, Pamphlets, 1905, no. 35. See also frequent descriptions of this sport fishing in SPO, 1906–1915, 'Reports of the Game and Fisheries Commission 1905–1914'; SPC, 1910, no. 13, 'Report of the Minister of Fisheries, 1909'; and *Port Arthur News*, Mar. 6, 1916.
189 *Thunder Bay Journal*, May 29, 1900; *Globe*, July 24, 1900; and *Port Arthur News*, Aug. 29, 1908, are good examples among scant specific information.
190 Scattered throughout Don Steer's *The Montreal River Area* (Sault Ste Marie: Sault Ste Marie Museum, 1991) are snippets of undated recreational information for this shore. Some early ones seem applicable to this period. See also SSMPL, Historical Files, binder no. 47; *Sault News* (Mich.), July 21, 1894; and *Sault Star*, Aug. 1, 31, 1901, Mar. 13, 1902, June 20, 1907, and Apr. 29, Aug. 17, 1912.
191 SSMPL, Historical Files, Clergue Scrapbook.
192 *Sault Star*, Aug. 2, 1906, Aug. 17, 1912, and Apr. 9, 1913; and Steer, comments as above.

193 Emo's rapid agricultural rise is described in the Emo Historical Committee's *The river of time: A history of Emo* (Altona, MB: Friesen Printers, 1978), and EPL, Local History Files. Similarly, details of the renewed growth at Fort Frances are to be found in 'A history of Fort Frances' (mimeo) put out by the Fort Frances Public Library and Museum, 1973, and the historical files of both the FFPL and FFM.

194 Thompson, 10–26.

195 Here, as elsewhere in this section, all references to electrical development come from Wightman and Wightman, 'The rise of electrical power,' 37–64; see particularly 38–45. Industrial details are taken from Gertrude Horan and Allan Shaw as well as from the LWM and KPL, Historical Files and numerous issues of both the local newspapers and the *Winnipeg Free Press.*

196 George Wice, *Carved from the wilderness: The intriguing story of Dryden* (Dryden: Alex Wilson Coldstream, 1967); DPL, Local History Files as well as articles in the local press and *Winnipeg Free Press.*

197 *Sault Star*, July 12, 1962; Katherine Punch, 'Sault Ste. Marie,' *Canadian Geographical Journal* 73 (1966): 202–3; and Emilia Kolcon-Lach, 'Early Italian settlement at Sault Ste. Marie, Ontario, 1898–1921,' M.A. dissertation, University of Western Ontario, London, 1979. For the lakehead cities, see 'Thunder Bay's People,' *Polyphony* 9 (1987): 5–114.

198 Van Every, 191–202; and McDowall, 9–50.

199 With reference to waterfront development, see, for example, *Sault Star*, Mar. 13 to May 8, 1902, June 3, 1909, and Feb. 3, May 13, Oct. 10, 1913. With reference to the city, the most ready source is Frances M. Heath, *Sault Ste. Marie, city by the Rapids* (Burlington: Windsor Publications, 1988), particularly chapters 4 and 5.

200 These and related events in this struggle are covered by Elizabeth Arthur in 'The Landing and the Plot,' *Lakehead University Review* 1 (1968): 1–17; Joseph Mauro in *Thunder Bay: A history of the Golden Gateway of the great north-west* (Thunder Bay: City of Thunder Bay, 1981); and Thorald E. Tronrud in *Guardians of Progress: Boosters and boosterism in Thunder Bay, 1870–1914* (Thunder Bay: Thunder Bay Historical Museum Society, 1993). Information from the latter figures strongly in the remaining endnotes that deal with the twin cities here.

201 *Winnipeg Free Press*, July 29 and Aug. 18, 1891, and *Fort William Journal*, Sept. 2, 1891, provide good examples of CPR expansion, while dozens of articles in these papers chronicle the rising elevator capacity. Summaries of the latter are to be found in Henry Sellers, 'The early history ... of grain,' 21–25, and BRL, Description and Travel, no. 2, 'The grain story' and History Files, Grain Elevators, no. 40, 'Historical facts ... grain elevators ... 1883–1964.' In addition to various snippets of information on the morphological changes of Fort William over these years gleaned from a variety of sources, information here comes from a

range of old maps and from field observations of the downtown and adjacent areas during residence at the Lakehead in the autumn of 1987.

202 Tronrud, *Guardians of Progress*, along with the same combination of reading, fieldwork, and map study as outlined above, as well as *Winnipeg Free Press*, Dec. 24, 1891 and Sept. 5, 1896; and *Sentinel*, July 15, 1892.

203 *Industrial Canada* 7 (1906): 369–70; LUA, Box XIV, no. 54, Mar. 21, 1906; and *Port Arthur News*, Mar. 20, 1906, Apr. 9, 1907, and Jan. 7, 25, 1913.

204 A.A. Anderson, 'The development of the harbours of Port Arthur and Fort William,' *Thunder Bay Historical Museum Society, Papers and Records* 20 (1983): 42–99; *Port Arthur News*, Mar. 22, Aug. 30, Sept. 16, Oct. 24, and Nov. 10, 1909; and TBM, Port Arthur Board of Trade Minutes, Feb. 14, 1912, and Subject Files, Blast Furnace.

205 Wightman and Wightman, 'The rise of electric power,' 41–3.

206 *Fort William Journal*, Sept. 2, 1899. This redirection of capital sources is very evident in BRL, 'Historical facts ... grain elevators ... 1883–1964,' for example. So is the CPR's declining interest in elevator ownership, which followed its withdrawal from grain shipping on the lakes, as seen in *Fort William Times Journal*, Aug. 27, 1902. On freight organization, see *Port Arthur News*, July 28, 1908.

207 Early hints at frustration felt in this matter can be found in *Sentinel*, Feb. 17, 1893; *Winnipeg Free Press*, Sept. 5, 1895; and *Fort William Journal*, May 14, 1895. Real trouble here rumbled on for years and became extreme during World War I (*Port Arthur News Chronicle*, Jan. 4, 1917.) Information on the actual creation and the history of the exchanges is derived from the *Fort William Industrial and Commercial Review* for December, 1913, and personal correspondence with Thorald E. Tronrud, Mar. 16, 1995.

208 Thorald J. Tronrud, 'Buying prosperity: The bonusing of factories at the Lakehead, 1885–1914,' *Urban History Review* 19 (1990): 1–13, is a succinct analysis of the situation here prior to war.

209 For a complete review of this infrastructure setting, see Wightman and Wightman, 'Road and highway development,' 369–73.

210 LWM, History Files, Lake Shipping; *Rainy Lake Herald*, May 11, 1899; *Rat Portage Miner*, Sept. 7, 1900, and May 8, June 9, 1903; *Kenora Miner*, June 5, 1906, and Mar. 25, 1910; *Canadian Rail and Marine World* (1906): 429, and (1913): 147; and *Rainy River Record*, Oct. 17, 1913.

211 *Sault News* (Mich.), Apr. 20, 1901; *Sault Star*, Sept. 12, 1901, and *Canadian Rail and Marine World* (1906): 167.

212 W.T. Easterbrook and Hugh G.J. Aitken, *Canadian economic history* (Toronto: Macmillan Canada, 1956), 482–92; Donald Creighton, *The story of Canada* (Toronto: Macmillan Canada, 1959), 193–5 and 228–30; and Lower, *The North American assault on the Canadian forest*, 192–4.

213 White, 193–4.

214 Morris Zaslow, *The northward expansion of Canada, 1914–1967* (Toronto: McClelland and Stewart, 1988), 42–3.

215 Ian M. Drummond, 'The electrification of Ontario,' in *Progress without planning*, 134–35; and Easterbrook and Aitken, 517–20.

216 H.A. Innis, *Settlement and the mining frontier*, vol. 9 in the Canadian Frontiers of Settlement Series, ed. W.A. Mackintosh and W.L.G. Joung (Toronto: Macmillan, 1936), 390–405; and Nancy M. Wightman and W. Robert Wightman, 'Beyond Rail and Road,' *Thunder Bay Historical Museum Society, Papers and Records* 21 (1993): 19–34.

217 White, 213–17.

218 Ian Radforth, *Bushworkers and bosses: Logging in Northern Ontario, 1900–1980* (Toronto: University of Toronto Press, 1987), 107–31.

219 Lambert and Pross, 235–46.

220 The issue of road development across the region as discussed here is laid out at more length in Wightman and Wightman, 'Road and highway development,' 373–7.

221 W.R. Wightman, *Forever on the fringe* (Toronto: University of Toronto Press, 1982), 140, touches on the issue of rural gene pools and social life, but the author is aware of no real historical study of the matter in northern communities. *A chronicle of Finnish settlements in the rural Thunder Bay Area* (Thunder Bay: Thunder Bay Finnish Canadian Historic Society, 1976) underlines the importance of these functions of community halls.

222 Wightman and Wightman, 'The rise of electric power,' 49; for examples of early rural telephone systems, see *Port Arthur News*, Jan. 6, 1910; *Fort Frances Times*, Mar. 23, 1922; *Fort William Times Journal*, May 16, 1922; *Sault Star*, Jan. 5, 1925; and *Dryden Observer*, June 3, 1927. A concise list of municipal telephone companies is given in SPO, 1925, no. 43, 'Report on Ontario telephone systems, 1924.'

223 AO, MU 1319, Heenan Papers (Report of Edge and Nichols, Nov. 10, 1914); and *Dryden Observer*, June 12, 1926.

224 *Fort William Times Journal*, Feb. 22 1922, and May 6, 1925.

225 Ibid., Oct. 16, 1924; *Fort Frances Times*, Oct. 16, 1924; and *Dryden Observer*, Oct. 10 and 24, 1924. Among these speculative companies, most numerous in the Lakehead area, were the Northern Land and Lumber Co. and the Pioneer Land Co., a subsidiary of the Pigeon River Lumber Co. of Port Arthur. The detailed property records of the latter, covering lots in fourteen townships, are to be found in LUA, Box XLIV, file 142 (a).

226 *Fort William Times Journal*, Nov. 28, 1924, reiterating a view first given in that paper on Feb. 4, 1922.

227 SPO, 1913–1917, no. 3, 'Reports of the Department of Lands and Forests for 1912–1916' make this point very well.

228 Unfortunately, the census records after 1911 lump the Goulais-Batchawana townships into an amorphous 'other' category. While development in these Indian Townships was limited, their exclusion from the Algoma West statistics here makes the latter overly conservative.

229 *Port Arthur News*, Apr. 20, 1914; *Fort Frances Times*, Mar. 9 1922; and *Sault Star*, Dec. 24, 1930.

230 SPO, 1921, no. 3, 'Report of the Department of Lands and Forests for 1920'; *Dryden Observer*, Sept. 5, 1919 and June 6, 1924; and *Fort Frances Times*, Mar. 9, 1922.

231 BRL, Local History files, 'Fifty years with Pass Lake homesteaders, 1924–72'; *Fort William Times Journal*, Sept. 26, 1922, Feb. 22, Oct. 11, Nov. 28, 1924, May 6, 1925, and Feb. 27, Mar. 9, 1928; and TBM, Fort William Board of Trade, Minutes, Apr. 16, 1928.

232 AO, RG 16, G-5-1, series 16-66, ms 597 (Algoma 1919 and 1920); *Dryden Observer*, Sept. 5, 1919; *Fort William Times Journal*, Mar. 13, 1922; and *Fort Frances Times*, July 20, 1922.

233 SPO, 1920, no. 7, 'Report of the Department of Agriculture for 1919'; *Farmers Advocate* 54 (1918): 1463–4; and *Kenora Miner*, June 20, 1914. The importance of these provincial agents and their support from government across the north was first recognized by Lower in *Settlement and the forest frontier in Eastern Canada*, 104–7. It is described elsewhere in the north in Wightman, *Forever on the fringe*, 158–62.

234 AO, RG 16, G-5-1, series 16-66, ms 597 (Algoma 1914); *Sault Star*, Jan. 27, May 26, 1915, and Feb. 6, 1923; *Farmers Advocate* 54 (1918): 1463–4; and *Fort Frances Times*, June 15, July 13, Sept. 28, 1916, Mar. 9, 1922, Apr. 3, June 21, 1923, and Mar. 29, 1928.

235 AO, RG 16, G-5-1, series 16-66, ms 597 (Algoma 1919, 1926); SSMPL, Vertical File, Algoma Agriculture; *Farm, Dairy and Rural Home* 38 (July 17, 1919): 2–3; *Farmers Advocate* 54 (1918): 1463–4; *Fort Frances Times*, Nov. 16, 1916, June 28, 1917, May 1, 1924, and Mar. 24, 1928; *Kenora Miner*, May 23, 1917; *Dryden Observer*, Sept. 5, 1919, and Jan. 22, 1926; and *Fort William Times Journal*, Feb. 3, 1922, and Dec. 10, 1927.

236 AO, RG 16, G-5-1, series 16-66, ms 597 (Algoma 1919–1923); *Fort Frances Times*, Apr. 12, May 24, 1917, and Mar. 29, 1928; *Sault Star*, July 26, 1918; *Kenora Miner*, Feb. 25 and Apr. 17, 1920; *Fort William Times Journal*, Feb. 3, Aug. 12, 1922, and Dec. 10, 1927; and *Dryden Observer*, Feb. 5, 22, 1924, Nov. 20, 1925, Mar. 11, 1927, and Jan. 4, 1928.

237 G.W. Collins, 'Seed potatoes in Northwestern Ontario,' *Ontario Agricultural College Review* 30 (1918): 310–11; and *Kenora Miner*, Oct. 21, 1914, and Sept. 5, 1919.

238 AO, RG 16, G-5-1, series 16-66, ms 597 (Algoma 1910–1920 and 1922); *Fort Frances Times*, May 29, 1919; *Fort William Times Journal*, Nov. 27, 1920; and *Dryden Observer*, Feb. 5, 1929.

239 *Sault Star*, June 5, 1913, and Dec. 18, 1914; and *Port Arthur News*, Mar. 11, 1913.

240 *Farm, Dairy and Rural Home* 38 (July 17, 1919); *Fort Frances Times*, June 28, 1917, and Aug. 21, 1919; *Farmers Advocate* 54 (1918): 1463–4; *Kenora Miner*, Feb. 24, 1917; and *Dryden Observer*, May 24, 1926.

241 AO, RG 16, G-5-1, series 16-66, ms 597 (Algoma 1912 and after); *Port Arthur News*, Mar. 10, 1914; *Fort William Times Journal*, May 1, 1917; *Fort Frances Times*, June 28, 1917, and Feb. 25, 1926; and *Dryden Observer*, Apr. 9, 1926.

242 *Fort William Times Journal*, Feb. 2, 1929; and *Fort Frances Times*, Feb. 25, 1926.

243 AO, RG 16, G-5-1, series 16-66, ms 597 (Algoma), particularly the report for 1916; *Sault Star*, July 5, 1919; *Fort Frances Times*, Oct. 11, 1922; and *Fort William Times Journal*, Dec. 10, 1927.

244 *Port Arthur News*, Sept. 19, 1914; *Fort Frances Times*, Oct. 1, 1914, Aug. 11, Sept. 1, 1921, and Sept. 20, 1923; *Rainy River Record*, Sept. 14, 1916, and Aug. 12, 1923; *Sault Star*, Oct. 14, 1919; *Kenora Miner*, Sept. 22, 1928; and *Fort William Times Journal*, June 16, 1929.

245 Wightman and Wightman, 'Agricultural settlement,' 57–62, cover this point and touch on many others here.

246 H.W. McElroy, 'Co-operation in the Rainy River Valley,' *Ontario Agricultural College Review* 26 (1914): 185–7; *Fort Frances Times*, Dec. 19, 1912, and Aug. 5, 1915; and *Kenora Miner*, Oct. 21, 1914.

247 *Fort Frances Times*, Aug. 5, 1915; *Sault Star*, Mar. 10, Nov. 2, 1917, and Aug. 17, 1924; *Farmers Advocate* 54 (1918): 1463–4; *Dryden Observer*, Oct. 8, 1920, and May 28, 1926; and *Fort William Times Journal*, Apr. 30, 1921.

248 *Fort William Times Journal*, Dec. 5, 1931.

249 EPL, Local History Files, Agriculture, 'Rainy River clover seed growers'; *Kenora Miner*, Oct. 21, 1914, and May 1, 1915; and *Dryden Observer*, July 11, Aug. 8 and Nov. 14, 1919.

250 *Fort Frances Times*, May 4, June 8, 1922, July 10, 1924, and Sept. 23, 1925; and *Dryden Observer*, Oct. 9, 1925.

251 SSMPL, Red Scrapbook, Soo Dairies.

252 See, for example, *Fort William Times Journal*, Feb. 15, 1919, Sept. 30, 1921, and Sept. 26, 1924. See also P.M., Enid Oliver, 'Slate River Valley, a history,' as one example of numerous local histories touching on rising milk routes.

253 *Port Arthur News*, Sept. 21, 1916; and *Fort William Times Journal*, May 31, June 2, 3, 1926, and Mar. 12, 1928.

254 *Fort Frances Times*, Jan. 25, Feb. 8, 15, 17, 22, Apr. 12, May 4, 24, 1917, Feb. 1, 1925, and Apr. 10, 1930; and *Rainy River Record*, Jan. 6, 1927, and Sept. 13, Dec. 15, 1928.

255 *Dryden Observer*, Feb. 5, 22, July 24, Nov. 21, 1924, Nov. 20, 27, 1925, Apr. 30, 1926, Mar. 11, 1927, and Jan. 7, 1928.

256 *Fort Frances Times*, Mar. 18, Aug. 5, 1915, June 15, 29, 1916, Apr. 24, 1919, and Apr. 23, 1925.

257 *Dryden Observer*, Sept. 15, 1919.

258 *Fort William Times Journal*, Aug. 2, 15, 1919; *Fort Frances Times*, Aug. 13, 1919; and *Sault Star*, Nov. 3, 1922, and May 11, 1923.

259 *Fort Frances Times*, Nov. 16, 1916, Jan. 25, 1917, Feb. 13, 19, Dec. 3, 1925, and Mar. 29, 1928; *Rainy River Record*, Nov. 6, 1930; *Dryden Observer*, Feb. 22, 1924; *Kenora Miner*, Sept. 26, 1923; and *Fort William Times Journal*, Oct. 23, 1922.

260 AO, RG 16, G-5-1, series 16-66, ms 597 (Algoma 1914 and after); *Sault Star*, Dec. 3, 1924, Aug. 2, 1928, and June 6, 1929; EPL, Local History Files, Agriculture; *Fort Frances Times*, Aug. 13, 1919, July 16, 1925, Aug. 5, 1926, and Mar. 29, Oct. 25, 1928; and *Rainy River Record*, Jan. 30 and Sept. 14, 1930.

261 *Kenora Miner*, Mar. 25, 1931; and *Fort William Times Journal*, Apr. 28, 1928, and Nov. 3, 1930.

262 On the growth of markets, see *Port Arthur News*, May 14 and Sept. 19, 1914; *Kenora Miner*, July 1, 1914; and *Sault Star*, May 1, 24, 1923, and Feb. 23, Aug. 23, 1924.

263 Comments here come from a wide range of sources including numerous local histories and Tweedsmuir historical scrapbooks in local libraries. What follows is no more than a sample of the more insightful. AO, RG 16, G-5-1, series 16-66, ms 597 (Algoma) and Pamphlets, 1923, no. 23; *Farmers Advocate* 54 (1918): 1463–4; *Sault Star*, Apr. 28, June 3, 1914, Sept. 24, 1924, and July 14, 1925; and SSMPL, Robert Beaton, 'A brief history of farming in the Township of Korah.'

264 *Sault Star*, Apr. 28, 1914; *Dryden Observer*, Aug. 3, 1913, Sept. 15, 1919, and Aug. 29, 1924; and *Kenora Miner*, Sept. 28, 1931.

265 Zaslow, The northward expansion of Canada, 70; and *Final Report, Canadian Commission on Pulpwood, 1923* (Ottawa: King's Printer 1924); 55–7.

266 Lower, *The North American assault on the Canadian forest*, 192–8; and Sinclair, 79–80.

267 *Fort William Times Journal*, Feb. 6, 1923.

268 Ibid., Sept. 13, 1926.

269 Radforth, 25–36 and 107–18; Edmund William Bradwin, *The bunkhouse man ... 1903–1914* (Toronto: University of Toronto Press, 1972), 55–61, 93–110, and 141–2; and MacKay, *The lumberjacks*, 221–24 and 228–37.

270 *Sault Star*, May 19, 1913, Mar. 25, 1926, and Mar. 6, 1928; and *Canada Lumberman*, Nov. 26, 1914.

271 Bertrand; Barr, 'Lumbering on the Pigeon River watershed,' 8; *Port Arthur News*, May 12, 1915; and *Fort William Times Journal*, Feb. 6, 1923.

272 LWM, Local History Files, Lumber Industry; and *Kenora Miner*, May 2, 1914, Apr. 17, 1915, May 26, Sept. 19, 1917, and Apr. 6, 1918.

273 FFM, Local History Files, Forest Industry; and *Fort Frances Times*, Feb. 10, 1916, Mar. 29, 1923, Apr. 2, 1925, and Apr. 11, 1929.

274 NAC, RG 33/13, vol. 2, G5 (Zavitz to Finlayson, Apr. 22, 1924).

275 Zaslow, *The northward expansion of Canada*, 77; Lower, *Settlement and the forest frontier*, 113–14; and 'The Lumber Industry in Canada, 1920,' Dominion Bureau of Statistics, Ottawa, 1923, 51–3.

276 A.R.M. Lower, in his *Settlement and the forest frontier*, 114, aptly dubbed this shift to pulpwood a 'revolution,' but the most insightful comment on its origins are in Sinclair, 82, and Gillis and Roach, 99.

277 Lambert and Pross, 264.

278 Ibid., 263–4; Gillis and Roach, 100; and Nelles, 376–7.

279 SPO, 1921, no. 67, 'A return of all letters and papers ... of the Riddell-Latchford Inquiry in 1920.'

280 In addition to a barrage of press reports in the *Sault Star*, *Fort William Times Journal*, and *Fort Frances Times*, 1920–1922, information here is distilled from the actual testimony before the Commission preserved in NAC, RG 33/13, vol. 2 G5 and vol. 3, H5.

281 *Fort William Times Journal*, June 7, 9, 10, 12, July 15, and Sept. 23, 26, 1921.

282 NAC, MG 27, II-F-7, vol. 25, no. 3; SPO, 1921, no. 67, 'A return of all letters and papers ... of the Reddell-Latchford Inquiry in 1920'; *Sault Star*, Apr. 29, 1920, and Jan. 16, 1922; *Fort William Times Journal*, Jan. 15–30, 1920; and *Fort Frances Times*, Aug. 4, Oct. 6, 1921, and Feb. 22, Mar. 9, 1922.

283 Backus, with two dealers in the Rainy River country, was openly accused by Mathieu of being deeply involved, but no charges followed (see *Fort Frances Times*, May 5, 1921). If Spanish River was not guilty of such illegalities, why did that company attempt to bar the Commission from examining its books? (See *Sault Star*, Feb. 15 and Mar. 4, 1921.)

284 Nelles, 377–9; MacKay, *Heritage lost*, 69; Lambert and Pross, 263; and Gillis and Roach, 104.

285 Radforth, 54. Radforth also makes this point in his 'Finnish lumber workers in Ontario, 1919–1946,' *Polyphony* 3, no. 2 (1981): 27.

286 *Fort William Times Journal*, Dec. 12, 1920, and Jan. 12, 1922; *Kenora Miner*, July 12, 1924; and *Dryden Observer*, Apr. 12, 1928.

287 TBPL, Local History Files, Pulp and Papers Industry; and N.M., Pamphlet File, Paul Barry, 'The Transit Zone at the top of Lake Superior.'

288 Thomas F. Waters, *The Superior north shore* (Minneapolis: University of Minnesota Press, 1987), 126–8; Alexander and Oliphant, 264–6; Woodside, 112–4; and *Sault Star*, Apr. 29, 1920, and Mar. 11, Aug. 31, 1922.

289 LWM, Local History File, Lumber Industry; *Fort William Times Journal*, Dec. 10, 1927; and *Sault Star*, Aug. 6, 1923.

290 Gillis and Roach, 104.

291 DPL, Local History File, Pulp and Paper Industry; *Sault Star*, May 3, 13, and Aug. 4, 1918, and reminiscent accounts June 22, 1927, Mar. 16, 1937, and July 29, 1971; and *Fort Frances Times*, Feb. 1, 1917.

292 Lambert and Pross, 269–72; Sinclair, 82; and Nelles, 391–5.

293 Nelles, 391–3; and *Kenora Miner*, Feb. 23, 1921, and Jan. 2, 16, 1924.

294 AO, RG 1, E-4-B, vol. 4, contains all records of transfers in holders for the Pic River and Black Sturgeon limits Dec. 1, 1916, May 12, 1917, and July 5, 1918. An interesting adjunct is SPO, 1921, no. 72, 'Return of all correspondence regarding the Pic River and Black Sturgeon limits since 1916,' which takes up 94 pages.

295 *Port Arthur News*, Jan. 15, Feb. 20 and 27, 1917; *Fort William Times Journal*, May 17, 1918, and July 27, Dec. 15, 1920, as well as Feb. 20 and 21, 1922.

296 NAC, RG 33/13, vol. 4, no. P7 (Jan. 19, 1924); *Sault Star*, Aug. 31, 1922, Oct. 2, 12, 1925, and Jan. 18, Apr. 9, 1927.

297 NAC, RG 39, vol. 594, no. 8, 25–6; TBM, Subject Files, Forest Industry; TBPL, Pamphlet File, Superior Pulpwood History; *Fort William Times Journal*, Sept. 17, 1923, Dec. 12, 1925, Dec. 11, 1926, and Dec. 14, 1929; and *Twin City Grain and Trade News*, Mar. 8, 1918.

298 The *Final Report, Canadian Royal Commission on Forestry* provides a useful review of the voluminous correspondence and statistical records preserved for Ontario in NAC, RG 33/13, vol. 2, G1, G2 and G5 and vol. 3, H5, as does the *Globe*, *Sault Star*, *Port Arthur News* and *Manitoba Free Press* for Jan. 14–19, 1924. In the secondary literature, the best summation is in Gillis and Roach, 202–4.

299 Nelles, 443; and Lambert and Pross, 269–76.

300 *Fort Frances Times*, May 28, Oct. 1, 8, 1925, and Apr. 20, June 30, 1927.

301 *Kenora Miner*, Feb. 29, 1922, Jan. 2, 16, Apr. 4, 1924, and Apr. 23, 1925.

302 *Dryden Observer*, June 16, Aug. 16, 1922, July 25, 1924, and Mar. 13, 1925; *Fort William Times Journal*, Oct. 9, 1923; and *Kenora Miner*, Dec. 15, 1928.

303 SPO, 1928, no. 3, 'Report of the Department of Lands and Forests for 1927'; *Fort William Times Journal*, Oct. 19, 1921; and *Kenora Miner*, Mar. 1, 1924.

304 *Fort William Times Journal*, July 27, Dec. 15, 1920, Dec. 16, 1922, and Dec. 14, 1929; and *Sault Star*, Jan. 7, 1920.

305 *Fort William Times Journal*, Feb. 20, 21, Mar. 20, Dec. 16, 1922, Apr. 19, 1924, Dec. 11, 1926, Dec. 10, 1927, Dec. 24, 1928, and Dec. 14, 1929.

306 Ibid., Nov. 16, 1916, Feb. 3, 1919, and July 9, Sept. 30, Dec. 15, 1920.

307 Ibid., Jan. 18, 1921, June 12, Dec. 16, 1922, Apr. 6, 1925, May 22, 1926, and Nov. 12, 1928.

308 Ibid., May 3, 1927.

309 Ibid., Jan. 10, May 11, 20, Dec. 16, 1920, Apr. 11, 1921, Mar. 8, Feb. 10, 1922, and Aug. 11, 13, Sept. 13, 25, 1923.

310 Ibid., Mar. 26, June 30, Nov. 25, 1924, May 21, July 27, 1925, Apr. 28, May 3, June 21, 27, Dec. 10, 1927, and Apr. 26, 1928.

311 Wightman and Wightman, 'The rise of electric power,' 39.

312 AO, RG 1, E-3-A, vol. 21 (May 1, 1918, July 17, 1923), E-4-B, vol. 4 (Dec. 17, 1917), vol. 5 (July 8, Dec. 19, 1920); and *Fort William Times Journal,* May 17, 1918, Mar. 20, 1922, and Jan. 15, 1924.

313 AO, RG 1, E-4-B, vol. 5 (July 8, 1922); and *Fort William Times Journal*, July 9, 27, 1920, July 2, 27, 1922, and Jan. 15, 1924.

314 AO, RG 1, E-4-B, vol. 5 (Nov. 8, 1923 and Apr. 19, 1928).

315 AO, RG 1, E-4-B, vol. 7 (Sept. 10, 1925); and *Fort William Times Journal*, June 13, Oct. 27, 1925, and Oct. 24, 1926.

316 AO, RG 1, E-4-B, vol. 5 (Dec. 11, 1920), vol. 7 (Sept. 10, 1925), E-7, vol. 3 (Memo, Nov. 19, 1930); *A history of the Port Arthur Forest District*, District Forest History Series, no. 4 (Toronto: Dept. of Lands and Forests, 1963), n.p.; SPO, 1924 and 1927, no. 3, 'Report of the Department of Lands and Forests for 1923 and 1926'; and *Fort William Times Journal*, July 20, Nov. 2, 1920, Apr. 7, 1921, May 27, 28, Oct. 28, 1921, and Oct. 3, 1922.

317 *Sault Star*, June 22, 1927, and reminiscent articles June 18, Oct. 20, 1928, Mar. 16, 1937, and July 29, 1971.

318 AO, RG 1, E-4-B, vol. 6 (Oct. 1921).

319 Radforth, *Bushworkers and bosses*, 17–19; and Zaslow, *The northward expansion of Canada*, 78–82.

320 *Fort Frances Times*, Jan. 26, 1928, and Jan. 31, 1929; and *Kenora Miner*, Dec. 5, 1928, and Jan. 17, 1931.

321 *Sault Star*, Oct. 20, 1928, Jan. 21, 1929, and Nov. 5, 1930.

322 *Fort William Times Journal*, Aug. 4, 28, Sept. 13, 1928, Jan. 28, Mar. 4, July 3, Dec. 14, 1929, and Apr. 12, Oct. 24, 1930.

323 Zaslow, *The northward expansion of Canada*, 72; and Gillis and Roach, 103–4.

324 Gillis and Roach, 100–2; MacKay, *Heritage lost*, 45–6 and 69; and Lambert and Pross, 201.

325 Gillis and Roach, 105.

326 Nelles, 429; and George, 52.

327 Middleton and Landon, 519–21.

328 Inwood, 200-2.

329 The best single source on this topic is Ann Balmer and John Peters, 'Magpie River hydroelectric development,' Historic Sites Document submitted to Acres International Limited, 1987, 11–18 and 94–104.

330 SPO, 1912 to 1923, no. 4, 'Reports of the Bureau of Mines 1911 to 1923'; *Sault Star*, Mar. 24, 1922, and oct. 2, 1924.

331 Nelles, 429; Inwood, 200–4; *Fort Frances Times*, Mar. 3, 1921; *Northern Miner*, Aug. 6, 1921; and *Sault Star*, Sept. 23, 1922.

332 *Port Arthur News*, July 22, 1915; *Fort William Times Journal*, May 3, 1922, and July 7, 1923; and *Northern Miner*, June 20, 1930.

333 SPO, 1915 and 1922, no. 4, 'Report of the Bureau of Mines for 1914 and 1921'; *Port Arthur News*, July 23, 1909; *Sault Star*, Oct. 14, 1914, May 14, 1915, and July 31, 1919; and *Northern Miner*, Aug. 5, 1916.

334 *Fort Frances Times*, Nov. 22, 1923, July 10, Oct. 30, 1924, and Jan. 29, Feb. 5, 1925; and *Northern Miner*, Aug. 8, Dec. 17, 1925, Dec. 18, 1926, and Feb. 20, 1930.

335 *Port Arthur News*, Mar. 16, 1909; *Dryden Observer*, June 26, 1913, July 14, 1922, and Aug. 31, 1928; and *Northern Miner*, Investors Ed., Apr., 1925.

336 *Port Arthur News*, Mar. 3, 1909; *Northern Miner*, May 29, 1919, Oct. 29, 1921, May 10, Nov. 15, 1928, and Apr. 25, June 6, Sept. 5, 26, 1929; and *Dryden Observer*, Aug. 31, 1928.

337 George, 60–1.

338 Waters, 92–3; and *Sault Star*, May 31, June 14, 1923, Jan. 16, 24, 1924, Feb. 23, May 22, 1926, Jan. 26, May 23, 1927, Aug. 22, 1928, Aug. 22, 1929, and Apr. 12, June 15, 1930.

339 *Sault Star*, Apr. 3, May 22, 1918, Mar. 9, 1921, Aug. 11, Nov. 13, 1922, Mar. 5, 1924, Aug. 31, 1925, and Apr. 10, 1928; and *Northern Miner*, Mar. 14, 16, 1922, Aug. 16, Sept. 6, 1924, and Aug. 21, 1926.

340 This point is made in Middleton and Landon, 521–4, but is most evident in the pages of the *Northern Miner* for these years.

341 *Fort William Times Journal*, Feb. 16, 1926.

342 *Northern Miner*, Mar. 20, 1926, and Jan. 5, 27, June 9, 1927. For a full account of transportation modes to these camps, see Wightman and Wightman, 'Beyond rail and road,' 20.

343 *Northern Miner*, Aug. 16, Nov. 22, Dec. 27, 1928, May 16, Dec. 12, 1929, and Feb. 20, 1930.

344 Ibid., Apr. 10, 1926, June 9, Nov. 10, 1927, July 5, Oct. 11, Nov. 10, Dec. 20, 27, 1928, Jan. 3, Apr. 11, July 25, Oct. 10, 1929, and Jan. 23, Mar. 6, 1930.

345 In 1897 an English syndicate staked at Red Lake and sank a shaft, but to no end, according to BRL, Local History Files, Red Lake Mines, L. Carson Brown, 'The Red Lake gold field,' 117. The same year, Indians of the Longlac area were reported in the *Winnipeg Free Press* of Jan. 22 to have discovered the occurrence of rich veins of gold-bearing ore in the vicinity of their community.
346 *Northern Miner*, Nov. 27, 1926, Feb. 26 and Sept. 8, 1927, May 31, 1928, June 6, 1929, May 1, 1930, and Jan. 23, 1931.
347 George, 60 and 62; and *Northern Miner*, Oct. 16 and Dec. 11, 16, 1930.
348 Waters, 186 and 193; and McCullough, 74.
349 Waters, 185; and McCullough, 42.
350 McCullough, 43–5; and *Sault Star*, June 20, 1920.
351 As Goodier, 284 and 301, makes clear, these postures and activities did much to sully the Company's public image in Canadian waters, particularly in these post-war years.
352 *Sault Star*, Jan. 26, 1926, and Mar. 1, 20, Apr. 4, 1922.
353 Ibid., Mar. 20 and May 3, 1923.
354 Don Steer, 5–18 and 28–30; and *Sault Star*, May 27, Dec. 9, 1924, and Apr. 5, 1928.
355 Goodier, 301; Waters, 191; *Port Arthur News*, Nov. 12, 1915; and *Fort William Times Journal*, Dec. 15, 1917.
356 Goodier, 302.
357 Goodier, 294 and 297–8; and Waters, 186–8.
358 SPO, 1920, no. 14, 'Report of the Fish and Game Commission for 1919'; and *Fort William Times Journal*, July 10, 1918.
359 NAC, RG 23, vol. 572, no. 704-8-8-3 (Desbaret to McDonald, July 11, 1917, McDonald to Desbaret, July 21, 1917, and McNabb to Rodd, Aug. 1, 1917); and *Fort William Times Journal*, July 20 and Dec. 15, 1917.
360 McCullough, 57; and *Fort William Times Journal*, Feb. 13, 1918.
361 TBM, Subject Files, CBC Interviews, Joe Thorstiensen, Beardmore, July 27, 1975, 1–3; and *Fort William Times Journal*, Feb. 13, 1918, and Aug. 19, 1920.
362 McCullough, 57; SPO, 1921, no. 83, 'A return of all papers relating to catch, markets, price to fishermen licence holders, profits from the government fishing operation on Lake Nipigon' (not printed); and *Fort William Times Journal*, Aug. 19, 1920.
363 TBM, Subject Files, CBC Interviews, Joe Thorstiensen, 1–3.
364 Ibid., 3.
365 Macins, 16.
366 *Kenora Miner*, Aug. 6, 1910, Feb. 19, 1919, July 25, 1923, Feb. 25, 1925, and Mar. 22, 1926.
367 Barr and Dyck, 64.

368 Ryan, 1–7; and BRL, Local History Files, fishing, 'Commercial fishing, Rainy River District' (mimeo), 1–6.

369 Lambert and Pross, 457; and McCullough, 86 and 97.

370 *Port Arthur News*, Mar. 28, Aug. 2, 1910, Mar. 23, 1912, and May 5, 1914.

371 NAC, RG 23, vol. 570, no. 704-6-3 (Petitions to Found, Feb. 13 and Dec. 13, 1912, and Board of Trade to Found, Sept. 25, Oct. 30, 1914); and *Kenora Miner*, May 7, 27 and June 24, 1914.

372 NAC, RG, 23, vol. 582, no. 704-31-2 (Found to Manion, July 17, 1919); SPO, 1921, no. 14, 'Report of the Fish and Game Commission for 1920'; *Fort Frances Times*, Apr. 17 and July 10, 1919; *Sault Star*, Jan. 22, July 14, 1921, and Dec. 19, 1922; and *Fort William Times Journal*, Dec. 7, 1921.

373 McCullough, 96–7; NAC, RG 23, vol. 1048, no. 721-8-3, pt. 1 (Found to American Fisheries Commission, Jan. 11, 1928); *Kenora Miner*, Apr. 3, 1926; and *Sault Star*, May 31, 1927.

374 *Fort Frances Times*, Aug. 24, 1922; and *Kenora Miner*, Sept. 9, 1920.

375 SPO, 1929, no. 3, 'Report of the Department of Lands and Forests for 1928.'

376 TBM, Subject Files, Tourism, 'A summer vacation' (1918), 34 p.; FFM, Local History Files, Tourism, 'Rainy River, Rainy Lake' (1923), 16 p.; *Sault Star*, July 16, 1921; *Kenora Miner*, Feb. 18, 1925; *Fort William Times Journal*, May 12, 1926; and *Fort Frances Times*, Apr. 29, 1926.

377 Donald F. Davis, 'Dependent motorization: Canada and the automobile to the 1930's,' *Journal of Canadian Studies* 21 (1986): 124–6; and FFM, Local History Files, Tourism (mimeo), 1928.

378 *Sault Star*, July 24, 1919.

379 Ibid., July 23, 1918, Sept. 4, 1920, July 16, 1921, Aug. 26, 1927, July 28, 1928, and June 18, 1929.

380 Ibid., June 12, 1922, Aug. 7, 11, 1923, Sept. 15, 1924, Apr. 7, June 25, 1925, and Aug. 26, 1930.

381 Ibid., July 16, 1921, June 5, 1925, Jan. 22, 1927, Sept. 27, 1928, and May 6, 1930.

382 Steer, 2–34; and *Sault Star*, June 28, 1921, June 5, Sept. 25, 1925, and June 4, 1930.

383 *Sault Star*, Aug. 3, 1922, May 31, 1923, and Sept. 27, 1928.

384 Ibid., Aug. 15, 1915, June 20, July 10, 1916, June 19, 1918, Aug. 12, 1921, June 5, 1923, and June 5, 1925.

385 Ibid., June 22, Nov. 8, 1922, and Jan. 5, 1923.

386 Ibid., Aug. 30, 1915, Aug. 30, 1919, and May 31, Nov. 29, 1923.

387 *Fort William Times Journal*, May 16, 1921, and June 24, Dec. 12, 1925.

388 These problems with trash fish are recorded as early as SPC, 1906, no. 22, 'Report of the Department of Marine and Fisheries 1905'; NAC, RG 23, vol. 329, no. 2834 (Duncan to Prince, May 15, 1910); and continue in the provincial overseer's

comments of the annual reports of Ontario's Fish and Game Commission for many years.

389 NAC, RG 23, vol. 808, no. 719-5-27, pt. 1 (McDonald to Found, Oct. 11, 1930).

390 Again, these problems are recorded in NAC, RG 23, vol. 329, no. 2834 (Duncan to Prince, May 15, 1910) and are the subject of later comments in the annual reports of Ontario's Fish and Game Commission.

391 *Fort William Times Journal*, May 16, 1921; and *Port Arthur News*, July 12, 1923, June 30, 1925, and Aug. 12, 1929.

392 *Fort William Times Journal*, Aug. 13, 1920, May 19, July 25, 1925, and May 12, July 18, Aug. 26, 1929.

393 Ibid., July 18, 1921, Aug. 15, 1922, Dec. 13, 1924, Nov. 25, 1927, and Aug. 31, 1928.

394 Ibid., Aug. 2, 1927.

395 Ibid., Mar. 16, 1922, July 24, 1925, and Mar. 3, 1927; and *Port Arthur News*, June 10, 1926.

396 *Kenora Miner*, Apr. 21, 1915, and Mar. 10, 1918.

397 Ibid., Mar. 22 and Sept. 20, 1919.

398 Ibid., Apr. 3, June 7, 1913, June 17, 1914, Mar. 24, 1923, and Feb. 18, 1927; and *Canadian Rail and Marine World* (1925): 330.

399 LWM, Local History Files, Tourism.

400 FFM, Local History Files, Tourism (mimeo), 1928.

401 Ibid.

402 FFM, Local History Files, Tourism; *Kenora Miner*, Dec. 5, 1923; *Fort Frances Times*, Aug. 12, 1926, and July 2, 1927; and *Rainy River Record*, July 3, 1930.

403 *Fort Frances Times*, July 30, 1914.

404 David Backes, 'Wilderness visions: Arthur Carhart's 1922 proposal for the Quetico-Superior Wilderness,' *Forest and Conservation History* 35 (1991): 128–37.

405 Lambert and Pross, 480–1.

406 Gerald Kellon and George Warecki, 'The battle for wilderness in Ontario: Saving Quetico-Superior, 1927 to 1960,' in *Patterns of the past*, ed. Roger Hall et al. (Toronto: Dundurn Press, 1988), 328–32.

407 G.R. Stevens, *History of the Canadian National Railways* (New York: Macmillan, 1973), 260–85.

408 Anderson, 46; and TBM, Subject Files, Longlac.

409 *Tracks beside the water*, 161; and Barr and Dyck, 62.

410 *Sault Star*, Aug. 31, 1911, Oct. 8, 23, 1920, Nov. 3, 16, 1923, and Dec. 19, 1928; *Dryden Observer*, June 26, 1913; and *Fort Frances Times*, June 28, 1927.

411 Hornepayne Municipal Office, Boxes 1 and 2.

412 D.F. Parrott, *The Red Lake gold rush* (Red Lake: n.p., 1976), 110–27; John Richthammer, *The end of the road* (Red Lake: Red Lake Festival Days, 1985), 58–60; MTL, Baldwin Room, *Northern Ontario Canada, 1926* (Toronto: n.p., 1927), 52–7; and *The river of time*, 28–9 and 217.

413 MTL, Balwin Room, *Northern Ontario Canada, 1926*, 51 and 53; FFM, Local History Files; *Kenora Miner*, Feb. 24 and Apr. 4, 1924; and *Dryden Observer*, Dec. 19, 1919, June 20, 1924, and Aug. 19, 1927.

414 *Tracks beside the water*, 13, 25, and 53; and *Fort William Times Journal* July 8, 9, 1915, and Sept. 27, 1923. For some discussion of railway YMCAs, see Ronald Melcher, 'Sports in the workplaces,' in *Not just a game*, ed. Jean Harvey and Hart Cantelon (Ottawa: University of Ottawa Press, 1988), 56–8.

415 SSMPL, Local History Files, no. 47, 'Sixty years a City,' Sault Ste Marie, 1962; and *Sault Star*, July 28, 1922.

416 *Sault Star*, Dec. 2, 1924.

417 Emilia Kolcon-Lach, 'Early Italian Settlement at Sault Ste. Marie, Ontario, 1898–1921,' M.A. dissertation, University of Western Ontario, London, 1978, 22–33, makes this point for the earlier immigrant population. *Sault Star*, Jan. 22, 1920, July 28, 1922, Dec. 2, 1924, and Dec. 22, 1950.

418 *Sault Star*, Dec. 2, 1920.

419 *Canadian Rail and Marine World* (1913): 540; and *Sault Star*, Apr. 5, Dec. 30, 1912, May 1, 14, 31, Oct. 1, 4, 7, Nov. 6, 18, Dec. 16, 1913, Mar. 9, 20, May 2, 9, June 29, July 21, 30, Aug. 25, 1914, Apr. 26, 28, 1916, and Aug. 31, 1920.

420 McDowell, 58–92; Inwood, 200–4; and *Sault Star*, 1912–30, especially, Dec. 17, 1930.

421 See 'Thunder Bay's people,' *Polyphony* 9 (1987): 1–114; or BRL, *Thunder Bay Mosaic*, 1–5.

422 Anderson, 46–7.

423 *Fort William Times Journal*, Apr. 24, 1920.

424 Ibid., Dec. 10, 1923.

425 BRL, Local History Files, 'Historical facts grain elevator construction and shipping, Lakehead Harbour, 1883–1964,' 12.

426 *Fort William Times Journal*, Aug. 2, Sept. 17, 1917, Oct. 29, 1918, and May 12, Sept. 26, 1922; and *Twin City Grain and Trade News*, Nov. 1, 1918.

427 *Industrial Canada* 14 (1914): 911–12; and *Port Arthur News*, Feb. 11, 1915.

428 BRL, Local History Files, 'The Port Arthur Shipbuilding Company'; *Port Arthur News* and *Fort William Times Journal*, 1915–1927, particularly the latter, Jan. 8, 1921, Feb. 4, 1925, and Dec. 11, 1926, for references to pulp and paper machinery.

429 *Fort William Times Journal*, Jan. 29, Sept. 11, 1918, Sept. 15, 1919, and Dec. 31, 1949.

430 Ibid., Aug. 2, Nov. 24, Dec. 15, 1917, and Jan. 19, Sept. 5, 1918.

431 Ibid., Nov. 14, 1918, Feb. 10, 1919, Feb. 27, 1920, Oct. 26, 1921, and Jan. 30, 1929.

432 TBM, Subject Files, Iron-ore Smelter, 1921; *Fort William Times Journal*, Apr. 19, May 9, 1921 and Jan. 12, 1922; and *Sault Star*, May 19, 1921.

433 AO, The Irving Papers, MU 1468, 30/36/03 (Borron to Irving, Oct. 10, 1896).

434 See, for example, SPC, 1917, no. 27, 'Report of the Department of Indian Affairs for 1916.'

435 SPC, 1901, no. 27, pt. II, 'Report of the Department of Indian Affairs for 1900'; and Census of Canada, population tables, 1931. Both sources offer frequent figures over these years but these never agree for corresponding years, and, in the case of the first set, differ markedly and inexplicably from one reporting to the next.

436 SPC, 1911 and 1913, no. 27, 'Report of the Department of Indian Affairs for 1910 and 1912.'

437 SPC, 1891, 1899, 1908, 1912 and 1919, no. 27, 'Reports of the Department of Indian Affairs for 1890, 1898, 1907, 1911 and 1918.'

438 NAC, RG 10, vol. 2824, no. 168-291-1 (Dec. 18, 1895, Feb. 5, 1899, and Jan. 3, 1900); and SPC, 1900, no. 14, 'Report of the Department of Indian Affairs for 1899.'

439 SPC, 1903 and 1906–7, no. 27, 'Report of the Department of Indian Affairs for 1902 and 1906.'

440 NAC, RG 10, vol. 2846, no. 174445 (Van Abbott to Indian Affairs, June 27, 1896) and vol. 2928, no. 191782 (MacRae to Indian Affairs, Oct. 19, 1897) as well as the steady stream of references to migration by members of this band in SPC, 1895 to 1910, in the 'Reports of the Department of Indian Affairs.'

441 NAC, RG 10, vol. 2926, no. 190934 (MacRae to Indian Affairs, Sept. 23, 1897) and vol. 3084, no. 275903 (Memo, Aug. 9, 1917); NMC, H2/440, (Sand Point, 1918); and SPC, 1894 and 1898, no. 14, 'Report of the Department of Indian Affairs for 1893 and 1897.'

442 References to this harvest each fall appear not only in most of the newspapers of the region but are often cited as a solid source of family income in the Sessional Papers. See, for example, 1906 and 1908, no. 27, 'Report of the Department of Indian Affairs for 1905 and 1907'; and *Winnipeg Free Press*, Aug. 18, 1891.

443 Thomas W. Dunk, 'Indian participation in the industrial economy on the north shore of Lake Superior, 1869–1940,' *Thunder Bay Historical Museum Society, Papers and Records* 15 (1987): 3–13, provides a good summary here.

444 TBPL, Local History Files, Railways.

445 White River Municipal Office, History Files, Mobert and Regan.

446 NAC, RG 10, vol. 1981, vol. 6124-6 (McLean to Beggs, Aug. 6 and Oct. 26, 1897), and vol. 2922, no. 189242 (Beggs to Indian Affairs, Sept. 14, 1899); and

SPC, 1902 and 1905, no. 27, 'Report of the Department of Indian Affairs for 1901 and 1904.'

447 NAC, RG 10, vol. 2928, no. 191782 (MacRae to Indian Affairs, Oct. 19, 1897); SPC 1895 and 1897, no. 14, 'Report of the Department of Indian Affairs for 1894 and 1896'; and SPC, 1906 and 1912, no. 24, 'Report of the Department of Indian Affairs for 1905 and 1911.'

448 Thomas W. Dunk gives some details here but the bulk of information is scattered. See, for example, NAC, RG 10, vol. 2928, no. 191782 (MacRae to Indian Affairs, Oct. 19, 1897); SPC, 1896, no. 14, 'Report of the Department of Indian Affairs for 1895'; and *Northern Miner*, Sept. 12, 1925, Oct. 11, 1928, and June 6, 1919.

449 SPC, 1893, no. 14, 'Report of the Department of Indian Affairs for 1892'; SPC, 1902 and 1906–7, no. 27, 'Report of the Department of Indian Affairs for 1901 and 1906'; and *Sault Star*, Apr. 12, 1923.

450 SPC, 1906, no. 27, 'Report of the Department of Indian Affairs for 1905'; and *Sault Star*, Nov. 7, 1907, and Apr. 12, 1923.

451 SPC. 1903, 1906 and 1919, no. 27, 'Reports of the Department of Indian Affairs for 1902, 1906 and 1918.'

452 Bradwin, 218–37; and Radforth, 25–34.

453 SPC, 1906–7, no. 27, 'Report of the Department of Indian Affairs for 1906.'

454 S.C. O'Grady, *Report of storage possibilities of Lac Seul* (Winnipeg: Department of the Interior, 1916), 1–17; and Wightman and Wightman, 'The rise of electric power,' 40–1. In the case of HEPC action on the Nipigon watershed, litigation and discussion towards an arbitrated settlement is currently under way.

455 For a discussion of the problems and their resolution on the Lake of the Woods, see the *Kenora Miner*, Jan. 17, 28, June 3, 1914, Sept. 11, 15, 1915, Feb. 2, 1916, June 13, 1917, Mar. 16, 1918, Mar. 2, 11, June 4, 1921, Nov. 19, 1924, and Apr. 27, 1927.

456 NAC, RG 10, vol. 1981, no. 6124-6 (McLean to Beggs, Aug. 6 and Oct. 26, 1897); AO, RG 1, A-I-7, box 8 (Irving to Crown Lands, Oct. 16, 1896), Irving Papers, MU 1468, 30/36/03 (Borron to Irving, Oct. 10, 1896), and MU 1469, 31/37/01 (Matheson to Pedley, Nov. 28, 1905); and *Kenora Miner*, Jan. 23, 1906.

457 NAC, RG 10, vol. 4061, no. 397, 171-14 (Order in Council, July 26, 1907) and vol. 4082, no. 487, 210-1 (inter-departmental correspondence, May 24 and June 5, 1917); and AO, RG 1, A-I-7, box 8 (Order in Council, July 26, 1907). See also *Port Arthur News*, Jan. 10, 1915; *Fort Frances Times*, Mar. 4, 1915, and Mar. 9, 30, Apr. 13, 1916; and *Rainy River Record*, Dec. 15, 1916, and May 19, 1917.

458 NAC, RG 10, vol. 2760, no. 15076-2 (Memo, July 14, 1894), vol. 3937, no. 120, 213 (McColl to Langevin, Oct. 10, 1894 and May 12, 1896), vol. 3990, no. 180, 397 (Stuart to Indian Affairs, Jan. 7, 1899 and Cohill to Indian Affairs, May 18, 1899); SPC, 1906–7, no. 27, 'Report of the Department of Indian Affairs for

1906'; *Tracks beside the water*, 345; *Sault Star*, Jan. 3, 1902, July 22, 1917, and Jan. 10, 25, 1930; and *Dryden Observer*, June 11, 1964.

459 This decline is very evident to anyone reading the increasingly brief, vague, and platitudinous 'Reports of the Department of Indian Affairs' after World War I or who attempts to piece together their condition from the thinning files of the same Department as preserved in the National Archives as RG 10.

4: The Malaise of Depression, Then War, 1930–1950

1 Principal sources used in this summary include: W.T. Easterbrook and Hugh G.J. Aitken, *Canadian economic history* (Toronto: Macmillan Canada, 1956); K.J. Rea. *The prosperous years: The economic history of Ontario, 1939–1973* (Toronto: University of Toronto Press, 1985); Edgar McInnis, *Canada: A political and social history* (Toronto: Holt, Rinehart and Winston, 1964); and Randall White, *Ontario 1610–1985: A political and economic history* (Toronto: Dundurn Press, 1985).

2 Joseph Schull, *Ontario since 1867* (Toronto: McClelland and Stewart, 1978), 283–311.

3 One could choose from a wide range of sources to make this point, but major ones include: A.R.M. Lower, *Settlement and the forest frontier in Eastern Canada*, pt. I, vol. 9 of Canadian Frontiers of Settlement, ed. W.A. Macintosh (Toronto: Macmillan Canada, 1936), 130–46; Richard S. Lambert and Paul Pross, *Renewing nature's wealth* (Toronto: Queen's Printers, 1967), 310–12; G.P. Glazebrook, *Life in Ontario: A social history* (Toronto: University of Toronto Press, 1968), 167; and Donald E. Pugh, 'Ontario's Great Clay Belt hoax,' *Canadian Geographical Journal* 90 (Jan. 1975): 19–24.

4 Save for Roy I. Wolfe, 'The summer resorts of Ontario in the nineteenth century,' *Ontario History* 54 (1962): 149–60, and Geoffrey Wall, 'Recreational land-use in Muskoka,' *Ontario Geography* 11 (1977): 11–29, little is available in the formal literature on tourism; on fishing only some scattered comments for the thirties can be found in A.B. McCullough, *The commercial fisheries of the Canadian Great Lakes* (Ottawa: National Historic Parks and Sites Branch, 1985), and on transportation see a recent paper by the authors, 'Road and highway development in Northwestern Ontario, 1850 to 1990' in the *Canadian Geographer* 36 (1992): 366–80.

5 Morris Zaslow, *The northward expansion of Canada, 1914–1967* (Toronto: McClelland and Stewart, 1988), 34.

6 Ibid., 457–63; and R.J. Burgar, 'Forest land-use evolution in Ontario's Upper Great Lakes Basin,' in *The Great Lakes forest: An environmental and social history*, ed. Susan L. Flader (Minneapolis: University of Minnesota Press, 1983), 188.

7 Lambert and Pross, 308.
8 Zaslow, 52, and Ivor G. Davis, 'Agriculture in the northern forest – The case of Northwestern Ontario,' *Lakehead University Review* 1 (1968): 132.
9 SPO, 1933, no. 3, 'Report of the Department of Lands and Forests for 1932' and subsequent annual reports to SPO, 1940, no. 3 for 1939.
10 See, for example, *Fort William Times Journal*, Feb. 20, 1936; and *Dryden Observer*, Mar. 13, 1936.
11 Burgar, 188.
12 Lambert and Pross, 425.
13 Zaslow, 57–63; and Davies, 133.
14 *Rainy River Record*, June 25, 1931.
15 *Dryden Observer*, May 12, 1933; and *Fort William Times Journal*, Aug. 17, 1932, and May 18, 1933.
16 *Sault Star*, Apr. 28, 1933; and *Fort Frances Times*, Sept. 12, 1933, and Mar. 15, 1935, are good examples.
17 *Kenora Miner*, Mar. 25, 1931, Apr. 12, 22, 1933, Mar. 17, 1934, and Mar. 22, 1935.
18 *Fort William Times Journal*, July 16, 1930, and Aug. 12, 1940; and *Sault Star*, Aug. 12, 15, 1930, Aug. 15, 1931, Sept. 10, 1937, Sept. 15, 1938, and Aug. 5, Sept. 12, 1940.
19 *Rainy River Record*, Aug. 17, Sept. 6, 1934, Sept. 12, 1935, and Aug. 7, 1939; *Fort Frances Times*, Aug. 25, 1932, Aug. 3, 1933, Sept. 5, 1935, and Aug. 3, 17, 1939; and *Fort William Times Journal*, Nov. 6, 1935, and Aug. 27, 1936.
20 See, for example, the *Kenora Miner*, Mar. 24, 1939.
21 *Fort William Times Journal*, June 10, 1932, and June 6, 1942; and *Kenora Miner*, May 3, 1940.
22 *Fort Frances Times*, May 25, 1933.
23 *Rainy River Record*, Oct. 12, 1932, Nov. 18, 1934, Jan. 24, 1935, and Dec. 9, 23, 1937; and *Fort Frances Times*, Mar. 14, 1935.
24 *Sault Star*, June 19, 1934; *Rainy River Record*, Dec. 10, 1936; and *Fort Frances Times*, Mar. 14, 1935.
25 Jack K. Knight, 'Agriculture in New Ontario,' *Ontario Agricultural College Review* 47 (1934): 37–41.
26 *Rainy River Record*, Apr. 25, Sept. 5, 1935, and Aug. 11, 1938; and *Fort Frances Times*, Aug. 11, 1938.
27 *Sault Star*, Aug. 27, 1954; and *Dryden Observer*, Mar. 25, 1931, and Feb. 21, 1936.
28 *Fort William Times Journal*, June 16, 1932, and Feb. 7, 1942.
29 Ibid., Nov. 3, 1930, and Apr. 12, 1937.
30 EPL, Local History Files, Agriculture; and *Fort Frances Times*, Oct. 28, 1937.

31 *Fort Frances Times*, Mar. 24, June 2, 1932, and Oct. 4, 1934.
32 Ibid., June 4, 1936, and June 10, 1937; and *Rainy River Record*, June 10, 1937, June 9, 1938, and June 8, 15, 1939.
33 *Sault Star*, Jan. 15, 1932; *Fort Frances Times*, Nov. 15, 1934; *Fort William Times Journal*, Dec. 19, 1936, and Nov. 5, 1937; and *Kenora Miner*, Aug. 28, 1936.
34 *Sault Star*, Nov. 30, 1934, and June 25, 1938; and *Rainy River Record*, Sept. 22, 1938.
35 *Fort William Times Journal*, May 16, 1936, and Oct. 2, 1937.
36 *Fort Frances Times*, Oct. 19, 1939.
37 Ibid., Mar. 23, 1939; *Rainy River Record*, July 27, 1939; and *Fort William Times Journal*, Feb. 10, 1940.
38 *Fort Frances Times*, Dec. 17, 24, 1931, Oct. 20, 1932, and Mar. 12, 1938.
39 *Fort William Times Journal*, Apr. 27, 1932, and Jan. 17, 1940.
40 Interestingly enough, prairie cattle had been commonly shipped by rail to eastern markets for years but must have gone to feed lots between their arrival in central Canada and their sale at the stockyards. Closer to home, drovers commonly bought cattle and shipped them south by boat from upper Huron, but no records of such operations exist at Sault Ste. Marie.
41 *Dryden Observer*, Dec. 6, 1935, and Feb. 14, 1936.
42 EPL, Local History Files, Agriculture; and *Fort Frances Times*, July 7, 1938.
43 Despite the increasing appearance of cars and trucks, the number of horses in the region grew by about 2,000 to almost 7,000 head by 1941, some being railed in to local sidings (*Fort Frances Times*, June 6, 1935). Most appear to have been heavy draft breeds intended sometimes for bush work but more often for the farm, due to an increase in cultivable acreage and the range of machinery in use (*Sault Star*, Apr. 10, 1934, and Sept. 12, 1935; and *Rainy River Record*, July 12, 1938).
44 FFM, Transportation File; *Fort Frances Times*, Feb. 14, Dec. 12, 1929, and Nov. 24, 1932; and *Rainy River Record*, Nov. 17, 1930, and Jan. 12, 1932.
45 Nancy M. Wightman and W. Robert Wightman, 'Road and highway development in northwestern Ontario, 1850 to 1990,' *Canadian Geographer* 36 (1992): 376.
46 See, for example, *Sault Star*, Nov. 25, 1939; *Fort Frances Times*, Dec. 2, 1940; and *Fort William Times Journal*, Nov. 29, 1941.
47 *Kenora Miner*, Feb. 3, 1939.
48 *Sault Star*, Feb. 2, 1920, Dec. 11, 21, 1939, and Dec. 3, 1940.
49 Nancy M. Wightman and W. Robert Wightman, 'The rise of electric power in northwestern Ontario: Its impact on regional development 1890–1990,' in *Geographic perspectives on the provincial norths*, ed. Margaret Johnston (Toronto: Copp Clark Longman, 1994), 47; and *Fort William Times Journal*, Jan. 19, 1928, Feb. 7, 28, 1929, and July 7, 1932.
50 Thomas F. Waters, *The Superior north shore* (Minneapolis: University of Minnesota Press, 1987); 191.

51 NAC, RG 23, vol. 928, no. 72-4-5 (14) (copy of these resolutions dated Sept. 21–2, 1933).

52 McCullough, 101; AO, RG 39, vol. 417 (Order in Council, Oct. 25, 1932); and NAC, RG 23, vol. 928. no. 721-4-5 (16) (Order in Council, June 11, 1937).

53 *Sault Star*, Oct. 18, 1940; for reactions at the hearings at the Lakehead see *Fort William Times Journal*, Oct. 21, 1940.

54 *Sault Star*, Jan. 15, 1938.

55 *Tracks beside the water* (Sioux Lookout: Sioux Lookout and District Historical Society, 1982), 157.

56 Larry Milbury, *Austin Airways: Canada's Oldest Airline* (Toronto: Canav Books, 1985), 42; *Kenora Miner*, Oct. 11 1933; *Fort William Times Journal*, Jan. 12, 1935; and *Sault Star*, Sept. 7, 1938, and Feb. 13, 1940.

57 NAC, RG 23, vol. 928, no. 721-4-5 (13) (McCallough to Rodd, Oct. 13, 1930); *Fort Frances Times*, Jan. 17, 1935; and *Kenora Miner*, June 14, 1935, and Mar. 10, Apr. 6, 1937.

58 McCullough, 56–8; John L. Goodier, 'Fishermen and their trade on Canadian Lake Superior: One hundred years,' *Inland Seas* 45 (1989): 302; and *Sault Star*, Oct. 17, 1931.

59 Goodier, 292–3; and *Sault Star*, Dec. 3, 1930, Dec. 26, 1933, June 25, 1935, Nov. 22, 1939, and Dec. 20, 1940.

60 Goodier, 294–6.

61 Waters, 191–2; Goodier, 294; and *Sault Star*, Jan. 16, 1934, and Oct. 16, 1940.

62 *Fort William Times Journal*, Dec. 14, 1935, May 11, 1937, and May 10, 1938.

63 Zaslow, 70; and A.R.M. Lower, *The North American assault on the Canadian forest* (Toronto: The Ryerson Press, 1938), 196.

64 Lambert and Pross, 324; and Lower, 199.

65 Lambert and Pross, 325; and NAC, RG 39, vol. 416 (Order in Council, Apr. 10, 1934).

66 Peter W. Sinclair, 'The North and North-West: Forestry and agriculture,' *Progress without planning*, ed. Ian M. Drummond (Toronto: University of Toronto Press, 1987): 80; and Ian Radforth, *Bushworkers and bosses* (Toronto: University of Toronto Press, 1987), 15.

67 *Sault Star*, Feb. 22, 1929, Dec. 17, 1931, Aug. 18, 1932, Dec. 26, 1933, and May 28, July 3, Nov. 9, 1935.

68 Ibid., Aug. 21, 1931, and Sept. 10, 1938.

69 AO, RG 1, E-12, vol. 21 (Lumber Mill Returns 1941); and LUPL, J.P. Bertrand, 'Timber wolves' (unpaginated typescript), Port Arthur, 1960; and *Fort William Timber Journal*, Dec. 6, 1939, and Sept. 14, 16, 19, Oct. 9, 1940.

70 HBC Arch., B421/a/1 (Hudson, 1933); AO, RG 1, E-7, vol. 4 (Order in Council, Oct. 18, 1937); *Fort William Times Journal*, June 9, 1931; and *Kenora Miner*, Aug. 23, 1933.

71 NAC, RG 39, vol. 417 (copy of *The Canadian Gazette*, July 23, 1932); and AO, RG 1, E-12, vol. 21 (Lumber Mill Returns 1941).
72 *Fort Frances Times*, Apr. 3, and Oct. 2, 1930.
73 Ibid., Sept. 1, 1932, Apr. 5, May 3, 1934, Nov. 28, 1935, Jan. 30, 1936, and Nov. 7, 1940.
74 *Sault Star*, Sept. 12, 1936; and *Fort Frances Times*, Jan. 11, Feb. 22, Oct. 24, 1940, July 17, Oct. 30, 1941, and Apr. 23, 1942.
75 SPO, 1930, no. 3, 'Report of the Department of Lands and Forests for 1929.'
76 Zaslow, 82.
77 *Sault Star*, Aug. 21, Oct. 4, 1930, and July 31, Aug. 8, 1931.
78 Ibid., Sept. 1, 11, 29, 1931, July 2, 1932, Oct. 11, 1933, Aug. 4, 1934, and Mar. 22, 1935.
79 *Fort William Times Journal*, Dec. 12, 1937, and Dec. 17, 1938.
80 Ibid., July 25, 1931, May 31, 1932, June 26, 1933, Nov. 28, 30, 1934, Mar. 11, 1935, and Oct. 23, 1936.
81 Ibid., June 6, Oct. 17, 1934, and Oct. 27, 1939; and *Sault Star*, Oct. 13, 1934.
82 *Fort Frances Times*, Jan. 31, 1929; *Kenora Miner*, Jan. 11, 1931; and *Fort William Times Journal*, Apr. 6 and July 11, 1931.
83 *Kenora Miner*, Feb. 22, 1933, June 23, 1936, and May 2, 1941; *Fort Frances Times*, Sept. 12, 1931, Oct. 12, 1933, Nov. 29, 1934, and Jan. 16, 1941; and *Sault Star*, May 1, 1941. Ontario and Minnesota as well as Great Lakes seem to have been reorganized and taken up by a cluster of newspaper producers with headquarters in Minneapolis, according to these records.
84 H.V. Nelles, *The politics of development: Forests, mines and hydro electric power in Ontario, 1849–1941* (Toronto: Macmillan Canada, 1974), 459–60; Sinclair, 83–4; and Lambert and Pross, 335–41.
85 Lambert and Pross, 339–41; and Nelles, 353–8.
86 AO, RG 1, E-7, vol. 4 (Order in Council, Aug. 23, 1937); and *Fort William Times Journal*, Aug. 25, 1937, and Feb. 6, 1940.
87 AO, RG 1, E-7, vol. 4 (Orders in Council, Jan. 16, Feb. 27, Sept. 14, 1937).
88 Ibid. (Orders in Council, Feb. 27 and Sept. 14, 1937); and *Fort William Times Journal*, Nov. 16, 1934, and Oct. 5, 1936.
89 AO, RG 1, E-7, vol. 4 (Order in Council, Dec. 22, 1937) and vol. 5 (Order in Council, Aug. 16, 1940).
90 Ibid., vol. 5 (Orders in Council, Feb. 5, Dec. 20, 1936 and Sept. 14, 1937).
91 Ibid., vol. 4 (Orders in Council, Jan. 16, Apr. 16 and Sept. 14, 1937) and vol. 5 (Order in Council, Aug. 16, 1940); and *Fort William Times Journal*, Jan. 25, 1937.
92 AO, RG 1, E-7, vol. 4, (Orders in Council, Jan. 16 and Apr. 16, 1937).
93 Ibid. (Order in Council, Aug. 13, 1937); *Fort Williams Times Journal*, Aug. 7, 1937; and *Sault Star*, Aug. 13, 1937.

94 As a result, all these agreements were cancelled or transferred by later Orders in Council, see AO, RG 1, E-7, vol. 5 (Orders in Council, Aug. 25 and 27, 1945); and *Sault Star*, Apr. 23, 1940.

95 *Fort William Times Journal*, Apr. 8, Oct. 25, 1937, and Jan. 4, 20, Feb. 21, May 6, 1938; and *Sault Star*, July 30, 1937, and Feb. 8, 1938.

96 Lambert and Pross, 342–5. Reports of the Inquiry appeared from time to time in the press. See, for example, *Fort William Times Journal*, Jan. 30, 1939 and Feb. 1, Apr. 28, 1940.

97 Nelles, 460; and *Fort William Times Journal*, Oct. 27 and Dec. 16, 1939.

98 AO, MU 1319, 1962, no. 4, Misc.; WPL, Local History, Binder no. 5; and *Sault Star*, Sept. 10, 1932.

99 *Sault Star*, Oct. 16, 1933, July 6, 1934, and Mar. 14, 1935.

100 Ibid., Dec. 5, 1934, and May 5, 1936; and WPL, Local History, Binder no. 5.

101 The best account of the various activities and capabilities of these firms is to be found in J.P. Bertrand.

102 AO, MU 1319, 1962, no. 4, Misc., RG 1, E-7, vol. 3 (Orders in Council, July 6 and Dec. 24, 1931); Jeanne Marcella, *A History of Jackfish* (Terrace Bay: Terrace Bay Library, 1987), 30; and *Fort William Times Journal*, Apr. 15, May 30, June 24, 1935, and May 31, Oct. 13, 1938.

103 Bertrand; and *Fort William Times Journal*, Oct. 17, 1940.

104 Lambert and Pross, 335–8.

105 However, some production still came from the immediate area, see *Sault Star*, Aug. 4, 1934, and Sept. 2, 1940.

106 A summary of information of this type is to be found in material appended to AO, RG 1, E-5, vol. 19 (Reports on Pulp and Paper Production, 1940).

107 Lambert and Pross, 325, 339.

108 Sinclair, 83.

109 *Sault Star*, Dec. 10, 1929, Dec. 5, 1934, Mar. 22, 1937, Oct. 2, 1939, and Aug. 27, 1940.

110 Zaslow, 97–8; and Radforth, 126–8.

111 Radforth, 124.

112 Ibid., 126–8; and *Fort William Times Journal*, June 20 to Dec. 14, 1933.

113 *Sault Star*, Jan. 26, Apr. 20 and Oct. 9, 12, 1934; and *Fort William Times Journal*, Nov. 3, 1934.

114 Radforth, 127–8; and *Fort William Times Journal*, Feb. 20, 1936.

115 Radforth, 129.

116 R. Peter Gillis and Thomas R. Roach, *Lost initiatives* (New York: Greenwood Press, 1986), 101–5; J.A. Brodie, 'Timber management in Ontario,' *Canadian Geographical Journal* 42 (Mar. 1951): 102–3; Lambert and Pross, 199–201; and Zaslow, 72–4.

117 *Sault Star*, Apr. 27, 1925, Apr. 21, 1927, May 31, 1928, and June 14, 17, 1929.

118 Lambert and Pross, 325; and Gillis and Roach, 101.

119 *Northern Miner*, Sept. 25, 1930, and July 9, 1931.

120 Ibid., Nov. 7, 1941.

121 Zaslow, 126; and T.A. Rickard, 'Gold and silver in Ontario,' *Canadian Mining Journal* 65 (1944): 696. As Peter George points out in his essay entitled 'Ontario's mining industry, 1870–1940,' in *Progress without planning*, ed. Ian Drummond, 61, the Canadian dollar price was somewhat lower than the U.S.$36 an ounce.

122 Nelles, 434–8; and George, 66–8.

123 See, for example, *Kenora Miner*, Mar. 23, 1931, and Jan. 3, 1933; or *Sault Star*, Jan. 17, 1933, and Jan. 24, 1935.

124 *Kenora Miner*, Aug. 19, 1931, and Oct. 6, 1939; and *Northern Miner*, Feb. 11, 1934, July 4, Sept. 5, 1935, Feb. 20, Aug. 13, 27, 1936, Jan. 7, May 13, 1937, and July 6, 1939.

125 NAC, RG 45, vol. 27, no. 2880, pt. 3 (Riddell to Lynch, Oct. 31, 1935); *Northern Miner*, May 17, Sept. 13, 1934, and Feb. 14, 21, June 27, 1935; and *Fort Frances Times*, July 13, 1938.

126 *Fort Frances Times*, July 13, 1938; *Northern Miner*, Feb. 20, 1930, Feb. 5, Mar. 26, 1931, Aug. 2, 1934, Jan. 17, Oct. 3, 17, 1935, and Sept. 10, Oct. 8, 22, 1936; and *Fort William Times Journal*, Sept. 16, 1935, and July 30, 1936.

127 *Northern Miner*, Jan. 26, 1932, Aug. 31, Dec. 16, 1933, May 3, 1934, Oct. 11, Nov. 22, Dec. 6, 1935, Nov. 5, Dec. 24, 1936, Jan. 14, Mar. 11, Apr. 29, June 10, July 13, Aug. 19, 1937, and Mar. 6, 1941; and *Fort William Times Journal*, Dec. 4, 1935.

128 *Northern Miner*, Dec. 11, 1930, July 2, 1932, Aug. 31, 1933, July 9, 1936, Nov. 16, 1939, July 18, 1940, and June 12, 1941; and *Sault Star*, Oct. 2, 1942.

129 *Northern Miner*, June 30, Aug. 20, Nov. 19, Dec. 10, 1931, and Feb. 2, 23, June 14, 1933; and *Sault Star* Apr. 12, 1930, July 8, 1932, and June 4, 1934.

130 *Northern Miner*, Feb. 7, Mar. 21, Apr. 11, 18, 1935, Mar. 19, May 14, July 16, Sept. 10, 17, 1936, June 17, Dec. 2, 1937, Aug. 17, 1939, and Feb. 29, 1940; and *Sault Star*, July 5, 1932, and June 4, 1934.

131 George, 62–3. Several general works have been published on both these areas, the most complete include: D.F. Parrott, *The Red Lake Gold Rush* (Red Lake: the author, 1983); and Edgar J.D. Lavoie, ... *And the Geraldton way* (Geraldton: Times Star Publishing Ltd., 1987).

132 *Northern Miner*, July 9, Oct. 8, Nov. 12, 1931, Nov. 10, Dec. 29, 1932, and Aug. 3, 1933.

133 Ibid., Apr. 26, 1934.

134 Ibid., Nov. 24, Dec. 1, 8, 22, 1938, July 6, 1939, Apr. 4, 1940, and Mar. 6, 1941.

135 Ibid., July 25, 1929, Dec. 16, 1930, Mar 5, Apr. 16, 1931, and Apr. 20, Sept. 14, Oct. 12, 1933.

136 Ibid., Apr. 5, July 5, and Aug. 16, 1934.

137 Ibid., Jan. 22, Feb. 12, Apr. 16, June 11, 1931 and Mar. 16, Sept. 7, 1933.

138 Ibid., Oct. 15, 1931, June 16, 23, Sept. 8, Oct. 20, 1932, and June 1, 22, 29, 1933.

139 G.B. Weiler, 'Some memories of the Thunder Bay gold rush of '34,' *Thunder Bay Historical Museum Society Papers and Records*, 8 (1980): 22–31; *Northern Miner*, Oct. 19, Nov. 23, 1933, and Sept. 13, 27, 1934; and *Sault Star*, Oct. 16, 1934.

140 *Northern Miner*, Dec. 24, 1936, and Dec. 2, 1937; and *Fort William Times Journal*, Dec. 19, 1936.

141 *Northern Miner*, July 28, 1938; and *Fort William Times Journal*, Dec. 16, 1939.

142 *Northern Miner*, Feb. 28 and Aug. 29, 1929; and *Sault Star*, Aug. 24, 1929.

143 *Sault Star*, May 17 and July 10, 1930.

144 *Northern Miner*, Feb. 19, 1931.

145 Duncan McDowall, *Steel at the Sault* (Toronto: University of Toronto Press, 1984), 163–4; and *Northern Miner*, Oct. 24, 1935.

146 McDowall, 153–63.

147 NAC, RG 45, vol. 32, no. 461 (Boulton to the Geological Survey, Jan. 24, 1936); and *Sault Star*, Feb. 16 and Mar. 3, 1937.

148 NAC, RG 45, vol. 73, no 4134-0 (Boulton to Copley, Mar. 7, 1933).

149 McDowall, 166; *Northern Miner*, Feb. 18, 25 and Aug. 5, 1937; and *Globe and Mail*, Dec. 30, 1937, and June 22, July 13, Aug. 24, Sept. 28, 1939.

150 *Sault Star*, Mar. 18, 1937; and *Northern Miner*, July 22, 1937.

151 *Northern Miner*, Sept. 28, 1939; and *Sault Star*, Sept. 27, 1939, and May 27, 1940.

152 *Sault Star*, Dec. 23, 1939; and *Northern Miner*, Oct. 24, 1940.

153 *Sault Star*, Mar. 30, 1938.

154 William Treadwell, 'The pellet makers,' *Canadian Geographical Journal* 72 (June 1966): 195; and *Northern Miner*, Apr. 7 and May 12, 1938.

155 Treadwell, 195.

156 *Northern Miner*, Mar. 2, 16, and May 26, 1939.

157 Treadwell, 196; and *Northern Miner*, Mar. 6, 1941.

158 For a further account of such developments in the region, see Wightman and Wightman, 'Road and highway development,' 366–80.

159 This rift, which Sir James Dunn spitefully augmented (see McDowall, 169), was fomented by Ontario's Hepburn government with its new policies of 'cut relief [and make-work projects], put the men back to work,' and, as H.V. Nelles, 440–1, notes, his unrelated demand that Ottawa cease natural resource taxation, in the spirit of Confederation, or add its contribution to the development of mining infrastructure.

160 See, for example, *Fort Frances Times*, May 12, 1931; *Dryden Observer*, Sept. 18, 1931; *Fort William Times Journal*, July 29, 1931; and *Sault Star*, June 14, 1932.

161 The press in these years frequently mentioned such sports events and the excellent relations between camp and community. Personal interviews with the elderly of the region, however, elicited stories of camp foremen who were particularly harsh, including one Scot who used his crews off hours to create his own golf course. Perhaps the best pictorial record of life under these circumstances is a large hand-lettered account by a haberdasher and photographer who sold clothing and took pictures of the work at and east of Nipigon. This remarkable set of albums is lodged in the Dorion Public Library.

162 For both a tabular reconstruction and more complete commentary on the rise of this industry in the northwest, see Wightman and Wightman, 'The rise of electric power,' 44–46. For a more succinct statement, see Zaslow, 92–4.

163 *Fort William Times Journal*, Jan. 5, 11, 16, 21, and Aug. 14, 1935; and Nancy M. Wightman and W. Robert Wightman, 'Beyond rail and road: The Red Lake–Pickle Lake gold fields, 1925–1954,' *Thunder Bay Historical Museum Society Papers and Records* 21 (1993): 29.

164 *Fort William Times Journal*, Nov. 2, 1937, and Aug. 11, 1938; *Sault Star*, Dec. 2, 3, 1937, and Aug. 12, 1938; and *Geraltdon Times Star*, Sept. 1, 1947.

165 *Kenora Miner*, Aug. 5, 1931.

166 *Fort Frances Times*, Dec. 17, 1931; and *Rainy River Record*, June 2, 1932.

167 Lori Nelson and Patty Nelson, *The summer people: A history of Kenora's tourist industry* (Kenora: Spoke Press, 1979), 58; and HBC Archives, B440/a/1 (Minaki Post, May 1932–3).

168 *Fort William Times Journal*, May 14, 1931, and Jan. 11, 1936.

169 *Sault Star*, Nov. 17, 1930, Nov. 13, 1931, and Jan. 10, 1935.

170 *Kenora Miner*, May 2, July 4, Aug. 8, 1934, and July 2, 1935.

171 *Fort Frances Times*, May 16, and July 25, 1935.

172 *Fort William Times Journal*, Jan. 11, 1936, and Dec. 18, 1937.

173 *Sault Star*, Jan. 10, 1935.

174 *Kenora Miner*, Mar. 31, 1939; and *Fort Frances Times*, Feb. 15, 1940.

175 *Fort William Times Journal*, Dec. 19, 1936, Dec. 18, 1937, and Jan. 12, 1941.

176 *Sault Star*, May 14, 1937, and Sept. 11, 1939.

177 Donald F. Davis, 'Dependent motorization: Canada and the automobile to the thirties,' *Journal of Canadian Studies* 21 (1986): 126.

178 *Evergreen reflections* (Vermilion Bay: The Nor-West Historical Society, 1986): 17, 112–14; Rae Kiebuzinski, *Yesterday the river* (Ear Falls: Ear Falls Historical Committee, 1975): 344; HBC Archives, B/273/a/1, (*Dinorwic Post*, July 1937–8); and *Dryden Observer*, June 28, Dec. 14, 1935, June 12, 1936, and Mar. 21, Aug. 22, 1941.

179 *Tracks beside the water* (Sioux Lookout: Sioux Lookout and District Historical Society, 1982): 170; and Kiebuzinski, 306.

180 *Fort William Times Journal*, Aug. 21, 1936, and Sept. 11, 1940.

181 See, for example, *Sault Star*, Oct. 23, 1933; *Kenora Miner*, Sept. 17, 1937; *Dryden Observer*, June 17, 1938; and *Fort William Times Journal*, July 12, 1940.

182 *Fort William Times Journal*, Jan. 29 and Feb. 2, 1949; and *Rainy River Record*, Feb. 10, 1949.

183 *Sault Star*, Dec. 22, 1950.

184 Ian M. Drummond, ed., *Progress without planning* (Toronto: University of Toronto Press, 1987), 21. See also *Sault Star*, May 18, Oct. 1940, and Sept. 20, Oct. 17, 1941; and *Fort William Times Journal*, July 31, Dec. 14, 1940, and Dec. 20, 1941.

185 *Sault Star*, Sept. 12, 1933, and July 9, 1936; and *Tracks beside the water*, 40.

186 Randall White, *Ontario 1610–1985: A political and economic history* (Toronto: Dundurn Press, 1985), 222–39; Sinclair, 83; and Nelles, 454.

187 In Sault Ste Marie, for example, a special employment agency was set up in December 1930 and soon had 1,300 registrants, according to the *Sault Star*, Aug. 8, 1931, and conditions were equally as bad at the Lakehead, from reports in the *Fort William Times Journal*, Dec. 12, 1930, and after.

188 *Fort William Times Journal*, Jan. 5, 21, and May 14, 1935.

189 For some measure of the uncertainty and rejection these unemployed faced, see *Fort William Times Journal*, May 27, 1931, and Oct. 7, 8, 20, 1932; and *Fort Frances Times*, Oct. 29 and Nov. 5, 1936.

190 See, for example, the rules applied as stated in the *Sault Star*, Aug. 8, 1935.

191 AO, Pamphlets, 1982, no. 68. The *Sault Star*, May 10, and Aug. 17, 30, 1932, is also very interesting on such arrangements.

192 Such cuts of 5 to 10 per cent, in preference to layoffs, occurred at the Sault Ste. Marie steel mills (*Sault Star*, Oct. 6, 1931) and generally across the pulp and paper industry, as earlier references have indicated.

193 *Sault Star*, June 14, 1932, July 7, 1935, and June 9, 1936, are regional examples of this tendency, which Drummond, in *Progress without Planning*, 21, indicates was much more widespread in the province.

194 *Sault Star*, May 9, 1929, June 12, 1930, and Sept. 11, 1933.

195 McDowall, 171–3.

196 *Sault Star*, Apr. 30, 1937, Aug. 28, 1939, and Nov. 11, 1940.

197 Ibid., Apr. 12, 1937, Dec. 2, 1938, Dec. 1, 1939, and June 23, 1940.

198 *Fort William Times Journal*, Nov. 14, 1936, Jan. 25, July 13, Sept. 17, 1937, Mar. 22, Nov. 16, 1938, Dec. 16, 1939, and June 1, 1940.

199 BRL, Historical Files, Shipbuilding, 'The Port Arthur Shipbuilding Company'; and *Fort William Times Journal*, Feb. 2, Aug. 19, Dec. 14, 1940, and Apr. 14, Dec. 10, 1941.

200 *Fort William Times Journal*, Apr. 3, 1941.
201 Ibid., Dec. 6, 1939, and Mar. 19, 1940.
202 *Fort Frances Times*, Oct. 24, 1940, and July 17, 1941; and *Kenora Miner*, Mar. 28 and Apr. 25, 1939.
203 *Fort Frances Times Journal*, June 8, 1931, May 16, 1936, and Dec. 16, 1939.
204 *Sault Star*, Feb. 8, 1938; and *Fort William Times Journal*, Feb. 21, 1938, and Dec. 16, 1939.
205 *Sault Star*, Feb. 9, 1934, and Mar. 1, 1940.
206 *Geraldton District Times*, Sept. 1, 1937; *Fort William Times Journal*, Oct. 24, 1936, and Aug. 31, 1938; *Kenora Miner*, Dec. 21, 1934; and *Red Lake News*, Aug. 7, 1937.
207 George, 62, comments on the dispersed pattern of mine villages here but does not appear to recognize the more eastern parallels that were historically evident in places like Timmins, but are most pronounced in the Sudbury Basin.
208 Robert Bothwell et al., *Canada, 1900–1945* (Toronto: University of Toronto Press, 1920), 361–6.
209 Schull, 314–15.
210 Bothwell et al., 357–8; and Rea, 163–4.
211 Rea, 162–3; and Easterbrook and Aitken, 535–6.
212 Rea, 163–6.
213 Philip Smith, *Harvest from the rock* (Toronto: University of Toronto Press, 1980), 281; and Rea, 163–5.
214 *Sault Star*, Oct. 2, 1942; and *Northern Miner*, May 7, 1942.
215 *Northern Miner*, Mar. 4, 18, and Sept. 9, 1943.
216 Ibid., Sept. 25, 1941, May 21, Sept. 24, Oct. 29, 1942, and Aug. 19, 1943.
217 Ibid., July 6, Aug. 13, 1944, and Apr. 5, 1945; and *Geraldton Times Star*, Sept. 1, 1947.
218 *Northern Miner*, Dec. 17, 31, 1942, and Jan. 4, July 26, 1945.
219 Ibid., July 26, 1945, Jan. 3, 10, 1946, Oct. 14, 1948, Oct. 20, 1949, and Oct. 19, 1950.
220 Ibid., Apr. 4, 1946.
221 Ibid., Oct. 9, 1947, and Nov. 24, 1949; and *Fort William Times Journal*, Dec. 20, 1947.
222 Rea, 164–5; Smith, 281; and *Northern Miner*, Sept. 3, 1942, Aug. 24, 1943, July 6, 1944, and Special Investors Edition, 1945.
223 *Northern Miner*, Feb. 4, 25, 1943.
224 Ibid., Aug. 24, 1943, and Apr. 5, May 17, 1945; *Fort William Times Journal*, Dec. 18, 1943; and *Geraldton Times Star*, Sept. 1, 1947.
225 *Northern Miner*, May 17, July 26, Dec. 20, 1945, Apr. 4, 1946, and Feb. 20, 1947.

226 Zaslow, 114; *Northern Miner*, Feb. 5, May 13, Dec. 2, 1948, and Jan. 26, Feb. 2, 9, June 8, Nov. 9, 1950; and *Geraldton Times Star*, Sept. 22, 1949. The dates for the opening and final closing of all these mines is listed in NAC, RG 14, B-10-5, no. 76.

227 *Northern Miner*, Special Investors Edition, 1945, June 13, 1946, Dec. 2, 1948, Oct. 20, 1949, and Oct. 19, 1950.

228 Smith, 282; and *Northern Miner*, Feb. 20, May 8, 1947, Feb. 19, Mar. 25, 1948, Jan. 2, 16, 20, 1949, and Mar. 23, 1950.

229 Rea, 167.

230 *Northern Miner*, Oct. 24, 1940, Dec. 30, 1948, and Oct. 19, 1950; *Sault Star*, Jan. 4, 1940, June 18, 1941, and Oct. 26, 1950; and *Fort William Times Journal*, Oct. 23, and Dec. 8, 1945.

231 Smith, 285–6; *Northern Miner*, Nov. 11 and 16, 1948; and *Sault Star*, Apr. 9, 20, 29, June 14, Aug. 2, 4, 18, 1949, and Apr. 6, June 1, 1950.

232 McDowall, 181–99; and Rea, 210–11.

233 *Northern Miner*, Mar. 12, 1942, and Apr. 15, 1943.

234 *Sault Star*, May 8 and Sept. 14, 1942; and *Northern Miner*, Apr. 15, May 6, 1943, and Nov. 9, 1944.

235 *Northern Miner*, Oct. 19, 1944.

236 Treadwell, 196.

237 Rea, 167; and *Northern Miner*, Feb. 18 and Mar. 18, 1943.

238 Treadwell, 196. Other figures for water removal vary from 150 billion in the *Fort Frances Times*, Apr. 30, 1942, to 110 trillion in Schull, 321. The latter may refer to the whole as opposed to the first stage of the project.

239 Rea, 167; Wightman and Wightman, 'The rise of electric power,' 46; and *Northern Miner*, Mar. 23, and Dec. 2, 1943.

240 *Northern Miner*, Oct. 3, 1944.

241 Ibid., June 14, Aug. 16, Nov. 18, 1945, and May 2, 30, Sept. 19, 1946.

242 McDowall, 214–31.

243 Rea, 168; *Northern Miner*, May 2, 30 1946, and Dec. 4, 1947; and *Fort Frances Times*, Dec. 4, 1947.

244 Treadwell, 196–7.

245 *Northern Miner*, Oct. 24, 1946, Nov. 25, 1948, May 26, 1949, and Oct. 19, 1950.

246 Ibid., Oct. 4, 1945, and May 12, June 16, 1949.

247 Rea, 168.

248 Bothwell, 337; *Fort Frances Times*, Aug. 8, 1940; *Fort William Times Journal*, May 10, 1941 and Jan. 17, 1942; and *Sault Star*, Apr. 11, 1942.

249 Radforth, 141–2; and *Sault Star*, Oct. 6, 1943.

250 *Sault Star*, May 26, 1943; and *Fort William Times Journal*, Nov. 12, 1943.

251 Chris M.V. Madsen, 'German prisoners of war in Canada during the Second World War,' M.A. dissertation, University of Western Ontario, London, 1992, Appendix I.

252 Ibid., 126–33. The opinions expressed here differ considerably from the positive memories, concerning the attitude and work of these men, of Mr. Allan Buel, a young forester with Kimberly-Clark at Longlac, as related during an interview with the authors in 1989 at his home in Manotick. *Sault Star*, Apr. 18, 1946.

253 *Northern Miner*, Sept. 24, 1942.

254 *Fort Frances Times*, Dec. 16, 1943, and Mar. 14, Aug. 22, 1946; *Fort Frances Times Journal*, Sept. 17, 1943, Feb. 9, 1944, and Dec. 8, 1945; and *Sault Star*, Apr. 3, May 26, 1943, and Aug. 16, 1945.

255 *Fort William Times Journal*, Sept. 21 and Dec. 8, 1945.

256 Rea, 188; and AO, RG 1, E-7, vol. 5, (Order in Council, May 5, 1943).

257 AO, RG 1, E-7, vol. 6, (Orders in Council, Aug. 25 and 27, 1943); and *Fort William Times Journal*, Aug. 28, 1943.

258 *Fort Frances Times*, Jan. 3 and Feb. 24, 1944.

259 Rea, 187–9; Lambert and Pross, 396; and *Fort William Times Journal*, Dec. 8 and 9, 1943.

260 Lambert and Pross, 397–402; and Rea, 189–90.

261 SPO, 1947, no. 37, 'Report of the Royal Commission on Forestry, 1947.'

262 Lambert and Pross, 402–3; and Rea, 190–1.

263 Rea, 190; *Sault Star*, Oct. 3, 1947; and SPO, 1943 and 1945, no. 3, 'Report of the Department of Lands and Forests for 1942 and for 1944.'

264 AO, RG 1, E-7, vol. 5 (separate Orders in Council, Aug. 27, 1945, for each licence and licensee).

265 *Fort Frances Times*, July 12, 1945; *Kenora Miner*, July 13, 1945; and *Dryden Observer*, Dec. 10, 1948.

266 *Fort William Times Journal*, Dec. 8, 1945, June 7, Nov. 2, 1946, and Dec. 16, 1948.

267 SPO, 1945, no. 3, 'Report of the Department of Lands and Forests for 1945'; *Sault Star*, Oct. 28, 1941; and *Fort William Times Journal*, Mar. 16, 1942, Nov. 22, 1944, July 25, Oct. 31, 1945, and Mar. 5, 1946.

268 Radforth, 20; *Dryden Observer*, Nov. 7, 1951; and *Fort William Times Journal*, Oct. 31, 1945.

269 Jean Boultbee, *Pic, pulp and people*, revised by Jesse Embree (Marathon: Township of Marathon, 1981), 42–71; *Fort William Times Journal*, Nov. 17, 1943, and Feb. 24, Mar. 16, 1944; and *Marathon Courier*, Feb. 1945.

270 Bertrand.

271 AO, Pamphlets, 1947, no. 52; *Fort William Times Journal*, Aug. 27, 1943, Jan. 11, Apr. 13, 16, 1946, and June 9, 10, 1948; and *Geraldton Times Star*, Sept. 1, 1947.

272 *Terrace Bay News*, Oct. 23, 1947.
273 Radforth, 144–8.
274 Ibid., 159–62.
275 Ibid., 162–5; *Fort William Times Journal*, Dec. 2, Aug. 2, and Sept. 8, 1947; *Northern Miner*, Feb. 27, 1948; and *Sault Star*, June 18, 1948.
276 *Fort William Times Journal*, Jan. 11, and Apr. 6, 16, 1949; and *Sault Star*, Mar. 29, 1949.
277 *Rainy River Record*, Mar. 12, 1944, and June 28, 1945; *Fort Frances Times*, Nov. 29, 1945; and *Dryden Observer*, Dec. 10, 1948.
278 *Fort William Times Journal*, June 29, 1945, and Sept. 4, 1948.
279 *Sault Star*, Oct. 20, 1948, and Mar. 17, Aug. 8, 1949.
280 Bertrand; and SPO, 1945, no. 3, 'Report of the Department of Lands and Forests for 1944.'
281 *Sault Star*, Aug. 27, 1948.
282 *Marathon Courier*, Feb., July 1945, Dec. 1946, and Mar. 1949; Terrace Bay Municipal Office, Historical Files; and *Geraldton Times Star*, Nov. 25, 1948, and Jan. 27, 1949. It is important, however, to recognize that these activities were not unique (*Fort William Times Journal*, Dec. 20, 1947). Companies like Great Lakes at Valora were also using trucks, sledges, and jammers (*Fort William Times Journal*, Aug. 28, 1947) while Brompton was using similar equipment on its limit, as well as three powerful tugs on Lake Nipigon (*Fort William Times Journal*, Feb. 14, 1948 and *Geraldton Times Star*, Nov. 25, 1948, and June 2, 1949).
283 *Marathon Courier*, Apr. and Sept. 1945.
284 *Fort William Times Journal*, Sept. 22, and Oct. 2, 1947.
285 Radforth, 191–2; *Geraldton Times Star*, Nov. 25, 1948; and *Marathon Courier*, Feb. and Mar., 1949.
286 Radforth, 168.
287 SPO, 1947, no. 37, 'Report of the Royal Commission on Forestry, 1947,' Forest Communities.
288 Radforth, 168–9.
289 *Port Arthur News Chronicle*, Aug. 14, 1947; *Geraldton Times Star*, Nov. 25, 1948; and *Marathon Courier*, Feb. and Mar., 1949.
290 For a thorough discussion of this reorganization, see Lambert and Pross, 361–82.
291 Lambert and Pross, 204–23, 365–6; and Rea, 190–1.
292 Lambert and Pross, 405–6; J.A. Brodie, 'Ontario has its picture taken,' *Sylva* 2 (1946): 51–6; and Burgar, 192.
293 SPO, 1941, no. 3, 'Report of the Department of Lands and Forests for 1940'; Lambert and Pross, 226–31; *Kenora Miner*, Aug. 4, 1936; *Sault Star*, Aug. 32, 1939, and May 9, 1940; and *Fort William Times Journal*, Aug. 17, 1939, and Apr. 10, 1944.

294 *Fort William Times Journal*, Dec. 8, 1945, and Apr. 29, 1946; and *Geraldton Times Star*, Oct. 3, 1946.

295 Lambert and Pross, 229–31; and *Fort William Times Journal*, Apr. 29, 1946, June 28, 1947, and Aug. 11, 31, 1949.

296 Lambert and Pross, 228–9; *Sault Star*, Aug. 31, 1949; and *Fort William Times Journal*, June 11, 1949.

297 Rea, 186; and Lambert and Pross, 394–5.

298 Rea, 187–91. While this author renders a good analysis, the weight he places on American capitalism seems exaggerated in the northwest, where the problem, as often as not, reflected an innate, conservative Canadian business outlook. It is only fair to recognize that some firms such as Ontario and Minnesota Pulp and Paper did undertake such planning at surprisingly early dates across their Seine, Manitou, Lake of the Woods, and English River concessions (*Fort Frances Times*, May 25, 1949). See also Lambert and Pross, 406–7.

299 All through the later decade, E.E. Johnson continued to harp on this issue and his own problems (*Fort William Times Journal*, Feb. 10, 1948, Apr. 6, July 19, Sept. 1, 1949, and Jan. 24, July 8, Oct.4, 5, 19, 1950).

300 Lambert and Pross, 407–8.

301 Ibid., 408; and Schull, 322–3.

302 *Fort William Times Journal*, May 11, 1946, and May 5, 1949; *Fort Frances Times*, May 1 and Nov. 27, 1947; and *Geraldton Times Star*, Dec. 1, 1949.

303 SPO, 1942, no. 3, 'Report of the Department of Lands and Forests for 1941.'

304 Bothwell, 377.

305 SPO, 1943, no. 9, 'Report of the Department of Game and Fisheries for 1941–42.'

306 *Sault Star*, June 19, Sept. 15, 1941, Mar. 3, 1942, and Sept. 9, 1943; and *Fort William Times Journal*, July 14, 1942.

307 Reports in the *Fort Frances Times*, *Rainy River Record*, *Kenora Miner*, *Fort William Times Journal*, and *Port Arthur News Chronicle*, as well as the *Sault Star*, make this case as clearly, as do ones like the *Dryden Observer*, Sept. 2, 1951, where even the tourist bureau closed for the duration in May 1942.

308 *Sault Star*, Aug. 9, 1941.

309 SPO, 1943, no. 3, 'Report of the Department of Lands and Forests for 1942'; and Lambert and Pross, 425–8.

310 SPO, 1942 and 1945, no. 3, 'Report of the Department of Lands and Forests for 1941 and 1944'; and *Dryden Observer*, May 5, 1944.

311 SPO, 1947, no. 48, 'First Report of the Department of Travel and Publicity for 1947–48'; *Fort Frances Times*, Mar. 28, 1946; *Kenora Miner*, Mar. 23, 1947; and *Fort William Times Journal*, Dec. 14, 1947.

312 Lambert and Pross, 452–4; SPO, 1947, no. 48, 'First Report of the Department of Travel and Publicity for 1946–47'; and SPO, 1948, no. 51, 'Report of the Department of Travel and Publicity for 1947.'

313 *Sault Star*, Mar. 27, 1948, and Aug. 15, 1949; and *Fort William Times Journal*, Feb. 2, 1949.

314 This point is best made in the *Dryden Observer*, Dec. 28, 1945, and the *Geraldton Times Star*, May 20, 1948, and with reference to older areas made clear in the *Kenora Miner*, Dec. 14, 1945, and Sept. 12, 1947, and *Fort William Times Journal*, Dec. 14, 1946.

315 Such sources mix automobile figures for border crossings without discrimination between tourist or non-tourist vehicles. They similarly give tourist numbers and commercial camp registrations under household head without distinguishing one from the other.

316 The heavy reliance on road access at and below the regional level is also noted by Rea, 160.

317 Such ships, ill maintained in the thirties, the victims of fire and post-war alternatives to lake vacationing, faded quickly into the background and disappeared. This decline is well documented in the U.W.O., R.C., Landon Collection, Scrapbooks.

318 *Rainy River Record*, Feb. 10, 1949; and *Dryden Observer*, Nov. 10, 1950.

319 FFM, Tourist Booklet; *Fort Frances Times*, Mar. 28, 1946; and *Sault Star*, June 14, 1948, and Apr. 15, 1950.

320 BRL, District History Files, no. 12; *Fort William Times Journal*, Dec. 14, 1946, Mar. 27, 1947, and Dec. 30, 1950; and *Geraldton Times Star*, May 20, 1948.

321 *Kenora Miner*, Dec. 23, 1947.

322 FFM, Tourist Booklet; *Sault Star*, Apr. 1, 1947; *Northern Miner*, Aug. 26, 1948; *Kenora Miner*, Dec. 12, 1950; and *Dryden Observer*, May 1, 1951.

323 SPO, 1948, no. 3, 'Report of the Department of Lands and Forests for 1948'; and G.E. Meyer, 'Kenora summer resort land in great demand,' *Sylva* 2, no. 3 (1946): 3–8.

324 See, for example, *Geraldton Times Star*, Dec. 31, 1946, Mar. 27, 1947, and May 20, 1948; *Dryden Observer*, Nov. 10, 1950; and *Fort William Times Journal*, Dec. 30, 1950.

325 George Wills and Iris Wills, *The auto camper's guide to Canada* (New York: Harper and Brothers, 1955): 3–5. For an example of the crowds that such campers were avoiding, see *Fort William Times Journal*, Dec. 14, 1946, which gives the attendance figure for Chippewa Park during the prior summer.

326 SPO, 1945, no. 3, 'Report of the Department of Lands and Forests for 1944'; and Lambert and Pross, 284–6.

327 Wills and Wills, 132–43.

328 Rea, 134.

329 Local histories for the region and many of the volumes of the Tweedsmuir Histories, carefully maintained by local chapters of the Women's Institute, make this point frequently.

330 NAC, RG 76, vol. 647, file A60239 (Maar to Immigration and Immigration to Maar, June 1946); BRL, Local History Files, Agriculture, Oliver and Paipoonge Townships; *Fort Frances Times*, Feb. 20, 1947; and *Fort William Times Journal*, Dec. 5, 1949.

331 *Dryden Observer*, July 27, 1947; and *Sault Star*, June 20, 1949.

332 *Sault Star*, June 24, 1944.

333 *Dryden Observer*, Sept. 28, 1948; *Port Arthur News Chronicle*, Oct. 12, 1948; *Rainy River Record*, Feb. 23, 1950; and *Sault Star*, Aug. 10, 1970 (reminiscent article).

334 These comments are based on observations made across the region during succeeding field seasons from 1986 to 1988.

335 Rea, 135–7; and G.F. Perkins, *Marketing milestones in Ontario, 1935–1960* (Toronto: Ontario Department of Agriculture, 1962), 1–7.

336 *Sault Star*, June 10, 1944; *Fort William Times Journal*, June 5, 1944; *Rainy River Record*, June 22, 1944; *Dryden Observer*, June 30, 1944; and *Fort Frances Times*, July 6, 1944.

337 *Rainy River Record*, Feb. 27, 1947, and Apr. 3, 1947; and *Fort Frances Times*, Feb. 10, 1949.

338 *Fort Frances Times*, Feb. 20, 1947.

339 Wightman and Wightman, 'The rise of electric power,' 47.

340 Rea, 135–6; *Fort Frances Times*, Apr. 25, 1940; and *Fort William Times Journal*, Sept. 12, 1944, and Aug. 16, 1946.

341 *Rainy River Record*, July 1, 1943, and June 6, 1946; *Fort Frances Times*, June 31, 1948, and June 19, 1951. For a parallel situation elsewhere in northern Ontario, see W.R. Wightman, *Forever on the fringe* (Toronto: University of Toronto Press, 1982), 186–7 and 197–8.

342 *Fort William Times Journal*, Feb. 7, 1942, Nov. 27, 1947, and Feb. 19, 1949.

343 Ibid., Apr. 29, 1948.

344 Ibid., Dec. 3, 1946, and Oct. 13, 1947.

345 *Rainy River Record*, Sept. 21, 1950.

346 *Fort William Times Journal*, June 6, 1942, and Dec. 19, 1944; *Rainy River Record*, Jan. 10, 1946, and Aug. 28, 1947; *Fort Frances Times*, June 5 and Dec. 11, 1947; and *Dryden Observer*, Jan. 4, 1948.

347 *Rainy River Record*, Sept. 15, and Oct. 27, 1949.

348 Rea, 138.

349 *Sault Star*, Sept. 20, 1948; and *Fort William Times Journal*, Oct. 1, 1949.

350 *Dryden Observer*, Sept. 11, 1946; *Kenora Miner*, Aug. 27 and Nov. 21, 1947; *Fort Frances Times*, Aug. 28, 1948; and *Rainy River Record*, Sept. 9, 1948.

351 SPO, 1944, no. 3, 'Report of the Department of Lands and Forests for 1943.'

352 These townships would appear to have included several in the northern tiers of the Dryden area, as well as some about Upsala and others along the northern and eastern extreme of those clustered behind Thunder Bay.

353 *Kenora Miner*, Dec. 21, 1945; and *Dryden Observer*, June 4, Sept. 3, 1948, and Oct. 14, 1949.

354 White, 247.

355 Mention has already been made of Dunn's determination to link any wartime expansion at Algoma Steel to this ability to turn such addition to plant to future domestic profit. Similar shifts at the Lakehead are exemplified by Northern Engineering and Supply's move from making shells to brass and iron castings (*Fort William Times Journal*, Feb. 4, 1946), Port Arthur Shipbuilding's shift from military vessels to Great Lakes freighters (*Fort William Times Journal*, Mar. 14, 1946), and Canada Car's return to the manufacture of rail cars and streetcars, and buses (*Fort William Times Journal*, Aug. 8, 1949 and May 6, 1950).

356 *Fort William Times Journal*, Feb. 29, 1944; *Sault Star*, June 17, 1943.

357 George Wice, *Carved from the wilderness: The intriguing story of Dryden* (Dryden: Alex Wilson Colstream Ltd., 1967), 44; and *Fort Frances Times*, July 17, 1947.

358 References to returning POW's are numerous. See, for example, Elinor Barr and Betty Dyck, *Ignace: A saga of the Shield* (Winnipeg: Prairie Publishing Co., 1979), 124; Boultbee, 41; and *Terrace Bay News*, Nov. 2, 1977.

359 *The River of time*, 167; and *Dryden Observer*, Sept. 26, 1947.

360 Ira M. Robinson, *New industrial towns on Canada's resource frontier*, Dept. of Geography Research Paper no. 73 (Chicago: University of Chicago Press, 1962), 47–8. For more details on improvement districts and their operation, see K. Crawford, *Single enterprise communities in Canada*, A report to the Central Mortgage and Housing Corporation by the Institute of Local Government, Queen's University (Ottawa: Queen's Printer, 1953), 46–50 and 65–70.

361 Oiva W. Saarinen, 'The influence of Thomas Adams and the British new town movement in the planning of Canadian resource communities,' in *The usable urban past*, ed. A.F.J. Artibise and Gilbert A. Stelter, Carleton Library Series (Toronto: Macmillan Canada, 1979), 270–5.

362 L.D. McCann, 'Canadian resource towns: A heartland-hinterland perspective,' in *Essays in Canadian urban process and form*, ed. Richard E. Preston and Lorn H. Russworm (Waterloo: University of Waterloo, 1980), 2: 220.

363 Oiva W. Saarinen, 'Single sector communities in Northern Ontario: The creation and planning of dependent towns,' in *Power and place: Canadian urban development in the North American context*, ed. Gilbert A. Stelter and Alan F.J. Artibise (Vancouver: University of British Columbia Press, 1986), 225–35.

364 The most comprehensive study here is Robert Robson, 'Ontario Hydro colonies: A study of frontier settlements,' *Laurentian University Review* 17, 2 (1985): 113–39; other worthwhile descriptions appear in 'A history of Ear Falls,' found in EFPL, Local History Files, as well as descriptions among the back issues of *Hydro News* read in the Ontario Hydro Public Reference Centre; the *Sault Star*, Apr. 4, 1929 and Oct. 1, Nov. 15, 1938, with reference to those of the Great Lakes Power Company; and the *Fort William Times Journal*, Dec. 14, 1946, specific to the Nipigon River villages.

365 By the mid-forties long articles with titles like 'Red Lake just grew' had begun to reflect public reaction in the *Northern Miner* of July 26, 1945, and Apr. 5, 1946. A Report of the Ontario Mining Commission, published in the *Fort William Times Journal*, Oct. 5, 1944, used Geraldton as its example of all the ills associated with unplanned mining communities.

366 Saarinen, 'Single sector communities,' 234, and Agnes W. Turcott, *Land of the big goose* (Altona, Man.: Friesen Printers, 1982), 51–98, which gives a detailed review of settlement events over the first half of this century.

367 *Fort William Times Journal*, Dec. 18, 1943; and *Northern Miner*, Sept. 14, 1944.

368 FFPL, Local History Files; and APL, Vertical Files, as well as a two-volume anonymous work, 'From canoes to Chryslers: A history of Atikokan, 1882 to 1982.'

369 *Northern Miner*, Sept. 14, 1944.

370 GPL, Local History Files; *Geraldton Times Star*, Mar. 7 and Apr. 18, 1946; *Northern Miner*, Feb. 20, 1947; and *Kenora Miner*, Dec. 22, 1950.

371 The importance of this date, when the Progressive Conservatives swept to power in Ontario with a 22-point program toward 'planned and responsible public resource management,' cannot be over-emphasized. See Rea, 17–19.

372 *Fort William Times Journal*, Oct. 5, 1944.

373 *Sault Star*, June 21, 1945; and *Dryden Observer*, July 27, 1945.

374 A.J. Auden, 'Nipigon Forest Village: A preliminary prospectus,' *Forest Chronicle* 20, 4 (1944): 209–61. A reprint of this article appears in AO, Pamphlets, 1944, no. 77.

375 *Sault Star*, June 21, 1945.

376 The best summary of this idea appears in a brief to the province by Frank F. Moran, reprinted in the *Fort William Times Journal*, Aug. 1, 1947.

377 Considerable insight into the reasoning behind this further change in thinking is to be gained in the LUPL, where certain contemporary records of the Lakehead Timberman's Association are to be found.

378 *Geraldton Times Star*, Jan. 26, 1950. Four years later a map in the *Fort William Times Journal*, Mar. 2, 1954, shows almost double that number of 'permanent woods communities' including several to the east on the A.C.R. north of Franz.

379 Much information here is distilled from interviews with Mr. Alan Buel and Mr. Dick Harkness (both now retired), the first a forester with Kimberly-Clark at Longlac, the second with Marathon Paper at Hillsport and Stevens in these years.
380 See, for example, the *Monitary Times*, Nov. 4, 1945; or P. Addison, 'North Shore expansion,' *Sylva* 2 (1945): 32–41.
381 RRPL, Local History Files, 'A History of the town of Red Rock.'
382 Boultbee, 50–71; TBPL, Local History Files; and *Terrace Bay News*, 1947–50.
383 BRL, History Files, Towns, no. 5; TBPL, 'A History of Terrace Bay'; and *Marathon Courier*, *Marathon Mercury*, 1947–50.
384 Saarinen, 'Single sector communities,' 246–8, makes this point very well in this discussion of Terrace Bay. However, an even stronger impression of the evolving concept can be gleaned from their individual town plans or from visiting them in turn.
385 Rea, 15–23; Schull, 314–25; Nelles, 353–8 and 459–60; Lambert and Pross, 335–41; and Sinclair, 83–4.

5: Modern Complications in the Northwest, 1950–1994

1 While some of this preamble reflects other authors, its essence is distilled from Robert Bothwell et al., *Canada since 1945* (Toronto: University of Toronto Press, 1989).
2 This promotion is most evident in the numerous official press releases on northern development as well as in publications and annual reports of the Department of Natural Resources, later the Ministry of Natural Resources.
3 This view of government responsiveness into the seventies is not shared by all authors, including R. Peter Gillis and Thomas Roach in *Lost initiatives: Canada's forest industry, forest policy and forest conservation* (New York: Greenman Press, 1986), 236–63. On the larger issue of excessive consumption and inadequate regard for the environment, see Geoffrey R. Weller, 'Resource development in Northern Ontario: A case study in hinterland politics,' in *Resources and the environment: Policy perspectives for Canada*, ed. O.P. Dwivedi (Toronto: McClelland and Stewart, 1980), 243–68.
4 Randall White, *Ontario, 1610–1985: A political and economic history* (Toronto: Dundurn Press, 1985), 245–7; and Joseph Schull, *Ontario since 1867* (Toronto: McClelland and Stewart, 1978), 334–9.
5 K.J. Rea, *The prosperous years: The economic history of Ontario, 1939–1975* (Toronto: University of Toronto Press, 1985), 159–60.
6 A general review of national conditions and events behind this dichotomy is to be found in Bothwell, 15–19 and 445–74.
7 Schull, 341.

8 Nancy M. Wightman and W. Robert Wightman, 'Beyond rail and road: The Red Lake–Pickle Lake gold fields, 1925–1954,' *Thunder Bay Historical Museum Society Records and Papers* 21 (1993): 32.
9 Bothwell, 220, however, makes the point that the operation of this program in Ontario was modest when compared with its lavish provisions for northern development in the western provinces.
10 For a much more detailed account of the above developments, see Nancy M. Wightman and W. Robert Wightman, 'Road and highway development in northwestern Ontario, 1950 to 1990,' *Canadian Geographer* 36 (1992): 377–9.
11 Donald MacKay, *The people's railway: A history of the Canadian National* (Toronto: Douglas and McIntyre, 1992), 146–59; and W. Kaye Lamb, *History of the Canadian Pacific Railway* (New York: Macmillan, 1977), 376–86. For a much less detailed appraisal, see Rea, 56–8 and 63–5.
12 Lamb, 384–5; and MacKay, 190.
13 *Sault Star*, May 1, 1956, July 31, 1963, and June 15, 1977.
14 Ibid., Nov. 23, 1961. Even in the nineties isolated hamlets north to Hearst receive basic service by a regular mixed train.
15 MacKay, 283–5; and Lamb, 374–5 and 422.
16 Rea, 59 and 63.
17 MacKay, 280–1.
18 MacKay, 173–95; and Lamb, 360–75.
19 For a more detailed discussion of the technical advantages of diesel, see O.S. Nock, *Railways of Canada* (London: Adam and Charles Black, 1973), 107–17.
20 *Sault Star*, June 27, 1953, and Nov. 6, 1974.
21 MacKay, 174–5; and Lamb, 382–6.
22 MacKay, 280; *Fort William Times Journal*, Sept. 17, 1954, and Oct. 6, 1955; *Marathon Mercury*, Sept. 23, 1954; *Northern Miner*, Sept. 2, 23, Oct. 7, 1954, Oct. 20, 1955, and July 26, 1966; and *Sault Star*, Apr. 26, 1966.
23 *Rainy River Record*, Apr. 3, 1952, Mar. 12, 1953, Aug. 28, 1960, Aug. 23, 1962, Feb. 14, 1963, and Nov. 26, 1964.
24 *White River Community Leader*, Jan. 3, 1969.
25 *Algoma News Review*, Dec. 12, 1973, and June 4, 1975.
26 MacKay, 261.
27 W.R. Wightman, *Forever on the fringe* (Toronto: University of Toronto Press, 1982), 178; A.G. Young, *Great Lakes Saga* (Owen Sound: Richardson, Bond and Wright, 1965), 109–46; and Lorenzo Marcolini, 'Canadian Pacific Steamship Line: Last of an era,' *Inland Seas* 22 (1966): 15. However, the best record is to be found in the U.W.O., Regional Collection, Landon Papers, Shipping Scrapbooks.
28 *Fort William Times Journal*, Dec. 3, 1949.

29 Gerald Millar and W.H. Van Allan, 'The Lakehead: An up-to-date harbour,' *Canadian Geographical Journal* 64 (1962): 174–9; Mark L. Thompson, *Steamboats and sailors of the Great Lakes* (Detroit: Wayne State University Press, 1991): 74; and *Fort William Times Journal*, Dec. 8, 1960.

30 Adrian O. Seaborne and Patricia N. Larrain, 'Changing patterns of trade through the Port of Thunder Bay,' *Canadian Geographer* 27 (1983): 285–68; *Northern Miner*, June 9, 1969, and Aug. 8, 1979; and *Sault Star*, Nov. 29, 1976, and Apr. 7, 1977.

31 Millar and Van Allan, 177.

32 *Fort William Times Journal*, Oct. 19, 1960; *Sault Star*, June 11, 1962; and Millar and Van Allan, 178.

33 Philip Smith, *It seems like only yesterday: Air Canada, the first 50 years* (Toronto: McClelland and Stewart, 1986), 16; and Rea, 67.

34 J.C. Dillon, *Early days: A record of the early days of the Provincial Air Service of Ontario* (Toronto: Department of Lands and Forests, 1961), 1–8; Richard S. Lambert and Paul Pross, *Renewing nature's wealth* (Toronto: Queen's Printer, 1967), 134–48; and Robert S. Grant, 'Ontario's Provincial Air Service,' *Canadian Geographical Journal* 19 (1979): 50–54.

35 Dillon, 11; Smith, 13–18; and Wightman and Wightman, 'Beyond rail and road,' 19–26.

36 Smith, 18–22; and Grant, 55. For an example of one such carrier, see Larry Milberry, *Austin Airways: Canada's oldest airlines* (Toronto: Canav Books, 1985).

37 Smith, 18 and 50.

38 *Fort William Times Journal*, Apr. 6, Aug. 23, 1946, and Mar. 14, June 30, 1947; and *Sault Star*, July 21, 1959. For a map showing the original Armstrong route, see David H. Collins, *Wings across time: The story of Air Canada* (Toronto: Griffin House, 1978), 8.

39 *Sault Star*, July 21, 1959, Aug. 1, 1961, and May 25, 1964; *Fort William Times Journal*, Dec. 31, 1953, and Mar. 5, 1955; and *Dryden Observer*, Mar. 21, Apr. 20, 1967, and July 3, 1969.

40 Rea, 63–4.

41 Ibid., 65; *Sault Star*, July 13, 1971, and Oct. 20, 1973; and *Geraldton Times Star*, July 11, 1968.

42 *Sault Star*, May 28, 1977.

43 For a complete discussion of this process of northern electrification, including a table showing the generating capacity of each power station, see Nancy M. Wightman and W. Robert Wightman, 'The rise of electrical power in northwestern Ontario, 1890–1990,' in *Geographical perspectives on the provincial norths*, ed. Margaret E. Johnston (Toronto: Copp Clark Longman, 1994), 34–57.

44 Rea, 72–3.
45 Schull, 339; Rea, 74–5; and *Sault Star*, Apr. 30, May 9, June 7, and Sept. 1, 1956.
46 Schull, 339–40; Rea, 75; and *Sault Star*, June 26, 1957.
47 Rea, 76; and *Dryden Observer*, Mar. 18, 1971.
48 Thomas Grindlay, *A history of the independent telephone industry in Ontario* (Toronto: The Ontario Telephone Commission, 1975), provides much detail here, but the issues are most succinctly summarized by Rea, 76–7.
49 *Sault Star*, June 26, 1957.
50 *Northern Miner*, July 22, 1965.
51 The sources for these generalizations are the columns of numerous local and regional newspapers in which references to media development are most numerous but lacking much descriptive detail.
52 Philip Smith, *Harvest from the rock: A history of mining in Ontario* (Toronto: Macmillan, 1986), 314; and Rea, 162.
53 *Northern Miner*, Nov. 29, 1951. An appreciation of these changes can best be gained by sampling the technical section and the machinery advertisements in this paper over the years.
54 *Northern Miner*, May 12, 1955, Mar. 21, 1957, Apr. 16, July 12, 23, 1959, and Nov. 24, 1960; and *Fort William Times Journal*, Mar. 15, 1964, and Apr. 21, 1970. Apparently this drive reached a new peak in 1972–3 (*Thunder Bay Chronicle Journal*, Apr. 29, 1980) and was again high at the end of the decade.
55 Rea, 181–4; and Lynne Mitchell, *An economic history of Northwestern Ontario*, Component Study no. 1, Design for Development (Toronto: Ministry of Northern Affairs, 1969), 33.
56 Philip Smith, *Harvest from the rock*, 326–8; Oiva Sarrinen, 'Mining in Northern Ontario,' in *Ontario: Perspectives on economy and environment*, ed. Bruce Mitchell (Waterloo: Department of Geography Publications, University of Waterloo, 1991), no. 34, 65; and *Northern Ontario manpower survey: Mineral and forest industries*, Component Study no. 6, Design for Development (Toronto: Ministry of Northern Affairs, 1977), 7–9.
57 William Treadwell, 'The pellet makers,' *Canadian Geographical Journal* 72 (1966): 196–8; *Fort William Times Journal*, Jan. 11, 1950, Sept. 28, 1953, and May 2, 1960; and *Northern Miner*, Feb. 26, Nov. 5, 1953, Feb. 4, 1954, and Feb. 4, May 5, 1960.
58 Treadwell, 198; and *Northern Miner*, Jan. 12, 1950, Feb. 26, Sept. 28, 1953, Mar. 6, Apr. 17, 1958, Aug. 6, 1959, and Feb. 4, May 2, 5, 1960.
59 *Northern Miner*, July 11, 18, 1957, Mar. 6, Apr. 17, July 13, 1958, and Sept. 6, 1962.
60 Ibid., May 5, 1960, Feb. 9, 1961, Nov. 28, 1963, and Apr. 9, 1964.

61 Ibid., Feb. 13, July 13, 1958; Jan. 8, 1959, Feb. 9, May 4, 1961, Sept. 6, 1962, and Jan. 17, 1963; and *Fort William Times Journal*, Apr. 12, 1960.

62 *Northern Miner*, Jan. 4, 1962, Nov. 28, 1963, Apr. 9, Sept. 24, 1964, and Feb. 9, Aug. 3, 24, 1967; and AOD, Historical Clipping Files, no. 1, 3 and 8.

63 *Northern Miner*, Jan. 21, 1971, Mar. 25, 1976, Mar. 24, 1977, Aug. 24, 1978, and Mar. 22, 1979; and *Thunder Bay Chronicle Journal*, Apr. 29, 1980.

64 *Dryden Observer*, Apr. 20 and Sept. 28, 1977; and *Northern Miner*, Mar. 22, 1979.

65 *Sault Star*, Apr. 5, 1951; and *Northern Miner*, Feb. 7, 1952.

66 AOD, Historical Clipping Files, nos. 3, 5, and 8; and *Northern Miner*, June 16, 1949, June 29, 1950, and Nov. 5, 1953.

67 Treadwell, 200; and *Northern Miner*, Mar. 10, Nov. 17, 1949, and June 24, 1950.

68 AOD, Historical Clipping Files, nos. 6 and 7; and *Sault Star*, May 3, 1954.

69 AOD, Historical Clipping Files, no. 7; and *Sault Star*, May 7, 1954.

70 AOD, Historical Clipping Files, no. 1; and *Northern Miner*, June 9, 1955, Feb. 19, 1959, Mar. 8, 1962, Sept. 24, 1964, Apr. 1, 1965.

71 These opportunities were both broad and demanding. They ranged from the needs of the rising petroleum industry for casings and pipe to those of the blossoming urban construction trades for structural steel to fit everything from telecommunication and hydro towers to rails and sheet steel.

72 Treadwell, 200; and *Northern Miner*, May 10, 1956.

73 AOD, Historical Clipping Files, no. 6; *Northern Miner*, Mar. 21, 1957; *Algoma News*, June 28, 1967; and *Sault Star*, June 10, 1970, and June 7, 1977.

74 *Sault Star*, Feb. 2, 1967. Although there was further drilling and discussion about opening, transporting, even beneficiating the magnetite of the Britannia property behind Goulais-Batchawana, it was never developed (*Northern Miner*, Mar. 8, 29, 1962, Mar. 7, 1963, and Feb. 13, 1964).

75 *Northern Miner*, Dec. 5, 1955, and June 7, 1956.

76 Ibid., Mar. 17, May 5, and June 30, 1955; and *Dryden Observer*, May 13, 1955.

77 *Fort William Times Journal*, Dec. 16, 1955; *Dryden Observer*, Dec. 20, 1955, and Jan. 19, Mar. 16, Nov. 23, 1967; and *Northern Miner*, Mar. 21, June 27, 1957, May 12, 1960, Mar. 2, 1961, Jan. 25, 1962, Sept. 23, 1965, Nov. 30, 1967, and Mar. 28, 1968.

78 *Northern Miner*, June 20, 1968, Dec. 14, 1972, Dec. 5, 1974, Nov. 18, 1978, and Apr. 29, 1980; and *Dryden Observer*, Jan. 30, 1969, and Nov. 29, 1973.

79 *Northern Miner*, Nov. 7, 1957, Feb. 5, Aug. 6, 1959, Sept. 15, 1960, and Feb. 9, June 15, 1961; *Fort William Times Journal*, Jan. 13, 1960; and *Geraldton Times Star*, Jan. 28, 1965.

80 Treadwell, 203.

81 *Northern Miner*, Dec. 26, 1969, May 22, 1975, and Apr. 7, 1977.

82 Treadwell, 197; and *Northern Miner*, June 28, 1956, Feb. 28, 1957, Jan. 23, July 17, 1958, Oct. 1, 1959, Feb. 25, 1960, Mar. 30, 1961, Sept. 4, 1964, Nov. 30, 1967, and Jan. 22, 1976.

83 Treadwell, 203; *Northern Miner*, Feb. 20, 1969, Aug. 12, 1971, Oct. 11, 1973, Mar. 7, Aug. 15, 1974, July 24, 1975, and Mar. 25, Nov. 18, 1976; and *Dryden Observer*, Feb. 12, 1972, and Oct. 4, Nov. 29, 1973.

84 Rea, 163; and Saarinen, 164.

85 See, for example, *Kenora Miner*, Nov. 2, 1951; and *Northern Miner*, Jan. 5, June 14, and Oct. 11, 1956.

86 *Fort William Times Journal*, Aug. 7, 1948; and *Northern Miner*, Aug. 12, 1948, and June 19, Oct. 2, 1952.

87 *Northern Miner*, Dec. 30, 1948, Mar. 12, June 11, Nov. 19, 1953, and Jan. 9, 1958.

88 For a summary of events here, see L. Carson Brown, 'Manitouwadge, cave of the great spirit,' *Canadian Geographical Journal* 67 (1963): 134–45 (as Brown notes, the real discoverer was J.E. Thompson of the Ontario Department of Mines in 1931 and a copy of Thompson's diary and field notes are to be found in the Manitouwadge Public Library); and *Northern Miner*, Dec. 24, and 31, 1953.

89 *Northern Miner*, Jan. 14, 28, Feb. 11 and July 8, 1954; *Manitouwadge Echo*, Dec. 16, 1964, and Feb. 26, 1969; and *Fort William Times Journal*, Mar. 2, and June 7, 17, 1954.

90 *Northern Miner*, Mar. 25, 1954, and Feb. 17, June 30, 1955; and *Fort William Times Journal*, June 17, 1954.

91 *Northern Miner*, Aug. 1, and Nov. 28, 1957; and *Sault Star*, Aug. 1, 1957.

92 *Northern Miner*, Aug. 8, Oct. 10, 1963, Mar. 19, 1964, June 15, July 13, 1967, and Sept. 1, Oct. 20, 1977; *Port Arthur News Chronicle*, July 19, 1963, and June 2, 1964; and *Manitouwadge Echo*, Sept. 9, 1964, Feb. 10, May 27, 1965, and July 13, 1967.

93 *Northern Miner*, Oct. 11, 1956, Apr. 4, May 23, June 27, 1957, Feb. 20, Apr. 24, 1958, Apr. 30, July 23, 1959, Jan. 21, Feb. 11, May 12, 1960, Apr. 2, 1964, and Aug. 17, 1967.

94 Ibid., Jan. 31, 1951, Nov. 7, 1955, Jan. 17, June 20, 1957, Sept. 13, 1962, Aug. 6, Oct. 15, 1964, Nov. 18, Dec. 16, 1965, Sept. 3, 1966, Dec. 21, 1967, Apr. 4, Oct. 3, 31, 1968, June 12, 19, 1969, Sept. 2, 1971, Dec. 14, 1972, Jan. 11, Mar. 1, 1973, and Jan. 17, 1974; and *Sault Star*, July 28, Oct. 15, 1956, and May 22, Aug. 8, 1964.

95 *Northern Miner*, Jan. 16, Oct. 22, Dec. 10, 1964, Feb. 23, 1967, June 12, July 3, Aug. 26, 1969, and Apr. 30, 1970; *Manitouwadge Echo,*, July 22, 1966; and *Thunder Bay Times News*, May 29, 1974.

96 Rea, 177.

97 *Northern Miner*, Jan. 9, 16, July 17, Dec. 4, 1969, Jan. 1, July 9, 1970, Jan. 28, July 8, 1971, July 19, 1973, Sept. 9, 1976, and June 26, 1980; *Dryden Observer*,

Jan. 16, 23, Feb. 13, 1969, Oct. 29, 1970, and Feb. 4, May 11, 1971; and *Sioux Lookout Bulletin*, Nov. 18, 1970.

98 *Northern Miner*, Mar. 12, 1953, and June 28, 1951. For a summary of mining events in this field, see Elinor Barr and Betty Dyck, *Ignace: A saga of the Shield* (Winnipeg: Prairie Publishing Co., 1979), 159–60.

99 *Northern Miner*, Oct. 9, 1969.

100 Ibid., Apr. 21, July 9, 16, 1970 and Mar. 16, 1972; *Dryden Observer*, Oct. 30, Nov. 6, 1969, Oct. 15, 1970 and July 20, 1972; and *Sault Star*, July 14, 1970.

101 *Northern Miner*, Oct. 20, 1970, Feb. 18, 1971, Apr. 19, 1973, Oct. 20, 1977, Apr. 19, June 29, 1978, and Apr. 12, 1979; *Dryden Observer*, June 28, 1973, and Oct. 24, 1974; and *Thunder Bay Chronicle Journal*, Apr. 29, 1978.

102 *Northern Miner*, Dec. 4, 1969, July 9, Dec. 3, 1970, June 3, July 8, 1971, Mar. 2, May 27, 1972, May 24, June 7, 1973, and May 30, 1974; *Dryden Observer*, Jan. 31, 1974, and Oct. 6, 1976; and *Sioux Lookout Bulletin*, Oct. 5, 1976.

103 *Northern Miner*, Oct. 7, 1976, May 19, 26, June 30, 1977, Dec. 7, 1978 and June 26, 1980; and *Thunder Bay Chronicle Journal*, Apr. 29, 1980.

104 Rea, 174–6.

105 *Rainy River Record*, Nov. 20, 1952, and Feb. 12, Apr. 19, Dec. 4, 1953; and *Northern Miner*, Nov. 6, 1952, and Mar. 26, 1953.

106 *Northern Miner*, Aug. 6, 1948, June 17, 1953, Nov. 4, 1954, and Aug. 18, 1955; *Fort William Times Journal*, June 17, 1953; and *Rainy River Record*, June 30, 1953.

107 *Northern Miner*, July 26, Aug. 23, and Dec. 27, 1956.

108 Ibid., July 26, 1955, and Feb. 8, 1962.

109 Ibid., Oct. 28, 1965, Nov. 30, 1967, Apr. 25, 1968, Jan. 20, Sept. 28, 1972, and May 8, 1981; *Sault Star*, Apr. 18, 1968; and *Thunder Bay Chronical Journal*, Apr. 29, 1980.

110 *Northern Miner*, Jan. 26, 1967, Mar. 21, Apr. 18, May 30, 1968, July 10, 1969, Dec. 21, 1972, Feb. 8, Apr. 19, Aug. 30, 1973, Mar. 21, Aug. 8, Oct. 10, 1974, July 15, Nov. 11, 1976, Apr. 21, 1977, and May 8, 1980.

111 Smith, *Harvest from the rock*, 281; and *Northern Miner*, Nov. 25, 1948, and Nov. 29, 1951.

112 Rea, 164; Smith, *Harvest from the rock*, 281–2, *Fort William Times Journal*, Feb. 20 and Aug. 7, 1970; and *Northern Miner*, Mar. 2, 1972, Mar. 3, 1977, and Oct. 18, 1979.

113 Smith, *Harvest from the rock*, 321; Rea, 164–5; Saarinen, 164; and *Northern Miner*, Mar. 21, 1968.

114 Rea, 165; and Smith, *Harvest from the rock*, 327. For the sequence of price jumps, see *Northern Miner*, Mar. 1, May 17, 1973, Oct. 12, 1976, Oct. 18, 1979, and Jan. 4, 1980; for a discussion of Canada's related monetary problems, see Bothwell, 295–8.

115 *Northern Miner*, June 12, 1950, Sept. 1, 1955, and Jan. 5, June 14, Oct. 11, 1956; *Fort Frances Times*, Oct. 5, 1949; and *Kenora Miner*, Nov. 2, 1951.
116 *Northern Miner*, Oct. 16, 1947, Sept. 9, 1948, Oct. 19, 1950, Jan. 15, 1953, Sept. 4, 1958, and June 1, 1972; *Fort William Times Journal*, Oct. 23, 1950; *Dryden Observer*, Jan. 26 and Apr. 20, 1951; and *Sioux Lookout Bulletin*, June 25, 1973.
117 *Northern Miner*, Jan. 25, 1951, July 18, 1963, and Nov. 8, 1973.
118 Ibid., May 17, 1954, and Apr. 2, 1964; *Geraldton Times Star*, June 4 and Nov. 4, 1970; and *Fort William Times Journal*, Dec. 29, 1951.
119 *Northern Miner*, Apr. 2, June 14, 21, Aug. 30, 1951, Jan. 10, Apr. 17, 1952, June 17, 1954, Feb. 10, 1955, Aug. 2, 1956, June 1, 1961, and June 10, 1965.
120 Ibid., Mar. 12, Apr. 23, 1959, Feb. 2, 1961, Feb. 21, Mar. 21, 1962, Mar. 7, July 4, 1974, and Dec. 25, 1975; and *Algoma News*, Oct. 2, 1974.
121 *Northern Miner*, Feb. 21, Mar. 21, 1962, Sept. 26, Nov. 21, 1963, Feb. 23, Sept. 28, 1967, Feb. 27, Mar. 27, 1969, and Apr. 5, Aug. 2, 1973; *Algoma News*, June 24, 1964, Jan. 26, 1966, and May 27, 1970; and *Sault Star*, Oct. 15, 1966, June 13, Sept. 23, 1967, Apr. 2, 1968, and Mar. 27, 1973.
122 For a good review of this gold field in the mid-sixties, see L. Carson Brown, 'The Red Lake gold field,' *Canadian Geographical Journal* 69 (1965): 114–25.
123 *Northern Miner*, Jan. 29, 1959, and June 9, 1960.
124 Ibid., May 27, 1965, Sept. 7, 1967, Mar. 21, May 30, 1968, Apr. 22, July 1, 1971, May 3, July 19, Aug. 1, Sept. 19, 1974, Mar. 3, Dec. 4, 1975, Apr. 8, June 10, 17, 1976, and July 31, 1980.
125 FFPL, Local History Files, Mine Centre; *Northern Miner*, Apr. 25, 1974, Feb. 17, Aug. 4, 1977, Mar. 23, 1978, and Jan. 4, 1979; and *Sioux Lookout Bulletin*, June 25, 1973, and Jan. 22, 1974.
126 *Northern Miner*, May 10, 1973, Sept. 25, Oct. 2, 1975, and Mar. 4, 1976.
127 *Terrace Bay News*, Oct. 17, 1979.
128 Rea, 214–16.
129 Royal Commission on the Northern Environment, 'The economic future of the forest products industry' (Toronto: Ministry of Natural Resources, 1981), 7–14.
130 Ontario, *Forest production policy options* (Toronto: Ministry of Natural Resources, 1972), 25–308; and *Thunder Bay Chronical Journal*, Apr. 29, 1980. The figure quoted here ignores those persons involved in harvesting as opposed to manufacturing operations.
131 Rea, 185.
132 *Kenora Miner*, Mar. 2, 1947; *Rainy River Record*, Dec. 30, 1954; *Fort Frances Times*, July 12, 1964; and *Dryden Observer*, Jan. 4 and Mar. 29, 1962.
133 Ian Radforth, 'Woodworkers and the mechanization of the pulpwood industry of Northern Ontario, 1952–1970,' *Canadian Historical Association Historical Papers* (1982): 80.

134 Rea, 186; *Kenora Miner*, Mar. 21, 1947; *Fort William Times Journal*, Apr. 29, 1960; and *Dryden Observer*, Dec. 6, 9, 1955, Jan. 17, 1958, Apr. 23, 1959, and Jan. 4, Mar. 29, 1962.

135 Such drives on the Kaministiquia, Nipigon, and White rivers were terminated in the sixties, while others on the Seine as well as on Lake of the Woods and the Wabigoon–Eagle chain came to an end in the following decade according to BRL, Wood Industries of Northwestern Ontario, file 94; WPL, Binder no. 3; *Sault Star*, Feb. 15, 1962; and *Nipigon Gazette*, Feb. 9, 1983. Records in the LUA for the Pigeon and Arrow River area suggest the end came here as early as the fifties, as did serious driving on the Black and any rivers in Algoma south to Sault Ste Marie.

136 Radforth, 74.

137 C.R. Silversides, 'The impact of forest operations and techniques upon forest operations in eastern Canada,' *Meddeletsor fra Norsk Institutt for Skagforskoring* 41.16 (1988): 241–4.

138 C.R. Silversides, 'Development in the technology of harvesting timber,' a paper given at the Tenth Commonwealth Forestry Conference, Britain, 1974, 5. For a more personal and laconic account of these developments, see our correspondence with Mr W.D. (Dick) Harkness, long-time chief forester at Marathon, and notes of an interview with Mr Allan F. Buell, then in a comparable role at Kimberly-Clark, which are now in the authors' hands but will be tendered to the Archives of Ontario.

139 Ian Radforth, *Bushworkers and bosses, logging in northern Ontario, 1900–1980* (Toronto: University of Toronto Press, 1987), 206–8; and Silversides, 'Developments in the technology of harvesting timber,' 3–4.

140 Silversides, 'The impact of forest operations,' 240 and 246–8, which gives a list of experiments and trials for such specialized equipment in the northwest as well as elsewhere to 1971.

141 Silversides, 'Developments in the technology of harvesting timber,' 5–9.

142 The only clearly documented attempt in the region at this latter system was by Domtar for its kraft operation at Red Rock (*Nipigon Gazette*, Aug. 15, 1979). While only sulphate processing could cope with this problem, there is no evidence the company adopted this chipwood technique.

143 *Fort William Times Journal*, Feb. 12, 1970.

144 Ian Radforth provides a very sound and balanced account of these matters in *Bushworkers and bosses*, 202–26.

145 Rea, 214.

146 *Manpower survey, northwestern Ontario* (Ottawa: Dept. of Immigration, 1977), 27; and Royal Commission on the Northern Environment, 8–9.

147 *Fort Frances Times*, July 12, 1945; *Kenora Miner*, July 13, 1945; and *Fort William Times Journal*, Dec. 15, 1954.

148 *Dryden Observer*, June 20, 1947, Jan. 19, July 13, Nov. 23, Dec. 1, 1951, and June 27, 1952.

149 *Fort William Times Journal*, Dec. 29, 1951, Mar. 2, 1954, and May 12, 1960.

150 Ibid., Dec. 29, 1951.

151 Ibid., Dec. 29, 1951, and Oct. 25, 1955; *Terrace Bay News*, June 12, 1958; and *Marathon Mercury*, Aug. 3, 1950, Oct. 11, 1951, Feb. 5, 1953, and Dec. 5, 1957.

152 *Sault Star*, Jan. 12, 1952, Aug. 7, 1955, Sept. 3, 1956, and Mar. 14, 1959.

153 *Dryden Observer*, June 11, 1964, Oct. 30, 1969, Mar. 14, Sept. 19, 1974, and Oct. 27, 1976; and *Terrace Bay News*, July 31, 1974, and Jan. 2, 1980.

154 See, for example, *Fort William Times Journal*, May 12, Nov. 7, 1960, and Apr. 21, 1970; and *Northern Affairs Newsletter*, June 1980.

155 *Sault Star*, Sept. 23, 1977.

156 *Fort William Times Journal*, Mar. 12, and Apr. 2, 28, 1970.

157 Ibid., Apr. 21, and May 6, 1970.

158 Ibid., May 28, 1967; *Nipigon Gazette*, Nov. 28, 1972; and *Dryden Observer*, Mar. 4, and Sept. 19, 1974.

159 *Fort William Times Journal*, Apr. 21, 1970.

160 Ibid., Oct. 25, 1953, and Mar. 28, 1967.

161 TBPL, History Files; *Fort William Times Journal*, June 19, 1948; and *Marathon Mercury*, Dec. 5, 1957.

162 Mitchell, 22.

163 *Rainy River Record*, Dec. 31, 1964.

164 Radforth, *Bushworkers and bosses*, 22–3.

165 *Sault Star*, July 19, 1966.

166 Rea, 216.

167 Department of Lands and Forests, Annual reports for 1969, 1970 and 1971; *Marathon Mercury*, May 7, 1962; and *Sault Star*, July 19, 1966.

168 AO, Pamphlets, 1966; MPL, History Files; *Marathon Mercury*, Dec. 31, 1963; and *Thunder Bay Chronicle Journal*, Apr. 29, 1980.

169 Rea, 216–17.

170 Bruce Mitchell, 'Provincial domain in environmental management and resource development' in *Resources and the environment: Policy perspectives for Canada*, ed. O.P. Dwivedi, 51.

171 NAC, RG 23, vol. 437, no. 702-4-15 (correspondence June and Nov. 1951); *Fort Frances Times*, June 26, and July 17, 1947; *Fort William Times Journal*, June 22, 1951; *Sault Star*, June 30, 1951; and *Rainy River Record*, Aug. 16 and Sept. 4, 1952.

172 *Fort Frances Times*, July 15, 1948; and *Rainy River Record*, June 28, 1951, and Feb. 26, Mar. 12, Nov. 27, Dec. 3, 1953.

173 NAC, RG 23, vol. 437, no. 702-4-16 (Lands and Forests to Council on Fisheries, Mar. 23, 1954); and *Fort William Times Journal*, Oct. 31, Dec. 20, 1950, and Mar. 17, July 28, 1951.

174 *Sault Star*, July 3, 1954.

175 *Rainy River Record*, Apr. 28, 1960, Sept. 5, 1963, Oct. 1, 1964, Dec. 27, 1968, Aug. 27, 1970, Feb. 4, 1971, and June 22, 1978.

176 *Sault Star*, Aug. 21, 1969, Sept. 12, 1973, and Mar. 31, 1977.

177 *Fort William Times Journal*, Dec. 20, 1967; and *Thunder Bay Chronicle Journal*, Nov. 23, 1970, Oct. 18, 1976, and Feb. 20, 1980.

178 *Terrace Bay News*, Feb. 16, 1961, and Apr. 7, 1967.

179 *Marathon Mercury*, Nov. 6, 1966, Mar. 22, 1967, and Apr. 19, 1976; *Terrace Bay News*, Dec. 5, 1968, Dec. 2, 1971, May 25, 1972, Mar. 12, Apr. 23, 1975, and Dec. 12, 1979; and *Fort William Times Journal*, Jan. 22, 1970.

180 *Dryden Observer*, Aug. 21, 1958, Jan. 22, Apr. 2, 1959, July 21, 1966, and Aug. 10, 1967.

181 *Fort William Times Journal*, Apr. 10, 1970; and *Dryden Observer*, May 24, June 21, 1973, and Oct. 23, 1975.

182 *Sault Star*, Nov. 29, 1976, and Jan. 6, 1977; and *Dryden Observer*, Jan. 5, Apr. 20, 27, May 11, July 6, and Sept. 14, 1977.

183 *Dryden Observer*, Aug. 16, 1978, and Feb. 14, 21, June 27, July 4, Aug. 15, Sept. 12, 1979.

184 *Sault Star*, Nov. 7, 1979.

185 Rea, 213.

186 Both Lambert and Pross, 421–2, and Rea, 214, make this point.

187 *Fort William Times Journal*, July 8, Oct. 4, 5, 19, 1950, Apr. 3, 1951, and Nov. 12, 1954.

188 While such formal arrangements for third parties are a part of the modern Forest Management Agreement, it is important to emphasize that firm and amicable agreements worked out as given situations dictated became an increasingly common feature of the industry in the northwest after the early fifties.

189 Radforth, *Bushworkers and bosses*, 15; Lambert and Pross, 421; and Tracy Tieman, *Sawmills in Ontario* (Toronto: Ministry of Natural Resources, 1986), 2–5.

190 Tieman, 2.

191 *Sault Star*, Oct. 4, 1962.

192 *Tracks beside the water* (Sioux Lookout: Sioux Lookout and District Historical Society, 1982), 41; *Fort William Times Journal*, Nov. 17, 1954; and *Rainy River Record*, Oct. 16, 1952, and Nov. 4, 1954.

193 *Fort William Times Journal*, Feb. 27, and Nov. 4, 1960; *Dryden Observer*, Aug. 17, 1961; *Sault Star*, Jan. 16, 1971; *Rainy River Record*, Jan. 10, Aug. 29, Oct. 10, 1963, Aug. 27, 1964, June 27, 1974, and Sept. 21, 1978; and *Nipigon Gazette*, Aug. 15, 1979.

194 KPL, Kenora Industrial File.

195 EFPL, Industries, Great Lakes Paper Co.; and *Dryden Observer*, Dec. 14, 1961, Feb. 24, 1966, May 18, Sept. 28, 1967, and Sept. 9, Nov. 30, 1969.

196 *Fort William Times Journal*, Aug. 8, 1960; *Sioux Lookout Bulletin*, Oct. 13, 1967 and Jan. 10, 1969; and *Dryden Observer*, Jan. 23, 1969.
197 *Sioux Lookout Bulletin*, Jan. 18, 1973, and May 6, July 10, 1974; and *Dryden Observer*, Oct. 12, 1972, Mar. 22, 1973, and Mar. 14, 1974.
198 *Sioux Lookout Bulletin*, Aug. 3, 1977; and *Dryden Observer*, Oct. 12, 1977.
199 *Fort William Times Journal*, Dec. 31, 1949; and personal interview with Mr Mac Squires, Woodlands Division, Abitibi-Price, Thunder Bay, Dec. 12, 1978.
200 A.J. Placz, *Q & O: Our Story* (Thorold: Quebec and Ontario Paper Co., 1988), 43; and *Sault Star*, Nov. 6, 1970.
201 TBPL, *K.C. News*, file, June, 1978; *Terrace Bay News*, Dec. 14, 1950, Apr. 24, 1969, and Oct. 17, 1973; *Fort William Times Journal*, Dec. 29, 1951, Aug. 13, 1952, Sept. 23, Nov. 12, 1954, and Apr. 21, 1970; and *Geraldton Times Star*, Feb. 4, 1963.
202 *Marathon Mercury*, May 24, 1956.
203 *The Echo*, Feb. 21, 1974; and *Sault Star*, Apr. 25, 1979.
204 SSMPL, Scrapbook no. 21; *Sault Star*, Dec. 21, 1956, Mar. 23, 1961, Feb. 14, 1962, Sept. 24, 1966, July 17, 1967, Aug. 7, 9, 1974, Nov. 12, 14, 1975, and Jan. 20, 1976; and *Algoma News*, Nov. 23, 30, and Dec. 30, 1977.
205 SSMPL, Vertical File, Weyerhauser/Roddis; and *Sault Star*, Sept. 2, 1953, Feb. 20, 1954, June 14, 1961, Aug. 27, 1966, Apr. 21, 1971, Apr. 17, 1972, Jan. 20, 1976, and Nov. 26, 1979.
206 G.F. Vosper, 'Logging in Lake Superior Provincial Park,' Ministry of Natural Resources, Ontario, Wawa District, 1984; *Sault Star*, July 11, Sept. 4, 1957, and Apr. 28, 1973; and personal interview with Mr Bob Gibbs, Woodlands Division, Ministry of Natural Resources, Sault Ste Marie, July 17, 1989.
207 *Rainy River Record*, June 27, 1974.
208 BRL, Historical Files, Northwestern Ontario, no. 99; *Nipigon Gazette*, Mar. 7, 1973; and personal interview with Ms C.S. Livingston, Chief Accountant, MacMillan Bloedel, Nipigon Plywood Mill, Aug. 11, 1988.
209 *Geraldton Times Star*, Feb. 4, 1963; *Marathon Mercury*, Apr. 14, 1963; *Terrace Bay News*, Nov. 15, 1972; and personal interview with Mr George Swan, Personnel Manager, Weldwood of Canada, Ltd., Longlac, Aug. 21, 1988.
210 For example, the Norply mill at Nipigon gained its timber from the unused poplar on adjacent Domtar concessions and sent all refuse to Red Rock; Weldwood at Longlac had similar agreements with both Kimberly-Clark and Marathon, the latter of which took all wood refuse, but Weyerhauser, having their own limits, sold their chips to the highest bidder, which was not always Abitibi in Sault Ste Marie.
211 Lambert and Pross, 370–5 and 404–12.

212 A map reflecting this pattern can be found in the *Ontario Resources Atlas* (Toronto: Department of Lands and Forests, 1954), 23.

213 R.J. Burgar, 'Forest land use evolution in Ontario's Upper Great Lakes Basin,' in *The Great Lakes Forest: An environmental and social history*, ed. Susan L. Flader (Minneapolis: University of Minnesota Press, 1983), 192; and Lambert and Pross, 404–5.

214 Lambert and Pross, 405; Department of Lands and Forests, Annual reports for 1949–1954; *Sault Star*, May 13, 1948.

215 *Toronto Star*, Aug. 28, 1976.

216 Lambert and Pross, 414–15.

217 Rea, 214.

218 Burgar, 192.

219 The exact quotation of his statement appears in Rea, 191.

220 *Sault Star*, May 23, 1950, Oct. 12, 1953, Mar. 24, 1961, Feb. 15, 1952, and Apr. 12, 1969.

221 Plasz, 43.

222 *Terrace Bay News*, July 31, 1974; and *Sioux Lookout Bulletin*, Aug. 14, 1974.

223 *The Link*, Dec. 1947, Mar. 1949, and Jan. 1956; *Fort William Times Journal*, Oct. 11, 1956; and *Sault Star*, Jan. 2, 1974.

224 AO, RG 1, E-10, Box 147, file 7-1-2 (Little to Scott, July 3, 17, 1951 and Aug. 1, 1952).

225 Ibid. (Little to Mapledoram, May 18, 1955, Sept. 26, 1956, and May, 1962).

226 *Dryden Observer*, Apr. 1, 1955 and July 20, Oct. 12, Apr. 1, 1965; *Fort William Times Journal*, Mar. 31, 1955; and *Sault Star*, Sept. 26, 1957.

227 *North Affairs Newsletter*, June 1980.

228 *Sault Star*, Apr. 24, 1956.

229 Provincial statistics produced annually for the period show no significant trend, as noted by Rea, 185.

230 Lambert and Pross, 404; and Gillis and Roach, 248.

231 *The forest resources of Ontario* (Toronto: Department of Lands and Forests, 1963).

232 The individual district background reports submitted in the late sixties during the preparation of the *Northwestern Ontario land use plan*, approved in 1972, make the fact quite clear.

233 Lambert and Pross, 248–9.

234 *Sault Star*, May 12, 1971.

235 Lambert and Pross, 367.

236 Ibid., 248–9; and *Sault Star*, Nov. 9, 1977, and June 21, 1979.

237 Lambert and Pross, 222–3.

238 Ibid., 229.

239 Ibid., 226–8 and 233; *Sault Star*, June 25, 1968, Apr. 1, 1969, and June 2, 1972; and *Lands and Forests Newsletter* 24 (1971): no. 14.

240 Lambert and Pross, 414–16.

241 Burgar, 192.

242 *Fort William Times Journal*, Dec. 29, 1951.

243 GPL, Forest Data File; *Fort William Times Journal*, May 11, 1946 and Mar. 2, 1954; *Rainy River Record*, May 21, 1953; *Sault Star*, June 29, 1957; *Mid-North News*, Nov. 27, 1958; *Dryden Observer*, Apr. 25, June 6, 1958, Apr. 9, Oct. 1, 1959, June 29, 1961, and Nov. 9, 1967; and *Thunder Bay News Chronicle*, July 31, 1974.

244 See, for example, *Fort William Times Journal*, May 5, 1952; *Sault Star*, June 1, 1954; *Dryden Observer*, Feb. 23, 1967; and *Thunder Bay News Chronicle*, June 12, 1977.

245 Lambert and Pross, 231; *Lands and Forests Newsletter* 23, (1970), no. 27; *Sault Star*, May 5, 1958, June 3, 1963, and Oct. 29, 1969; *Geraldton Times Star*, Nov. 4, 1970, and July 31, 1974; *Fort William Times Journal*, Dec. 29, 1951, and Mar. 2, 1954; and *Sioux Lookout Bulletin*, May 14, 1970.

246 Planting statistics derived from the annual reports of the Department of Lands and Forests for 1955 to 1960–61. Comments on scarification and site preparation are to be found in these same reports but are also exemplified in KPL, Forestry File; BRL, Northwestern Ontario, file 22; *Sault Star*, June 12, 1960, July 19, 26, 1961, and July 2, 1964; *Fort William Times Journal*, Dec. 29, 1951.

247 Gillis and Roach, 250–1; and *Sault Star*, May 13, 1972.

248 *Department of Lands and Forests' Annual Reports*, 1963–66; *Sault Star*, May 5, 1968, June 10, 26, 1971, and Jan. 10, 1980; *Fort William Times Journal*, Apr. 21, 1970; *Geraldton Times Star*, Oct. 30, 1969; and *Lands and Forests Newsletter* 23 (1970), no. 27.

249 See, for example, BRL, Northwestern Ontario, file 26; *Dryden Observer*, Dec. 29, 1966, and May 14, 1970; *Thunder Bay News Chronicle*, July 31, 1974; and *Rainy River Record*, Dec. 21, 1978.

250 *Report of the forest study unit* (Toronto: Department of Lands and Forests, 1967); *Design for development ... policy recommendations* (Toronto: Department of Treasury and Economics, 1970); and *Forest production policy options for Ontario* (Toronto: Ministry of Natural Resources, 1972).

251 K.A. Anson, *Forest management in Ontario* (Toronto: Ministry of Natural Resources, 1976), especially 2–8.

252 Rea, 192–3.

253 A well-balanced review of national conditions and events behind this dichotomy is to be found in Bothwell, 15–19 and 445–74.

254 In addition to periodic comments in the regional press on pricing patterns, the annual reports of the Department of Lands and Forests trace the Great Lakes' market returns into the late fifties. Real improvement, however, came only with the seventies.

255 *Sault Star*, Sept. 6, 1946, June 10, 1948, and May 16, 1949.

256 NAC, RG 23, vol. 1612, no. 784-8-11, pt. 1 (Memo of Oct. 12, 1959); Thomas F. Waters, *The Superior north shore* (Minneapolis: University of Minnesota Press, 1987), 186–8; *Fort William Times Journal*, Dec. 14, 1946; and *Sault Star*, Aug. 27, 1959.

257 As far as the authors can discover, this blanket category for inland lakes went undefined from the late thirties until 1964, when the annual report of the Department of Lands and Forests for that year offered clarification.

258 NAC, RG 23, vol. 784-8-11, pt. 3 (Report of Dr. W.A. Kennedy, Jan. 25, 1960); and Waters, 160, support A.B. McCullough, *The commercial fisheries of the Canadian Great Lakes* (Ottawa: National Historic Parks and Sites Board, 1985), 80.

259 *Sault Star*, May 22 and June 10, 1948.

260 Lambert and Pross, 459–60; John L. Goodier, 'Fishermen and their trade on Canadian Lake Superior: One hundred years,' *Inland Seas* 45 (1989): 303; McCullough, 88–9; Waters, 152–60; and a series of searching articles in the *Sault Star*, Apr. 25–30 and Aug. 29, 1956, which blame years of over-fishing, among other causes.

261 Lambert and Pross, 511–15; Waters, 153–4; and McCullough, 102–3.

262 Waters, 153, and numerous regional press reports; see especially the *Sault Star*, May 3, 1951, Apr. 23, 1953, Apr. 10, July 3, 1954, and Apr. 26, July 28, 1956.

263 Lambert and Pross, 514–15; Waters, 154–5; and further *Sault Star* articles of July 25, 26, 1957, Sept. 25, 1958, Aug. 6, 1959, July 17, Nov. 24, 1961, Apr. 30, Aug. 24, Sept. 22, 1962, as well as Oct. 30, 1967, and Oct. 12, 1977.

264 Yearly updates are given in the annual reports of the Department of Lands and Forests for 1962–66.

265 *Sault Star*, June 4, 1962.

266 Ibid., July 17, 1963.

267 Department of Lands and Forests' Annual report for 1963.

268 *Sault Star*, June 12, and July 7, 1961.

269 *Sault Star*, May 31, and July 28, 1956.

270 Ministry of Natural Resources, Annual report for 1974; *Fort William Times Journal*, Nov. 22, 1954, and Apr. 12, 1957; *Sault Star*, Oct. 4, 1962, July 10, 1964, Jan. 16, 1967, Sept. 17, 1971, and May 19, 1976.

271 NAC, RG 23, vol. 1613, no. 704-8-11, pt. 2 (Memo, Oct. 12, 1961); *Fort William Times Journal*, Nov. 22, 1954; and *Sault Star*, Dec. 9, 14, 1961, May 5, Sept. 17, 1971, and Mar. 18, 1980.

272 NAC, RG 33-79, vol. 6, pt. 3 (Minutes and Correspondence for hearings of the Royal Commission on Freshwater Fishing at Kenora, Port Arthur, and Sault Ste Marie, Nov./Dec., 1965).

273 Department of Lands and Forests, Annual reports for 1950, 1953, and 1961.

274 NAC, RG 23, vol. 437, no. 702-4-16 (Lands and Forests to Ontario Council of Great Lakes Fishermen, Mar. 23, 1954); and RG 33-79, vol. 6, pt. 3, p. 1003-20 (Port Arthur Hearings, Dec. 1965); and *Fort William Times Journal*, Dec. 20, 1950.

275 Early reaction to such concern can be seen in the formation of the Ontario Water Resources Commission in 1957, the increasing press coverage of such pollution through the sixties, and the signing of the initial Great Lakes Quality Agreement in 1972.

276 Department of Lands and Forests, Annual Report for 1956; and the *Rainy River Record*, July 17, 1958, and Dec. 22, 1977.

277 *Dryden Observer*, Feb. 16 and 23, 1951.

278 Sybil Willard, *The pioneers and the present ... the Township of Barclay, 1882–1982* (Dryden: Alex Coldstream Ltd. for the Barclay Historical Society, 1983), 93–4; and *Tracks beside the water*, 517 and 623.

279 Both these large inventories/assessments appear for a sequence of years in the Department of Lands and Forests annual reports for 1960–8.

280 NAC, RG 33-79, pt. 3, pp. 1020-5, 1050 and 2055 (Port Arthur Hearings, Dec., 1965); and E.S. Rogers, *Ojibway fisheries in northwestern Ontario* (Toronto: Ministry of Natural Resources, 1972), 1–42.

281 *Fort William Times Journal*, Mar. 1 and 27, 1870; and *Dryden Observer*, Sept. 27, 1978.

282 AO, Pamphlets, 1978, no. 105; and Rogers, 35–42.

283 Rea, 134–8.

284 M.J. Troughton, 'The failure of agricultural settlement in northern Ontario,' *Nordia* 17 (1983): 145–7; and I.G. Davies, 'Agriculture in the northern forest, the case of northwestern Ontario,' *Lakehead University Review*, 1 (1968): 140.

285 *Fort Frances Times*, Nov. 2, 1947; *Fort William Times Journal*, Dec. 5, 1949; *Rainy River Record*, Apr. 23, 30, 1953, and Dec. 1, 1960; and *Sault Star*, Aug. 1, 1956.

286 Davies, 143 and 153; Richard C. Benson, 'Part-time farming in a physically marginal area of Northern Ontario,' in *Part-time farming: Problem or resource in rural development*, ed. A.M. Fuller and Julius Mage (Norwich: Geo Abstracts Ltd., 1976), 27–8; Lynne Mitchell, 11; and Troughton, 145.

287 Davies, 140–1; and Troughton, 143–4.

288 Radforth, 'Woodworkers and the mechanization of the pulpwood logging industry,' 71–6.

289 *Rainy River Record*, Mar. 9, 1961, Mar. 22, 1973, and Mar. 16, 1978; *Dryden Observer*, Mar. 26, 1959, and June 11, 1964; and *Fort William Times Journal*, Aug. 3, 1960.

290 Lambert and Pross, 308.

291 An excellent summary of this report is to be found in the *Sault Star*, Nov. 19, 1961.

292 Michael Fox and Sandra L. Macenko, *The agriculture-forest interface: An overview of land use change*, Working Paper no. 38 (Ottawa: Canada Land Directorate, 1985), 27–30; and Anthony M. Fuller, *The development of the ARDA farm enlargement and consolidation program in Ontario, 1966–75*, Studies in Rural Adjustment no. 75 (Guelph: Centre for Resource Development, 1975): 1–8.

293 J.L. Nowland and J.A. McKeague, 'Canada's limited agricultural land resource,' in *Managing Canada's renewable resources*, ed. R.R. Krueger and B. Mitchell (Toronto: Methuen Press, 1977), 115.

294 Robert S. Dilley, 'Farming on the margin,' in *Geographic perspectives on the provincial norths*, ed. Margaret E. Johnston (Toronto: Copp Clark Longman, 1994), 185.

295 Anthony M. Fuller, *The development of the ARDA farm enlargement and consolidation program*, 1–8.

296 Personal interview with Mr A. Grant Mitchell, retired Agricultural Representative for Algoma, July 14, 1989.

297 Fuller, *The development of the ARDA ... program*, 90–4.

298 Personal interview with Mr A. Grant Mitchell, July 14, 1989.

299 Much of the information to the end of the paragraph comes from Fuller, *The development of the ARDA ... program*, 35–43.

300 *Rainy River Record*, May 30, 1963.

301 Dilley, 190–2; and Lynne Mitchell, 11.

302 *Rainy River Record*, Nov. 23, 1950, Apr. 7, 1955, Dec. 31, 1959, Jan. 7, 28, Feb. 4, Apr. 7, 1960, May 25, 1961, and Feb. 28, 1963. While mention of copying Manitoulin's blueprint for success is made in these references, a full discussion of what was involved on the island is to be found in Wightman, *Forever on the fringe*, 181–8 and 197–200.

303 *Rainy River Record*, Jan. 7, 28, Feb. 4, Apr. 7, Oct. 6, 1960, and Feb. 2, 1961.

304 *Rainy River Record*, Feb. 28, 1963, Jan. 26, July 27, 1967, Oct. 31, 1968, Sept. 24, 1970, and Nov. 15, 1979.

305 Fox and Macenko, 27; Fuller, *The development of the ARDA ... program*, 89; Troughton, 149–50; and J.S. Wolfe and L. Bodnar, *Unrealized potential: An examination of the role of government in the past, present and future of agriculture in northern Ontario*, Pub. 117 (Guelph: School of Rural Planning and Development, 1983) 36–8.

306 The complex problems of abandonment among both agricultural owners and bush operators is more thoroughly documented and so better described in process for the Manitoulin Island in Wightman, *Forever on the fringe*, 189–92.

307 *Rainy River Record*, Oct. 26, 1967, supplies a summary review of this problem with feed grains and the rules surrounding this northwestern subsidy.

308 For more information on these urban-related agricultural and horticultural demands, see Elving J.S. Josephson, 'A study of the changing scale and degree of specialization in the Slate River Valley,' B.A. dissertation, Lakehead University, Thunder Bay, 1972.

309 Kates, Peat, Marwick and Co., *Northwestern Ontario's tourist industry* (Toronto: Department of Tourism and Information, 1968), 2–4.

310 *Thunder Bay Chronicle Journal*, Mar. 22, 1980.

311 Balmer, Crapo and Assoc., *Tourism development in Ontario: a framework for opportunity* (Toronto: Ministry of Industry and Tourism, 1976), 29; and *Rainy River Record*, Jan. 30, 1969.

312 FFM, Tourism file; *Sault Star*, Sept. 13, 1968; *Dryden Observer*, Oct. 11, 1971; and *Geraldton Times Star*, Nov. 10, 1974.

313 *Fort Frances Times*, Mar. 9, 1955; *Sault Star*, Aug. 11, 1975, and June 8, 1959; *Dryden Observer*, June 8, 1961; and *Thunder Bay Times News*, Dec. 2, 1970.

314 *A history of the Port Arthur Forest District* (Toronto: Department of Lands and Forests, 1963), n.p.; *Sault Star*, Mar. 27, 1948, and June 21, 1963; *Fort William Times Journal*, May 19, 1951; and *Rainy River Record*, May 2, 1963, and May 14, 1964.

315 Wightman and Wightman, 'Road and highway development,' 377–9; and *Sault Star*, July 16, 1959, Aug. 11, 1962, and Sept. 7, Nov. 14, 1963.

316 Adelaide Leitch, 'Wilderness Park–Lake Superior,' *Canadian Geographical Journal* 55 (1957): 43–4; and *Sault Star*, June 16, 1959.

317 *Fort William Times Journal*, Mar. 13, 1954, and Nov. 30, 1963; *Marathon Mercury*, May 19, 1960, June 1, 1961, and May 23, 1962; and *Sault Star*, June 24 and Aug. 5, 1961.

318 *Rainy River Record*, Feb. 17, 1955, and Apr. 27, 1961; and *Fort William Times Journal*, Nov. 30, 1963.

319 Wightman and Wightman, 'Road and highway development,' 377–9.

320 For examples of such early motel construction, see *Sault Star*, Aug. 5, 1961, and Aug. 23, 1962; and *Terrace Bay News*, July 13, Oct. 26, and Dec. 20, 1962.

321 D.E. Hallman, 'Tourism and outdoor recreation in northwestern Ontario: An overview,' *Lakehead University Review* 6 (1973): 52–61; FFM, Tourism file; 'Fort Frances District, background information for the northwestern Ontario strategic land use plan,' Ministry of Natural Resources, Fort Frances, 1980, 84–7; *Sault*

Star, June 25, 1955, July 21, 28, 1962, and Aug. 7, 1973; and *Nipigon Gazette*, June 12, 1980.

322 See, for example, NAC, RG 23, vol. 928, no. 721-4-5, pt. 19 (Sault Ste Marie City Council to Minister of Fisheries, Apr. 20, 1950); *Sault Star*, Apr. 15, 1950; *Rainy River Record*, Aug. 7 and Sept. 25, 1969; *Fort William Times Journal*, Apr. 4, 1970; and *Fort William Times News*, Sept. 6, 1970.

323 FFM, Tourism file; SSMPL, Algoma District, file no. 4; Hallman, 59; and *Sault Star*, July 9, 1966.

324 FFM, Tourism file; Kates, Peat, Marwick and Co., 16; *Rainy River Record*, Sept. 12, 1973; and *Fort Frances Times*, Apr. 17, 1975.

325 *The history of the Port Arthur Forest District*, n.p.; 'Fort Frances District, background information,' 84–7; *Fort William Times Journal*, Feb. 9, 1960, and Apr. 11, 1963; *Sault Star*, Sept. 2, 1961, Jan. 2, 1962, Aug. 15, 1966, June 17, Aug. 15, 1970, Aug. 25, 1977, and Aug. 3, 9, 1978; and *Terrace Bay News*, July 12, 1974.

326 Hallman, 60; and *Background information and approaches to policy: Northwestern Ontario Planning Region* (Toronto: Ministry of Natural Resources, 1974), map. 29.

327 With Hallman, 54–6, the *Sault Star*, July 26, 1957, reflects the rise in car camping.

328 Kates, Peat, Marwick and Co., 25 and table 4.

329 *Background information and approaches to policy*, 27–30; Kates, Peat, Marwick and Co., 20 and table 4; *Fort William Times Journal*, Oct. 18, 1955; and *Sault Star*, July 24, 1964, and Apr. 23, July 2, 1969.

330 'Fort Frances District, background information,' 87; *Dryden Observer*, May 16, 1974; and *Rainy River Record*, June 6, 1974.

331 Lambert and Pross, 477–99.

332 For a quick reference to the later sixties, see ibid., map 482–3, prior to 1970. However, the principal sources here are appropriate road maps in the AO, Map Collection, supplemented by those preserved in the Serge Sauer Map Library, University of Western Ontario.

333 *Sault Star*, Apr. 21 and June 24, 1975.

334 For a quick summary of Quetico's evolution, see Lambert and Pross, 284–99 (selectively) and 479–81. However, for a detailed appreciation of both the history of the park and the philosophy espoused, see George Michael Warecki, 'The Quetico-Superior Council and the Battle for Wilderness in Quetico Provincial Park, 1909–1960,' M.A. dissertation, University of Western Ontario, London, 1983; Bruce M. Littlejohn, 'Quetico country wilderness highway to wilderness recreation,' *Canadian Geographical Journal* 71 (1965): 40, 55, and 79–81; and Martha Straditto, 'The Quetico heritage,' *Beaver* (1984): 32–77. The most

complete treatment of the bitter struggle for park policy reform, however, is the recent volume by Gerald Killan, *Protected places: A history of Ontario's Provincial Parks System* (Toronto: Dundurn Press, 1993), 226 pp.

335 *Marathon Mercury*, Apr. 3, 1963; and *Sault Star*, July 13, 1971, as well as the *Pukaskwa National Park management plan summary* (Ottawa: Parks Canada, 1982): 1–5.

336 While the regional press and libraries are full of snippets on these developments, there are as yet no summary articles or editorials to which the reader can be referred or official studies with statistical substantiation to elaborate the case.

337 O.S. Nock, *The Algoma Central Railway* (London: Adam and Charles Black, 1975) gives a solid account of the acquisition of rolling stock; and *Sault Star*, Sept. 29, Oct. 18, 1949, Sept. 17, 1951, and Sept. 25, 1957.

338 *Sault Star*, Oct. 3, Nov. 6, 1970, Mar. 9, Oct. 6, 1972, Oct. 6, 1973, Nov. 6, 1974, and Aug. 3, 1978.

339 Ibid., Oct. 6, 1972, and Sept. 16, 1979. The authors enjoyed all these tours in the eighties.

340 *Kenora Miner*, Jan. 27, 1950, and Jan. 29, 1961; and *Sault Star*, Feb. 11, 1974.

341 *Sault Star*, Jan. 8, 1972.

342 Ibid., Aug. 28, 1959, July 18, 1966, Nov. 28, 1970, and Aug. 13, 1980.

343 *Thunder Bay Chronical Journal*, Jan. 21 and Apr. 29, 1980.

344 Rea, 240.

345 John Abbott, 'Sault Ste. Marie: Explorations in the origin and evolution of municipal government,' *Laurentian University Review* 17, no. 2 (1985): 57–68; and *Sault Star*, Oct. 18, 1963.

346 *Sault Star*, Dec. 3, 1956, June 14, 1957, and Mar. 16, 1962; and a personal interview with Mr James T. Melville, Vice-President, Algoma Steel Corp., Sault Ste Marie, July 11, 1989.

347 *Sault Star*, May 11, 1959, May 8, June 15, 1961, Nov. 30, 1963, and Sept. 15, 1971.

348 Ibid., Aug. 1, 1981.

349 *Globe and Mail*, June 28, 1961.

350 *Sault Star*, Sept. 16, 1974.

351 SSMM, *Summary report of the International Joint Commission on boundary waters pollution* (Ottawa: 1968), 29–43.

352 *Sault Star*, June 8, 1959, July 30, 1970, Apr. 23, 1973, and May 31, 1975.

353 Ibid., June 13, 1972, July 22, 23, 1976, and June 6, 1978.

354 SSMPL, Historical Files, C.A. Sweet, 'A Sault Ste. Marie time chart, 1975–1971' (mimeo); and *Sault Star*, Sept. 2, 1971.

355 Lambert and Pross, 229; and *Sault Star*, Sept. 27, 1976.

356 *Sault Star*, July 9, 1963.
357 Ibid., Oct. 28, 1970 and Aug. 31, Oct. 31, 1973.
358 Ibid., July 3, 1972, Apr. 19, 1973, and Aug. 30, 1976.
359 BRL, Historical Files, Thunder Bay, no. 1, 'A capsule history of Thunder Bay' (mimeo) and no. 19.
360 *Thunder Bay Mosaic* (Thunder Bay: Thunder Bay Multicultural Association, 1983): 11–69; and 'Thunder Bay's people,' ed. Antonio Pucci and John Potestro, *Polyphony* 9 (1987): especially 10–20.
361 *Fort William Times Journal*, Feb. 4, Dec. 14, 1946, Sept. 12, 1952, Oct. 18, 1960, and Apr. 21, 1970.
362 Ibid., Feb. 17, Mar. 7, Oct. 27, Dec. 29, 1951, Apr. 10, 1953, July 30, 1954, Feb. 4, Sept. 27, 1955, May 11, 1960, and Jan. 21, Apr. 21, May 19, 1970; and *Northern Ontario Business*, Apr., 1981.
363 Ibid., Mar. 14, Dec. 14, 1946, Dec. 10, 1949, and Dec. 29, 1951.
364 *Thunder Bay Chronicle Journal*, Apr. 29, 1980.
365 *Fort William Times Journal*, Dec. 4, 1946, Feb. 16, 1949, Feb. 17, 1951, and Feb. 13, 1952.
366 Ibid., Apr. 2, 1952, July 23, 1953, and Mar. 19, 1960; and *Thunder Bay Chronical Journal*, Apr. 29, 1980.
367 BRL, Historical Files, Thunder Bay, no. 19; *Fort William Times Journal*, June 25, 1952, Jan. 18, 1955, and Apr. 12, July 11, 1960; *Sault Star*, Nov. 29, 1976, and Apr. 7, 1977; *Northern Miner*, Aug. 18, 1979; and *Thunder Bay Chronicle Journal*, Apr. 29, 1980.
368 Seaborne and Larrain, 288; BRL, Historical Files, Thunder Bay, no. 1; and *Transport, Thunder Bay* 1 (summer, 1983): 4.
369 Personal interview with Mr James E. Hill, Manager, Port Developments, Thunder Bay Harbour Commission, Nov. 17, 1987.
370 BRL, Historical Files, Thunder Bay, no. 19.
371 Geoffrey R. Weller, 'The politics and administration of amalgamation, the case of Thunder Bay,' *Laurentian University Review* 17, no. 2 (1985): 69–85.
372 This conclusion is based on the study of statistical tables in *The Lakehead and Northwestern Ontario: An economic survey* (Toronto: Regional Development Branch, Department of Treasury and Economics, 1969); and *The Northern Ontario statistical profile* (Toronto: Department of Northern Affairs and Development, 1976).
373 TBPL, Clipping Files; Jeanne Marcella, *A history of Jackfish* (Terrace Bay: Terrace Bay Library, 1987), 7; and personal interviews with Mr K.P. Zurby, Clerk of the Township of Michipicoten and an employee who grew up in Brient, Wawa, Aug. 16, 1988.

374 *Tracks beside the water*, 13, 138–40, and 185.

375 C.M. Wallace, 'Communities in the northern Ontario frontier,' in *At the end of the shift: Mines and single industry towns in Northern Ontario*, ed. Matt Bray and Ashley Thomson (Toronto: Dundurn Press, 1991), 15–18, especially 10–13, Oiva Saarinen, 'Single industry communities in Northern Ontario: The creation and planning of dependent towns,' in *Power and place: Canadian urban development in the North American context*, ed. G.A. Stelter and A. Artibise (Vancouver: University of British Columbia Press, 1986), 228; and Gilbert A. Stelter and Alan F.J. Artibise, 'Canadian resource towns in historical perspective,' in *Shaping the urban landscape*, ed. Stelter and Artibise (Ottawa: Carleton University Press, 1982), 415–20.

376 Robert Robson, 'Ontario Hydro colonies: A study of frontier settlement,' *Laurentian University Review* 17, no. 2 (1985): 115–25; and personal interview with Mr W.L. Harris, President, Great Lakes Power Ltd., Sault Ste Marie, July 19, 1988.

377 *Northern Miner*, Nov. 29, 1951, and Nov. 25, 1956; and *Fort William Times Journal*, June 11, 1953.

378 Robert Robson, 'Building resource towns: Government intervention in Ontario in the 1950s,' in *At the end of the shift*, ed. Bray and Thomson, 97–9.

379 *Fort William Times Journal*, Nov. 12, 1954; *Northern Miner*, Nov. 25, 1954, Nov. 29, 1956, and Apr. 12, 1960; and *The Echo*, July 11, 1968.

380 LPL, History File, Longlac; *Evergreen reflections* (Vermilion Bay: The Nor-West Historical Society, 1986), 7; *The Link* (Fall 1956); *The Echo*, July 11, 1968; *Kimberly-Clark Newsletter* 5, no. 5, (Aug. 1976); and *Northern Affairs Newsletter*, 6, no. 4 (Dec. 1983).

381 *Northern Miner*, Nov. 26, 1970.

382 Robson, 'Building resource towns,' 99. In addition to specific references recorded earlier for the Anglo-Canadian project at Sioux Lookout, much more detailed correspondence of this and related matters is to be found in AO, RG 1, A-vi-1. For the Ear Falls case, see EFPL, History File, Griffith Mines as well as the *Dryden Observer*, Nov. 10, 1966, and Apr. 13, Sept. 14, 1967.

383 Robson, 'Building resource towns,' 101–2; *Sault Star*, July 26, 1966, and Feb. 3, 1967; *Marathon Mercury*, May 23, 1962; and *Northern Miner*, Mar. 30, 1967.

384 Robson, 'Building resource towns,' 103; and *Northern Miner*, Mar. 30, 1967, and July 9, 1970.

385 *Northern Miner*, Jan. 20 and Nov. 26, 1970.

386 *Sault Star*, Apr. 18, 1968; *Sioux Lookout Bulletin*, Apr. 7, 1970; and *Fort William Times Journal*, Apr. 7, 1970.

387 *Northern Miner*, Feb. 12, 1970; *Sioux Lookout Bulletin*, Apr. 7, 1970; and *Dryden Observer*, Oct. 5, 1970, Nov. 18, 1971, June 28, 1973, Jan. 31, 1974, and July 24, 1975.

388 SLPL, Historical Files, contain actual copies of these preliminary assessments; *Dryden Observer*, Oct. 14, 1973 and Mar. 4, 1975; and *Northern Miner*, Mar. 27, and July 24, 1975.

389 The available record on these subjects in the local press and local repositories is too voluminous to consider listing here or describing in the text, even by example.

390 Much of this impression is gleaned from B.A. dissertations in the Department of Geography at Lakehead University, Thunder Bay, by Elving J.N. Josephson (1972), Kevin Des Rosiers (1978), and Ray F. Fulton (1981) and also from personal interviews with Mr Clarence D. Haverson, Agricultural Representative, Thunder Bay District, Thunder Bay, Nov. 21, 1987; Mr A. Grant Mitchell, retired Agricultural Representative, Algoma District, Sault Ste Marie; and Mr William J. Wierzbicki, Planning Office, Sault Ste Marie, July 12, 1989.

391 As well as expressing the views of numerous municipal clerks in Rainy River and some in the Kenora district, this summary relies heavily on personal interviews with Mr Bruce Ward, Agricultural Representative, Rainy River District, Emo, July 18, 1986, and his counterpart, Mr Elmer Lick, Dryden, Aug. 19, 1988.

392 This is not to suggest that concern for these matters was not felt by many within the society or its forest industry before this period but to underline that such persons were not in the majority or in positions to make their collective views a strong force in moulding the regional attitude.

393 *Lake Superior Strategic Fisheries Plan, 1986–2000* (Toronto: Ministry of Natural Resources, 1987), 14.

394 Personal interview, Mr Mike Petzold, Lake Superior Fisheries Management Unit, Ministry of Natural Resources, Sault Ste Marie, July 25, 1994.

395 *Sault Star*, Sept. 7, 1977, and Aug. 11, 1980; and *Thunder Bay Chronicle Journal*, June 11, 1989.

396 Personal interview, Mr Mike Petzold and statistics supplied by him. The only possible threat to this fishery would come through the return of the lamprey, which again has infested the St Marys River (see *Sault Star*, Sept. 6, 1984; *London Free Press*, Mar. 28, 1989; and *Manitoulin Expositor*, Oct. 18, 1989).

397 Personal interview, Mr Richard Salmon, Lake Nipigon Fisheries Assessment Unit, Ministry of Natural Resources, Nipigon, July 21, 1994.

398 From the statistics supplied by Mr Salmon, however, it is not clear whether these two species were first added to the catch as of 1983 or to the statistics of that date, although the former seems the more likely explanation.

399 Personal interview, Mr Richard Salmon.

400 Personal interviews, Mr John Maffei, Senior Technical Officer, Ministry of Natural Resources, Kenora, July 18, 1994; and Mr Don Pento, District Supervisor, Ministry of Natural Resources, Red Lake, July 20, 1994.

401 *Red Lake District Fisheries Plan, 1985–2000* (Toronto: Ministry of Natural Resources, 1984), 7–8.

402 Personal interviews, Mr John Maffei and Mr Don Pento.

403 *Rainy River Record*, Dec. 22, 1977.

404 *Background information, Fort Frances Fisheries Management Plan, 1985–2000* (Fort Frances: Ministry of Natural Resources, 1984), 3–4.

405 Personal interview, Mr Eric Archer, Technical Officer, Ministry of Natural Resources, Fort Frances, July 14, 1994.

406 Personal interview, Mr John Maffei.

407 *Northern Miner*, Jan. 15, 1981, June 16, 1986, Jan. 5, 1987, and Mar. 6, July 31, Sept. 4, 18, Dec. 1, 1989.

408 Ibid., May 1, 1980, June 18, 1981, Mar. 17, 1983, and June 2, 1984.

409 Ibid., June 2, Nov. 29, 1984, Oct. 17, 1988, and July 31, Oct. 9, 1989; and *Globe and Mail*, May 5, 1994.

410 *Thunder Bay Chronical Journal*, Jan. 4, 1980; and *Northern Miner*, Nov. 16, 1987, and June 12, 1993.

411 Personal interview, Mr M.J. Lavigne Jr, Resident Geologist, Thunder Bay District, Ministry of Northern Development and Mines, Thunder Bay, July 11, 1994.

412 *The Mining Act, Regulations, March, 1992* (Toronto: Ministry of Northern Development and Mines, 1992); and personal interview, Mr Jim Murphy, District Abatement Supervisor, Thunder Bay District, Northwestern Region, Ministry of the Environment, Thunder Bay, July 12, 1994.

413 *Northern Miner*, Nov. 27, 1980.

414 Ibid., Jan. 16, 1981, Apr. 23, Nov. 25, 1982, and Jan. 30, 1989.

415 Ibid., Nov. 25, 1985.

416 Ibid., Jan. 31, 1980, Jan. 28, 1981, Jan. 27, 1982, Apr. 26, 1984, Jan 10, 1985, and Mar. 3, 1986.

417 Algoma Steel Corporation, *Annual report for 1980* (Sault Ste Marie, 1981); and *Northern Miner*, Nov. 25, 1982.

418 *Northern Miner*, Nov. 30, 1978.

419 Algoma Central Railway, *Annual report for 1988* (Sault Ste Marie, 1989), 7; *Sault Star*, Jan 23 and Nov. 26, 1986; *Algoma News*, Aug. 3, 1988; and *Northern Miner*, Sept. 4, 1989.

420 Algoma Steel Incorporated, *Annual reports for 1992 and for 1993* (Sault Ste Marie, 1992, 1993); and personal interviews with Mr Stan Black, President, Algoma Central Railway, Sault Ste Marie, July 25, 1994; and Mr Paul Findlay, Chief Council, Algoma Steel Inc., Sault Ste Marie, July 25, 1994.

421 Algoma Steel Incorporated, *Annual Report for 1993* (Sault Ste Marie, 1993); and personal interview, Mr Kenn Cutts, Economic Development Officer, Superior East Development Association, Wawa, July 6, 1994.

422 Personal interviews, Mr Stan Black and Mr Paul Findlay.

423 The Wawa mines gained this sad accolade of being the only remaining operation when Dofasco closed both its Adams and Sherman properties in northeastern Ontario; see the *Northern Miner*, Mar. 13, 1989.

424 Ibid., Nov. 22, 1984, Dec. 7, 1987, Feb. 8, 1988, and Mar. 6, 1989; and *Dryden Observer*, Dec. 26, 1979, and Nov. 12, 1986.

425 *Northern Miner*, Apr. 19, June 29, 1978, Nov. 29, 1979, May 1, 1980, and Mar. 4, June 8, 1991; *Thunder Bay Chronicle Journal*, Apr. 29, 1978; and *Dryden Observer*, Nov. 28, 1979.

426 Personal discussion, Office personnel, Ministry of Northern Development and Mines, Wawa, July 22, 1994; and *Northern Miner*, Dec. 6, 1984, Oct. 2, 1989, and Aug. 9, 1993.

427 *Northern Miner*, Jan. 24, May 8, July 17, 1980, May 5, 14, Dec. 10, 1981, Dec. 2, 1982, Apr. 17, May 8, 1989, and Jan. 1, 1990; and *Thunder Bay Chronicle Journal*, Apr. 29, 1980, Aug. 1, 1992, and Jan. 14, 1993.

428 *Northern Miner*, July 17, 1980, Jan. 9, 1983, July 18, Sept. 30, Oct. 2, 1985, Feb. 24, July 21, Nov. 10, 1986, Mar. 16, Dec. 7, 1987, and Aug. 1, 8, 1988; *Thunder Bay Times News*, July 12, 1982; *Marathon Mercury*, Nov. 13, 1985; and *Terrace Bay-Schreiber News*, July 30 and Oct. 8, 1991.

429 Personal Interview, Aurel J. Gauthier, Clerk-Treasurer, Municipality of Schreiber, July 21, 1994.

430 *Northern Miner*, July 31, 1980, Mar. 7, 1985, Mar. 17, 1988, Feb. 26, Oct. 15, 1990, Apr. 22, 1991, Mar. 16, 1992, and Mar. 20, 1993.

431 Ibid., Apr. 26, Nov. 22, 1984, Mar. 7, June 6, 1985, Apr. 14, 1986, July 6, 1987, Jan. 1, Mar. 6, Apr. 17, 1989, and Jan. 1, 1990; and *Thunder Bay Chronical Journal*, June 2, 1993.

432 *Northern Miner*, June 16, 1986, Mar. 23, 1987, Jan. 18, 1988, and Mar. 6, Oct. 30, 1989.

433 Ibid., Dec. 7, 1987, and May 22, Dec. 25, 1989; and personal interview, Mr M.J. Lavigne Jr.

434 *Northern Miner*, Mar. 4, 1976, Oct. 23, 1980, May 31, June 14, 1984, Mar. 30, June 16, Aug. 2, 1986, July 13, Aug. 17, Oct. 26, 1987, and Mar. 21, 1988; *Terrace Bay-Schreiber News*, May 21, 1980; and *Nipigon Gazette*, Mar. 10, 1982.

435 *Northern Miner*, Jan. 4, Aug. 16, 1979, Feb. 21, Nov. 30, 1980, Mar. 5, Apr. 20, 1981, Dec. 11, 22, 1983, and Feb. 15, June 13, 1988.

436 Ibid., Feb. 10, June 1, 1983, June 2, 1984, Jan. 17, 1985, Mar. 17, 1986, Mar. 28, June 13, Sept. 5, 1988, May 1, July 3, Nov. 6, 13, 1989, June 4, 1990, Sept. 23, Dec. 23, 1991, and Mar. 12, 1994.

437 Ibid., July 27, Nov. 23, 1987, Mar. 14, July 25, 1988, July 24, 1989, Jan. 7, Oct. 7, 14, 1991, Apr. 13, 1992, and Feb. 15, May 13, Aug. 2, 1993; and *Thunder Bay Chronicle Journal*, Dec. 21, 1993.

438 Much has been written on Hemlo in book, monograph, and article format and is easily available to the reader who desires greater details. Simple references will suffice here. *Northern Miner*, Aug. 13, Sept. 3, Oct. 1, 1981, and July 29, Oct. 7, 28, Nov. 11, Dec. 16, 1982.

439 Ibid., Aug. 26, Nov. 18, Dec. 16, 1982, Jan. 13, July 14, Dec. 22, 1983, Jan. 19, Apr. 12, July 19, 1984; and Apr. 4, 25, June 6, 1985; *Sault Star*, Jan. 12, 1983; *Thunder Bay Times News*, Dec. 23, 1983.

440 *Northern Miner*, Aug. 1, 1985, Mar. 17, 1986, and Oct. 12, Aug. 21, 1989; *Marathon Mercury*, Sept. 11, 1983; and *Thunder Bay Times News*, Oct. 3, 1987.

441 *Northern Miner*, Feb. 27, Apr. 24, 1989, June 10, 1991, July 6, 1992, and June 27, 1993.

442 *Thunder Bay Chronicle Journal*, Apr. 29, 1980. While collective projections for the northern regions of the province were uncertain for the eighties (see Rea, 217), those making specific comments on the northwest were more optimistic (see Royal Commission on the Northern Environment, 8).

443 *Thunder Bay Chronicle Journal*, July 15, 1982, Apr. 23, 1983, Jan. 6, 1984, Apr. 21, 1987, Apr. 20, 1989, Apr. 30, 1991, and Apr. 21, June 19, 1992; *Dryden Observer*, Nov. 2, 1983, Oct. 14, 1989, and Apr. 14, 1993; and *Marathon Mercury*, Jan. 27, 1983.

444 *Marathon Mercury*, Feb. 9, and Mar. 2, 1983; and *Terrace Bay-Schreiber News*, Apr. 2, 1983.

445 *Sault Star*, Feb. 10, and Mar. 23, 1984.

446 *Thunder Bay Chronicle*, Apr. 19, June 3, 1983, Apr. 30, 1993, and Mar. 11, 1994.

447 Personal interview, Mr D. Bruce Strapp, Executive Director, Sault Ste Marie Economic Development Corporation, Sault Ste Marie, July 27, 1994; *Thunder Bay Chronicle Journal*, Jan. 6, 1991; and *Thunder Bay Business*, Mar. 1993. (Negotiations between Belgravia and the receivers for St Marys Paper were completed in August, according to CBC Northern Ontario Radio, Aug. 18, 1994. Discussions followed for an employee purchase of 40 per cent of the company, and certain wage reductions, with settlement of the entire matter completed in late autumn 1994.)

448 *Thunder Bay Chronicle Journal*, Feb. 11, Apr. 4, 21, Mar. 17, and Aug. 8, 25, 1992; and *Terrace Bay-Schreiber News*, Oct. 26, and Nov. 2, 1993.

449 This certainly has been the case at Kenora, Fort Frances, and Red Rock (see *Globe and Mail*, Jan. 30 and Mar. 11, 1994). Information indicative of the same move at Avenor's operation in Dryden and Thunder Bay and at James River, Marathon, surfaced in interviews with Mr J.F. Dayman, Economic Development Officer, Dryden, July 19, 1994, and Mr Angus MacIntyre, Economic Development Officer, Marathon, July 22, 1994. The current unsubstantiated rumour in Terrace Bay

suggests that Kimberly-Clark has quietly put that mill up for outright sale at a figure of $340 million.

450 *Thunder Bay Chronicle Journal*, Dec. 23, 1993.

451 *Northern Affairs Newsletter* 3, June, 1980; *Lakehead Living*, Apr. 24, 1984, and Mar. 4, 1990; and *Thunder Bay Times News*, Sept. 19, 1989.

452 Personal interview, Mr David Rennie, Human Resources Officer, St Marys Paper Co., Sault Ste Marie, July 18, 1989; *Thunder Bay Chronicle Journal*, Feb. 27, Apr. 29, and Dec. 19, 1980; *Thunder Bay Times News*, Sept. 29, 1984; and *Sault Star*, May 2, 1979, and Mar. 15, 1982.

453 *Terrace Bay-Schreiber News*, Jan. 2, 1980; and *Nipigon Gazette*, Mar. 12, 1981, and June 7, 1982.

454 *Terrace Bay-Schreiber News*, Apr. 2, 1983; *Marathon Mercury*, June 1, 1983, Aug. 29, 1984, and Dec. 17, 1989; and *Thunder Bay Times News*, June 30, 1988.

455 Personal interview, Mr D. Bruce Strapp; *Thunder Bay Times News*, Jan. 31, and Sept. 19, 1989; *Thunder Bay Chronical Journal*, Oct. 12, 1990; and *Terrace Bay-Schreiber News*, July 13, 1993.

456 *Lakehead Living*, Mar. 4, 1990; and *Thunder Bay Chronicle Journal*, Apr. 30, Sept. 25, Oct. 19, 1991, and Dec. 23, 1993. As one editor noted, at the opening of 1990 the only facility of this type was at Thorold. Now eleven are in operation in Ontario, with two more under construction (*Thunder Bay Chronicle Journal*, July 2, 1992).

457 Personal interviews with Mr J.F. Dayman; Mr David Hamilton, Mayor of Thunder Bay, Thunder Bay, July 12, 1994; Mr Jim Murphy; and Mr R.L. Stewart, District Supervisor, Ministry of the Environment and Energy, Sault Ste Marie, July 25, 1994.

458 Personal interview, Mr Jim Murphy.

459 FFPL, Pulp and Paper file, 1986.

460 FFPL, 'Fort Frances/International Falls: Working together for a better environment,' Boise Cascade, 1993.

461 *Thunder Bay Chronicle Journal*, Feb. 7, Apr. 11, 30, 1991, and Dec. 10, 1992; and *Nipigon Gazette*, Apr. 12, 1993.

462 Personal interview, Mr Jim Murphy; and *Thunder Bay Chronicle Journal*, June 19, 1992. See also J.R. Ralston, 'A municipal and industrial strategy for abatement in Ontario,' in *Making a great Lake Superior*, ed. Jake Vander Wal and Paul D. White (Thunder Bay: Lakehead Centre for Northern Studies, 1992), 286–94.

463 Personal interview, Mr R.L. Stewart; *Sault Star*, June 22, 1985; and *Report of the Ministry of Natural Resources for 1991*. For an interesting review of the RAP concept and of the problem and progress at each of these sites, see John H. Hartig, 'Remedial action plans for the Great Lakes today and tomorrow' and the series of

short statements by Ljubica Peltier et al. in the subsequent 'Lake Superior areas of contention' in *Making a great Lake Superior*, ed. Vander Wal and White, 163–82. In addition, some useful comments on RAPs, their aims and precepts, appear in Karl Schaefer and Ken Cullis, 'Tourism and the remedial action plan in the Nipigon Bay area of concern,' in *Communities, resources and tourism in the North*, ed. Margaret E. Johnston and Wolfgang Haider (Thunder Bay: Lakehead Centre for Northern Studies, 1993), 135–50.

464 *Terrace Bay-Schreiber News*, Sept. 3, 1991; and *Thunder Bay Times News*, Sept. 3, 1991.

465 *Dryden Observer*, Mar. 12, 1992; *Marathon Mercury*, Aug. 22, 1992; and *Terrace Bay-Schreiber News*, Sept. 1, 1992.

466 *Thunder Bay Post*, Feb. 9, 1993; *Thunder Bay Chronicle Journal*, Feb. 17, 1993; and *Globe and Mail*, Mar. 1, 1993.

467 *Thunder Bay Chronicle Journal*, July 21, 1991. This issue is at the heart of numerous comments in northwestern Ontario's 'aging' mills, which seem otherwise to have been kept moderately up-to-date.

468 The Dryden operation works off the same woodroom electronic sorting system as the pulp mill, which enables a very effective and efficient separation of the incoming roundwood. In contrast, the larger but equally profitable Domtar mill at White River is a completely separate operation with its own exclusive saw-log woodland sources.

469 Boise Cascade Canada Ltd., *Annual report for 1991*; and *Thunder Bay Chronical Journal*, Oct. 24, 1991.

470 Personal interviews with Mr W.D. Harkness, retired vice president and manager, Woodlands, American Can of Canada Ltd., Marathon, July 25, 1994; Mr Bill Davidson, Forester, Kimberly-Clark, Woodland Division, Longlac, July 7, 1994; Mr John E. Munroe, Area Forester, Ministry of Natural Resources, Atikokan, July 14, 1994; Mr J.D. Steele, Unit Forester, Ministry of Natural Resources, Dryden, July 20, 1994; Mr Fred Dewsberry, Forester, Ministry of Natural Resources, Thunder Bay, July 21, 1994. For a history of the earlier rise of the Buchanan Group, see *Thunder Bay Chronicle Journal*, Mar. 27, 1987.

471 Personal interviews with Mr Ralph T. Forfar, Registered Consultant Forester, Sault Ste Marie, July 27, 1994; and Mr Doug Afford, Forester, Ministry of Natural Resources, Sault Ste Marie, July 27, 1994. This information is supplemented by G.F. Vosper's four reports for the MNR in 1984 on various aspects of activity within and around Lake Superior Provincial Park, found in SSMPL.

472 Personal interview, Mr John O'Brien, Human Resources Manager, Weldwood of Canada Ltd., Longlac, July 7, 1994.

473 *Thunder Bay Chronicle Journal*, Dec. 14, 1986 and Feb. 10, Mar 16, 1987; *Northern Ontario Business*, Nov. 7, 1986, and Mar. 4, 1987; and *Thunder Bay*

Times News, Aug. 19, 1988. The latter facility was taken over by the South Korean company Shin Ho with an intent to reopen it as a particleboard mill; when this idea fell through, the company considered, but later shelved, plans for a market pulp mill elsewhere in the city (see *Thunder Bay Times News*, Aug. 19, 1988; and *Thunder Bay Chronicle Journal*, Feb. 9, 1990, and Apr. 4, 1992).

474 Personal interview, Mr Kenn Cutts. The first proposed strandboard mill was slated for Atikokan, but its Chinese capital was redirected by that government (see *Thunder Bay Times News*, Jan. 12, 1989).

475 Personal interview, Mr John Maffei and confirmed by Mr H.D. Harkness.

476 Personal interview, Mr D. Bruce Strapp, July 28, 1994.

477 Personal interviews with Mr Malcolm F. Squires, Divisional Forester, Abitibi-Price, Thunder Bay, Nov. 12, 1987; and Mr R.D. Scott, Forest Management Supervisor, Ministry of Natural Resources, Thunder Bay, Nov. 20, 1987.

478 Personal interview, Mr C.K. Sumi, Timber Management Planner, Ministry of Natural Resources, Thunder Bay, July 11, 1994.

479 Personal interview, Mr Bill Davidson; *Terrace Bay-Schreiber News*, Jan. 2 and Aug. 13, 1985; and *Marathon Mercury*, Aug. 27, 1986.

480 Personal interviews with Mr Don Pento, District manager, Ministry of Natural Resources, Red Lake, July 19, 1994; and Mr C.K. Sumi.

481 *Thunder Bay Chronicle Journal*, May 28, 1987, and May 18, Sept. 7, 1988; and *Thunder Bay Business*, Mar. 1993.

482 Radforth, *Bushworkers and bosses*, 227–30; and *Fort Frances Times*, Dec. 20, 1978, and Mar. 7, Sept. 26, 1979.

483 Personal interview, Mr J.D. Steele; *Thunder Bay Chronicle Journal*, Apr. 25, 1990, Feb. 1, 1992, and Oct. 19, 1993; and *Business North*, July 12, 1992.

484 Personal interviews with Mr R.G. Cox, Woodlands Manager, Boise-Cascade Canada, Fort Frances, July 14, 1994, Mr John Maffei; and Mr Fred Dewsberry.

485 For a statement from the viewpoint of the interest groups, see George B. Priddle, 'Forest management in Ontario,' in *Ontario: Geographical perspectives on the economy and environment*, ed. Bruce Mitchell, Department of Geography Publication Series no. 34 (Waterloo: University of Waterloo, 1991), 189–203.

486 *Wood fibre supply and demand in Northern Ontario*, A report by F.L.C. Reed and Associates for Abitibi-Price, American Can, Boise-Cascade, Domtar, Great Lakes, Kimberly-Clark, Ontario Paper, Reed and Spruce Falls Power and Paper (Vancouver, Apr. 21, 1980), a very reasonable summary of which appears in *Thunder Bay Chronicle Journal*, Apr. 29, 1980.

487 Burgar, 192.

488 'Forest Management Agreements,' brochure, Ministry of Natural Resources, Toronto, 1987, 5–9.

489 Personal interviews with Mr John E. Munroe and Mr Don Pento.

490 Personal interview, Mr C.K. Sumi.

491 *The Report of the Ministry of Natural Resources* for 1981, 1987, and 1989.

492 *Diversity: Forest, people and communities – a comprehensive forest policy framework for Ontario*, Report of the Ontario Forest Policy Panel to the Minister of Natural Resources (Toronto: Queen's Printer, 1993), 147 pp.

493 *The Reports of the Ministry of Natural Resources* for 1981 to 1986.

494 Gordon L. Baskerville, *An audit of management of the Crown forest of Ontario*, A report to the Minister of Natural Resources, Aug. 1, 1986 (Toronto: Queen's Printer, 1986), 97 pp. See also *Thunder Bay Chronicle Journal*, Oct. 31, and Nov. 2, 3, 4, 1987; and *Thunder Bay Times News*, Dec. 26, 1987.

495 *Globe and Mail*, Apr. 21, 1994.

496 Questions are now being raised by wildlife personnel over clear-cut size, since much of the northern half of the area now under harvesting is not moose but woodland caribou range, an animal that is much better provided for, in this age when forest fires are so diligently controlled, by clear-cuts as large as 100,000 hectares (see 'Woodland Caribou and logging in Ontario, questions and answers,' a pamphlet first circulated by the MNR in Nov. 1995 and accompanied by a more detailed ministerial fact sheet).

497 *Hearings on a class environmental assessment for timber management on Crown Lands in Ontario*, The Report to the Environmental Assessment Board (Toronto: Queen's Printer, 1994): 550 pp.

498 *An Act to revise the Crown Timber Act to provide for the sustainability of Crown Forests in Ontario*, Bill 171, 3rd Session, 35th Legislature, Ontario, 43, Elizabeth II, 1994.

499 Killan, 166–9.

500 Ibid., 235–8 and 307–10.

501 It would appear several others might have remained closed but for confusion in the printed literature. Of the two others that avoided this fate, MacLeod did so with help from Geraldton and Sioux Narrows through the efforts of the local Indian Band. For an excellent review of the whole austerity issue, see Killan, 289–322, and for a list of parks to be closed early, *Manitoulin Recorder*, Aug. 17, 1994.

502 Killan, 323–4.

503 Much of the above is a distillation from the authors' field observations, interviews, and research in northwestern Ontario, which experience now extends back a decade, combined with Killan, 323–74.

504 Personal interview, Mr Ronald LeeKam, Park Planner, Northwest Region, Ministry of Natural Resources, Thunder Bay, July 11, 1994, and popular pamphlets by that ministry on its evolving policy and programs, including *Ontario's Provincial Parks class environmental assessment for Provincial Park management*, Special report no. 1 (Toronto: Ministry of Natural Resources, 1992): 17 pp.

505 Personal interview, Ronald LeeKam. For an appreciation of some of the local conflicts and problems being talked over, see *Thunder Bay Chronicle Journal*, July 9 and 10, 1994.

506 Personal interview, Ms Sharon Otiquam, Chief of Management Services, Pukaskwa National Park, Heron Bay, July 22, 1994.

507 *Sault Star*, Jan. 18 and 25, 1979.

508 'Old Fort William, its history and its programs,' prepared by Ann Martin in 1987 and updated by Marty Mascarin in 1993, an in-house document read in the Library at Old Fort William in the summer of 1994.

509 *Thunder Bay Chronicle Journal*, Mar. 22, 1980.

510 *London Free Press* (citing the *Toronto Star*), Feb. 4, 1994. For a useful comment on the broader Canadian and provincial problem, see T.D. Hinch and R.W. Butler, 'Tourism development concerns in northern and eastern Ontario: A survey of professionals,' in *Communities, resources and tourism in the north*, 109–34.

511 *Thunder Bay Chronicle Journal*, Apr. 12, 1980; *Northern Affairs Newsletter* 3, no. 4 (1980) and 6, no. 2 (1983); and *Sault Star*, June 15, 1985.

512 *London Free Press*, Feb. 4, 1994; and *Thunder Bay Times News*, July 21, 1994.

513 *Lakehead Living*, Dec. 27, 1980, and Feb. 1, 1983; and *Thunder Bay Chronicle Journal*, Feb. 2, 1988, and Mar. 10, 1989.

514 This summation comes from numerous interviews with local businessmen, tourist operators, economic development officers, and municipal officials, confirmed by field observations of the regional industry since 1985.

515 This view, commonly expressed in the summer of 1994, was most forcefully put in personal interviews with Mr J.F. Daymen (Dryden), Mr Angus MacIntyre (Marathon), Mr Kenn Cutts (Wawa), and Mr D. Bruce Strapp (Sault Ste Marie).

516 At Kenora, related recreational literature, which points to a cooperative association of the Evergreen Mountain operation with major hotels and resort accommodations in the town, is quite explicitly directed at this Manitoba market.

517 Personal interviews with Mr Angus MacIntyre and Mr D. Bruce Strapp, who, with numerous other sources, provided considerable tourist literature for the Superior north shore and west Algoma area; and *Sault Star*, Sept. 17, 1980, Mar. 24, Sept. 23, Nov. 11, 1982, Dec. 16, 1983, and May 21, 1985; *Northern Affairs Newsletter* (Special Travel Edition), 1980; and *Thunder Bay Times News*, Jan. 12, 1985, Feb. 16, 1987, and Feb. 10, 1992.

518 Personal interview, Mr D. Bruce Strapp; *Thunder Bay Times News*, July 9, 1994.

519 *Thunder Bay Chronicle Journal*, July 9, 1994.

520 Unless otherwise indicated, the information in the following section was gained from personal interviews with Mr Calvin Holden (Thunder Bay), Oct. 12, 1987; Mr Elmer Lick (Dryden), Aug. 14, 1988; Mr A. Grant Mitchell (retired, Sault Ste Marie), July 14, 1989; and Mr Bruce Ward (Emo), July 10, 1986, and July 15,

1994, all of whom were Agricultural Representatives with the Ontario Ministry of Agriculture and Food, as well as Mr Dael Bierworth, Manager of Field Services for the Northwest for the same Ministry, July 11, 1994.

521 These figures are derived from *Agricultural statistics for Ontario, 1992* (Toronto: Ministry of Agriculture and Food, 1993), table 33.

522 *Dryden Observer*, July 29 and Oct. 28, 1987.

523 Wightman and Wightman, 'The rise of electric power,' 52–3.

524 Personal interviews with Mr J.F. Dayman and Mr Eric Rutherford, Reeve, Township of Beardmore, Beardmore, July 8, 1994.

525 *Globe and Mail*, May 5, 1994; and *Thunder Bay Times News*, July 21, 1994.

526 *Sault Star*, Dec. 17, 1982.

527 Personal interview, Mr Stan Black; *Globe and Mail*, July 29, 1994; and *Sault Star*, July 9, 20, and 30, 1994.

528 Personal interview with Mr Paul Heayn, Treasurer, Town of Dryden, Dryden, July 20, 1994, and well as Mr David Hamilton and Mr D. Bruce Strapp.

529 *Terrace Bay-Schreiber News*, June 15, 1993.

530 Personal interviews with Mr David Hamilton and Mr D. Bruce Strapp; *Sault Star*, Nov. 3, 1982, Feb. 19, 1983, and July 17, 1994; *Thunder Bay Chronicle Journal*, Apr. 23, 1983; and *Northern Ontario Business*, Oct. 1989.

531 Personal interviews with Mr William J. Wierzbicki, Planning Office, City of Sault Ste Marie, Sault Ste Marie, July 8, 1989; Mr R.L. Stewart; and Mr David Hamilton.

532 *Thunder Bay Times News*, July 29, 1987; and *Thunder Bay Chronicle Journal*, Feb. 1, 4, and Mar. 25, 1993. For the most recent history of this old company, see David A. Benedet, *Port Arthur Built: A history of the Port Arthur Shipbuilding Co.* (Thunder Bay: Pascol Engineering, 1994), 148 pp.

533 *Northern Business*, Apr. 1981 and Feb. 1993; *Thunder Bay Chronicle Journal*, Jan. 10, 1982, Feb. 8, July 12, 1983, Jan. 18, Mar. 20, Nov. 21, 1984, Mar. 6, Oct. 29, 1986, Dec. 5, 19, 1992, and June 11, 1993; and *Lakehead Living*, May 24, 1983.

534 *Northern Business*, Nov. 1993.

535 Personal interview, Mr James E. Hill, Manager, Port Development, Thunder Bay Harbour Commission, Thunder Bay, Nov. 7, 1987; *Thunder Bay Magazine*, Apr. 1986; and *Thunder Bay Chronicle Journal*, Jan. 30, 1992.

536 *Globe and Mail*, Mar. 31 and Apr. 23, 1994.

537 Personal interview, Mr James T. Melville; *Sault Star*, Oct. 13, 15, 1982, Mar. 18, 1983, and Feb. 16, Apr. 4, June 5, 10, 1985; *Globe and Mail*, July 23, 1983; and *Toronto Sunday Star*, Mar. 1, 1987.

538 Personal interview, Mr R.L. Stewart, who also noted that such work must continue in the late nineties.

539 *Sault Star*, Feb. 16, 1985; *Northern Miner*, Sept. 4, 1989.
540 *Sault Star*. Aug. 1, 1981, Oct. 13, 15, 1982, June 5, 10, 1985, and July 10, 1990; *Globe and Mail*, July 23, 1983, and Mar 7, 1994; and *Toronto Sunday Star*, Mar. 1, 1987.
541 Personal interview, Mr Paul Findlay.
542 CBC, Northern Ontario Radio interview with Mr Glen Manchester, Director of Finance and Comptroller, Algoma Steel Inc., July 26, 1994.
543 In interviews during the summer of 1994, this was the common concern of municipal officials and economic development officers in towns and villages across the region.
544 Interview, Mr J.F. Dayman, and quite evident in the graphs of recent community profiles, such as the one completed for the combined area of Kenora, Keewatin, Jaffray, and Melick in October 1993.
545 Personal interview, Mr Edward V. Hoshizaki, Economic Development Officer, Sioux Lookout, July 20, 1994.
546 *Sault Star*, Nov. 19, 1981, Oct. 1, 1987, and Dec. 9, 1991; *Algoma News Review*, Aug. 3, 1988; and *Toronto Star*, Oct. 1, 1987.
547 Telephone interview with Mr Harold Nicholas of Nicholas Technical Services, July 26, 1994.
548 *Bear News*, Mar. 5, 1988.
549 Personal interview, Mr Dennis V. Smith, Treasurer, Township of Wicksteed, Hornepayne, Aug. 7, 1988; *Northern Affairs Newsletter* 5, no. 4 (1982); and *Thunder Bay Times News*, Aug. 22, 1984.
550 *Thunder Bay Chronicle Journal*, Feb. 11, Mar. 17, Apr. 21, Aug. 8, 25, 1992, and Aug. 12, 1993.
551 Personal interview, Mr Dennis V. Brown, Alderman, Town of Atikokan, Atikokan, July 14, 1994; Warren Paulson, *The little town that could* (Atikokan: Atikokan Economic Development Corporation, 1993), 1–6; and R.E. Michels, 'Atikokan Ten Years Later,' A presentation to the Northwestern Ontario Planning Conference, Thunder Bay, Sept. 18, 1987 (copy obtained through Mr Dennis V. Brown).
552 *Thunder Bay Times News*, Aug. 6, 1980; and *Northern Affairs Newsletter* 6, no. 2 (1983).
553 *Dryden Observer*, July 29, 1987.
554 *Northern Miner*, Dec. 6, 1984, Oct. 2, 1989, and Aug. 9, 1993; *Thunder Bay Chronicle Journal*, Sept. 1, 1993; and *Marathon Mercury*, July 20, 1994.
555 *Marathon Mercury*, June 1, Aug. 24, 1983, July 18, Nov. 28, 1984, Feb. 5, 1986, and June 24, Aug. 19, 1987.
556 Personal interview, Mr Ross Mitchell, Chief Administrative Officer, Town of Marathon, Marathon, July 26, 1988.
557 *Thunder Bay Times News*, Dec. 12, 1986, and *Marathon Mercury*, Mar. 6, 1989.

558 *Final report and recommendations of the Advisory Committee on resource dependent communities in Northern Ontario* (Toronto: Ministry of Northern Development and Mines, 1986), 70 pp.

559 Personal interview, Mr Dael Bierworth.

560 The historical remarks on Indian administration are taken from a very fine eleven-page summary presented in the introduction to the finding aid for RG 10 (Indian Affairs) in NAC.

561 One need go no further than the pages of the national press, which for more than a decade has featured regular articles on Native concerns.

562 In their travels in preparation of this book, the authors witnessed the late stages and aftermath of this problem around Kenora and saw its frightening effects on Osnaburgh House at the height of the problem there.

563 For the exact working of the rules relating to the forest industry, see *Hearings on a class environmental assessment for timber management on Crown lands in Ontario*, 13–15. For the examples of the impact of recent changes in the Mining Act, which also treat the matter, see *Northern Miner*. Mar. 6, Oct. 30, 1989, Oct. 15, 1990, and Sept. 9, 1991.

564 *Kenora Miner*, May 12, 1978; and *Northern Ontario Business*, Sept. 1985.

565 Personal interview, Mr Richard Salmon.

566 *Sault Star*, May 30, 1994.

567 SSMM, C. Syrette et al., 'Batchawana band history, 1850–1977,' unpublished manuscript dated 1977, 65 pp.

568 Personal interview, Ms Sharon Otiquam, Chief of Management Services, Pukaskwa National Park, Heron Bay, July 22, 1994; and *Pukaskwa Management Plan Review, Public Consultation Newsletter* 2 (Summer 1991).

569 Discussions with Mr John H. Peters, Ontario Hydro, Toronto, who is deeply involved in these negotiations on behalf of this provincial utility.

570 *Red Lake District Fisheries Plan, 1985–2000*, 6–9; and personal interview, Mr Don Pento. Some more general information on this issue can be found in Rogers, 36 pp.

571 Wayne R. McKenney, 'The Sioux Lookout medical program,' *Beaver* (Spring, 1973): 52–7; John Eyles et al., 'Fair share for the zone: Allocating health-care resources for the Native population of the Sioux Lookout Zone,' *Canadian Geographer* 30 (1994): 134–50; Toby Maloney, 'Native network spreads news in Northern Ontario,' *Canadian Geographical Journal* 90 (July 1987): 6–4; as well as a personal interview at *Wawatay* in Aug. 1987 and a more general one on town expansion with Mr Edward V. Hoshizaki.

572 The authors here couch their comments in the light of childhood memories of conditions on the Manitoulin Island in the forties and fifties and the progress they found on reserves there, when researching and writing *Forever on the fringe* in the seventies.

Bibliography

Published Sources

Abbott, John. 'Sault Ste. Marie: Explorations in the origins and evolution of municipal government,' *Laurentian University Review* 17 (1985): 57–68

Addison, P. 'North shore expansion,' *Sylva* 2 (1945): 32–41

Agassiz, Lewis. *Lake Superior: With a narrative of a tour* ... New York: Arno and the New York Times, 1970

Alcock, F.J. 'Past and present fur trade routes to the Canadian Northwest,' *Geographical Review* 10 (1920): 57–83

Alexander, W.J., and W.L. Oliphant. 'The big tow,' *Inland Seas* 17 (1961): 264–72

Algoma Central Railway. *Annual Report for 1988*. Sault Ste Marie, 1989

Algoma Steel Corporation. *Annual Report for 1980*. Sault Ste Marie, 1981

Algoma Steel Incorporated. *Annual Reports for 1992 and for 1993*. Sault Ste Marie, 1992 and 1993

Alwin, John A. 'The uncelebrated boats of the Albany,' *Beaver* (Spring 1975): 47–53

Anderson, A.A. 'The development of the harbours of Port Arthur and Fort William,' *Thunder Bay Historical Museum Society Papers and Records* 11 (1983): 42–8

Anson, K.A. *Forest management in Ontario*. Toronto: Ministry of Natural Resources, 1976

Arthur, Elizabeth. 'The Landing and the Plot,' *Lakehead University Review* 1 (1968): 1–17

– *The Thunder Bay District, 1821–1892*. Toronto: University of Toronto Press, 1973

– 'Orientation and disorientation at Rainy River,' *Ontario History* 72 (1981): 195–218

– 'Beyond Superior: Ontario's new-found land.' In *Patterns of the past*, ed. Roger Hall et al., 130–49, Toronto: Dundurn Press, 1988

Auden, A.J. 'Nipigon Forest Village, a preliminary prospectus,' *Forest Chronicle* 20 (4) (1944): 209–61

Backes, David. 'Wilderness visions: Arthur Carhart's 1922 proposal for the Quetico-Superior wilderness,' *Forest and Conservation History* 35 (1991): 128–37

Balmer, Crapo, and Associates. *Tourism development in Ontario: A framework for opportunity*. Toronto: Ministry of Industry and Tourism, 1976

Bancroft, William L. 'Memoirs of Captain Samuel Ward with a sketch of the early commerce of the upper lakes,' *Michigan Pioneer and Historical Collections* 21 (1912–13); 336–66

Barr, Elinor, 'Lumbering in the Pigeon River watershed,' *Thunder Bay Historical Museum Society Papers and Records* 4 (1976): 3–9

– *Silver Islet, striking it rich in Lake Superior*. Toronto: Natural Heritage/Natural History, 1988

Barr, Elinor, and Betty Dyck. *Ignace: A saga of the Shield*. Winnipeg: Prairie Publishing Co., 1979

Barry, James P. 'The Wolseley Expedition crosses the Great Lakes,' *Inland Seas* 24 (1968): 91–107

Baskerville, Gordon L. *An audit of management of the Crown forest of Ontario*. A report to the Minister of Natural Resources, Aug. 1, 1986. Toronto: Queen's Printer, 1986

Bayliss, Joseph, and Estelle Bayliss. *Historic St. Joseph Island*. Cedar Rapids, IA: The Torch Press, 1938

Beeson, Lewis, ed. 'Sault Ste. Marie in the 1850s,' *Michigan History* 39 (1955): 281–97

Bell, Robert. 'The mineral region of Lake Superior,' *The Canadian Naturalist Quarterly and Journal of Science* n.s. 7 (1875): 49–51

Benedet, David A. *Port Arthur Built: A history of the Port Arthur Shipbuilding Co.* Thunder Bay: Pascol Engineering, 1994

Benson, Richard C. 'Part-time farming in a physically marginal area of northern Ontario.' In *Part-time farming: Problem or resource in rural development*, ed. A.M. Fuller and Julius Mage, 114–25. Norwich: Geo Abstracts Ltd., 1976

Berton, Pierre. *The last spike: The great railway, 1881–1885*. Toronto: McClelland and Stewart, 1972

Bertrand, J.P. *Highway of destiny: An epic story of Canadian development*. New York: Vantage Press, 1959

Bleasdale, R. 'Manitowaning: An experiment in Indian settlement,' *Ontario History* 66 (1974): 147–57

Bigsby, John J. *The shoe and canoe or pictures of travel in the Canadas*. 2 vols. London: Chapman and Hall, 1850

Boise Cascade Canada Ltd. *Annual Report*. 1991

Bothwell, Robert, et al. *Canada, 1900–1945*. Toronto: University of Toronto Press, 1920

– *Canada since 1945*. Toronto: University of Toronto Press, 1989

Boultbee, Jean. *Pic, pulp and people*. Revised by Jesse Embree. Marathon: Township of Marathon, 1981

Bradwin, Edmund William. *The bunkhouse man: A study of work and play in the camps of Canada, 1903–1904*. Toronto: University of Toronto Press, 1972

Brock, Gordon. *The province of northern Ontario*. Cobalt: Highway Book Shop, 1978

Brodie, J.A. 'Ontario has its picture taken,' *Sylva* 2 (1946): 51–6

– 'Timber management in Ontario,' *Canadian Geographical Journal* 42 (Mar. 1951): 101–17

Brown, L. Carson. 'Manitouwadge, cave of the great spirit,' *Canadian Geographical Journal* 67 (1963): 134–45

– 'The Red Lake gold field,' *Canadian Geographical Journal* 69 (1965): 114–25

Brown, R.C. 'The doctrine of usefulness: Natural resources and national parks policy, 1887–1914.' In *Canadian parks in perspective*, ed. J.G. Nelson, 46–62. Montreal: Harvest House, 1969

Burgar, R.J. 'Forest land-use evolution in Ontario's Upper Great Lakes basin.' In *The Great Lakes forest: An environmental and social history*, ed. Susan L. Flader, 177–93. Minneapolis: University of Minnesota Press, 1983

Burpee, L. 'From sea to sea,' *Canadian Geographical Journal* 16 (Jan. 1938): 3–32

Campbell, Marjorie Wilkins. *The North West Company*. Toronto: Macmillan Canada, 1973

Canada. Department of Energy, Mines and Resources. 'Posts of the Canadian fur trade,' *The National Atlas of Canada*, 4th ed., 79–80. Ottawa: Department of Energy, Mines and Resources, 1975

– Department of Immigration. *Manpower survey: Northwestern Ontario*. Ottawa: Department of Immigration, 1977

– Parks Canada. *Pukaskwa National Park management plan summary*. Ottawa: Parks Canada, 1982

Canadian Commission on Pulpwood. *Final report, 1923*. Ottawa: King's Printer, 1924

Canadian Indian treaties and surrenders. Ottawa: King's Printer, 1921

Capp, Edward H. *The story of Baw-a-ting, being the annals of Sault Ste. Marie*. Sault Ste Marie: Sault Star Press, 1903

Careless, J.M.S. 'Frontierism, metropolitanism and Canadian history,' *Canadian Historical Review* 35 (1954): 1–21

– 'Two River Empires: An historical analysis,' *American Review of Canadian Studies* 5 (1975): 28–46

– 'Metropolis and region: The interplay between city and region in Canadian history before 1914,' *Urban History Review* 3 (78) (1979): 99–118

– *Frontier and metropolis: Regions, cities and identities in Canada before 1914*. Toronto: University of Toronto Press, 1989

Carruthers, George. *Paper making: The first century of paper making in Canada.* Toronto: Garden City Press, 1947

Carter, James L., and Ernest H. Rankin. *The journey of Charles W. Penny in 1840.* Marquette: The John M. Longyear Research Library, 1970

Chase, Lew Allen. 'Early copper mines in Michigan,' *Michigan History* 29 (1945): 22–30

A chronicle of Finnish settlements in the rural Thunder Bay area. Thunder Bay: Thunder Bay Finnish Canadian Historic Society, 1976

Chubb, Michael. 'Tourism patterns and determinants in the Great Lakes Region,' *Geo Journal* 19 (1989): 297–302

Collins, David H. *Wings across time: The story of Air Canada.* Toronto: Griffin House, 1978

Collins, G.W. 'Seed potatoes in northwestern Ontario,' *Ontario Agricultural Review* 30 (1918): 310–11

Cottam, S. Barry. 'Indian title as a celestial institution.' In *Aboriginal resource use in Canada: Historical and legal aspects*, ed. Kerry Abel and Jean Friesan, 247–65. Winnipeg: University of Manitoba Press, 1991

Crawford, K. *Single enterprise communities in Canada.* A report to the Central Mortgage and Housing Corporation by the Institute of Local Government, Queen's University. Ottawa: Queen's Printer, 1953

Crawford, Robert. *The answer to the pamphlet entitled 'The question of the terminus.'* Collingwood: The Enterprise Press, 1874

Creighton, Donald. *The empire of the St. Lawrence.* Toronto: Macmillan Canada, 1956

– *The story of Canada.* Toronto: Macmillan Canada, 1959

– 'The decline and fall of the empire of the St. Lawrence,' *Canadian Historical Association Historical Papers* (1969): 14–26

Cumberland, Barlow. *The northern lakes of Canada: Georgian Bay, Great Manitoulin Channel, Mackinac, Sault Ste. Marie, Lake Superior.* Toronto: Hunter Rose Co., 1886

Currie, A.W. *The Grand Trunk Railway of Canada.* Toronto: University of Toronto Press, 1957

Cuthbertson, A. *Freshwater: A history and a narrative of the Great Lakes.* Toronto: Macmillan Canada, 1931

Davidson, Gordon Charles. *The North West Company.* San Francisco: University of California Publications in History, 1918

Davis, Donald. 'Dependent motorization: Canada and the automobile to the 1930s,' *Journal of Canadian Studies* 21 (1986): 106–31

Davis, I.G. 'Agriculture in the northern forest – The case of northwestern Ontario,' *Lakehead University Review* 1 (1968): 129–53

– 'Thunder Bay and northwestern Ontario,' *Lakehead University Review* 6 (1973): 3–37

Davis, Marion M. 'Stories of St. Helena Island,' *Michigan History Magazine* 10 (1926): 411–46

– 'Three Islands,' *Michigan History Magazine* 12 (1928): 518–35

Dennis, Keith. 'Oliver Dounais – The Silver King,' *Thunder Bay Historical Museum Society Papers and Records* 2 (1974): 12–21

Dilley, Robert S. 'Farming on the margin.' In *Geographic perspectives on the provincial norths*, ed. Margaret E. Johnston, 180–98. Toronto: Copp Clark Longman, 1994

– 'Thunder Bay Tourism: Opportunities and attitudes.' In *Communities, resources and tourism in the north*, ed. Margaret E. Johnston and Wolfgang Haider, 109–15. Thunder Bay: Lakehead Centre for Northern Studies, 1994

Dillon, J.C. *Early Days: A record of the early days of the Provincial Air Service of Ontario*. Toronto: Department of Lands and Forests, 1961

Disturnell, John. *A trip through the lakes of North America*. New York: J. Disturnell 1863

– *Lake Superior guide*. Philadelphia: 1874

Dobie, John. 'Commercial fishing on the Lake of the Woods,' *Minnesota History* (June 1957): 272–6

Doughty, Arthur G. 'The awakening of Canadian interest in the northwest,' *Canadian Historical Association Reports* (1928): 5–11

Douglas, James. 'The native copper mines of Lake Superior,' *Canadian Naturalist* 7 (1875): 318–36

Drummond, Ian M. 'The electrification of Ontario.' In *Progress without planning*, ed. Ian. M. Drummond, 134–47. Toronto: University of Toronto Press, 1987

Dunk, Thomas W. 'Indian participation in the industrial economy on the north shore of Lake Superior, 1869 to 1940,' *Thunder Bay Historical Museum Society Papers and Records* 15 (1987): 3–13

Easterbrook, W.T., and Hugh G.J. Aitken. *Canadian economic history*. Toronto: Macmillan Canada, 1956

Elliott, John. 'A position paper on the impact of technology and employment problems in single industry towns in northern Ontario,' *Laurentian University Review* 16 (1984): 113–19

Emery, George. 'Adam Oliver, Ingersoll and the Thunder Bay district, 1850–82,' *Ontario History* 68 (1976): 25–43

Evans, A. Margaret. 'The Mowat era.' In *Profiles of a province*, 97–106. Toronto: The Ontario Historical Society, 1967

Evergreen reflections. Vermilion Bay: The Nor-West Historical Society, 1986

Eyles, John, et al. 'Fair share for the zone: Allocating health-care resources for the native population of the Sioux Lookout Zone,' *Canadian Geographer* 30 (1994): 134–50

Fell, C.P. 'The newsprint industry.' In *The Canadian economy and its problems*, ed. H.A. Innes and A.F.W. Plumptre, 40–54. Toronto: Canadian Institute of International Affairs, 1934

Fenwick, A.R. 'Wings over the bush,' *Canadian Geographical Journal* 29 (Summer 1944): 157–83

Fowle, Otto. *Sault Ste. Marie and its great waterway*. New York: The Knickerbocker Press, 1925

Fox, Michael, and Sandra L. Mackenko. *The agriculture-forest interface: An overview of land use change*, Working Paper no. 38. Ottawa: Canada Land Directorate, 1985

Freeman, Donald B., and Frances L. Dungey. 'A spatial duopoly: Competition in the western Canadian fur trade, 1770–1830,' *Journal of Historical Geography* 7 (1981): 252–70

Fuller, Anthony M. *The development of the ARDA farm enlargement and consolidation program in Ontario, 1966–75*. Studies in Rural Adjustment, no. 75. Guelph: The Centre for Resource Development, 1975

– 'The development of farm life and farming in Ontario.' In *Farming and the rural community in Ontario*, ed. Anthony M. Fuller, 1–28. Toronto: University of Toronto Press, 1985

Galbraith, John S. 'The Hudson's Bay land controversy, 1863–1869,' *Mississippi Valley Historical Review* 36 (1949): 457–78

– 'British American competition in the border fur trade of the 1820s,' *Minnesota History* 36 (1959): 241–9

George, Peter. 'Ontario's mining industry, 1870–1940.' In *Progress without planning*, ed. Ian M. Drummond, 52–76. Toronto: University of Toronto Press, 1987

Gillis, R. Peter, and Thomas R. Roach. *Lost initiatives: Canada's forest industries, forest policy and forest conservation*. New York: Greenman Press, 1986

Glazebrook, G.T. *Life in Ontario: A social history*. Toronto: University of Toronto Press, 1968

Gluek, Alvin C. *Minnesota and the manifest destiny of the Canadian northwest*. Toronto: University of Toronto Press, 1965

'Gold mines of the Lake of the Woods,' *Canadian Mining Review* 3 (5) (1885): 7

Goode, G.B. 'The Report of the Commissioner of Fish and Fisheries for 1887, part III: The fisheries of Lake Superior,' *The commercial fisheries and fishery industry of the United States*, 33–69. Washington: 1891

Goodier, J.L. 'The nineteenth century fisheries of the Hudson's Bay Company trading posts on Lake Superior: A biogeographical study,' *Canadian Geographer* 28 (1984): 324–46

– 'Fishermen and their trade on the Canadian Great Lakes: One hundred years,' *Inland Seas* 45 (1989): 284–306

Gorman, W.J. 'Steep Rock iron mine,' *Canadian Geographical Journal* 25 (Fall 1942): 246–62

Gough, Barry M. 'Canada's adventure in China, 1784–1821,' *Canadian Geographical Journal* 93 (Dec. 1977): 28–37

Grant, G.M. *Ocean to ocean; Sandford Fleming's expedition through Canada in 1872.* Toronto: J. Campbell, 1873

Grant, Robert S. 'Ontario's provincial air service,' *Canadian Geographical Journal* 19 (1979): 50–5

Great Lake Saga. Chicago: Beer and Company, 1898

Grindlay, Thomas. *A history of the independent telephone industry in Ontario.* Toronto: The Ontario Telephone Commission, 1975

Gusson, H.T. 'Deadly disease attacks white pine,' *Ontario Agricultural College Review* 32 (1930): 49–52, 66, 68

Hall, Anthony. 'Native limited identities and newcomer metropolitanism in Upper Canada, 1814–1867.' In *Old Ontario: Essays in honour of J.M.S. Careless*, ed. David Keane and Colin Read, 149–73. Toronto: Dundurn Press, 1990

– 'The St. Catharines Milling and Lumber Company versus the Queen.' In *Aboriginal resource use in Canada: Historical and legal aspects*, ed. Kerry Abel and Jean Friesen, 267–85. Winnipeg: University of Manitoba Press, 1991

Hallman, D.E. 'Tourism and outdoor recreation in northwestern Ontario: An overview,' *Lakehead University Review* 6 (1973): 52–61

Halverson, Lynn L. 'The commercial fisheries of the Michigan waters of Lake Superior,' *Michigan History* 39 (1955): 1–17

Hartig, John H. 'Remedial action plans for the Great Lakes today and tomorrow.' In *Making a great Lake Superior*, ed. Jake Vander Wal and Paul D. White, 163–82. Thunder Bay: Lakehead Centre for Northern Studies, 1992

Heath, Frances M. 'Sault Ste. Marie: City by the Rapids.' Burlington: Windsor Press, 1988

Hill, Douglas. *The opening of the Canadian west.* London: William Heinemann, 1967

Hilton, S.A. 'Silos and silage for dairy cattle,' *Ontario Agricultural College Review* 24 (1921): 122–5

Hinch, T.D., and R.W. Butler. 'Tourism development concerns in northern and eastern Ontario: A survey of professionals.' In *Communities, resources and tourism in the north*, ed. Margaret E. Johnston and Wolfgang Haider, 109–34. Thunder Bay: Lakehead Centre for Northern Studies, 1993

Holmquist, June D. 'Commercial fishing on Lake Superior in the 1890s,' *Minnesota History* 34 (1955): 243–9

Holzkamm, Tim E., at al. 'Rainy River sturgeon: An Ojibway resource in the fur trade economy,' *Canadian Geographer* 32 (1988): 194–205

Horan, Gertrude. *A history of Rat Portage, Kenora, 1879–1906*. Kenora: 1954
Hubbard, Bella. *Memorials of half a century in Michigan and the Lakes region*. New York: The Knickerbocker Press, 1888
Hybels, Robert J. 'Lake Superior copper fever,' *Michigan History* 34 (1950): 97–119
Innis, Harold A. 'Interrelations between the fur trade of Canada and the United States,' *Mississippi Valley Historical Review* 20 (1933): 321–32
– *Settlement and the mining frontier*. In Canadian Frontiers of Settlement Series, vol. 9, ed. W.A. Mackintosh and W.L.G. Joung. Toronto: Macmillan, 1936
– *The fur trade in Canada*. Rev. ed. Toronto: University of Toronto Press, 1962
Inwood, Kris. 'The iron and steel industry.' In *Progress without planning*, ed. Ian M. Drummond, 185–207. Toronto: University of Toronto Press, 1987
Jackson, H.M. 'The saga of Sioux Lookout,' *Sylva* 3 (1947): 11–18
Johnston, R.N. 'Aircraft in forest field work at Sioux Lookout Ontario in 1921,' *Ontario Agricultural College Review* 24 (1922): 365–6
Jones, R.L. *A history of agriculture in Ontario: 1613–1800*. Toronto: University of Toronto Press, 1946
Kates, Peat, Marwick and Co. *Northwestern Ontario's tourist industry*. Toronto: Prepared for the Department of Tourism and Information, 1968
Kaups, M. 'North shore commercial fishing, 1849–1870,' *Minnesota History* 59 (1978): 43–58
Kehoe, J.J. 'The Sault Ste. Marie ship canal,' *Canadian Magazine of Politics, Science, Arts and Literature* 1 (1893): 589–94
Keller, R.H. 'An economic history of Indian treaties in the Great Lakes region,' *American Indian Journal* 4 (2) (1978): 2–20
Kellon, Gerald, and George Warecki. 'The battle for wilderness in Ontario: Saving Quetico-Superior, 1927 to 1960.' In *Patterns of the past*, ed. Roger Hall et al., 329–55. Toronto: Dundurn Press, 1988
Kerr, Donald. 'The geography of the Canadian iron and steel industry,' *Economic Geography* 35 (1959): 151–63
Kiebuzinski, Rae. *Yesterday the river*. Ear Falls: Ear Falls Historical Committee, 1975
Killan, Gerald. *Protected places: A history of Ontario's provincial parks system*. Toronto: Dundurn Press, 1993
Kingston, William H.G. *Western wanderings or a pleasure tour through the Canadas*. Montreal: Benjamin Dawson, 1856
Kirkwood, A., and J.J. Murphy. *The undeveloped lands of northern and western Ontario*. Toronto: Hunter Rose Company, 1878
Knight, Jack K. 'Agriculture in New Ontario,' *Ontario Agricultural College Review* 47 (1934): 137–41

Konarek, J. 'Algoma Central and Hudson Bay Railway, the beginnings,' *Ontario History* 62 (1970): 73–81

Lamb, W. Kaye. *History of the Canadian Pacific Railway*. New York: Macmillan, 1977

Lambert, Richard S., and Paul Pross. *Renewing nature's wealth*. Toronto: Hunter Rose Company, 1967

Landon, Fred. *Lake Huron*. New York: Bobbs-Merrill Company, 1944

– 'The Keefer Lakehead Terminal,' *Inland Seas* 18 (1962): 267–72

Lapping, M.B. 'The status of northern agriculture in Canada: A cold wind blowing,' *Nordia* 17 (1983): 47–51

Lavender, David S. *The first in the wilderness*. Garden City, New York: Doubleday, 1964

Lavoie, Edgar J.D. *And the Geraldton way: A history of Geraldton and district up to 1947*. Geraldton: Times Star Publishing Ltd., 1987

Lawrie, A.H., and J.F. Rahrer. *Lake Superior: A case study of the lake and its fisheries*. Technical report no. 9. Ann Arbor: Great Lakes Fisheries Commission, 1973

Leitch, Adelaide. 'Wilderness Park – Lake Superior,' *Canadian Geographical Journal* 55 (1957): 42–5

Leslie, A.P. 'D.D.T. in Ontario forests,' *Canadian Geographical Journal* 31 (Oct. 1945): 186–97

Littlejohn, Bruce M. 'Quetico country: Wilderness highway to wilderness recreation,' *Canadian Geographical Journal* 71 (1965): 40–55, 79–91

Logan, W.E. *Remarks on the mining region of Lake Superior*. Montreal: Lovell and Gibson, 1847

Longstreth, Thomas M. *The Lake Superior country*. Toronto: McClelland and Stewart, 1924

Lower, A.R.M. 'The assault on the Laurentian barrier, 1850–1870,' *Canadian Historical Review* 10 (1929): 294–307

– *Settlement and the forest frontier in Eastern Canada*. Part 1, vol. IX of Canadian Frontiers of Settlement, ed. W.A. Macintosh. Toronto: Macmillan, 1936

– *The North American assault on the Canadian forest*. Toronto: The Ryerson Press, 1938

McCalla, Douglas. 'The commercial policies on the Toronto Board of Trade, 1850–1860,' *Canadian Historical Review* 50 (1969): 51–67

McCann, L.D. 'Canadian resource towns: A heartland–hinterland perspective.' In *Essays in Canadian urban process and form*, vol. 2, ed. E. Preston and Lorn H. Russworm, 213–66. Waterloo: University of Waterloo, 1980

McCullough, A.B. *The commercial fisheries of the Canadian Great Lakes*. Ottawa: Environment Canada, Parks Service, 1989

MacDonald, Graham A. 'The ancient fisheries at Sault Ste. Marie,' *Canadian Geographical Journal* 94 (1977): 54–8
– 'The Agawa outpost, Lake Superior,' *Beaver* (Autumn 1978): 38–43
– 'Commercial civility and old Sault Ste. Marie,' *Beaver* (Autumn 1981): 19–26, 52–9
Macdonell, Allan. *The North-west Transportation, Navigation and Railway Company.* Toronto: Lovell and Gibson, 1858
McDougall, Duncan M. 'Immigration into Canada 1951–1920,' *Canadian Journal of Economics and Political Science* 27 (1961): 162–75
McDowall, Duncan. *Steel at the Sault: Francis H. Clergue, James Dunn and the Algoma Steel Corporation, 1901–56.* Toronto: University of Toronto Press, 1984
McElroy, H.W. 'Co-operation in the Rainy River Valley,' *Ontario Agricultural College Review* 26 (1914): 185–7
MacInnes, T.R.L. 'History of Indian administration in Canada,' *Canadian Journal of Economics and Political Science* 12 (1945): 387–94
McInnis, Edgar. *Canada: A political and social history.* Toronto: Holt, Rinehart Winston, 1964
Macins, Val. *The fisheries of Lake of the Woods.* Toronto: Ministry of Natural Resources, Sport Fisheries Branch, 1972
MacKay, Donald. *The lumberjacks.* Toronto: McGraw-Hill Ryerson, 1978
– *Heritage lost: The crisis in Canada's forests.* Toronto: Macmillan Canada, 1985
– *The people's railway: A history of the Canadian National.* Toronto: Douglas and McIntyre, 1992
McKellar, Peter. 'How Nipigon Bay lost the CPR shipping port on the Great Lakes,' *Thunder Bay Historical Society* (1911–12): 25–7
– 'The Otter Head tin swindle,' *Thunder Bay Historical Society* (1912–13): 11–13
– 'Early Mining,' *Thunder Bay Historical Society* (1918): 15–17
McKenney, Thomas L. *Sketches of a tour to the lakes: Of the character and the customs of the Chippeway Indians and of incidents connected with the Treaty of Fond du Lac.* Facsimile of 1827 edition. Minneapolis: Ross and Harness, 1959
McKenney, Wayne R. 'The Sioux Lookout medical program,' *Beaver* (Spring 1973): 52–7
MacLeod, D. Peter. 'The Anishinabeg point of view: The history of the Great Lakes Region in 1800 and nineteenth-century Mississaugi, Odawa and Ojiwa historiography,' *Canadian Historical Review* 73 (1992): 195–210
Maloney, Toby. 'Native network spreads news in northern Ontario,' *Canadian Geographical Journal* 90 (July 1987): 6– 14
Manore, Jack. 'Mr. Dawson's Road,' *Beaver* 71 (Mar. 1991): 6–11
Marcella, Jeanne. *A History of Jackfish.* Terrace Bay: Terrace Bay Library, 1987
Marcolini, Lorenzo. 'Canadian Pacific Steamship Line: Last of an era,' *Inland Seas* 22 (1966): 3–16

Masters, D.D. 'T.C. Keefer and the development of Canadian transportation,' *Canadian Historical Association Reports* (1940): 36–48

Mauro, Joseph M. *Thunder Bay: A history of the Golden Gateway of the great northwest.* Thunder Bay: City of Thunder Bay, 1981

Melcher, Ronald. 'Sports in the workplaces.' In *Not just a game*, ed. Jean Harvey and Hart Cantelon, 56–8. Ottawa: University of Ottawa Press, 1988

Meyer, G.E. 'Kenora summer resort land in great demand,' *Sylva* 2 (3) (1946): 3–8

Middleton, Jesse Edgar, and Fred Landon. *The province of Ontario: A history, 1615–1927.* Vol. 1. Toronto: Dominion Publishing Co., 1926

Milbury, Larry. *Austin Airways: Canada's oldest airline.* Toronto: Canav Books, 1985

Millar, Gerald, and W.H. Van Allan. 'The Lakehead: An up-to-date harbour,' *Canadian Geographical Journal* 64 (1962): 174–9

Miller, W.G. 'Mines and mining.' In *Canada and its provinces*, vol. 18, ed. Adam Shortt and A.G. Doughty, 613–45. Toronto: Publishers Association of Canada, 1914

Mills, James Cooke. 'The gateway to the inland sea: The Sault Ste. Marie canal and its importance to Canada,' *Canadian Magazine of Politics, Science, Arts and Literature* 38 (1912): 31–2

'Mining on the Lake of the Woods,' *Canadian Mining Review* 3 (3) (1885): 6

Mitchell, Bruce. 'Provincial domain in environmental management and resource development.' In *Resources and the environment: Policy perspectives for Canada*, ed. O.P. Dwivedi, 49–76. Toronto: McClelland and Stewart, 1980

Mitchell, Lynne. *An economic history of northwestern Ontario.* Component Study no. 1: Design for Development. Toronto: Ministry of Northern Affairs, 1969

Moodie, D. Wayne. 'The trading post settlement of the Canadian northwest, 1774–1821,' *Journal of Historical Geography* 13 (1987): 360–74

Morgan, F. 'Wild rice harvest,' *Beaver* (Autumn 1960): 24–31

Moris, J.L. *Indians of Ontario.* Toronto: Department of Lands and Forests, 1943

Morse, Eric W. *Fur trade canoe routes of Canada: Then and now.* Toronto: University of Toronto Press, 1969

Nelles, H.V. *The politics of development: Forests, mines and hydro electric power in Ontario, 1849–1941.* Toronto: Macmillan Canada, 1974

Nelson, Lori, and Patty Nelson. *The summer people: A history of Kenora's tourist industry.* Kenora: Spoke Press, 1979

Neumeyer, Elizabeth. 'Michigan Indians battle against removal,' *Michigan History* 55 (1971): 275–88

Newell, Dianne. 'Silver mining in the Thunder Bay District, 1865–85,' *Thunder Bay Historical Museum Society Papers and Records* 13 (1985): 28–43

– *Technology on the frontier: Mining in old Ontario.* Vancouver: University of British Columbia Press, 1986

Nicholson, Norman L. *The boundaries of Canadian confederation.* Toronto: Carleton Library Series, 1979

Nock, O.S. *Railways of Canada.* London: Adam and Charles Black, 1973

– *Algoma Central Railway.* London: Adam Charles Block, 1975

Noel, S.J.R. *Patrons, clients, brokers: Ontario society and politics, 1791–1896.* Toronto: University of Toronto Press, 1990

North-Western Ontario: Its boundaries, resources and communications. Toronto: Hunter Rose and Co., 1879

Nowland, J.L., and J.A. McKeague. 'Canada's limited agricultural land resource.' In *Managing Canada's renewable resources*, ed. R.R. Kreuger and B. Mitchell, 109–18. Toronto: Methuen Press, 1977

Nute, Grace L. 'The American Fur Company's fishing enterprises on Lake Superior,' *Mississippi Valley Historical Review* 12 (1926): 483–503

– 'Posts of the Minnesota fur trade area, 1660–1855,' *Minnesota History* 11 (1930): 353–85

– *Lake Superior.* New York: Bobbs-Merrill Company, 1944

O'Grady, S.C. *Report of storage possibilities of Lac Seul.* Winnipeg: Department of the Interior, 1916

Ontario. *An Act to revise the Crown Timber Act to provide for the sustainability of Crown Forests in Ontario.* Bill 171, 3rd Session, 35th Legislature, Ontario, 43, Elizabeth II, 1994

– Department of Lands and Forests. *Ontario Resources Atlas.* Toronto: Department of Lands and Forests, 1954

– Department of Lands and Forests. *The forest resources of Ontario.* Toronto: Department of Lands and Forests, 1963

– Department of Lands and Forests. *A history of the Port Arthur Forest District.* District History Series no. 4. Toronto: Department of Lands and Forests, 1963

– Department of Lands and Forests. *A history of the Sioux Lookout Forest District.* District History Series no. 6. Toronto: Department of Lands and Forests, 1963

– Department of Lands and Forests. *Report of the forestry study unit.* Toronto: Department of Lands and Forests, 1967

– Department of Northern Affairs and Development. *The northern Ontario statistical profile.* Toronto: Department of Northern Affairs and Development, 1976

– Department of Treasury and Economics. *The Lakehead and northwestern Ontario: An economic survey.* Toronto: The Regional Development Branch, Department of Treasury and Economics, 1969

– Department of Treasury and Economics. *Design for development: Northwestern Ontario Region, Phase 2, policy recommendations.* Toronto: Department of Treasury and Economics, 1970

– Environmental Assessment Board. *Hearings on a class environmental assessment for timber management on Crown lands in Ontario.* The Report to the Environmental Assessment Board. Toronto: Queen's Printer, 1994
– Ministry of Agriculture and Food. *Agricultural statistics for Ontario, 1992.* Toronto: Ministry of Agriculture and Food, 1993
– Ministry of Natural Resources. *Forest production policy options.* Toronto: Ministry of Natural Resources, 1972
– Ministry of Natural Resources. *Background information and approaches to policy: Northwestern Ontario Planning Region.* Toronto: Ministry of Natural Resources, 1974
– Ministry of Natural Resources. *Background information, Fort Frances Fisheries Management Plan, 1985–2000.* Fort Frances: Ministry of Natural Resources, 1984
– Ministry of Natural Resources. *Red Lake District Fisheries Plan, 1985–2000.* Toronto: Ministry of Natural Resources, 1984
– Ministry of Natural Resources. *Lake Superior Strategic Fisheries Plan, 1986–2000.* Toronto: Ministry of Natural Resources, 1987
– Ministry of Natural Resources. *Ontario's Provincial Parks class environmental assessment for Provincial Park management.* Special report no. 1. Toronto: Ministry of Natural Resources, 1992
– Ministry of Natural Resources. *Diversity: Forest, people and communities – A comprehensive forest policy framework for Ontario.* The report of the Ontario Forest Policy Panel to the Minister of Natural Resources. Toronto: Queen's Printer, 1993
– Ministry of Northern Affairs. *Northern Ontario manpower survey: Mineral and forest industries.* Component Study no. 6: Design for Development. Toronto: Ministry of Northern Affairs, 1977
– Ministry of Northern Development and Mines. *Final report and recommendations of the Advisory Council on resource dependent communities in northern Ontario.* Toronto: Ministry of Northern Development and Mines, 1986
– Ministry of Northern Development and Mines. 'A brief history of mining and mineral legislation in Ontario,' *Ontario mines and minerals: A green paper*, 36–9. Toronto: Ministry of Northern Development and Mines, 1988
– Ministry of Northern Development and Mines. *The Mining Act, Regulation, March 1992.* Toronto: Ministry of Northern Development and Mines, 1992
– Royal Commission on the Northern Environment. 'The economic future of the forest products industry,' 7–14. Toronto: Ministry of Natural Resources, 1981
Osborne, Brian S., and Donald Swainson. *The Sault Ste. Marie Canal: Three centuries of development.* Ottawa: Environment Canada, Parks Branch, 1983
Owram, Doug. *Promise of Eden: The Canadian expansionist movement and the idea of the West, 1852–1900.* Toronto: University of Toronto Press, 1980

Parker, Keith. 'Colonization roads and commercial policy,' *Ontario History* 67 (1975): 31–8

Parrot, D.F. *The Red Lake gold rush.* Red Lake: author, 1976

Paterson, Murray, and Robert G. Ruggles. 'Ontario Hydro in northern Ontario: An environmental perspective,' *Laurentian University Review* 16 (1984): 121–49

Pattison, Irma E. *An historical chronology of highway legislation in Ontario, 1774–1961.* Toronto: Department of Highways, 1964

Pattulo, George R. *Northwestern Ontario, The districts of Thunder Bay and Algoma: A brief description.* Port Arthur: Evening Herald Publishing Co., 1883

Paulson, Warren. *The little town that could.* Atitokan: Atikokan Economic Development Corporation, 1993

Peltier, Ljubica, et al. 'Lake Superior areas of contention,' In *Making a great Lake Superior*, ed. Jake Vander Wal and Paul D. White, 175–9. Thunder Bay: Lakehead Centre for Northern Studies, 1992

Perkins, G.F. *Marketing milestones in Ontario, 1935–1960.* Toronto: Ontario Department of Agriculture, 1962

Placz, A.J. *Quebec Ontario, our story.* Thorold: 1988

Priddle, George B. 'Forest management in Ontario.' In *Ontario: Geographical perspectives on the economy and environment*, ed. Bruce Mitchell, 189–203. Department of Geography Publication Series, no. 34. Waterloo: University of Waterloo, 1991

'Professor Bell on the Nipigon Territory,' *The Canadian Naturalist and Quarterly Journal of Science* n.s. 5 (1870): 118–20

Pucci, Antonio, and John Potestro, eds. 'Thunder Bay's people,' *Polyphony* 9 (1987): 1–114

Pugh, Donald E. 'Ontario's Great Clay Belt hoax,' *Canadian Geographical Journal* 90 (Jan. 1975): 19–24

Punch, Katherine. 'Sault Ste. Marie,' *Canadian Geographical Journal* 73 (1966): 198–207

The question of the terminus of the branch of the Pacific Railway on the north shore of Lake Superior. Ottawa: McLean, Rogers and Co., 1874

Quimby, George I. *Indian life in the Upper Lakes region, 11,000 BC to AD 1800.* Chicago: University of Chicago Press, 1960

Radforth, Ian. 'Finnish lumber workers in Ontario, 1919–1946,' *Polyphony* 3 (2) (1981): 23–34

– 'Woodworkers and the mechanization of the pulpwood industry of northern Ontario, 1952–1970,' *Canadian Historical Association Historical Papers* (1982): 73–101

– *Bushworkers and bosses: Logging in northern Ontario, 1900–1980.* Toronto: University of Toronto Press, 1987

Ralston, J.R. 'A municipal and industrial strategy for abatement in Ontario.' In *Making a great Lake Superior*, ed. Jake Vander Wal and Paul D. White, 286–94. Thunder Bay: Lakehead Centre for Northern Studies, 1992

Ray, Arthur J. *Indians in the fur trade, 1660–1870.* Toronto: University of Toronto Press, 1974

– 'Some conservation schemes of the Hudson's Bay Company, 1821–1850: An examination of the problems of resource management in the fur trade,' *Journal of Historical Geography* 1 (1975): 49–68

– 'Periodic shortages, native welfare and the Hudson's Bay Company, 1670–1930.' In *Interpreting Canada's north*, ed. Kenneth S. Coates and William R. Morrison, 94–112. Toronto: Copp Clark Pitman, 1989

– *The Canadian fur trade in the industrial age*. Toronto: University of Toronto Press, 1990

Rea, K.J. *The prosperous years: The economic history of Ontario, 1939–1973.* Toronto: University of Toronto Press, 1985

Rector, W.G. *Log transport in the Lake State lumber industry, 1840–1914*, Glendale, CA: The Arthur H. Clark Co., 1953

Regehr, T.D. *The Canadian Northern Railway*. Toronto: Macmillan Canada, 1976

Reid, Paddy C.S. *The archaeology of northwestern Ontario; the prehistoric and fur trade period.* Toronto: Ministry of Culture and Recreation, Historical Planning and Research Branch, 1980

Rice, Doreen. 'Sault Ste. Marie ferries,' *Inland Seas* 20 (1964): 115

Rich, E.E. *The history of the Hudson's Bay Company, 1670–1870.* Vol. 2. London: The Hudson's Bay Company Historical Society, 1959

Richthammer, John. *The end of the road.* Red Lake: Red Lake Festival Days, 1985

Rickard, T.A. 'Gold and silver in Ontario,' *Canadian Mining Journal* 65 (1944): 688–96

Rigier, A., and K.H. Loftas. 'Effects of fisheries exploitation on salmonid communities in olagotrophic lakes,' *Journal of the Fisheries Board of Canada* 29 (1972): 956–65

The river of time: A history of Emo. Altona, MB: Friesen Printers, 1978

Robinson, Ira M. *New industrial towns on Canada's resource frontier.* Department of Geography Research Paper no. 73. Chicago: University of Chicago Press, 1962

Robinson, P.J. 'Yonge Street and the North West Company,' *Canadian Historical Review* 24 (1943): 253–65

Robson, Robert. 'Ontario Hydro colonies: A study of frontier settlements,' *Laurentian University Review* 17 (2) (1985): 113–39

– 'Building resource towns: Government intervention in Ontario in the 1950s.' In *At the end of the shift*, ed. Matt Bray and Ashley Thomson, 97–9. Toronto: Dundurn Press, 1992

Rogers, E.S. *Ojibway fisheries in northwestern Ontario*. Toronto: Ministry of Natural Resources, 1972

Rohe, Randal E. 'The upper Great Lakes lumber era,' *Inland Seas* 40 (1984): 16–20

Roland, Walpole. *Algoma West: Its mines, scenery and industrial resources*. Toronto: Warwick and Sons, 1887

Russell, A.L. 'A brief history of Port Arthur harbour,' *Thunder Bay Historical Society Papers* (1915): 21–6

Saarinen, Oiva. 'The influence of Thomas Adams and the British new town movement in the planning of Canadian resource communities.' In *The usable urban past*, Carleton Library Series, ed. A.F.J. Artibise and Gilbert A. Stelter, 268–93. Toronto: Macmillan Canada, 1979

– 'Geographical perspectives on Finnish-Canadian immigration and settlement,' *Polyphony* 3 (1981): 16–22

– 'Single sector communities in northern Ontario: The creation and planning of dependent towns.' In *Power and place: Canadian urban development in the North American context*, ed. Gilbert A. Stelter and Alan F.J. Artibise, 217–64. Vancouver: University of British Columbia Press, 1986

– 'Mining in northern Ontario,' *Ontario: Perspectives on economy and environment*, 153–68. Department of Geography Publications Series, no. 34. Waterloo: University of Waterloo, 1991

Schaefer, Karl, and Ken Cullis. 'Tourism and the remedial action plan in the Nipigon Bay area of concern.' In *Communities, resources and tourism in the North*, ed. Margaret E. Johnston and Wolfgang Haider, 135–50. Thunder Bay: Lakehead Centre for Northern Studies, 1993

Schull, Joseph. *Ontario since 1867*. Toronto: McClelland and Stewart, 1978

Scollie, Brent F. 'The population of Thunder Bay, 1884–1901,' *Thunder Bay Historical Museum Society Papers and Records* 7 (1979): 21–9

Scott, Don. 'Northern alienation.' In *The government and politics of Ontario*, ed. D.C. MacDonald, 235–47. Toronto: Macmillan Canada, 1975

Seaborne, Adrian O., and Patricia N. Larrain. 'Changing patterns of trade through the Port of Thunder Bay,' *Canadian Geographer* 27 (1983): 285–91

Sellers, Harry. 'The early history of the handling and transportation of grain in the District of Thunder Bay,' *Thunder Bay Historical Society Papers* (1909–10): 21–6

Shaw, Allan. *The days between 1876–1926*. Kenora: Spoke Press, 1973

Shchepanek, Michael J. 'Trade posts of the Moose–Michipicoten trade route,' *Canadian Geographical Journal* 83 (1971): 66–9

Silversides, C.R. 'The impact of forest operations and techniques upon forest operations in eastern Canada,' *Meddelestor fra Norsk Institutt for Skagforskoring* 41.16 (1988): 241–4

Sinclair, Peter W. 'The north and north-west: Forestry and agriculture.' In *Progress without planning*, ed. Ian M. Drummond, 77–90. Toronto: University of Toronto Press, 1987

Smith, Philip. *Harvest from the rock: A history of mining in Ontario*. Toronto: Macmillan Canada, 1968

– *It seems like only yesterday: Air Canada, the first 50 years*. Toronto: McClelland and Stewart, 1986

Smith, R.M. 'King's Highways of Ontario,' *Canadian Geographical Journal* 16 (1931): 159–93

– 'Northern Ontario: Limits of land settlement for the good citizen,' *Canadian Geographical Journal* 23 (1941): 182–211

Smith, Shirlee A. 'James Sutherland, inland trader,' *Beaver* (Winter 1975): 18–23

Spragge, George W. 'Colonization roads in Canada West 1850–1867,' *Ontario History* 49 (1957): 1–17

Stanley, George F.G. 'The Indian background of Canadian history,' *Canadian Historical Association Reports* (1952): 14–21

– *Toil and trouble: Military expeditions to Red River*. Toronto: Dundurn Press, 1989

Steer, Don. *The Montreal River Harbour area: A history and description from oral and printed sources*. Sault Ste Marie: Sault Ste Marie Museum, 1991

Stelter, Gilbert A., and Alan F.J. Artibise. 'Canadian resource towns in historical perspective.' In *Shaping the urban landscape*, ed. Gilbert A. Stelter and Alan F.J. Artibise, 413–35. Ottawa: Carleton University Press, 1982

Stevens, G.R. *History of the Canadian National Railways*. New York: Macmillan, 1973

Straditto, Martha. 'The Quetico heritage,' *Beaver* (1984): 32–77

Studness, Charles M. 'Economic opportunities and the westward migration of Canadians during the late nineteenth century,' *Canadian Journal of Economics and Political Science* 30 (1964): 570–84

Suomi, L. *Dryden District forest history, 1882–1940*. District Forest History Series, no. 12. Toronto: Department of Lands and Forests, 1960

Surtees, R.J. 'The development of an Indian policy in Canada,' *Ontario History* 61 (1969): 87–98

Swainson, Donald. 'The Northwest Transportation Company: Personalities and attitudes,' *Transaction of the History and Science Society of Manitoba* ser. 3, 26 (1969–70): 59–77

Thomas, Lewis H. 'The Hind and Dawson expeditions, 1857–58,' *Beaver* (Winter 1958): 39–45

Thompson, M. *Rainy River: Our town, our lives*. Rainy River: n.p., 1979

Thompson, Mark L. *Steamboats and sailors of the Great Lakes*. Detroit: Wayne State University Press, 1991

Thunder Bay Mosaic. Thunder Bay: Thunder Bay Multicultural Association, 1983

Tieman, Tracy. *Sawmills in Ontario.* Toronto: Ministry of Natural Resources, 1986

Todd, John. 'The Nipigon Tramway,' *Canadian Rail* (Oct. 1977): 309–17

Tracks beside the water – Sioux Lookout. Sioux Lookout: Sioux Lookout Historical Society, 1967

Treadwell, William. 'The pellet makers,' *Canadian Geographical Journal* 72 (June 1966): 186–205

Tronrud, Thorald J. 'Frontier social structure: The Canadian Lakehead, 1871 and 1881,' *Ontario History* 79 (1987): 145–65

– 'Buying prosperity: The bonusing of factories at the Lakehead,' *Urban History Review* 19 (1990): 1–13

– *Guardians of progress: Boosters and boosterism in Thunder Bay, 1870–1914.* Thunder Bay: Thunder Bay Historical Museum Society, 1993

Troughton, M.J. 'The failure of agricultural settlement in northern Ontario,' *Nordia* 17 (1983): 141–9

Turcott, Agnes W. *Land of the big goose.* Altona, MB: Friesen Printers, 1982

Van Every, Margaret. 'Francis Hector Clergue and the rise of Sault Ste. Marie as an industrial centre,' *Ontario History* 56 (1964): 191–202

Van Oosten, John. 'Michigan's commercial fisheries of the Great Lakes,' *Michigan History Magazine* 22 (1938): 107–45

Van Steen, Marcus. 'The Trans-Canada Highway makes road building history north of Lake Superior,' *Canadian Geographical Journal* 65 (1962): 174–81

Varjo, Uuno. 'Development of Finnish communities in the vicinity of Thunder Bay, Ontario,' *Nordia* 19 (1985): 81–113

Voorhis, E. *Historic forts and trading posts of the French regime and of the English fur trading companies.* Ottawa: Department of the Interior, 1930

Wall, Geoffrey. 'Recreational land use in Muskoka,' *Ontario Geography* 11 (1977): 11–28

Wallace, C.M. 'Communities in the northern Ontario frontier.' In *At the end of the shift: Mines and single industry towns in northern Ontario*, ed. Matt Bray and Ashley Thomson, 5–18. Toronto: Dundurn Press, 1992

Waters, Thomas F. *The Superior north shore.* Minneapolis: University of Minnesota Press, 1987

Weiler, G.B. 'Some memories of the Thunder Bay gold rush of '34,' *Thunder Bay Historical Museum Society Papers and Records* 8 (1980): 22–31

Weiller, John. *The Michipicoten Hudson's Bay Company Post, 1821–1904.* Research report no. 3. Toronto: Ministry of Culture and Recreation, Ontario Historical Sites Branch, 1973

Weller, Geoffrey R. 'Resource development in northern Ontario: A case study in hinterland politics.' In *Resources and the environment: Policy perspectives for Canada*, ed. O.P. Dwivedi, 243–68. Toronto: McClelland and Stewart, 1980

– 'The politics and administration of amalgamation: The case of Thunder Bay,' *Laurentian University Review* 17 (2) (1985): 69–86

Wells, J.J. 'History of Fort William,' *Thunder Bay Historical Society Papers* (1912–1913): 15–25

White, Randall. *Ontario, 1610–1985: A political and economic history*. Toronto: Dundurn Press, 1985

Wice, George. *Carved from the wilderness: The intriguing story of Dryden*. Dryden: Alex Wilson Colstream Ltd., 1967

Wiegman, Carl. *Trees to news: A chronicle of the Ontario Paper Company's origins and development*. Toronto: McClelland and Stewart, 1953

Wightman, Nancy M., and Robert W. Wightman. 'Agricultural settlement in northwestern Ontario to 1930,' *Thunder Bay Historical Museum Society Papers and Records* 17 (1989): 44–63

– 'The Mica Bay Affair: conflict on the upper-lakes mining frontier,' *Ontario History* 83 (1991): 193–208

– 'A most promising mining country: Northwestern Ontario, 1845–1900,' *Thunder Bay Historical Museum Society Papers and Records* 19 (1991): 35–50

– 'Road and highway development in northwestern Ontario, 1850 to 1990,' *Canadian Geographer* 36 (1992): 366–80

– 'Beyond rail and road: The Red Lake–Pickle Lake gold fields, 1925–1954,' *Thunder Bay Historical Museum Society Papers and Records* 21 (1993): 19–34

– 'The rise of electric power in northwestern Ontario: Its impact on regional development, 1890–1990.' In *Geographic perspectives on the provincial norths*, ed. Margaret Johnston, 34–57. Toronto: Copp Clark Longman, 1994

Wightman, W.R. *Forever on the fringe: Six studies in the development of the Manitoulin Island*. Toronto: University of Toronto Press, 1982

– 'The Canadian steam packet service on the Upper Lakes,' *Inland Seas* 46 (1990): 248–64

Willard, Sybil. *The pioneers and the present: A history of the Township of Barclay, 1882–1982*. Dryden: Alex Coldstream Ltd. for the Barclay Historical Society, 1983

Wills, George, and Iris Wills. *The auto camper's guide to Canada*. New York: Harper and Brothers, 1955

Wilson, J. Donald. 'A note on the Shingwauk Industrial Home for Indians,' *Journal of the Canadian Church History Society* 4 (1974): 66–71

Wolfe, J.S., and L. Bodnar. *Unrealized potential: An examination of the role of government in the past, present and future of agriculture in northern Ontario*. Guelph: School of Rural Planning and Development, Pub. 117, 1983

Wolfe, R.I. 'The summer cottage in Ontario,' *Economic Geography* 27 (1951): 10–32

– 'The summer resorts of Ontario in the nineteenth century,' *Ontario History* 54 (1962): 149–60

– 'About cottages and cottaging,' *Landscape* 15 (1965): 5–8

– 'The changing pattern of tourism in Ontario.' In *Profiles of a province*, 173–7. Toronto: The Ontario Historical Society, 1967

Wood fibre supply and demand in northern Ontario. A report by F.L.C. Reed and Associates for Abitibi-Price, American Can, Boise Cascade, Domtar, Great Lakes, Kimberly-Clark, Ontario Paper, Reed, and Spruce Falls Power and Paper. Vancouver: Apr. 21, 1980

Woodside, Tom. *A history of the Sault Ste. Marie Forest District.* District Forest History Series, no. 20. Toronto: Department of Lands and Forests, 1965

Young, A.G. *Great Lakes saga.* Owen Sound: Richardson, Bond and Wright, 1965

Young, W.D. *Democracy and discontent.* Toronto: Ryerson Press, 1969

Zaslow, Morris. 'The Ontario boundary question.' In *Profiles of a province*, 107–17. Toronto: The Ontario Historical Society, 1967

– *The opening of the Canadian north, 1870–1914.* Toronto: McClelland and Stewart, 1971

– 'Edward Barnes Borron, 1820–1915; Northern pioneer and public servant extraordinary.' In *Aspects of nineteenth century Ontario*, ed. F.H. Armstrong et al., 297–311. Toronto: University of Western Ontario Press, 1974

– *Reading the rocks: The story of the Geological Survey of Canada, 1842–1972.* Toronto: Macmillan Canada, 1975

– *The northward expansion of Canada, 1914–1967.* Toronto: McClelland and Stewart, 1988

Theses, Reports, and Papers

Balmer, Ann, and John Peters. 'Magpie River hydroelectric development.' Historic Sites Document submitted to Acres International Ltd., 1987

Bertrand, J.P. 'Timber wolves.' Typescript. Port Arthur, 1960

'Forest management agreements.' Toronto: Ministry of Natural Resources, 1987

'Fort Frances District: Background information for the northwestern Ontario strategic land use plan.' Fort Frances: Ministry of Natural Resources, 1980

Harrington, Carolyn J. 'The influence of location on the development of an Indian Community at the Rapids of the St. Marys River.' M.A. dissertation, University of Western Ontario. London, 1979

'A history of Fort Frances.' Mimeo. Fort Frances Public Library and Museum, 1973

Josephson, Elving J.S. 'A study of the changing scale and degree of specialization in the Slate River Valley.' B.A. dissertation, Lakehead University. Thunder Bay, 1972

Kolcon-Lach, Emilia. 'Early Italian settlement at Sault Ste. Marie, Ontario, 1898–1921.' M.A. dissertation, University of Western Ontario. London, 1979

Leighton, James Douglas. 'The development of a federal Indian policy in Canada, 1840–1890.' Ph.D. dissertation, University of Toronto. Toronto, 1975

'The lumber industry in Canada 1920.' Ottawa: Dominion Bureau of Statistics, 1923

MacDonald, G.A. 'East of Superior: A history of the Lake Superior Provincial Park Region.' Wawa: Ministry of Natural Resources, Parks Branch, 1974

– 'The Saulteur-Ojibway fisheries at Sault Ste. Marie, 1740–1920.' M.A. dissertation, University of Waterloo. Waterloo, 1978

McEachran, Ute. 'The reorganization of the fur trade after the merger of the Hudson's Bay Company and North West Company, 1821–1826.' Discussion paper no. 39. Department of Geography, York University, Toronto, 1988

Madsen, Chris M.V. 'German prisoners of war in Canada during the Second World War.' M.A. dissertation, University of Western Ontario. London, 1992

Martelli, John. 'Regional protest and alienation: The case of northern Ontario.' M.A. dissertation, University of Western Ontario. London, 1993

Martin, Ann. 'Old Fort William: Its history and its programs.' Old Fort William Library, Thunder Bay, 1987; updated by Marty Mascarin, 1993

Michels, R.E. 'Atikokan Ten Years Later.' Presentation to the Northwestern Ontario Planning Conference, Sept. 18, 1987, Thunder Bay

Mountain, James A. 'The inhospitable shore: An historical resource study of Neys Provincial Park.' Parks Branch, Ministry of Natural Resources, North Central Region, n.d.

Peters, John. 'Historical position paper on northwestern Ontario.' Report for the Ministry of Culture and Recreation, 1970s

– 'Commercial fishing in Lake Huron, 1800 to 1915.' M.A. dissertation, University of Western Ontario. London, 1981

Ryan, P.A. 'A history of commercial fishing on Lac des Mille Lacs, 1885–1985.' Report No. 1986-2. Ministry of Natural Resources, Thunder Bay District, 1986

Silversides, C.R. 'Development in the technology of harvesting timber.' Paper given at the Tenth Commonwealth Forestry Conference, Britain, 1974

Timothy, Dallen J. 'Ethnic islands in the Thunder Bay frontier: A study of four Finnish settlements.' M.A. dissertation, University of Western Ontario. London, 1993

Vosper, G.F. 'Logging in Lake Superior Provincial Park.' Ministry of Natural Resources, Wawa District, 1984

Warecki, George Michael. 'The Quetico-Superior Council and the battle for wilderness in Quetico Provincial Park, 1909–1960.' M.A. dissertation, University of Western Ontario. London, 1983

Weller, G.R. 'Algoma and Superior: Prospects for political separations in northern Ontario and northern Michigan.' Paper presented at annual meeting of the Western Social Science Association, Denver, CO, 1982

Whiteside, J.F. 'The Toronto Stock Exchange to 1900: Its membership and the development of the share market.' M.A. dissertation, Trent University. Peterborough, 1979

'Woodland caribou and logging in Ontario: Questions and answers.' Ministry of Natural Resources, Toronto, Nov. 1993

Wright, Anna Margaret. 'The westward expansion of Upper Canada, 1841–1867.' M.A. dissertation, Queen's University. Kingston, 1940

Index